Plate 3. Command ship from *The Last Starfighter*. The texture-mapped ship has 450,000 polygons. (Copyright © 1984 Digital Productions. Courtesy of G. Demos.)

(a)

Plate 4. (a) The cockpit of an F5 flight simulator; the pilot's view is projected onto a dome surrounding the cockpit. (b) The view from the cockpit of the flight simulator. The fighter jet is modeled geometrically, whereas the terrain is photo-textured. (Courtesy of R. Economy, General Electric Company.)

(b)

Introduction to Computer Graphics

Introduction to Computer Graphics

James D. Foley
Georgia Institute of Technology

Andries van Dam
Brown University

Steven K. Feiner
Columbia University

John F. Hughes
Brown University

Richard L. Phillips
*Los Alamos National Laboratory
and The University of Michigan*

▲▼▼
ADDISON–WESLEY

Boston • San Francisco • New York • Toronto • Montreal
London • Munich • Paris • Madrid
Capetown • Sydney • Tokyo • Singapore • Mexico City

Sponsoring Editor   *Peter S. Gordon*
Senior Production Supervisor   *Jim Rigney*
Copy Editors   *Lyn Dupré and Joyce Grandy*
Text Designer   *Sandra Rigney*
Technical Art Consultant   *Joseph K. Vetere*
Illustrators   *C&C Associates and Tech Graphics*
Cover Designer   *Eileen Hoff*
Senior Manufacturing Manager   *Roy Logan*
Marketing Manager   *Robert Donegan*

Cover images from "Luxo Jr.," by J. Lasseter, W. Reeves, E. Ostby, and S. Leffler. (Copyright © 1986 Pixar.) "Luxo" is a trademark of Jac Jacobsen Industrier.

This book is an abridged and modified version of *Computer Graphics: Principles and Practice,* Second Edition, by Foley, van Dam, Feiner, and Hughes, published in 1990 in the Addison-Wesley Systems Programming Series, IBM Editorial Board, consulting editors.

Library of Congress Cataloging-in-Publication data

Introduction to computer graphics / James D. Foley . . . [et al.] .].
    p. cm.
  Includes bibliographical references and index.
  ISBN 0-201-60921-5
  1. Computer graphics. I. Foley, James D., 1942–
T385.I538 1993
006.6—dc20   93-16677
                                                        CIP

Reprinted with corrections, May 1997.

Text printed on recycled and acid-free paper.

ISBN 0201609215

14 1516171819 MA   05 04 03 02

14th Printing   July 2002

To Marylou, Heather, Jenn, my parents, and my teachers

Jim

To Debbie, my father, my mother in memoriam, and my children Elisa, Lori, and Katrin

Andy

To Jenni, my parents, and my teachers

Steve

To my family, my teacher Rob Kirby, and my father in memoriam

John

And to all of our students.

———————————

To Thomas Carlyle who, upon learning that his charwoman had inadvertently burned his just-finished manuscript of *The French Revolution*, began writing it again.

Dick

Preface

This book is an adaptation of *Computer Graphics: Principles and Practice*, Second Edition (*CGPP*), by Foley, van Dam, Feiner, and Hughes. *Introduction to Computer Graphics* was created by abridging and modifying that comprehensive teaching and reference work to suit the needs of different courses and different professional requirements. While this book is half the size of its parent, it is not merely a shorter version of it. Indeed, it features new material and, in some cases, a different approach to exposition, all added with the needs of its intended audience in mind.

This book is designed to be used in a one- to two-semester course in computer graphics in any four-year college or university and, assuming only a small amount of mathematical preparation, for a one-semester course in community colleges or other two-year institutions. *Introduction to Computer Graphics* is also an ideal book for the professional who wants to learn the rudiments of this dynamic and exciting field, whether to become a practitioner or simply to gain an appreciation of the far-ranging applications of computer graphics.

This book is not meant to supplant *CGPP* as being more current or in any way more comprehensive. There are chapters, however, where, because of the dizzying pace at which the field is moving, older material was dropped and hardware performance and cost figures were updated. One such example can be found in Chapter 4, where the statement from *CGPP*—which, bear in mind was just published in 1990—that "… a graphics workstation typically consists of a CPU capable of executing at least several million instructions per second (MIPS) …" was updated to reflect the fact that 20–100 MIPS are now commonplace.

Other major differences and strengths of *Introduction to Computer Graphics* are:

- The computer language used throughout the book, both in pseudocoded program fragments and complete working programs, is modern ANSI C. The use of C, rather than Pascal as in *CGPP*, is consistent with both current teaching and professional practice, especially in graphics.

- As a direct benefit of the use of C in the book, there is now a one-to-one correspondence between the data types and functions of the code used in this book with those of the SRGP and SPHIGS software packages that are available (free of charge to adopters) to accompany the book (see page 559).

- The SPHIGS package mentioned above has been substantially enhanced with many new features, such as multiple light sources, improved rendering, and improved pick correlation for better interactive manipulation.

- The book features several worked-out examples, some of which are quite extensive. These examples are strategically located in chapters where they best enhance the exposition of difficult concepts. One such example is a complete working program for interactively defining Bézier parametric cubic curves.

- The importance of computer graphics to the emerging field of multimedia is introduced by describing some examples, complete with figures, and providing their supporting references.

- A mathematical preliminaries section has been added to the chapter on Geometrical Transformations. This section provides sufficient information for the reader to understand and use all subsequent mathematically oriented material in the book.

Potential Syllabi

There are several paths that a reader can take through this book. A few are suggested here, but it is entirely feasible to select one suiting the reader's circumstances. Even the order of study can be permuted. For example, the material on hardware could come either earlier or later in a syllabus than is suggested by Chapter 4's ordinal positioning.

A minimal one-semester course emphasizing 2D graphics.   Where the goal is to provide a good, but not rigorous, overview of elements of mostly 2D graphics, this course of study will be appropriate for students in a two- or four-year college or university.

Chapter	Sections
1	All
2	Sect. 2.1–2.2
3	Sect. 3.1–3.3, 3.9–3.9.3
4	Sect. 4.1, 4.2, 4.3, and 4.5
5	Sect. 5.1 (as appropriate), 5.2, 5.3, 5.4

Chapter	Sections
6	Sect. 6.1, 6.2, 6.3, 6.4.1, 6.4.2
8	All
9	Sect. 9.1, 9.2.1–9.2.3
11	Sect. 11.1–11.2
12	Selected reading to demonstrate advanced capabilities

A one-semester course providing an overview of 2D and 3D graphics. This syllabus will provide a strong foundation in graphics for readers who are mathematically well prepared.

Chapter	Sections
1	All
2	All
3	Sects. 3.1–3.5, 3.8–3.11, 3.14–3.15
4	Sect. 4.1, 4.2, 4.3, and 4.5
5	Sect. 5.1 (as appropriate), 5.2–5.5, 5.7, 5.8
6	Sect. 6.1–6.5, Sect. 6.6 (except 6.6.4), 6.7
7	Sect. 7.1–7.5, 7.10, and 7.11.6
8	All
9	Sect. 9.1, 9.2.1–9.2.3, 9.2.7, 9.3.1–9.3.2
11	All
12	All
13	Sect. 13.1–13.2, possibly 13.4
14	Sect. 14.1–14.2, possibly 14.5–14.7

A two-semester course covering 2D and 3D graphics, modeling, and rendering. All chapters (possibly omitting selected topics from Chapters 9 and 10) plus selected topics from *CGPP*.

Since many readers of *Introduction to Computer Graphics* will be interested in consulting its more advanced and comprehensive parent, the preface to *CGPP* follows this one. There the reader will find a discussion of *CGPP*'s important features and suggestions for structuring courses based on that book.

Electronic Instructor's Manual

An Electronic Instructor's Manual (EIM), which supplements this book, is available from Brown University. Information on how to obtain the EIM is acquired by sending e-mail to eim@cs.brown.edu. No message body is necessary; just enter EIM (or eim) on the Subject line. The e-mail reply will contain a description of the contents of the EIM and how to obtain any part of it. It is necessary to have Internet ftp access to retrieve the EIM. No other distribution method is available.

The EIM comprises four parts. They are:

- **Expanded versions of the syllabi suggested above.** The rationale for each syllabus is described on a step-by-step basis. Also, where appropriate, aids to teaching the material are suggested.
- **Selected ANSI C source code from the book.** Program fragments as well as complete working programs are provided. In general, an instructor must have SRGP and SPHIGS for this code to be useful.
- **All the artwork from the book.** With the exception of stripped-in half-tones, each figure is provided as either an Encapsulated Postscript (EPS) or Tagged Image File Format (TIFF) file. These figures will be useful for preparation of lecture slides. The artwork files are organized by chapter so that an instructor can obtain just the figures needed for a particular syllabus.
- **Freely available software resources.** In addition to the SRGP and SPHIGS packages which supplement the text, there are many packages available that the instructor may wish to obtain for use in the course. Packages such as SIPP (SImple Polygon Processor) and Rayshade, a ray tracing program, implement many of the realistic rendering techniques described in the text. Information on how to obtain these and other packages is provided.

Acknowledgments

First, it should be stated that while all the authors of *CGPP* participated to some degree in the preparation of this book, I assume full responsibility for any new errors introduced in the adaptation process.

David Sklar was a guest author for *CGPP*, and much of the material he contributed to that book remains here in Chapters 2 and 7. He was also helpful to me in locating electronic versions of computer code and artwork from the original book.

Peter Gordon, my editor, always had timely, wise, and calming advice throughout the duration of this project. Jim Rigney, my production supervisor, spent lots of helpful hours teaching me the "tricks of the trade."

Many people helped with various aspects of the book. Among them are Yvonne Martinez, Chuck Hansen, Tom Rokicki, David Cortesi, Janick (J.) Bergeron, Henry McGilton, Greg Cockroft, Mike Hawley, Ed Catmull, Loren Carpenter, Harold Borkin, Alan Paeth, Jim White, and Bert Herzog.

A special thank you is owed to Ed Angel of The University of New Mexico and his courageous students for beta—make that alpha—testing of a first draft of the book in the fall of 1992.

Finally, without D.C. this would never have happened.

Santa Fe, N.M.   R.L.P.

Preface to Computer Graphics: Principles and Practice, Second Edition

> Interactive graphics is a field whose time has come. Until recently it was an esoteric specialty involving expensive display hardware, substantial computer resources, and idiosyncratic software. In the last few years, however, it has benefited from the steady and sometimes even spectacular reduction in the hardware price/performance ratio (e.g., personal computers for home or office with their standard graphics terminals), and from the development of high-level, device-independent graphics packages that help make graphics programming rational and straightforward. Interactive graphics is now finally ready to fulfill its promise to provide us with pictorial communication and thus to become a major facilitator of man/machine interaction. (From preface, *Fundamentals of Interactive Computer Graphics*, James Foley and Andries van Dam, 1982)

This assertion that computer graphics had finally arrived was made before the revolution in computer culture sparked by Apple's Macintosh and the IBM PC and its clones. Now even preschool children are comfortable with interactive-graphics techniques, such as the desktop metaphor for window manipulation and menu and icon selection with a mouse. Graphics-based user interfaces have made productive users of neophytes, and the desk without its graphics computer is increasingly rare.

At the same time that interactive graphics has become common in user interfaces and visualization of data and objects, the rendering of 3D objects has become dramatically more realistic, as evidenced by the ubiquitous computer-generated commercials and movie special effects. Techniques that were experimental in the early eighties are now standard practice, and more remarkable "photorealistic" effects are around the corner. The simpler kinds of pseudorealism, which took hours of computer time per image in the early eighties, now are done routinely at animation rates (ten or more frames/second) on personal computers. Thus "real-time" vector displays in 1981 showed moving wire-frame objects made of tens of thousands of vectors without hidden-edge removal; in 1990 real-time raster displays can show not only the same kinds of line drawings but also moving objects composed of as many as one hundred thousand triangles rendered with Gouraud or Phong shading and specular highlights and with full hidden-surface removal. The highest-performance systems provide real-time texture mapping, antialiasing, atmospheric attenuation for fog and haze, and other advanced effects.

Graphics software standards have also advanced significantly since our first edition. The SIGGRAPH Core '79 package, on which the first edition's SGP package was based, has all but disappeared, along with direct-view storage tube and refresh vector displays. The much more powerful PHIGS package, supporting storage and editing of structure hierarchy, has become an official ANSI and ISO standard, and it is widely available for real-time geometric graphics in scientific and engineering applications, along with PHIGS+, which supports lighting, shading, curves, and surfaces. Official graphics standards complement lower-level, more efficient de facto standards, such as Apple's QuickDraw, X Window System's Xlib 2D integer raster graphics package, and Silicon Graphics' GL 3D library. Also widely available are implementations of Pixar's RenderMan interface for photorealistic rendering and PostScript interpreters for hardcopy page and screen image description. Better graphics software has been used to make dramatic improvements in the "look and feel" of user interfaces, and we may expect increasing use of 3D effects, both for aesthetic reasons and for providing new metaphors for organizing and presenting, and navigating through information.

Perhaps the most important new movement in graphics is the increasing concern for modeling objects, not just for creating their pictures. Furthermore, interest is growing in describing the time-varying geometry and behavior of 3D objects. Thus graphics is increasingly concerned with simulation, animation, and a "back to physics" movement in both modeling and rendering in order to create objects that look and behave as realistically as possible.

As the tools and capabilities available become more and more sophisticated and complex, we need to be able to apply them effectively. Rendering is no longer the bottleneck. Therefore researchers are beginning to apply artificial-intelligence techniques to assist in the design of object models, in motion planning, and in the layout of effective 2D and 3D graphical presentations.

Today the frontiers of graphics are moving very rapidly, and a text that sets out to be a standard reference work must periodically be updated and expanded. This book is almost a total rewrite of the *Fundamentals of Interactive Computer Graphics,* and although this second edition contains nearly double the original 623 pages, we remain painfully aware of how much material we have been forced to omit.

Major differences from the first edition include the following:

- The vector-graphics orientation is replaced by a raster orientation.

- The simple 2D floating-point graphics package (SGP) is replaced by two packages—SRGP and SPHIGS—that reflect the two major schools of interactive graphics programming. SRGP combines features of the QuickDraw and Xlib 2D integer raster graphics packages. SPHIGS, based on PHIGS, provides the fundamental features of a 3D floating-point package with hierarchical display lists. We explain how to do applications programming in each of these packages and show how to implement the basic clipping, scan-conversion, viewing, and display list traversal algorithms that underlie these systems.

- User-interface issues are discussed at considerable length, both for 2D desktop metaphors and for 3D interaction devices.

- Coverage of modeling is expanded to include NURB (nonuniform rational B-spline) curves and surfaces, a chapter on solid modeling, and a chapter on advanced modeling techniques, such as physically based modeling, procedural models, fractals, L-grammar systems, and particle systems.

- Increased coverage of rendering includes a detailed treatment of antialiasing and greatly expanded chapters on visible-surface determination, illumination, and shading, including physically based illumination models, ray tracing, and radiosity.

- Material is added on advanced raster graphics architectures and algorithms, including clipping and scan-conversion of complex primitives and simple image-processing operations, such as compositing.

- A brief introduction to animation is added.

This text can be used by those without prior background in graphics and only some background in Pascal programming, basic data structures and algorithms, computer architecture, and simple linear algebra. An appendix reviews the necessary mathematical foundations. The book covers enough material for a full-year course, but is partitioned into groups to make selective coverage possible. The reader, therefore, can progress through a carefully designed sequence of units, starting with simple, generally applicable fundamentals and ending with more complex and specialized subjects.

Basic Group

Chapter 1 provides a historical perspective and some fundamental issues in hardware, software, and applications. Chapters 2 and 3 describe, respectively, the use and the implementation of SRGP, a simple 2D integer graphics package. Chapter 4 introduces graphics hardware, including some hints about how to use hardware in implementing the operations described in the preceding chapters. The next two chapters, 5 and 6, introduce the ideas of transformations in the plane and 3-space, representations by matrices, the use of homogeneous coordinates to unify linear and affine transformations, and the description of 3D views, including the transformations from arbitrary view volumes to canonical view volumes. Finally, Chapter 7 introduces SPHIGS, a 3D floating-point hierarchical graphics package that is a simplified version of the PHIGS standard, and describes its use in some basic modeling operations. Chapter 7 also discusses the advantages and disadvantages of the hierarchy available in PHIGS and the structure of applications that use this graphics package.

User Interface Group

Chapters 8-10 describe the current technology of interaction devices and then address the higher-level issues in user-interface design. Various popular user-interface paradigms are described and critiqued. In the final chapter user-interface software, such as window managers, interaction technique-libraries, and user-interface management systems, is addressed.

Model Definition Group

The first two modeling chapters, 11 and 12, describe the current technologies used in geometric modeling: the representation of curves and surfaces by parametric functions, especially cubic splines, and the representation of solids by various techniques, including boundary representations and CSG models. Chapter 13 introduces the human color-vision system, various color-description systems, and conversion from one to another. This chapter also briefly addresses rules for the effective use of color.

Image Synthesis Group

Chapter 14, the first in a four-chapter sequence, describes the quest for realism from the earliest vector drawings to state-of-the-art shaded graphics. The artifacts caused by aliasing are of crucial concern in raster graphics, and this chapter discusses their causes and cures in considerable detail by introducing the Fourier transform and convolution. Chapter 15 describes a variety of strategies for visible-surface determination in enough detail to allow the reader to implement some of the most important ones. Illumination and shading algorithms are covered in detail in Chapter 16. The early part of this chapter discusses algorithms most commonly found in current hardware, while the remainder treats texture, shadows, transparency, reflections, physically based illumination models, ray tracing, and radiosity methods. The last chapter in this group, Chapter 17, describes both image manipulations, such as scaling, shearing, and rotating pixmaps, and image storage techniques, including various image-compression schemes.

Advanced Techniques Group

The last four chapters give an overview of the current state of the art (a moving target, of course). Chapter 18 describes advanced graphics hardware used in high-end commercial and research machines; this chapter was contributed by Steven Molnar and Henry Fuchs, authorities on high-performance graphics architectures. Chapter 19 describes the complex raster algorithms used for such tasks as scan-converting arbitrary conics, generating antialiased text, and implementing page-description languages, such as PostScript. The final two chapters survey some of the most important techniques in the fields of high-level modeling and computer animation.

The first two groups cover only elementary material and thus can be used for a basic course at the undergraduate level. A follow-on course can then use the more advanced chapters. Alternatively, instructors can assemble customized courses by picking chapters out of the various groups.

For example, a course designed to introduce students to primarily 2D graphics would include Chapters 1 and 2, simple scan conversion and clipping from Chapter 3, a technology overview with emphasis on raster architectures and interaction devices from Chapter 4, homogeneous mathematics from Chapter 5, and

3D viewing only from a "how to use it" point of view from Sections 6.1 to 6.3. The User Interface Group, Chapters 8-10, would be followed by selected introductory sections and simple algorithms from the Image Synthesis Group, Chapters 14, 15, and 16.

A one-course general overview of graphics would include Chapters 1 and 2, basic algorithms from Chapter 3, raster architectures and interaction devices from Chapter 4, Chapter 5, and most of Chapters 6 and 7 on viewing and SPHIGS. The second half of the course would include sections on modeling from Chapters 11 and 13, on image synthesis from Chapters 14, 15, and 16, and on advanced modeling from Chapter 20 to give breadth of coverage in these slightly more advanced areas.

A course emphasizing 3D modeling and rendering would start with Chapter 3 sections on scan converting, clipping of lines and polygons, and introducing antialiasing. The course would then progress to Chapters 5 and 6 on the basic mathematics of transformations and viewing, Chapter 13 on color, and then cover the key Chapters 14, 15, and 16 in the Image Synthesis Group. Coverage would be rounded off by selections in surface and solid modeling, Chapter 20 on advanced modeling, and Chapter 21 on animation from the Advanced Techniques Group.

Graphics Packages

The SRGP and SPHIGS graphics packages, designed by David Sklar, coauthor of the two chapters on these packages, are available from the publisher for the IBM PC (ISBN 0-201-54700-7), the Macintosh (ISBN 0-201-54701-5), and UNIX workstations running X11, as are many of the algorithms for scan conversion, clipping, and viewing.

Acknowledgments

This book could not have been produced without the dedicated work and the indulgence of many friends and colleagues. We acknowledge here our debt to those who have contributed significantly to one or more chapters; many others have helped by commenting on individual chapters, and we are grateful to them as well. We regret any inadvertent omissions. Katrina Avery and Lyn Dupré did a superb job of editing. Additional valuable editing on multiple versions of multiple chapters was provided by Debbie van Dam, Melissa Gold, and Clare Campbell. We are especially grateful to our production supervisor, Bette Aaronson, our art director, Joe Vetere, and our editor, Keith Wollman, not only for their great help in producing the book, but also for their patience and good humor under admittedly adverse circumstances—if we ever made a promised deadline during these frantic five years, we can't remember it!

Computer graphics has become too complex for even a team of four main authors and three guest authors to be expert in all areas. We relied on colleagues and students to amplify our knowledge, catch our mistakes and provide constructive criticism of form and content. We take full responsibility for any remaining sins of omission and commission. Detailed technical readings on one or more chapters were provided by John Airey, Kurt Akeley, Tom Banchoff, Brian Barsky, David

Bates, Cliff Beshers, Gary Bishop, Peter Bono, Marvin Bunker, Bill Buxton, Edward Chang, Norman Chin, Michael F. Cohen, William Cowan, John Dennis, Tom Dewald, Scott Draves, Steve Drucker, Tom Duff, Richard Economy, David Ellsworth, Nick England, Jerry Farrell, Robin Forrest, Alain Fournier, Alan Freiden, Christina Gibbs, Melissa Gold, Mark Green, Cathleen Greenberg, Margaret Hagen, Griff Hamlin, Pat Hanrahan, John Heidema, Rob Jacob, Abid Kamran, Mike Kappel, Henry Kaufman, Karen Kendler, David Kurlander, David Laidlaw, Keith Lantz, Hsien-Che Lee, Aaron Marcus, Nelson Max, Deborah Mayhew, Barbara Meier, Gary Meyer, Jim Michener, Jakob Nielsen, Mark Nodine, Randy Pausch, Ari Requicha, David Rosenthal, David Salesin, Hanan Samet, James Sanford, James Sargent, Robin Schaufler, Robert Scheifler, John Schnizlein, Michael Shantzis, Ben Shneiderman, Ken Shoemake, Judith Schrier, John Sibert, Dave Simons, Jonathan Steinhart, Maureen Stone, Paul Strauss, Seth Tager, Peter Tanner, Brice Tebbs, Ben Trumbore, Yi Tso, Greg Turk, Jeff Vroom, Colin Ware, Gary Watkins, Chuck Weger, Kevin Weiler, Turner Whitted, George Wolberg, and Larry Wolff.

Several colleagues, including Jack Bresenham, Brian Barsky, Jerry Van Aken, Dilip DaSilva (who suggested the uniform midpoint treatment of Chapter 3) and Don Hatfield, not only read chapters closely but also provided detailed suggestions on algorithms.

Welcome word-processing relief was provided by Katrina Avery, Barbara Britten, Clare Campbell, Tina Cantor, Joyce Cavatoni, Louisa Hogan, Jenni Rodda, and Debbie van Dam. Drawings for Chapters 1–3 were ably created by Dan Robbins, Scott Snibbe, Tina Cantor, and Clare Campbell. Figure and image sequences created for this book were provided by Beth Cobb, David Kurlander, Allen Paeth, and George Wolberg (with assistance from Peter Karp). Plates II.21–37, showing a progression of rendering techniques, were designed and rendered at Pixar by Thomas Williams and H.B. Siegel, under the direction of M.W. Mantle, using Pixar's PhotoRealistic RenderMan software. Thanks to Industrial Light & Magic for the use of their laser scanner to create Plates II.24–37, and to Norman Chin for computing vertex normals for Color Plates II.30–32. L. Lu and Carles Castellsagué wrote programs to make figures.

Jeff Vogel implemented the algorithms of Chapter 3, and he and Atul Butte verified the code in Chapters 2 and 7. David Sklar wrote the Mac and X11 implementations of SRGP and SPHIGS with help from Ron Balsys, Scott Boyajian, Atul Butte, Alex Contovounesios, and Scott Draves. Randy Pausch and his students ported the packages to the PC environment.

We have installed an automated electronic mail server to allow our readers to obtain machine-readable copies of many of the algorithms, suggest exercises, report errors in the text and in SRGP/SPHIGS, and obtain errata lists for the text and software. Send email to "graphtext @ cs.brown.edu" with a Subject line of "Help" to receive the current list of available services.

Atlanta, GA	J.D.F.
Providence, RI	A.v.D.
New York, NY	S.K.F.
Providence, RI	J.F.H.

About the Authors

James Foley (Ph.D., University of Michigan) is founder and Director of the Graphics, Visualization & Usability Center at Georgia Institute of Technology, where he is also Professor of Computer Science and Professor of Electrical Engineering. Coauthor with Andries van Dam of *Fundamentals of Interactive Computer Graphics*, Dr. Foley is a member of ACM, ACM SIGGRAPH, ACM SIGCHI, the Human Factors Society, IEEE, and the IEEE Computer Society. He is editor-in-chief of *ACM Transactions on Graphics*, and serves on the editorial boards of *Computers and Graphics* and *Presence*. His research interests are UIDE (the User Interface Design Environment, a model-based user interface development tool), user interface software, information visualization, multimedia, and human factors of the user interface. Dr. Foley is a Fellow of the IEEE, and a member of Phi Beta Kappa, Tau Beta Pi, and Sigma Xi.

Andries van Dam (Ph.D., University of Pennsylvania) was one of the founders and the first chairman of the computer science department at Brown University. He is currently L. Herbert Ballou University Professor and professor of computer science at Brown, and senior consulting scientist at BLOC Development and Electronic Book Technologies, and on Technical Advisory Boards for ShoGraphics and Microsoft. A member of the IEEE Computer Society and ACM, he is also cofounder of ACM SIGGRAPH. Dr. van Dam helped found and was an editor of *Computer Graphics and Image Processing* and of *ACM Transactions on Graphics*. Coauthor of the widely used book *Fundamentals of Interactive Computer Graphics* with James Foley and of *Pascal on the Macintosh: A Graphical Approach* with David Niguidula, he has, in addition, published over eighty papers. In 1984 he received an IEEE Centennial Medal; in 1988 the state of Rhode Island Governor's Science and Technology Award; in 1990, the NCGA Academic Award; and in 1991, the SIGGRAPH Steven A. Coons Award. Dr. van Dam's research interests include hypermedia, electronic books, and high-performance workstations for teaching and research.

Steven Feiner (Ph.D., Brown University) is associate professor of computer science at Columbia University where he directs the computer graphics and user interface laboratory. His current research focuses on picture synthesis, applications of artificial intelligence to computer graphics, user interfaces, animation, virtual worlds, and hypermedia systems. He is also involved with the development of knowledge-based systems that automate the design and layout of graphical user interfaces. Dr. Feiner is on the editorial boards of *Electronic Publishing* and *ACM Transactions on Information Systems*, and is a member of ACM SIGGRAPH and the IEEE Computer Society. In 1991 he received an ONR Young Investigator Award. Dr. Feiner's work has been published in over forty papers and presented in numerous tutorials and panels.

John Hughes (Ph.D., University of California, Berkeley) is an assistant professor of computer science at Brown University where he codirects the computer graphics group with Andries van Dam. His research interests include the application of mathematics to computer graphics for scientific and mathematical visualization, automated computer animation, foundations of computer graphics, and interactive illustration. He is a member of ACM SIGGRAPH and the IEEE Computer Society. Recent papers have appeared in *Computer Graphics* and *Topology*, and his work on sphere eversions was described in a cover article for *Science News*.

Richard Phillips (Ph.D., University of Michigan) is principally responsible for this adaptation of *CGPP*. Dr. Phillips is Professor Emeritus of Electrical and Computer Engineering, and Aerospace Engineering at the University of Michigan. There, as founding director of the Computer Aided Engineering Network, he was instrumental in establishing a several hundred node workstation network for student and faculty use in the College of Engineering. He was also founding director of the Center for Information Technology Integration. He is currently a technical staff member at Los Alamos National Laboratory, where his current research interests are scientific visualization, multimedia workstations, distributed computing, and multimedia digital publication. He is a member of IEEE and ACM and serves on the editorial board of *Computers and Graphics*.

Contents

Introduction to Computer Graphics

1 Introducing: Computer Graphics

Welcome to computer graphics, arguably the most exciting area of computer science. Computer graphics is a branch of computer science, yes, but its appeal reaches far beyond that relatively specialized field. In its short lifetime, computer graphics has attracted some of the most creative people in the world to its fold. They come from all disciplines—art, science, music, dance, film making, and many others. To name a few, Disney animators used computer graphics to give the ballroom scene in *Beauty and the Beast* its special appeal. Merce Cunningham, the choreographer, uses computer graphics to produce labanotation scores—scripts from which dancers learn their steps. David Em, a respected conventional-medium artist, now uses computer graphics extensively in his work. In fact, since the excitement and diversity of computer graphics can be best conveyed by consideration of its applications, let us look at several in more detail.

1.1 A FEW USES OF COMPUTER GRAPHICS

Computer graphics is used today in many different areas of industry, business, government, education, and entertainment. The list of applications is enormous, and is growing rapidly as computers with graphics capabilities become commodity products. Here is a brief look at some of these areas.

■ **User interfaces.** You may not be aware of it, but you have probably already used computer graphics. If you have worked on a Macintosh or an IBM-compatible computer running Windows 3.1, you are practically a seasoned graphics user.

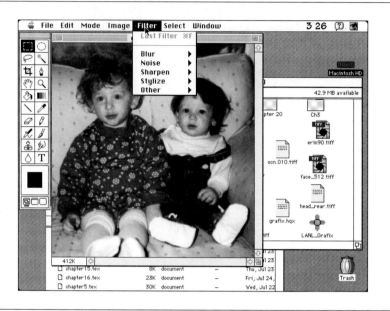

Figure 1.1   A Macintosh screen, showing windows, a menu, and desktop icons.

After all, most applications that run on personal computers and workstations have user interfaces (similar to the one shown in Fig. 1.1) that rely on desktop window systems to manage multiple simultaneous activities, and on a pointing capability to allow users to select menu items, icons, and objects on the screen. Word-processing, spreadsheet, and desktop-publishing programs are typical applications that take advantage of such user-interface techniques. As we shall see, computer graphics plays an integral role in both the input and output functions of user interfaces.

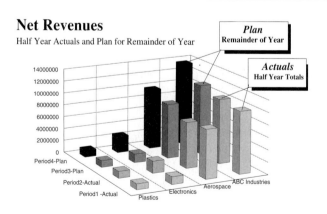

Figure 1.2   Business data shown as a 3D bar graph.

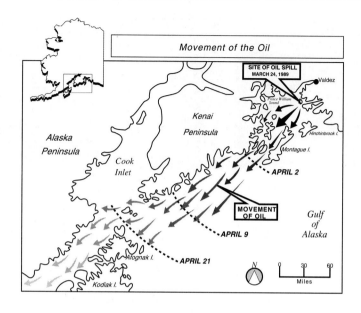

Figure 1.3   Use of a cartographic background to depict geographically related data. (Courtesy of Tom Poiker, Simon Fraser University.)

- **Interactive plotting in business, science, and technology.** The next most common use of graphics today is to create 2D and 3D graphs of mathematical, physical, and economic functions; histograms, bar and pie charts; task-scheduling charts; inventory and production charts; and the like. All these graphs are used to present meaningfully and concisely the trends and patterns gleaned from data, so as to clarify complex phenomena and to facilitate informed decision making. Figure 1.2 shows a typical example of a 3D plot of business data.

- **Cartography.** Computer graphics is used to produce both accurate and schematic representations of geographical and other natural phenomena from measurement data. Examples include geographic maps, relief maps, exploration maps for drilling and mining, oceanographic charts, weather maps, contour maps, and population-density maps. Figure 1.3 shows a map that was produced to illustrate some aspects of the 1989 Exxon *Valdez* oil spill disaster. This map is an example of *thematic* mapping, where data values—such as movement of the spilled oil—are overlaid on a map background.

- **Medicine.** Computer graphics is playing an ever-increasing role in fields such as diagnostic medicine and surgery planning. In the latter case, surgeons use graphics as an aid to guiding instruments and to determining precisely where diseased tissue should be removed. One application of computer graphics in diagnosis is shown in Fig. 1.4. There we see three images derived from magnetic resonance imaging (MRI) of a human brain. From a series of parallel scans of the type

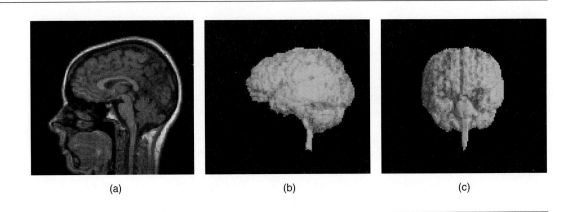

(a)   (b)   (c)

Figure 1.4   A 3D representation of the human brain constructed from MRI scans. A series of images of the type shown in (a) are processed to produce the 3D scenes shown in (b), a side view, and (c), the rear view. (Courtesy of John George, Los Alamos National Laboratory.)

in part (a), diagnosticians can synthesize a 3D representation of the brain, shown in parts (b) and (c). The user can manipulate the model interactively to reveal detailed information about the brain's condition. Another, especially exciting, medical application of computer graphics is shown in Fig. 1.5. There we see 3D plots of data obtained by illuminating living tissue with laser light, a technique known as *optical biopsy*. In this case, normal (part a) and cancerous (part b) canine livers exhibit greatly differing optical signatures, offering the hope of nonsurgical diagnosis.

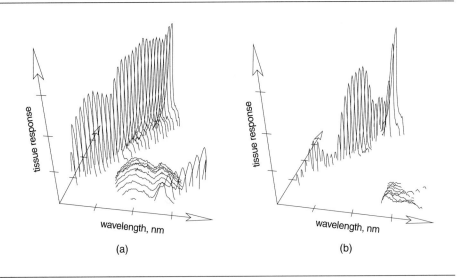

(a)   (b)

Figure 1.5   Results of an optical biopsy. (a) Signature of normal liver tissue. (b) Signature of cancerous liver tissue. (Courtesy of Thomas Loree, Los Alamos National Laboratory.)

■ **Computer-aided drafting and design.** In computer-aided design (CAD), users employ interactive graphics to design components and systems of mechanical, electrical, electromechanical, and electronic devices, including structures such as buildings, automobile bodies, airplane and ship hulls, very large-scale integrated (VLSI) chips, and telephone and computer networks. Usually, the emphasis is on interacting with a computer-based model of the component or system being designed, but sometimes the user merely wants to produce precise drawings of components and assemblies, as for online drafting or architectural blueprints. Figure 1.6 shows an example of architectural CAD; it is a drawing of a power plant.

■ **Multimedia systems**. Computer graphics plays a critical role in the rapidly expanding area of multimedia systems. As the name implies, multimedia involves more than one communications medium. Conventionally, in such systems, we see text, graphics, and sound, but there can be many other media [PHIL91]. Figure 1.7 shows how nonconventional multimedia components could be used in education. The figure is derived from a hypothetical multimedia textbook of computer graphics [PHIL92]. Part (a) shows the procedure for drawing a 2D line segment (we

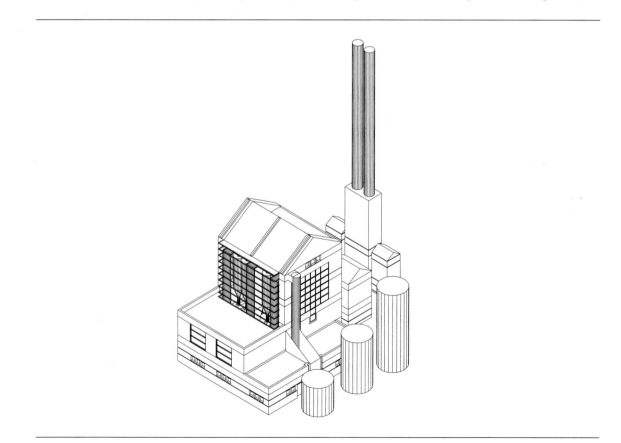

Figure 1.6   Drawing of a power plant produced by an architectural CAD system. (Courtesy of Harold Borkin, Architecture and Planning Research Lab, University of Michigan.)

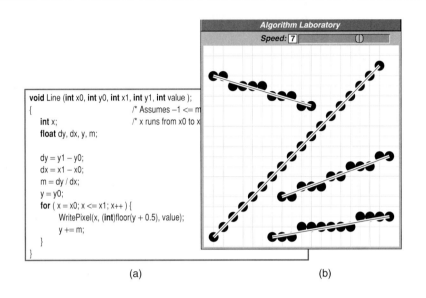

```
void Line (int x0, int y0, int x1, int y1, int value );
{                                      /* Assumes –1 <= m
    int x;                             /* x runs from x0 to x
    float dy, dx, y, m;

    dy = y1 – y0;
    dx = x1 – x0;
    m = dy / dx;
    y = y0;
    for ( x = x0; x <= x1; x++ ) {
        WritePixel(x, (int)floor(y + 0.5), value);
        y += m;
    }
}
```

(a)   (b)

Figure 1.7   An interactive algorithm from a multimedia textbook. (a) The computer code that implements the algorithm. (b) An interactive sketching panel, which appears when the reader points to the code. Specifying the endpoints of a line causes the code to be executed.

shall discuss the meaning of this code in Chapter 3). The code is *live* as it appears on the multimedia page; that is, by pointing at it, the reader can execute it. An algorithm laboratory panel, shown in part (b), appears, which lets the reader try out a variety of endpoint conditions, and watch the algorithm in action.

■   **Simulation and animation for scientific visualization and entertainment.** Computer-produced animated movies and displays of the time-varying behavior of real and simulated objects are becoming increasingly popular for scientific and engineering visualization (see Color Plate 1). We can use them to study abstract mathematical entities as well as mathematical models of such phenomena as fluid flow, relativity, nuclear and chemical reactions, physiological system and organ function, and deformation of mechanical structures under various kinds of loads. Another advanced-technology area is the production of elegant special effects in movies (see Color Plates 2 and 3). Sophisticated mechanisms are available to model the objects and to represent light and shadows.

1.2 A BRIEF HISTORY OF COMPUTER GRAPHICS

This book concentrates on fundamental principles and techniques that were derived in the past and are still applicable today—and generally will be applicable in the future. In this section, we take a brief look at the historical development of computer graphics, to place today's systems in context. Fuller treatments of the interesting evolution of this field are presented in [PRIN71], [MACH78], [CHAS81], and [CACM84]. It is easier to chronicle the evolution of hardware than that of software, since hardware evolution has had a greater influence on how the field developed. Thus, we begin with hardware.

Even in the early days of computing, there was crude plotting on hardcopy devices such as Teletypes and lineprinters. The Whirlwind Computer, developed in 1950 at MIT, had computer-driven cathode ray tube (CRT) displays for output, both for operator use and for cameras producing hardcopy. The beginnings of modern interactive graphics are found in Ivan Sutherland's seminal doctoral work on the Sketchpad drawing system [SUTH63]. He introduced data structures for storing symbol hierarchies built up via easy replication of standard components, a technique akin to the use of plastic templates for drawing circuit symbols. Sutherland also developed interaction techniques that used the keyboard and light pen (a hand-held pointing device that senses light emitted by objects on the screen) for making choices, pointing, and drawing, and formulated many other fundamental ideas and techniques still in use today. Indeed, many of the features introduced in Sketchpad are found in the PHIGS graphics package discussed in Chapter 7.

At the same time, it was becoming clear to computer, automobile, and aerospace manufacturers that CAD and computer-aided manufacturing (CAM) activities had enormous potential for automating drafting and other drawing-intensive activities. The General Motors DAC system [JACK64] for automobile design and the Itek Digitek system [CHAS81] for lens design were pioneering programs that showed the utility of graphical interaction in the iterative design cycles common in engineering. By the mid-sixties, a number of research projects and commercial products had appeared.

Since, at that time, computer input/output (I/O) was done primarily in batch mode using punched cards, hopes were high for a breakthrough in interactive user–computer communication. Interactive graphics, as "the window on the computer," was to be an integral part of vastly accelerated interactive design cycles. The results were not nearly so dramatic, however, since interactive graphics remained beyond the resources of all but the most technology-intensive organizations.

Thus, until the early 1980s, computer graphics was a small, specialized field, largely because the hardware was expensive and graphics-based application programs were few. Then, personal computers with built-in raster graphics displays— such as the Apple Macintosh and the IBM PC and its clones—popularized the use of **bitmap graphics** for user–computer interaction. A **bitmap** is a ones and zeros representation of the rectangular array of points, called **pixels** or **pels** (short for *picture elements*), on the screen. Once bitmap graphics became affordable, an explosion of easy-to-use and inexpensive graphics-based applications soon followed. Graphics-based user interfaces allowed millions of new users to control simple, low-cost application programs, such as spreadsheets, word processors, and drawing programs.

The concept of a **desktop** became a popular metaphor for organizing screen space. By means of a **window manager**, the user could create, position, and resize rectangular screen areas on the desktop, called **windows,** that acted as virtual graphics terminals, each running an application. This approach allowed users to switch among multiple activities just by pointing at the desired window, typically with a pointing device called a **mouse**. Like pieces of paper on a messy desk, windows could overlap arbitrarily. Also part of this desktop metaphor were displays of icons that represented not just data files and application programs, but also common office objects—such as file cabinets, mailboxes, printers, and trashcans—that performed the computer-operation equivalents of their real-life counterparts (see Fig. 1.1).

Direct manipulation of objects via **pointing and clicking** replaced much of the typing of the arcane commands used in earlier computers. Thus, users could select icons to activate the corresponding programs or objects, or select buttons on pull-down or pop-up screen menus to make choices. Today, almost all interactive application programs, even those for manipulating text (e.g., word processors) or numerical data (e.g., spreadsheet programs), use graphics extensively in the user interface and for visualizing and manipulating the application-specific objects.

1.2.1 Output Technology

The display devices developed in the mid-sixties and in common use until the mid-eighties are called **vector, stroke, line drawing,** or **calligraphic displays.** The term *vector* is used as a synonym for *line* here; a *stroke* is a short line, and characters are made of sequences of such strokes. A typical vector system consists of a display processor connected as an I/O peripheral to the central processing unit (CPU), a display buffer memory, and a CRT. The essence of a vector system is that the electron beam, which writes on the CRT's phosphor coating (see Chapter 4), is deflected from endpoint to endpoint, as dictated by the arbitrary order of the display commands; this technique is called **random scan** (see Fig. 1.10b). Since the light output of the phosphor decays in tens or at most hundreds of microseconds, the display processor must cycle through the display list to **refresh** the phosphor at least 30 times per second (30 Hz) to avoid flicker.

The development, in the early seventies, of inexpensive raster graphics based on television technology contributed more to the growth of the field than did any other technology. **Raster displays** store the display **primitives** (such as lines, characters, and solidly shaded or patterned areas) in a refresh buffer in terms of the primitives' component pixels, as shown in Fig. 1.8. In some raster displays, a hardware display controller (as shown in the figure) receives and interprets sequences of output commands; in simpler, more common systems, such as those in personal computers, the display controller exists only as a software component of the graphics library and the refresh buffer is just a piece of the CPU's memory that can be read out by the image display subsystem (often called the **video controller**) that produces the actual image on the screen.

The complete image on a raster display is formed from the **raster**, which is a set of horizontal **scan lines**, each a row of individual pixels; the raster is thus stored as a matrix of pixels representing the entire screen area. The entire image is scanned out sequentially by the video controller, one scan line at a time, from top to bottom and then back to the top (as shown in Fig. 1.9). At each pixel, the beam's

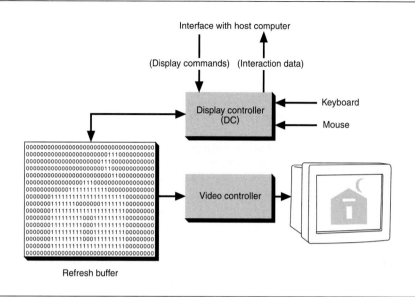

Figure 1.8   Architecture of a raster display.

intensity is set to reflect the pixel's intensity; in color systems, three beams are controlled—one each for the red, green, and blue primary colors—as specified by the three color components of each pixel's value (see Chapters 4 and 11). In Fig. 1.10, part (a) shows the difference between random and raster scan for displaying a simple 2D line drawing of a house. In part (b), the vector arcs are notated with arrowheads showing the random deflection of the beam. Dashed lines denote deflection of the beam, which is not turned on (it is **blanked**), so that no vector is drawn. Part (c) shows the unfilled house rendered by rectangles, polygons, and

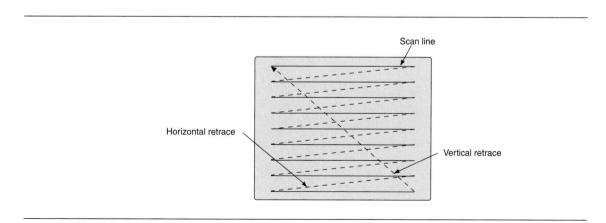

Figure 1.9   Raster scan.

arcs, whereas part (d) shows a filled version. Note the jagged appearance of the lines and arcs in the raster scan images of parts (c) and (d); we shall discuss that visual artifact shortly.

Since, in a raster system the entire grid of, say, 1024 lines of 1024 pixels must be stored explicitly, the availability of inexpensive solid-state random-access memory (RAM) for bitmaps in the early seventies was the breakthrough needed to make raster graphics the dominant hardware technology. **Bilevel** (also called **monochrome**) CRTs draw images in black and white or black and green; some plasma panels use black and orange. Bilevel bitmaps contain a single bit per pixel, and the entire bitmap for a screen with a resolution of 1024 by 1024 pixels is only 2^{20} bits, or about 128,000 bytes. Low-end color systems have 8 bits per pixel, allowing 256 colors simultaneously; more expensive systems have 24 bits per pixel, allowing a choice of any of 16 million colors; and refresh buffers with 32 bits per pixel, and screen resolution of 1280 by 1024 pixels, are available even on personal computers. Of the 32 bits, 24 are devoted to representing color, and 8 to control purposes, as discussed in Chapter 4. A typical 1280 by 1024 color system with 24 bits per pixel requires 3.75 MB of RAM—inexpensive by today's standards. The term *bitmap*, strictly speaking, applies only to 1-bit-per-pixel bilevel systems; for multiple-bit-per-pixel systems, we use the more general term **pixmap** (short for *pixel map*). Since pixmap in common parlance refers both to the contents of the refresh buffer and to the buffer memory itself, we use the term **frame buffer** when we mean the actual buffer memory.

The major advantages of raster graphics over *vector graphics* include lower cost and the ability to display areas filled with solid colors or patterns—an especially rich means of communicating information that is essential for realistic images of 3D objects.

The major disadvantage of raster systems compared to vector systems arises from the discrete nature of the pixel representation. First, primitives such as lines and polygons are specified in terms of their endpoints (vertices) and must be scan-converted into their component pixels in the frame buffer. The term **scan conversion** derives from the notion that the programmer specifies endpoint or vertex coordinates in random-scan mode, and this information must be reduced by the system to pixels for display in raster-scan mode. Scan conversion is commonly done with software in personal computers and low-end workstations, where the microprocessor CPU is responsible for all graphics.

Another drawback of raster systems arises from the nature of the raster itself. Whereas a vector system can draw continuous, smooth lines (and even smooth curves) from essentially any point on the CRT face to any other, the raster system can display mathematically smooth lines, polygons, and boundaries of curved primitives such as circles and ellipses only by approximating them with pixels on the raster grid. This approximation can cause the familiar problem of "jaggies" or "staircasing," as shown in Fig. 1.10(c) and (d). This visual artifact is a manifestation of a sampling error called **aliasing** in signal-processing theory; such artifacts occur when a function of a continuous variable that contains sharp changes in intensity is approximated with discrete samples. Modern computer graphics is concerned with techniques for antialiasing on gray-scale or color systems. These

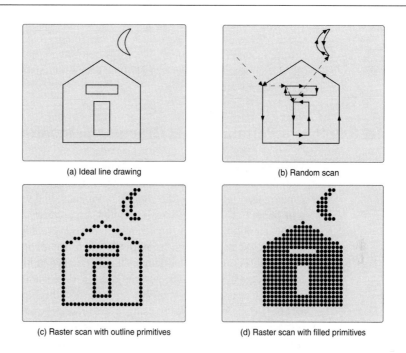

(a) Ideal line drawing   (b) Random scan

(c) Raster scan with outline primitives   (d) Raster scan with filled primitives

Figure 1.10   Random scan versus raster scan. We symbolize the screen as a rounded rectangle filled with a light gray shade that denotes the white background; the image is drawn in black on this background.

techniques specify gradations in intensity of neighboring pixels at edges of primitives, rather than set pixels to maximum or zero intensity only; see Chapter 3 for further discussion of this important topic.

1.2.2 Input Technology

Input technology has also improved greatly over the years. The clumsy, fragile light pen of vector systems has been replaced by the ubiquitous mouse (first developed by office-automation pioneer Doug Engelbart in the mid-sixties [ENGE68]); the data tablet; and the transparent, touch-sensitive panel mounted on the screen. Even fancier input devices that supply not just (x, y) locations on the screen, but also 3D and even higher-dimensional input values (degrees of freedom), are becoming common, as discussed in Chapter 8. Audio communication also has exciting potential, since it allows hands-free input and natural output of simple instructions, feedback, and so on. With the standard input devices, the user can specify operations or picture components by typing or drawing new information, or by pointing to existing information on the screen. These interactions require no knowledge of programming and only a little keyboard use: The user makes choices simply by selecting menu buttons or icons, answers questions by checking options or typing a few characters in a form, places copies of predefined symbols on the screen, draws by indicating consecutive endpoints to be connected by straight lines or interpolated by smooth curves, paints by moving the cursor over the screen, and fills closed areas bounded by polygons or paint contours with shades of gray, colors, or various patterns.

1.2.3 Software Portability and Graphics Standards

As we have seen, steady advances in hardware technology have made possible the evolution of graphics displays from one-of-a-kind special output devices to the standard user interface to the computer. We may well wonder whether software has kept pace. For example, to what extent have we resolved early difficulties with overly complex, cumbersome, and expensive graphics systems and application software? We have moved from low-level, device-dependent packages supplied by manufacturers for their particular display devices to higher-level, device-independent packages. These packages can drive a wide variety of display devices, from laser printers and plotters to film recorders and high-performance interactive displays. The main purpose of using a device-independent package in conjunction with a high-level programming language is to promote application-program portability. The package provides this portability in much the same way as does a high-level, machine-independent language (such as FORTRAN, Pascal, or C): by isolating the programmer from most machine peculiarities, and by providing language features readily implemented on a broad range of processors.

A general awareness of the need for standards in such device-independent graphics arose in the mid-seventies and culminated in a specification for a **3D Core Graphics System** (the Core, for short) produced by an **ACM SIGGRAPH**[1] Committee in 1977 [GSPC77], and refined in 1979 [GSPC79].

The Core specification fulfilled its intended role as a baseline specification. Not only did Core have many implementations, but it also was used as input to official (governmental) standards projects within both **ANSI** (the **American National Standards Institute**) and **ISO** (**the International Standards Organization**). The first graphics specification to be standardized officially was **GKS**, the **Graphical Kernel System** [ANSI85], an elaborated, cleaned-up version of the Core that, unlike the Core, was restricted to 2D. In 1988, **GKS-3D** [INTE88], a 3D extension of GKS, became an official standard, as did a much more sophisticated but even more complex graphics system called **PHIGS (Programmer's Hierarchical Interactive Graphics System** [ANSI88]). GKS supports the grouping of logically related primitives—such as lines, polygons, and character strings—and

---

[1] SIGGRAPH is the Special Interest Group on Graphics, one of the professional groups within the Association for Computing Machinery (ACM). ACM is one of the two major professional societies for computer professionals; the IEEE Computer Society is the other. SIGGRAPH publishes a research journal and sponsors an annual conference that features presentations of research papers in the field and an equipment exhibition. The IEEE Computer Society also publishes a research journal in graphics.

their attributes into collections called **segments**; these segments cannot be nested. PHIGS, as its name implies, does support nested hierarchical groupings of 3D sub-primitives, called **structures**. In PHIGS, all primitives, including invocations of structures, are subject to geometric transformations (scaling, rotation, and translation) to accomplish dynamic movement. PHIGS also supports a retained database of structures that the programmer can edit selectively; PHIGS automatically updates the screen whenever the database has been altered. PHIGS has been extended with a set of features for modern, pseudorealistic rendering[2] of objects on raster displays; this extension is called **PHIGS+** [PHIG88] prior to its submission to ANSI/ISO, and **PHIGS PLUS** within ISO [PHIG92]. PHIGS implementations are large packages, due to the many features and to the complexity of the specification. PHIGS and especially PHIGS PLUS implementations run fastest when there is hardware support for their transformation, clipping, and rendering features.

In addition to official standards promulgated by national, international or professional organization standards bodies, there are non-official standards. These so-called industry or de facto standards are developed, promoted, and licensed by individual companies or by consortia of companies and universities. Well-known industry graphics standards include Adobe's PostScript, Silicon Graphics' OpenGL, Ithaca Software's HOOPS, and the MIT-led X-Consortium's X Window System and its client-server protocol extensions for 3D graphics, PEX (see Chapter 7). Industry standards may be more prevalent and therefore more important commercially than official standards because they can be updated more rapidly, particularly those that are a key commercial product of a company and therefore have considerable resources behind them.

This book discusses graphics software standards at length. We first study, in Chapter 2, **SRGP** (the Simple Raster Graphics Package), which borrows features from Apple's popular QuickDraw integer raster graphics package [ROSE85] and MIT's X Window System [SCHE88] for output, and from GKS and PHIGS for input. Having looked at simple applications in this low-level raster graphics package, we then study the scan-conversion and clipping algorithms that such packages use to generate images of primitives in the frame buffer. Then, after building a mathematical foundation for 2D and 3D geometric transformations in Chapter 5, and for parallel and perspective viewing in 3D in Chapter 6, we study a far more powerful package called **SPHIGS** (Simple PHIGS) in Chapter 7. SPHIGS is a subset of PHIGS that operates on primitives defined in a floating-point, abstract, 3D world-coordinate system independent of any type of display technology, and that supports some simple PHIGS PLUS features. We orient our discussion to PHIGS and PHIGS PLUS because we believe that they will have much more influence on interactive 3D graphics than will GKS-3D, especially given the increasing availability of hardware that supports real-time transformations and rendering of pseudo realistic images.

---

[2] A *pseudorealistic rendering* is one that simulates the simple laws of optics describing how light is reflected by objects. *Photorealistic rendering* uses more accurate approximations to the way objects reflect and refract light; these approximations require more computation but produce images that are more nearly photographic in quality.

1.3 THE ADVANTAGES OF INTERACTIVE GRAPHICS

Graphics provides one of the most natural means of communicating with a computer, since our highly developed 2D and 3D pattern-recognition abilities allow us to perceive and process pictorial data rapidly and efficiently. In many design, implementation, and construction processes today, the information that pictures can give is virtually indispensable. Scientific visualization became an important field in the late 1980s, when scientists and engineers realized that they could not interpret the prodigious quantities of data produced by supercomputers without summarizing the data and highlighting trends and phenomena in various kinds of graphical representations.

Interactive computer graphics is the most important means of producing pictures since the invention of photography and television; it has the added advantage that, with the computer, we can make pictures not only of concrete, real-world objects, but also of abstract, synthetic objects and of data that have no inherent geometry, such as survey results. Furthermore, we are not confined to static images. Although static pictures are a good means of communicating information, dynamically varying pictures are frequently even more effective, especially for time-varying phenomena, both real (e.g., the deflection of an aircraft wing in supersonic flight, or the development of a human face from childhood through old age) and abstract (e.g., growth trends, such as nuclear energy use in the United States, or population movement from cities to suburbs and back to the cities).

With **motion dynamics,** objects can be moved and tumbled with respect to a stationary observer. The objects can also remain stationary and the viewer can move around them, pan to select the portion in view, and zoom in or out for more or less detail, as though looking through the viewfinder of a rapidly moving video camera. In many cases, both the objects and the camera are moving. A typical example is the flight simulator (Color Plates 4a and 4b), which combines a mechanical platform supporting a mock cockpit with display screens for windows. Computers control platform motion, gauges, and the simulated world of both stationary and moving objects through which the pilot navigates. Amusement parks also offer motion-simulator rides through simulated terrestrial and extraterrestrial landscapes. Video arcades offer graphics-based dexterity games and race car-driving simulators, video games exploiting interactive motion dynamics (see Color Plate 5).

Update dynamics is the actual change of the shape, color, or other properties of the objects being viewed, or modeled. For instance, a system can display the deformations of an airplane structure in flight or the state changes in a block diagram of a nuclear reactor in response to the operator's manipulation of graphical representations of the many control mechanisms. The smoother the change, the more realistic and meaningful the result.

Interactive computer graphics thus permits extensive, high-bandwidth user–computer interaction. Such interactions significantly enhance our ability to understand data, to perceive trends, and to visualize real or imaginary objects.

1.4 CONCEPTUAL FRAMEWORK FOR INTERACTIVE GRAPHICS

The high-level conceptual framework shown in Fig. 1.11 can be used to describe almost any interactive graphics system. At the hardware level (not shown explicitly in the diagram), a computer receives input from interaction devices, and outputs images to a display device. The software has three components. The first, the **application program**, creates, stores into, and retrieves from the second component, the **application model,** which represents the data or objects to be pictured on the screen. The application program also handles user input. This program produces views by sending to the third component, the **graphics system**, a series of graphics output commands that contain both a detailed geometric description of *what* is to be viewed and the attributes describing *how* the objects should appear. The graphics system is responsible for actually producing the picture from the detailed descriptions and for passing the user's input to the application program for processing.

The graphics system is thus an intermediary between the application program and the display hardware that effects an **output transformation** from objects in the application model to a view of the model. Symmetrically, it effects an **input transformation** from user actions to inputs to the application program that will cause the application to make changes in the model or picture. The fundamental task of the designer of an interactive graphics application program is to specify what classes of data items or objects are to be generated and represented pictorially, and how the user and the application program are to interact to create and modify the model and its visual representation. Most of the programmer's task concerns creating and editing the model and handling user interaction, rather than actually creating views, since that task is handled by the graphics system.

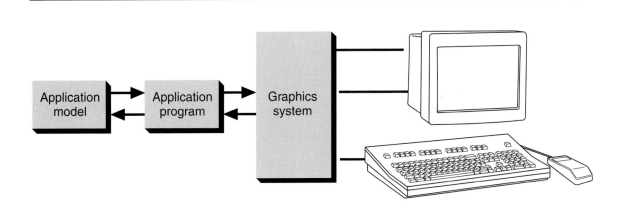

Figure 1.11   Conceptual framework for interactive graphics.

1.4.1 Application Modeling

The application model captures all the data and objects, as well as the relationships among them that are relevant to the display and interaction part of the application program and to any nongraphical postprocessing modules. Examples of such post processing modules are analyses of the transient behavior of a circuit or of the stresses in an aircraft wing, simulation of a population model or a weather system, and pricing computations for a building. In the class of applications typified by painting programs such as MacPaint and PCPaint, the intent of the program is to produce an image by letting the user set or modify individual pixels. Here, an explicit application model is not needed—the picture is both means and end, and the displayed bitmap or pixmap serves in effect as the application model.

More typically, however, there is an identifiable application model represent-ing application objects through a combination of data and procedural description that is independent of a particular display device. Procedural descriptions are used, for example, to define fractals, as described in Section 14.11. A data model can be as rudimentary as an array of data points or as complex as a linked list representing a network data structure or a relational database storing a set of relations. We often speak of storing the **application model** in the **application database;** the terms are used interchangeably here. Models typically store descriptions of primitives (points, lines, curves, and polygons in 2D or 3D, and polyhedra and free-form sur-faces in 3D) that define the shape of components of the object; object **attributes** such as line style, color, or surface texture; and **connectivity** relationships and positioning data that describe how the components fit together.

Geometric data in the application model often are accompanied by nongeo-metric textual or numeric property information useful to a postprocessing program or to the interactive user. Examples of such data in CAD applications include man-ufacturing data; price and supplier data; thermal, mechanical, electrical, or elec-tronic properties; and mechanical or electrical tolerances.

1.4.2 Display of the Model

The application program creates the application model either as a result of prior computation, as in an engineering or scientific simulation on a supercomputer, or as part of an interactive session at the display device during which the user guides the construction process step by step to choose components and geometric and nongeometric property data. The user can ask the application program at any time to show a view of the model that it has created so far. (The word *view* is used inten-tionally here, both in the sense of a visual rendering of geometric properties of the objects being modeled and in the technical database sense of a 2D presentation of properties of a subset of the model.)

Models are application-specific and are created independently of any particu-lar display system. Therefore, the application program must convert a description of the portion of the model to be viewed from the internal representation of the geometry (whether stored explicitly in the model or derived on the fly) to whatever procedure calls or commands the graphics system uses to create an image. This conversion process has two phases. First, the application program traverses the application database that stores the model in order to extract the portions to be viewed, using some selection or query criteria. Then, the extracted data or geometry, plus attributes, are converted to a format that can be sent to the graphics system. The selection criteria can be geometric (e.g., the portion of the model to be viewed has been shifted via the graphics equivalent of a pan or zoom camera operation), or they can be similar to traditional database query criteria.

The data extracted during the database traversal must either be geometric or converted to geometric data; the data can be described to the graphics system in terms of both the primitives that the system can display directly and the attributes that control the primitives' appearance. Display primitives typically match those stored in geometric models: lines, rectangles, polygons, circles, ellipses, and text in 2D; and polygons, polyhedra, and text in 3D.

The graphics system typically consists of a set of output subroutines corresponding to the various primitives, attributes, and other elements. These are collected in a **graphics-subroutine library** or **package** that can be called from high-level languages such as C, Pascal, or LISP. The application program specifies geometric primitives and attributes to these subroutines, and the subroutines then drive the specific display device and cause it to display the image. Much as conventional I/O systems create logical I/O units to shield the application programmer from the messy details of hardware and device drivers, graphics systems create a **logical display device**. This abstraction of the display device pertains both to the output of images and to interaction via logical input devices. For example, the mouse, data tablet, touch panel, 2D joystick, or trackball can each be treated as the **locator** logical input device that returns an (x, y) screen location. The application program can ask the graphics system either to **sample** the input devices (i.e., ask their current values) or to wait at a specified point until an **event** is generated when the user activates a device being waited on.

1.4.3 Interaction Handling

The typical application-program schema for interaction handling is the **event-driven loop**. It is easily visualized as a finite-state machine with a central wait state and transitions to other states that are caused by user-input events. Processing a command may entail nested event loops of the same format that have their own states and input transitions. An application program may also sample input devices such as the locator by asking for their values at any time; the program then uses the returned value as input to a processing procedure that also changes the state of the application program, the image, or the database. The event-driven loop is characterized by the following pseudocode schema:

```
generate initial display, derived from application model as appropriate
do {
    enable selection of commands or objects
    /* Program pauses indefinitely in wait state until user acts */
    wait for user selection
```

```
switch ( on selection ) {
    process selection to complete command or process completed command,
    updating model and screen as needed
}
}
while ( !quit )  /* User has not selected the "quit" option */
```

Let us examine the application's reaction to input in more detail. The application program typically responds to user interactions in one of two modes. First, the user action may require only that the screen be updated—for example, the system may respond by highlighting a selected object or by making available a new menu of choices. The application then needs only to update its internal state and to call the graphics package to update the screen; it does not need to update the database. If, however, the user action calls for a change in the model—for example, addition or deletion of a component—the application must update the model and then call the graphics package to update the screen from the model. Either the entire model is retraversed to regenerate the image from scratch or, with more sophisticated incremental-update algorithms, the screen is updated selectively. It is important to understand that no significant change can take place in the objects on the screen without a corresponding change in the model. The screen is indeed the window on the computer in that the user, in general, is manipulating not an image, but rather the model that is literally and figuratively behind the image. Only in painting and image-enhancement applications are the model and the image identical. Therefore, it is the application's job to interpret user input. The graphics system has no responsibility for building or modifying the model, either initially or in response to user interaction; its only job is to create images from geometric descriptions and to pass along the user's input data.

The event-loop model, although fundamental to current practice in computer graphics, is limited in that the user–computer dialogue is a *sequential*, ping-pong model of alternating user actions and computer reactions. In the future, we may expect to see more of *parallel* conversations, in which simultaneous input and output using multiple communications channels—for example, both graphics and voice—take place. Formalisms, not to mention programming-language constructs, for such free-form conversations are not yet well developed; we shall not discuss them further here.

SUMMARY

Graphical interfaces have replaced textual interfaces as the standard means for user–computer interaction. Graphics has also become a key technology for communicating ideas, data, and trends in most areas of commerce, science, engineering, and education. With graphics, we can create artificial (or virtual) worlds, each a computer-based exploratorium for examining objects and phenomena in a natural and intuitive way that exploits our highly developed skills in visual pattern recognition.

Until the late eighties, the bulk of computer-graphics applications dealt with 2D objects; 3D applications were relatively rare, both because 3D software is intrinsically far more complex than is 2D software and because a great deal of computing power is required to render pseudorealistic images. Therefore, until recently, real-time user interaction with 3D models and pseudorealistic images was feasible on only extremely expensive high-performance workstations with dedicated, special-purpose graphics hardware. The spectacular progress of VLSI semiconductor technology that was responsible for the advent of inexpensive microprocessors and memory led in the early eighties to the creation of personal-computer interfaces based on 2D bitmap graphics. That same technology has made it possible, less than a decade later, to create subsystems of only a few chips that do real-time 3D animation with color-shaded images of complex objects, typically described by thousands of polygons. These subsystems can be added as 3D accelerators to workstations or even to personal computers that use commodity microprocessors. It is clear that an explosive growth of 3D applications will parallel the current growth in 2D applications. Furthermore, topics such as photorealistic rendering, which once were considered exotic, are now part of the state of the art and are available routinely in graphics software and increasingly in graphics hardware.

Much of the task of creating effective graphic communication, whether 2D or 3D, lies in modeling the objects whose images we want to produce. The graphics system acts as the intermediary between the application model and the output device. The application program is responsible for creating and updating the model based on user interaction; the graphics system does the best-understood, most routine part of the job when it creates views of objects and passes user events to the application. The growing literature on various types of physically based modeling shows that graphics is evolving to include a great deal more than rendering and interaction handling. Images and animations are no longer merely illustrations in science and engineering—they have become part of the content of science and engineering and are influencing how scientists and engineers conduct their daily work.

Exercises

1.1   List the interactive graphics programs you use on a routine basis in your knowledge work: writing, calculating, graphing, programming, debugging, and so on. Which of these programs would work almost as well on an alphanumerics-only terminal? Which would be nearly useless without graphics capability? Explain your answers.

1.2   The phrase **look and feel** has been applied extensively to the user interface of graphics programs. Itemize the major components—such as icons, windows, scroll bars, and menus—of the look of the graphics interface of your favorite word-processing or window-manager program. List the graphics capabilities that these components require. What opportunities do you see for applying color and 3D depictions to the look? For example, how might a "cluttered office" be a more powerful spatial metaphor for organizing and accessing information than is a "messy desktop"?

1.3   In a vein similar to that of Exercise 1.2, what opportunities do you see for dynamic icons to augment or even to replace the static icons of current desktop metaphors?

1.4   Break down your favorite graphics application into its major modules, using the conceptual model of Fig. 1.11 as a guide. How much of the application actually deals with graphics per se? How much deals with data-structure creation and maintenance? How much deals with calculations, such as simulation?

1.5   The terms *simulation* and *animation* are often used together and even interchangeably in computer graphics. This usage is natural when we are visualizing the behavioral (or structural) changes over time in a physical or abstract system. Construct three examples of systems that could benefit from such visualizations. Specify what form the simulations would take and how they would be executed. Give an example that distinguishes a *simulation* from an *animation*.

1.6   As a variation on Exercise 1.5, create a high-level design of a graphical exploratorium for a nontrivial topic in science, mathematics, or engineering. Discuss how the interaction sequences would work and what facilities the user should have for experimentation.

1.7   Without peeking at Chapter 3, construct a straightforward algorithm for scan converting a line in the first quadrant, whose slope is less than or equal to 45°.

1.8   Aliasing is a serious problem in that it produces unpleasant or even misleading visual artifacts. Name situations in which these artifacts matter, and those situations in which they do not. Discuss various ways to minimize the effects of jaggies, and explain what the "costs" of those remedies might be.

2 Programming in the Simple Raster Graphics Package (SRGP)

In Chapter 1, we saw that vector and raster displays are two substantially different hardware technologies for creating images on the screen. Raster displays are the dominant hardware technology, because they support several features that are essential to the majority of modern applications. First, raster displays can fill areas with a uniform color or a repeated pattern in two or more colors; vector displays can, at best, only simulate filled areas with closely spaced sequences of parallel vectors. Second, raster displays store images in a way that allows manipulation at a fine level: Individual pixels can be read or written, and arbitrary portions of the image can be copied or moved.

The first graphics package we discuss, **SRGP** (Simple Raster Graphics Package), is device-independent and exploits raster capabilities. SRGP's repertoire of primitives (lines, rectangles, circles and ellipses, and text strings) is similar to that of the popular Macintosh QuickDraw raster package and that of the Xlib package of the X Window System. SRGP's interaction-handling features, on the other hand, are a subset of those of SPHIGS, the higher-level graphics package for displaying 3D primitives (covered in Chapter 7). SPHIGS (Simple PHIGS) is a simplified dialect of the standard PHIGS graphics package (Programmer's Hierarchical Interactive Graphics System) designed for both raster and vector hardware. Although SRGP and SPHIGS were written specifically for this text, they are also very much in the spirit of mainstream graphics packages, and most of what you will learn here is immediately applicable to commercial packages. In this book, we introduce both packages; for a more complete description, you should consult the reference manuals distributed with the software packages.

We start our discussion of SRGP by examining the operations that applications perform in order to draw on the screen: the specification of primitives and of

21

the attributes that affect their image. (Since graphics printers display information essentially as raster displays do, we need not concern ourselves with them until we look more closely at hardware in Chapter 4.) Next we learn how to make applications interactive by using SRGP's input functions. Then we cover the utility of pixel manipulation, available only in raster displays. We conclude by discussing some limitations of integer raster graphics packages such as SRGP.

Although our discussion of SRGP assumes that it controls the entire screen, the package has been designed to run in window environments (see Chapter 10), in which case it controls the interior of a window as though it were a virtual screen. The application programmer therefore need not be concerned about the details of running under control of a window manager.

2.1 DRAWING WITH SRGP

2.1.1 Specification of Graphics Primitives

Drawing in integer raster graphics packages such as SRGP is like plotting graphs on graph paper with a very fine grid. The grid varies from 80 to 120 points per inch on conventional displays to 300 or more on high-resolution displays. The higher the resolution, the better the appearance of fine detail. Figure 2.1 shows a display screen (or the surface of a printer's paper or film) ruled in SRGP's integer Cartesian coordinate system. Note that pixels in SRGP lie at the intersection of grid lines.

The origin (0, 0) is at the bottom left of the screen; positive x increases toward the right and positive y increases toward the top. The pixel at the upper-right corner is (width−1, height−1), where width and height are the device-dependent dimensions of the screen.

On graph paper, we can draw a continuous line between two points located anywhere on the paper; on raster displays, however, we can draw lines only between grid points, and a line must be approximated by intensifying the grid-point pixels lying on it or near to it. Similarly, solid figures such as filled polygons or circles are created by intensifying the pixels in their interiors and on their boundaries. Since specifying each pixel of a line or a closed figure would be far too onerous, graphics packages let the programmer specify primitives such as lines and polygons via their vertices; the package then fills in the details using scan-conversion algorithms, discussed in Chapter 3.

SRGP supports a basic collection of primitives: lines, polygons, circles and ellipses, and text.[1] To specify a primitive, the application sends the coordinates defining the primitive's shape to the appropriate SRGP primitive-generator function. It is legal for a specified point to lie outside the screen's bounded rectangular area; of course, only those portions of a primitive that lie inside the screen bounds will be visible.

---

[1] Specialized functions that draw a single pixel or an array of pixels are described in the SRGP reference manual.

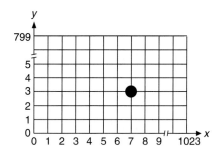

Figure 2.1 Cartesian coordinate system of a screen 1024 pixels wide by 800 pixels high. Pixel (7, 3) is shown.

We use ANSI C with the following typesetting conventions. C keywords, built-in types, and user-defined types are in boldface. Variables used in the text body are italicized. Symbolic constants are in uppercase type. Comments are inside /*…*/ delimiters, and pseudocode is italicized. For brevity, declarations of constants and variables are omitted when obvious. Boolean variables are of type **unsigned char** with TRUE and FALSE being defined as 1 and 0, respectively. Once defined, new types such as **point**, will be used in later code fragments without restatement.

Lines and polylines. The following SRGP function draws a line from $(x1, y1)$ to $(x2, y2)$:

```
void SRGP_lineCoord ( int x1, int y1, int x2, int y2 );
```

Thus, to plot a line from (0, 0) to (100, 300), we simply call

```
SRGP_lineCoord (0, 0, 100, 300);
```

Because it is often more natural to think in terms of endpoints rather than of individual x and y coordinates, SRGP provides an alternative line-drawing function:

```
void SRGP_line ( point pt1, point pt2 );
```

Here "point" is a defined type, a struct of two integers holding the point's x and y values:

```
typedef struct {
    int x, y;
} point;
```

A sequence of lines connecting successive vertices is called a **polyline**. Although polylines can be created by repeated calls to the line-drawing functions, SRGP includes them as a special case. There are two polyline functions, analogous to the

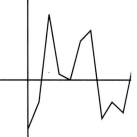

Figure 2.2
Graphing a data array.

coordinate and point forms of the line-drawing functions. These take arrays as parameters:

> **void** SRGP_polyLineCoord (**int** vertexCount, **vertexCoordinateList** xArray,
>   **vertexCoordinateList** yArray);
> **void** SRGP_polyLine (**int** vertexCount, **vertexList** vertices);

where *vertexCoordinateList* and *vertexList* are types defined by the SRGP package—arrays of integers and points, respectively.

The first parameter in both of these polyline calls tells SRGP how many vertices to expect. In the first call, the second and third parameters are integer arrays of paired *x* and *y* values, and the polyline is drawn from vertex (xArray[0], yArray[0]), to vertex (xArray[1], yArray[1]), to vertex (xArray[2], yArray[2]), and so on. This form is convenient, for instance, when plotting data on a standard set of axes, where *xArray* is a predetermined set of values of the independent variable and *yArray* is the set of data being computed or input by the user.

As an example, let us plot the output of an economic analysis program that computes month-by-month trade figures and stores them in the 12-entry integer data array *balanceOfTrade*. We will start our plot at (200, 200). To be able to see the differences between successive points, we will graph them 10 pixels apart on the *x* axis. Thus, we will create an integer array, *months*, to represent the 12 months, and will set the entries to the desired *x* values, 200, 210,..., 310. Similarly, we must increment each value in the data array by 200 to put the twelve *y* coordinates in the right place. Then, the graph in Fig. 2.2 is plotted with the following code:

```
/* Plot the axes */
SRGP_lineCoord (175, 200, 320, 200);
SRGP_lineCoord (200, 140, 200, 280);

/* Plot the data */
SRGP_polyLineCoord (12, months, balanceOfTrade);
```

We can use the second polyline form to draw shapes by specifying pairs of *x* and *y* values together as points, passing an array of such points to SRGP. We create the bowtie shape in Fig. 2.3 by calling

```
SRGP_polyLine (7, bowtieArray);
```

The table in Fig. 2.3 shows how *bowtieArray* was defined.

Markers and polymarkers.   It is often convenient to place *markers* (e.g., dots, asterisks, or circles) at the data points on graphs. SRGP therefore offers companions to the line and polyline functions. The following functions will create a marker symbol centered at (*x*, y):

> **void** SRGP_markerCoord (**int** x, **int** y);
> **void** SRGP_marker (**point** pt);

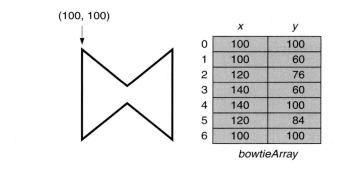

(100, 100)

	x	y
0	100	100
1	100	60
2	120	76
3	140	60
4	140	100
5	120	84
6	100	100

bowtieArray

Figure 2.3   Drawing a polyline.

The marker's style and size can be changed as well, as will be explained in Section 2.1.2. To create a sequence of identical markers at a set of points, we call either of

> **void** SRGP_polyMarkerCoord(**int** vertexCount, **vertexCoordinateList** xArray,
>   **vertexCoordinateList** yArray);
> **void** SRGP_polyMarker (**int** vertexCount, **vertexList** vertices);

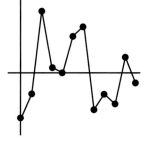

Figure 2.4
Graphing the data array
using markers.

Thus, the following additional call will add markers to the graph of Fig. 2.2 to produce Fig. 2.4:

> SRGP_polyMarkerCoord (12, months, balanceOfTrade);

Polygons and rectangles.   To draw an outline polygon, we either can specify a polyline that closes on itself, by making the first and last vertices identical (as we did to draw the bowtie in Fig. 2.3), or we can use the following specialized SRGP call:

> **void** SRGP_polygon (**int** vertexCount, **vertexList** vertices);

This call automatically closes the figure by drawing a line from the last vertex to the first. To draw the bowtie in Fig. 2.3 as a polygon, we use the following call, where bowtieArray is now an array of only six points:

> SRGP_polygon (6, bowtieArray);

Any rectangle can be specified as a polygon having four vertices, but an upright rectangle (one whose edges are parallel to the screen's edges) can also be specified with the SRGP *rectangle* primitive using only two vertices (the lower-left and the upper-right corners):

> **void** SRGP_rectangleCoord (**int** leftX, **int** bottomY, **int** rightX, **int** topY);
> **void** SRGP_rectanglePt (**point** bottomLeft, **point** topRight);
> **void** SRGP_rectangle (**rectangle** rect);

The *rectangle* struct stores the bottom-left and top-right corners:

```
typedef struct {
    point  bottomLeft, topRight;
} rectangle;
```

Thus the following call draws an upright rectangle 101 pixels wide and 151 pixels high:

```
SRGP_rectangleCoord (50, 25, 150, 175);
```

SRGP provides the following utilities for creating rectangles and points from coordinate data.

```
point SRGP_defPoint ( int x, int y );
rectangle SRGP_defRectangle ( int leftX, int bottomY, int rightX, int topY );
```

Our example rectangle could thus have been drawn by

```
rect = SRGP_defRectangle ( 50, 25, 150, 175 );
SRGP_rectangle (rect);
```

Circles and ellipses.   Figure 2.5 shows circular and elliptical arcs drawn by SRGP. Since circles are a special case of ellipses, we use the term **ellipse arc** for all these forms, whether circular or elliptical, closed or partial arcs. SRGP can draw only standard ellipses, those whose major and minor axes are parallel to the coordinate axes.

Although there are many mathematically equivalent methods for specifying ellipse arcs, it is convenient for the programmer to specify arcs via the upright rectangles in which they are inscribed (Fig. 2.6); these upright rectangles are called *bounding boxes* or *extents*.

The general ellipse function is

```
void SRGP_ellipseArc ( rectangle extentRect, float startAngle, float endAngle );
```

The width and height of the extent determine the shape of the ellipse. Whether the arc is closed depends on a pair of angles that specify where the arc starts and

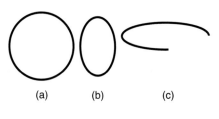

(a)   (b)   (c)

Figure 2.5   Drawings of ellipse arcs. (a) Circular, (b) Elliptical closed, (c) Elliptical.

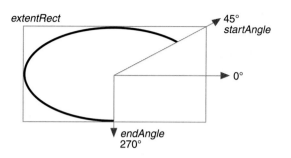

Figure 2.6   Specifying ellipse arcs.

ends. For convenience, each angle is measured in *rectangular degrees* that run counterclockwise, with 0° corresponding to the positive portion of the *x* axis, 90° to the positive portion of the *y* axis, and 45° to the "diagonal" extending from the origin to the top-right corner of the rectangle. Clearly, rectangular degrees are equivalent to circular degrees only if the extent is a square. The general relationship between rectangular angles and circular angles is

$$rectangular\ angle = \arctan\left(\tan(\ circular\ angle\ ) \cdot \frac{width}{height}\right) + adjust\ ,$$

where the angles are in radians, and

$$adjust \quad = \quad 0,\ \text{for}\ \ 0 \leq circular\ angle < \frac{\pi}{2}$$

$$adjust \quad = \quad \pi,\ \text{for}\ \ \frac{\pi}{2} \leq circular\ angle < \frac{3\pi}{2}$$

$$adjust \quad = \quad 2\pi,\ \text{for}\ \ \frac{3\pi}{2} \leq circular\ angle < 2\pi\ .$$

2.1.2 Attributes

Line style and line width.   The appearance of a primitive can be controlled by specification of its **attributes.**[2] The SRGP attributes that apply to lines, polylines, polygons, rectangles, and ellipse arcs are *line style*, *line width*, *color*, and *pen style*.

Attributes are set *modally*; that is, they are global state variables that retain their values until they are changed explicitly. Primitives are drawn with the attributes in effect at the time the primitives are specified; therefore, changing an attribute's value in no way affects previously created primitives—only those that are specified after the change in attribute value are affected. Modal attributes are convenient because they spare programmers from having to specify a long list of

---

[2] The descriptions here of SRGP's attributes often lack fine detail, particularly on interactions between different attributes. The detail is omitted because the exact effect of an attribute is a function of its implementation, and, for performance reasons, different implementations are used on different systems; for these details, consult the implementation-specific reference manuals.

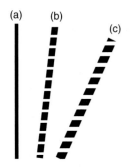

(a)   (b)

(c)

Figure 2.7
Lines of various widths and
styles.

parameters for each primitive (there may be dozens of different attributes in a production system).

Line style and line width are set by calls to

void SRGP_setLineStyle (**lineStyle** CONTINUOUS / DASHED / DOTTED / ...);[3]
void SRGP_setLineWidth (**int** widthValue);

The width of a line is measured in screen units—that is, in pixels. Each attribute has a default: line style is CONTINUOUS, and width is 1. Figure 2.7 shows lines in a variety of widths and styles; the code that generated the figure is shown in Prog. 2.1.

We can think of line style as a bit mask used to write pixels selectively as the primitive is scan-converted by SRGP. A zero in the mask indicates that this pixel should not be written and thus preserves its original value in the frame buffer. One can think of this pixel of the line as transparent, in that it lets the original pixel *underneath* show through. CONTINUOUS thus corresponds to the string of all 1s, and DASHED to the string 1111001111001111[....], the dash being twice as long as the transparent interdash segments.

Each attribute has a default; for example, the default for line style is CONTINUOUS, that for line width is 1, and so on. In the early code examples, we did not set the line style for the first line we drew; thus, we made use of the line-style default. In practice, however, making assumptions about the current state of attributes is not safe, and in the code examples that follow, we set attributes explicitly in each function, so as to make the functions modular and thus to facilitate debugging and maintenance. In Section 2.1.4, we will see that it is even safer for the programmer to save and restore attributes explicitly for each function.

Program 2.1

Code used to generate Fig. 2.7.

```
SRGP_setLineWidth (5);
SRGP_lineCoord (55, 5, 55, 295);          /* Line a */
SRGP_setLineStyle(DASHED);
SRGP_setLineWidth(10);
SRGP_lineCoord(105, 5, 155, 295);         /* Line b */
SRGP_setLineWidth(15);
SRGP_setLineStyle(DOTTED);
SRGP_lineCoord(155, 5, 285, 255);         /* Line c */
```

Attributes that can be set for the marker primitive are

void SRGP_setMarkerSize (**int** sizeValue);
void SRGP_setMarkerStyle (**markerStyle** MARKER_CIRCLE
        / MARKER_SQUARE / ...);

Marker size specifies in pixels the length of the sides of the square extent of each marker. The complete set of marker styles is presented in the reference manual; the circle style is the default shown in Fig. 2.4.

---

[3] Here and in the following text, we use a shorthand notation. In SRGP, these symbolic constants are actually values of an enumerated data type **lineStyle**.

Color.   Each of the attributes presented so far affects only some of the SRGP primitives, but the integer-valued color attribute affects all primitives. Obviously, the meaning of color attribute depends heavily on the underlying hardware; the two color values found on every system are 0 and 1. On bilevel systems, the appearance of the colors is easy to predict: color-1 pixels are black and color-0 pixels are white for black-on-white devices, green is 1 and black is 0 for green-on-black devices, and so on.

The integer color attribute does not specify a color directly; rather, it is an index into SRGP's **color table**, each entry of which defines a color or gray-scale value in a manner that the SRGP programmer need not know. There are 2^d entries in the color table, where d is the *depth* (number of bits stored for each pixel) of the frame buffer. On bilevel implementations, the color table is hardwired; on most color implementations, however, SRGP allows the application to modify the table. See the reference manual for details. Some of the uses for the indirectness provided by color tables are explored in Chapter 4.

An application can use either of two methods to specify colors. An application for which machine independence is important should use the integers 0 and 1 directly; the application will then run on all bilevel and color displays. If the application assumes color support or is written for a particular display device, it can use the implementation-dependent *color names* supported by SRGP. These names are symbolic integer constants that show where certain standard colors have been placed within the default color table for that display device. For instance, a black-on-white implementation provides the two color names COLOR_BLACK (1) and COLOR_WHITE (0); we use these two values in the sample code fragments in this chapter. Note that color names are not useful to applications that modify the color table. We select a color by calling

void SRGP_setColor (**int** colorIndex);

2.1.3 Filled Primitives and Their Attributes

Primitives that enclose areas (the so-called *area-defining* primitives) can be drawn in two ways: *outlined* or *filled*. The functions described in the preceding section generate the former style: closed outlines with unfilled interiors. SRGP's filled versions of area-defining primitives draw the interior pixels with no outline. Figure 2.8 shows SRGP's repertoire of filled primitives, including the filled ellipse arc, or *pie slice*, in part (b).

Note that SRGP does not draw a contrasting outline, such as a 1-pixel-thick solid boundary, around the interior; applications wanting such an outline must draw it explicitly. There is also a subtle issue of whether pixels on the border of an area-defining primitive should actually be drawn, that is, whether only pixels that lie strictly in the interior should be drawn. This problem will be discussed in detail in Section 3.4.

To generate a filled polygon, we use *SRGP_fillPolygon* or *SRGP_fillPolygonCoord,* with the same parameter lists used in the unfilled versions of these calls. We define the other area-filling primitives in the same way, by prefixing "fill"

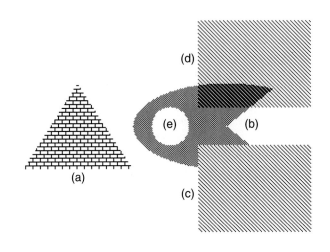

Figure 2.8   Bitmap patterns of filled primitives. (a–c) Opaque. (d) Transparent. (e) Solid.

Program 2.2

Code used to generate Fig. 2.8.

```
SRGP_setFillStyle(BITMAP_PATTERN_OPAQUE);
SRGP_setFillBitmapPattern(BRICK_BIT_PATTERN);            /* Brick pattern */
SRGP_fillPolygon(3, triangle_coords);                   /* a */

SRGP_setFillBitmapPattern(MEDIUM_GRAY_BIT_PATTERN);     /* 50 percent gray */
SRGP_fillEllipseArc(ellipseArcRect, 60.0, 290);         /* b */

SRGP_setFillBitmapPattern(DIAGONAL_BIT_PATTERN);
SRGP_fillRectangle(opaqueFilledRect);                   /* c */

SRGP_setFillStyle(BITMAP_PATTERN_TRANSPARENT);
SRGP_fillRectangle(transparentFilledRect);              /* d */

SRGP_setFillStyle(SOLID);
SRGP_setColor(COLOR_WHITE);
SRGP_fillEllipse(circleRect);                           /* e */
```

to their names. Since polygons may be concave or even self-intersecting, we need a rule for specifying which regions are interior, and thus should be filled, and which are exterior. SRGP polygons follow the *odd-parity* rule. To determine whether a region lies inside or outside a given polygon, choose as a test point any point inside the particular region. Next, choose a ray that starts at the test point, extends infinitely in any direction, and does not pass through any vertices. If this ray intersects the polygon outline an odd number of times, the region is considered to be interior (Fig. 2.9).

SRGP does not actually perform this test for each pixel while drawing; rather, this package uses the optimized polygon scan-conversion technique described in

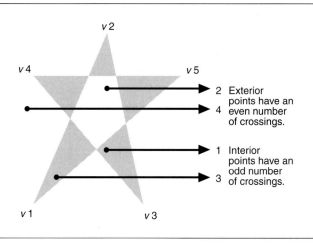

Figure 2.9   Odd-parity rule for determining interior of a polygon.

Chapter 3, in which the odd-parity rule is efficiently applied to an entire span of adjacent pixels which lie either inside or outside. Also, the odd-parity ray-intersection test is used in a process called **pick correlation** to determine the object a user is selecting with the cursor, as described in Chapter 7.

Fill style and fill pattern for areas.   The fill-style attribute can be used to control the appearance of a filled primitive's interior in four different ways, using

> **void** SRGP_setFillStyle (**drawStyle** SOLID / BITMAP_PATTERN_OPAQUE /
> BITMAP_PATTERN_TRANSPARENT / PIXMAP_PATTERN);

The first option, SOLID, produces a primitive uniformly filled with the current value of the color attribute (Fig. 2.8e, with color set to COLOR_WHITE). The second two options, BITMAP_PATTERN_OPAQUE and BITMAP_PATTERN_-TRANSPARENT, fill primitives with a regular, nonsolid pattern, the former rewriting all pixels underneath in either the current color or in another color (Fig. 2.8c), the latter rewriting some pixels underneath the primitive in the current color but letting others show through (Fig. 2.8d). The last option, PIXMAP_PATTERN, writes patterns containing an arbitrary number of colors, always in opaque mode.

Bitmap fill patterns are bitmap arrays of 1s and 0s chosen from a table of available patterns by specifying

> **void** SRGP_setFillBitmapPattern (**int** patternIndex);

Each entry in the pattern table stores a unique pattern; the ones provided with SRGP, shown in the reference manual, include gray-scale tones (ranging from nearly black to nearly white) and various regular and random patterns. In transparent mode, these patterns are generated as follows. Consider any pattern in the pattern table as a small bitmap—say, 8 by 8—to be repeated as needed (*tiled*) to fill the primitive. On a bilevel system, the current color (in effect, the *foreground* color) is written where there are 1s in the pattern; where there are 0s—the *holes*—the corresponding pixels of the original image are not written, and thus *show through* the partially transparent primitive written on top. Thus, the bitmap pattern acts as a *memory write-enable mask* for patterns in transparent mode, much as the line-style bit mask did for lines and outline primitives.

In the more commonly used BITMAP_PATTERN_OPAQUE mode, the 1s are written in the current color, but the 0s are written in another color, the *background color*, previously set by

    void SRGP_setBackgroundColor (**int** colorIndex);

On bilevel displays, each bitmap pattern in OPAQUE mode can generate only two distinctive fill patterns. For example, a bitmap pattern of mostly 1s can be used on a black-and-white display to generate a dark-gray fill pattern if the current color is set to black (and the background to white), and a light-gray fill pattern if the current color is set to white (and the background to black). On a color display, any combination of a foreground and a background color may be used for a variety of two-tone effects. A typical application on a bilevel display always sets the background color whenever it sets the foreground color, since opaque bitmap patterns are not visible if the two are equal; an application could create a SetColor function to set the background color automatically to contrast with the foreground whenever the foreground color is set explicitly.

Figure 2.8 was created by the code fragment shown in Prog. 2.2. The advantage of having two-tone bitmap patterns is that the colors are not specified explicitly, but rather are determined by the color attributes in effect, and thus can be generated in any color combination. The disadvantage, and the reason that SRGP also supports pixmap patterns, is that only two colors can be generated. Often, we would like to fill an area of a display with more than two colors, in an explicitly specified pattern. In the same way that a bitmap pattern is a small bitmap used to tile the primitive, a small pixmap can be used to tile the primitive, where the pixmap is a pattern array of color-table indices. Since each pixel is explicitly set in the pixmap, there is no concept of holes, and therefore there is no distinction between transparent and opaque filling modes. To fill an area with a color pattern, we select a fill style of PIXMAP_PATTERN and use the corresponding pixmap pattern-selection function:

    void SRGP_setFillPixmapPattern (**int** patternIndex);

Since both bitmap and pixmap patterns generate pixels with color values that are indices into the current color table, the appearance of filled primitives changes if the programmer modifies the color-table entries. The SRGP reference manual discusses how to change or add to both the bitmap and pixmap pattern tables. Also, although SRGP provides default entries in the bitmap pattern table, it does not give a default pixmap pattern table, since there is an indefinite number of color pixmap patterns that might be useful.

Application screen background. We have defined **background color** as the color of the 0 bits in bitmap patterns used in opaque mode, but the term *background* is used in another, unrelated way. Typically, the user expects the screen to display primitives on some uniform *application screen background pattern* that covers an opaque window or the entire screen. The application screen background pattern is often solid color 0, since SRGP initializes the screen to that color upon initialization. However, the background pattern is sometimes nonsolid or solid of some other color; in these cases, the application is responsible for setting up the application screen background by drawing a full-screen rectangle of the desired pattern, before drawing any other primitives.

A common technique to *erase* primitives is to redraw them in the application screen background pattern, rather than to redraw the entire image each time a primitive is deleted. However, this *quick-and-dirty* updating technique yields a damaged image when the erased primitive overlaps with other primitives.

For example, assume that the screen background pattern in Fig. 2.8 is solid white and that we erase the rectangle in part (c) by redrawing it using solid COLOR_WHITE. This technique would leave a white gap in the filled ellipse arc (part b) underneath. *Damage repair* involves going back to the application database and respecifying primitives (see Exercise 2.8).

2.1.4 Saving and Restoring Attributes

As you can see, SRGP supports a variety of attributes for its various primitives. Attributes can be saved for later restoration; this feature is especially useful in designing application functions that perform their actions without side effects— that is, without affecting the global attribute state. For convenience, SRGP allows the inquiry and restoration of the entire set of attributes—called the *attribute group*—via

```
void  SRGP_inquireAttributes ( attributeGroup *group );
void  SRGP_setAttributes ( attributeGroup group );
```

The application program has access to all fields of the SRGP-defined "attribute-Group" record so the record returned by the inquiry function can be used later for selective restoration.

2.1.5 Text

Specifying and implementing text drawing is always complex in a graphics package because of the large number of options and attributes text can have. Among these are the style or **font** of the characters (Times, Helvetica, Bodoni, etc.), their appearance (roman, **bold**, *italic*, underlined, etc.), their size (typically measured in **points**[4]) and widths, the intercharacter spacing, the spacing between consecutive lines, the angle at which characters are drawn (horizontal, vertical, or at a specified angle), and so on.

[4] A point is a unit commonly used in the publishing industry; it is equal to approximately 1/72 inch.

The most rudimentary facility, typically found in simple hardware and software, is fixed-width, monospace character spacing, in which all characters occupy the same width and have equal spacing between them. At the other end of the spectrum, proportional spacing varies both the width of characters and the spacing between them to make the text legible and aesthetically pleasing. Books, magazines, and newspapers all use proportional spacing, as do most raster graphics displays and laser printers. SRGP provides in-between functionality: Text is horizontally aligned and character widths vary, but space between characters is constant. With this simple form of proportional spacing, the application can annotate graphics diagrams, interact with the user via textual menus, dialog boxes, and fill-in forms, and even implement simple word processors. Text-intensive applications, however, such as desktop-publishing programs for high-quality documents, need specialized packages that offer more control over text specification and attributes than does SRGP. PostScript [ADOB85] offers many such advanced features and has become an industry standard for describing text and other primitives with a large variety of options and attributes. Text in SRGP is generated by a call to

> **void** SRGP_text (**point** origin, **char** *text);

The location of a text primitive is controlled by specification of its **origin**, also known as its **anchor point.** The x coordinate of the origin marks the left edge of the first character, and the y coordinate specifies where the baseline of the string should appear. (The **baseline** is the hypothetical line on which characters rest, as shown in the textual menu button of Fig. 2.10. Some characters, such as "y" and "q," have a tail, called the **descender**, that goes below the baseline.)

A text primitive's appearance is determined by only two attributes— the current color and the font. The font is an index into an implementation-dependent table of fonts in various sizes and styles:

> **void** SRGP_setFont (**int** valueIndex);

Each character in a font is defined as a rectangular bitmap, and SRGP draws a character by filling a rectangle using the character's bitmap as a pattern, in bitmap-pattern-transparent mode. The 1s in the bitmap define the character's interior, and the 0s specify the surrounding space and gaps such as the hole in "o." (Some more sophisticated packages define characters in pixmaps, allowing a character's interior to be patterned.)

Formatting text.   Because SRGP implementations offer a restricted repertoire of fonts and sizes, and because implementations on different hardware rarely offer equivalent repertoires, an application has limited control over the height and width of text strings. Since text-extent information is needed in order to produce well balanced compositions (for instance, to center a text string within a rectangular frame), SRGP provides the following function for querying the extent of a given string using the current value of the font attribute:

> **void** SRGP_inquireTextExtent(**char** *text, **int** *width, **int** *height, **int** *descent);

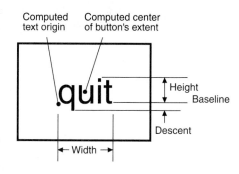

Computed text origin   Computed center of button's extent

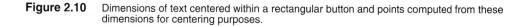

Height
Baseline
Descent
Width

Figure 2.10   Dimensions of text centered within a rectangular button and points computed from these dimensions for centering purposes.

Although SRGP does not support bitmap opaque mode for writing characters, such a mode can be simulated easily. As an example, the function in Prog. 2.3 shows how extent information and text-specific attributes can be used to produce black text, in the current font, centered within a white enclosing rectangle, as shown in Fig. 2.10. The function first creates the background button rectangle of the specified size, with a separate border, and then centers the text within it. Exercise 2.9 is a variation on this theme.

Program 2.3

Code used to generate Fig. 2.10.

```
void MakeQuitButton( rectangle buttonRect )
{
    point  centerOfButton, textOrigin;
    int  width, height, descent;

    SRGP_setFillStyle(SOLID);
    SRGP_setColor(COLOR_WHITE);
    SRGP_fillRectangle(buttonRect);
    SRGP_setColor(COLOR_BLACK);
    SRGP_setLineWidth(2);
    SRGP_Rectangle(buttonRect);
    SRGP_inquireTextExtent("quit", &width, &height, &descent);
    centerOfButton.x = (buttonRect.bottomLeft.x + buttonRect.topRight.x)/2;
    centerOfButton.y = (buttonRect.bottomLeft.y + buttonRect.topRight.y)/2;
    textOrigin.x = centerOfButton.x − (width/2);
    textOrigin.y = centerOfButton.y − (height/2);
    SRGP_text(textOrigin, "quit" );
}
```

2.2 BASIC INTERACTION HANDLING

Now that we know how to draw basic shapes and text, our next step is to learn how to write interactive programs that communicate effectively with the user, via input devices such as the keyboard and the mouse. First, we look at general guidelines for making effective and pleasant-to-use interactive programs; then we discuss the fundamental notion of logical (abstract) input devices. Finally, we look at SRGP's mechanisms for dealing with various aspects of interaction handling.

2.2.1 Human Factors

The designer of an interactive program must deal with many matters that do not arise in a noninteractive, batch program. They are the so-called **human factors** of a program, such as its interaction style (often called **look and feel**) and its ease of learning and of use, and they are as important as its functional completeness and correctness. Techniques for user–computer interaction that exhibit good human factors are studied in more detail in Chapter 8. The guidelines discussed there include these:

- Provide *simple and consistent* interaction sequences.
- *Do not overload the user* with too many different options and styles.
- *Show the available options clearly* at every stage of the interaction.
- *Give appropriate feedback* to the user.
- Allow the user to *recover gracefully* from mistakes.

We attempt to follow these guidelines for good human factors in our sample programs. For example, we typically use menus to allow the user to indicate which function to execute next, by using a mouse to pick a text button in a menu of such buttons. Also common are palettes (iconic menus) of basic geometric primitives, application-specific symbols, and fill patterns. Menus and palettes satisfy our first three guidelines in that their entries prompt the user with a list of available options and provide a single, consistent way of choosing among these options. Unavailable options may be either deleted temporarily or *grayed out* by being drawn in a low-intensity gray-scale pattern rather than a solid color (see Programming Project 2.14).

Feedback occurs at every step of a menu operation to satisfy the fourth guideline: The application program will *highlight* the menu choice or object selection—for example, display it in inverse video or framed in a rectangle—to draw attention to it. The package itself may also provide an *echo* in which an immediate response to the manipulation of an input device is given. For example, characters appear immediately at the position of the cursor as keyboard input is typed; as the mouse is moved on the table or desktop, a cursor echoes the corresponding location on the screen. Graphics packages offer a variety of cursor shapes that can be used by the application program to reflect the state of the program. In many display systems, the cursor shape can be varied dynamically as a function of the cursor's position on the screen. In many word-processing programs, for example, the cursor is shown as an arrow in menu areas and as a blinking vertical bar in text areas.

Graceful error recovery, our fifth guideline, is usually provided through *cancel* and *undo/redo* features. They require the application program to maintain a record of operations and their inverse, corrective actions.

2.2.2 Logical Input Devices

Device types in SRGP.   A major goal in designing graphics packages is device independence, which enhances portability of applications. SRGP achieves this goal for graphics output by providing primitives specified in terms of an abstract integer coordinate system, thus shielding the application from the need to set the individual pixels in the frame buffer. To provide a level of abstraction for graphics input, SRGP supports a set of **logical input devices** that shield the application from the details of the physical input devices available. Two logical devices are supported by SRGP:

- **Locator**, a device for specifying screen coordinates and the state of one or more associated buttons
- **Keyboard**, a device for specifying character string input

SRGP maps the logical devices onto the physical devices available (e.g., the locator could map to a mouse, joystick, tablet, or touch-sensitive screen). This mapping of logical to physical is familiar from conventional procedural languages and operating systems, in which I/O devices such as terminals, disks, and tape drives are abstracted to logical data files to achieve both device-independence and simplicity of application programming.

Device handling in other packages.   SRGP's input model is essentially a subset of the GKS and PHIGS input models. SRGP implementations support only one logical locator and one keyboard device, whereas GKS and PHIGS allow multiple devices of each type. Those packages also support additional device types: the **stroke** device (returning a polyline of cursor positions entered with the physical locator), the **choice** device (abstracting a function-key pad and returning a key identifier), the **valuator** (abstracting a slider or control dial and returning a floating-point number), and the **pick** device (abstracting a pointing device, such as a mouse or data tablet, with an associated button to signify a selection, and returning the identification of the logical entity picked). Other packages, such as QuickDraw and the X Window System, handle input devices in a more device-dependent way that gives the programmer finer control over an individual device's operation, at the cost of greater application-program complexity and reduced portability to other platforms.

Chapter 8 elaborates further on the properties of logical devices. Here, we briefly summarize modes of interacting with logical devices in general, and then examine SRGP's interaction functions in more detail.

2.2.3 Sampling Versus Event-Driven Processing

Two fundamental techniques are used to receive information created by user interactions. In **sampling** (also called **polling**), the application program queries the current value of a logical input device (called the **measure** of the device) and continues execution. The sampling is performed regardless of whether the device's measure has changed since the last sampling; indeed, only by continuous sampling of the device will changes in the device's state be known to the application. This mode is costly for interactive applications, because they would spend most of their CPU cycles in tight sampling loops waiting for measure changes.

An alternative to the CPU-intensive polling loop is the **interrupt-driven** interaction; in this technique, the application enables one or more devices for input and then continues normal execution until interrupted by some input **event** (a change in a device's state caused by user action); control then passes asynchronously to an interrupt procedure, which responds to the event. For each input device, an **event trigger** is defined; the event trigger is the user action that causes an event to occur. Typically, the trigger is a button push, such as a press of the mouse button (**mouse down**) or a press of a keyboard key.

To free applications programmers from the tricky and difficult aspects of asynchronous transfer of control, many graphics packages, including GKS, PHIGS, and SRGP, offer **event-driven** interaction as a synchronous simulation of interrupt-driven interaction. In this technique, an application enables devices and then continues execution. In the background, the package monitors the devices and stores information about each event in an event queue (Fig. 2.11). The application, at its convenience, checks the event queue and processes the events in temporal order. In effect, the application specifies when it would like to be *interrupted*.

When an application checks the event queue, it specifies whether it would like to enter a wait state. If the queue contains one or more event reports, the head event (representing the event that occurred earliest) is removed, and its information is made available to the application. If the queue is empty and a wait state is not desired, the application is informed that no event is available and that it is free to continue execution. If the queue is empty and a wait state is desired, the application pauses until the next event occurs or until an application-specified maximum-wait-time interval passes. In effect, event mode replaces polling of the input devices with the much more efficient waiting on the event queue.

In summary, in sampling mode, the device is polled and an event measure is collected, regardless of any user activity. In event mode, the application either gets an event report from a prior user action or waits until a user action (or timeout) occurs. It is this *respond only when the user acts* behavior of event mode that is the essential difference between sampled and event-driven input. Event-driven programming may seem more complex than sampling, but you are already familiar with a similar technique used with the scanf function in an interactive C program:

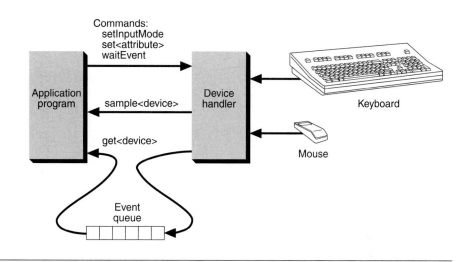

Commands:
setInputMode
set<attribute>
waitEvent

Application
program

Device
handler

sample<device>

get<device>

Keyboard

Mouse

Event
queue

Figure 2.11   Sampling versus event-handling using the event queue.

C enables the keyboard, and the application waits in the scanf until the user has completed entering a line of text. Some environments allow the scanf statement to access characters that were typed and queued before the scanf was issued.

Simple event-driven programs in SRGP and in similar packages follow the reactive *ping-pong* interaction introduced in Section 1.4.3 and pseudocoded in Prog. 2.4; this interaction can be nicely modeled as a finite-state automaton. More complex styles of interaction, allowing simultaneous program and user activity, are discussed in Chapter 8.

Program 2.4

Event-driven interaction scheme.

```
initialize, including generating the initial image;
activate interactive device(s) in event mode;
do {          /* main event loop */
    wait for user-triggered event on any of several devices;
    switch ( which device caused event ) {
        case DEVICE_1: collect DEVICE_1 event measure data, process, respond;
        case DEVICE_2: collect DEVICE_2 event measure data, process, respond;
        ...
    }
}
while ( user does not request quit );
```

Event-driven applications typically spend most of their time in a wait state, since interaction is dominated by *think time* during which the user decides what to do next; even in fast-paced game applications, the number of events a user can generate in a second is a fraction of what the application could handle. Since SRGP typically implements event mode using true (hardware) interrupts, the wait state effectively uses no CPU time. On a multitasking system, the advantage is obvious: The event-mode application requires CPU time only for short bursts of activity immediately following user action, thereby freeing the CPU for other tasks.

One other point, about correct use of event mode, should be mentioned. Although the queueing mechanism does allow program and user to operate asynchronously, the user should not be allowed to get too far ahead of the program, because each event should result in an echo as well as some feedback from the application program. It is true that experienced users have learned to use **typeahead** to type in parameters such as file names or even operating-system commands while the system is processing earlier requests, especially if at least a character-by-character echo is provided immediately. In contrast, **mouseahead** for graphical commands is generally not as useful (and is much more dangerous), because the user usually needs to see the screen updated to reflect the application model's current state before the next graphical interaction.

2.2.4 Sample Mode

Activating, deactivating, and setting the mode of a device. The following function is used to activate or deactivate a device; taking a device and a mode as parameters:

> **void** SRGP_setInputMode (**inputDevice** LOCATOR / KEYBOARD,
>   **inputMode** INACTIVE / SAMPLE / EVENT);

Thus, to set the locator to sample mode, we call

> SRGP_setInputMode (LOCATOR, SAMPLE);

Initially, both devices are inactive. Placing a device in a mode in no way affects the other input device—both may be active simultaneously and even then need not be in the same mode.

The locator's measure. The locator is a logical abstraction of a mouse or data tablet, returning the cursor position as a screen (x, y) coordinate pair, the number of the button that most recently experienced a transition, and the state of the buttons as a **chord** array (since multiple buttons can be pressed simultaneously). The second field lets the application know which button caused the trigger for that event.

```
typedef struct {
    point  position;
    enum {
        UP, DOWN
        } buttonChord[MAX_BUTTON_COUNT];        /*Typically 1–3*/
    int buttonOfMostRecentTransition;
    } locatorMeasure;
```

Having activated the locator in sample mode with the SRGP_setInputMode function, we can ask its current measure using

> **void** SRGP_sampleLocator (**locatorMeasure** *measure);

Let us examine the prototype sampling application shown in Prog. 2.5, a simple *painting* loop involving only button 1 on the locator. Such painting entails leaving a trail of paint where the user has dragged the locator while holding down button 1; the locator is sampled in a loop as the user moves it. First, we must detect when the user starts painting by sampling the button until it is depressed; then we place the paint (a filled rectangle in our simple example) at each sample point until the user releases the button.

Program 2.5

Sampling loop for painting.

```
set up color/pattern attributes, and brush size in halfBrushHeight and halfBrushWidth
SRGP_setInputMode(LOCATOR, SAMPLE);

/* First, sample until the button goes down.*/
do {
    SRGP_sampleLocator(locMeasure);
} while (locMeasure.buttonChord[0] == UP);

/*Perform the painting loop:
        Continuously place brush and then sample, until button is released.*/
do {
    rect = SRGP_defRectangle( locMeasure.position.x – halfBrushWidth,
                locMeasure.position.y – halfBrushHeight,
                locMeasure.position.x + halfBrushWidth,
                locMeasure.position.y + halfBrushHeight );
    SRGP_fillRectangle (rect );
    SRGP_sampleLocator( &locMeasure );
} while ( locMeasure.buttonChord[0] == DOWN );
```

The results of this sequence are crude: The paint rectangles are arbitrarily close together or far apart, with their density completely dependent on how far the locator was moved between consecutive samples. The sampling rate is determined essentially by the speed at which the CPU runs the operating system, the package, and the application.

Sample mode is available for both logical devices; however, the keyboard device is almost always operated in event mode, so techniques for sampling it are not addressed here.

2.2.5 Event Mode

Using event mode for initiation of sampling loop.   Although the two sampling loops of the painting example (one to detect the button-down transition, the other to paint until the button-up transition) certainly do the job, they put an unnecessary load on the CPU. Although overloading may not be a serious concern in a personal computer, it is not advisable in a system running multiple tasks, let alone doing time-sharing. Although it is certainly necessary to sample the locator repetitively for the painting loop itself (because we need to know the position of the locator at all times while the button is down), we do not need to use a sampling loop to wait for the button-down event that initiates the painting interaction. Event mode, discussed next, can be used when there is no need for measure information while waiting for an event.

SRGP_waitEvent. At any time after SRGP_setInputMode has activated a device in event mode, the program may inspect the event queue by entering the wait state with

> **inputDevice** SRGP_waitEvent (**int** maxWaitTime);

The function returns immediately if the queue is not empty; otherwise, the parameter specifies the maximum amount of time (measured in $1/60$ second) for which the function should wait for an event to fill the queue. A negative *maxWaitTime* (specified by the symbolic constant INDEFINITE) causes the function to wait indefinitely, whereas a value of zero causes it to return immediately, regardless of the state of the queue.

   The function returns the identity of the device that issued the head event, as LOCATOR, KEYBOARD, or NO_DEVICE. The special value NO_DEVICE is returned if no event was available within the specified time limit—that is, if the device timed out. The device type can then be tested to determine how the head event's measure should be retrieved (described later in this section).

The keyboard device.   The trigger event for the keyboard device depends on the **processing mode** in which the keyboard device has been placed. EDIT mode is used when the application receives strings (e.g., file names, commands) from the user, who types and edits the string and then presses the Return key to trigger the event. In RAW mode, used for interactions in which the keyboard must be monitored closely, every key press triggers an event. The application uses the following function to set the processing mode:

> **void** SRGP_setKeyboardProcessingMode (**keyboardMode** EDIT / RAW);

In EDIT mode, the user can type entire strings, correcting them with the backspace key as necessary, and then use the Return (or Enter) key as trigger. This mode is used when the user is to type in an entire string, such as a file name or a figure label. All control keys except backspace and Return are ignored, and the measure is the string as it appears at the time of the trigger. In RAW mode, on the other hand, each character typed, including control characters, is a trigger and is returned individually as the measure. This mode is used when individual keyboard characters act as commands—for example, for moving the cursor, for simple editing operations, or for video-game actions. RAW mode provides no echo, whereas EDIT mode echoes the string on the screen and displays a **text cursor** (such as an underscore or block character) where the next character to be typed will appear. Each backspace causes the text cursor to back up and to erase one character.

   When SRGP_waitEvent returns the device code KEYBOARD, the application obtains the measure associated with the event by calling

> **void** SRGP_getKeyboard (**char** *measure , **int** buffersize);

When the keyboard device is active in RAW mode, its measure is always exactly one character in length. In this case, the first character of the measure string returns the RAW measure.

The program shown in Prog. 2.6 demonstrates the use of EDIT mode. It receives a list of file names from the user, deleting each file so entered. When the user enters a null string (by pressing Return without typing any other characters), the interaction ends. During the interaction, the program waits indefinitely for the user to enter the next string.

Although this code explicitly specifies where the text prompt is to appear, it does not specify where the user's input string is typed (and corrected with the backspace). The location of this keyboard echo is specified by the programmer, as discussed in Section 2.2.7.

The locator device. The trigger event for the locator device is a press or release of a mouse button. When SRGP_waitEvent returns the device code LOCATOR, the application obtains the measure associated with the event by calling

> **void** SRGP_getLocator (**locatorMeasure** *measure);

Typically, the **position** field of the measure is used to determine in which area of the screen the user designated the point. For example, if the locator cursor is in a rectangular region where a menu button is displayed, the event should be interpreted as a request for some action; if it is in the main drawing area, the point might be inside a previously drawn object to indicate it should be selected, or in an *empty* region to indicate where a new object should be placed.

Program 2.6

EDIT-mode keyboard interaction.

```
#define KEYMEASURE_SIZE 80
SRGP_setInputMode(KEYBOARD, EVENT);        /* Assume only keyboard is active */
SRGP_setKeyboardProcessingMode(EDIT);
pt = SRGP_defPoint( 100, 100 );
SRGP_text( pt, "Specify one or more files to be deleted; to exit press Return\n" );

/* main event loop */
do {
    inputDev = SRGP_waitEvent( INDEFINITE );
    SRGP_getKeyboard( measure , KEYMEASURE_SIZE );
    if (strcoll(measure, "" ))
        DeleteFile(measure);                   /* DeleteFile does confirmation, etc. */
}
while ( strcoll(measure, "" ) );
```

The pseudocode shown in Prog. 2.7 (similar to that shown previously for the keyboard) implements another use of the locator, letting the user specify points at which markers are to be placed. The user terminates the marker-placing loop by pressing the locator button while the cursor points to a screen button, a rectangle containing the text *quit*.

In this example, only the user's pressing of locator button 1 is significant; releases of the button are ignored. Note that the button must be released before the next button-press event can take place—the event is triggered by a transition, not by a button state. Furthermore, to ensure that events coming from the other buttons do not disturb this interaction, the application tells SRGP which buttons are to trigger a locator event, by calling

> **void** SRGP_setLocatorButtonMask (**int** activeButtons);

Values for the button mask are LEFT_BUTTON_MASK, MIDDLE_BUTTON_- MASK, and RIGHT_BUTTON_MASK. A composite mask is formed by logically or'ing individual values. The default locator-button mask is 1, but no matter what the mask is, all buttons always have a measure. On implementations that support fewer than three buttons, references to any nonexistent buttons are simply ignored by SRGP, and these buttons' measures always contain UP.

The function PickedQuitButton compares the measure position against the bounds of the quit button rectangle and returns a Boolean value signifying whether the user picked the quit button. This process is a simple example of **pick correlation,** as discussed in Section 2.2.6.

<table>
<tr>
<td>Program 2.7

Locator interaction.</td>
<td>

```
#define QUIT 0
create the on-screen Quit button;
SRGP_setLocatorButtonMask( LEFT_BUTTON_MASK );
SRGP_setInputMode( LOCATOR, EVENT );          /* Assume only locator is active */
/* main event loop */
terminate = FALSE;
do {
    inputDev = SRGP_waitEvent( INDEFINITE );
    SRGP_getLocator( &measure );
    if (measure.buttonChord[QUIT] == DOWN ) {
        if PickedQuitButton( measure.position ) terminate  = TRUE;
        else
            SRGP_marker( measure.position );
    }
}
while ( !terminate );
```

</td>
</tr>
</table>

Waiting for multiple events.   The code fragments in Progs. 2.6 and 2.7 did not illustrate event mode's greatest advantage: the ability to wait for more than one device at the same time. SRGP queues events of enabled devices in chronological order and lets the application program take the first one off the queue when SRGP_waitEvent is called. Unlike hardware interrupts, which are processed in order of priorities, events are thus processed strictly in temporal order. The application examines the returned device code to determine which device caused the event.

The function shown in Prog. 2.8 allows the user to place any number of small circle markers anywhere within a rectangular drawing area. The user places a marker by pointing to the desired position and pressing button 1, then requests that the interaction be terminated either by pressing button 3 or by typing "q" or "Q".

Program 2.8

Use of several devices simultaneously.

```
#define PLACE_BUTTON 0
#define QUIT_BUTTON 2

generate initial screen layout;
SRGP_setInputMode( KEYBOARD, EVENT );
SRGP_setKeyboardProcessingMode( RAW );
SRGP_setInputMode( LOCATOR, EVENT );
SRGP_setLocatorButtonMask( LEFT_BUTTON_MASK | RIGHT_BUTTON_MASK );
                                          /* Ignore 2nd button */
/* Main event loop */
terminate = FALSE;
do {
    device = SRGP_waitEvent( INDEFINITE );
    switch ( device ) {
        case KEYBOARD:
            SRGP_getKeyboard( keyMeasure, lbuf );
            terminate = (keyMeasure[0] == 'q') || (keyMeasure[0] == 'Q');
            break;
        case LOCATOR: {
            SRGP_getLocator( &locMeasure );
            switch ( locMeasure.buttonOfMostRecentTransition ) {
                case PLACE_BUTTON:
                    if (( locMeasure.buttonChord[PLACE_BUTTON] == DOWN )
                        && InDrawingArea( locMeasure.position ))
                            SRGP_marker( locMeasure.position );
                    break;
                case QUIT_BUTTON:
                    terminate = TRUE;
                    break;
            }   /* button case */
        }    /* locator case */
    }   /* device case */
}
while (!terminate );
```

2.2.6 Pick Correlation for Interaction Handling

A graphics application customarily divides the screen area into regions dedicated to specific purposes. When the user presses the locator button, the application must determine exactly what screen button, icon, or other object was selected, if any, so that it can respond appropriately. This determination, called **pick correlation**, is a fundamental part of interactive graphics.

An application program using SRGP performs pick correlation by determining in which region the cursor is located, and then which object within that region, if any, the user is selecting. Points in an empty subregion might be ignored (if the point is between menu buttons in a menu, for example) or might specify the desired position for a new object (if the point lies in the main drawing area). Since a great many regions on the screen are upright rectangles, almost all the work for pick correlation can be done by a simple, frequently used Boolean function that checks whether a given point lies in a given rectangle. The GEOM package distributed with SRGP includes this function (GEOM_ptInRect) as well as other utilities for coordinate arithmetic. (For more information on pick correlation, see Section 7.11.2.)

Let us look at a classic example of pick correlation. Consider a painting application with a **menu bar** across the top of the screen. This menu bar contains the names of pull-down menus, called menu **headers**. When the user picks a header (by placing the cursor on top of the header's text string and pressing a locator button), the corresponding **menu body** is displayed on the screen below the header and the header is highlighted. After the user selects an entry on the menu (by releasing the locator button), the menu body disappears and the header is unhighlighted. The rest of the screen contains the main drawing area in which the user can place and pick objects. The application, in creating each object, assigns it a unique positive integer identifier (ID) that is returned by the pick-correlation function for further processing of the object.

Program 2.9

High-level interaction scheme for menu handling.

```
void HighLevelInteractionHandler( locatorMeasure measureOfLocator )
{
    if ( GEOM_pointInRect( measureOfLocator.position, menuBarExtent ) {
        /* Find out which menu's header, if any, the user selected;
              Then, pull down that menu's body */
        menuID = CorrelateMenuBar( measureOfLocator.position );
        if ( menuID > 0 ) {
            chosenItemIndex = PerformPulldownMenuInteraction( menuID );
            if (chosenItemIndex > 0 )
                PerformActionChosenFromMenu(menuID, chosenItemIndex);
        }
    else        /* The user picked within the drawing area; detect what and respond */
    {
        objectID = CorrelateDrawingArea( measureOfLocator.position );
        if ( objectID > 0 ) ProcessObject( objectID );
    }
}
```

When a point is obtained from the locator via a button-down event, the high-level interaction-handling schema shown in Prog. 2.9 is executed; it is essentially a dispatching procedure that uses pick correlation within the menu bar or the main drawing area to divide the work among menu- and object-picking functions. First, if the cursor was in the menu bar, a subsidiary correlation procedure determines whether the user selected a menu header. If so, a procedure (detailed in Section 2.3.1) is called to perform the menu interaction; it returns an index specifying which item within the menu's body (if any) was chosen. The menu ID and item index together uniquely identify the action that should be taken in response. If the cursor was not in the menu bar but rather in the main drawing area, another subsidiary correlation procedure is called to determine what object was picked, if any. If an object was picked, a processing procedure is called to respond appropriately.

The function CorrelateMenuBar performs a finer correlation by calling GEOM_pointInRect once for each menu header in the menu bar; it accesses a data structure storing the rectangular screen extent of each header. The function CorrelateDrawingArea must do more sophisticated correlation because, typically, objects in the drawing area may overlap and are not necessarily rectangular.

2.2.7 Setting Device Measure and Attributes

Each input device has its own set of attributes, and the application can set these attributes to custom-tailor the feedback the device presents to the user. (The button mask presented earlier is also an attribute; it differs from those presented here in that it does not affect feedback.) Like output-primitive attributes, input-device attributes are set modally by specific functions. Attributes can be set at any time, whether or not the device is active.

In addition, each input device's measure, normally determined by the user's actions, can also be set by the application. Unlike input-device attributes, an input device's measure is reset to a default value when the device is deactivated; thus, upon reactivation, devices initially have predictable values, a convenience to the programmer and to the user. This automatic resetting can be overridden by explicitly setting a device's measure while it is inactive.

Locator echo attributes.   Several types of echoes are useful for the locator. The programmer can control both echo type and cursor shape with

> **void** SRGP_setLocatorEchoType (**echoType** NO_ECHO / CURSOR /
> RUBBER_LINE /RUBBER_RECT);

The default is CURSOR, and SRGP implementations supply a cursor table from which an application selects a desired cursor shape (see the reference manual). A common use of the ability to specify the cursor shape dynamically is to provide feedback by changing the cursor shape according to the region in which the cursor lies. RUBBER_LINE and RUBBER_RECT echo are commonly used to specify a line or box. With these echoes set, SRGP automatically draws a continuously updated line or rectangle as the user moves the locator. The line or rectangle is defined by two points, the anchor point (another locator attribute) and the current locator position. Figure 2.12 illustrates the use of these two modes for user specification of a line and a rectangle.

In Fig. 2.12(a), the echo is a cross-hair cursor, and the user is about to press the locator button. The application initiates a rubber echo, anchored at the current locator position, in response to the button press. In parts (b) and (c), the user's movement of the locator device is echoed by the rubber primitive. The locator position in part (c) is returned to the application when the user releases the button, and the application responds by drawing a line or rectangle primitive and restoring normal cursor echo (see part d).

The anchor point for rubber echo is set with

> **void** SRGP_setLocatorEchoRubberAnchor (**point** position);

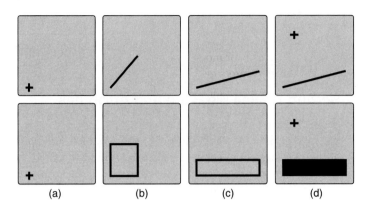

(a)   (b)   (c)   (d)

Figure 2.12   Rubber-echo scenarios.(a)Button press imitates echo. (b) Rubber primitive echoes locator device. (c) Locator position returns to application. (d) Application draws line and restores echo.

An application typically uses the *position* field of the measure obtained from the most recent locator-button–press event as the anchor position, since that button press typically initiates the rubber-echo sequence.

Locator measure control.   The *position* portion of the locator measure is automatically reset to the center of the screen whenever the locator is deactivated. Unless the programmer explicitly resets it, the measure (and feedback position, if the echo is active) is initialized to that same position when the device is reactivated. At any time, whether the device is active or inactive, the programmer can reset the locator's measure (the *position* portion, not the fields concerning the buttons) by using

   void SRGP_setLocatorMeasure (**point** position);

Resetting the measure while the locator is inactive has no immediate effect on the screen, but resetting it while the locator is active changes the echo (if any) accordingly. Thus, if the program wants the cursor to appear initially at a position other than the center when the locator is activated, a call to SRGP_setLocatorMeasure with that initial position must precede the call to SRGP_setInputMode. This technique is commonly used to achieve continuity of cursor position: The last measure before the locator was deactivated is stored, and the cursor is returned to that position when it is reactivated.

Keyboard attributes and measure control.   Unlike the locator, whose echo is positioned to reflect movements of a physical device, there is no obvious screen position for a keyboard device's echo. The position is thus an attribute (with an implementation-specific default value) of the keyboard device that can be set via

   void SRGP_setKeyboardEchoOrigin (**point** origin);

The default measure for the keyboard is automatically reset to the null string when the keyboard is deactivated. Setting the measure explicitly to a nonnull initial value just before activating the keyboard is a convenient way to present a default input string (displayed by SRGP as soon as echoing begins) that the user can accept as is or modify before pressing the Return key, thereby minimizing typing. The keyboard's measure, a character string, is set via

void SRGP_setKeyboardMeasure (**char** *measure);

2.3 RASTER GRAPHICS FEATURES

By now, we have introduced most of the features of SRGP. This section discusses the remaining facilities that take particular advantage of raster hardware, especially the ability to save and restore pieces of the screen as they are overlaid by other images, such as windows or temporary menus. Such image manipulations are done under control of window- and menu-manager application programs. We also introduce offscreen bitmaps for storing windows and menus, and we discuss the use of clipping rectangles.

2.3.1 Canvases

The best way to make complex icons or menus appear and disappear quickly is to create them once in memory and then to copy them onto the screen as needed. Raster graphics packages do this by generating the primitives in invisible, offscreen bitmaps or pixmaps of the requisite size, called **canvases** in SRGP, and then copying the canvases to and from display memory. This technique is, in effect, a type of buffering. Moving blocks of pixels back and forth is faster, in general, than is regenerating the information, given the existence of the fast SRGP_copyPixel operation that we shall discuss soon.

An SRGP canvas is a data structure that stores an image as a 2D array of pixels. It also stores some control information concerning the size and attributes of the image. Each canvas represents its image in its own Cartesian coordinate system, which is identical to that of the screen shown in Fig. 2.1; in fact, the screen is itself a canvas, special solely because it is the only canvas that is displayed. To make an image stored in an off-screen canvas visible, the application must copy it onto the screen canvas. Beforehand, the portion of the screen image on which the new image—for example, a menu—will appear can be saved by copying the pixels in that region to an offscreen canvas. When the menu selection has taken place, the screen image is restored by copying back these pixels.

At any given time, there is one *currently active* canvas: the canvas into which new primitives are drawn and to which new attribute settings apply. This canvas may be the screen canvas (the default we have been using) or an offscreen canvas. The coordinates passed to the primitive functions are expressed in terms of the local coordinate space of the currently active canvas. Each canvas also has its own complete set of SRGP attributes, which affect all drawing on that canvas and are set to the standard default values when the canvas is created. Calls to attribute-set-ting functions modify only the attributes in the currently active canvas. It is conve-nient to think of a canvas as a virtual screen of program-specified dimensions, having its own associated pixmap, coordinate system, and attribute group. These properties of the canvas are sometimes called the **state** or **context** of the canvas.

When SRGP is initialized, the **screen canvas** is automatically created and made active. All our programs thus far have generated primitives into only that canvas. It is the only canvas visible on the screen, and its ID is SCREEN_CAN-VAS, an SRGP constant. A new offscreen canvas is created by calling the follow-ing function, which returns the (integer) ID allocated for the new canvas:

int SRGP_createCanvas (**int** width, **int** height);

Like the screen, the new canvas's local coordinate system origin $(0, 0)$ is at the bot-tom-left corner, and the top-right corner at $(width-1, height-1)$. A 1 by 1 canvas is therefore defined by width and height of 1, and its bottom-left and top-right cor-ners are both $(0, 0)$! This is consistent with our treatment of pixels as being at grid intersections: The single pixel in a 1 by 1 canvas is at $(0, 0)$.

A newly created canvas is automatically activated and its pixels are initialized to color 0 (as is done for the screen canvas before any primitives are displayed). Once a canvas is created, its size cannot be changed. Also, the programmer cannot control the number of bits per pixel in a canvas, since SRGP uses as many bits per pixel as the hardware allows. The attributes of a canvas are kept as part of its *local* state information; thus, the program does not need to save the attributes of the cur-rently active canvas explicitly before creating a new active canvas.

The application selects a previously created canvas to be the currently active canvas via

void SRGP_useCanvas (**int** canvasID);

Activation of canvas in no way implies that canvas is made visible; to be seen, an image in an offscreen canvas must be copied onto the screen canvas (using the SGRP_copyPixel function described shortly).

Canvases are deleted by the following function, which may not be used to delete the screen canvas or the currently active canvas:

void SRGP_deleteCanvas (**int** canvasID);

The following functions allow inquiry of canvas size; one returns the rectangle that defines the canvas coordinate system (the bottom-left point always being $(0, 0)$), and the other returns the width and height as separate quantities.

rectangle SRGP_inquireCanvasExtent (**int** canvasID);
void SRGP_inquireCanvasSize (**int** canvasID, *width, *height);

Let us examine the way canvases can be used for the implementation of Per-formPulldownMenuInteraction, the function called by the high-level interaction handler presented in Prog. 2.9. The function is implemented by the pseudocode of

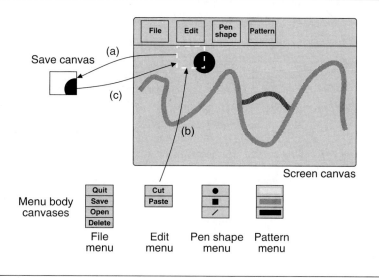

Figure 2.13 Saving and restoring area covered by menu body.

Prog. 2.10, and its sequence of actions is illustrated in Fig. 2.13. Each menu has a unique ID (returned by the CorrelateMenuBar function) that can be used to locate a data record containing the following information about the appearance of the menu body.

- The ID of the canvas storing the menu's body

- The rectangular area (called *menuBodyScreenExtent* in the pseudocode), specified in screen-canvas coordinates, in which the menu's body should appear when the user pulls down the menu by clicking in its header.

Program 2.10

Pseudocode for Perform-PulldownMenuInteraction

```
int  PerformPulldownMenuInteraction( int menuID );
/* The saving/copying of rectangular regions of canvases is described later */
{
    highlight the menu header in the menu bar;
    menuBodyScreenExtent = screen-area rectangle at which menu body should appear
        save the current pixels of the menuBodyScreenExtent in a temporary canvas
            /* See Fig. 2.13a */
    copy menu body image from body canvas to menuBodyScreenExtent
            /* See Fig. 2.13b and C code in Prog. 2.11 */
    wait for button-up signaling the user made a selection, then get locator measure
    copy saved image from temporary canvas back to menuBodyScreenExtent
            /* See Fig. 2.13c */
    if ( GEOM_pointInRect(measureOfLocator.position, menuBodyScreenExtent )
        calculate and return index of chosen item, using y coord of measure position
    else
        return 0;
}
```

2.3.2 Clipping Rectangles

To protect other portions of the canvas, it often is desirable to restrict the effect of graphics primitives to a subregion of the active canvas. To facilitate this operation, SRGP maintains a **clip rectangle** attribute. All primitives are clipped to the boundaries of this rectangle; that is, primitives (or portions of primitives) lying outside the clip rectangle are not drawn. Like any attribute, the clip rectangle can be changed at any time, and its most recent setting is stored with the canvas's attribute group. The default clipping rectangle (what we have used so far) is the full canvas; it can be made smaller than the canvas, but it cannot extend beyond the canvas boundaries. The relevant set and inquiry calls for the clip rectangle are

> **void** SRGP_setClipRectangle (**rectangle** clipRect);
> **rectangle** SRGP_inquireClipRectangle ();

A painting application like that presented in Section 2.2.4 would use the clip rectangle to restrict the placement of paint to the drawing region of the screen, ensuring that the surrounding menu areas are not damaged. Although SRGP offers only a single upright rectangle clipping boundary, some more sophisticated software such as PostScript offers multiple, arbitrarily shaped clipping regions.

2.3.3 The SRGP_copyPixel Operation

The powerful SRGP_copyPixel command is a typical raster command that is often called bitBlt (bit block transfer) or pixBlt (pixel Blt) when implemented directly in hardware; it first became available in microcode on the pioneering ALTO bitmap workstation at Xerox Palo Alto Research Center in the early 1970s [INGA81]. This command is used to copy an array of pixels from a rectangular region of a canvas, the *source* region, to a *destination* region in the currently active canvas (see Fig. 2.14). The SRGP facility provides only restricted functionality in that the destination rectangle must be of the same size as the source. In more powerful versions, the source can be copied to a destination region of a different size, being automatically scaled to fit. Also, additional features may be available, such as **masks** to selectively shield desired source or destination pixels from copying, and **halftone patterns** that can be used to **screen** (i.e., shade) the destination region.

SRGP_copyPixel can copy between any two canvases and is specified as follows:

> **void** SRGP_copyPixel (**int** sourceCanvasID, **rectangle** sourceRect,
>   **point** destCorner);

The *sourceRect* specifies the source region in an arbitrary canvas, and *destCorner* specifies the bottom-left corner of the destination rectangle inside the currently active canvas, each in their own coordinate systems. The copy operation is subject to the same clip rectangle that prevents primitives from generating pixels into protected regions of a canvas. Thus, the region into which pixels are ultimately copied is the intersection of the extent of the destination canvas, the destination region, and the clip rectangle, shown as the striped region in Fig. 2.15.

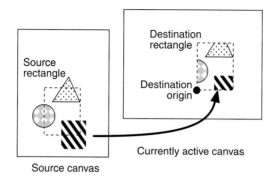

Figure 2.14   SRGP_copyPixel.

To show the use of copyPixel in handling pull-down menus, we shall implement the fourth statement of pseudocode—*copy menu body image*—from the PerformPulldownMenuInteraction function (Prog. 2.10). In the third statement of the pseudocode, we saved in an offscreen canvas the screen region where the menu body is to go; now we wish to copy the menu body to the screen.

The C code is shown in Prog. 2.11. We must be sure to distinguish between the two rectangles, which are of identical size but that are expressed in different coordinate systems. The first rectangle, which we call *menuBodyExtent* in the code, is simply the extent of the menu body's canvas in its own coordinate system. This extent is used as the source rectangle in the SRGP_copyPixel operation that puts the menu on the screen. The *menuBodyScreenExtent* is a rectangle of the same size that specifies in screen coordinates the position in which the menu body should appear; that extent's bottom-left corner is horizontally aligned with the left

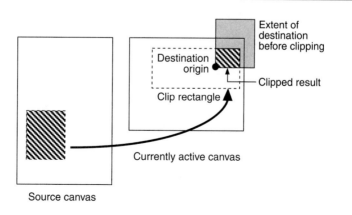

Figure 2.15   Clipping during copyPixel.

side of the menu header, and its top-right corner abuts the bottom of the menu bar. (Figure 2.13 symbolizes the Edit menu's screen extent as a dashed outline, and its body extent as a solid outline.) The bottom-left corner of the *menuBodyScreenExtent* is used to specify the destination for the SRGP_copyPixel that copies the menu body (Fig. 2.15). It is also the source rectangle for the initial save of the screen area to be overlaid by the menu body and the destination of the final restore.

Notice that the application's state is saved and restored to eliminate side effects. We set the screen clip rectangle to SCREEN_EXTENT before copying; alternatively, we could set it to the exact *menuBodyScreenExtent*.

Program 2.11

Code for copying the menu body to the screen.

```
/* This code fragment copies a menu-body image onto screen,
      at the screen position stored in the body's record */

/* Save the ID of the currently active canvas, which needn't be the screen */
saveCanvasID = SRGP_inquireActiveCanvas();

/* Save the screen canvas' clip-rectangle attribute value */
SRGP_useCanvas( SCREEN_CANVAS );
saveClipRectangle = SRGP_inquireClipRectangle();

/* temporarily set screen clip rectangle to allow writing to all of the screen */
SRGP_setClipRectangle( SCREEN_EXTENT );

/* Copy menu body from its canvas to its proper area below menu bar header */
SRGP_copyPixel( menuCanvasID, menuBodyExtent,
      menuBodyScreenExtent.bottomLeft );

/* Restore screen attributes and active canvas */
SRGP_setClipRectangle( saveClipRectangle );
SRGP_useCanvas( saveCanvasID );
```

2.3.4 Write Mode or RasterOp

SRGP_copyPixel can do more than just move an array of pixels from a source region to a destination. It can also execute a logical (bitwise) operation between each corresponding pair of pixels in the source and destination regions, then place the result in the destination region. This operation can be symbolized as

$$D \leftarrow S \textbf{ op } D$$

where **op**, frequently called the *RasterOp* or *write mode*, consists in general of the 16 Boolean operators. Only the most common of these—**replace, or, xor**, and **and**—are supported by SRGP; these operators are shown for a 1-bit-per-pixel image in Fig. 2.16.

Write mode affects not only SRGP_copyPixel, but also any new primitives written onto a canvas. Each pixel (either of a source rectangle of a SRGP_copyPixel or of a primitive) is stored in its memory location, either it is written in destructive **replace** mode or its value is logically combined with the previously stored value of the pixel. (This bitwise combination of source and destination values is similar to the way a CPU's hardware performs arithmetic or logical operations on the contents of a memory location during a read–modify–write memory cycle.) Although **replace** is by far the most common mode, **xor** is quite useful for generating dynamic objects, such as cursors and rubberband echoes, as we discuss shortly.

We set the write-mode attribute with:

> **void** SRGP_setWriteMode (**writeMode** WRITE_REPLACE / WRITE_XOR /
> WRITE_OR / WRITE_AND);

Since all primitives are generated according to the current write mode, the SRGP programmer must be sure to set this mode explicitly and not to rely on the default setting of WRITE_REPLACE.

To see how RasterOp works, we look at how SRGP actually stores and manipulates pixels; only here do hardware and implementation considerations intrude on the abstract view of raster graphics that we have maintained so far.

RasterOps are performed on the pixel values, which are indices into the color table, not on the hardware color specifications stored as entries in the color table. Thus, for a bilevel, 1-bit-per-pixel system, the RasterOp is done on two indices of 1 bit each. For an 8-bit-per-pixel color system, the RasterOp is done as a bitwise logical operation on two 8-bit indices.

Although the interpretation of the four basic operations on 1-bit-per-pixel monochrome images shown in Fig. 2.16 is natural enough, the results of all but **replace** mode are not nearly so natural for n-bit-per-pixel images ($n > 1$), since a bitwise logical operation on the source and destination indices yields a third index whose color value may be wholly unrelated to the source and destination colors.

The **replace** mode involves writing over what is already on the screen (or other canvas). This destructive write operation is the normal mode for drawing

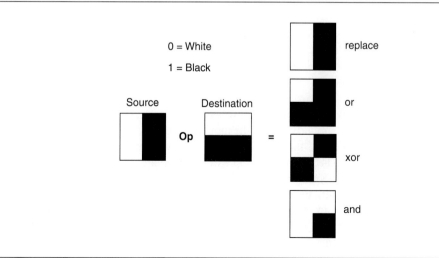

Figure 2.16   Write modes for combining source and destination pixels.

primitives, and it is customarily used to move and pop windows. It can also be used to *erase* old primitives by drawing over them in the application screen background pattern.

The **or** mode on bilevel displays makes a nondestructive addition to what is already on the canvas. With color 0 as white background and color 1 as black foreground, **or**ing a gray fill pattern onto a white background changes the underlying bits to show the gray pattern. But **or**ing the gray pattern over a black area has no effect on the screen. Thus, **or**ing a light-gray paint swath over a polygon filled with a brick pattern merely fills in the bricks with the brush pattern; it does not erase the black edges of the bricks, as **replace** mode would. Painting is often done in **or** mode for this reason (see Exercise 2.6).

The **xor** mode on bilevel displays can be used to invert a destination region. For example, to highlight a button selected by the user, we set **xor** mode and generate a filled rectangle primitive with color 1, thereby toggling all pixels of the button: 0 **xor** 1 = 1, 1 **xor** 1 = 0. To restore the button's original status, we simply stay in **xor** mode and draw the rectangle a second time, thereby toggling the bits back to their original state. This technique is also used internally by SRGP to provide the locator's rubber-line and rubber-rectangle echo modes (see Example 2.1).

On many bilevel graphics displays, the **xor** technique is used by the underlying hardware (or in some cases software) to display the locator's cursor image in a nondestructive manner. There are some disadvantages to this simple technique: When the cursor is on top of a background with a fine pattern that is almost 50 percent black and 50 percent white, it is possible for the cursor to be only barely noticeable. Therefore, many bilevel displays and most color displays use **replace** mode for the cursor echo and use a black cursor with a white border so it will show up against any background. Not being able to **xor** complicates the echo hardware or software (see Exercise 2.4).

The **and** mode can be used, for example, to reset pixels selectively in the destination region to color 0, thereby "erasing" them.

Example 2.1

Problem: Implement a rubber-echo interaction, without using the built-in locator echo. Watch for artifacts, especially upon initiation and termination of the interaction loop.

Answer: We will implement a rubberband box echo. The rubberline echo can be implemented similarly. While the mouse is moving, and the final locator value has not been selected, the interaction function will track the mouse and draw the rubber-echo. The interaction loop will be called after the user has pressed a mouse button. The interaction will allow dragging of the current point, with appropriate rubber-echo, until the user releases the button, indicating the end of the interaction.

On return from our function, we need to restore the state to what it was on function entry, so that the caller is insulated from the details of our function's implementation.

To create the echo, the essential idea is to draw the echo shape (rectangle) using **xor** mode, so that by redrawing the same shape, it may be erased, with no special concern for what it was drawn over. To have the echo image appear, we must draw the entity once. To restore the display to its state prior to the echo, we have to draw exactly the same shape a second time so that it does not leave some trace on the screen.

Since we must collect locator data to update the echo, we will echo the rubber-band before we sample the locator the first time, and then repeatedly, in a loop, sample, erase the old echo, and redraw the updated echo. As we sample, we check the buttons' status, before erasing and redrawing, to see whether the interaction should terminate. In addition, although not essential, it is useful to check whether the mouse has actually moved since the last sample, and do the erase-redraw only if it has moved.

The following C code implements this approach to the problem (the function buttons_are_down() is not shown, but it simply checks the state of the mouse buttons):

Code that implements rubber-echo interaction.

```
void RubberRectInteract ( point anchor_pt, point curr_pt, int drag_flag,
            int buttonmask, locatorMeasure *final_loc, rectangle *final_rect)
{
    attributeGroup  save_attributes;
    locatorMeasure  curr_loc;
    int  some_button_down;
    rectangle  curr_rect;

    SRGP_inquireAttributes( &save_attributes );
    SRGP_setLineStyle( CONTINUOUS );
    SRGP_setFillStyle( SOLID );
    SRGP_setInputMode( LOCATOR, SAMPLE );
    SRGP_setWriteMode( WRITE_XOR );

    SRGP_setLocatorEchoType( CURSOR )                /* or NO_ECHO */;
    SRGP_setLocatorMeasure( curr_pt );               /* for good measure */

    /*
    *  We want the rectangle to be insensitive to whether
    *  the anchor is lower and to left of current point —
    *  the GEOM_ utility function assures this.
    */
    curr_rect = GEOM_rectFromDiagPoints( anchor_pt, curr_pt );
    /* Now we make the rubberband box first appear: */
    SRGP_rectangle( curr_rect );

    while( (buttons_are_down( buttonmask, curr_loc.button_chord )) ) {
        SRGP_sampleLocator( &curr_loc );
    /* We update echo only if the mouse has moved; */
        if (curr_loc.position.x != curr_pt.x || curr_loc.position.y != curr_pt.y) {
            SRGP_rectangle( curr_rect );
    /* At this point, last box we drew disappears */
            curr_pt = curr_loc.position;
            curr_rect = GEOM_rectFromDiagPoints( anchor_pt, curr_pt );
```

```
                    SRGP_rectangle( curr_rect );
        /* Now box appears from anchor to new position */
                }
        }

        /* At this point, we have drawn the box to the last point once */
        /* Thus, we must erase it by drawing it again:            */
            SRGP_rectangle( curr_rect );
            *final_loc = curr_loc;
            *final_rect = curr_rect;

        /* Now restore state as of function entry: */
            SRGP_setInputMode( LOCATOR, INACTIVE );
            SRGP_setAttributes( save_attributes );
        }
```

2.4 LIMITATIONS OF SRGP

Although SRGP is a powerful package supporting a large class of applications, inherent limitations make it less than optimal for some applications. Most obviously, SRGP provides no support for applications displaying 3D geometry. Also, more subtle limitations affect even many 2D applications:

- The machine-dependent integer coordinate system of SRGP is too inflexible for those applications that require the greater precision, range, and convenience of floating-point.

- As with most other 2D raster graphics libraries, SRGP stores an image in a canvas in a semantics-free manner as a matrix of unconnected pixel values rather than as a collection of graphics objects (primitives), and thus does not support object-level operations, such as *delete, move,* or *change color.* Because SRGP keeps no record of the actions that produced the current screen image, it also cannot refresh a screen if the image is damaged by other software, nor can it re–scan-convert the primitives to produce an image for display on a device with a different resolution.

2.4.1 Application Coordinate Systems

In Chapter 1, we introduced the notion that, for most applications, drawings are only a means to an end and that the primary role of the application database is to support such processes as analysis, simulation, verification, and manufacturing. The database must therefore store geometric information using the range and precision required by these processes, independent of the coordinate system and resolution of the display device. For example, a VLSI CAD/CAM program may need to represent circuits that are 1 to 2 centimeters (cm) long at a precision of half a micron, whereas an astronomy program may need a range of 1 to 10^9 light-years with a precision of a million miles. For maximum flexibility and range, many applications use floating-point *world coordinates* for storing geometry in their database.

Such an application could do the mapping from world to device coordinates itself; however, considering the complexity of this mapping (which we shall discuss in Chapter 6), it is convenient to use a graphics package that accepts primitives specified in world coordinates and maps them to the display device in a machine-independent manner. The recent availability of inexpensive floating-point chips offering roughly the performance of integer arithmetic has significantly reduced the time penalty associated with the use of floating point—the flexibility makes it well worth its cost to the applications that need it.

For 2D graphics, the most common software that provides floating-point coordinates is Adobe's PostScript, used both as the standard page-description language for driving hardcopy printers and (in an extension called Display PostScript) as the graphics package for windowing systems on some workstations. For 3D floating point graphics, PHIGS and PHIGS+ are now widely available, and various 3D extensions to PostScript are appearing.

2.4.2 Storage of Primitives for Respecification

Consider what happens when an application using SRGP needs to redraw a picture at a different size, or at the same size on a display device with a different resolution (such as a higher-resolution printer). Because SRGP has no record of the primitives it has drawn, the application must respecify the entire set of primitives to SRGP after scaling the coordinates.

If SRGP were enhanced to retain a record of all specified primitives, the application could let SRGP regenerate them from its own storage. SRGP could then support another commonly needed operation, refreshing the screen. On some graphics systems, the application's screen image can be damaged by messages from other users or applications; unless the screen canvas can be refreshed from a redundantly stored copy in an offscreen canvas, respecification of the primitives is the only way to repair the damage.

The most important advantage of having the package store primitives is the support of editing operations that are the essence of drawing or construction applications, a class of programs that is quite different from the painting applications illustrated in this chapter's examples. A **painting program** allows the user to paint arbitrary swaths using a brush of varying size, shape, color, and pattern. More complete painting programs also allow placement of such predefined shapes as rectangles, polygons, and circles. Any part of the canvas can be subsequently edited at a pixel level; portions of an object can be covered with paint, or arbitrary rectangular regions of the canvas can be copied or moved elsewhere. The user cannot point to a previously drawn shape or to a painted swath and then delete or move it as a coherent, indivisible object. This limitation exists because a painting program allows an object, once placed on the canvas, to be mutilated and fragmented, losing its identity as a coherent object. For example, what would it mean for the user to point to a fragment of an object that had been split into pieces that were independently positioned in various areas of the screen? Would the user be referring to the fragment itself, or to the entire original object? In essence, the ability to affect individual pixels makes pick correlation—and therefore object picking and editing—impossible.

A **drawing program,** conversely, allows the user to pick and edit any object at any time. These applications, also called **layout editors** or **graphical illustrators**, allow a user to position standard shapes (also called *symbols*, *templates*, or *objects*) and then to edit the layout by deleting, moving, rotating, scaling these shapes, and changing their attributes. Similar interactive programs that allow users to assemble complex 3D objects from simpler ones are called **geometric editors** or **construction programs.**

Scaling, screen refreshing, and object-level editing all require the storage and respecification of primitives by the application or by the graphics package. If the application stores the primitives, it can perform the respecification; however, these operations are more complex than they may seem at first glance. For example, a primitive can be deleted trivially by erasing the screen and respecifying all the primitives (except, of course, the deleted one); however, a more efficient method is to erase the primitive's image by drawing the application screen background on top of it and then to respecify any primitives that may have been damaged. Because these operations are both complex and frequently needed, there is good reason for moving their functionality into the graphics package itself.

An object-level, geometric graphics package, such as PHIGS, lets the application define objects using a 2D or 3D floating-point coordinate system. The package stores objects internally, allows the application to edit the stored objects, and updates the screen whenever necessary due to an editing operation. The package also performs pick correlation, producing an object ID when given a screen coordinate. Because these packages manipulate objects, they cannot permit pixel-level manipulations (copyPixel and write mode)—this is the price of preserving object coherence. Thus, neither a raster graphics package without primitive storage nor a geometric graphics package with primitive storage satisfies all needs. Chapter 7 discusses the pros and cons of the retention of primitives in the graphics package.

Image scaling via pixel replication.   If neither the application nor the package has a record of the primitives (as is typical of most painting programs), scaling cannot be done by respecifying the primitives with scaled endpoint coordinates. All that can be done is to scale the contents of the canvas using read-pixel and write-pixel operations. The simple, fast way to scale up a bitmap/pixmap image (to make it larger) is via **pixel replication,** where each pixel is replaced by an N by N block of pixels, thus enlarging the image by a scale factor of N.

With pixel replication, the image becomes larger, but it also becomes coarser, since no new information is provided beyond that contained in the original pixel-level representation. Moreover, pixel replication can increase an image's size by only an integer factor. We must use a second technique—area sampling and filtering (discussed in Chapter 3)—to scale up or down properly. Filtering works best on pixmaps with depth greater than 1.

The problem of image scaling arises frequently, particularly when an image created by a painting program is to be printed. Let's consider sending a canvas to a printer that provides twice the resolution of the screen. Each pixel is now one-half its original size; thus, we can show the original image with the same number of pixels at half the size, or we can use pixel replication to produce an image of the original size without taking advantage of the finer resolution of the printer. Either way, something is lost—size or quality—and the only scaling method that does not sacrifice quality is respecification.

SUMMARY

In this chapter, we have discussed a simple but powerful raster graphics package, SRGP. It lets the application program draw 2D primitives subject to various attributes that affect the appearance of those primitives. Drawing can be performed directly onto the screen canvas or onto an offscreen canvas of any desired size. Drawing can be restricted to a rectangular region of a canvas via the clip rectangle attribute. Besides the standard 2D shapes, SRGP also supports intra- and intercanvas copying of rectangular regions. Copying and drawing can be affected by the write-mode attribute, allowing a destination pixel's current value to play a role in the determination of its new value.

SRGP also introduces the notion of logical input devices, which are high-level abstractions of physical input devices. The SRGP keyboard device abstracts the physical keyboard, and the locator device abstracts such devices as the mouse, the data tablet, and the joystick. Logical devices may operate either in sampled (polled) mode or in event mode. In event mode, a user action triggers the placing of an event report on the event queue, which the application may examine at its own convenience. In sample mode, the application continuously examines the device's measure for important changes.

Because SRGP scan converts primitives to their component pixels and does not store their original geometry, the only editing SRGP permits is the alteration of individual pixels, by drawing new primitives or by using the copyPixel operation on blocks of pixels. Object manipulations such as moving, deleting, or resizing must be done by the application program itself, which must respecify the updated image to SRGP.

Other systems offer a different set of features for graphics. For example, the PostScript language offers floating-point primitives and attributes, including far more general curved shapes and clipping facilities. PHIGS is a subroutine package that offers manipulation of hierarchically modeled objects, defined in a 3D floating-point world-coordinate system. These objects are stored in an editable database; the package automatically regenerates the image from this stored representation after any editing operation.

SRGP is a subroutine package, and many developers are finding that an interpreted language such as Adobe's PostScript provides maximal power and flexibility. Also, opinions differ on which should become standard—subroutine packages (integer or floating-point, with or without retention of primitives) or display languages such as PostScript that do not retain primitives. Each has its appropriate application domain, and we expect each to persist for some time.

In the next chapter, we see how SRGP does its drawing via scan conversion and clipping. In the following chapters, after an overview of hardware, we discuss the mathematics of transformations and 3D viewing in preparation for learning about PHIGS.

Exercises

2.1   SRGP runs in window environments but does not allow the application to take advantage of multiple windows: The screen canvas is mapped to a single window on the screen, and no other canvases are visible. What changes would you make to the SRGP design and application–programmer interface to allow an application to take advantage of a window system?

2.2   An SRGP application can be fully machine-independent only if it uses solely the two colors 0 and 1. Develop a strategy for enhancing SRGP so that SRGP simulates color when necessary, allowing an application to be designed to take advantage of color but still to operate in a useful way on a bilevel display. Discuss the problems and conflicts that any such strategy creates.

2.3   Implement an animation sequence in which several trivial objects move and resize. First, generate each frame by erasing the screen and then specifying the objects in their new positions. Then, try double-buffering: Use an offscreen canvas as a buffer into which each frame is drawn before being copied to the screen canvas. Compare the results of the two methods. Also, consider the use of SRGP_-copyPixel. Under what restricted circumstances is it useful for animation?

2.4   Implement nondestructive cursor tracking without using SRGP's built-in cursor echo. Use a bitmap or pixmap pattern to store a cursor's image, with 0s in the pattern representing transparency. Implement an **xor** cursor on a bilevel display, and a replace-mode cursor on a bilevel or color display. To test the tracking, you should perform a sampling loop with the SRGP locator device and move the cursor over an area containing information written previously.

2.5   Consider implementing the following feature in a painting application. The user can paint an **xor** swath that inverts the colors under the brush. It might seem that this is easily implemented by setting the write mode and then executing the code of Prog. 2.5. What complications arise? Propose solutions.

2.6   Some painting applications provide a *spray-painting* mode, in which passing the brush over an area affects a random minority of the pixels in the area. Each time the brush passes over an area, different pixels are touched, so with each pass of the brush, the *denser* the paint becomes. Implement a spray-painting interaction for a bilevel display. (*Beware*: The most obvious algorithms produce streaks or fail to provide increasing density. You will have to create a library of sparse bitmaps or patterns; see the SRGP reference manual for information on making custom patterns.)

2.7   Implement transparent-background text for bilevel displays, without using SRGP's built-in text primitive. Use an offscreen canvas to store the bitmap shape for each character, but support no more than six characters—this is not a lesson in font design! (*Hint*: You may have to use two different algorithms to support both colors 0 and 1.)

2.8   A drawing program can update the screen after a deletion operation by filling the deleted object's shape with the application screen background pattern. This technique, of course, may damage other objects on the screen. Why is it not sufficient to repair the damage by simply respecifying all objects whose rectangular extents intersect the extent of the deleted object? Discuss solutions to the problem of optimizing damage repair.

2.9   Implement a function that draws a button with text centered within an opaque rectangle with a thin border. Allow the caller to specify the colors for the text, background, and border; the screen position at which the center of the button should be placed; a pair of min/max dimensions for both width and height; and the font and the text string itself. If the string cannot fit on one line within the button at its maximum length, break the string at appropriate places (e.g., spaces) to make multiline text for the button.

2.10 Implement an onscreen valuator logical input device that allows the user to specify a temperature by using the mouse to vary the length of a simulated column of mercury. The device's attributes should include the range of the measure, the initial measure, the desired granularity of the measure (e.g., accuracy to 2° F), and the desired length and position of the thermometer's screen image. To test your device, use an interaction that simulates an indefinite waitEvent in which the only active device is the valuator.

2.11 Imagine customizing an SRGP implementation by adding an onscreen valuator device (like that described in Exercise 2.10) to the input model and supporting it for both event and sample modes. What kinds of problems might arise if the implementation is installed on a workstation having only one physical locator device? Propose solutions.

2.12 Implement a *rounded-rectangle* primitive—a rectangle whose corners are rounded, each corner being an ellipse arc of 90 rectangular degrees. Allow the application to have control of the radii of the ellipse arc. Support both outlined and filled versions.

**Programming
Projects**

2.13 Implement the pull-down menu package whose high-level design is presented in code fragments in Sections 2.2.6, 2.3.1, and 2.3.3. Have the package initialize the menu bar and menu bodies by reading strings from an input file. Allow the program to deactivate a menu to make the header disappear, and to activate a menu (with its horizontal position on the menu bar as a parameter) to make that menu appear.

2.14 Enhance your menu package from Project 2.13 by implementing disabling of selected menu items. Disabled items in a menu body should appear "grayed out"; since SRGP does not support the drawing of text using a pen style, on a bilevel display you must paint over solid text using a write mode in order to achieve this effect.

2.15 Enhance your menu package from Exercise 2.13 by highlighting the item to which the locator currently points while the user is choosing an item from the menu body.

2.16 Implement a layout application that allows the user to place objects in a square subregion of the screen. Ellipses, rectangles, and equilateral triangles should be supported. The user will click on a screen button to select an object type or to initiate an action (redraw screen, save scene to file, restore scene from file, or quit).

2.17 Add object editing to your layout application from Exercise 2.16. The user must be able to delete, move, and resize or rescale objects. Use this simple pick-correlation method: Scan the objects in the application database and choose the first object whose rectangular extent encloses the locator position. (Show that this naive method has a disturbing side effect: It is possible for a visible object to be unpickable!) Be sure to give the user feedback by highlighting the currently selected object.

2.18 Add an extra half-dimension to your layout application from Exercise 2.16 by implementing overlap priority. The user must be able to push/pop an object (force its priority to be the very lowest/highest). Enhance pick correlation to use overlap priority to resolve conflicts. How does the push/pop functionality, along with the use of priority by the pick correlator, allow the user to override the inaccuracy of naive pick correlation?

2.19 Optimize the screen-update algorithm of your layout application from Exercise 2.16 using the results of Exercise 2.8, so that a minimum number of objects is respecified in response to an edit operation.

2.20 Enhance your layout application from Exercise 2.16 so that the keyboard and locator are enabled simultaneously, to provide keyboard abbreviations for common operations. For example, pressing the "d" key could delete the currently selected object.

2.21 Design and implement analytical techniques for pick correlation for the three types of objects supported by your layout application from Exercise 2.16. Your new techniques should provide full accuracy; the user should no longer have to use pop/push to pick a visible low-priority object.

3

Basic Raster Graphics Algorithms for Drawing 2D Primitives

A raster graphics package approximates mathematical (*ideal*) primitives, described in terms of vertices on a Cartesian grid, by sets of pixels of the appropriate intensity of gray or color. These pixels are stored as a bitmap or pixmap in CPU memory or in a frame buffer. In the previous chapter, we studied the features of SRGP, a typical raster graphics package, from an application programmer's point of view. The purpose of this chapter is to look at SRGP from a package implementor's point of view—that is, in terms of the fundamental algorithms for scan converting primitives to pixels, subject to their attributes, and for clipping them against an upright clip rectangle. Examples of scan-converted and clipped primitives are shown in Fig. 3.1.

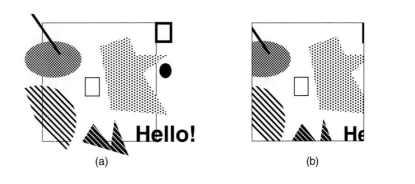

(a)   (b)

Figure 3.1   Clipping SRGP primitives to a rectangular clip region. (a) Primitives and the clipping rectangle. (b) Clipped results.

More advanced algorithms that handle features not supported in SRGP are used in more sophisticated and complex packages. The algorithms in this chapter are discussed in terms of the 2D integer Cartesian grid, but most of the scan-conversion algorithms can be extended to floating point, and the clipping algorithms can be extended both to floating point and to 3D. The final section introduces the concept of antialiasing—that is, minimizing jaggies by making use of a system's ability to vary a pixel's intensity.

3.1 OVERVIEW

3.1.1 Implications of Display-System Architecture

The fundamental conceptual model of Chapter 1 presents a graphics package as the system that mediates between the application program (and its application data structure/model) and the display hardware. The package gives the application program a device-independent interface to the hardware, as shown in Fig. 3.2, where SRGP's functions are partitioned into those forming an output pipeline and those forming an input pipeline.

In the **output pipeline,** the application program takes descriptions of objects in terms of primitives and attributes stored in or derived from an application model or data structure, and specifies them to the graphics package, which in turn clips and scan converts them to the pixels seen on the screen. The package's primitive-generation functions specify *what* is to be generated, the attribute functions specify *how* primitives are to be generated, the SRGP_copyPixel function specifies *how* images are to be modified, and the canvas-control functions specify *where* the images are to be generated. In the **input pipeline,** a user interaction at

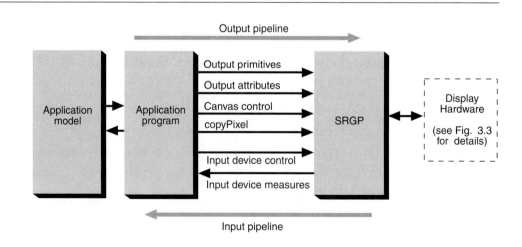

Figure 3.2   SRGP as intermediary between the application program and the graphics system, providing output and input pipelines.

the display end is converted to measure values returned by the package's sampling or event-driven input functions to the application program; the input pipeline typically uses those values to modify the model or the image on the screen. Functions relating to input include those to initialize and control input devices and those to obtain the latter's measures during interaction. We do not cover either SRGP's canvas management or its input handling in this book, since these topics have little to do with raster graphics and are primarily data-structure and low-level systems-software issues, respectively.

An SRGP implementation must communicate with a potentially wide variety of display devices. Some display systems are attached as peripherals with their own internal frame buffers and display controllers. These display controllers are processors specialized to interpret and execute drawing commands that generate pixels into the frame buffer. Other, simpler systems are refreshed directly from the memory used by the CPU. Output-only subsets of the package may drive raster hardcopy devices. These various types of hardware architectures will be discussed in more detail in Chapter 4. In any display-system architecture, the CPU must be able to read and write individual pixels in the frame buffer. It is also convenient to be able to move rectangular blocks of pixels to and from the frame buffer to implement the copyPixel (bitBlt) type of operation. This facility is used not for generating primitives directly but to make portions of offscreen bitmaps or pixmaps visible and to save and restore pieces of the screen for window management, menu handling, scrolling, and so on.

Whereas all implementations for systems that refresh from CPU memory are essentially identical because all the work is done in software, implementations for display controller and hardcopy systems vary considerably, depending on what the respective hardware devices can do by themselves and what remains for the software to do. Naturally, in any architecture, software scan conversion must be used to generate both primitives and attributes not directly supported in hardware. Let us look briefly at the range of architectures and implementations.

Displays with frame buffers and display controllers. SRGP has the least amount of work to do if it drives a display controller that does its own scan conversion and handles all of SRGP's primitives and attributes directly. In this case, SRGP needs only to convert its internal representation of primitives, attributes, and write modes to the formats accepted by the display peripheral that actually draws the primitives (Fig. 3.3a).

The display-controller architecture is most powerful when memory mapping allows the CPU to access the frame buffer directly, and the display controller to access the CPU's memory. The CPU can then read and write individual pixels and copyPixel blocks of pixels with normal CPU instructions, and the display controller can scan convert into offscreen canvases and also use its copyPixel instruction to move pixels between the two memories or within its own frame buffer. When the CPU and the display controller can run asynchronously, there must be synchronization to avoid memory conflicts. Often, the display controller is controlled by the CPU as a coprocessor. If the display peripheral's display controller can only scan convert into its own frame buffer and cannot write pixels into CPU memory,

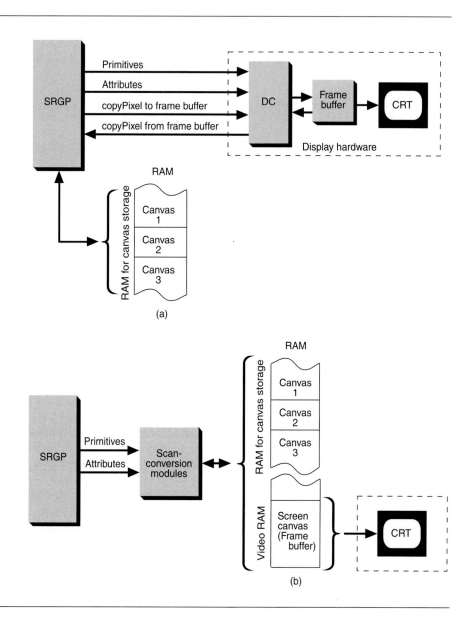

Figure 3.3   SRGP driving two types of display systems. (a) Display peripheral with display controller and frame buffer. (b) No display controller, memory-shared frame buffer.

we need a way to generate primitives in an offscreen canvas. The package then uses the display controller for scan conversion into the screen canvas but must do its own software scan conversion for offscreen canvases. The package can, of course, copyPixel images scan converted by the hardware from the frame buffer to offscreen canvases.

Displays with frame buffers only. For displays without a display controller, SRGP does its own scan conversion into both offscreen canvases and the frame buffer. A typical organization for such an SRGP implementation that drives a shared-memory frame buffer is shown in Fig. 3.3 (b). Note that we show only the parts of memory that constitute the frame buffer and store the canvases managed by SRGP; the rest of the memory is occupied by all the usual software and data, including, of course, SRGP itself.

Hardcopy devices. As will be explained in Chapter 4, hardcopy devices range in their capabilities along the same spectrum as display systems. The simplest devices accept only one scan line at a time and rely on the software to provide that scan line exactly when it is to be imaged on film or on paper. For such simple hardware, SRGP must generate a complete bitmap or pixmap and scan it out one line at a time to the output device. Slightly smarter devices can accept an entire frame (page) at a time. Yet more powerful equipment has built-in scan-conversion hardware, often called raster image processors (RIPs). At the high end of the scale, PostScript printers have internal *engines* that read PostScript programs describing pages in a device-independent fashion; they interpret such programs to produce the primitives and attributes that are then scan converted. The fundamental clipping and scan-conversion algorithms are essentially independent of the raster device's output technology; therefore, we need not address hardcopy devices further in this chapter.

3.1.2 The Output Pipeline in Software

Here we examine the output pipeline driving simple frame-buffer displays only in order to address the problems of software clipping and scan conversion. The various algorithms introduced are discussed at a general, machine-independent level, so they apply to both software and hardware (or microcode) implementations.

As each output primitive is encountered by SRGP, the package *scan converts* the primitive: Pixels are written in the current canvas according to their applicable attributes and current write mode. The primitive is also **clipped** to the clip rectangle; that is, pixels belonging to the primitive that are outside the clip region are not displayed. There are several ways of doing clipping. The obvious technique is to clip a primitive prior to scan conversion by computing its analytical intersections with the clip-rectangle boundaries; these intersection points are then used to define new vertices for the clipped version of the primitive. The advantage of clipping before scan converting is, of course, that the scan converter must deal with only the clipped version of the primitive, not with the original (possibly much larger) one. This technique is used most often for clipping lines, rectangles, and polygons, for which clipping algorithms are fairly simple and efficient.

The simplest, brute-force clipping technique, called **scissoring,** is to scan convert the entire primitive but to write only the visible pixels in the clip-rectangle region of the canvas. In principle, this procedure checks each pixel's coordinates against the (x, y) bounds of the rectangle before writing that pixel. In practice, there are shortcuts that obviate having to check adjacent pixels on a scan line, as we shall see later. This type of clipping is thus accomplished on the fly; if the bounds check can be done quickly (e.g., by a tight inner loop running completely in microcode or in an instruction cache), this approach may actually be faster than first clipping the primitive and then scan converting the resulting, clipped portions. It also generalizes to arbitrary clip regions.

A third technique is to generate the entire collection of primitives into a temporary canvas and then to copyPixel only the contents of the clip rectangle to the destination canvas. This approach is wasteful of both space and time, but it is easy to implement and is often used for text.

Raster displays invoke clipping and scan-conversion algorithms each time an image is created or modified. Hence, these algorithms not only must create visually satisfactory images but also must execute as rapidly as possible. As discussed in detail in later sections, scan-conversion algorithms use *incremental methods* to minimize the number of calculations (especially multiplies and divides) performed during each iteration; further, these calculations employ integer rather than floating-point arithmetic. Speed can be increased even further by using multiple parallel processors to scan convert simultaneously entire output primitives or pieces of them.

3.2 SCAN CONVERTING LINES

A scan-conversion algorithm for lines computes the coordinates of the pixels that lie on or near an ideal, infinitely thin straight line imposed on a 2D raster grid. In principle, we would like the sequence of pixels to lie as close to the ideal line as possible and to be as straight as possible. Consider a 1-pixel-thick approximation to an ideal line; what properties should it have? For lines with slopes between -1 and 1 inclusive, exactly 1 pixel should be illuminated in each column; for lines with slopes outside this range, exactly 1 pixel should be illuminated in each row. All lines should be drawn with constant brightness, independent of length and orientation, and as rapidly as possible. There should also be provisions for drawing lines that are more than 1 pixel wide, centered on the ideal line, that are affected by line-style and pen-style attributes, and that create other effects needed for high quality illustrations. For example, the shape of the endpoint regions should be under programmer control to allow beveled, rounded, and mitered corners. We would even like to be able to minimize the jaggies due to the discrete approximation of the ideal line, by using antialiasing techniques that exploit the ability to set the intensity of individual pixels on n-bits-per-pixel displays.

For now, we consider only 1-pixel-thick lines that have exactly 1 bilevel pixel in each column (or row for lines with slope $> \pm 1$). Later in the chapter, we will consider thick primitives and deal with styles.

To visualize the geometry, we recall that SRGP represents a pixel as a circular dot centered at that pixel's (x, y) location on the integer grid. This representation is a convenient approximation to the more or less circular cross-section of the CRT's electron beam, but the exact spacing between the beam spots on an actual display

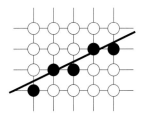

Figure 3.4
A scan-converted line
showing intensified pixels
as black circles.

can vary greatly among systems. In some systems, adjacent spots overlap; in others, there may be space between adjacent vertical pixels; in most systems, the spacing is tighter in the horizontal than in the vertical direction. Another variation in coordinate-system representation arises in systems, such as the Macintosh, that treat pixels as being centered in the rectangular box between adjacent grid lines instead of on the grid lines themselves. In this scheme, rectangles are defined to be all pixels interior to the mathematical rectangle defined by two corner points. This definition allows zero-width (null) canvases: The rectangle from (x, y) to (x, y) contains no pixels, unlike the SRGP canvas, which has a single pixel at that point. For now, we continue to represent pixels as disjoint circles centered on a uniform grid, although we shall make some minor changes when we discuss antialiasing.

Figure 3.4 shows a highly magnified view of a 1-pixel-thick line and of the ideal line that it approximates. The intensified pixels are shown as filled circles, and the nonintensified pixels are shown as unfilled circles. On an actual screen, the diameter of the roughly circular pixel is larger than the interpixel spacing, so our symbolic representation exaggerates the discreteness of the pixels.

Since SRGP primitives are defined on an integer grid, the endpoints of a line have integer coordinates. In fact, if we first clip the line to the clip rectangle, a line intersecting a clip edge may actually have an endpoint with a noninteger coordinate value. The same is true when we use a floating-point raster graphics package. (We will discuss these noninteger intersections in Section 3.2.3.) Assume that our line has slope $|m| \leq 1$; lines at other slopes can be handled by suitable changes in the development that follows. Also, the most common lines—those that are horizontal, are vertical, or have a slope of ± 1—can be handled as trivial special cases because these lines pass through only pixel centers (see Exercise 3.1).

3.2.1 The Basic Incremental Algorithm

The simplest strategy for scan converting lines is to compute the slope m as $\Delta y/\Delta x$, to increment x by 1 starting with the leftmost point, to calculate $y_i = mx_i + B$ for each x_i, and to intensify the pixel at $(x_i, \text{Round}(y_i))$, where $\text{Round}(y_i) = \text{Floor}(0.5 + y_i)$. This computation selects the closest pixel—that is, the pixel whose distance to the true line is smallest. This brute-force strategy is inefficient, however, because each iteration requires a floating-point (or binary fraction) multiply, addition, and invocation of Floor. We can eliminate the multiplication by noting that

$$y_{i+1} = mx_{i+1} + B = m(x_i + \Delta x) + B = y_i + m\Delta x,$$

and if $\Delta x = 1$, then $y_{i+1} = y_i + m$.

Thus, a unit change in x changes y by m, which is the slope of the line. For all points (x_i, y_i) on the line (*not* the points on our rasterization of the line), we know that if $x_{i+1} = x_i + 1$, then $y_{i+1} = y_i + m$; that is, the values of x and y are defined in terms of their previous values (see Fig. 3.5). This is what defines an incremental algorithm: At each step, we make incremental calculations based on the preceding step.

We initialize the incremental calculation with (x_0, y_0), the integer coordinates of an endpoint. Note that this incremental technique avoids the need to deal with

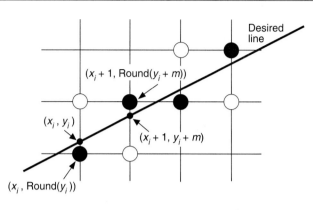

Figure 3.5   Incremental calculation of (x_i, y_i).

the y intercept, B, explicitly. If $|m| > 1$, a step in x creates a step in y that is greater than 1. Thus, we must reverse the roles of x and y by assigning a unit step to y and incrementing x by $\Delta x = \Delta y/m = 1/m$. Line, the function in Prog. 3.1, implements the incremental technique. The start point must be the left endpoint. Also, it is limited to the case $-1 \le m \le 1$, but other slopes may be accommodated by symmetry. Checking for the special cases of horizontal, vertical, or diagonal lines is omitted.

WritePixel, used by Line, is a low-level function provided by the device level software; it places a value into a canvas for a pixel whose coordinates are given as the first two arguments.[1] We assume here that we scan convert only in replace mode; for SRGP's other write modes, we must use a low-level ReadPixel function to read the pixel at the destination location, logically combine that pixel with the source pixel, and then write the result into the destination pixel with WritePixel.

This algorithm is often referred to as a **digital differential analyzer (DDA)** algorithm. The DDA is a mechanical device that solves differential equations by numerical methods: It traces out successive (x, y) values by simultaneously incrementing x and y by small steps proportional to the first derivative of x and y. In our case, the x increment is 1, and the y increment is $dy/dx = m$. Since real variables have limited precision, summing an inexact m repetitively introduces cumulative error buildup and eventually a drift away from a true Round(y_i); for most (short) lines, this will not present a problem.

Program 3.1

The incremental line scan-conversion algorithm.

```
void   Line(int x0, int y0, int x1, int y1, int value)
{                              /* Assumes −1 ≤ m ≤ 1, x0 < x1 */
    int    x;                  /* x runs from x0 to x1 in unit increments.*/
    float  dy, dx, y, m;

    dy = y1 − y0;
    dx = x1 − x0;
```

---

[1] If such a low-level function is not available, the SRGP_pointCoord function may be used, as described in the SRGP reference manual.

```
m = dy / dx;
y = y0;
for (x = x0; x <= x1; x++) {
    WritePixel(x, (int) floor(y + 0.5), value);    / *Set pixel to value */
    y += m;                                         / *Step y by slope m */
}
}
```

3.2.2 Midpoint Line Algorithm

The drawbacks of function Line are that rounding y to an integer takes time and that the variables y and m must be real or fractional binary because the slope is a fraction. Bresenham developed a classic algorithm [BRES65] that is attractive because it uses only integer arithmetic, thus avoiding the Round function, and allows the calculation for (x_{i+1}, y_{i+1}) to be performed incrementally—that is, by using the calculation already done at (x_i, y_i). A floating-point version of this algorithm can be applied to lines with arbitrary real-valued endpoint coordinates. Furthermore, Bresenham's incremental technique may be applied to the integer computation of circles as well, although it does not generalize easily to arbitrary conics. We therefore use a slightly different formulation, the *midpoint technique*, first published by Pitteway [PITT67] and adapted by Van Aken [VANA84] and other researchers. For lines and integer circles, the midpoint formulation, as Van Aken shows [VANA85], reduces to the Bresenham formulation and therefore generates the same pixels. Bresenham showed that his line and integer circle algorithms provide the best-fit approximations to true lines and circles by minimizing the error (distance) to the true primitive [BRES77]. Kappel discusses the effects of various error criteria in [KAPP85].

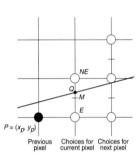

Figure 3.6
The pixel grid for the midpoint line algorithm, showing the midpoint M, and the E and NE pixels to choose between.

We assume that the line's slope is between 0 and 1. Other slopes can be handled by suitable reflections about the principal axes. We call the lower-left endpoint (x_0, y_0), and the upper-right endpoint (x_1, y_1).

Consider the line in Fig. 3.6, where the previously selected pixel appears as a black circle and the two pixels from which to choose at the next stage are shown as unfilled circles. Assume that we have just selected the pixel P at (x_P, y_P) and now must choose between the pixel one increment to the right (called the east pixel, E) or the pixel one increment to the right and one increment up (called the northeast pixel, NE). Let Q be the intersection point of the line being scan-converted with the grid line $x = x_P + 1$. In Bresenham's formulation, the difference between the vertical distances from E and NE to Q is computed, and the sign of the difference is used to select the pixel whose distance from Q is smaller as the best approximation to the line. In the midpoint formulation, we observe on which side of the line the midpoint M lies. It is easy to see that, if the midpoint lies above the line, pixel E is closer to the line; if the midpoint lies below the line, pixel NE is closer to the line. The line may pass between E and NE, or both pixels may lie on one side, but in any case, the midpoint test chooses the closest pixel. Also, the error—that is, the vertical distance between the chosen pixel and the actual line—is always $\leq 1/2$.

The algorithm chooses NE as the next pixel for the line shown in Fig. 3.6. Now all we need is a way to calculate on which side of the line the midpoint lies.

Let us represent the line by an implicit function[2] with coefficients a, b, and c: $F(x, y) = ax + by + c = 0$. (The b coefficient of y is unrelated to the y intercept B in the slope-intercept form.) If $dy = y_1 - y_0$, and $dx = x_1 - x_0$, the slope-intercept form can be written as

$$y = \frac{dy}{dx} x + B;$$

therefore,

$$F(x, y) = dy \cdot x - dx \cdot y + B \cdot dx = 0.$$

Here $a = dy$, $b = -dx$, and $c = B \cdot dx$ in the implicit form.[3]

It can easily be verified that $F(x, y)$ is zero on the line, positive for points below the line, and negative for points above the line. To apply the midpoint criterion, we need only to compute $F(M) = F(x_P + 1, y_P + \frac{1}{2})$ and to test its sign. Because our decision is based on the value of the function at $(x_P + 1, y_P + \frac{1}{2})$, we define a decision variable $d = F(x_P + 1, y_P + \frac{1}{2})$. By definition, $d = a(x_P + 1) + b(y_P + \frac{1}{2}) + c$. If $d > 0$, we choose pixel NE; if $d < 0$, we choose E; and if $d = 0$, we can choose either, so we pick E.

Next, we ask what happens to the location of M and therefore to the value of d for the next grid line; both depend, of course, on whether we chose E or NE. If E is chosen, M is incremented by one step in the x direction. Then,

$$d_{\text{new}} = F(x_P + 2, y_P + \tfrac{1}{2}) = a(x_P + 2) + b(y_P + \tfrac{1}{2}) + c,$$

but

$$d_{\text{old}} = a(x_P + 1) + b(y_P + \tfrac{1}{2}) + c.$$

Subtracting d_{old} from d_{new} to get the incremental difference, we write $d_{\text{new}} = d_{\text{old}} + a$.

We call the increment to add after E is chosen Δ_E; $\Delta_E = a = dy$. In other words, we can derive the value of the decision variable at the next step incrementally from the value at the current step without having to compute $F(M)$ directly, by merely adding Δ_E.

If NE is chosen, M is incremented by one step each in both the x and y directions. Then,

$$d_{\text{new}} = F(x_P + 2, y_P + \tfrac{3}{2}) = a(x_P + 2) + b(y_P + \tfrac{3}{2}) + c.$$

Subtracting d_{old} from d_{new} to get the incremental difference, we write

$$d_{\text{new}} = d_{\text{old}} + a + b.$$

We call the increment to add to d after NE is chosen Δ_{NE}; $\Delta_{NE} = a + b = dy - dx$.

Let us summarize the incremental midpoint technique. At each step, the algorithm chooses between two pixels based on the sign of the decision variable calcu-

---

[2] This functional form extends nicely to the implicit formulation of circles.

[3] It is important for the proper functioning of the midpoint algorithm to choose a to be positive; we meet this criterion if dy is positive, since $y_1 > y_0$.

lated in the previous iteration; then it updates the decision variable by adding either Δ_E or Δ_{NE} to the old value, depending on the choice of pixel.

Since the first pixel is simply the first endpoint (x_0, y_0), we can directly calculate the initial value of d for choosing between E and NE. The first midpoint is at $(x_0 + 1, y_0 + \frac{1}{2})$, and

$$F(x_0 + 1, y_0 + \tfrac{1}{2}) = a(x_0 + 1) + b(y_0 + \tfrac{1}{2}) + c$$

$$= ax_0 + by_0 + c + a + b/2$$

$$= F(x_0, y_0) + a + b/2.$$

But (x_0, y_0) is a point on the line and $F(x_0, y_0)$ is therefore 0; hence, d_{start} is just $a + b/2 = dy - dx/2$. Using d_{start}, we choose the second pixel, and so on. To eliminate the fraction in d_{start}, we redefine our original F by multiplying it by 2; $F(x, y) = 2(ax + by + c)$. This multiplies each constant and the decision variable (and the increments Δ_E and Δ_{NE}) by 2 but does not affect the sign of the decision variable, which is all that matters for the midpoint test.

The arithmetic needed to evaluate d_{new} for any step is simple integer addition. No time-consuming multiplication is involved. Further, the inner loop is quite simple, as seen in the midpoint algorithm of Prog. 3.2. The first statement in the loop, the test of d, determines the choice of pixel, but we actually increment x and y to that pixel location after updating the decision variable (for compatibility with the circle algorithms). Note that this version of the algorithm works for only those lines with slope between 0 and 1; generalizing the algorithm is left as Exercise 3.2. In [SPRO82], Sproull gives an elegant derivation of Bresenham's formulation of this algorithm as a series of program transformations from the original brute-force algorithm. No equivalent of that derivation for circles has yet appeared, but the midpoint technique does generalize, as we shall see.

Program 3.2

The midpoint line scan-conversion algorithm.

```
void   MidpointLine(int x0, int y0, int x1, int y1, int value)
{
    int    dx, dy, incrE, incrNE, d, x, y;

    dx = x1 – x0;
    dy = y1 – y0;
    d = dy * 2 – dx;            /* Initial value of d */
    incrE = dy * 2;             /* Increment used for move to E */
    incrNE = (dy – dx) * 2;      /* Increment used for move to NE */
    x = x0;
    y = y0;
    WritePixel(x, y, value);     /* The start pixel */
    while (x < x1) {
        if (d <= 0) {            /* Choose E */
            d += incrE;
            x++;
        } else {                 /*Choose NE*/
            d += incrNE;
            x++;
            y++;
```

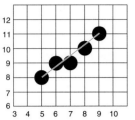

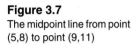

Figure 3.7
The midpoint line from point (5,8) to point (9,11)

```
        }
        WritePixel(x, y, value);        /* The selected pixel closest to the line */
    }
}
```

For a line from point (5, 8) to point (9, 11), the successive values of d are 2, 0, 6, and 4, resulting in the selection of NE, E, NE, and then NE, respectively, as shown in Fig. 3.7. The line appears abnormally jagged because of the enlarged scale of the drawing and the artificially large interpixel spacing used to make the geometry of the algorithm clear. For the same reason, the drawings in the following sections also make the primitives appear blockier than they look on an actual screen.

Example 3.1

Problem: Develop and program an enhanced version of the midpoint line algorithm that looks ahead two pixels rather than only one.

Answer: An alternative to using the midpoint line algorithm for scan converting lines is the double-step algorithm introduced by Wu and Rokne [WU87]. Like the midpoint algorithm, this technique is incremental; (x_{i+1}, y_{i+1}) can be computed from (x_i, y_i) using only integer arithmetic. The midpoint algorithm first determines the direction (slope) of the line, then it proceeds by using a decision variable to choose between two alternative pixels at each step. The double-step algorithm reduces the number of decisions, i.e., choices for the next pixel, by two. It accomplishes this by looking for the next *pair* of pixels rather than just the next pixel. Wu [WU87] showed that four patterns can occur:

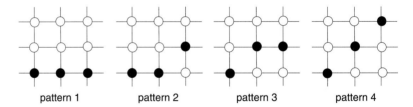

pattern 1　　　　pattern 2　　　　pattern 3　　　　pattern 4

Wu showed that pattern 1 and pattern 4 cannot occur on the same line. Furthermore, if the slope of the line is greater than $\frac{1}{2}$, pattern 1 cannot occur. Similarly, if the slope of the line is less than $\frac{1}{2}$, pattern 4 can not occur. Thus, by testing the slope, the choice is narrowed to one of three patterns: 1, 2, 3 or 2, 3, 4. Let us look at the case where the slope is between 0 and $\frac{1}{2}$. This excludes pattern 4, as already indicated. A determination needs to be made whether pattern 1, or either pattern 2 or 3 is used to fill in the raster image. The decision variable d is initially set to $d = 4dy - dx$. Then for each increment (step of two raster units), testing whether $d < 0$ determines whether pattern 1 is used. If d is greater than or equal to 0, then a determination must be made between patterns 2 and 3. This is simply the test: $d < 2dy$. To increment d, we use the following rule:

$$d_{i+1} = d_i + 4dy \qquad \text{if } d_i < 0 \text{ (pattern 1),}$$
$$d_{i+1} = d_i + 4dy - 2dx \quad \text{otherwise (pattern 2 or 3).}$$

The midpoint line algorithm can be modified to take advantage of this improvement as follows:

Code that implements enhanced midpoint line algorithm.

```
void DoubleStep( int x0, int y0, int x1, int y1 )
{
    int current_x, incr_1, incr_2, cond, dx, dy, d;

    /* Inner loop code for the case where (0 < slope < 1/2)
       Routine DrawPixels needs both the pattern and the current x position.
       This is because the last pixel might need only a single pixel drawn and not
       the entire pattern.  By drawing the entire pattern, the line might extend too far */

    /* Set up the initialization for the inner loop */
        dx = x1 − x0;
        dy = y1 − y0;
        current_x = x0;
        incr_1 = 4*dy;
        incr_2 = 4*dy − 2*dx;
        cond = 2 * dy;
        d = 4*dy − dx;

        while( current_x < x1 ) {                /* still more scan converting needed */
            if ( d < 0 ) {                       /* first decision */
                DrawPixels(PATTERN_1,current_x);
                d += incr_1;
            } else {
                if ( d < cond )                  /* wasn't the first case, is it 2 or 3 */
                    DrawPixels(PATTERN_2, current_x);
                else
                    DrawPixels(PATTERN_3, current_x);
                    d += incr_2;
            }
            current_x += 2;
        }
}
```

Like the midpoint algorithm, all computations can be done using integer additions and multiplications by 2. If the display is multilevel, rather than discriminating between patterns 2 and 3, one can simply draw them both at half-intensity, getting a form of antialiasing for free! Wyvill [WYVI90] noted that one can take advantage of the symmetry about the midpoint and scan convert the line from both endpoints simultaneously, thereby doubling the speed of the algorithm. The complete algorithm for the symmetric double-step line algorithm, coded in C, can be found in [WYVI90].

3.2.3 Additional Issues

Endpoint order. Among the complications to consider is that we must ensure that a line from P_0 to P_1 contains the same set of pixels as the line from P_1 to P_0, so that the appearance of the line is independent of the order of specification of the endpoints. The only place where the choice of pixel is dependent on the direction of the line is where the line passes exactly through the midpoint and the decision variable is zero; going left to right, we chose to pick E for this case. By symmetry, while going from right to left, we would also expect to choose W for $d = 0$, but that would choose a pixel one unit up in y relative to the one chosen for the left-to-right scan. We therefore need to choose SW when $d = 0$ for right-to-left scanning. Similar adjustments need to be made for lines at other slopes.

The alternative solution of switching a given line's endpoints as needed so that scan conversion always proceeds in the same direction does not work when we use line styles. The line style always *anchors* the specified write mask at the start point, which would be the bottom-left point, independent of line direction. That does not necessarily produce the desired visual effect. In particular, for a dot-dash line pattern of, say, 111100, we would like to have the pattern start at whichever start point is specified, not automatically at the bottom-left point. Also, if the algorithm always put endpoints in a canonical order, the pattern might go left to right for one segment and right to left for the adjoining segment, as a function of the second line's slope; this would create an unexpected discontinuity at the shared vertex, where the pattern should follow seamlessly from one line segment to the next.

Starting at the edge of a clip rectangle.   Another issue is that we must modify our algorithm to accept a line that has been analytically clipped by one of the algorithms in Section 3.9. Figure. 3.8(a) shows a line being clipped at the left edge, $x = x_{min}$, of the clip rectangle. The intersection point of the line with the edge

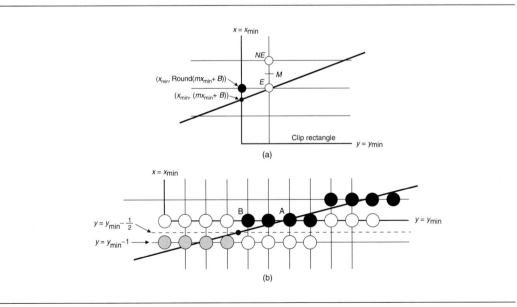

(a)

(b)

Figure 3.8   Starting the line at a clip boundary. (a) Intersection with a vertical edge. (b) Intersection with a horizontal edge (gray pixels are on the line but are outside the clip rectangle).

has an integer x coordinate but a real y coordinate. The pixel at the left edge, $(x_{min}, \text{Round}(mx_{min} + B))$, is the same pixel that would be drawn at this x value for the unclipped line by the incremental algorithm.[4] Given this initial pixel value, we must next initialize the decision variable at the midpoint between the E and NE positions in the next column over. It is important to realize that this strategy produces the correct sequence of pixels, while clipping the line at the x_{min} boundary and then scan converting the clipped line from $(x_{min}, \text{Round}(mx_{min} + B))$ to (x_1, y_1) using the integer midpoint line algorithm would not—that clipped line has a different slope!

The situation is more complicated if the line intersects a horizontal rather than a vertical edge, as shown in Fig. 3.8(b). For the type of shallow line shown, there will be multiple pixels lying on the scan line $y = y_{min}$ that correspond to the bottom edge of the clip region. We want to count each of these pixels as inside the clip region, but simply computing the analytical intersection of the line with the $y = y_{min}$ scan line and then rounding the x value of the intersection point would produce pixel A, not the leftmost point of the span of pixels shown, pixel B. From the figure, it is clear that the leftmost pixel of the span, B, is the one that lies just above and to the right of the place on the grid where the line first crosses above the midpoint $y = y_{min} - \frac{1}{2}$. Therefore, we simply find the intersection of the line with the horizontal line $y = y_{min} - \frac{1}{2}$, and round up the x value; the first pixel, B, is then the one at $(\text{Round}(x_{y_{min}-\frac{1}{2}}), y_{min})$.

Finally, the incremental midpoint algorithm works even if endpoints are specified in a floating-point raster graphics package; the only difference is that the increments are now reals, and the arithmetic is done with reals.

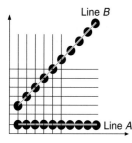

Figure 3.9
Varying intensity of raster lines as a function of slope.

Varying the intensity of a line as a function of slope. Consider the two-scan converted lines in Fig. 3.9. Line B, the diagonal line, has a slope of 1 and hence is $\sqrt{2}$ times as long as A, the horizontal line. Yet the same number of pixels (10) is drawn to represent each line. If the intensity of each pixel is I, then the intensity per unit length of line A is I, whereas for line B it is only $I/\sqrt{2}$; this discrepancy is easily detected by the viewer. On a bilevel display, there is no cure for this problem, but on an n-bits-per-pixel system we can compensate by setting the intensity to be a function of the line's slope. Antialiasing, discussed in Section 3.14, achieves an even better result by treating the line as a thin rectangle and computing appropriate intensities for the multiple pixels in each column that lie in or near the rectangle.

Treating the line as a rectangle is also a way to create thick lines. In Section 3.7, we show how to modify the basic scan-conversion algorithms to deal with thick primitives and with primitives whose appearance is affected by line-style and pen-style attributes.

Outline primitives composed of lines. Knowing how to scan convert lines, how do we scan convert primitives made from lines? Polylines can be scan-converted one line segment at a time. Scan converting rectangles and polygons as area

---

[4] When $mx_{min} + B$ lies exactly halfway between horizontal grid lines, we actually must round down. This is a consequence of choosing pixel E when $d = 0$.

defining primitives could be done a line segment at a time, but that would result in some pixels being drawn that lie outside a primitive's area—see Sections 3.4 and 3.5 for special algorithms to handle this problem. Care must be taken to draw shared vertices of polylines only once, since drawing a vertex twice causes it to change color or to be set to background when writing in **xor** mode to a screen, or to be written at double intensity on a film recorder. In fact, other pixels may be shared by two line segments that lie close together or cross as well. See Exercise 3.7 for a discussion of this issue and of the difference between a polyline and a sequence of connected line segments.

3.3 SCAN CONVERTING CIRCLES

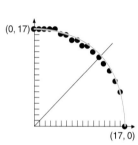

Although SRGP does not offer a circle primitive, the implementation will benefit from treating the circular ellipse arc as a special case because of its eight-fold symmetry, both for clipping and for scan conversion. The equation of a circle centered at the origin is $x^2 + y^2 = R^2$. Circles not centered at the origin may be translated to the origin by integer amounts and then scan-converted, with pixels written with the appropriate offset. There are several easy but inefficient ways to scan convert a circle. Solving for y in the implicit circle equation, we get the explicit $y = f(x)$ as

$$y = \pm\sqrt{R^2 - x^2}.$$

Figure 3.10
A quarter circle generated with unit steps in x, and with y calculated and then rounded. Unique values of y for each x produce gaps.

To draw a quarter circle (the other quarters are drawn by symmetry), we can increment x from 0 to R in unit steps, solving for $+y$ at each step. This approach works, but it is inefficient because of the multiply and square-root operations. Furthermore, the circle will have large gaps (unless R is large) for values of x close to R, because the slope of the circle becomes infinite there (see Fig. 3.10). A similarly inefficient method, that does, however, avoid the large gaps, is to plot $(R\cos\theta, R\sin\theta)$ by stepping θ from 0° to 90°.

3.3.1 Eight-Way Symmetry

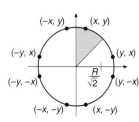

We can improve the drawing process of the previous section by taking greater advantage of the symmetry in a circle. Consider first a circle centered at the origin. If the point (x, y) is on the circle, then we can trivially compute seven other points on the circle, as shown in Fig. 3.11. Therefore, we need to compute only one 45° segment to determine the circle completely. For a circle centered at the origin, the eight symmetrical points can be displayed with function CirclePoints (the function is easily generalized to the case of circles with arbitrary origins):

Figure 3.11
Eight symmetrical points on a circle.

```
void CirclePoints (float x, float y, int value)
{
    WritePixel (x, y, value);
    WritePixel (y, x, value);
    WritePixel (y, -x, value);
```

```
            WritePixel (x, −y, value);
            WritePixel (−x, −y, value);
            WritePixel (−y, −x, value);
            WritePixel (−y, x, value);
            WritePixel (−x, y, value);
        }
```

We do not want to call CirclePoints when $x = y$, because each of four pixels would be set twice; the code is easily modified to handle that boundary condition.

3.3.2 Midpoint Circle Algorithm

Bresenham [BRES77] developed an incremental circle generator that is more efficient than the methods we have discussed. Conceived for use with pen plotters, the algorithm generates all points on a circle centered at the origin by incrementing all the way around the circle. We derive a similar algorithm, again using the midpoint criterion, which, for the case of integer center point and radius, generates the same, optimal set of pixels. Furthermore, the resulting code is essentially the same as that specified in patent 4,371,933 [BRES83].

We consider only 45° of a circle, the second octant from $x = 0$ to $x = y = R/\sqrt{2}$, and use the CirclePoints function to display points on the entire circle. As with the midpoint line algorithm, the strategy is to select which of two pixels is closer to the circle by evaluating a function at the midpoint between the two pixels. In the second octant, if pixel P at (x_p, y_p) has been previously chosen as closest to the circle, the choice of the next pixel is between pixel E and pixel SE (see Fig. 3.12).

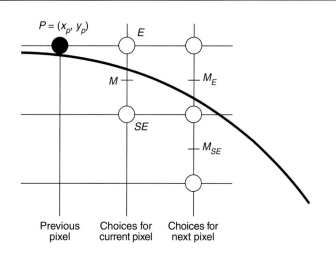

Figure 3.12   The pixel grid for the midpoint circle algorithm showing M and the pixels E and SE to·choose between.

Let $F(x, y) = x^2 + y^2 - R^2$; this function is 0 on the circle, positive outside the circle, and negative inside the circle. It can be seen that if the midpoint between the pixels E and SE is outside the circle, then pixel SE is closer to the circle. On the other hand, if the midpoint is inside the circle, pixel E is closer to the circle.

As for lines, we choose on the basis of the decision variable d, which is the value of the function at the midpoint,

$$d_{\text{old}} = F(x_P + 1, y_P - \tfrac{1}{2}) = (x_P + 1)^2 + (y_P - \tfrac{1}{2})^2 - R^2.$$

If $d_{\text{old}} < 0$, E is chosen, and the next midpoint will be one increment over in x. Then,

$$d_{\text{new}} = F(x_P + 2, y_P - \tfrac{1}{2}) = (x_P + 2)^2 + (y_P - \tfrac{1}{2})^2 - R^2,$$

and $d_{\text{new}} = d_{\text{old}} + (2x_P + 3)$; therefore, the increment $\Delta_E = 2x_P + 3$.

If $d_{\text{old}} \geq 0$, SE is chosen,[5] and the next midpoint will be one increment over in x and one increment down in y. Then

$$d_{\text{new}} = F(x_P + 2, y_P - \tfrac{3}{2}) = (x_P + 2)^2 + (y_P - \tfrac{3}{2})^2 - R^2.$$

Since $d_{\text{new}} = d_{\text{old}} + (2x_P - 2y_P + 5)$, the increment $\Delta_{SE} = 2x_P - 2y_P + 5$.

Recall that, in the linear case, Δ_E and Δ_{NE} were constants; in the quadratic case, however, Δ_E and Δ_{SE} vary at each step and are functions of the particular values of x_P and y_P at the pixel chosen in the previous iteration. Because these functions are expressed in terms of (x_P, y_P), we call P the **point of evaluation**. The Δ functions can be evaluated directly at each step by plugging in the values of x and y for the pixel chosen in the previous iteration. This direct evaluation is not expensive computationally, since the functions are only linear.

In summary, we do the same two steps at each iteration of the algorithm as we did for the line: (1) Choose the pixel based on the sign of the variable d computed during the previous iteration, and (2) update the decision variable d with the Δ that corresponds to the choice of pixel. The only difference from the line algorithm is that, in updating d, we evaluate a linear function of the point of evaluation.

All that remains now is to compute the initial condition. By limiting the algorithm to integer radii in the second octant, we know that the starting pixel lies on the circle at $(0, R)$. The next midpoint lies at $(1, R - \tfrac{1}{2})$, therefore, and $F(1, R - \tfrac{1}{2}) = 1 + (R^2 - R + \tfrac{1}{4}) - R^2 = \tfrac{5}{4} - R$. Now we can implement the algorithm directly, as in Prog. 3.3. Notice how similar in structure this algorithm is to the line algorithm.

The problem with this version is that we are forced to do real arithmetic because of the fractional initialization of d. Although the function can be easily modified to handle circles that are not located on integer centers or do not have integer radii, we would like a more efficient, purely integer version. We thus do a simple program transformation to eliminate fractions.

First, we define a new decision variable, h, by $h = d - \tfrac{1}{4}$, and we substitute $h + \tfrac{1}{4}$ for d in the code. Now the initialization is $h = 1 - R$, and the comparison

---

[5] Choosing SE when $d = 0$ differs from our choice in the line algorithm and is arbitrary. The reader may wish to simulate the algorithm by hand to see that, for $R = 17$, one pixel is changed by this choice.

Program 3.3

The midpoint circle scan-conversion algorithm.

```
void   MidpointCircle(int radius, int value)
{
    int    x, y;
    float  d;

    x = 0;                        /*Initialization*/
    y = radius;
    d = 5.0 / 4 – radius;
    CirclePoints(x, y, value);
    while (y > x) {
        if (d < 0) {              /*Select E*/
            d += x * 2.0 + 3;
            x++;
        } else {                  /*Select SE*/
            d += (x – y) * 2.0 + 5;
            x++;
            y—;
        }
        CirclePoints(x, y, value);
    }
}
```

$d < 0$ becomes $h < -\frac{1}{4}$. However, since h starts out with an integer value and is incremented by integer values (Δ_E and Δ_{SE}), we can change the comparison to just $h < 0$. We now have an integer algorithm in terms of h; for consistency with the line algorithm, we will substitute d for h throughout. The final, fully integer algorithm is shown in Prog. 3.4.

Program 3.4

The integer midpoint circle scan-conversion algorithm.

```
void   MidpointCircle(int radius, int value)
{
    int    x, y, d;

    x = 0;                        /*Initialization.*/
    y = radius;
    d = 1 – radius;
    CirclePoints(x, y, value);
    while (y > x) {
        if (d < 0) {              /*Select E*/
            d += x * 2 + 3;
            x++;
        } else {                  /*Select SE*/
            d += (x – y) * 2 + 5;
            x++;
            y—;
        }
        CirclePoints(x, y, value);
    }
}
```

Figure 3.13 shows the second octant of a circle of radius 17 generated with the algorithm, and the first octant generated by symmetry (compare the results to Fig. 3.10).

Second-order differences.   We can improve the performance of the midpoint circle algorithm by using the incremental computation technique even more extensively. We noted that the Δ functions are linear equations, and we computed them directly. Any polynomial can be computed incrementally, however, as we did with the decision variables for both the line and the circle. In effect, we are calculating **first-** and **second-order partial differences,** a useful technique that we will encounter again in Chapter 9. The strategy is to evaluate the function directly at two adjacent points, to calculate the difference (which, for polynomials, is always a polynomial of lower degree), and to apply that difference in each iteration.

If we choose E in the current iteration, the point of evaluation moves from (x_P, y_P) to $(x_P + 1, y_P)$. As we saw, the first-order difference is $\Delta_{E\text{old}}$ at $(x_P, y_P) = 2x_P + 3$. Therefore,

$$\Delta_{E\text{new}} \text{ at } (x_P + 1, y_P) = 2(x_P + 1) + 3,$$

and the second-order difference is $\Delta_{E\text{new}} - \Delta_{E\text{old}} = 2.$
Similarly, $\Delta_{SE\text{old}}$ at $(x_P, y_P) = 2x_P - 2y_P + 5$. Therefore,

$$\Delta_{SE\text{new}} \text{ at } (x_P + 1, y_P) = 2(x_P + 1) - 2y_P + 5,$$

and the second-order difference is $\Delta_{SE\text{new}} - \Delta_{SE\text{old}} = 2.$
If we choose SE in the current iteration, the point of evaluation moves from (x_P, y_P) to $(x_P + 1, y_P - 1)$. Therefore,

$$\Delta_{E\text{new}} \text{ at } (x_P + 1, y_P - 1) = 2(x_P + 1) + 3,$$

and the second-order difference is $\Delta_{E\text{new}} - \Delta_{E\text{old}} = 2.$ Also,

$$\Delta_{SE\text{new}} \text{ at } (x_P + 1, y_P - 1) = 2(x_P + 1) - 2(y_P - 1) + 5,$$

and the second-order difference is $\Delta_{SE\text{new}} - \Delta_{SE\text{old}} = 4.$
The revised algorithm then consists of the following steps: (1) Choose the pixel based on the sign of the variable d computed during the previous iteration; (2) update the decision variable d with either Δ_E or Δ_{SE}, using the value of the corresponding Δ computed during the previous iteration; (3) update the Δ's to take into account the move to the new pixel, using the constant differences computed previously; and (4) do the move. Δ_E and Δ_{SE} are initialized using the start pixel (0, R). The revised function using this technique is shown in Prog. 3.5.

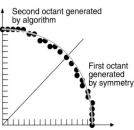

Second octant generated by algorithm

First octant generated by symmetry

Figure 3.13
Second octant of circle generated with midpoint algorithm, and first octant generated by symmetry.

Program 3.5

The midpoint circle scan-conversion algorithm using second-order differences.

```
void   MidpointCircle(int radius, int value)
{
    /*This function uses second-order partial differences to compute increments*/
    /* in the decision variable.  Assumes center of circle is at origin*/
    int    x, y, d, deltaE, deltaSE;
```

```
x = 0;                          /*Initialization*/
y = radius;
d = 1 − radius;
deltaE = 3;
deltaSE = 5 − radius * 2;
CirclePoints(x, y, value);
while (y > x) {
    if (d < 0) {                /*Select E*/
        d += deltaE;
        deltaE += 2;
        deltaSE += 2;
        x++;
    } else {                    /*Select SE*/
        d += deltaSE;
        deltaE += 2;
        deltaSE += 4;
        x++;
        y—;
    }
    CirclePoints(x, y, value);
}
}
```

3.4 FILLING RECTANGLES

The task of filling primitives can be broken down into two parts: the decision of which pixels to fill (this depends on the shape of the primitive, as modified by clipping), and the easier decision of with what value to fill them. We first discuss filling unclipped primitives with a solid color; we will deal with pattern filling in Section 3.6. In general, determining which pixels to fill consists of taking successive scan lines that intersect the primitive and filling in *spans* of adjacent pixels that lie inside the primitive from left to right.

To fill a rectangle with a solid color, we set each pixel lying on a scan line running from the left edge to the right edge to the same pixel value; that is, we fill each span from x_{min} to x_{max}. Spans exploit a primitive's **spatial coherence:** the fact that primitives often do not change from pixel to pixel within a span or from scan line to scan line. We exploit coherence in general by looking for only those pixels at which changes occur. For a solidly shaded primitive, all pixels on a span are set to the same value, which provides **span coherence.** The solidly shaded rectangle also exhibits strong *scan-line coherence* in that consecutive scan lines that intersect the rectangle are identical; later, we also use **edge coherence** for the edges of general polygons. We take advantage of various types of coherence not only for scan converting 2D primitives, but also for rendering 3D primitives, as will be discussed in Section 13.1.

The capability to treat multiple pixels in a span identically is especially important because we should write the frame buffer one word at a time to minimize the number of time-consuming memory accesses. For a bilevel display, we thus write 16 or 32 pixels at a time; if spans are not word-aligned, the algorithm must do suitable masking of words containing fewer than the full set of pixels. The need for writing memory efficiently is entirely similar for implementing copyPixel, as will be discussed briefly in Section 3.13. In our code, we concentrate on defining spans and ignore the issue of writing memory efficiently; see Chapter 4 and Exercise 3.10.

Rectangle scan conversion is thus simply a nested **for** loop:

```
for ( y from ymin to ymax of the rectangle ) {    /* By scan line */
    for ( x from xmin to xmax ) {                 /* By pixel in span */
        WritePixel(x, y, value);
    }
}
```

An interesting problem arises in this straightforward solution, similar to the problem of scan converting a polyline with line segments that share pixels. Consider two rectangles that share a common edge. If we scan convert each rectangle in turn, we will write the pixels on the shared edge twice, which is undesirable, as noted earlier. This problem is a manifestation of a larger problem of area-defining primitives, that of defining which pixels belong to a primitive and which pixels do not. Clearly, those pixels that lie in the mathematical interior of an area-defining primitive belong to that primitive. But what about those pixels on the boundary? If we were looking at a single rectangle (or just thinking about the problem in a mathematical way), a straightforward answer would be to include the pixels on the boundary; but since we want to avoid the problem of scan converting shared edges twice, we must define some rule that assigns boundary pixels uniquely.

A simple rule is to say that a boundary pixel—that is, a pixel lying on an edge—is not considered part of the primitive if the halfplane defined by that edge and containing the primitive lies below a nonvertical edge or to the left of a vertical edge. Thus, pixels on left and bottom edges will be drawn, but pixels that lie on top and right edges will not be drawn. A shared vertical edge therefore *belongs* to the rightmost of the two sharing rectangles. In effect, spans within a rectangle represent an interval that is closed on the left end and open on the right end.

A number of points must be made about this rule. First, it applies to arbitrary polygons as well as to rectangles. Second, the bottom-left vertex of a rectangle still would be drawn twice—we need another rule to deal with that special case, as will be discussed in the next section. Third, we may apply the rule also to unfilled rectangles and polygons. Fourth, the rule causes each span to be missing its rightmost pixel, and each rectangle to be missing its topmost row. These problems illustrate that there is no *perfect* solution to the problem of not writing pixels on (potentially) shared edges twice, but implementors generally consider that it is better (visually less distracting) to have missing pixels at the right and top edge than it is to have pixels that disappear or are set to unexpected colors in **xor** mode.

3.5 FILLING POLYGONS

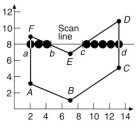

Figure 3.14
Polygon and scan line 8.

The general polygon scan-conversion algorithm described next handles both convex and concave polygons, even those that are self-intersecting or have interior holes. It operates by computing spans that lie between left and right edges of the polygon. The span extrema are calculated by an incremental algorithm that computes a scan line-edge intersection from the intersection with the previous scan line. Figure 3.14, which illustrates the basic polygon scan-conversion process, shows a polygon and one scan line passing through it. The intersections of scan line 8 with edges *FA* and *CD* lie on integer coordinates, whereas those for *EF* and *DE* do not; the intersections are marked in the figure by vertical tick marks labeled *a* through *d*.

We must determine which pixels on each scan line are within the polygon, and we must set the corresponding pixels (in this case, spans from $x = 2$ through 4 and 9 through 13) to their appropriate values. By repeating this process for each scan line that intersects the polygon, we scan convert the entire polygon, as shown for another polygon in Fig. 3.15.

Figure 3.15(a) shows the pixels defining the extrema of spans in black and the interior pixels on the span in gray. A straightforward way of deriving the extrema is to use the midpoint line scan-conversion algorithm on each edge and to keep a table of span extrema for each scan line, updating an entry if a new pixel is produced for an edge that extends the span. Note that this strategy produces some extrema pixels that lie outside the polygon; they were chosen by the scan-conversion algorithm because they lie closest to an edge, without regard to the side of the

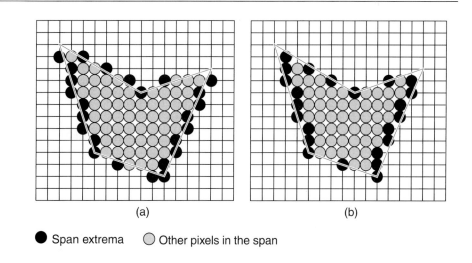

(a)   (b)

● Span extrema   ○ Other pixels in the span

Figure 3.15   Spans for a polygon. Extrema shown in black, interior pixels in gray. (a) Extrema computed by midpoint algorithm. (b) Extrema interior to polygon.

edge on which they lie—the line algorithm has no notions of interior and exterior. We do not want to draw such pixels on the outside of a shared edge, however, because they would intrude into the regions of neighboring polygons, and this result would look odd if these polygons had different colors. It is obviously preferable to draw only those pixels that are strictly interior to the region, even when an exterior pixel would be closer to the edge. We must therefore adjust the scan conversion algorithm accordingly; compare Fig. 3.15(a) with Fig. 3.15(b), and note that a number of pixels outside the ideal primitive are not drawn in part (b).

With this technique, a polygon does not intrude (even by a single pixel) into the regions defined by other primitives. We can apply the same technique to unfilled polygons, for consistency, or we can choose to scan convert rectangles and polygons a line segment at a time, in which case unfilled and filled polygons do not contain the same boundary pixels!

As with the original midpoint algorithm, we use an incremental algorithm to calculate the span extrema on one scan line from those at the previous scan line without having to compute the intersections of a scan line with each polygon edge analytically. In scan line 8 of Fig. 3.14, for instance, there are two spans of pixels within the polygon. The spans can be filled in by a three-step process:

1. Find the intersections of the scan line with all edges of the polygon.
2. Sort the intersections by increasing x coordinate.
3. Fill in all pixels between pairs of intersections that lie interior to the polygon, using the odd-parity rule to determine that a point is inside a region: Parity is initially even, and each intersection encountered thus inverts the parity bit—draw when parity is odd, do not draw when it is even.

The first two steps of the process, finding intersections and sorting them, are treated in the next section. Let us look now at the span-filling strategy. In Fig. 3.14, the sorted list of x coordinates is (2, 4.5, 8.5, 13). Step 3 requires four elaborations:

3.1 Given an intersection with an arbitrary, fractional x value, how do we determine which pixel on either side of that intersection is interior?
3.2 How do we deal with the special case of intersections at integer pixel coordinates?
3.3 How do we deal with the special case in step 3.2 for shared vertices?
3.4 How do we deal with the special case in step 3.2 in which the vertices define a horizontal edge?

To handle case 3.1, we say that if we are approaching a fractional intersection to the right and are inside the polygon, we round down the x coordinate of the intersection to define the interior pixel; if we are outside the polygon, we round up to be inside. We handle case 3.2 by applying the criterion we used to avoid conflicts at shared edges of rectangles: If the leftmost pixel in a span has integer x coordinate, we define it to be interior; if the rightmost pixel has integer x coordinate, we define it to be exterior. For case 3.3, we count the y_{min} vertex of an edge in in the parity calculation but not the y_{max} vertex; therefore, a y_{max} vertex is drawn only if it is the y_{min} vertex for the adjacent edge. Vertex A in Fig. 3.14, for example, is counted once in the parity calculation because it is the y_{min} vertex for edge FA but the y_{max} vertex for edge AB. Thus, both edges and spans are treated as intervals that are closed at their minimum value and open at their maximum value. Clearly, the opposite rule would work as well, but this rule seems more natural since it treats the minimum endpoint as an entering point, and the maximum as a leaving point. When we treat case 3.4—horizontal edges—the desired effect is that, as with rectangles, bottom edges are drawn but top edges are not. As we will show in the next section, this happens automatically if we do not count the edges' vertices, since they are neither y_{min} nor y_{max} vertices.

Let us apply these rules to scan line 8 in Fig. 3.14, which hits no vertices. We fill in pixels from point a, pixel $(2, 8)$, to the first pixel to the left of point b, pixel $(4, 8)$, and from the first pixel to the right of point c, pixel $(9, 8)$, to 1 pixel to the left of point d, pixel $(12, 8)$. For scan line 3, vertex A counts once because it is the y_{min} vertex of edge FA but the y_{max} vertex of edge AB; this causes odd parity, so we draw the span from there to 1 pixel to the left of the intersection with edge CB, where the parity is set to even and the span is terminated. Scan line 1 hits only vertex B; edges AB and BC both have their y_{min} vertices at B, which is therefore counted twice and leaves the parity even. This vertex acts as a null span—enter at the vertex, draw the pixel, exit at the vertex. Although such local minima draw a single pixel, no pixel is drawn at a local maximum, such as the intersection of scan line 9 with the vertex F, shared by edges FA and EF. Both vertices are y_{max} vertices and therefore do not affect the parity, which stays even.

3.5.1 Horizontal Edges

We deal properly with horizontal edges by not counting their vertices, as we can see by examining various cases in Fig. 3.16. Consider bottom edge AB. Vertex A is a y_{min} vertex for edge JA, and AB does not contribute. Therefore, the parity is odd and the span AB is drawn. Vertical edge BC has its y_{min} at B, but again AB does not contribute. The parity becomes even, and the span is terminated. At vertex J, edge IJ has a y_{min} vertex but edge JA does not, so the parity becomes odd and the span is drawn to edge BC. The span that starts at edge IJ and hits C sees no change at C because C is a y_{max} vertex for BC, so the span continues along bottom edge CD; at D, however, edge DE has a y_{min} vertex, so the parity is reset to even and the span ends. At I, edge IJ has its y_{max} vertex and edge HI also does not contribute, so parity stays even and the top edge IH is not drawn. At H, however, edge GH has a y_{min} vertex, the parity becomes odd, and the span is drawn from H to the pixel to the left of the intersection with edge EF. Finally, there is no y_{min} vertex at G, nor is there one at F, so top edge FG is not drawn.

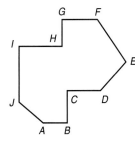

Figure 3.16
Horizontal edges in a polygon.

The preceding algorithm deals with shared vertices in a polygon, with edges shared by two adjacent polygons, and with horizontal edges. It allows self-intersecting polygons. As noted, it does not work perfectly, in that it omits pixels. Worse, it cannot totally avoid writing shared pixels multiple times without keeping a history: Consider edges shared by more than two polygons or a y_{min} vertex shared by two otherwise disjoint triangles (see Exercise 3.11).

3.5.2 Slivers

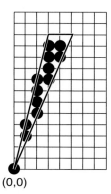

(0,0)

Figure 3.17
Scan converting slivers of
polygons.

There is another problem with our scan-conversion algorithm, one that is not resolved as satisfactorily as is that of horizontal edges: Polygons with edges that lie sufficiently close together create a **sliver**—a polygonal area so thin that its interior does not contain a distinct span for each scan line. Consider, for example, the triangle from (0, 0) to (3, 12) to (5, 12) to (0, 0), shown in Fig. 3.17. Because of the rule that only pixels that lie interior or on a left or bottom edge are drawn, there will be many scan lines with only a single pixel or no pixels. The problem of having *missing* pixels is yet another example of the *aliasing* problem, that is, of representing a continuous signal with a discrete approximation. If we had multiple bits per pixel, we could use antialiasing techniques, as introduced for lines in Section 3.14. Antialiasing would involve softening our rule *draw only pixels that lie interior or on a left or bottom edge*, to allow boundary pixels and even exterior pixels to take on intensity values that vary as a function of distance between a pixel's center and the primitive; multiple primitives can then contribute to a pixel's value.

3.5.3 Edge Coherence and the Scan-Line Algorithm

Step 1 in our procedure—calculating intersections—must be done cleverly lest it be slow. In particular, we must avoid the brute-force technique of testing each polygon edge for intersection with each new scan line. Very often, only a few of the edges are of interest for a given scan line. Furthermore, we note that many edges intersected by scan line i are also intersected by scan line $i + 1$. This *edge coherence* occurs along an edge for as many scan lines as intersect the edge. As we move from one scan line to the next, we can compute the new x intersection of the edge on the basis of the old x intersection, just as we computed the next pixel from the current pixel in midpoint line scan conversion, by using

$$x_{i+1} = x_i + 1/m,$$

where m is the slope of the edge. In the midpoint algorithm for scan converting lines, we avoided fractional arithmetic by computing an integer decision variable and checking only its sign to choose the pixel closest to the mathematical line; here, we would like to use integer arithmetic to do the required rounding for computing the closest interior pixel.

Consider lines with a slope greater than +1 that are left edges; right edges and other slopes are handled by similar, though somewhat trickier, arguments, and vertical edges are special cases. (Horizontal edges are handled implicitly by the span rules, as we saw.) At the (x_{min}, y_{min}) endpoint, we need to draw a pixel. As y is incremented, the x coordinate of the point on the ideal line will increase by $1/m$, where $m = (y_{max} - y_{min})/(x_{max} - x_{min})$ is the slope of the line. This increase will result in x having an integer and a fractional part, which can be expressed as a fraction with a denominator of $y_{max} - y_{min}$. As we iterate this process, the fractional part will overflow and the integer part will have to be incremented. For example, if the slope is $\frac{5}{2}$, and x_{min} is 3, then the sequence of x values will be 3, $3\frac{2}{5}$, $3\frac{4}{5}$, $3\frac{6}{5}$ = $4\frac{1}{5}$, and so on. When the fractional part of x is zero, we can draw the pixel (x, y) that lies on the line, but when the fractional part of x is nonzero, we need to round up in order to get a pixel that lies strictly inside the line. When the fractional part of x becomes greater than 1, we increment x and subtract 1 from the fractional part; we must also move 1 pixel to the right. If we increment to lie exactly on a pixel, we draw that pixel but must decrement the fraction by 1 to have it be less than 1.

We can avoid the use of fractions by keeping track only of the numerator of the fraction and observing that the fractional part is greater than 1 when the numerator is greater than the denominator. We implement this technique in the algorithm of Prog. 3.6, using the variable *increment* to keep track of successive additions of the numerator until it *overflows* past the denominator, when the numerator is decremented by the denominator and x is incremented.

Program 3.6

Scan converting left edge of a polygon.

```
void   LeftEdgeScan(int xmin, int ymin, int xmax, int ymax, int value)
{
    int   x, y, numerator, denominator, increment;

    x = xmin;
    numerator = xmax – xmin;
    denominator = ymax – ymin;
    increment = denominator;

    for (y = ymin; y < ymax; y++) {
        WritePixel(x, y, value);
        increment += numerator;
        if (increment > denominator) {
            /* Overflow, so round up to next pixel and decrement the increment */
            x += 1;
            increment –= denominator;
        }
    }
}
```

We now develop a **scan-line algorithm** that takes advantage of this edge coherence and, for each scan line, keeps track of the set of edges it intersects and the intersection points in a data structure called the **active-edge table** (AET). The edges in the AET are sorted on their x intersection values so that we can fill the spans defined by pairs of (suitably rounded) intersection values—that is, the span extrema. As we move to the next scan line at $y + 1$, the AET is updated. First, edges currently in the AET but not intersected by this next scan line (i.e., those whose $y_{max} = y$) are deleted. Second, any new edges intersected by this next scan line (i.e., those edges whose $y_{min} = y + 1$) are added to the AET. Finally, new x intersections are calculated, using the preceding incremental edge algorithm, for edges that were in the AET but are not yet completed.

To make the addition of edges to the AET efficient, we initially create a global **edge table** (ET) containing all edges sorted by their smaller y coordinate. The ET is typically built by using a bucket sort with as many buckets as there are scan

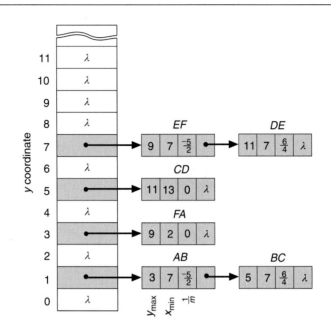

Figure 3.18   Bucket-sorted edge table for polygon of Fig. 3.14.

lines. Within each bucket, edges are kept in order of increasing x coordinate of the lower endpoint. Each entry in the ET contains the y_{max} coordinate of the edge, the x coordinate of the bottom endpoint (x_{min}), and the x increment used in stepping from one scan line to the next, $1/m$. Figure 3.18 shows how the six edges from the polygon of Fig. 3.14 would be sorted, and Fig. 3.19 shows the AET at scan lines 9 and 10 for that polygon. (In an actual implementation, we would probably add a flag indicating left or right edge.)

Once the ET has been formed, the following processing steps for the scan-line algorithm are completed:

1. Set y to the smallest y coordinate that has an entry in the ET, that is, y for the first nonempty bucket.

2. Initialize the AET to be empty.

3. Repeat until the AET and ET are empty:

    3.1 Move from ET bucket y to the AET those edges whose $y_{min} = y$ (entering edges).

    3.2 Remove from the AET those entries for which $y = y_{max}$ (edges not involved in the next scan line), then sort the AET on x (made easier because ET is presorted).

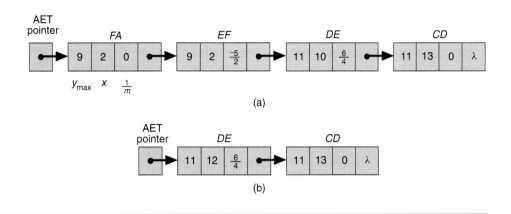

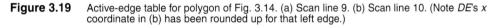

Figure 3.19   Active-edge table for polygon of Fig. 3.14. (a) Scan line 9. (b) Scan line 10. (Note *DE*'s *x* coordinate in (b) has been rounded up for that left edge.)

3.3   Fill in desired pixel values on scan line *y* by using pairs of *x* coordinates from the AET.

3.4   Increment *y* by 1 (to the coordinate of the next scan line).

3.5   For each nonvertical edge remaining in the AET, update *x* for the new *y*.

This algorithm uses both edge coherence to calculate *x* intersections and scan-line coherence (along with sorting) to calculate spans. Since the sorting works on a small number of edges and since the resorting of step 3.1 is applied to a mostly or completely sorted list, either insertion sort or even bubble sort may be used. In Chapters 13 and 14, we will see how to extend this algorithm to handle multiple polygons during visible surface determination, including the case of handling polygons that are transparent.

For purposes of scan conversion, triangles and trapezoids can be treated as special cases of polygons, since they have only two edges for any scan line (given that horizontal edges are not scan-converted explicitly). Indeed, since an arbitrary polygon can be decomposed into a mesh of triangles sharing vertices and edges (see Exercise 3.14), we could scan convert general polygons by first decomposing them into triangle meshes and then scan converting the component triangles. Such triangulation is a classic problem in computational geometry [PREP85] and is easy to do for convex polygons; doing it efficiently for nonconvex polygons is difficult.

Note that the calculation of spans is cumulative. That is, when the current iteration of the scan-conversion algorithm in step 3.5 generates multiple pixels falling on the same scan line, the span extrema must be updated appropriately. (Dealing with span calculations for edges that cross and for slivers takes a bit of special casing.) We can either compute all spans in one pass, then fill the spans in a second pass, or compute a span and fill it when completed. Another benefit of using spans is that clipping can be done at the same time as span arithmetic: The spans may be individually clipped at the left and right edges of the clip rectangle.

3.6 PATTERN FILLING

In the previous sections, we filled the interiors of SRGP's area-defining primitives with a solid color by passing the color in the **value** field of the WritePixel function. Here, we consider filling with a pattern, which we do by adding extra control to the part of the scan-conversion algorithm that actually writes each pixel. For pixmap patterns, this control causes the color value to be picked up from the appropriate position in the pixmap pattern, as shown next. To write bitmap patterns transparently, we do a WritePixel with foreground color at a pixel for a 1 in the pattern, and we inhibit the WritePixel for a 0, as with line style. If, on the other hand, the bitmap pattern is applied in opaque mode, the 1s and 0s select foreground and background color, respectively.

3.6.1 Pattern Filling Using Scan Conversion

The main issue for filling with patterns is the relation of the area of the pattern to that of the primitive. In other words, we need to decide where the pattern is *anchored* so that we know which pixel in the pattern corresponds to the current pixel of the primitive.

The first technique is to anchor the pattern at a vertex of a polygon by placing the leftmost pixel in the pattern's first row there. This choice allows the pattern to move when the primitive is moved, a visual effect that would be expected for patterns with a strong geometric organization, such as the cross-hatches often used in drafting applications. But there is no distinguished point on a polygon that is obviously right for such a relative anchor, and no distinguished points at all on smoothly varying primitives such as circles. Therefore, the programmer must specify the anchor point as a point on or within the primitive. In some systems, the anchor point may even be applied to a group of primitives.

The second technique, used in SRGP, is to consider the entire screen as being tiled with the pattern and to think of the primitive as consisting of an outline or filled area of transparent bits that let the pattern show through. The standard position for such an absolute anchor is the screen origin. The pixels of the primitive are then treated as 1s that are **and**ed with the pattern. A side effect of this technique is that the pattern does not *stick to* the primitive if the primitive is moved slightly. Instead, the primitive moves as though it were a cutout on a fixed, patterned background, and thus its appearance may change as it is moved; for regular patterns without a strong geometric orientation, users may not even be aware of this effect. In addition to being computationally efficient, absolute anchoring allows primitives to overlap and abut seamlessly.

To apply the pattern to the primitive, we index it with the current pixel's (x, y) coordinates. Since patterns are defined as small M by N bitmaps or pixmaps, we use modular arithmetic to make the pattern repeat. The *pattern*[0, 0] pixel is considered coincident with the screen origin,[6] and we can write, for example, a bit-map pattern in transparent mode with the statement

$$\textbf{if} \, (\, \text{pattern} \, [x \, \% \, M, \, y \, \% \, N] \,)\text{WritePixel(x, y, value)}$$

If we are filling an entire span in **replace** write mode, we can copy a whole row of the pattern at once, assuming a low-level version of a copyPixel facility is avail-able to write multiple pixels. Let us say, for example, that the pattern is an 8 by 8 matrix. It thus repeats for every span of 8 pixels. If the leftmost point of a span is byte-aligned—that is, if the x value of the first pixel mod 8 is 0—then the entire first row of the pattern can be written out with a copyPixel of a 1 by 8 array; this procedure is repeated as many times as is necessary to fill the span. If either end of the span is not byte-aligned, the pixels not in the span must be masked out. Imple-mentors spend much time making special cases of raster algorithms particularly efficient; for example, they test up-front to eliminate inner loops, and they write hand-tuned assembly-language code for inner loops that takes advantage of special hardware features such as instruction caches or particularly efficient loop instruc-tions.

3.6.2 Pattern Filling Without Repeated Scan Conversion

So far, we have discussed filling in the context of scan conversion. Another tech-nique is to scan convert a primitive first into a rectangular work area, and then to write each pixel from that bitmap to the appropriate place in the canvas. This so-called *rectangle write* to the canvas is simply a nested **for** loop in which a 1 writes the current color and a 0 writes nothing (for transparency) or writes the back-ground color (for opacity). This two-step process is twice as much work as filling during scan conversion, and therefore it is not worthwhile for primitives that are encountered and scan-converted only once. It pays off, however, for primitives that would otherwise be scan-converted repeatedly. This is the case for characters in a given font and size, which can be scan-converted ahead of time from their outlines. For characters defined only as bitmap fonts, or for other objects, such as icons and application symbols, that are painted or scanned in as bitmap images, scan conver-sion is not used in any case, and the rectangle write of their bitmaps is the only applicable technique. The advantage of a pre–scan-converted bitmap lies in the fact that clearly it is faster to write each pixel in a rectangular region, without hav-ing to do any clipping or span arithmetic, than to scan convert the primitive each time from scratch while doing such clipping.

But since we have to write a rectangular bitmap into the canvas, why not just copyPixel the bitmap directly, rather than writing 1 pixel at a time? For bilevel dis-plays, writing current color 1, copyPixel works fine: For transparent mode, we use **or** write mode; for opaque mode, we use **replace** write mode. For multilevel dis-plays, we cannot write the bitmap directly with a single bit per pixel, but must con-vert each bit to a full n-bit color value that is then written.

---

[6] In window systems, the pattern is often anchored at the origin of the window coordinate system.

Some systems have a more powerful copyPixel that can make copying subject to one or more source-read or destination-write masks. We can make good use of such a facility for transparent mode (used for characters in SRGP) if we can specify the bitmap as a destination-write mask and the source as an array of constant (current) color. Then pixels are written in the current color only where the bitmap write mask has 1s; the bitmap write mask acts as an arbitrary clip region. In a sense, the explicit nested for loop for implementing the rectangle write on *n*-bits-per-pixel systems simulates this more powerful *copyPixel with write mask* facility.

Now consider another variation. We wish to draw a filled letter, or some other shape, not with a solid interior but with a patterned one. For example, we would like to create a thick letter "P" with a 50 percent gray stipple pattern (graying out the character), or a house icon with a two-tone brick-and-mortar pattern. How can we write such an object in opaque mode without having to scan convert it each time? The problem is that *holes* interior to the region where there are 0s in the bitmap should be written in background color, whereas holes outside the region (such as the cavity in the "P") must still be written transparently so as not to affect the image underneath. In other words, we want 0s in the shape's interior to signify background color, and 0s in its exterior, including any cavities, to belong to a write mask used to protect pixels outside the shape. If we scan convert on the fly, the problem that the 0s mean different things in different regions of the bitmap does not arise, because we never look at pixels outside the shape's boundary.

We use a four-step process to avoid repeated scan conversion, as shown in the mountain scene of Fig. 3.20(a). Using the outline of our icon shown in part (b), the first step is to create a *solid* bitmap to be used as a write mask/clipping region, with pixels interior to the object set to 1s, and those exterior set to 0s; this is depicted in part (c), where white represents background pixels (0s) and black represents 1s. This scan conversion is done only once. As the second step, any time a patterned copy of the object is needed, we write the solid bitmap transparently in background color (in **replace** mode) to the canvas. This clears to background color a region of the shape of the object, as shown in part (d), where the house-shaped region is set to white background within the existing mountain image. The third step is to create a patterned version of the object's solid bitmap by doing a copyPixel of a pattern rectangle—part (e)—to the solid bitmap, using **and** mode. This turns some pixels internal to the object's shape from 1s to 0s—part (f)— and can be seen as clipping out a piece of the arbitrarily large pattern in the shape of the object. Finally, we again write this new bitmap transparently to the same place in the canvas, but this time in the current, foreground color, as shown in part (g). As in the first write to the canvas, all pixels outside the object's region are 0s, to protect pixels outside the region, whereas 0s inside the region do not affect the previously written (white) background; only where there are 1s is the (black) foreground written. To write the house with a solid red-brick pattern with gray mortar, we would write the solid bitmap in gray and the patterned bitmap in red; the pattern would have 1s everywhere except for small bands of 0s representing the mortar. In effect, we have reduced the rectangular write function that had to write two colors subject to a write mask to two write functions that write transparently or copyPixel with a write mask.

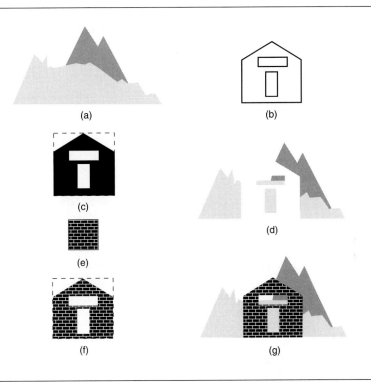

Figure 3.20   Writing a patterned object in opaque mode with two transparent writes. (a) Mountain scene. (b) Outline of house icon. (c) Bitmap for solid version of house icon. (d) Clearing the scene by writing background. (e) Brick pattern. (f) Brick pattern applied to house icon. (g) Writing the screen transparently with patterned house icon.

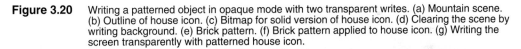

3.7 THICK PRIMITIVES

Conceptually, we produce thick primitives by tracing the scan-converted single-pixel outline primitive. We place the center of a brush of a specified cross-section (or another distinguished point, such as the upper-left corner of a rectangular brush) at each pixel chosen by the scan-conversion algorithm. A single-pixel-wide line can be conceived as being drawn with a brush the size of a single pixel. However, this simple description masks a number of tricky questions. First, what shape is the brush? Typical implementations use circular and rectangular brushes. Second, what is the orientation of a noncircular brush? Does the rectangular pen always stay upright, so that the brush has constant width, or does it turn as the primitive turns, so that the vertical axis of the brush is aligned with the tangent to the primitive? What do the ends of a thick line look like, both ideally and on the integer grid? What happens at the vertex of a thick polygon? How do line style and pen style interact? We shall answer the simpler questions in this section. The others are discussed in Chapter 19 of [FOLE90].

There are four basic methods for drawing thick primitives, illustrated in Figs. 3.21 through 3.24. We show the ideal primitives for these lines in black-on-white outline, the pixels generated to define the 1-pixel-thick scan-converted primitive in black, and the pixels added to form the thick primitive in gray. The reduced-scale versions show what the thick primitive actually looks like at still rather low resolution, with all pixels set to black. The first method is a crude approximation that uses more than 1 pixel for each column (or row) during scan conversion. The second traces the pen's cross-section along the single-pixel outline of the primitive. The third draws two copies of a primitive a thickness t apart and fills in the spans between these inner and outer boundaries. The fourth approximates all primitives by polylines and then uses a thick line for each polyline segment.

Let us look briefly at each of these methods and consider its advantages and disadvantages. All the methods produce effects that are satisfactory for many, if not most, purposes, at least for viewing on the screen. For printing, the higher resolution should be used to good advantage, especially since the speed of an algorithm for printing is not as critical as for online primitive generation. We can then use more complex algorithms to produce better-looking results. A package may even use different techniques for different primitives. For example, QuickDraw traces an upright rectangular pen for lines, but fills spans between confocal ellipse boundaries.

3.7.1 Replicating Pixels

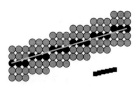

Figure 3.21
Thick line drawn by column replication.

A quick extension to the scan-conversion inner loop to write multiple pixels at each computed pixel works reasonably well for lines; here pixels are duplicated in columns for lines with $-1 <$ slope < 1 and in rows for all other lines. The effect, however, is that the line ends are always vertical or horizontal, which is not pleasing for rather thick lines, as Fig. 3.21 shows.

The pixel-replication algorithm also produces noticeable gaps in places where line segments meet at an angle, and misses pixels where there is a shift from horizontal to vertical replication as a function of the slope. This latter anomaly shows up as abnormal thinness in ellipse arcs at the boundaries between octants, as in Fig. 3.22.

Furthermore, the thickness of lines that are horizontal or vertical differs from that of lines at an angle, for which the *thickness* of the primitive is defined as the distance between the primitive's boundaries perpendicular to its tangent. Thus, if the thickness parameter is t, a horizontal or vertical line has thickness t, whereas one drawn at $45°$ has an average thickness of $t/\sqrt{2}$. This difference is another result of having fewer pixels in the line at an angle, as first noted in Section 3.2.3; it decreases the brightness contrast with horizontal and vertical lines of the same thickness. Still another problem with pixel replication is the generic problem of even-numbered widths: We cannot center the duplicated column or row about the selected pixel, so we must choose a side of the primitive to have an *extra* pixel. Altogether, pixel replication is an efficient but crude approximation that works best for primitives that are not very thick.

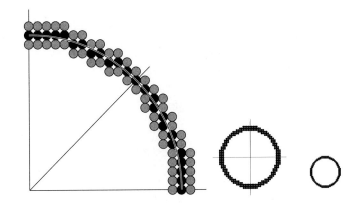

Figure 3.22   Thick circle drawn by column replication.

3.7.2 The Moving Pen

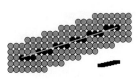

Figure 3.23
Thick line drawn by tracing
a rectangular pen.

Choosing a rectangular pen whose center or corner travels along the single-pixel outline of the primitive works reasonably well for lines; it produces the line shown in Fig. 3.23. Notice that this line is similar to that produced by pixel replication but is thicker at the endpoints. As with pixel replication, because the pen stays vertically aligned, the perceived thickness of the primitive varies as a function of the primitive's angle, but in the opposite way: The width is thinnest for horizontal segments and thickest for segments with slope of ± 1. An ellipse arc, for example, varies in thickness along its entire trajectory, being of the specified thickness when the tangent is nearly horizontal or vertical, and thickened by a factor of $\sqrt{2}$ around $\pm 45°$ (see Fig. 3.24). This problem would be eliminated if the square turned to follow the path, but it is much better to use a circular cross-section so that the thickness is angle-independent.

Now let us look at how to implement the moving-pen algorithm for the simple case of an upright rectangular or circular cross-section. The easiest solution is to copyPixel the required solid or patterned cross-section (also called **footprint**) so that its center or corner is at the chosen pixel; for a circular footprint and a pattern drawn in opaque mode, we must, in addition, mask off the bits outside the circular region, which is not an easy task unless our low-level copyPixel has a write mask for the destination region. The brute-force copyPixel solution writes pixels more than once, since the pen's footprints overlap at adjacent pixels. A better technique that also handles the circular-cross-section problem is to use the spans of the footprint to compute spans for successive footprints at adjacent pixels. As in filling area-defining primitives, such combining of spans on a raster line is merely a union or merge of line segments, entailing keeping track of the minimum and maximum x of the accumulated span for each raster line.

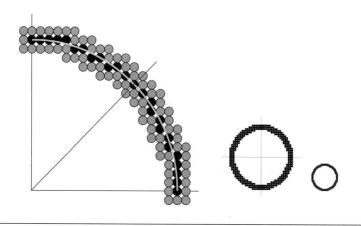

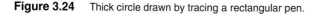

Figure 3.24   Thick circle drawn by tracing a rectangular pen.

Other methods for displaying thick primitives, such as filling areas between inner and outer boundaries constructed at a distance $t/2$ on either side of a single pixel trajectory, are discussed in Chapters 3 and 19 of [FOLE90].

3.8 CLIPPING IN A RASTER WORLD

As we noted in the introduction to this chapter, it is essential that both clipping and scan conversion be done as rapidly as possible, in order to provide the user with quick updates resulting from changes to the application model. Clipping can be done analytically, on the fly during scan conversion, or as part of a copyPixel with the desired clip rectangle from a canvas storing unclipped primitives to the destination canvas. This third technique would be useful when a large canvas can be generated ahead of time and the user can then examine pieces of it for a significant period of time by panning the clip rectangle, without updating the contents of the canvas.

Combining clipping and scan conversion, called *scissoring*, is easy to do for filled or thick primitives as part of span arithmetic: Only the extrema need to be clipped, and no interior pixels need be examined. Scissoring shows yet another advantage of span coherence. Also, if an outline primitive is not much larger than the clip rectangle, not many pixels, relatively speaking, will fall outside the clip region. For such a case, it may well be faster to generate each pixel and to clip it (i.e., to write it conditionally) than to do analytical clipping beforehand. In particular, although the bounds test is in the inner loop, the expensive memory write is avoided for exterior pixels, and both the incremental computation and the testing may run entirely in a fast memory, such as a CPU instruction cache or a display controller's microcode memory.

Other tricks may be useful. For example, one may *home in* on the intersection of a line with a clip edge by doing the standard midpoint scan-conversion algorithm on every *i*th pixel and testing the chosen pixel against the rectangle bounds until the first pixel that lies inside the region is encountered. Then the algorithm has to back up, find the first pixel inside, and do the normal scan conversion thereafter. The last interior pixel could be similarly determined, or each pixel could be tested as part of the scan-conversion loop and scan conversion stopped the first time the test failed. Testing every eighth pixel works well, since it is a good compromise between having too many tests and too many pixels to back up.

For graphics packages that operate in floating point, it is best to clip analytically in the floating-point coordinate system and then to scan convert the clipped primitives, being careful to initialize decision variables correctly, as we did for lines in Section 3.2.3. For integer graphics packages such as SRGP, there is a choice between preclipping and then scan converting or doing clipping during scan conversion. Since it is relatively easy to do analytical clipping for lines and polygons, clipping of those primitives is often done before scan conversion, while it is faster to clip other primitives during scan conversion. Also, it is quite common for a floating-point graphics package to do analytical clipping in its coordinate system and then to call lower-level scan-conversion software that actually generates the clipped primitives; this integer graphics software could then do an additional raster clip to rectangular (or even arbitrary) window boundaries. Because analytic clipping of primitives is both useful for integer graphics packages and essential for 2D and 3D floating-point graphics packages, we discuss the basic analytical clipping algorithms in this chapter.

3.9 CLIPPING LINES

This section treats analytical clipping of lines against rectangles; algorithms for clipping other primitives are handled in subsequent sections. Although there are specialized algorithms for rectangle and polygon clipping, it is important to note that SRGP primitives built out of lines (i.e., polylines, unfilled rectangles, and polygons) can be clipped by repeated application of the line clipper. Furthermore, circles may be piecewise linearly approximated with a sequence of very short lines, so that boundaries can be treated as a single polyline or polygon for both clipping and scan conversion. Conics are represented in some systems as ratios of parametric polynomials (see Chapter 9), a representation that also lends itself readily to an incremental, piecewise linear approximation suitable for a line-clipping algorithm. Clipping a rectangle against a rectangle results in at most a single rectangle. Clipping a convex polygon against a rectangle results in at most a single convex polygon, but clipping a concave polygon may produce more than one concave polygon. Clipping a circle against a rectangle results in as many as four arcs.

Lines intersecting a rectangular clip region (or any convex polygon) are always clipped to a single line segment; lines lying on the clip rectangle's border

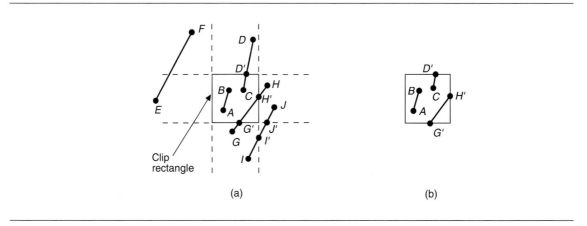

(a)   (b)

Figure 3.25   Cases for clipping lines.

are considered inside and hence are displayed. Figure 3.25 shows several examples of clipped lines.

3.9.1 Clipping Endpoints

Before we discuss clipping lines, let us look at the simpler problem of clipping individual points. If the x coordinate boundaries of the clip rectangle are at x_{min} and x_{max}, and the y coordinate boundaries are at y_{min} and y_{max}, then four inequalities must be satisfied for a point at (x, y) to be inside the clip rectangle:

$$x_{min} \leq x \leq x_{max}, y_{min} \leq y \leq y_{max}.$$

If any of the four inequalities does not hold, the point is outside the clip rectangle.

3.9.2 Clipping Lines by Solving Simultaneous Equations

To clip a line, we need to consider only its endpoints, not its infinitely many interior points. If both endpoints of a line lie inside the clip rectangle (e.g., AB in Fig. 3.25), the entire line lies inside the clip rectangle and can be **trivially accepted.** If one endpoint lies inside and one outside (e.g., CD in the figure), the line intersects the clip rectangle and we must compute the intersection point. If both endpoints are outside the clip rectangle, the line may (or may not) intersect with the clip rectangle (EF, GH, and IJ in the figure), and we need to perform further calculations to determine whether there are any intersections, and if there are, where they occur.

   The brute-force approach to clipping a line that cannot be trivially accepted is to intersect that line with each of the four clip-rectangle edges to see whether any intersection points lie on those edges; if so, the line cuts the clip rectangle and is partially inside. For each line and clip-rectangle edge, we therefore take the two mathematically infinite lines that contain them and intersect them. Next, we test whether this intersection point is *interior*—that is, whether it lies within both the clip rectangle edge and the line; if so, there is an intersection with the clip rectangle. In Fig. 3.25, intersection points G' and H' are interior, but I' and J' are not.

When we use this approach, we must solve two simultaneous equations using multiplication and division for each <edge, line> pair. Although the slope-intercept formula for lines learned in analytic geometry could be used, it describes infinite lines, whereas in graphics and clipping we deal with finite lines (called *line segments* in mathematics). In addition, the slope-intercept formula does not deal with vertical lines—a serious problem, given our upright clip rectangle. A parametric formulation for line segments solves both problems:

$$x = x_0 + t(x_1 - x_0),\ y = y_0 + t(y_1 - y_0).$$

These equations describe (x, y) on the directed line segment from (x_0, y_0) to (x_1, y_1) for the parameter t in the range [0, 1], as simple substitution for t confirms. Two sets of simultaneous equations of this parametric form can be solved for parameters t_{edge} for the edge and t_{line} for the line segment. The values of t_{edge} and t_{line} can then be checked to see whether both lie in [0, 1]; if they do, the intersection point lies within both segments and is a true clip-rectangle intersection. Furthermore, the special case of a line parallel to a clip-rectangle edge must also be tested before the simultaneous equations can be solved. Altogether, the brute-force approach involves considerable calculation and testing; it is thus inefficient.

3.9.3 The Cohen–Sutherland Line-Clipping Algorithm

The more efficient Cohen–Sutherland algorithm performs initial tests on a line to determine whether intersection calculations can be avoided. First, endpoint pairs are checked for trivial acceptance. If the line cannot be trivially accepted, *region checks* are done. For instance, two simple comparisons on x show that both endpoints of line EF in Fig. 3.25 have an x coordinate less than x_{min} and thus lie in the region to the left of the clip rectangle (i.e., in the outside halfplane defined by the left edge); therefore, line segment EF can be **trivially rejected** and needs to be neither clipped nor displayed. Similarly, we can trivially reject lines with both endpoints in regions to the right of x_{max}, below y_{min}, and above y_{max}.

If the line segment can be neither trivially accepted nor rejected, it is divided into two segments at a clip edge, so that one segment can be trivially rejected. Thus, a segment is iteratively clipped by testing for trivial acceptance or rejection, and is then subdivided if neither test is successful, until what remains is completely inside the clip rectangle or can be trivially rejected. The algorithm is particularly efficient for two common cases. In the first case of a large clip rectangle enclosing all or most of the display area, most primitives can be trivially accepted. In the second case of a small clip rectangle, almost all primitives can be trivially rejected. This latter case arises in a standard method of doing pick correlation in which a small rectangle surrounding the cursor, called the **pick window,** is used to clip primitives to determine which primitives lie within a small (rectangular) neighborhood of the cursor's **pick point** (see Section 7.11.2).

To perform trivial accept and reject tests, we extend the edges of the clip rectangle to divide the plane of the clip rectangle into nine regions (see Fig. 3.26). Each region is assigned a 4-bit code, determined by where the region lies with respect to the outside halfplanes of the clip-rectangle edges. Each bit in the outcode is set to either 1 (true) or 0 (false); the 4 bits in the code correspond to the following conditions:

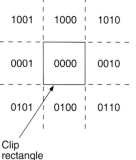

	1001	1000	1010	
	0001	0000	0010	
	0101	0100	0110	

Clip
rectangle

Figure 3.26
Region outcodes.

First bit   outside halfplane of top edge, above top edge $y > y_{max}$

Second bit   outside halfplane of bottom edge, below bottom edge $y < y_{min}$

Third bit   outside halfplane of right edge, to right of right edge $x > x_{max}$

Fourth bit   outside halfplane of left edge, to left of left edge $x < x_{min}$

Since the region lying above and to the left of the clip rectangle, for example, lies in the outside halfplane of the top and left edges, it is assigned a code of 1001. A particularly efficient way to calculate the outcode derives from the observation that bit 1 is the sign bit of $(y_{max} - y)$; bit 2 is that of $(y - y_{min})$; bit 3 is that of $(x_{max} - x)$; and bit 4 is that of $(x - x_{min})$. Each endpoint of the line segment is then assigned the code of the region in which it lies. We can now use these endpoint codes to determine whether the line segment lies completely inside the clip rectangle or in the outside halfplane of an edge. If both 4-bit codes of the endpoints are zero, then the line lies completely inside the clip rectangle. However, if both endpoints lie in the outside halfplane of a particular edge, as for *EF* in Fig. 3.25, the codes for both endpoints each have the bit set showing that the point lies in the outside halfplane of that edge. For *EF,* the outcodes are 0001 and 1001, respectively, showing with the fourth bit that the line segment lies in the outside halfplane of the left edge. Therefore, if the logical **and** of the codes of the endpoints is not zero, the line can be trivially rejected.

If a line cannot be trivially accepted or rejected, we must subdivide it into two segments such that one or both segments can be discarded. We accomplish this subdivision by using an edge that the line crosses to cut the line into two segments: The section lying in the outside halfplane of the edge is thrown away. We can choose any order in which to test edges, but we must, of course, use the same order each time in the algorithm; we shall use the top-to-bottom, right-to-left order of the outcode. A key property of the outcode is that bits that are set in a nonzero outcode correspond to edges crossed: If one endpoint lies in the outside halfplane of an edge and the line segment fails the trivial-rejection tests, then the other point must lie on the inside halfplane of that edge and the line segment must cross it. Thus, the algorithm always chooses a point that lies outside and then uses an outcode bit that is set to determine a clip edge; the edge chosen is the first in the top-to-bottom, right-to-left order—that is, it is the leftmost bit that is set in the outcode.

The algorithm works as follows. We compute the outcodes of both endpoints and check for trivial acceptance and rejection. If neither test is successful, we find an endpoint that lies outside (at least one will), and then test the outcode to find the edge that is crossed and to determine the corresponding intersection point. We can then clip off the line segment from the outside endpoint to the intersection point by replacing the outside endpoint with the intersection point, and compute the outcode of this new endpoint to prepare for the next iteration.

For example, consider the line segment *AD* in Fig. 3.27. Point *A* has outcode 0000, and point *D* has outcode 1001. The line can be neither trivially accepted nor rejected. Therefore, the algorithm chooses *D* as the outside point, whose outcode shows that the line crosses the top edge and the left edge. By our testing order, we first use the top edge to clip *AD* to *AB,* and we compute *B*'s outcode as 0000. In the next iteration, we apply the trivial acceptance/rejection tests to *AB,* and it is trivially accepted and displayed.

Line *EI* requires multiple iterations. The first endpoint, *E*, has an outcode of 0100, so the algorithm chooses it as the outside point and tests the outcode to find that the first edge against which the line is cut is the bottom edge, where *EI* is clipped to *FI*. In the second iteration, *FI* cannot be trivially accepted or rejected. The outcode of the first endpoint, *F,* is 0000, so the algorithm chooses the outside point *I* that has outcode 1010. The first edge clipped against is therefore the top edge, yielding *FH*. *H*'s outcode is determined to be 0010, so the third iteration results in a clip against the right edge to *FG*. This is trivially accepted in the fourth and final iteration and displayed. A different sequence of clips would have resulted if we had picked *I* as the initial point: On the basis of its outcode, we would have clipped against the top edge first, then the right edge, and finally the bottom edge.

In the code of Prog. 3.7, we use a C structure with fields as members to represent the outcode, because this representation is more natural than is an array of four integers. We use an external function to calculate the outcode for modularity; to improve performance, we would, of course, put this code in line.

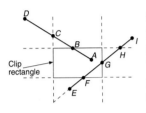

Figure 3.27
Illustration of Cohen–Sutherland line clipping.

Program 3.7

Cohen–Sutherland line-clipping algorithm.

```
typedef struct {
    unsigned all;
    unsigned left:4;
    unsigned right:4;
    unsigned bottom:4;
    unsigned top:4;
} outcode;

void   CohenSutherlandLineClipAndDraw(float x0, float y0, float x1, float y1,
                    float xmin, float xmax, float ymin, float ymax, int value)
/* Cohen-Sutherland clipping algorithm for line P0 = (x0, y0) to P1 = (x1, y1) and */
/* clip rectangle with diagonal from  (xmin, ymin) to (xmax, ymax) */
{
    boolean   accept, done;
    outcode outcode0, outcode1, outcodeOut;
    float   x, y;

    accept = FALSE;
    done = FALSE;
    outcode0 = CompOutCode(x0, y0, xmin, xmax, ymin, ymax);
    outcode1 = CompOutCode(x1, y1, xmin, xmax, ymin, ymax);
    do {
```

```
        if (outcode0.all == 0 && outcode1.all == 0) {
            accept = TRUE;
            done = TRUE;
        } else if ((outcode0.all & outcode1.all) != 0)
            done = TRUE;          /* Logical intersection is true, so trivial reject and exit */
        else {
            if (outcode0.all != 0)
                outcodeOut = outcode0;
            else
                outcodeOut = outcode1;
            if (outcodeOut.top) {                    /* Divide line at top of clip rectangle */
                x = x0 + (x1 − x0) * (ymax − y0) / (y1 − y0);
                y = ymax;
            } else if (outcodeOut.bottom) {    /* Divide line at bottom of clip rectangle */
                x = x0 + (x1 − x0) * (ymin − y0) / (y1 − y0);
                y = ymin;
            } else if (outcodeOut.right) {  /* Divide line at right edge of clip rectangle */
                y = y0 + (y1 − y0) * (xmax − x0) / (x1 − x0);
                x = xmax;
            } else if (outcodeOut.left) {        /* Divide line at left edge of clip rectangle */
                y = y0 + (y1 − y0) * (xmin − x0) / (x1 − x0);
                x = xmin;
            }
            if (outcodeOut.all == outcode0.all) {
                x0 = x;
                y0 = y;
                outcode0 = CompOutCode(x0, y0, xmin, xmax, ymin, ymax);
            } else {
                x1 = x;
                y1 = y;
                outcode1 = CompOutCode(x1, y1, xmin, xmax, ymin, ymax);
            }
        }                         /* Subdivide */
    } while (!done);
    if (accept)
        MidpointLineReal(x0, y0, x1, y1, value);     /* Version for float coordinates */
}

outcode CompOutCode (float x, float y,
        float xmin, float xmax, float ymin, float ymax)
{
    outcode code;
    code.top = 0, code.bottom = 0, code.right = 0, code.left = 0, code.all = 0;
    if (y > ymax) {
        code.top = 8;
        code.all += code.top;
    } else if (y < ymin) {
        code.bottom = 4;
        code.all += code.bottom;
    }
```

```
        if (x > xmax) {
            code.right = 2;
            code.all += code.right;
        } else if (x < xmin) {
            code.left = 1;
            code.all += code.left;
        }
        return code;
    }
```

We can improve the efficiency of the algorithm slightly by not recalculating slopes (see Exercise 3.22). Even with this improvement, however, the algorithm is not the most efficient one. Because testing and clipping are done in a fixed order, the algorithm will sometimes perform needless clipping. Such clipping occurs when the intersection with a rectangle edge is an **external intersection**, that is, when it does not lie on the clip-rectangle boundary (e.g., point *H* on line *EI* in Fig. 3.27). The Nicholl, Lee, and Nicholl [NICH87] algorithm, by contrast, avoids calculating external intersections by subdividing the plane into many more regions; it is discussed in Chapter 19 of [FOLE90]. An advantage of the much simpler Cohen–Sutherland algorithm is that its extension to a 3D orthographic view volume is straightforward, as can be seen in Section 6.6.3.

3.9.4 A Parametric Line-Clipping Algorithm

The Cohen–Sutherland algorithm is probably still the most commonly used line-clipping algorithm because it has been around the longest and has been published widely. In 1978, Cyrus and Beck published an algorithm that takes a fundamentally different and generally more efficient approach to line clipping [CYRU78]. The Cyrus–Beck technique can be used to clip a 2D line against a rectangle or an arbitrary convex polygon in the plane, or a 3D line against an arbitrary convex polyhedron in 3D space. Liang and Barsky later independently developed a more efficient parametric line-clipping algorithm that is especially fast in the special cases of upright 2D and 3D clip regions [LIAN84]. In addition to taking advantage of these simple clip boundaries, they introduced more efficient trivial rejection tests that work for general clip regions. Here we follow the original Cyrus–Beck development to introduce parametric clipping. Since we are concerned only with upright clip rectangles, however, we reduce the Cyrus–Beck formulation to the more efficient Liang–Barsky case at the end of the development.

Recall that the Cohen–Sutherland algorithm, for lines that cannot be trivially accepted or rejected, calculates the (*x*, *y*) intersection of a line segment with a clip edge by substituting the known value of *x* or *y* for the vertical or horizontal clip edge, respectively. The parametric line algorithm, however, finds the value of the parameter *t* in the parametric representation of the line segment for the point at which that segment intersects the infinite line on which the clip edge lies. Because all clip edges are, in general, intersected by the line, four values of *t* are calculated. A series of simple comparisons is used to determine which (if any) of the four

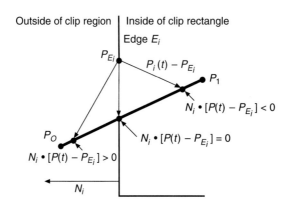

Figure 3.28   Dot products for three points outside, inside, and on the boundary of the clip region.

values of t correspond to actual intersections. Only then are the (x, y) values for one or two actual intersections calculated. In general, this approach saves time over the Cohen–Sutherland intersection-calculation algorithm because it avoids the repetitive looping needed to clip to multiple clip-rectangle edges. Also, calculations in 1D parameter space are simpler than those in 3D coordinate space. Liang and Barsky improve on Cyrus–Beck by examining each t value as it is generated, to reject some line segments before all four t values have been computed.

The Cyrus–Beck algorithm is based on the following formulation of the intersection between two lines. Figure 3.28 shows a single edge E_i of the clip rectangle and that edge's outward normal N_i (i.e., outward to the clip rectangle)[7], as well as the line segment from P_0 to P_1 that must be clipped to the edge. Either the edge or the line segment may have to be extended to find the intersection point.

As before, this line is represented parametrically as

$$P(t) = P_0 + t(P_1 - P_0),$$

where $t = 0$ at P_0 and $t = 1$ at P_1. Now, pick an arbitrary point P_{Ei} on edge E_i and consider the three vectors $P(t) - P_{Ei}$ from P_{Ei} to three designated points on the line from P_0 to P_1: the intersection point to be determined, an endpoint of the line on the inside halfplane of the edge, and an endpoint on the line in the outside halfplane of the edge. We can distinguish in which region a point lies by looking at the value of the dot product $N_i \cdot [P(t) - P_{Ei}]$. This value is negative for a point in the inside halfplane, zero for a point on the line containing the edge, and positive for a point that lies in the outside halfplane. The definitions of inside and outside halfplanes of an edge correspond to a counterclockwise enumeration of the edges of the clip region, a convention we shall use throughout this book. Now we can solve for the value of t at the intersection of P_0P_1 with the edge:

---

[7] Cyrus and Beck use inward normals, but we prefer to use outward normals for consistency with plane normals in 3D, which are outward. Our formulation, therefore, differs only in the testing of a sign.

$$N_i \cdot [P(t) - P_{E_i}] = 0.$$

First, substitute for $P(t)$:

$$N_i \cdot [P_0 + t(P_1 - P_0) - P_{E_i}] = 0.$$

Next, group terms and distribute the dot product:

$$N_i \cdot [P_0 - P_{E_i}] + N_i \cdot t[P_1 - P_0] = 0.$$

Let $D = (P_1 - P_0)$ be the vector from P_0 to P_1, and solve for t:

$$t = \frac{N_i \cdot [P_0 - P_{E_i}]}{-N_i \cdot D}. \tag{3.1}$$

Note that this gives a valid value of t only if the denominator of the expression is nonzero. For this to be true, the algorithm checks that

$N_i \neq 0$ (that is, the normal should not be 0; this could occur only as a mistake),

$D \neq 0$ (that is, $P_1 \neq P_0$),

$N_i \cdot D \neq 0$ (that is, the edge E_i and the line from P_0 to P_1 are not parallel. If they were parallel, there can be no single intersection for this edge, so the algorithm moves on to the next case).

Equation (3.1) can be used to find the intersections between P_0P_1 and each edge of the clip rectangle. We do this calculation by determining the normal and an arbitrary P_{E_i}—say, an endpoint of the edge—for each clip edge, then using these values for all line segments. Given the four values of t for a line segment, the next step is to determine which (if any) of the values correspond to internal intersections of the line segment with edges of the clip rectangle. As a first step, any value of t outside the interval $[0, 1]$ can be discarded, since it lies outside P_0P_1. Next, we need to determine whether the intersection lies on the clip boundary.

We could simply try sorting the remaining values of t, choosing the intermediate values of t for intersection points, as suggested in Fig. 3.29 for the case of line 1. But how do we distinguish this case from that of line 2, in which no portion of the line segment lies in the clip rectangle and the intermediate values of t correspond to points not on the clip boundary? Also, which of the four intersections of line 3 are the ones on the clip boundary?

The intersections in Fig. 3.29 are characterized as *potentially entering* (PE) or *potentially leaving* (PL) the clip rectangle, as follows: If moving from P_0 to P_1 causes us to cross a particular edge to enter the edge's inside halfplane, the intersection is PE; if it causes us to leave the edge's inside halfplane, it is PL. Notice that, with this distinction, two interior intersection points of a line intersecting the clip rectangle have opposing labels.

Formally, intersections can be classified as PE or PL on the basis of the angle between P_0P_1 and N_i: If the angle is less than 90°, the intersection is PL; if it is greater than 90°, it is PE. This information is contained in the sign of the dot product of N_i and P_0P_1:

$$N_i \cdot D < 0 \Rightarrow \text{PE (angle greater than 90)},$$

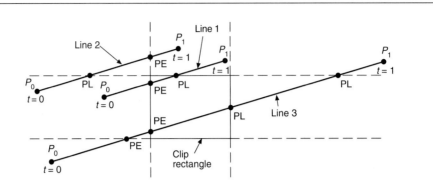

Figure 3.29   Lines lying diagonal to the clip rectangle.

$$N_i \cdot D > 0 \Rightarrow \text{PL (angle less than 90)}.$$

Notice that $N_i \cdot D$ is merely the denominator of Eq. (3.1), which means that, in the process of calculating t, the intersection can be trivially categorized. With this categorization, line 3 in Fig. 3.29 suggests the final step in the process. We must choose a (PE, PL) pair that defines the clipped line. The portion of the infinite line through P_0P_1 that is within the clipping region is bounded by the PE intersection with the largest t value, which we call t_E, and the PL intersection with the smallest t value, t_L. The intersecting line segment is then defined by the range (t_E, t_L). But because we are interested in intersecting P_0P_1, not the infinite line, the definition of the range must be further modified so that $t = 0$ is a lower bound for t_E and $t = 1$ is an upper bound for t_L. What if $t_E > t_L$? This is exactly the case for line 2. It means that no portion of P_0P_1 is within the clip rectangle, and the entire line is rejected. Values of t_E and t_L that correspond to actual intersections are used to calculate the corresponding x and y coordinates.

The completed algorithm for upright clip rectangles is pseudocoded in Prog. 3.8. The complete version of the code, adapted from [LIAN84], can be found in [FOLE90] as Fig. 3.45.

Program 3.8

Pseudocode for Cyrus–Beck parametric line-clipping algorithm.

```
{
    precalculate Nᵢ and select a P_Eᵢ for each edge

    for ( each line segment to be clipped ){
        if (P₁ = P₀)
            line is degenerate so clip as a point;
        else {
            t_E = 0;
            t_L = 1;
            for ( each candidate intersection with a clip edge ){
                if (Nᵢ · D != 0) {         /* Ignore edges parallel to line */
                    calculate t;
```

```
                    use sign of N_i · D to categorize as PE or PL;
                    if (PE) t_E = max(t_E, t);
                    if (PL) t_L = min(t_L, t);
                }
            }
            if (t_E > t_L)
                return nil;
            else
                return P(t_E) and P(t_L) as true clip intersections;
        }
    }
}
```

In summary, the Cohen–Sutherland algorithm is efficient when outcode test-ing can be done cheaply (for example, by doing bitwise operations in assembly language) and trivial acceptance or rejection is applicable to the majority of line segments. Parametric line clipping wins when many line segments need to be clipped, since the actual calculation of the coordinates of the intersection points is postponed until needed, and testing can be done on parameter values. This param-eter calculation is done even for endpoints that would have been trivially accepted in the Cohen–Sutherland strategy, however. The Liang–Barsky algorithm is more efficient than the Cyrus–Beck version because of additional trivial rejection testing that can avoid calculation of all four parameter values for lines that do not intersect the clip rectangle. For lines that cannot be trivially rejected by Cohen–Sutherland because they do not lie in an invisible halfplane, the rejection tests of Liang–Bar-sky are clearly preferable to the repeated clipping required by Cohen–Sutherland. The Nicholl et al. algorithm [NICH87] is generally preferable to either Cohen–Sutherland or Liang–Barsky but does not generalize to 3D, as does parametric clipping. Speed-ups to Cohen–Sutherland are discussed in [DUVA90].

3.10 CLIPPING CIRCLES

To clip a circle against a rectangle, we can first do a trivial accept/reject test by intersecting the circle's extent (a square of the size of the circle's diameter) with the clip rectangle, using the algorithm in the next section for polygon clipping. If the circle intersects the rectangle, we divide it into quadrants and do the trivial accept or reject test for each. These tests may lead in turn to tests for octants. We can then compute the intersection of the circle and the edge analytically by solving their equations simultaneously, and then scan convert the resulting arcs using the appropriately initialized algorithm with the calculated (and suitably rounded) start-ing and ending points. If scan conversion is fast, or if the circle is not too large, it is probably more efficient to scissor on a pixel-by-pixel basis, testing each boundary pixel against the rectangle bounds before it is written. An extent check would cer-tainly be useful in any case. If the circle is filled, spans of adjacent interior pixels on each scan line can be filled without bounds checking by clipping each span and then filling its interior pixels.

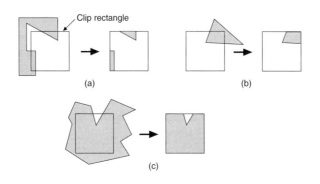

Figure 3.30   Examples of polygon clipping. (a) Multiple components. (b) Simple convex case. (c) Concave case with many exterior edges.

3.11 CLIPPING POLYGONS

An algorithm that clips a polygon must deal with many different cases, as shown in Fig. 3.30. The case in part (a) is particularly noteworthy in that the concave polygon is clipped into two separate polygons. All in all, the task of clipping seems rather complex. Each edge of the polygon must be tested against each edge of the clip rectangle; new edges must be added, and existing edges must be discarded, retained, or divided. Multiple polygons may result from clipping a single polygon. We need an organized way to deal with all these cases.

3.11.1 The Sutherland–Hodgman Polygon-Clipping Algorithm

Sutherland and Hodgman's polygon-clipping algorithm [SUTH74b] uses a *divide and conquer* strategy: It solves a series of simple and identical problems that, when combined, solve the overall problem. The simple problem is to clip a polygon against a single infinite clip edge. Four clip edges, each defining one boundary of the clip rectangle (Fig. 3.31), successively clip a polygon against a clip rectangle.

Note the difference between this strategy for a polygon and the Cohen–Sutherland algorithm for clipping a line: The polygon clipper clips against four edges in succession, whereas the line clipper tests the outcode to see which edge is crossed and clips only when necessary. The actual Sutherland–Hodgman algorithm is in fact more general: A polygon (convex or concave) can be clipped against any convex clipping polygon; in 3D, polygons can be clipped against convex polyhedral volumes defined by planes. The algorithm accepts a series of polygon vertices $v_1, v_2, \ldots, v_n$. In 2D, the vertices define polygon edges from v_i to v_{i+1} and from v_n to v_1. The algorithm clips against a single, infinite clip edge and outputs another

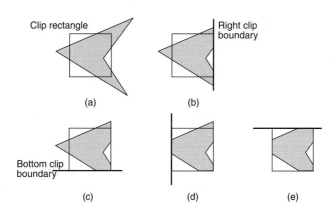

Clip rectangle

Right clip
boundary

(a)

(b)

Bottom clip
boundary

(c)

(d)

(e)

Figure 3.31   Polygon clipping, edge by edge. (a) Before clipping. (b) Clip on right. (c) Clip on bottom. (d) Clip on left. (e) Clip on top; polygon is fully clipped.

series of vertices defining the clipped polygon. In a second pass, the partially clipped polygon is then clipped against the second clip edge, and so on.

The algorithm moves around the polygon from v_n to v_1 and then on back to v_n, at each step examining the relationship between successive vertices and the clip edge. At each step, zero, one, or two vertices are added to the output list of vertices that defines the clipped polygon. Four possible cases must be analyzed, as shown in Fig. 3.32.

Let us consider the polygon edge from vertex s to vertex p in Fig. 3.32. Assume that start point s has been dealt with in the previous iteration. In case 1, when the polygon edge is completely inside the clip boundary, vertex p is added to the output list. In case 2, the intersection point i is output as a vertex because the edge intersects the boundary. In case 3, both vertices are outside the boundary, so there is no output. In case 4, the intersection point i and vertex p are both added to the output list.

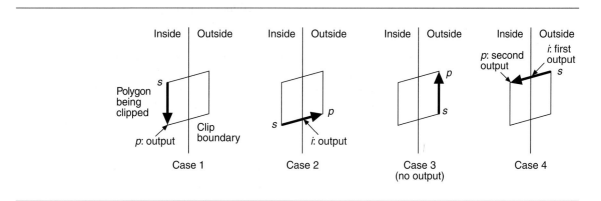

Figure 3.32   Four cases of polygon clipping.

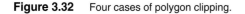

Function SutherlandHodgmanPolygonClip( ) in Prog. 3.9 accepts an array, *inVertexArray,* of vertices and creates another array, *outVertexArray,* of vertices. To keep the code simple, we show no error checking on array bounds, and we use the function Output( ) to place a vertex into *outVertexArray.* The function Intersect( ) calculates the intersection of the polygon edge from vertex *s* to vertex *p* with *clip-Boundary,* which is defined by two vertices on the clip polygon's boundary. The function Inside( ) returns TRUE if the vertex is on the inside of the clip boundary, where "inside" is defined as "to the left of the clip boundary when one looks from the first vertex to the second vertex of the clip boundary." This sense corresponds to a counterclockwise enumeration of edges. To calculate whether a point lies outside a clip boundary, we can test the sign of the dot product of the normal to the clip boundary and the polygon edge, as described in Section 3.9.4. (For the simple case of an upright clip rectangle, we need only test the sign of the horizontal or vertical distance to its boundary.)

Sutherland and Hodgman show how to structure the algorithm so that it is reentrant [SUTH74b]. As soon as a vertex is output, the clipper calls itself with that vertex. Clipping is performed against the next clip boundary, so that no intermediate storage is necessary for the partially clipped polygon: In essence, the polygon is passed through a *pipeline* of clippers. Each step can be implemented as special-purpose hardware with no intervening buffer space. This property (and its generality) makes the algorithm suitable for today's hardware implementations. In the algorithm as it stands, however, new edges may be introduced on the border of the clip rectangle. Consider Fig. 3.30(a)—a new edge is introduced by connecting the left top of the triangle and the left top of the rectangle. A postprocessing phase could eliminate these edges.

Program 3.9

Sutherland-Hodgman polygon-clipping algorithm.

```
typedef struct vertex {
    float  x, y;
} vertex;

typedef vertex edge[2];
typedef vertex vertexArray[MAX];          /* MAX is a declared constant */

void   Intersect(vertex first, vertex second, vertex *clipBoundary,
                 vertex *intersectPt)
{
    if (clipBoundary[0].y == clipBoundary[1].y) {        /* horizontal*/
        intersectPt->y = clipBoundary[0].y;
        intersectPt->x = first.x + (clipBoundary[0].y − first.y) *
            (second.x − first.x) / (second.y − first.y);
    } else {                                             /* vertical */
        intersectPt->x = clipBoundary[0].x;
        intersectPt->y = first.y + (clipBoundary[0].x − first.x) *
            (second.y − first.y) / (second.x − first.x);
    }
}
```

```
        }


boolean    Inside(vertex testVertex, vertex *clipBoundary)
{
    if (clipBoundary[1].x > clipBoundary[0].x)              /* bottom */
        if (testVertex.y >= clipBoundary[0].y) return TRUE;
    if (clipBoundary[1].x < clipBoundary[0].x)              /* top */
        if (testVertex.y <= clipBoundary[0].y) return TRUE;
    if (clipBoundary[1].y > clipBoundary[0].y)              /* right */
        if (testVertex.x <= clipBoundary[1].x) return TRUE;
    if (clipBoundary[1].y < clipBoundary[0].y)              /* left */
        if (testVertex.x >= clipBoundary[1].x) return TRUE;
    return FALSE;
}


void    Output(vertex newVertex, int *outLength, vertex *outVertexArray)
{
    (*outLength)++;
    outVertexArray[*outLength − 1].x = newVertex.x;
    outVertexArray[*outLength − 1].y = newVertex.y;
}


void    SutherlandHodgmanPolygonClip(vertex *inVertexArray,
        vertex *outVertexArray, int inLength, int *outLength, vertex *clip_boundary)
{
    vertex s, p, i;
    int    j;

    *outLength = 0;
    s = inVertexArray[inLength − 1];       /* Start with the last vertex in inVertexArray */
    for (j = 0; j < inLength; j++) {
        p = inVertexArray[j];      /* Now s and p correspond to the vertices in Fig. 3.33 */
        if (Inside(p, clip_boundary)) {                            /* Cases 1 and 4 */
            if (Inside(s, clip_boundary))
                Output(p, outLength, outVertexArray);             /* Case 1 */
            else {                                                 /* Case 4 */
                Intersect(s, p, clip_boundary, &i);
                Output(i, outLength, outVertexArray);
                Output(p, outLength, outVertexArray);
            }
        } else if (Inside(s, clip_boundary)) {                     /* Cases 2 and 3 */
            Intersect(s, p, clip_boundary, &i);                    /* Case 2 */
            Output(i, outLength, outVertexArray);
        }                                                  /* No action for case 3 */
        s = p;                                 /* Advance to next pair of vertices */
    }
}
```

3.12 GENERATING CHARACTERS

3.12.1 Defining and Clipping Characters

There are two basic techniques for defining characters. The most general but most computationally expensive way is to define each character as a curved or polygonal outline and to scan convert it as needed. We first discuss the other, simpler way, in which each character in a given font is specified as a small rectangular bitmap. Generating a character then entails simply using a copyPixel to copy the character's image from an offscreen canvas, called a **font cache**, into the frame buffer at the desired position.

The font cache may actually be in the frame buffer, as follows. In most graphics systems in which the display is refreshed from a private frame buffer, that memory is larger than is strictly required for storing the displayed image. For example, the pixels for a rectangular screen may be stored in a square memory, leaving a rectangular strip of *invisible* screen memory. Alternatively, there may be enough memory for two screens, one of which is being refreshed and one of which is being drawn in, to double-buffer the image. The font cache for the currently displayed font(s) is frequently stored in such invisible screen memory because the display controller's copyPixel works fastest within local image memory. A related use for such invisible memory is for saving screen areas temporarily obscured by popped-up images, such as windows, menus, and forms.

The bitmaps for the font cache are usually created by scanning in enlarged pictures of characters from typesetting fonts in various sizes; a typeface designer can then use a paint program to touch up individual pixels in each character's bitmap as necessary. Alternatively, the type designer may use a paint program to create, from scratch, fonts that are especially designed for screens and low-resolution printers. Since small bitmaps do not scale well, more than one bitmap must be defined for a given character in a given font just to provide various standard sizes. Furthermore, each type face requires its own set of bitmaps; therefore, a distinct font cache is needed for each font loaded by the application.

Bitmap characters are clipped automatically by SRGP as part of its implementation of copyPixel. Each character is clipped to the destination rectangle on a pixel-by-pixel basis, a technique that lets us clip a character at any row or column of its bitmap. For systems with slow copyPixel operations, a much faster, although cruder, method is to clip the character or even the entire string on an all-or-nothing basis by doing a trivial accept of the character or string extent. Only if the extent is trivially accepted is the copyPixel applied to the character or string. Even for systems with a fast copyPixel, it is still useful to do trivial accept/reject testing of the string extent as a precursor to clipping individual characters during the copyPixel operation.

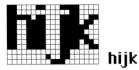

Figure 3.33
Portion of an example of a font cache.

SRGP's simple bitmap font-cache technique stores the characters side by side in a canvas that is quite wide but is only as tall as the tallest character; Fig. 3.33 shows a portion of the cache, along with discrete instances of the same characters at low resolution. Each loaded font is described by a struct (declared in Prog. 3.10) containing a reference to the canvas that stores the characters' images, along with information on the height of the characters and the amount of space to be placed between adjacent characters in a text string. (Some packages store the space between characters as part of a character's width, to allow variable intercharacter spacing.)

Program 3.10

Type declarations for the font cache.

```
typedef struct charLocation {
    int leftX, width;               /*Horizontal location, width of image in font cache*/
} charLocation;

typedef struct fontCacheDescriptor {
    canvasIndexInteger cache;
    int descenderHeight, totalHeight;    /*Height is a constant; width varies*/
    int interCharacterSpacing;           /*Measured in pixels*/
    charLocation locationTable[128];
} fontCacheDescriptor;
```

As described in Section 2.1.5, descender height and total height are constants for a given font—the former is the number of rows of pixels at the bottom of the font cache used only by descenders, and the latter is simply the height of the font-cache canvas. The width of a character, on the other hand, is not considered a constant; thus, a character can occupy the space that suits it, rather than being forced into a fixed-width character box. SRGP puts a fixed amount of space between characters when it draws a text string, the amount being specified as part of each font's descriptor. A word-processing application can display lines of text by using SRGP to display individual words of text, and can right-justify lines by using variable spacing between words and after punctuation to fill out lines so that their rightmost characters are aligned at the right margin. This application involves using the text-extent inquiry facilities to determine where the right edge of each word is, in order to calculate the start of the next word. Needless to say, SRGP's text-handling facilities are really too crude for sophisticated word processing, let alone for typesetting programs, since such applications require far finer control over the spacing of individual letters to deal with such effects as sub- and superscripting, kerning, and printing text that is not horizontally aligned.

3.12.2 Implementing a Text Output Primitive

In the code of Prog. 3.11, we show how SRGP text is implemented internally: Each character in the given string is placed individually, and the space between characters is dictated by the appropriate field in the font descriptor. Note that complexities such as dealing with mixed fonts in a string must be handled by the application program.

Program 3.11

Implementation of character placement for SRGP's text primitive.

```
void SRGP_characterText(point origin, char *stringToPrint,
        fontCacheDescriptor  fontInfo)
/* origin is where to place the character in the current canvas*/
{
```

```
    rectangle fontCacheRectangle;
    char charToPrint;
    int i;
    charLocation *fp;

/*Origin specified by the application is for baseline and does not include descender.*/
    origin.y −= fontInfo.descenderHeight;

    for (i = 0; i < strlen(stringToPrint); i++) {
        charToPrint = stringToPrint[i];
        fp = &fontInfo.locationTable[charToPrint];
/*Find the rectangular region within the cache wherein the character lies.*/
        fontCacheRectangle.bottomLeft = SRGP_defPoint(fp−>leftX, 0);
        fontCacheRectangle.topRight = SRGP_defPoint(fp−>leftX + fp−>width − 1,
            fontInfo.totalHeight − 1);
        SRGP_copyPixel(fontInfo.cache, fontCacheRectangle, origin);
/*Update the origin to move past the new character plus intercharacter spacing*/
        origin.x += fp−>width + interCharacterSpacing;
    }
}
```

We mentioned that the bitmap technique requires a distinct font cache for each combination of font, size, and face for each different resolution of display or output device supported. A single font in eight different point sizes and four faces (normal, bold, italic, bold italic) thus requires 32 font caches! One way to resolve this storage problem is to represent characters in an abstract, device-independent form using polygonal or curved outlines of their shapes defined with floating-point parameters, and then to transform them appropriately. Polynomial functions called **splines** (see Chapter 9) provide smooth curves with continuous first and higher derivatives and are commonly used to encode text outlines. Although each character definition takes up more space than its representation in a font cache, multiple sizes may be derived from a single stored representation by suitable scaling; also, italics may be quickly approximated by shearing the outline. Another major advantage of storing characters in a completely device-independent form is that the outlines may be arbitrarily translated, rotated, scaled, and clipped (or used as clipping regions themselves).

The storage economy of splined characters is not quite so great as this description suggests. For instance, not all point sizes for a character may be obtained by scaling a single abstract shape, because the shape for an aesthetically pleasing font is typically a function of point size; therefore, each shape suffices for only a limited range of point sizes. Moreover, scan conversion of splined text requires far more processing than does the simple copyPixel implementation, because the device-independent form must be converted to pixel coordinates on the basis of the current size, face, and transformation attributes. Thus, the font-cache technique is still the most common for personal computers and even is used for many workstations. A strategy that offers the best of both methods is to store the fonts in outline form but to convert the ones being used in a given application to their bitmap equivalents—for example, to build a font cache on the fly. A more detailed discussion of splined text can be found in [FOLE90], Section 19.4.

3.13 SRGP_COPYPIXEL

If only WritePixel and ReadPixel low-level functions are available, the SRGP_-copyPixel function can be implemented as a doubly nested for loop for each pixel. For simplicity, assume first that we are working with a bilevel display and do not need to deal with the low-level considerations of writing bits that are not word-aligned. In the inner loop of our simple SRGP_copyPixel, we do a ReadPixel of the source and destination pixels, logically combine them according to the SRGP write mode, and then WritePixel the result. Treating **replace** mode, the most common write mode, as a special case allows a simpler inner loop that does only a ReadPixel/WritePixel of the source into the destination, without having to do a logical operation. The clip rectangle is used during address calculation to restrict the region into which destination pixels are written.

3.14 ANTIALIASING

3.14.1 Increasing Resolution

The primitives drawn so far have a common problem: They have jagged edges. This undesirable effect, known as **the jaggies** or **staircasing**, is the result of an all-or-nothing approach to scan conversion in which each pixel either is replaced with the primitive's color or is left unchanged. Jaggies are an instance of a phenomenon known as **aliasing**. The application of techniques that reduce or eliminate aliasing is referred to as **antialiasing**, and primitives or images produced using these techniques are said to be **antialiased**. [FOLE90], in Chapter 14, discusses basic ideas from signal processing that explain how aliasing got its name, why it occurs, and how to reduce or eliminate it when creating pictures. Here, we content ourselves with a more intuitive explanation of why SRGP's primitives exhibit aliasing, and describe how to modify the line scan-conversion algorithm developed in this chapter to generate antialiased lines.

Consider using the midpoint algorithm to draw a 1-pixel-thick black line, with slope between 0 and 1, on a white background. In each column through which the line passes, the algorithm sets the color of the pixel that is closest to the line. Each time the line moves between columns in which the pixels closest to the line are not in the same row, there is a sharp jag in the line drawn into the canvas, as is clear in Fig. 3.34(a). The same is true for other scan-converted primitives that can assign only one of two intensity values to pixels.

Suppose we now use a display device with twice the horizontal and vertical resolution. As shown in Fig. 3.34(b), the line passes through twice as many columns and therefore has twice as many jags, but each jag is half as large in x and

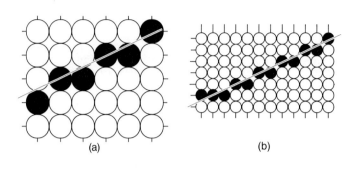

(a)　　　　　　　　　　　　　　　　(b)

Figure 3.34　(a) Standard midpoint line on a bilevel display. (b) Same line on a display that has twice the linear resolution.

in y. Although the resulting picture looks better, the improvement comes at the price of quadrupling the memory cost, memory bandwidth, and scan-conversion time. Increasing resolution is an expensive solution that only diminishes the problem of jaggies—it does not eliminate the problem. In the following sections, we look at antialiasing techniques that are less costly, yet result in significantly better images.

3.14.2 Unweighted Area Sampling

The first approach to improving picture quality can be developed by recognizing that, although an ideal primitive such as the line has zero width, the primitive we are drawing has nonzero width. A scan-converted primitive occupies a finite area on the screen—even the thinnest horizontal or vertical line on a display surface is 1 pixel thick and lines at other angles have widths that vary over the primitive. Thus, we think of any line as a rectangle of a desired thickness covering a portion of the grid, as shown in Fig. 3.35. It follows that a line should not set the intensity of only a single pixel in a column to black, but rather should contribute some amount of intensity to each pixel in the columns whose area it intersects. (Such varying intensity can be shown on only those displays with multiple bits per pixel, of course.) Then, for 1-pixel-thick lines, only horizontal and vertical lines would affect exactly 1 pixel in their column or row. For lines at other angles, more than 1 pixel would now be set in a column or row, each to an appropriate intensity.

But what is the geometry of a pixel? How large is it? How much intensity should a line contribute to each pixel it intersects? It is computationally simple to assume that the pixels form an array of nonoverlapping square tiles covering the screen, centered on grid points, rather than disjoint circles as earlier in the chapter. [When we refer to a primitive overlapping all or a portion of a pixel, we mean that it covers (part of) the tile; to emphasize this we sometimes refer to the square as the *area represented by the pixel*.] We also assume that a line contributes to each pixel's intensity an amount proportional to the percentage of the pixel's tile it covers. A fully covered pixel on a black-and-white display will be colored black,

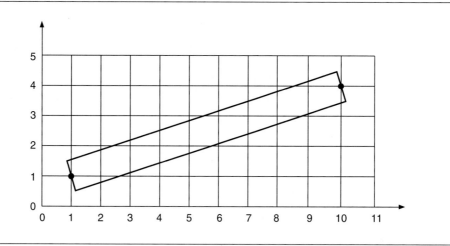

Figure 3.35   Line of nonzero width from point (1,1) to point (10,4).

whereas a partially covered pixel will be colored a gray whose intensity depends on the line's coverage of the pixel. This technique, as applied to the line shown in Fig. 3.35, is shown in Fig. 3.36.

For a black line on a white background, pixel (2, 1) is about 70 percent black, whereas pixel (2, 2) is about 25 percent black. Pixels such as (2, 3) not intersected by the line are completely white. Setting a pixel's intensity in proportion to the amount of its area covered by the primitive softens the harsh, on–off characteristic of the edge of the primitive and yields a more gradual transition between full on and full off. This blurring makes a line look better at a distance, despite the fact

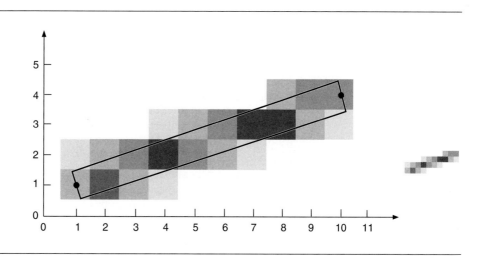

Figure 3.36   Intensity of a pixel is proportional to its area covered by the line.

that it spreads the on–off transition over multiple pixels in a column or row. A rough approximation to the area overlap can be found by dividing the pixel into a finer grid of rectangular subpixels, then counting the number of subpixels inside the line—for example, below the line's top edge or above its bottom edge. (See Exercise 3.25.)

We call the technique of setting intensity proportional to the amount of area covered **unweighted area sampling**. This technique produces noticeably better results than does setting pixels to full intensity or zero intensity, but there is an even more effective strategy called **weighted area sampling**. To explain the difference between the two forms of area sampling, we note that unweighted area sampling has the following three properties. First, the intensity of a pixel intersected by a line edge decreases as the distance between the pixel center and the edge increases: The farther away a primitive is, the less influence it has on a pixel's intensity. This relation obviously holds because the intensity decreases as the area of overlap decreases, and that area decreases as the line's edge moves away from the pixel's center and toward the boundary of the pixel. When the line covers the pixel completely, the overlap area and therefore the intensity are at a maximum; when the primitive edge is just tangent to the boundary, the area and therefore the intensity are zero.

A second property of unweighted area sampling is that a primitive cannot influence the intensity at a pixel at all if the primitive does not intersect the pixel—that is, if it does not intersect the square tile represented by the pixel. A third property of unweighted area sampling is that equal areas contribute equal intensity, regardless of the distance between the pixel's center and the area; only the total amount of overlapped area matters. Thus, a small area in the corner of the pixel contributes just as much as does an equal-sized area near the pixel's center.

3.14.3 Weighted Area Sampling

In weighted area sampling, we keep unweighted area sampling's first and second properties (intensity decreases with decreased area overlap, and primitives contribute only if they overlap the area represented by the pixel), but we alter the third property. We let equal areas contribute unequally: A small area closer to the pixel center has greater influence than does one at a greater distance. A theoretical basis for this change is given in [FOLE90], Chapter 14, where weighted area sampling is discussed in the context of filtering theory.

To retain the second property, we must make the following change in the geometry of the pixel. In unweighted area sampling, if an edge of a primitive is quite close to the boundary of the square tile we have used to represent a pixel until now, but does not actually intersect this boundary, it will not contribute to the pixel's intensity. In our new approach, the pixel represents a circular area larger than the square tile; the primitive *will* intersect this larger area; hence, it will contribute to the intensity of the pixel. Note that this means that the areas associated with adjacent pixels actually overlap.

To explain the origin of the adjectives *unweighted* and *weighted*, we define a **weighting function** that determines the influence on the intensity of a pixel of a

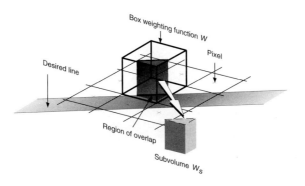

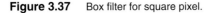

Figure 3.37   Box filter for square pixel.

given small area dA of a primitive, as a function of dA's distance from the center of the pixel. This function is constant for unweighted area sampling, and decreases with increasing distance for weighted area sampling. Think of the weighting function as a function, $W(x, y)$, on the plane, whose height above the (x, y) plane gives the weight for the area dA at (x, y). For unweighted area sampling with the pixels represented as square tiles, the graph of W is a box, as shown in Fig. 3.37.

The figure shows square pixels, with centers indicated by crosses at the intersections of grid lines; the weighting function is shown as a box whose base is that of the current pixel. The intensity contributed by the area of the pixel covered by the primitive is the total of intensity contributions from all small areas in the region of overlap between the primitive and the pixel. The intensity contributed by each small area is proportional to the area multiplied by the weight. Therefore, the total intensity is the integral of the weighting function over the area of overlap. The volume represented by this integral, W_S, is always a fraction between 0 and 1, and the pixel's intensity I is $I_{max} \cdot W_S$. In Fig. 3.37, W_S is a wedge of the box. The weighting function is also called a **filter function**, and the box is also called a **box filter.** For unweighted area sampling, the height of the box is normalized to 1, so that the box's volume is 1, which causes a thick line covering the entire pixel to have an intensity $I = I_{max} \cdot 1 = I_{max}$.

Now let us construct a weighting function for weighted area sampling; it must give less weight to small areas farther away from the pixel center than it does to those closer. Let us pick a weighting function that is the simplest decreasing function of distance; for example, we choose a function that has a maximum at the center of the pixel and decreases linearly with increasing distance from the center. Because of rotational symmetry, the graph of this function forms a circular cone. The circular base of the cone (often called the **support** of the filter) should have a radius larger than you might expect; filtering theory shows that a good choice for the radius is the unit distance of the integer grid. Thus, a primitive fairly far from a pixel's center can still influence that pixel's intensity; also, the supports associated with neighboring pixels overlap, and therefore a single small piece of a primitive

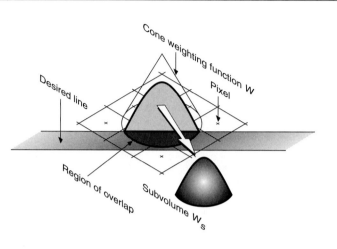

Figure 3.38   Cone filter for circular pixel with diameter of two grid units.

may actually contribute to several different pixels (Fig. 3.38). This overlap also ensures that there are no areas of the grid not covered by some pixel, which would be the case if the circular pixels had a radius of only one-half of a grid unit.[8]

As with the box filter, the sum of all intensity contributions for the cone filter is the volume under the cone and above the intersection of the cone's base and the primitive; this volume W_S is a vertical section of the cone, as shown in Fig. 3.38. As with the box filter, the height of the cone is first normalized so that the volume under the entire cone is 1; this allows a pixel whose support is completely covered by a primitive to be displayed at maximum intensity. Although contributions from areas of the primitive far from the pixel's center but still intersecting the support are rather small, a pixel whose center is sufficiently close to a line receives some intensity contribution from that line. Conversely, a pixel that, in the square-geometry model, was entirely covered by a line of unit thickness[9] is not quite as bright as it used to be. The net effect of weighted area sampling is to decrease the contrast between adjacent pixels in order to provide smoother transitions. In particular, with weighted area sampling, a horizontal or vertical line of unit thickness has more than 1 pixel intensified in each column or row, which would not be the case for unweighted area sampling.

The conical filter has two useful properties: rotational symmetry and linear decrease of the function with radial distance. We prefer rotational symmetry

[8] As noted in Section 3.2, pixels displayed on a CRT are roughly circular in cross-section, and adjacent pixels typically overlap; the model of overlapping circles used in weighted area sampling, however, is not directly related to this fact and holds even for display technologies, such as LCD screens or plasma panels, in which the physical pixels are actually nonoverlapping square tiles.

[9] We now say a "a line of unit thickness" rather than "a line 1 pixel thick" to make it clear that the unit of line width is still that of the SRGP grid, whereas the pixel's support has grown to have a two-unit diameter.

because it not only makes area calculations independent of the angle of the line, but also is theoretically optimal. Note, however, that the cone's linear slope (and its radius) are only an approximation to the optimal filter function, although the cone filter is still better than the box filter [FOLE90]. Optimal filters are computationally most expensive, box filters least, and therefore cone filters are a very reasonable compromise between cost and quality. We could integrate the cone filter into our scan-conversion algorithms rather easily. Details of this process can be found in [FOLE90].

3.15 ADVANCED TOPICS

We have only touched on the concepts of clipping and scan conversion in this chapter. In practice, many complex situations arise that require the application of advanced approaches. These are discussed fully in Chapter 19 of [FOLE90], but it will be useful to enumerate some of them here.

Clipping.   While the clipping algorithms we have discussed in this chapter will perform correctly in most cases, they will not always do so efficiently. In addition, in some situations they will not be precise or even give the correct answer. Some of the improved algorithms are the Nicholl–Lee–Nicholl approach to 2D clipping, which exhibits a dramatic speedup over both the Liang–Barsky and Cohen–Sutherland algorithms. Also, clipping situations arise that we have not even considered, such as clipping general polygons against other general polygons. For this situation the Weiler polygon algorithm is useful.

Scan-converting primitives.   We have only considered scan-conversion of simple primitives—lines, circles, and polygons. Not only are there more accurate and efficient algorithms for these objects, but there are methods for scan-converting more complicated primitives, as well, including ellipses, elliptical arcs, cubic curves, and general conic sections. There are also algorithms for thick primitives, where the boundary is not just a mathematical region, but has arbitrary width. Included in this class of problems is how to attractively and efficiently join thick line segments. Finally, filling self-intersecting polygons, where it is not clear which is inside and which is outside, must often be considered.

Antialiasing.   The situations requiring antialiasing are much more numerous than for the straight line cases we have considered. Also, we must have a more complete knowledge of sampling theory in order to antialias correctly. Special algorithms are required for circles, conic sections, general curves, as well as rectangles, polygons, and line ends.

Text.   Text is a highly specialized entity, and our earlier techniques are usually not sufficient. In this chapter, we discussed using a font cache to store characters that could then be copied directly to the bitmap, but we also observed certain limitations of this approach: A different cache may be needed for each size of text, and the intercharacter spacing is fixed. Furthermore, although versions of bold or italic text can be created from this font cache, they are usually unsatisfactory. Even if we have a precise geometric drawing of a character, such as might be provided by a font designer, we cannot scan convert it on a stroke-by-stroke basis. The results will generally be unacceptable. Rather, specialized techniques have been developed to display text, including antialiasing.

Filling algorithms.   Sometimes, after drawing a sequence of primitives, we may wish to color them in, or we may wish to color in a region defined by a freehand drawing. For example, it may be easier to make a mosaic pattern by creating a grid of lines and then filling it in with various colors than it is to lay down the colored squares evenly in the first place. Note that, when the first technique is used, no 2D primitives are drawn: We use only the 2D areas that happen to make up the background after the lines are drawn. Thus, determining how large a region to color amounts to detecting when a border is reached. Algorithms to perform this operation are called *fill algorithms*. Among those used are *boundary fill*, *flood fill*, and *tint fill* algorithms. Each has a special purpose and many graphics systems offer them all.

SUMMARY

In this chapter, we have taken our first look at the fundamental clipping and scan-conversion algorithms that are the meat and potatoes of raster graphics packages. We have covered only the basics here; many elaborations and special cases must be considered for robust implementations. You should consult Chapters 14, 17, and 19 of [FOLE90] for a fuller treatment of these issues.

The most important idea of this chapter is that, since speed is essential in interactive raster graphics, incremental scan-conversion algorithms using only integer operations in their inner loops are usually the best. The basic algorithms can be extended to handle thickness, as well as patterns for boundaries or for filling areas. Whereas the basic algorithms that convert single-pixel-wide primitives try to minimize the error between chosen pixels on the Cartesian grid and the ideal primitive defined on the plane, the algorithms for thick primitives can trade off quality and *correctness* for speed. Although much of 2D raster graphics today still operates, even on color displays, with single-bit-per-pixel primitives, we expect that techniques for real-time antialiasing will soon become prevalent.

Exercises

3.1   Implement the special-case code for scan converting horizontal and vertical lines, and lines with slopes of ±1.

3.2   Modify the midpoint algorithm for scan converting lines (Prog. 3.2) to handle lines at any angle.

3.3   Show why the point-to-line error is always $\leq \frac{1}{2}$ for the midpoint line scan-conversion algorithm.

3.4   Modify the midpoint algorithm for scan converting lines of Exercise 3.2 to handle endpoint order and intersections with clip edges, as discussed in Section 3.2.3.

3.5   Modify the midpoint algorithm for scan converting lines (Exercise 3.2) to write pixels with varying intensity as a function of line slope.

3.6   Modify the midpoint algorithm for scan converting lines (Exercise 3.2) to deal with endpoints that do not have integer coordinates—this is easiest if you use floating point throughout your algorithm. As a more difficult exercise, handle lines of *rational* endpoints using only integers.

3.7   Show how polylines may share more than vertex pixels. Develop an algorithm that avoids writing pixels twice. *Hint*: Consider scan conversion and writing to the canvas in **xor** mode as separate phases.)

3.8   Develop an alternative to the midpoint circle scan-conversion algorithm of Section 3.3.2 based on a piecewise-linear approximation of the circle with a polyline.

3.9   Develop an algorithm for scan converting unfilled rounded rectangles with a specified radius for the quarter-circle corners.

3.10 Write a scan-conversion function for solidly filled upright rectangles at arbitrary screen positions that writes a bilevel frame buffer efficiently, an entire word of pixels at a time.

3.11 Construct examples of pixels that are *missing* or written multiple times, using the rules of Section 3.5. Try to develop alternative, possibly more complex, rules that do not draw shared pixels on shared edges twice, yet do not cause pixels to be missing. Are these rules worth the added overhead?

3.12 Implement the pseudocode of Section 3.5 for polygon scan conversion, taking into account in the span bookkeeping of potential sliver polygons.

3.13 Develop scan-conversion algorithms for triangles and trapezoids that take advantage of the simple nature of these shapes. Such algorithms are common in hardware.

3.14 Investigate triangulation algorithms for decomposing an arbitrary, possibly concave or self-intersecting, polygon into a mesh of triangles whose vertices are shared. Does it help to restrict the polygon to being, at worse, concave without self-intersections or interior holes? (See also [PREP85].)

3.15 Extend the midpoint algorithm for scan converting circles (Prog. 3.4) to handle filled circles and circular wedges (for pie charts), using span tables.

3.16 Implement both absolute and relative anchor algorithms for polygon pattern filling, discussed in Section 3.7, and contrast them in terms of visual effect and computational efficiency.

3.17 Apply the technique of Fig. 3.20 for writing characters filled with patterns in opaque mode. Show how having a copyPixel with a write mask may be used to good advantage for this class of problems.

3.18 Implement a technique for drawing various symbols such as cursor icons represented by small bitmaps so that they can be seen regardless of the background on which they are written. *Hint*: Define a mask for each symbol that "encloses" the symbol—that is, that covers more pixels than the symbol—and that draws masks and symbols in separate passes.

3.19 Implement thick-line algorithms using the techniques listed in Section 3.7. Contrast their efficiency and the quality of the results they produced.

3.20 Extend the midpoint algorithm for scan converting circles (Prog. 3.4) to handle thick circles.

3.21 Implement a thick-line algorithm that accommodates line style as well as pen style and pattern.

3.22 Modify the Cohen–Sutherland line-clipping algorithm of Prog. 3.7 to avoid recalculation of slopes during successive passes. Also, redefine the *outcode* struct to be the union of the **unsigned int** *all* and the four one-bit flags, *left*, *right*, *bottom*, and *top*.

3.23 Consider a convex polygon with n vertices being clipped against a clip rectangle. What is the maximum number of vertices in the resulting clipped polygon? What is the minimum number? Consider the same problem for a concave polygon. How many polygons might result? If a single polygon results, what is the largest number of vertices it might have?

3.24 Explain why the Sutherland–Hodgman polygon-clipping algorithm works for only convex clipping regions.

3.25 Devise a strategy for subdividing a pixel and counting the number of subpixels covered (at least to a significant degree) by a line, as part of a line-drawing algorithm using unweighted area sampling.

4 Graphics Hardware

In this chapter, we describe how the important hardware elements of a computer graphics display system work. Section 4.1 covers hardcopy technologies: printers, pen plotters, laser printers, ink-jet plotters, and film recorders. The basic technological concepts behind each type of device are described briefly, and a concluding section compares the various devices. Section 4.2, on display technologies, discusses monochrome and color shadow-mask CRTs, liquid-crystal displays (LCDs), and electroluminescent displays. Again, a concluding section discusses the pros and cons of the various display technologies.

Raster display systems, which can use any of the display technologies discussed here, are described in Section 4.3. A simple, straightforward raster system is first introduced, and is then enhanced with respect to graphics functionality and integration of raster- and general-purpose processors into the system address space. Section 4.4 describes the role of the look-up table and video controller in image display, color control, and image mixing. Section 4.5 follows, with a discussion of user interaction devices such as tablets, mice, touch panels, and so on. Again, operational concepts rather than technological details are stressed. Section 4.6 briefly treats image-input devices, such as film scanners, by means of which an existing image can be input to a computer.

Figure 4.1 shows the relation of these devices to one another. The key element is the integrated CPU and display processor known as a **graphics workstation**, typically consisting of a CPU capable of executing 20–100 million instructions per second (MIPS) and a display with resolution of at least 1000×800, or more. The local-area network connects multiple workstations for file sharing, electronic mail, and access to shared peripherals such as high-quality film recorders, large disks, gateways to other networks, and higher-performance computers.

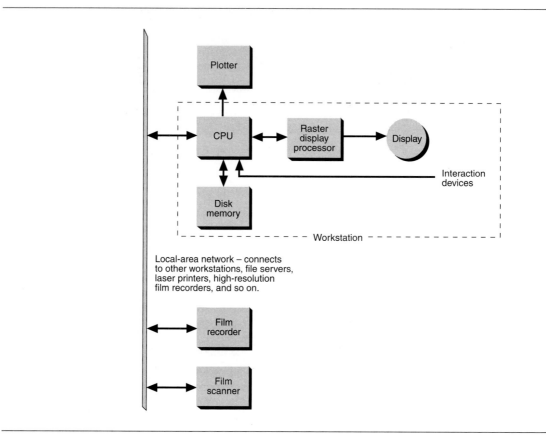

Figure 4.1   Components of a typical interactive graphics system.

4.1 HARDCOPY TECHNOLOGIES

In this section, we discuss various hardcopy technologies, then summarize their characteristics. However, several important terms must be defined first.

The image quality achievable with display devices depends on both the addressability and the dot size of the device. **Dot size** (also called **spot size**) is the diameter of a single dot created on the device. **Addressability** is the number of individual dots per inch that can be created; it may differ in the horizontal and vertical directions. Addressability in x is just the reciprocal of the distance between the centers of dots at addresses (x, y) and $(x + 1, y)$; addressability in y is defined similarly. **Interdot distance** is the reciprocal of addressability.

It is usually desirable that dot size be somewhat greater than the interdot distance, so that smooth shapes can be created. Figure 4.2 illustrates this reasoning.

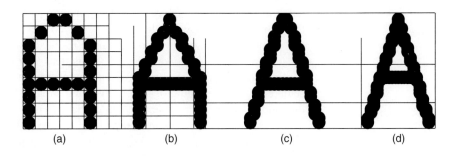

(a)   (b)   (c)   (d)

Figure 4.2   The effects of various ratios of the dot size to the interdot distance. (a) Interdot spacing equal to dot size. (b) Interdot spacing one-half dot size. (c) Interdot spacing one-third dot size. (d) Interdot spacing one-quarter dot size.

Tradeoffs arise here, however: Dot size several times the interdot distance allows very smooth shapes to be printed, whereas a smaller dot size allows finer detail.

Resolution, which is related to dot size and can be no greater than address-ability, is the number of distinguishable lines per inch that a device can create. Resolution is defined as the closest spacing at which adjacent black and white lines can be distinguished by observers (this again implies that horizontal and vertical resolution may differ). If 40 black lines interleaved with 40 white lines can be distinguished across one inch, the resolution is 80 lines per inch (also referred to as 40 line-pairs per inch). Resolution also depends on the cross-sectional intensity distribution of a spot. A spot with sharply delineated edges yields higher resolution than does one with edges that trail off.

Many of the devices to be discussed can create only a few colors at any one point. Additional colors can be obtained with dither patterns, described in Chapter 11, at the cost of decreased spatial resolution of the resulting image.

Dot-matrix printers use a print head of from 7 to 24 **pins** (thin, stiff pieces of wire), each of which can be individually *fired*, to strike a ribbon against the paper. The print head moves across the paper one step at a time, the paper is advanced one line, and the print head makes another pass across the paper. Hence, these printers are raster output devices, requiring scan conversion of vector images prior to printing.

Colored ribbons can be used to produce color hardcopy. Two approaches are possible. The first is using multiple print heads, each head with a different color ribbon. Alternatively and more commonly, a single print head is used with a multi-colored ribbon.

More colors than are actually on the ribbon can be created by overstriking two different colors at the same dot on the paper. The color on top may be somewhat stronger than that underneath. Up to eight colors can be created at any one dot by overstriking with three colors—typically cyan, magenta, and yellow. However, the black resulting from striking all three is quite muddy, so a true black is often added to the ribbon.

One type of plotter is the **pen plotter**, which moves a pen over a piece of paper in random, vector-drawing style. In drawing a line, the pen is positioned at the start of the line, lowered to the paper, moved in a straight path to the endpoint of the line, raised, and moved to the start of the next line.

There are two basic varieties of pen plotters. The **flatbed plotter** moves the pen in x and y on a sheet of paper spread out on a table and held down by electrostatic charge, by vacuum, or simply by being stretched tightly. A carriage moves longitudinally over the table. On the carriage a pen mount moves latitudinally along the carriage; the pen can be raised and lowered. Flatbed plotters are available in sizes from 12 by 18 inches to 6 by 10 feet and larger.

In contrast, **drum plotters** move the paper along one axis and the pen along the other axis. Typically, the paper is stretched tightly across a drum. Pins on the drum engage prepunched holes in the paper to prevent slipping. The drum can rotate both forward and backward. By contrast, many **desktop plotters** move the paper back and forth between pinch rollers, while the pen moves across the paper (Fig. 4.3).

Laser printers scan a laser beam across a positively-charged rotating drum coated with selenium. The areas hit by the laser beam lose their charge, and the positive charge remains only where the copy is to be black. A negatively charged powdered toner adheres to the positively charged areas of the drum and is then transferred to blank paper to form the copy. In color xerography, this process is repeated three times, once for each primary color. Figure 4.4 is a partial schematic of a monochrome laser printer. The positive charge is either present or not present at any one spot on the drum, and there is either black or not black at the corresponding spot on the copy. Hence, the laser printer is a two-level monochrome device or an eight-color color device.

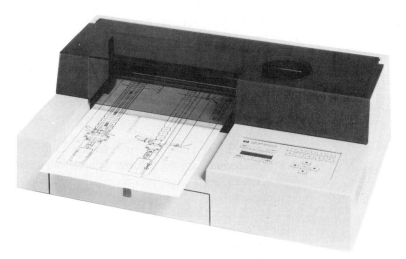

Figure 4.3   A desktop plotter. (Courtesy of Hewlett-Packard Company.)

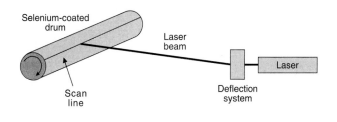

Figure 4.4 Organization of a laser printer (the toner-application mechanism and the paper feeder are not shown).

Laser printers have a microprocessor to do scan conversion and to control the printer. An increasing number of laser printers accept the PostScript document and image description language as a de facto standard [ADOB85]. PostScript provides a procedural description of an image to be printed, and can also be used to store image descriptions. Most laser printers work with 8.5-by-11-inch or 8.5-by-14-inch paper, but considerably wider (30-inch) laser printers are available for engineering drawing and map-making applications.

Ink-jet printers spray cyan, magenta, yellow, and sometimes black ink onto paper. In most cases, the ink jets are mounted on a head in a printer-like mechanism. The print head moves across the page to draw one scan line, returns while the paper advances by one inter–scan-line spacing, and draws the next scan line. Slight irregularities in interline spacing can arise if the paper transport moves a bit too much or too little. Also, all the colors are deposited simultaneously, unlike the multipass laser plotters and printers. Most ink-jet printers are limited to on–off (i.e., bilevel) control of each pixel: A few have a variable dot-size capability.

Thermal-transfer printers, another raster hardcopy device, use finely spaced (typically 200-per-inch) heating nibs to transfer pigments from colored wax paper to plain paper. The wax paper and plain paper are drawn together over the strip of heating nibs, which are selectively heated to cause the pigment transfer. For color printing (the most common use of this technology), the wax paper is on a roll of alternating cyan, magenta, yellow, and black strips, each of a length equal to the paper size. Because the nibs heat and cool very rapidly, a single color hardcopy image can be created in less than 1 minute. Some thermal-transfer printers accept a video signal and digital bitmap input, making them convenient for creating hardcopy of video images.

Thermal sublimation dye transfer printers work similarly to the thermal transfer printers, except the heating and dye transfer process permit 256 intensities each of cyan, magenta, and yellow to be transferred, creating high-quality full-color images with a spatial resolution of 200 dots per inch. The process is slower than wax transfer, but the quality is near-photographic—making this type of printer the clear choice for producing full-color pre-press proofs.

A **camera** that photographs an image displayed on a **cathode-ray tube (CRT)** can be considered another hardcopy device. This is the most common hardcopy technology we discuss that yields a large number of colors at a single resolution point because film can capture many different colors.

There are two basic techniques for color film recorders. In one, the camera records the color image directly from a color CRT. Image resolution is limited because of the shadow mask of the color monitor (see Section 4.2) and the need to use a raster scan with the color monitor. In the other approach, a black-and-white CRT is photographed through color filters, and the different color components of the image are displayed in sequence. This technique yields very high-quality raster or vector images. Colors are mixed by double-exposing parts of the image through two or more filters, usually with different CRT intensities.

Input to film recorders can be a raster video signal, a bitmap, or vector-style instructions. Either the video signal can drive a color CRT directly, or the red, green, and blue components of the signal can be electronically separated for time-sequential display through filters. In either case, the video signal must stay constant during the entire recording cycle, which can be up to 1 minute if relatively slow (low-sensitivity) film is being used.

Table 4.1 summarizes the differences among color hardcopy devices. Considerable detail on the technology of hardcopy devices can be found in [DURB88]. The current pace of technological innovation is, of course, so great that the relative advantages and disadvantages of some of these devices will surely change. Also, some of the technologies are available in a wide range of prices and performances. Film recorders and pen plotters, for instance, can cost from about $500 to $100,000.

Table 4.1   A Comparison of Several Color Hardcopy Technologies*

Property	Pen Plotter	Dot Matrix	Laser	Ink Jet	Photo
Color levels per dot	to 16	8	8	8–many	many
Addressability, points per in.	1000+	to 250	to 1500	to 200	to 800
Dot size, thousandths of in.	15–6	18–10	5	20–8	20–6
Relative cost range	L–M	VL	M-H	L–M	M–H
Relative cost per image	L	VL	M	L	H
Image quality	L–M	L	H	M	M–H
Speed	L	L–M	M	M	L

*VL = very low, L = low, M = medium, H = high.

Note that, of all the color devices, only the film recorder, thermal sublimation dye transfer printers, and some ink-jet printers can capture a wide range of colors. All the other technologies use essentially a binary on–off control for the three or four colors they can record directly. Note also that color control is tricky: There is no guarantee that the eight colors on one device will look anything like the eight colors on the display or on another hardcopy device. See Section 13.4 of [FOLE90] for a discussion of the difficulties inherent to color reproduction.

4.2 DISPLAY TECHNOLOGIES

Interactive computer graphics demands display devices whose images can be changed quickly. Nonpermanent image displays allow an image to be changed, making possible dynamic movement of portions of an image. The CRT is by far the most common display device and will remain so for some time. However, solid-state technologies are being developed that may, in the long term, substantially reduce the dominance of the CRT.

The **monochromatic** CRTs used for graphics displays are essentially the same as those used in black-and-white home television sets. Figure 4.5 shows a highly stylized cross-sectional view of a CRT. The electron gun emits a stream of electrons that is accelerated toward the phosphor-coated screen by a high positive voltage applied near the face of the tube. On the way to the screen, the electrons are forced into a narrow beam by the focusing mechanism and are directed toward a particular point on the screen by the magnetic field produced by the deflection coils. When the electrons hit the screen, the phosphor emits visible light. Because the phosphor's light output decays exponentially with time, the entire picture must be **refreshed** (redrawn) many times per second, so that the viewer sees what appears to be a constant, unflickering picture.

The refresh rate for raster-scan displays is independent of picture complexity. The refresh rate for vector systems depends directly on picture complexity (number of lines, points, and characters): The greater the complexity, the longer the time taken by a single refresh cycle and the lower the refresh rate.

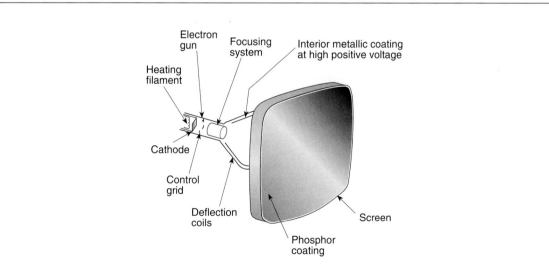

Figure 4.5   Cross-section of a CRT (not to scale).

The stream of electrons from the heated cathode is accelerated toward the phosphor by a high voltage, typically 15,000 to 20,000 volts, which determines the velocity achieved by the electrons before they hit the phosphor. The control-grid voltage determines how many electrons are actually in the electron beam. The more negative the control-grid voltage is, the fewer the electrons that pass through the grid. This phenomenon allows the spot's intensity to be controlled, because the light output of the phosphor decreases as the number of electrons in the beam decreases.

The focusing system concentrates the electron beam so that the beam converges to a small point when it hits the phosphor coating. It is not enough for the electrons in the beam to move parallel to one another. They would diverge because of electron repulsion, so the focusing system must make them converge to counteract the divergence. With the exception of this tendency to diverge, focusing an electron beam is analogous to focusing a light beam.

When the electron beam strikes the phosphor-coated screen of the CRT, the individual electrons are moving with kinetic energy proportional to the acceleration voltage. Some of this energy is dissipated as heat, but the rest is transferred to the electrons of the phosphor atoms, making them jump to higher quantum-energy levels. In returning to their previous quantum levels, these excited electrons give up their extra energy in the form of light, at frequencies (i.e., colors) predicted by quantum theory. Any given phosphor has several different quantum levels to an unexcited state. Further, electrons on some levels are less stable and return to the unexcited state more rapidly than others. A phosphor's **fluorescence** is the light emitted as these very unstable electrons lose their excess energy while the phosphor is being struck by electrons. **Phosphorescence** is the light given off by the return of the relatively more stable excited electrons to their unexcited state once the electron beam excitation is removed. With typical phosphors, most of the light emitted is phosphorescence, since the excitation and hence the fluorescence usually last just a fraction of a microsecond. A phosphor's **persistence** is defined as the time from the removal of excitation to the moment when phosphorescence has decayed to 10 percent of the initial light output. The range of persistence of different phosphors can reach many seconds, but for most phosphors used in graphics equipment it is usually 10 to 60 microseconds. This light output decays exponentially with time. Characteristics of phosphors are detailed in [SHER93].

The **refresh rate** of a CRT is the number of times per second the image is redrawn; it is typically 60 per second or higher for raster displays. As the refresh rate decreases, **flicker** develops because the eye can no longer integrate the individual light impulses coming from a pixel. The refresh rate above which a picture stops flickering and fuses into a steady image is called the **critical fusion frequency**, or **CFF**. The process of fusion is familiar to all of us; it occurs whenever we watch television or motion pictures. A flicker-free picture appears constant or steady to the viewer, even though, in fact, any given point is *off* much longer than it is *on*.

One determinant of the CFF is the phosphor's persistence: The longer the persistence, the lower the CFF. The relation between fusion frequency and persistence is nonlinear: Doubling persistence does not halve the CFF. As persistence increases into the several-second range, the fusion frequency becomes quite small. At the other extreme, even a phosphor with absolutely no persistence at all can be used, since all the eye really requires is to see some light for a short period of time, repeated at a frequency above the CFF.

The **horizontal scan rate** is the number of scan lines per second that the circuitry driving a CRT is able to display. The rate is approximately the product of the refresh rate and the number of scan lines. For a given scan rate, an increase in the refresh rate means a decrease in the number of scan lines.

The **bandwidth** of a monitor has to do with the speed with which the electron gun can be turned on or off. To achieve a horizontal resolution of n pixels per scan line, it must be possible to turn the electron gun on at least $n/2$ times and off another $n/2$ times in one scan line, in order to create alternating on and off lines. Consider a raster scan of 1000 lines by 1000 pixels, displayed at a 60-Hz refresh rate. A simple calculation shows that the time required to draw one pixel is the inverse of the quantity (1000 pixels/line $\times$ 1000 lines/frame $\times$ 60 frames/sec), about 16 nanoseconds. Actually, because there is some overhead associated with each vertical and horizontal refresh cycle, one pixel is drawn in about 11 nanoseconds [WHIT84]. Thus, the period of an on–off cycle is about 22 nanoseconds, which corresponds to a frequency of 45 MHz. This frequency is the minimum bandwidth needed to achieve 1000 lines (500 line-pairs) of resolution, but is not the actual bandwidth because we have ignored the effect of spot size. The nonzero spot size must be compensated for with a higher bandwidth, which causes the beam to turn on and off more quickly, giving the pixels sharper edges than they would have otherwise. It is not unusual for the actual bandwidth of a 1000×1000 monitor to be 100 MHz.

Color television sets and color raster displays use some form of **shadow-mask CRT**. Here, the inside of the tube's viewing surface is covered with closely spaced groups of red, green, and blue phosphor dots. The dot groups are so small that light emanating from the individual dots is perceived by the viewer as a mixture of the three colors. Thus, a wide range of colors can be produced by each group, depending on how strongly each individual phosphor dot is excited. A shadow mask, which is a thin metal plate perforated with many small holes and mounted close to the viewing surface, is carefully aligned so that each of the three electron beams (one each for red, green, and blue) can hit only one type of phosphor dot. The dots thus can be excited selectively.

Figure 4.6 shows one of the most common types of shadow-mask CRT, a **delta–delta CRT**. The phosphor dots are arranged in a triangular **triad** pattern, as are the three electron guns. The guns are deflected together, and are aimed (converged) at the same point on the viewing surface. The shadow mask has one small hole for each triad. The holes are precisely aligned with respect to both the triads and the electron guns, so that each dot in the triad is exposed to electrons from only one gun. High-precision delta–delta CRTs are particularly difficult to keep in alignment. An alternative arrangement, the **precision in-line delta CRT**, is easier to converge and to manufacture, and is the current technology of choice for high-precision (1000-scan-line) monitors. However, because the delta–delta CRT provides higher resolution, it is likely to reemerge as the dominant technology for

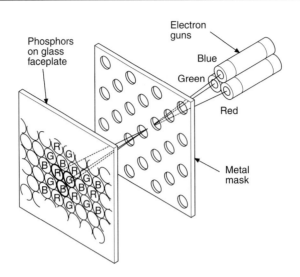

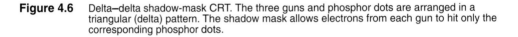

Figure 4.6   Delta–delta shadow-mask CRT. The three guns and phosphor dots are arranged in a triangular (delta) pattern. The shadow mask allows electrons from each gun to hit only the corresponding phosphor dots.

high-definition television (HDTV). Still in the research laboratory but likely to become commercially viable is the **flat-panel color CRT**, in which the electron beams move parallel to the viewing surface, and are then turned 90° to strike the surface.

The need for the shadow mask and triads imposes a limit on the resolution of color CRTs not present with monochrome CRTs. In very high-resolution tubes, the triads are placed on about 0.21-millimeter centers; those in home television tubes are on about 0.60-millimeter centers (this distance is also called the **pitch** of the tube). Because a finely focused beam cannot be guaranteed to hit exactly in the center of a shadow-mask hole, the beam diameter (defined as the diameter at which the intensity is 50 percent of the maximum) must be about 7/4 times the pitch. Thus, on a mask with a pitch of 0.25-millimeter (0.01 inch), the beam is about 0.018 inch across, and the resolution can be no more than about $1/0.018 = 55$ lines per inch. On a 0.25-millimeter pitch, 19-inch (diagonal measure) monitor, which is about 15.5 inches wide by 11.6 inches high [CONR85], the resolution achievable is thus only $15.5 \times 55 = 850$ by $11.6 \times 55 = 638$. This value compares with a typical addressability of 1280×1024, or 1024×800. As illustrated in Fig. 4.2, a resolution somewhat less than the addressability is useful.

Most high-quality shadow-mask CRTs have diagonals of 15 to 21 inches, with slightly curved faceplates that create optical distortions for the viewer. Several types of flat-face CRTs are becoming available.

A **liquid-crystal display (LCD)** is made up of six layers, as shown in Fig. 4.7. The front layer is a vertical polarizer plate. Next is a layer with thin grid wires

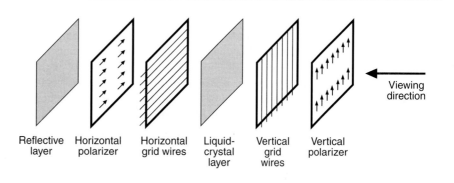

Reflective   Horizontal   Horizontal   Liquid-   Vertical   Vertical
layer   polarizer   grid wires   crystal   grid   polarizer
                    layer   wires

Viewing direction

Figure 4.7   The layers of a liquid-crystal display (LCD), all of which are sandwiched together to form a thin panel.

electrodeposited on the surface adjoining the crystals. Next is a thin (about 0.0005-inch) liquid-crystal layer, then a layer with horizontal grid wires on the surface next to the crystals, then a horizontal polarizer, and finally a reflector.

The liquid-crystal material is made up of long crystalline molecules. The individual molecules normally are arranged in a spiral fashion such that the direction of polarization of polarized light passing through is rotated 90°. Light entering through the front layer is polarized vertically. As the light passes through the liquid crystal, the polarization is rotated 90° to horizontal, so the light now passes through the rear horizontal polarizer, is reflected, and returns through the two polarizers and crystal.

When the crystals are in an electric field, they all line up in the same direction, and thus have no polarizing effect. Hence, crystals in the electric field do not change the polarization of the transmitted light, so the light remains vertically polarized and does not pass through the rear polarizer: The light is absorbed, so the viewer sees a dark spot on the display.

A dark spot at point (x_1, y_1) is created via matrix addressing. The point is selected by applying a negative voltage $-V$ to the horizontal grid wire x_1 and a positive voltage $+V$ to the vertical grid wire y_1: Neither $-V$ nor $+V$ is large enough to cause the crystals to line up, but their difference is large enough to do so. Now the crystals at (x_1, y_1) no longer rotate the direction of polarization of the transmitted light, so it remains vertically polarized and does not pass through the rear polarizer: The light is absorbed, so the viewer sees a dark spot on the display.

Active matrix LCD panels have a transistor at each (x, y) grid point. The transistors are used to cause the crystals to change their state quickly, and also to control the degree to which the state has been changed. These two properties allow LCDs to be used in miniature television sets with continuous-tone images. The crystals can also be dyed to provide color. Most important, the transistor can serve as a memory for the state of a cell and can hold the cell in that state until it is changed. That is, the memory provided by the transistor enables a cell to remain on all the time and hence to be brighter than it would be if it had to be refreshed periodically. Color LCD panels with resolutions up to 800×1000 on a 14-inch diagonal panel have been built.

Advantages of LCDs are low cost, low weight, small size, and low power consumption. In the past, the major disadvantage was that LCDs were passive, reflecting only incident light and creating no light of their own (although this can be corrected with backlighting): Any glare washed out the image. In recent years, use of active panels has removed this concern. In fact, laptop computers with color displays—unavailable until recently—use both active and nonactive LCD technology. Also, because LCD displays are small and light, they can be used in head-mounted displays such as that discussed in Section 8.1.6. As color LCD screens increase in size and decrease in cost, they will ultimately pose a threat to the dominance of the color CRT—but not for many years.

Electroluminescent (EL) displays consist of the same gridlike structure as used in LCD and plasma displays. Between the front and back panels is a thin (typically 500-nanometer) layer of an electroluminescent material, such as zinc sulfide doped with manganese, that emits light when in a high electric field (about 106 volts per centimeter). A point on the panel is illuminated via the matrix-addressing scheme, with several hundred volts placed across the horizontal and vertical selection lines. Color electroluminescent displays are also available.

These displays are bright and can be switched on and off quickly, and transistors at each pixel can be used to store the image. Typical panel sizes are 6 by 8 inches up to 12 by 16 inches, with 70 addressable dots per inch. These displays' major disadvantage is that their power consumption is higher than that of the LCD panel. However, their brightness has led to their use in some portable computers.

Most large-screen displays use some form of **projection CRT**, in which the light from a small (several-inch-diameter) but very bright monochrome CRT is magnified and projected from a curved mirror. Color systems use three projectors with red, green, and blue filters. A shadow-mask CRT does not create enough light to be projected onto a large (2-meter-diagonal) screen.

The General Electric **light-valve projection system** is used for very large screens, where the light output from the projection CRT would not be sufficient. A light valve is just what its name implies: a mechanism for controlling how much light passes through a valve. The light source can have much higher intensity than a CRT can. In the most common approach, an electron gun traces an image on a thin oil film on a piece of glass. The electron charge causes the film to vary in thickness. Light from the high-intensity source is directed at the glass, and is refracted in different directions because of the variation in the thickness of the oil film. Special optics project light that is refracted in certain directions on the screen, while other light is not projected. Color is possible with these systems, through use of either three projectors or a more sophisticated set of optics with a single projector. More details are given in [SHER93].

Table 4.2 summarizes the characteristics of three major display technologies. The pace of technological innovation is such, however, that some of the relationships may change over the next few years. Also, note that the liquid-crystal comparisons are for passive addressing; with active matrix addressing, gray levels and colors are achievable.

More detailed information on these display technologies is given in [APT85; BALD85; CONR85; PERR85; SHER93; and TANN85].

Table 4.2

Comparison of Display Technologies

Property	CRT	Electro-luminescent	Liquid Crystal
Power consumption	fair	fair–good	excellent
Screen size	excellent	good	fair
Depth	poor	excellent	excellent
Weight	poor	excellent	excellent
Ruggedness	fair–good	good–excellent	excellent
Brightness	excellent	excellent	fair–good
Addressability	good–excellent	good	fair–good
Contrast	good–excellent	good	fair
Intensity levels per dot	excellent	fair	fair
Viewing angle	excellent	good	poor
Color capability	excellent	good	good
Relative cost range	low	medium–high	low

4.3 RASTER-SCAN DISPLAY SYSTEMS

The basic concepts of raster graphics systems were presented in Chapter 1, and Chapter 2 provided further insight into the types of operations possible with a raster display. In this section, we discuss the various elements of a raster display, stressing two fundamental ways in which various raster systems differ one from another.

First, most raster displays have some specialized hardware to assist in scan converting output primitives into the pixmap, and to perform the raster operations of moving, copying, and modifying pixels or blocks of pixels. We call this hardware a **graphics display processor**. The fundamental difference among display systems is how much the display processor does versus how much must be done by the graphics subroutine package executing on the general-purpose CPU that drives the raster display. Note that the graphics display processor is also sometimes called a **graphics controller** (emphasizing its similarity to the control units for other peripheral devices) or a **display coprocessor**. The second key differentiator in raster systems is the relationship between the pixmap and the address space of the general-purpose computer's memory, whether the pixmap is part of the general-purpose computer's memory or is separate.

In Section 4.3.1, we introduce a simple raster display consisting of a CPU, containing the pixmap as part of its memory, and a video controller driving a CRT. There is no display processor, so the CPU does both the application and graphics work. In Section 4.3.2, a graphics processor with a separate pixmap is introduced, and a wide range of graphics-processor functionalities is discussed in Section 4.3.3. Section 4.3.4 discusses ways in which the pixmap can be integrated back into the CPU's address space, given the existence of a graphics processor.

4.3.1 Simple Raster Display System

The simplest and most common raster display system organization is shown in Fig. 4.8. The relation between memory and the CPU is exactly the same as in a non-graphics computer system. However, a portion of the memory also serves as the pixmap. The video controller displays the image defined in the frame buffer, accessing the memory through a separate access port as often as the raster-scan rate dictates. In many systems, a fixed portion of memory is permanently allocated to the frame buffer, whereas some systems have several interchangeable memory areas (sometimes called **pages** in the personal-computer world). Yet other systems can designate (via a register) any part of memory for the frame buffer.

The application program and graphics subroutine package share the system memory and are executed by the CPU. The graphics package includes scan-conversion procedures, so that when the application program calls, say, SRGP_lineCoord ($x1$, $y1$, $x2$, $y2$), the graphics package can set the appropriate pixels in the frame buffer (details on scan-conversion procedures were given in Chapter 3). Because the frame buffer is in the address space of the CPU, the graphics package can easily access it to set pixels and to implement the PixBlt instructions described in Chapter 2.

The video controller cycles through the frame buffer, one scan line at a time, typically 60 times per second. Memory reference addresses are generated in synchrony with the raster scan, and the contents of the memory are used to control the CRT beam's intensity or color. The video controller is organized as shown in

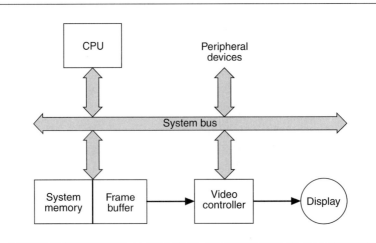

Figure 4.8   A common raster display system architecture. A dedicated portion of the system memory is dual-ported, so that it can be accessed directly by the video controller, without the system bus being tied up.

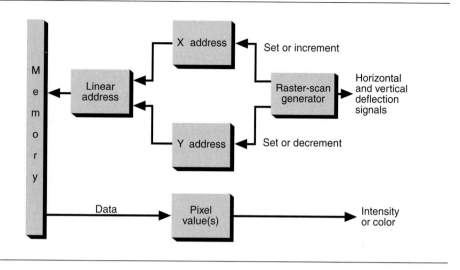

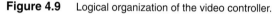

Figure 4.9   Logical organization of the video controller.

Fig. 4.9. The raster-scan generator produces deflection signals that generate the raster scan; it also controls the X and Y address registers, which in turn define the memory location to be accessed next.

Assume that the frame buffer is addressed in x from 0 to x_{max} and in y from 0 to y_{max}; then, at the start of a refresh cycle, the X address register is set to zero and the Y register is set to y_{max} (the top scan line). As the first scan line is generated, the X address is incremented up through x_{max}. Each pixel value is fetched and is used to control the intensity of the CRT beam. After the first scan line, the X address is reset to zero and the Y address is decremented by one. The process continues until the last scan line ($y = 0$) is generated.

In this simplistic situation, one memory access is made to the frame buffer for each pixel to be displayed. For a high-resolution display of 1000 pixels by 1000 lines refreshed 60 times per second, a simple way to estimate the time available for displaying a single 1-bit pixel is to calculate $1/(1000 \times 1000 \times 60) = 16$ nanoseconds. This calculation ignores the fact that pixels are not being displayed during horizontal and vertical retrace.[1] But typical RAM memory chips have cycle times around 80 nanoseconds: They cannot support one access every 16 nanoseconds! Thus, the video controller must fetch multiple pixel values in one memory cycle. In the case at hand, the controller might fetch 16 bits in one memory cycle, thereby taking care of 16 pixels $\times$ 16 ns/pixel = 256 nanoseconds of refresh time. The 16 bits are loaded into a register on the video controller, then are shifted out to control the CRT beam intensity, one every 16 nanoseconds. In the 256 nanoseconds this takes, there is time for about three memory cycles: one for the video controller and

---

[1] In a raster scan system there is a certain amount of time during which no image is being traced: the horizontal retrace time, which occurs once per scan line, and the vertical retrace time, which occurs once per frame.

two for the CPU. This sharing may force the CPU to wait for memory accesses, potentially reducing the speed of the CPU proportionately. Of course, cache memory on the CPU chip can ameliorate this problem. Another approach is to use non-traditional memory-chip organizations for frame buffers. For example, turning on all the pixels on a scan line in one access time reduces the number of memory cycles needed to scan convert into memory, especially for filled areas. The video RAM (VRAM) organization, developed by Texas Instruments, can read out all the pixels on a scan line in one cycle, thus reducing the number of memory cycles needed to refresh the display.

We have thus far assumed monochrome, 1-bit-per-pixel bitmaps. This assumption is fine for some applications, but is grossly unsatisfactory for others. Additional control over the intensity of each pixel is obtained by storing multiple bits for each pixel: 2 bits yield four intensities, and so on. The bits can be used to control not only intensity, but also color. How many bits per pixel are needed for a stored image to be perceived as having continuous shades of gray? Five or 6 bits are often enough, but 8 or more bits can be necessary. Thus, for color displays, a somewhat simplified argument suggests that three times as many bits are needed: 8 bits for each of the three additive primary colors red, blue, and green.

While systems with 24 bits per pixel are relatively inexpensive, many color applications do not require 2^{24} different colors in a single picture (which typically has only 2^{18} to 2^{20} pixels). Moreover, there is often need for both a small number of colors in a given picture or application and the ability to change colors from picture to picture or from application to application. Also, in many image-analysis and image-enhancement applications, it is desirable to change the visual appearance of an image without changing the underlying data defining the image, in order, say, to display all pixels with values below some threshold as black, to expand an intensity range, or to create a pseudocolor display of a monochromatic image.

For these various reasons, the video controller of raster displays often includes a **video look-up table** (also called a **look-up table**, or **LUT**). The look-up table has as many entries as there are pixel values. A pixel's value is used not to control the beam directly, but rather as an index into the look-up table. The table entry's value is used to control the intensity or color of the CRT. A pixel value of 67 would thus cause the contents of table entry 67 to be accessed and used to control the CRT beam. This look-up operation is done for each pixel on each display cycle, so the table must be accessible quickly, and the CPU must be able to load the look-up table on program command.

In Fig. 4.10, the look-up table is interposed between the frame buffer and the CRT display. The frame buffer has 8 bits per pixel, and the look-up table therefore has 256 entries.

The simple raster display system organization of Fig. 4.8 is used in many inexpensive personal computers. Such a system is inexpensive to build, but has a number of disadvantages. First, scan conversion in software is slow. For instance, the (x, y) address of each pixel on a line must be calculated, then must be translated into a memory address consisting of a byte and bit-within-byte pair. Although each of the individual steps is simple, each is repeated many times. Software-based scan

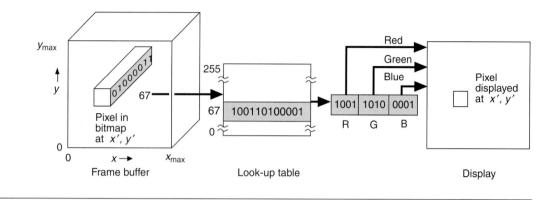

Figure 4.10 Organization of a video look-up table. A pixel with value 67 (binary 01000011) is displayed on the screen with the red electron gun at 9/15 of maximum, green at 10/15, and blue at 1/15. This look-up table is shown with 12 bits per entry. Up to 24 bits are common.

conversion slows down the overall pace of user interaction with the application, potentially creating user dissatisfaction.

The second disadvantage of this architecture is that as the number of pixels or the refresh rate of the display increases, the number of memory accesses made by the video controller also increases, thus decreasing the number of memory cycles available to the CPU. The CPU is thus slowed down, especially with an architecture where the frame buffer must be accessed over the system bus. With the dual-porting of part of the system memory shown in Fig. 4.8, the slowdown occurs only when the CPU is accessing the frame buffer, usually for scan conversion or raster operations. These two disadvantages must be weighed against the ease with which the CPU can access the frame buffer and against the architectural simplicity of the system.

4.3.2 Raster Display System with Peripheral Display Processor

The raster display system with a peripheral display processor is a common architecture (see Fig. 4.11) that avoids the disadvantages of the simple raster display by introducing a separate graphics processor to perform graphics functions such as scan conversion and raster operations, and a separate frame buffer for image refresh. We now have two processors: the general-purpose CPU and the special-purpose display processor. We also have three memory areas: the system memory, the display-processor memory, and the frame buffer. The system memory holds data plus those programs that execute on the CPU: the application program, graphics package, and operating system. Similarly, the display-processor memory holds data plus the programs that perform scan conversion and raster operations. The frame buffer contains the displayable image created by the scan-conversion and raster operations.

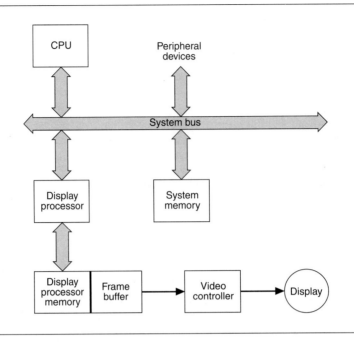

Figure 4.11   Raster system architecture with a peripheral display processor.

In simple cases, the display processor can consist of specialized logic to perform the mapping from 2D (x, y) coordinates to a linear memory address. In this case, the scan-conversion and raster operations are still performed by the CPU, so the display-processor memory is not needed; only the frame buffer is present. Most peripheral display processors also perform scan conversion. In this section, we present a prototype system. Its features are a (sometimes simplified) composite of many typical commercially available systems, such as the plug-in graphics cards used with IBM PC-compatible computers.

The frame buffer is $1024 \times 1024 \times 8$ bits per pixel, and there is a 256-entry look-up table of 12 bits, 4 each for red, green, and blue. The origin is at lower left, but only the first 768 rows of the pixmap (y in the range of 0 to 767) are displayed. The display has six status registers, which are set by various instructions and affect the execution of other instructions. These are the CP (made up of the X and Y position registers), FILL, INDEX, WMODE, MASK, and PATTERN registers. Their operation is explained next.

Some of the instructions for the simple raster display are as follows:

Move (x, y) The X and Y registers that define the current position (CP) are set to x and y. Because the pixmap is 1024×1024, x and y must be between 0 and 1023.

MoveR (dx, dy) The values dx and dy are added to the X and Y registers, thus defining a new CP. The dx and dy values must be between -1024 and $+1023$, and are represented in 2's-complement notation. The addition may cause overflow and hence a wraparound of the X and Y register values.

Line (x, y) A line is drawn from CP to (x, y), and this position becomes the new CP.

LineR (dx, dy) A line is drawn from CP to CP + (dx, dy), and this position becomes the new CP.

Point (x, y) The pixel at (x, y) is set, and this position becomes the new CP.

PointR (dx, dy) The pixel at CP + (dx, dy) is set, and this position becomes the new CP.

Rect (x, y) A rectangle is drawn between the CP and (x, y). The CP is unaffected.

RectR (dx, dy) A rectangle is drawn between the CP and CP + (dx, dy). The parameter dx can be thought of as the rectangle width, and dy as the height. The CP is unaffected.

Text $(n, address)$ The n characters at memory location *address* are displayed, starting at the CP. Characters are defined on a 7-by-9-pixel grid, with 2 extra pixels of vertical and horizontal spacing to separate characters and lines. The CP is updated to the lower-left corner of the area in which character $n + 1$ would be displayed.

Circle $(radius)$ A circle is drawn centered at the CP. The CP is unaffected.

Polygon $(n, address)$ Stored at address is a vertex list $(x_1, y_1, x_2, y_2, x_3, y_3, \ldots, x_n, y_n)$. A polygon is drawn starting at (x_1, y_1), through all the vertices up to (x_n, y_n), and then back to (x_1, y_1). The CP is unaffected.

AreaFill $(flag)$ The flag is used to set the FILL flag in the raster display. When the flag is set to ON (by a nonzero value of *flag*), all the areas created by the commands Rect, RectR, Circle, CircleSector, Polygon are filled in as they are created, using the pattern defined with the Pattern command.

RasterOp $(dx, dy, xdest, ydest)$ A rectangular region of the frame buffer, from CP to CP + (dx, dy), is combined with the region of the same size with lower-left corner at $(xdest, ydest)$, overwriting that region. The combination is controlled by the WMODE register.

The commands and immediate data are transferred to the display processor via a first-in, first-out (**FIFO**) buffer (i.e., a queue) in a dedicated portion of the CPU address space. The graphics package places commands into the queue, and the display accesses the instructions and executes them. Pointers to the start and end of the buffer are also in specific memory locations, accessible to both the CPU and display. The pointer to the start of the buffer is modified by the display processor each time a byte is removed; the pointer to the end of the buffer is modified by the CPU each time a byte is added. Appropriate testing is done to ensure that an empty buffer is not read and that a full buffer is not written. Direct memory access is used to fetch the addressed data for the instructions.

A queue is more attractive for command passing than is a single instruction register or location accessed by the display. First, the variable length of the instructions favors the queue concept. Second, the CPU can get ahead of the display, and queue up a number of display commands. When the CPU has finished issuing display commands, it can proceed to do other work while the display empties out the queue.

Programming the display is similar to using the SRGP package of Chapter 2. Several programming examples are presented in Chapter 4 of [FOLE90].

4.3.3 Additional Display-Processor Functionality

Our simple display processor performs only some of the graphics-related operations that might be implemented. The temptation faced by the system designer is to offload the main CPU more and more by adding functionality to the display processor, such as by using a local memory to store lists of display instructions, by doing clipping and the window-to-viewport transformation, and perhaps by providing pick-correlation logic and automatic feedback when a graphical element is picked. Ultimately, the display processor becomes another general-purpose CPU doing general interactive graphics work, and the designer is again tempted to provide special-function hardware to offload the display processor.

This **wheel of reincarnation** was identified by Myer and Sutherland in 1968 [MYER68]. Their point was that there is a tradeoff between special-purpose and general-purpose functionality. Special-purpose hardware usually does the job faster than does a general-purpose processor. On the other hand, special-purpose hardware is more expensive and cannot be used for other purposes. This tradeoff is an enduring theme in graphics system design.

If clipping (Chapter 3) is added to the display processor, then output primitives can be specified to the processor in coordinates other than device coordinates. This specification can be done in floating-point coordinates, although some display processors operate on only integers (this is changing rapidly as inexpensive floating-point chips become available). If only integers are used, the coordinates used by the application program must be integer, or the graphics package must map floating-point coordinates into integer coordinates. For this mapping to be possible, the application program must give the graphics package a rectangle guaranteed to enclose the coordinates of all output primitives specified to the package. The rectangle must then be mapped into the maximum integer range, so that everything within the rectangle is in the integer coordinate range.

If the subroutine package is 3D, then the display processor can perform the far more complex 3D geometric transformations and clipping described in Chapters 5 and 6. Also, if the package includes 3D surface primitives, such as polygonal areas, the display processor can also perform the visible surface-determination and rendering steps discussed in Chapters 13 and 14. Chapter 18 of [FOLE90] discusses some of the fundamental approaches to organizing general- and special-purpose VLSI chips to perform these steps quickly. Many commercially available displays provide these features.

Another function that is often added to the display processor is local segment storage, also called **display list storage**. Display instructions, grouped into named segments and having unclipped integer coordinates, are stored in the display processor memory, permitting the display processor to operate more autonomously from the CPU.

What exactly can a display processor do with these stored segments? It can transform and redraw them, as in zooming or scrolling. Local dragging of segments into new positions can be provided. Local picking can be implemented by having the display processor compare the cursor position to all the graphics primitives (more efficient ways of doing this are discussed in Chapter 7). Regeneration, required to fill in the holes created when a segment is erased, can also be done from segment storage. Segments can be created, deleted, edited, and made visible or invisible.

Segments can also be copied or referenced, both reducing the amount of information that must be sent from the CPU to the display processor and economizing on storage in the display processor itself. It is possible to build up a complex hierarchical data structure using this capability, and many commercial display processors with local segment memory can copy or reference other segments. When the segments are displayed, a reference to another segment must be preceded by saving the display processor's current state, just as a subroutine call is preceded by saving the CPU's current state. References can be nested, giving rise to a **structured display file or hierarchical display list,** as in PHIGS [ANSI88], which is discussed further in Chapter 7.

Although this raster display system architecture with its graphics display and separate frame buffer has many advantages over the simple raster display system of Section 4.3.1, it also has some disadvantages. If the display processor is accessed by the CPU as a peripheral on a direct-memory-access port then there is considerable operating-system overhead each time an instruction is passed to it (this is not an issue for a display processor whose instruction register is memory-mapped into the CPU's address space, since then it is easy for the graphics package to set up the registers directly).

The raster-operation command is a particular difficulty. Conceptually, it should have four potential source–destination pairs: system memory to system memory, system memory to frame buffer, frame buffer to system memory, and frame buffer to frame buffer (here, the frame buffer and display processor memory of Fig. 4.11 are considered identical, since they are in the same address space). In display-processor systems, however, the different source–destination pairs are handled in different ways, and the system-memory-to-system-memory case may not exist. This lack of symmetry complicates the programmer's task and reduces flexibility. For example, if the offscreen portion of the pixmap becomes filled with menus, fonts, and so on, then it is difficult to use main memory as an overflow area. Furthermore, because the use of pixmaps is so pervasive, failure to support raster operations on pixmaps stored in main memory is not really viable.

The display processor defined earlier in this section, like many real display processors, moves raster images between the system memory and frame buffer via I/O transfers on the system bus. Unfortunately, this movement can be too slow for real-time operations, such as animating, dragging, and popping up windows and menus: The time taken in the operating system to initiate the transfers and the transfer rate on the bus get in the way. This problem can be partially relieved by increasing the display processor's memory to hold more offscreen pixmaps, but then that memory is not available for other purposes—and there is almost never enough memory anyway!

4.3.4 Raster Display System with Integrated Display Processor

We can ameliorate many of the shortcomings of the peripheral display processor discussed in the previous section by dedicating a special portion of system memory to be the frame buffer and by providing a second access port to the frame buffer from the video controller, thus creating the **single-address-space (SAS)** display system architecture shown in Fig. 4.12. Here the display processor, the CPU, and the video controller are all on the system bus, and thus all can access system memory. The origin and, in some cases, the size of the frame buffer are held in registers, making double-buffering a simple matter of reloading the origin register: The results of scan conversion can go either into the frame buffer for immediate display or elsewhere in system memory for later display. Similarly, the source and destination for raster operations performed by the display processor can be anywhere in system memory (now the only memory of interest to us). This arrangement is also attractive because the CPU can directly manipulate pixels in the frame buffer simply by reading or writing the appropriate bits.

SAS architecture has, however, a number of shortcomings. Contention for access to the system memory is the most serious. One solution to this problem is to use a CPU chip containing instruction- or data-cache memories, thus reducing the CPU's dependence on frequent and rapid access to the system memory. Of course, these and other solutions can be integrated in various ingenious ways, as discussed in more detail in [FOLE90], Chapter 18.

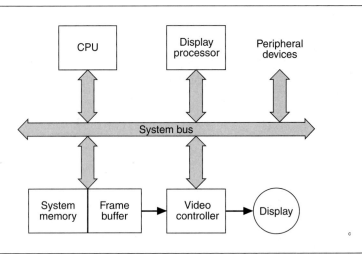

Figure 4.12   A common single-address-space (SAS) raster display system architecture with an integral display processor. The display processor may have a private memory for algorithms and working storage. A dedicated portion of the system memory is dual-ported so that it can be accessed directly by the video controller, without the system bus being tied up.

Another design complication arises if the CPU has a virtual address space, as do the commonly used Motorola 680x0 and Intel 80x86 families, and various reduced-instruction-set-computer (RISC) processors. In this case memory addresses generated by the display processor must go through the same dynamic address translation as other memory addresses do. In addition, many CPU architectures distinguish between a kernel operating system virtual address space and an application program virtual address space. It is often desirable for the frame buffer (canvas 0 in SRGP terminology) to be in the kernel space, so that the operating system's display device driver can access it directly. However, the canvases allocated by the application program must be in the application space. Therefore, display instructions that access the frame buffer must distinguish between the kernel and application address spaces. If the kernel is to be accessed, then the display instruction must be invoked by a time-consuming operating system service call rather than by a simple subroutine call.

Despite these potential complications, more and more raster display systems do in fact have a single-address-space architecture, typically of the type in Fig. 4.12. The flexibility of allowing both the CPU and display processor to access any part of memory in a uniform and homogeneous way is very compelling, and does simplify programming.

4.4 THE VIDEO CONTROLLER

The most important task for the video controller is the constant refresh of the display. There are two fundamental types of refresh: **interlaced** and **noninterlaced**. The former is used in broadcast television and in raster displays designed to drive regular televisions. The refresh cycle is broken into two fields, each lasting $\frac{1}{60}$ second; thus, a full refresh lasts $\frac{1}{30}$ second. All odd-numbered scan lines are displayed in the first field, and all even-numbered ones are displayed in the second. The purpose of the interlaced scan is to place some new information in all areas of the screen at a 60-Hz rate, since a 30-Hz refresh rate tends to cause flicker. The net effect of interlacing is to produce a picture whose effective refresh rate is closer to 60 than to 30 Hz. This technique works as long as adjacent scan lines do in fact display similar information; an image consisting of horizontal lines on alternating scan lines would flicker badly. Most video controllers refresh at 60 or more Hz and use a noninterlaced scan.

The output from the video controller has one of three forms: RGB, monochrome, or NTSC. For RGB (red, green, blue), separate cables carry the red, green, and blue signals to control the three electron guns of a shadow-mask CRT, and another cable carries the synchronization to signal the start of vertical and horizontal retrace. There are standards for the voltages, wave shapes, and synchronization timings of RGB signals. For 480-scan-line monochrome signals, RS-170 is the standard; for color, RS-170A; for higher-resolution monochrome signals, RS-343. Frequently, the synchronization timings are included on the same cable as the green signal, in which case the signals are called composite video. Monochrome signals use the same standards but have only intensity and synchronization cables, or merely a single cable carrying composite intensity and synchronization.

NTSC (National Television System Committee) video is the signal format used in North American commercial television. Color, intensity, and synchronization information is combined into a signal with a bandwidth of about 5 MHz, broadcast as 525 scan lines, in two fields of 262.5 lines each. Just 480 lines are visible; the rest occur during the vertical retrace periods at the end of each field. A monochrome television set uses the intensity and synchronization information; a color television set also uses the color information to control the three color guns. The bandwidth limit allows many different television channels to broadcast over the frequency range allocated to television. Unfortunately, this bandwidth limits picture quality to an effective resolution of about 350×350. Nevertheless, NTSC is the standard for low-cost videotape-recording equipment. More expensive recorders store separate components of the color signal in analog or digital form. European and Russian television broadcast and videotape standards are two 625-scan-line, 50-Hz standards, SECAM and PAL.

Some video controllers superimpose a programmable cursor, stored in a 16×16 or 32×32 pixmap, on top of the frame buffer. This avoids the need to PixBlt the cursor shape into the frame buffer each refresh cycle, slightly reducing CPU overhead. Similarly, some video controllers superimpose multiple small, fixed-size pixmaps (called **sprites**) on top of the frame buffer. This feature is used often in video games.

4.4.1 Video Mixing

Another useful video-controller function is video mixing. Two images, one defined in the frame buffer and the other by a video signal coming from camera, recorder, or other source, can be merged to form a composite image. Examples of this merging are seen regularly on television news, sports, and weather shows. Figure 4.13 shows the generic system organization.

There are two types of mixing. In one, a graphics image is set into a video image. The chart or graph displayed over the shoulder of a newscaster is typical of this style. The mixing is accomplished with hardware that treats a designated

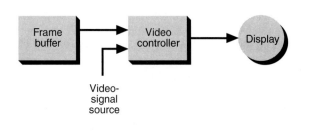

Figure 4.13   A video controller mixing images from frame buffer and video-signal source.

pixel value in the frame buffer as a flag to indicate that the video signal should be shown instead of the signal from the frame buffer. Normally, the designated pixel value corresponds to the background color of the frame-buffer image, although interesting effects can be achieved by using some other pixel value instead.

The second type of mixing places the video image on top of the frame-buffer image, as when a weather reporter stands in front of a full-screen weather map. The reporter is actually standing in front of a backdrop, whose color (typically blue) is used to control the mixing: Whenever the incoming video is blue, the frame buffer is shown; otherwise, the video image is shown. This technique works well as long as the reporter is not wearing a blue tie or shirt!

4.5 INPUT DEVICES FOR OPERATOR INTERACTION

In this section, we describe the workings of the most common input devices. We present a brief and high-level discussion of how the types of devices available work. In Chapter 8, we discuss the advantages and disadvantages of the various devices, and also describe some more advanced devices.

Our presentation is organized around the concept of **logical devices**, introduced in Chapter 2 as part of SRGP and discussed further in Chapter 7. There are five basic logical devices: the **locator**, to indicate a position or orientation; the **pick**, to select a displayed entity; the **valuator,** to input a single real number; the **keyboard**, to input a character string; and the **choice**, to select from a set of possible actions or choices. The logical-device concept defines equivalence classes of devices on the basis of the type of information the devices provide to the application program.

4.5.1 Locator Devices

Tablet.   A tablet (or **data tablet)** is a flat surface, ranging in size from about 6 by 6 inches up to 48 by 72 inches or more, which can detect the position of a movable stylus or puck held in the user's hand. Figure 4.14 shows a small tablet with both a stylus and puck (hereafter, we generally refer only to a stylus, although the discussion is relevant to either). Most tablets use an electrical sensing mechanism to determine the position of the stylus. In one such arrangement, a grid of wires on $\frac{1}{4}$- to $\frac{1}{2}$-inch centers is embedded in the tablet surface. Electromagnetic signals generated by electrical pulses applied in sequence to the wires in the grid induce an electrical signal in a wire coil in the stylus. The strength of the signal induced by each pulse is used to determine the position of the stylus. The signal strength is also used to determine roughly how far the stylus or cursor is from the tablet (*far, near,* (i.e., within about $\frac{1}{2}$ inch of the tablet), or *touching*). When the answer is *near* or *touching,* a cursor is usually shown on the display to provide visual feedback to the user. A signal is sent to the computer when the stylus tip is pressed against the tablet, or when any button on the puck (pucks have up to 16 buttons) is pressed. The

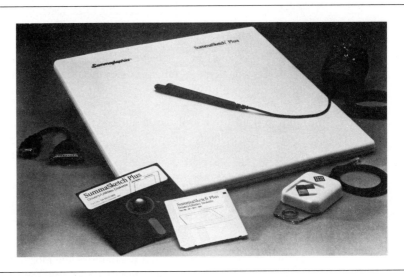

Figure 4.14   A data tablet with both a stylus and a puck. The stylus has a pressure-sensitive switch on the tip, which closes when the stylus is pressed. The puck has several pushbuttons for command entry, and a cross-hair cursor for accuracy in digitizing drawings that are placed on the tablet. (Courtesy of Summagraphics Corporation.)

tablet's (x, y) position, button status, and nearness state (if the nearness state is *far*, then no (x, y) position is available) is normally obtained 30 to 60 times per second.

Relevant parameters of tablets and other locator devices are their resolution (number of distinguishable points per inch), linearity, repeatability, and size or range. These parameters are particularly crucial for digitizing maps and drawings; they are of less concern when the device is used only to position a screen cursor, because the user has the feedback of the screen cursor position to guide his hand movements, and because the resolution of a typical display is much less than that of even inexpensive tablets. Other tablet technologies use sound (sonic) coupling and resistive coupling.

Several types of tablets are transparent, and thus can be back-lit for digitizing X-ray films and photographic negatives, and can also be mounted directly over a CRT. The resistive tablet is especially suited for this, as it can be curved to the shape of the CRT.

Mouse.   A mouse is a small hand-held device whose relative motion across a surface can be measured. Mice differ in the number of buttons and in how relative motion is detected. Many important uses of mice for various interaction tasks are discussed in Section 8.1. The motion of the roller in the base of a **mechanical mouse** is converted to digital values that are used to determine the direction and magnitude of movement. The **optical mouse** is used on a special pad having a grid of alternating light and dark lines. A light-emitting diode (LED) on the bottom of the mouse directs a beam of light down onto the pad, from which it is reflected and sensed by detectors on the bottom of the mouse. As the mouse is moved, the reflected light beam is broken each time a dark line is crossed. The number of pulses so generated, which is equal to the number of lines crossed, is used to report mouse movements to the computer.

Because mice are relative devices, they can be picked up, moved, and then put down again without any change in reported position. (A series of such movements is often called *stroking* the mouse.) The relative nature of the mouse means that the computer must maintain a *current mouse position*, which is incremented or decremented by mouse movements.

Trackball. The trackball is often described as an upside-down mechanical mouse. The motion of the trackball, which rotates freely within its housing, is sensed by potentiometers or shaft encoders. The user typically rotates the trackball by drawing the palm of his hand across the ball. Various switches are usually mounted within finger reach of the trackball itself and are used in ways analogous to the use of mouse and tablet-puck buttons.

Joystick. The joystick (Fig. 4.15) can be moved left or right, forward or backward; again, potentiometers sense the movements. Springs are often used to return the joystick to its home center position. Some joysticks, including the one pictured, have a third degree of freedom: The stick can be twisted clockwise and counterclockwise.

It is difficult to use a joystick to control the absolute position of a screen cursor directly, because a slight movement of the (usually) short shaft is amplified five or ten times in the movement of the cursor. This makes the screen cursor's movements quite jerky and does not allow quick and accurate fine positioning. Thus, the joystick is often used to control the velocity of the cursor movement rather than the absolute cursor position. This means that the current position of the screen cursor is changed at rates determined by the joystick.

Figure 4.15   A joystick with a third degree of freedom. The joystick can be twisted clockwise and counterclockwise. (Courtesy of Measurement Systems, Inc.)

Touch panel.   Mice, trackballs, and joysticks all take up work-surface area. The touch panel allows the user to point at the screen directly with a finger to move the cursor around on the screen. Several different technologies are used for touch panels. Low-resolution panels (from 10 to 50 resolvable positions in each direction) use a series of infrared LEDs and light sensors (photodiodes or phototransistors) to form a grid of invisible light beams over the display area. Touching the screen breaks one or two vertical and horizontal light beams, thereby indicating the finger's position. If two parallel beams are broken, the finger is presumed to be centered between them; if one is broken, the finger is presumed to be on the beam.

A capacitively coupled touch panel can provide about 100 resolvable positions in each direction. When the user touches the conductively coated glass panel, electronic circuits detect the touch position from the impedance change across the conductive coating [INTE85].

The most significant touch-panel parameters are resolution, the amount of pressure required for activation (not an issue for the light-beam panel), and transparency (again, not an issue for the light-beam panel). An important issue with some of the technologies is parallax: If the panel is $\frac{1}{2}$ inch away from the display, then users touch the position on the panel that is aligned with their eyes and the desired point on the display, not at the position on the panel directly perpendicular to the desired point on the display.

Users are accustomed to some type of tactile feedback, but touch panels of course offer none. It is thus especially important that other forms of immediate feedback be provided, such as an audible tone or highlighting of the designated target or position.

4.5.2 Keyboard Devices

The **alphanumeric keyboard** is the prototypical text input device. Several different technologies are used to detect a key depression, including mechanical contact closure, change in capacitance, and magnetic coupling. The important functional characteristic of a keyboard device is that it creates a code, e.g., ASCII, uniquely corresponding to a pressed key. It is sometimes desirable to allow *chording* (pressing several keys at once) on an alphanumeric keyboard, to give experienced users rapid access to many different commands. This is in general not possible with the standard **coded keyboard**, which returns an ASCII code per keystroke and returns nothing if two keys are pressed simultaneously (unless the additional keys were shift, control, or other special keys). In contrast, an **unencoded keyboard** returns the identity of all keys that are pressed simultaneously, thereby allowing chording.

4.5.3 Valuator Devices

Most valuator devices that provide scalar values are based on potentiometers, like the volume and tone controls of a stereo set. Valuators are usually rotary potentiometers (dials), typically mounted in a group of eight or ten. Simple rotary potentiometers can be rotated through about 330°; this may not be enough to provide both adequate range and resolution. Continuous-turn potentiometers can be rotated freely in either direction, and hence are unbounded in range. Linear potentiometers, which are of necessity bounded devices, are used infrequently in graphics systems.

4.5.4 Choice Devices

Function keys are the most common choice device. They are sometimes built as a separate unit, but more often are integrated with a keyboard. Other choice devices are the **buttons** found on many tablet pucks and on the mouse. Choice devices are generally used to enter commands or menu options in a graphics program. Dedicated-purpose systems can use function keys with permanent key-cap labels. So that labels can be changeable or "soft," function keys can include a small LCD or LED display next to each button or in the key caps themselves. Yet another alternative is to place buttons on the bezel of the display, so that button labels can be shown on the display itself, right next to the physical button.

4.6 IMAGE SCANNERS

Although data tablets can be used to digitize existing line drawings manually, this is a slow, tedious process, unsuitable for more than a few simple drawings—and it does not work at all for half-tone images. Image scanners provide an efficient solution. A television camera used in conjunction with a digital frame grabber is an inexpensive way to obtain moderate-resolution (1000×1000, with multiple intensity levels) raster images of black-and-white or color photographs. Slow-scan charge-coupled-device (CCD) television cameras can create a 2000×2000 image in about 30 seconds. An even lower-cost approach uses a scan head, consisting of a grid of light-sensing cells, mounted on the print head of a printer; it scans images at a resolution of about 80 units per inch. These resolutions are not acceptable for high-quality publication work, however. In such cases, a **photo scanner** is used. The photograph is mounted on a rotating drum. A finely collimated light beam is directed at the photo, and the amount of light reflected is measured by a photocell. For a negative, transmitted light is measured by a photocell inside the drum, which is transparent. As the drum rotates (Fig. 4.16), the light source slowly moves from one end to the other, thus doing a raster scan of the entire photograph. For colored photographs, multiple passes are made, using filters in front of the photocell to separate out various colors. The highest-resolution scanners use laser light sources, and have resolutions greater then 2000 units per inch.

Another class of scanner uses a long thin strip of CCDs, called a *CCD array.* A drawing is digitized by passing it under the CCD array, incrementing the drawing's movement by whatever resolution is required. Thus, a single pass, taking 1 or 2 minutes, is sufficient to digitize a large drawing. Resolution of the CCD array is 200 to 1000 units per inch, which is less than that of the photo scanner.

Line drawings can easily be scanned using any of the approaches we have described. The difficult part is distilling some meaning from the collection of

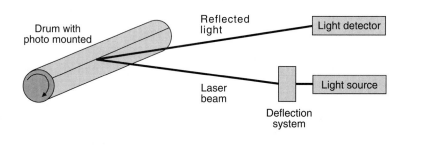

Figure 4.16   A photo scanner. The light source is deflected along the drum axis, and the amount of reflected light is measured.

pixels that results. **Vectorizing** is the process of extracting lines, characters, and other geometric primitives from a raster image. This task requires appropriate algorithms, not scanning hardware, and is essentially an image-processing problem involving several steps. First, thresholding and edge enhancement are used to clean up the raster image—to eliminate smudges and smears and to fill in gaps. Feature-extraction algorithms are then used to combine adjacent *on* pixels into geometric primitives such as straight lines. At a second level of complexity, pattern-recognition algorithms are used to combine the simple primitives into arcs, letters, symbols, and so on. User interaction may be necessary to resolve ambiguities caused by breaks in lines, dark smudges, and multiple lines intersecting near one another.

A more difficult problem is organizing a collection of geometric primitives into meaningful data structures. A disorganized collection of lines is not particularly useful as input to a CAD or topographic (mapping) application program. The higher-level geometric constructs represented in the drawings need to be recognized. Thus, the lines defining the outline of a country should be organized into a polygon primitive, and the small "+" representing the center of an arc should be grouped with the arc itself. There are partial solutions to these problems. Commercial systems depend on user intervention when the going gets tough, although algorithms are improving continually.

Exercises

4.1   If long-persistence phosphors decrease the fusion frequency, why not use them routinely?

4.2   Write a program to display test patterns on a raster display. Three different patterns should be provided: (1) horizontal lines 1 pixel wide, separated by 0, 1, 2, or 3 pixels; (2) vertical lines 1 pixel wide, separated by 0, 1, 2, or 3 pixels; and (3) a grid of 1-pixel dots on a grid spaced at 5-pixel intervals. Each pattern should be displayable in white, red, green, or blue, as well as alternating color bars. How does what you observe when the patterns are displayed relate to the discussion of raster resolution?

4.3   How long would it take to load a 512 by 512 by 1 bitmap, assuming that the pixels are packed 8 to a byte and that bytes can be transferred and unpacked at the rate of 100,000 bytes per second? How long would it take to load a 1024 by 1280 by 1 bitmap?

4.4   Design the logic of a hardware unit to convert from 2D raster addresses to byte plus bit-within-byte addresses. The inputs to the unit are as follows: (1) (x, y), a raster address; (2) *base*, the address of the memory byte that has raster address $(0, 0)$ in bit 0; and (3) x_{max}, the maximum raster x address (0 is the minimum). The outputs from the unit are as follows: (1) *byte*, the address of the byte that contains (x, y) in one of its bits; and (2) *bit*, the bit within *byte* which contains (x, y). What simplifications are possible if $x_{max} + 1$ is a power of 2?

5 Geometrical Transformations

This chapter introduces the basic 2D and 3D geometrical transformations used in computer graphics. The translation, scaling, and rotation transformations discussed here are essential to many graphics applications and will be referred to extensively in succeeding chapters.

The transformations are used directly by application programs and within many graphics subroutine packages. A city-planning application program would use translation to place symbols for buildings and trees at appropriate positions, rotation to orient the symbols, and scaling to size the symbols. In general, many applications use the geometric transformations to change the position, orientation, and size of objects (also called **symbols** or **templates**), in a drawing. In Chapter 6, 3D rotation, translation, and scaling will be used as part of the process of creating 2D renditions of 3D objects. In Chapter 7, we shall see how a contemporary graphics package uses transformations as part of its implementation and also makes them available to application programs.

5.1 MATHEMATICAL PRELIMINARIES

This section reviews the most important mathematics used in this book—especially vectors and matrices. It is by no means intended as a comprehensive discussion of linear algebra or geometry; nor is it meant to introduce you to these subjects. Rather, the assumption we make in this section is that you have had the equivalent of one year of college mathematics, but that your familiarity with subjects like algebra and geometry has faded somewhat. If you are already comfortable with the topics covered in this section, you can safely skip ahead to Section 5.2. If your familiarity with the concepts described here is not current, or if you have not seen them before, we hope that this section will serve as a handy "cookbook" that you can refer to as you work through the rest of the book. For those of you who are uncertain of your ability to grasp and apply the concepts reviewed here, be assured that every vector and matrix operation is simply a shorthand notation for its equivalent algebraic form. Because this notation is so convenient and powerful, however, we urge you to take the time to become comfortable with it. We have found that a program such as *Mathematica*™ [WOLF91]—which allows you to perform interactively both symbolic and numeric operations with vectors and matrices—is a valuable learning tool. Readers interested in exploring this material in more detail should consult [BANC83; HOFF61; MARS85].

5.1.1 Vectors and Their Properties

It may be that your first introduction to the concept of a vector was in a course in physics or mechanics, perhaps using the example of the speed and direction of flight of a baseball as it leaves a bat. At that moment, the ball's state can be represented by a line segment with an arrowhead. The line segment points in the direction of motion of the ball and has a length denoting its speed. This directed line segment represents the *velocity vector* of the ball. The velocity vector is but one example of the many such vectors which occur in physical problems. Other examples of vectors are force, acceleration, and momentum.

The notion of a vector has proved to be of great value both in physics and mathematics. We use vectors extensively in computer graphics. We use them to represent the position of points in a world-coordinate dataset, the orientation of surfaces in space, the behavior of light interacting with solid and transparent objects, and for many other purposes. We shall encounter vectors in many succeeding chapters. We shall note where and how we use vectors as we proceed to describe their properties.

Whereas some texts choose to describe vectors exclusively from a geometrical standpoint, we shall emphasize their dual nature and exploit their algebraic definition as well. This orientation leads us to the concise and compact formulations of linear algebra, which we favor for the mathematics of computer graphics. We shall, however, point out geometric interpretations when to do so serves as an aid to understanding certain concepts.

There are more rigorous definitions, but for our purposes we can say a **vector** is an *n*-tuple of real numbers, where *n* is 2 for 2D space, 3 for 3D space, etc. We shall denote vectors by italicized letters,[1] usually *u*, *v*, or *w* in this section. Vectors are amenable to two operations: addition of vectors, and multiplication of vectors

---

[1] In the remainder of this volume, we have done our best to adhere to the notational conventions that appear in the research literature, although these are by no means consistent from one paper to the next. Because of this variation in practice, you will sometimes see uppercase letters used to denote vectors, and sometimes lowercase letters.

by real numbers, called **scalar multiplication**.[2] The operations have certain properties. Addition is commutative, it is associative, and there is a vector, traditionally called 0, with the property that, for any vector v, $0 + v = v$. The operations also have inverses (i.e., for every vector v, there is another vector w with the property that $v + w = 0$; w is written "$-v$"). Scalar multiplication satisfies the rules $(\alpha\beta)v = \alpha(\beta v)$, $1v = v$, $(\alpha + \beta)\,v = \alpha v + \beta v$, and $\alpha(v + w) = \alpha v + \alpha w$.

Addition is defined componentwise, as is scalar multiplication. Vectors are written vertically, so that a sample 3D vector is

$$\begin{bmatrix} 1 \\ 3 \\ 1 \end{bmatrix}.$$

We can sum elements

$$\begin{bmatrix} 1 \\ 3 \\ 1 \end{bmatrix} + \begin{bmatrix} 2 \\ 3 \\ 6 \end{bmatrix} = \begin{bmatrix} 3 \\ 6 \\ 7 \end{bmatrix}.$$

Most of computer graphics is done in 2D space, 3D space, or, as we shall see in Sections 5.7 and 6.6.4, 4D space.

It is important at this point to make a distinction between vectors and points. While we can think of a point as being defined by a vector that is drawn to it, this representation requires us to specify *from* where the vector is drawn, i.e., define what we usually call an origin. There are many operations one can perform on points, however, that do not require an origin, and there are vector operations, e.g., multiplication, that are undefined when applied to points. It is best, therefore, not to confuse the nature of vectors and points, but treat them as separate concepts. However, there are operations—like forming a vector from the difference of two points—that always make perfect sense.

Having been forewarned about the distinction between vectors and points, we can, nonetheless, discover useful properties by treating points as vectors. As an example, consider 2D space with a specified origin. We can define addition of vectors by the well-known **parallelogram rule**: To add the vectors v and w, we take an arrow from the origin to w, translate it such that its base is at the point v, and define $v + w$ as the new endpoint of the arrow. If we also draw the arrow from the origin to v, and do the corresponding process, we get a parallelogram, as shown in Fig. 5.1. Scalar multiplication by a real number α is defined similarly: We draw an arrow from the origin to the point v, stretch it by a factor of α, holding the end at the origin fixed, and then αv is defined to be the endpoint of the resulting arrow. Of course, the same definitions can be made for 3D space.

Given the two operations available in a vector space, there are natural calculations to do with vectors. One of these calculations is forming **linear combinations**. A linear combination of the vectors $v_1, \ldots, v_n$ is any vector of the form $\alpha_1 v_1 + \alpha_2 v_2 + \ldots + \alpha_n v_n$. Linear combinations of vectors are used for describing many

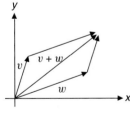

Figure 5.1
Addition of vectors in the plane.

---

[2] Scalars (i.e., real numbers) will be denoted by Greek letters, typically by those near the start of the alphabet.

objects. In Chapter 9 we shall encounter applications of linear combinations for the representation of curves and surfaces.

5.1.2 The Vector Dot Product

Given two n-dimensional vectors

$$\begin{bmatrix} x_1 \\ \cdot \\ \cdot \\ \cdot \\ x_n \end{bmatrix} \quad \text{and} \quad \begin{bmatrix} y_1 \\ \cdot \\ \cdot \\ \cdot \\ y_n \end{bmatrix},$$

we define their **inner product** or **dot product** to be $x_1 y_1 + \ldots + x_n y_n$. The dot product of vectors v and w is generally denoted by $v \cdot w$.

The distance from the point (x, y) in the plane to the origin $(0, 0)$ is $\sqrt{x^2 + y^2}$. In general, the distance from the point $(x_1, \ldots, x_n)$ to the origin in n-space is $\sqrt{x_1^2 + \ldots + x_n^2}$. If we let v be the vector

$$\begin{bmatrix} x_1 \\ \cdot \\ \cdot \\ \cdot \\ x_n \end{bmatrix},$$

we can see that this is just $\sqrt{v \cdot v}$. This is our definition of the **length** of an n-dimensional vector. We denote this length by $\| v \|$. The distance between two points in the standard n-space is defined similarly: The distance between P and Q is the length of the vector $Q - P$.

5.1.3 Properties of the Dot Product

The dot product has several nice properties. First, it is symmetric: $v \cdot w = w \cdot v$. Second, it is **nondegenerate**: $v \cdot v = 0$ only when $v = 0$. Third, it is **bilinear**: $v \cdot (u + \alpha w) = v \cdot u + \alpha(v \cdot w)$.

The dot product can be used to generate vectors whose length is 1 (this is called **normalizing a vector**). To normalize a vector, v, we simply compute $v' = v \, / \, \| v \|$. The resulting vector has length 1, and is called a **unit vector**.

Dot products can also be used to measure angles. The **angle between the vectors** v and w is

$$\cos^{-1} \left(\frac{v \cdot w}{\| v \| \, \| w \|} \right).$$

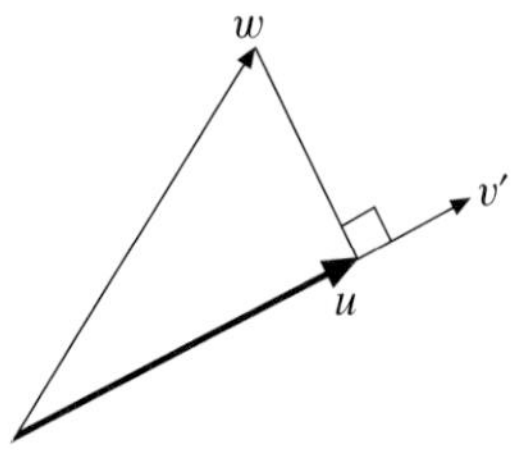

Figure 5.2
The projection of w onto the unit vector v' is a vector u, whose length is $\| w \|$ times the cosine of the angle between u and v'.

Note that, if v and w are unit vectors, then the division is unnecessary.

If we have a unit vector v' and another vector w, and we project w perpendicularly onto v', as shown in Fig. 5.2, and call the result u, then the length of u should be the length of w multiplied by $\cos\theta$, where θ is the angle between v and w. That is to say,

$$
\begin{aligned}
\| u \| &= \| w \| \cos\theta \\
&= \| w \| \left(\frac{v \cdot w}{\| v \| \; \| w \|} \right) \\
&= v \cdot w,
\end{aligned}
$$

since the length of v is 1. This gives us a new interpretation of the dot product: The dot product of v and w is the length of the projection of w onto v, provided that v is a unit vector. We shall encounter many applications of the dot product, especially in Chapter 14, where it is used in describing how light interacts with surfaces.

5.1.4 Matrices

A **matrix** is a rectangular array of numbers, which we frequently use in operations on points and vectors. You can think of a matrix as representing a rule for transforming its operands by a linear transformation. Its elements—generally real numbers—are doubly indexed, and by convention the first index indicates the row and the second indicates the column. Mathematical convention dictates that the indices start at 1; certain programming languages use indices that start at 0. We leave it to programmers in those languages to shift all indices by 1. Thus, if A is a matrix, then $a_{3,2}$ refers to the element in the third row, second column. When symbolic indices are used, as in a_{ij}, the comma between them is omitted.

A vector in n-space, which we have been writing in the form

$$
\begin{bmatrix}
x_1 \\
\cdot \\
\cdot \\
\cdot \\
x_n
\end{bmatrix},
$$

can be considered to be an $n \times 1$ matrix and is called a **column vector**. We shall use matrices, and their associated operations (Sections 5.1.5–5.1.8), throughout much of the book. Matrices play an important role in geometrical transformations (this chapter), 3D viewing (Chapter 6), 3D graphics packages (Chapter 7), and the description of curves and surfaces (Chapter 9).

5.1.5 Matrix Multiplication

Matrices are multiplied according to the following rule: If A is an $n \times m$ matrix with entries a_{ij}, and B is a $m \times p$ matrix with entries b_{ij}, then AB is defined, and is an $n \times p$ matrix with entries c_{ij}, where $c_{ij} = \sum_{s=1}^{m} a_{is} b_{sj}$. If we think of the columns of B as individual vectors, $B_1, \ldots, B_p$, and the rows of A as vectors $A_1, \ldots, A_m$ as well (but rotated 90° to be horizontal), then we see that c_{ij} is just $A_i \cdot B_j$. The usual properties of multiplication hold, except that matrix multiplication is not commutative: AB is, in general, different from BA. But multiplication distributes over addition: $A(B + C) = AB + AC$, and there is an identity element for multiplication—namely, the **identity matrix**, I, which is a square matrix with all entries 0 except for 1s on the diagonal (i.e., the entries are δ_{ij}, where $\delta_{ij} = 0$ unless $i = j$, and $\delta_{ii} = 1$). See Example 5.1 for a graphical depiction of matrix multiplication.

5.1.6 Determinants

The **determinant** of a square matrix is a single number that is formed from the elements of the matrix. Computation of the determinant is somewhat complicated, because the definition is recursive. The determinant of the 2×2 matrix $\begin{bmatrix} a & c \\ b & d \end{bmatrix}$ is just $ad - bc$. The determinant of an $n \times n$ matrix is defined in terms of determinants of smaller matrices. If we let A_{1i} denote the determinant of the $(n-1) \times (n-1)$ matrix that we obtain by deleting the first row and ith column from the $n \times n$ matrix A, then the determinant of A is defined by

$$\det A = \sum_{i=1}^{n} (-1)^{1+i} A_{1i} \, .$$

One special application of the determinant works in 3D space: the **cross-product**. We compute the cross-product of two vectors,

$$v = \begin{bmatrix} v_1 \\ v_2 \\ v_3 \end{bmatrix} \quad \text{and} \quad w = \begin{bmatrix} w_1 \\ w_2 \\ w_3 \end{bmatrix},$$

by taking the determinant of the matrix,

$$\begin{bmatrix} i & j & k \\ v_1 & v_2 & v_3 \\ w_1 & w_2 & w_3 \end{bmatrix},$$

where the letters i, j, and k represent unit vectors directed along the three coordinate axes. The result is then a linear combination of the variables i, j, and k, yielding the vector

$$\begin{bmatrix} v_2 w_3 - v_3 w_2 \\ v_3 w_1 - v_1 w_3 \\ v_1 w_2 - v_2 w_1 \end{bmatrix},$$

which is denoted by $v \times w$. It has the property that it is perpendicular to the plane defined by v and w, and its length is the product $\|v\| \, \|w\| \, |\sin \theta|$, where θ is the angle between v and w. We shall exploit the properties of the cross-product in Chapter 9, where we show it can be used to determine the plane equation of a polygon.

5.1.7 Matrix Transpose

An $n \times k$ matrix can be flipped along its diagonal (upper left to lower right) to make a $k \times n$ matrix. If the first matrix has entries a_{ij} ($i = 1,\ldots, n; j = 1,\ldots, k$), then the resulting matrix has entries b_{ij} ($i = 1,\ldots, k; j = 1,\ldots, n$), with $b_{ij} = a_{ji}$. This new matrix is called the **transpose** of the original matrix. The transpose of A is written A^{T}. If we consider a vector in n-dimensional space as an $n \times 1$ matrix, then its transpose is a $1 \times n$ matrix (sometimes called a row vector). Using the transpose, we can give a new description of the dot product; namely, $u \cdot v = u^T v$.

5.1.8 Matrix Inverse

Matrix multiplication differs from ordinary multiplication in another way: A matrix may not have a multiplicative inverse. In fact, inverses are defined for only square matrices, and not even all of these have inverses. To be precise, only those square matrices whose determinants are nonzero have inverses.

If A and B are $n \times n$ matrices, and $AB = BA = I$, where I is the $n \times n$ identity matrix, then B is said to be the inverse of A, and is written A^{-1}. For $n \times n$ matrices with real-number entries, it suffices to show that either $AB = I$ or $BA = I$ — if either is true, the other is as well.

If we are given an $n \times n$ matrix, the preferred way to find its inverse is by Gaussian elimination, especially for any matrix larger than 3×3. A good reference for this method, including working programs for implementation, is [PRES88].

Example 5.1

We shall see in Section 5.7 the importance of 4×4 matrices in computer graphics; they are used extensively in 3D transformations.

Problem:

a.   Find the matrix product $C = AB$ of

$$A = \begin{bmatrix} 1 & 0 & 0 & 0 \\ 0 & 1 & 0 & 0 \\ 0 & 0 & 0 & 0 \\ 0 & 0 & \frac{1}{k} & 1 \end{bmatrix} \quad \text{and} \quad B = \begin{bmatrix} \cos\theta & 0 & \sin\theta & 0 \\ 0 & 1 & 0 & m \\ -\sin\theta & 0 & \cos\theta & n \\ 0 & 0 & 0 & 1 \end{bmatrix}.$$

As we shall discover in Sections 6.5 and 5.7, these matrices specify a perspective projection and a rotation and two translations, respectively.

b.   Write a C function that returns the matrix product C of two 4×4 matrices A and B.

Answer:

a.   The matrix multiplication rule, defined in Section 5.1.5, can be illustrated as follows:

$$c_{ij} = \sum_{s=1}^{m} a_{is} b_{sj}$$

$$\begin{bmatrix} b_{11} & b_{12} & b_{13} & b_{14} \\ b_{21} & b_{22} & b_{23} & b_{24} \\ b_{31} & b_{32} & b_{33} & b_{34} \\ b_{41} & b_{42} & b_{43} & b_{44} \end{bmatrix},$$

$$\begin{bmatrix} a_{11} & a_{12} & a_{13} & a_{14} \\ a_{21} & a_{22} & a_{23} & a_{24} \\ a_{31} & a_{32} & a_{33} & a_{34} \\ a_{41} & a_{42} & a_{43} & a_{44} \end{bmatrix} \begin{bmatrix} c_{11} & c_{12} & c_{13} & c_{14} \\ c_{21} & c_{22} & c_{23} & c_{24} \\ c_{31} & c_{32} & c_{33} & c_{34} \\ c_{41} & c_{42} & c_{43} & c_{44} \end{bmatrix}$$

where we have selected the c_{43} element for evaluation. Thus, the equation for multiplication shows that we should multiply elements from the fourth row of A with elements from the third column of B. Performing this operation leads to the result that $c_{43} = \cos\theta/k$. By applying this procedure for every element of C, we find the resulting matrix to be

$$
C = \begin{bmatrix}
\cos\theta & 0 & \sin\theta & 0 \\
0 & 1 & 0 & m \\
0 & 0 & 0 & 0 \\
-\dfrac{\sin\theta}{k} & 0 & \dfrac{\cos\theta}{k} & \dfrac{n}{k}+1
\end{bmatrix}.
$$

b.
```
typedef struct Matrix4Struct {
    double element[4][4];
}Matrix4;

/* multiply together matrices c = ab */
/* note that c must not point to either of the input matrices */
Matrix4 *V3MatMul(a, b, c)
Matrix4 *a, *b, *c;
{
    int    i, j, k;
    for (i = 0; i < 4; i++) {
        for (j = 0; j < 4; j++) {
            c->element[i][j] = 0.0;
            for (k = 0; k < 4; k++)
                c->element[i][j] +=
                    a->element[i][k] * b->element[k][j];
        }
    }
    return (c);
}
```

5.2 2D TRANSFORMATIONS

We can **translate** points in the (x, y) plane to new positions by adding translation amounts to the coordinates of the points. For each point $P(x, y)$ to be moved by d_x units parallel to the x axis and by d_y units parallel to the y axis, to the new point $P'(x', y')$, we can write

$$x' = x + d_x, \qquad y' = y + d_y. \tag{5.1}$$

If we define the column vectors

$$P = \begin{bmatrix} x \\ y \end{bmatrix}, \quad P' = \begin{bmatrix} x' \\ y' \end{bmatrix}, \quad T = \begin{bmatrix} d_x \\ d_y \end{bmatrix}, \tag{5.2}$$

then Eq. (5.1) can be expressed more concisely as

$$P' = P + T. \tag{5.3}$$

We could translate an object by applying Eq. (5.2) to every point of the object. Because each line in an object is made up of an infinite number of points, however, this process would take an infinitely long time. Fortunately, we can translate all the points on a line by translating only the line's endpoints and by drawing a new line between the translated endpoints; this observation also applies to scaling (stretching) and rotation. Figure 5.3 shows the effect of translating the outline of a house by $(3, -4)$.

Points can be **scaled** (stretched) by s_x along the x axis and by s_y along the y axis into new points by the multiplications

$$x' = s_x \cdot x, \qquad y' = s_y \cdot y. \tag{5.4}$$

In matrix form, this is

$$\begin{bmatrix} x' \\ y' \end{bmatrix} = \begin{bmatrix} s_x & 0 \\ 0 & s_y \end{bmatrix} \cdot \begin{bmatrix} x \\ y \end{bmatrix} \quad \text{or} \quad P' = S \cdot P, \tag{5.5}$$

where S is the matrix in Eq. (5.5).

In Fig. 5.4, the house is scaled by $\frac{1}{2}$ in x and by $\frac{1}{4}$ in y. Notice that the scaling is about the origin: The house is smaller *and* is closer to the origin. If the scale factors were greater than 1, the house would be both larger and farther from the origin. Techniques for scaling about some point other than the origin are discussed in Section 5.3. The proportions of the house have also changed: A **differential** scaling, in which $s_x \neq s_y$, has been used. With a **uniform** scaling, in which $s_x = s_y$, the proportions are unaffected.

Points can be **rotated** through an angle θ about the origin. A rotation is defined mathematically by

$$x' = x \cdot \cos\theta - y \cdot \sin\theta, \qquad y' = x \cdot \sin\theta + y \cdot \cos\theta. \tag{5.6}$$

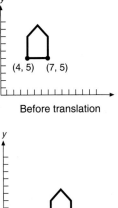

Before translation

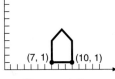

After translation

Figure 5.3
Translation of a house.

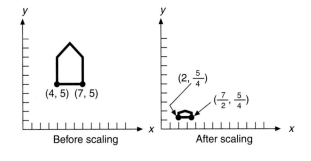

Before scaling   After scaling

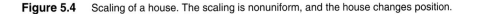

Figure 5.4   Scaling of a house. The scaling is nonuniform, and the house changes position.

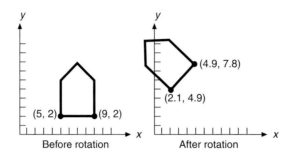

Figure 5.5   Rotation of a house. The house also changes position.

In matrix form, we have

$$\begin{bmatrix} x' \\ y' \end{bmatrix} = \begin{bmatrix} \cos\theta & -\sin\theta \\ \sin\theta & \cos\theta \end{bmatrix} \cdot \begin{bmatrix} x \\ y \end{bmatrix} \quad \text{or} \quad P' = R \cdot P, \tag{5.7}$$

where R is the rotation matrix in Eq. (5.7). Figure 5.5 shows the rotation of the house by 45°. As with scaling, rotation is about the origin; rotation about an arbitrary point is discussed in Section 5.3.

Positive angles are measured **counterclockwise** from x toward y. For negative (clockwise) angles, the identities $\cos(-\theta) = \cos\theta$ and $\sin(-\theta) = -\sin\theta$ can be used to modify Eqs. (5.6) and (5.7).

Equation (5.6) is easily derived from Fig. 5.6, in which a rotation by θ transforms $P(x, y)$ into $P'(x', y')$. Because the rotation is about the origin, the distances from the origin to P and to P', labeled r in the figure, are equal. By simple trigonometry, we find that

$$x = r \cdot \cos\phi, \quad y = r \cdot \sin\phi \tag{5.8}$$

and

$$x' = r \cdot \cos(\theta + \phi) = r \cdot \cos\phi \cdot \cos\theta - r \cdot \sin\phi \cdot \sin\theta,$$
$$y' = r \cdot \sin(\theta + \phi) = r \cdot \cos\phi \cdot \sin\theta + r \cdot \sin\phi \cdot \cos\theta. \tag{5.9}$$

Substituting Eq. (5.8) into Eq. (5.9) yields Eq. (5.6).

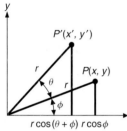

Figure 5.6
Derivation of the rotation equation.

5.3 HOMOGENEOUS COORDINATES AND MATRIX REPRESENTATION OF 2D TRANSFORMATIONS

The matrix representations for translation, scaling, and rotation are, respectively,

$$P' = T + P, \tag{5.3}$$

$$P' = S \cdot P, \tag{5.5}$$

$$P' = R \cdot P. \tag{5.7}$$

Unfortunately, translation is treated differently from scaling and rotation. We would like to be able to treat all three transformations in a consistent way, so that they can be combined easily.

If points are expressed in **homogeneous coordinates**, all three transformations can be treated as multiplications. Homogeneous coordinates were first developed in geometry [MAXW46; MAXW51] and have been applied subsequently in graphics [ROBE65; BLIN77b; BLIN78a]. Numerous graphics subroutine packages and display processors work with homogeneous coordinates and transformations.

In homogeneous coordinates, we add a third coordinate to a point. Instead of being represented by a pair of numbers (x, y), each point is represented by a triple (x, y, W). At the same time, we say that two sets of homogeneous coordinates (x, y, W) and (x', y', W') represent the same point if and only if one is a multiple of the other. Thus, $(2, 3, 6)$ and $(4, 6, 12)$ are the same points represented by different coordinate triples. That is, each point has many different homogeneous coordinate representations. Also, at least one of the homogeneous coordinates must be nonzero: $(0, 0, 0)$ is not allowed. If the W coordinate is nonzero, we can divide through by it: (x, y, W) represents the same point as $(x/W, y/W, 1)$. When W is nonzero, we normally do this division, and the numbers x/W and y/W are called the Cartesian coordinates of the homogeneous point. The points with $W = 0$ are called points at infinity, and will not appear often in our discussions.

Triples of coordinates typically represent points in 3-space, but here we are using them to represent points in 2-space. The connection is this: If we take all the triples representing the same point—that is, all triples of the form (tx, ty, tW), with $t \neq 0$—we get a line in 3-space. Thus, each homogeneous *point* represents a *line* in 3-space. If we **homogenize** the point (divide by W), we get a point of the form $(x, y, 1)$. Thus, the homogenized points form the plane defined by the equation $W = 1$ in (x, y, W)-space. Figure 5.7 shows this relationship. Points at infinity are not represented on this plane.

Because points are now three-element column vectors, transformation matrices, which multiply a point vector to produce another point vector, must be 3×3. In the 3×3 matrix form for homogeneous coordinates, the translation equations (5.1) are

$$\begin{bmatrix} x' \\ y' \\ 1 \end{bmatrix} = \begin{bmatrix} 1 & 0 & d_x \\ 0 & 1 & d_y \\ 0 & 0 & 1 \end{bmatrix} \cdot \begin{bmatrix} x \\ y \\ 1 \end{bmatrix}. \tag{5.10}$$

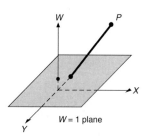

Figure 5.7

The *XYW* homogeneous coordinate space, with the $W = 1$ plane and point $P(X, Y, W)$ projected onto the $W = 1$ plane.

We caution you that certain graphics textbooks, including [FOLE82], use a convention of premultiplying matrices by row vectors, rather than postmultiplying by column vectors. Matrices must be transposed to go from one convention to the other, just as the row and column vectors are transposed:

$$(P \cdot M)^T = M^T \cdot P^T.$$

Equation (5.10) can be expressed differently as

$$P' = T(d_x, d_y) \cdot P, \tag{5.11}$$

where

$$T(d_x, d_y) = \begin{bmatrix} 1 & 0 & d_x \\ 0 & 1 & d_y \\ 0 & 0 & 1 \end{bmatrix}. \tag{5.12}$$

What happens if a point P is translated by $T(d_{x1}, d_{y1})$ to P' and then translated by $T(d_{x2}, d_{y2})$ to P''? The result that we expect intuitively is a net translation $T(d_{x1} + d_{x2}, d_{y1} + d_{y2})$. To confirm this intuition, we start with the givens:

$$P' = T(d_{x1}, d_{y1}) \cdot P, \tag{5.13}$$
$$P'' = T(d_{x2}, d_{y2}) \cdot P'. \tag{5.14}$$

Now, substituting Eq. (5.13) into Eq. (5.14), we obtain

$$P''= T(d_{x2}, d_{y2}) \cdot (T(d_{x1}, d_{y1}) \cdot P) = (T(d_{x2}, d_{y2}) \cdot T(d_{x1}, d_{y1})) \cdot P. \tag{5.15}$$

The matrix product $T(d_{x2}, d_{y2}) \cdot T(d_{x1}, d_{y1})$ is

$$\begin{bmatrix} 1 & 0 & d_{x2} \\ 0 & 1 & d_{y2} \\ 0 & 0 & 1 \end{bmatrix} \cdot \begin{bmatrix} 1 & 0 & d_{x1} \\ 0 & 1 & d_{y2} \\ 0 & 0 & 1 \end{bmatrix} = \begin{bmatrix} 1 & 0 & d_{x1} + d_{x2} \\ 0 & 1 & d_{y1} + d_{y2} \\ 0 & 0 & 1 \end{bmatrix}. \tag{5.16}$$

The net translation is indeed $T(d_{x1} + d_{x2}, d_{y1} + d_{y2})$. The matrix product is variously referred to as the **compounding**, **catenation**, **concatenation**, or **composition** of $T(d_{x1}, d_{y1})$ and $T(d_{x2}, d_{y2})$. Here, we shall normally use the term *composition*.

Similarly, the scaling equations Eq. (5.4) are represented in matrix form as

$$\begin{bmatrix} x' \\ y' \\ 1 \end{bmatrix} = \begin{bmatrix} s_x & 0 & 0 \\ 0 & s_y & 0 \\ 0 & 0 & 1 \end{bmatrix} \cdot \begin{bmatrix} x \\ y \\ 1 \end{bmatrix}. \tag{5.17}$$

Defining

$$S(s_x, s_y) = \begin{bmatrix} s_x & 0 & 0 \\ 0 & s_y & 0 \\ 0 & 0 & 1 \end{bmatrix}, \tag{5.18}$$

we have

$$P' = S(s_x, s_y) \cdot P. \tag{5.19}$$

Just as successive translations are additive, we expect that successive scalings should be multiplicative. Given

$$P' = S(s_{x1}, s_{y1}) \cdot P, \tag{5.20}$$

$$P'' = S(s_{x2}, s_{y2}) \cdot P', \tag{5.21}$$

and, substituting Eq. (5.20) into Eq. (5.21), we get

$$P'' = S(s_{x2}, s_{y2}) \cdot (S(s_{x1}, s_{y1}) \cdot P) = (S(s_{x2}, s_{y2}) \cdot S(s_{x1}, s_{y1})) \cdot P. \tag{5.22}$$

The matrix product $S(s_{x2}, s_{y2}) \cdot S(s_{x1}, s_{y1})$ is

$$\begin{bmatrix} s_{x2} & 0 & 0 \\ 0 & s_{y2} & 0 \\ 0 & 0 & 1 \end{bmatrix} \cdot \begin{bmatrix} s_{x1} & 0 & 0 \\ 0 & s_{y1} & 0 \\ 0 & 0 & 1 \end{bmatrix} = \begin{bmatrix} s_{x1} \cdot s_{x2} & 0 & 0 \\ 0 & s_{y1} \cdot s_{y2} & 0 \\ 0 & 0 & 1 \end{bmatrix}. \tag{5.23}$$

Thus, the scalings are indeed multiplicative.

Finally, the rotation equations (5.6) can be represented as

$$\begin{bmatrix} x' \\ y' \\ 1 \end{bmatrix} = \begin{bmatrix} \cos\theta & -\sin\theta & 0 \\ \sin\theta & \cos\theta & 0 \\ 0 & 0 & 1 \end{bmatrix} \cdot \begin{bmatrix} x \\ y \\ 1 \end{bmatrix}. \tag{5.24}$$

Letting

$$R(\theta) = \begin{bmatrix} \cos\theta & -\sin\theta & 0 \\ \sin\theta & \cos\theta & 0 \\ 0 & 0 & 1 \end{bmatrix}, \tag{5.25}$$

we have

$$P' = R(\theta) \cdot P. \tag{5.26}$$

Showing that two successive rotations are additive is left to you as Exercise 5.2.

In the upper-left 2×2 submatrix of Eq. (5.25), consider each of the two rows as vectors. The vectors can be shown to have three properties:

1. Each is a unit vector.
2. Each is perpendicular to the other (their dot product is zero).
3. The first and second vectors will be rotated by $R(\theta)$ to lie on the positive x and y axes, respectively (in the presence of conditions 1 and 2, this property is equivalent to the submatrix having a determinant of 1).

The first two properties are also true of the columns of the 2×2 submatrix. The two directions are those into which vectors along the positive x and y axes are rotated. These properties suggest two useful ways to go about deriving a rotation matrix when we know the effect desired from the rotation. A matrix having these properties is called **special orthogonal**.

A transformation matrix of the form

$$\begin{bmatrix} r_{11} & r_{12} & t_x \\ r_{21} & r_{22} & t_y \\ 0 & 0 & 1 \end{bmatrix}, \tag{5.27}$$

where the upper 2×2 submatrix is orthogonal, preserves angles and lengths. That is, a unit square remains a unit square, and becomes neither a rhombus with unit sides, nor a square with nonunit sides. Such transformations are also called **rigid-body** transformations, because the body or object being transformed is not

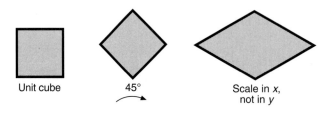

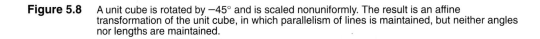

Unit cube   45°   Scale in *x*, not in *y*

Figure 5.8   A unit cube is rotated by −45° and is scaled nonuniformly. The result is an affine transformation of the unit cube, in which parallelism of lines is maintained, but neither angles nor lengths are maintained.

distorted in any way. An arbitrary sequence of rotation and translation matrices creates a matrix of this form.

What can be said about the product of an arbitrary sequence of rotation, translation, and scale matrices? They are called **affine transformations**, and have the property of preserving parallelism of lines, but not of lengths and angles. Figure 5.8 shows the results of applying a −45° rotation and then a nonuniform scaling to the unit cube. It is clear that neither angles nor lengths have been preserved by this sequence, but parallel lines have remained parallel. Further rotation, scale, and translation operations will not cause the parallel lines to cease being parallel. $R(\theta)$, $S(s_x, s_y)$, and $T(d_x, d_y)$ are also affine.

Another type of primitive transformation, the **shear transformation**, is also affine. Two-dimensional shear transformations are of two kinds: a shear along the *x* axis and a shear along the *y* axis. Figure 5.9 shows the effect of shearing the unit cube along each axis. The operation is represented by the matrix

$$SH_x = \begin{bmatrix} 1 & a & 0 \\ 0 & 1 & 0 \\ 0 & 0 & 1 \end{bmatrix}. \tag{5.28}$$

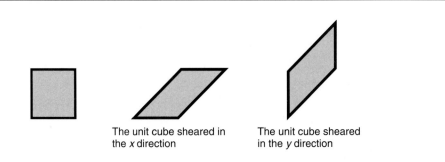

The unit cube sheared in the *x* direction   The unit cube sheared in the *y* direction

Figure 5.9   The primitive-shear operations applied to the unit cube. In each case, the lengths of the oblique lines are now greater than 1.

The term a in the shear matrix is the proportionality constant. Notice that the product $SH_x\,[x\ \ y\ \ 1]^T$ is $[x + ay\ \ y\ \ 1]^T$, clearly demonstrating the proportional change in x as a function of y.

Similarly, the matrix

$$SH_y = \begin{bmatrix} 1 & 0 & 0 \\ b & 1 & 0 \\ 0 & 0 & 1 \end{bmatrix} \tag{5.29}$$

shears along the y axis.

5.4 COMPOSITION OF 2D TRANSFORMATIONS

The idea of composition was introduced in Section 5.3. Here, we use composition to combine the fundamental R, S, and T matrices to produce desired general results. The basic purpose of composing transformations is to gain efficiency by applying a single composed transformation to a point, rather than applying a series of transformations, one after the other.

Consider the rotation of an object about some arbitrary point P_1. Because we know how to rotate only about the origin, we convert our original (difficult) problem into three separate (easy) problems. Thus, to rotate about P_1, we need a sequence of three fundamental transformations:

1. Translate such that P_1 is at the origin.
2. Rotate.
3. Translate such that the point at the origin returns to P_1.

This sequence is illustrated in Fig. 5.10, in which our house is rotated about $P_1(x_1, y_1)$. The first translation is by $(-x_1, -y_1)$, whereas the later translation is by the inverse (x_1, y_1). The result is rather different from that of applying just the rotation.

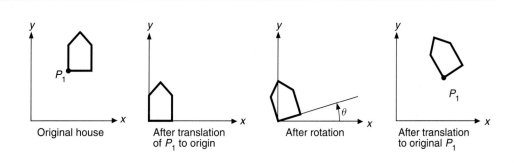

| Original house | After translation of P_1 to origin | After rotation | After translation to original P_1 |

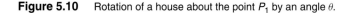

Figure 5.10 Rotation of a house about the point P_1 by an angle θ.

The net transformation is

$$T(x_1, y_1) \cdot R(\theta) \cdot T(-x_1, -y_1) = \begin{bmatrix} 1 & 0 & x_1 \\ 0 & 1 & y_1 \\ 0 & 0 & 1 \end{bmatrix} \cdot \begin{bmatrix} \cos\theta & -\sin\theta & 0 \\ \sin\theta & \cos\theta & 0 \\ 0 & 0 & 1 \end{bmatrix} \cdot \begin{bmatrix} 1 & 0 & -x_1 \\ 0 & 1 & -y_1 \\ 0 & 0 & 1 \end{bmatrix}$$

$$= \begin{bmatrix} \cos\theta & -\sin\theta & x_1(1-\cos\theta) + y_1\sin\theta \\ \sin\theta & \cos\theta & y_1(1-\cos\theta) - x_1\sin\theta \\ 0 & 0 & 1 \end{bmatrix}. \qquad (5.30)$$

A similar approach is used to scale an object about an arbitrary point P_1. First, translate such that P_1 goes to the origin, then scale, then translate back to P_1. In this case, the net transformation is

$$T(x_1, y_1) \cdot S(s_x, s_y) \cdot T(-x_1, -y_1) = \begin{bmatrix} 1 & 0 & x_1 \\ 0 & 1 & y_1 \\ 0 & 0 & 1 \end{bmatrix} \cdot \begin{bmatrix} s_x & 0 & 0 \\ 0 & s_y & 0 \\ 0 & 0 & 1 \end{bmatrix} \cdot \begin{bmatrix} 1 & 0 & -x_1 \\ 0 & 1 & -y_1 \\ 0 & 0 & 1 \end{bmatrix}$$

$$= \begin{bmatrix} s_x & 0 & x_1(1-s_x) \\ 0 & s_y & y_1(1-s_y) \\ 0 & 0 & 1 \end{bmatrix}. \qquad (5.31)$$

Suppose that we wish to scale, rotate, and position the house shown in Fig. 5.11 with P_1 as the center for the rotation and scaling. The sequence is to translate P_1 to the origin, to perform the scaling and rotation, and then to translate from the origin to the new position P_2 where the house is to be placed. A data structure that records this transformation might contain the scale factor(s), rotation angle, and translation amounts, and the order in which the transformations were applied, or it might simply record the composite transformation matrix:

$$T(x_2, y_2) \cdot R(\theta) \cdot S(s_x, s_y) \cdot T(-x_1, -y_1). \qquad (5.32)$$

If M_1 and M_2 each represent a fundamental translation, scaling, or rotation, when is $M_1 \cdot M_2 = M_2 \cdot M_1$? That is, when do M_1 and M_2 commute? In general, of

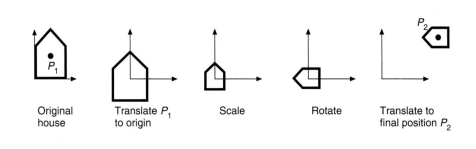

| Original house | Translate P_1 to origin | Scale | Rotate | Translate to final position P_2 |

Figure 5.11   Rotation of a house about the point P_1, and placement such that what was at P_1 is at P_2.

course, matrix multiplication is *not* commutative. However, it is easy to show that, in the following special cases, commutativity holds:

M_1	M_2
Translate	Translate
Scale	Scale
Rotate	Rotate
Scale (with $s_x = s_y$)	Rotate

In these cases, we do not have to be concerned about the *order* of matrix composition.

5.5 THE WINDOW-TO-VIEWPORT TRANSFORMATION

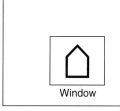

Window

World coordinates

Maximum range
of screen
coordinates

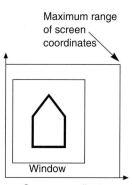

Window

Screen coordinates

Figure 5.12
The window in world coordinates and the viewport in screen coordinates determine the mapping that is applied to all the output primitives in world coordinates.

Some graphics packages allow the programmer to specify output primitive coordinates in a floating-point **world-coordinate** system, using whatever units are meaningful to the application program: angstroms, microns, meters, miles, light-years, and so on. The term *world* is used because the application program is representing a world that is being interactively created or displayed to the user.

Given that output primitives are specified in world coordinates, the graphics subroutine package must be told how to map world coordinates onto screen coordinates (we use the specific term *screen coordinates* to relate this discussion specifically to SRGP, but hardcopy output devices might be used, in which case the term *device coordinates* would be more appropriate). We could do this mapping by having the application programmer provide the graphics package with a transformation matrix to effect the mapping. Another way is to have the application programmer specify a rectangular region in world coordinates, called the **world-coordinate window**, and a corresponding rectangular region in screen coordinates, called the **viewport**, into which the world-coordinate window is to be mapped. The transformation that maps the window into the viewport is applied to all of the output primitives in world coordinates, thus mapping them into screen coordinates. Figure 5.12 shows this concept. As you can see in this figure, if the window and viewport do not have the same height-to-width ratio, a *non*uniform scaling occurs. If the application program changes the window or viewport, then new output primitives drawn onto the screen will be affected by the change. Existing output primitives are not affected by such a change.

The modifier *world-coordinate* is used with *window* to emphasize that we are not discussing a *window-manager window*, which is a different and more recent concept, and which unfortunately has the same name. Whenever there is no ambiguity as to which type of window is meant, we shall drop the modifier.

If SRGP were to provide world-coordinate output primitives, the viewport would be on the current canvas, which defaults to canvas 0, the screen. The application program would be able to change the window or the viewport at any time, in which case subsequently specified output primitives would be subjected to a new

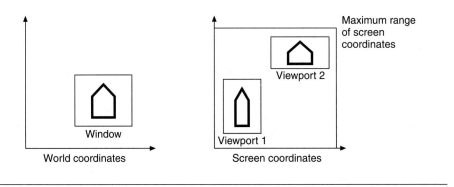

Figure 5.13   The effect of drawing output primitives with two viewports. Output primitives specifying the house were first drawn with viewport 1, the viewport was changed to viewport 2, and then the application program again called the graphics package to draw the output primitives.

transformation. If the change included a different viewport, then the new output primitives would be located on the canvas in positions different from those of the old ones, as shown in Fig. 5.13.

A window manager might map SRGP's canvas 0 into less than a full-screen window, in which case not all of the canvas or even of the viewport would necessarily be visible.

Given a window and viewport, what is the transformation matrix that maps the window from world coordinates into the viewport in screen coordinates? This matrix can be developed as a three-step transformation composition, as suggested in Fig. 5.14. The window, specified by its lower-left and upper-right corners, is first translated to the origin of world coordinates. Next, the size of the window is scaled to be equal to the size of the viewport. Finally, a translation is used to position the viewport. The overall matrix M_{wv}, obtained by composition of the two translation matrices and the scaling matrix, is:

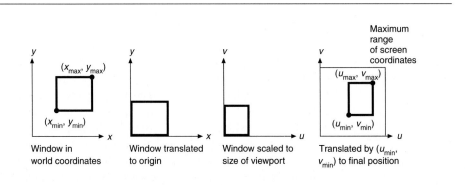

Figure 5.14   The steps used in transforming a world-coordinate window into a viewport.

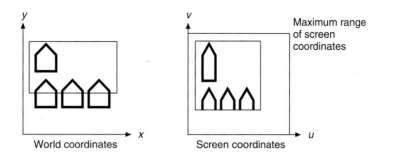

Figure 5.15   Output primitives in world coordinates are clipped against the window. Those that remain are displayed in the viewport.

$$M_{\mathrm{wv}} = T\left(u_{\min}, v_{\min}\right) \cdot S\left(\frac{u_{\max} - u_{\min}}{x_{\max} - x_{\min}}, \frac{v_{\max} - v_{\min}}{y_{\max} - y_{\min}}\right) \cdot T\left(-x_{\min}, -y_{\min}\right)$$

$$= \begin{bmatrix} 1 & 0 & u_{\min} \\ 0 & 1 & v_{\min} \\ 0 & 0 & 1 \end{bmatrix} \cdot \begin{bmatrix} \dfrac{u_{\max} - u_{\min}}{x_{\max} - x_{\min}} & 0 & 0 \\ 0 & \dfrac{v_{\max} - v_{\min}}{y_{\max} - y_{\min}} & 0 \\ 0 & 0 & 1 \end{bmatrix} \cdot \begin{bmatrix} 1 & 0 & -x_{\min} \\ 0 & 1 & -y_{\min} \\ 0 & 0 & 1 \end{bmatrix}$$

$$= \begin{bmatrix} \dfrac{u_{\max} - u_{\min}}{x_{\max} - x_{\min}} & 0 & -x_{\min} \cdot \dfrac{u_{\max} - u_{\min}}{x_{\max} - x_{\min}} + u_{\min} \\ 0 & \dfrac{v_{\max} - v_{\min}}{y_{\max} - y_{\min}} & -y_{\min} \cdot \dfrac{v_{\max} - v_{\min}}{y_{\max} - y_{\min}} + v_{\min} \\ 0 & 0 & 1 \end{bmatrix}. \qquad (5.33)$$

Multiplying $P = M_{\mathrm{wv}} \, [x \ \ y \ \ 1]^{\mathrm{T}}$ gives the expected result:

$$P = \left[(x - x_{\min}) \cdot \frac{u_{\max} - u_{\min}}{x_{\max} - x_{\min}} + u_{\min} \quad (y - y_{\min}) \cdot \frac{v_{\max} - v_{\min}}{y_{\max} - y_{\min}} + v_{\min} \quad 1 \right]. \quad (5.34)$$

   Many graphics packages combine the window–viewport transformation with clipping of output primitives against the window. The concept of clipping was introduced in Chapter 3; Fig. 5.15 illustrates clipping in the context of windows and viewports.

5.6 EFFICIENCY

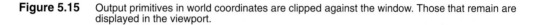

The most general composition of R, S, and T operations produces a matrix of the form

$$M = \begin{bmatrix} r_{11} & r_{12} & t_z \\ r_{21} & r_{22} & t_y \\ 0 & 0 & 1 \end{bmatrix}. \qquad (5.35)$$

The upper 2×2 submatrix is a composite rotation and scale matrix, whereas t_x and t_y are composite translations. Calculating $M \cdot P$ as a vector multiplied by a 3×3 matrix takes nine multiplies and six adds. The fixed structure of the last row of Eq. (5.35), however, simplifies the actual operations to

$$x' = x \cdot r_{11} + y \cdot r_{12} + t_x, \tag{5.36}$$

$$y' = x \cdot r_{21} + y \cdot r_{22} + t_y,$$

reducing the process to four multiplies and four adds—a significant speedup, especially since the operation can be applied to hundreds or even thousands of points per picture. Thus, although 3×3 matrices are convenient and useful for composing 2D transformations, we can use the final matrix most efficiently in a program by exploiting its special structure. Some hardware matrix multipliers have parallel adders and multipliers, thereby diminishing or removing this concern.

5.7 MATRIX REPRESENTATION OF 3D TRANSFORMATIONS

Just as 2D transformations can be represented by 3×3 matrices using homogeneous coordinates, 3D transformations can be represented by 4×4 matrices, provided that we use homogeneous-coordinate representations of points in 3-space as well. Thus, instead of representing a point as (x, y, z), we represent it as (x, y, z, W), where two of these quadruples represent the same point if one is a nonzero multiple of the other; the quadruple $(0, 0, 0, 0)$ is not allowed. As in 2D, a standard representation of a point (x, y, z, W) with $W \neq 0$ is given by $(x/W, y/W, z/W, 1)$. Transforming the point to this form is called **homogenizing**, as before. Also, points whose W coordinate is zero are called points at infinity. There is a geometrical interpretation as well. Each point in 3-space is being represented by a line through the origin in 4-space, and the homogenized representations of these points form a 3D subspace of 4-space that is defined by the single equation $W = 1$.

The 3D coordinate system used in this text is **right-handed**, as shown in Fig. 5.16. By convention, positive rotations in a right-handed system are such that, when looking from a positive axis toward the origin, a 90° *counterclockwise* rotation will transform one positive axis into the other. This table follows from this convention:

Axis of rotation is	Direction of positive rotation
x	y to z
y	z to x
z	x to y

(out of page)

Figure 5.16
The right-handed
coordinate system

These positive directions are also depicted in Fig. 5.16. Be warned that not all graphics texts follow this convention.

We use a right-handed system here because it is the standard mathematical convention, even though it is convenient in 3D graphics to think of a left-handed system superimposed on the face of a display (see Fig. 5.17), since a left-handed system gives the natural interpretation that larger z values are farther from the viewer. Notice that, in a left-handed system, positive rotations are *clockwise* when we are looking from a positive axis toward the origin. This definition of positive rotations allows the same rotation matrices given in this section to be used for either right- or left-handed coordinate systems. Conversion from right to left and from left to right is discussed in Section 5.9.

Translation in 3D is a simple extension from that in 2D:

$$T(d_x, d_y, d_z) = \begin{bmatrix} 1 & 0 & 0 & d_x \\ 0 & 1 & 0 & d_y \\ 0 & 0 & 1 & d_z \\ 0 & 0 & 0 & 1 \end{bmatrix}. \tag{5.37}$$

That is, $T(d_x, d_y, d_z) \cdot [x \ y \ z \ 1]^T = [x + d_x \ y + d_y \ z + d_z \ 1]^T$.

Scaling is similarly extended:

$$S(s_x, s_y, s_z) = \begin{bmatrix} s_x & 0 & 0 & 0 \\ 0 & s_y & 0 & 0 \\ 0 & 0 & s_z & 0 \\ 0 & 0 & 0 & 1 \end{bmatrix}. \tag{5.38}$$

Checking, we see that $S(s_x, s_y, s_z) \cdot [x \ y \ z \ 1]^T = [s_x \cdot x \ s_y \cdot y \ s_z \cdot z \ 1]^T$.

The 2D rotation of Eq. (5.26) is just a 3D rotation about the z axis, which is

$$R_z(\theta) = \begin{bmatrix} \cos\theta & -\sin\theta & 0 & 0 \\ \sin\theta & \cos\theta & 0 & 0 \\ 0 & 0 & 1 & 0 \\ 0 & 0 & 0 & 1 \end{bmatrix}. \tag{5.39}$$

This observation is easily verified: A 90° rotation of $[1 \ 0 \ 0 \ 1]^T$, which is the unit vector along the x axis, should produce the unit vector $[0 \ 1 \ 0 \ 1]^T$ along the y axis. Evaluating the product

$$\begin{bmatrix} 0 & -1 & 0 & 0 \\ 1 & 0 & 0 & 0 \\ 0 & 0 & 1 & 0 \\ 0 & 0 & 0 & 1 \end{bmatrix} \cdot \begin{bmatrix} 1 \\ 0 \\ 0 \\ 1 \end{bmatrix} \tag{5.40}$$

gives the predicted result of $[0 \ 1 \ 0 \ 1]^T$.

The x-axis rotation matrix is

$$R_x(\theta) = \begin{bmatrix} 1 & 0 & 0 & 0 \\ 0 & \cos\theta & -\sin\theta & 0 \\ 0 & \sin\theta & \cos\theta & 0 \\ 0 & 0 & 0 & 1 \end{bmatrix}. \tag{5.41}$$

The y-axis rotation matrix is

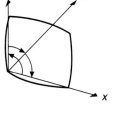

Figure 5.17
The left-handed coordinate system, with a superimposed display screen.

$$R_y(\theta) = \begin{bmatrix} \cos\theta & 0 & \sin\theta & 0 \\ 0 & 1 & 0 & 0 \\ -\sin\theta & 0 & \cos\theta & 0 \\ 0 & 0 & 0 & 1 \end{bmatrix}. \tag{5.42}$$

The columns (and the rows) of the upper-left 3×3 submatrix of $R_z(\theta)$, $R_x(\theta)$, and $R_y(\theta)$ are mutually perpendicular unit vectors and the submatrix has a determinant of 1, which means the three matrices are special orthogonal, as discussed in Section 5.3. Also, the upper-left 3×3 submatrix formed by an arbitrary sequence of rotations is special orthogonal. Recall that orthogonal transformations preserve distances and angles.

All these transformation matrices have inverses. We obtain the inverse for T by negating d_x, d_y, and d_z; and that for S, by replacing s_x, s_y, and s_z by their reciprocals; we obtain the inverse for each of the three rotation matrices by negating the angle of rotation.

The inverse of any orthogonal matrix B is just B's transpose: $B^{-1} = B^T$. In fact, taking the transpose does not need to involve even exchanging elements in the array that stores the matrix—it is necessary only to exchange row and column indexes when accessing the array. Notice that this method of finding an inverse is consistent with the result of negating θ to find the inverse of R_x, R_y, and R_z.

Any number of rotation, scaling, and translation matrices can be multiplied together. The result always has the form

$$M = \begin{bmatrix} r_{11} & r_{12} & r_{13} & t_x \\ r_{21} & r_{22} & r_{23} & t_y \\ r_{31} & r_{32} & r_{33} & t_z \\ 0 & 0 & 0 & 1 \end{bmatrix}. \tag{5.43}$$

As in the 2D case, the 3×3 upper-left submatrix R gives the aggregate rotation and scaling, whereas T gives the subsequent aggregate translation. We achieve some computational efficiency by performing the transformation explicitly as

$$\begin{bmatrix} x' \\ y' \\ z' \end{bmatrix} = R \cdot \begin{bmatrix} x \\ y \\ z \end{bmatrix} + T, \tag{5.44}$$

where R and T are submatrices from Eq. (5.43).

Corresponding to the two-dimensional shear matrices in Section 5.2 are three 3D shear matrices. The (x, y) shear is

$$SH_{xy}(sh_x, sh_y) = \begin{bmatrix} 1 & 0 & sh_x & 0 \\ 0 & 1 & sh_y & 0 \\ 0 & 0 & 1 & 0 \\ 0 & 0 & 0 & 1 \end{bmatrix}. \tag{5.45}$$

Applying SH_{xy} to the point $[x\ y\ z\ 1]^T$, we have $[x + sh_x \cdot z\quad y + sh_y \cdot z\quad z\quad 1]^T$. Shears along the x and y axes have a similar form.

So far, we have focused on transforming individual points. We transform lines, these being defined by two points, by transforming the endpoints. Planes, if they are defined by three points, may be handled the same way, but usually they are defined by a plane equation, and the coefficients of this plane equation must be transformed differently. We may also need to transform the plane normal. Let a plane be represented as the column vector of plane-equation coefficients $N = [A \ B \ C \ D]^T$. Then, a plane is defined by all points P such that $N \cdot P = 0$, where the symbol "$\cdot$" is the vector dot product and $P = [x \ y \ z \ 1]^T$. This dot product gives rise to the familiar plane equation $A \ x + B \ y + C \ z + D = 0$, which can also be expressed as the product of the row vector of plane-equation coefficients times the column vector P: $N^T \cdot P = 0$. Now suppose that we transform all points P on the plane by some matrix M. To maintain $N^T \cdot P = 0$ for the transformed points, we would like to transform N by some (to be determined) matrix Q, giving rise to the equation $(Q \cdot N)^T \cdot M \cdot P = 0$. This expression can in turn be rewritten as $N^T \cdot Q^T \cdot M \cdot P = 0$, using the identity $(Q \cdot N)^T = N^T \cdot Q^T$. The equation will hold if $Q^T \cdot M$ is a multiple of the identity matrix. If the multiplier is 1, this situation leads to $Q^T = M^{-1}$, or $Q = (M^{-1})^T$. Thus, the column vector N' of coefficients for a plane transformed by M is given by

$$N' = (M^{-1})^T \cdot N. \tag{5.46}$$

The matrix $(M^{-1})^T$ does not need to exist, in general, because the determinant of M might be zero. This situation would occur if M includes a projection (we might want to investigate the effect of a perspective projection on a plane).

If just the normal of the plane is to be transformed (e.g., to perform the shading calculations discussed in Chapter 14) and if M consists of only the composition of translation, rotation, and uniform scaling matrices, then the mathematics is even simpler. The N' of Eq. (5.46) can be simplified to $[A' \ B' \ C' \ 0]^T$. (With a zero W component, a homogeneous point represents a point at infinity, which can be thought of as a direction.)

5.8 COMPOSITION OF 3D TRANSFORMATIONS

In this section, we discuss how to compose 3D transformation matrices, using an example that will be useful in Section 6.5. The objective is to transform the directed line segments P_1P_2 and P_1P_3 in Fig. 5.18 from their starting position in part (a) to their ending position in part (b). Thus, point P_1 is to be translated to the origin, P_1P_2 is to lie on the positive z axis, and P_1P_3 is to lie in the positive y-axis half of the (y, z) plane. The lengths of the lines are to be unaffected by the transformation.

Two ways to achieve the desired transformation are presented. The first approach is to compose the primitive transformations T, R_x, R_y, and R_z. This approach, although somewhat tedious, is easy to illustrate, and understanding it will help us to build an understanding of transformations. The second approach, using the properties of special orthogonal matrices described in Section 5.7, is explained more briefly but is more abstract.

To work with the primitive transformations, we again break a difficult problem into simpler subproblems. In this case, the desired transformation can be done in four steps:

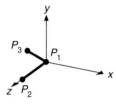

(a) Initial position

1. Translate P_1 to the origin.
2. Rotate about the y axis such that P_1P_2 lies in the (y, z) plane.
3. Rotate about the x axis such that P_1P_2 lies on the z axis.
4. Rotate about the z axis such that P_1P_3 lies in the (y, z) plane.

Step 1: Translate P_1 to the origin. The translation is

$$T(-x_1, -y_1, -z_1) = \begin{bmatrix} 1 & 0 & 0 & -x_1 \\ 0 & 1 & 0 & -y_1 \\ 0 & 0 & 1 & -z_1 \\ 0 & 0 & 0 & 1 \end{bmatrix}. \tag{5.47}$$

Applying T to P_1, P_2, and P_3 gives

(b) Final position

$$P_1' = T(-x_1, -y_1, -z_1) \cdot P_1 = \begin{bmatrix} 0 \\ 0 \\ 0 \\ 1 \end{bmatrix}, \tag{5.48}$$

Figure 5.18
Transforming P_1, P_2, and P_3 from their initial position (a) to their final position (b).

$$P_2' = T(-x_1, -y_1, -z_1) \cdot P_2 = \begin{bmatrix} x_2 - x_1 \\ y_2 - y_1 \\ z_2 - z_1 \\ 1 \end{bmatrix}, \tag{5.49}$$

$$P_3' = T(-x_1, -y_1, -z_1) \cdot P_3 = \begin{bmatrix} x_3 - x_1 \\ y_3 - y_1 \\ z_3 - z_1 \\ 1 \end{bmatrix}, \tag{5.50}$$

Step 2: Rotate about the y axis. Figure 5.19 shows P_1P_2 after step 1, along with the projection of P_1P_2 onto the (x, z) plane. The angle of rotation is $-(90 - \theta) = \theta - 90$. Then

$$\cos(\theta - 90) = \sin\theta = \frac{z_2'}{D_1} = \frac{z_2 - z_1}{D_1},$$

$$\sin(\theta - 90) = -\cos\theta = -\frac{x_2'}{D_1} = -\frac{x_2 - x_1}{D_1}, \tag{5.51}$$

where

$$D_1 = \sqrt{(z_2')^2 + (x_2')^2} = \sqrt{(z_2 - z_1)^2 + (x_2 - x_1)^2}. \tag{5.52}$$

When these values are substituted into Eq. (5.42), we get

$$P_2'' = R_y(\theta - 90) \cdot P_2' = [0 \ \ y_2 - y_1 \ \ D_1 \ \ 1]^T. \tag{5.53}$$

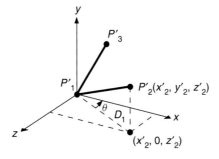

Figure 5.19 Rotation about the y axis: The projection of $P_1'P_2'$, which has length D_1, is rotated into the z axis. The angle θ shows the positive direction of rotation about the y axis: The actual angle used is $-(90 - \theta)$.

As expected, the x component of P_2'' is zero, and the z component is the length D_1.

Step 3: Rotate about the x axis. Figure 5.20 shows P_1P_2 after step 2. The angle of rotation is ϕ, for which

$$\cos\phi = \frac{z_2''}{D_2}, \quad \sin\phi = \frac{y_2''}{D_2}, \tag{5.54}$$

where $D_2 = |P_1''P_2''|$, the length of the line $P_1''P_2''$. But the length of line $P_1''P_2''$ is the same as the length of line P_1P_2, because rotation and translation transformations preserve length, so

$$D_2 = |P_1''P_2''| = |P_1P_2| = \sqrt{(x_2 - x_1)^2 + (y_2 - y_1)^2 + (z_2 - z_1)^2}. \tag{5.55}$$

The result of the rotation in step 3 is

$$P_2''' = R_x(\phi) \cdot P_2'' = R_x(\phi) \cdot R_y(\theta - 90) \cdot P_2'$$

$$= R_x(\phi) \cdot R_y(\theta - 90) \cdot T \cdot P_2 = [0 \quad 0 \quad |P_1P_2| \quad 1]^T. \tag{5.56}$$

That is, P_1P_2 now coincides with the positive z axis.

Step 4: Rotate about the z axis. Figure 5.21 shows P_1P_2 and P_1P_3 after step 3, with P_2''' on the z axis and P_3''' at the position

$$P_3''' = [x_3''' \quad y_3''' \quad z_3''' \quad 1]^T = R_x(\phi) \cdot R_y(\theta - 90) \cdot T(-x_1, -y_1, -z_1) \cdot P_3. \tag{5.57}$$

The rotation is through the positive angle α, with

$$\cos\alpha = y_3'''/D_3, \quad \sin\alpha = x_3'''/D_3, \quad D_3 = \sqrt{x_3'''^2 + y_3'''^2}. \tag{5.58}$$

Step 4 achieves the result shown in Fig. 5.18(b).

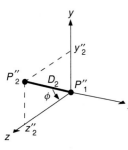

Figure 5.20
Rotation about the x axis: $P_1''P_2''$ is rotated into the z axis by the positive angle ϕ. D_2 is the length of the line segment. The line segment $P_1''P_3''$ is not shown, because it is not used to determine the angles of rotation. Both lines are rotated by $R_x(\phi)$.

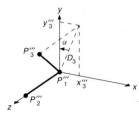

Figure 5.21
Rotation about the *z* axis: The projection of $P_1'P_3'$, whose length is D_3, is rotated by the positive angle α into the *y* axis, bringing the line itself into the (*y*, *z*) plane. D_3 is the length of the projection.

The composite matrix

$$R_z(\alpha) \cdot R_x(\phi) \cdot R_y(\theta - 90) \cdot T(-x_1, -y_1, -z_1) = R \cdot T \qquad (5.59)$$

is the required transformation, with $R = R_z(\alpha) \cdot R_x(\phi) \cdot R_y(\theta - 90)$. We leave it to you to apply this transformation to P_1, P_2, and P_3, to verify that P_1 is transformed to the origin, P_2 is transformed to the positive *z* axis, and P_3 is transformed to the positive *y* half of the (*y*, *z*) plane.

The second way to obtain the matrix R is to use the properties of orthogonal matrices discussed in Section 5.3. Recall that the unit row vectors of R rotate into the principal axes. Replacing the second subscripts of Eq. (5.43) with *x*, *y*, and *z* for notational convenience

$$R = \begin{bmatrix} r_{1_x} & r_{2_x} & r_{3_x} \\ r_{1_y} & r_{2_y} & r_{3_y} \\ r_{1_z} & r_{2_z} & r_{3_z} \end{bmatrix}. \qquad (5.60)$$

Because R_z is the unit vector along P_1P_2 that will rotate into the positive *z* axis,

$$R_z = [r_{1_z} \ r_{2_z} \ r_{3_z}]^T = \frac{P_1P_2}{|P_1P_2|}. \qquad (5.61)$$

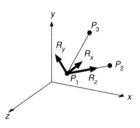

Figure 5.22
The unit vectors R_x, R_y, and R_z, which are transformed into the principal axes.

In addition, the R_x unit vector is perpendicular to the plane of P_1, P_2, and P_3 and will rotate into the positive *x* axis, so that R_x must be the normalized cross-product of two vectors in the plane:

$$R_x = [r_{1_x} \ r_{2_x} \ r_{3_x}]^T = \frac{P_1P_3 \times P_1P_2}{|P_1P_3 \times P_1P_2|}. \qquad (5.62)$$

Finally,

$$R_y = [r_{1_y} \ r_{2_y} \ r_{3_y}]^T = R_z \times R_x \qquad (5.63)$$

will rotate into the positive *y* axis. The composite matrix is given by

$$\begin{bmatrix} r_{1x} & r_{2_x} & r_{3_x} & 0 \\ r_{1y} & r_{2_y} & r_{3_y} & 0 \\ r_{1z} & r_{2_z} & r_{3_z} & 0 \\ 0 & 0 & 0 & 1 \end{bmatrix} \cdot T(-x_1, -y_1, -z_1) = R \cdot T, \qquad (5.64)$$

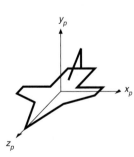

Figure 5.23
An airplane in the (x_p, y_p, z_p) coordinate system.

where R and T are as in Eq. (5.59). Figure 5.22 shows the individual vectors R_x, R_y, and R_z.

Now consider another example. Figure 5.23 shows an airplane defined in the x_p, y_p, z_p coordinate system and centered at the origin. We want to transform the airplane so that it heads in the direction given by the vector *DOF* (direction of flight), is centered at *P*, and is not banked, as shown in Fig. 5.24. The transformation to do this reorientation consists of a rotation to head the airplane in the proper direction, followed by a translation from the origin to *P*. To find the rotation matrix, we just determine in what direction each of the x_p, y_p, and z_p axes is

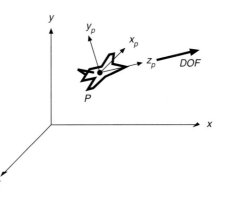

Figure 5.24 The airplane of Fig. 5.23 positioned at point P, and headed in direction DOF.

heading in Fig. 5.24, make sure the directions are normalized, and use these directions as column vectors in a rotation matrix.

The z_p axis must be transformed to the DOF direction, and the x_p axis must be transformed into a horizontal vector perpendicular to DOF—that is, in the direction of $y \times DOF$, the cross-product of y and DOF. The y_p direction is given by $z_p \times x_p = DOF \times (y \times DOF)$, the cross-product of z_p and x_p; hence, the three columns of the rotation matrix are the normalized vectors $|y \times DOF|$, $|DOF \times (y \times DOF)|$, and $|DOF|$:

$$
R = \begin{bmatrix} & & & 0 \\ |y \times DOF| & |DOF \times (y \times DOF)| & |DOF| & 0 \\ & & & 0 \\ 0 & 0 & 0 & 1 \end{bmatrix}. \quad (5.65)
$$

The situation if DOF is in the direction of the y axis is degenerate, because there is an infinite set of possible vectors for the horizontal vector. This degeneracy is reflected in the algebra, because the cross-products $y \times DOF$ and $DOF \times (y \times DOF)$ are zero. In this special case, R is not a rotation matrix.

5.9 TRANSFORMATIONS AS A CHANGE IN COORDINATE SYSTEM

We have been discussing transforming a set of points belonging to an object into another set of points, when both sets are in the same coordinate system. With this approach, the coordinate system stays unaltered and the object is transformed with respect to the origin of the coordinate system. An alternative but equivalent way of thinking about a transformation is as a change of coordinate systems. This view is useful when multiple objects, each defined in its own local coordinate system, are combined and we wish to express these objects' coordinates in a single, global coordinate system. We shall encounter this situation in Chapter 7.

Let us define $M_{i \leftarrow j}$ as the transformation that converts the representation of a point in coordinate system j into its representation in coordinate system i.

We define $P^{(i)}$ as the representation of a point in coordinate system i, $P^{(j)}$ as the representation of the point in system j, and $P^{(k)}$ as the representation of the point in coordinate system k; then,

$$P^{(i)} = M_{i \leftarrow j} \cdot P^{(j)} \text{ and } P^{(j)} = M_{j \leftarrow k} \cdot P^{(k)}. \tag{5.66}$$

Substituting, we obtain

$$P^{(i)} = M_{i \leftarrow j} \cdot P^{(j)} = M_{i \leftarrow j} \cdot M_{j \leftarrow k} \cdot P^{(k)} = M_{i \leftarrow k} \cdot P^{(k)}, \tag{5.67}$$

so

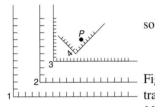

$$M_{i \leftarrow k} = M_{i \leftarrow j} \cdot M_{j \leftarrow k}. \tag{5.68}$$

Figure 5.25 shows four different coordinate systems. We see by inspection that the transformation from coordinate system 2 to 1 is $M_{1 \leftarrow 2} = T(4, 2)$. Similarly, $M_{2 \leftarrow 3} = T(2, 3) \cdot S(0.5, 0.5)$ and $M_{3 \leftarrow 4} = T(6.7, 1.8) \cdot R(45°)$. Then, $M_{1 \leftarrow 3} = M_{1 \leftarrow 2} \cdot M_{2 \leftarrow 3} = T(4, 2) \cdot T(2, 3) \cdot S(0.5, 0.5)$. The figure also shows a point that is $P^{(1)} = (10, 8)$, $P^{(2)} = (6, 6)$, $P^{(3)} = (8, 6)$, and $P^{(4)} = (4, 2)$ in coordinate systems 1 through 4, respectively. It is easy to verify that $P^{(i)} = M_{i \leftarrow j} \cdot P^{(j)}$ for $1 \le i, j \le 4$.

We also notice that $M_{i \leftarrow j} = M_{j \leftarrow i}^{-1}$. Thus, $M_{2 \leftarrow 1} = M_{1 \leftarrow 2}^{-1} = T(-4, -2)$. Because $M_{1 \leftarrow 3} = M_{1 \leftarrow 2} \cdot M_{2 \leftarrow 3}, M_{1 \leftarrow 3}^{-1} = M_{2 \leftarrow 3}^{-1} \cdot M_{1 \leftarrow 2}^{-1} = M_{3 \leftarrow 2} \cdot M_{3 \leftarrow 1}$.

In Section 5.7, we discussed left- and right-handed coordinate systems. The matrix that converts from points represented in one to points represented in the other is its own inverse, and is

$$M_{R \leftarrow L} = M_{L \leftarrow R} = \begin{bmatrix} 1 & 0 & 0 & 0 \\ 0 & 1 & 0 & 0 \\ 0 & 0 & -1 & 0 \\ 0 & 0 & 0 & 1 \end{bmatrix}. \tag{5.69}$$

The approach used in previous sections—defining all objects in the world-coordinate system, then transforming them to the desired place—implies the somewhat unrealistic notion that all objects are initially defined on top of one another in the same world system. It is more natural to think of each object as being defined in its own coordinate system and then being scaled, rotated, and translated by redefinition of its coordinates in the new world-coordinate system. In this second point of view, we think naturally of separate pieces of paper, each with an object on it, being shrunk or stretched, rotated, or placed on the world-coordinate plane. We can also, of course, imagine that the plane is being shrunk or stretched, tilted, or slid relative to each piece of paper. Mathematically, all these views are identical.

Consider the simple case of translating the set of points that define the house shown in Fig. 5.10 to the origin. This transformation is $T(-x_1, -y_1)$. Labeling the two coordinate systems as in Fig. 5.26, we can see that the transformation that maps coordinate system 1 into 2—that is, $M_{2 \leftarrow 1}$—is $T(x_1, y_1)$, which is just

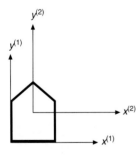

Figure 5.25
The point P and the coordinate systems 1, 2, 3, and 4.

Figure 5.26
The house and the two coordinate systems. Coordinates of points on the house can be represented in either coordinate system.

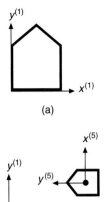

(a)

(b)

Figure 5.27
(a) The original house in its coordinate system. (b) The transformed house in its coordinate system, with respect to the original coordinate system.

$T(-x_1, -y_1)^{-1}$. Indeed, the general rule is that the transformation that transforms a set of points in a single coordinate system is just the inverse of the corresponding transformation to change the coordinate system in which a point is represented. This relation can be seen in Fig. 5.27, which is derived directly from Fig. 5.11. The transformation for the points represented in a single coordinate system is just

$$T(x_2, y_2) \cdot R(\theta) \cdot S(s_x, s_y) \cdot T(-x_1, -y_1). \tag{5.32}$$

In Fig. 5.27, the coordinate-system transformation is just

$$M_{5 \leftarrow 1} = M_{5 \leftarrow 4}\, M_{4 \leftarrow 3}\, M_{3 \leftarrow 2}\, M_{2 \leftarrow 1}$$

$$= (T(x_2, y_2) \cdot R(\theta) \cdot S(s_x, s_y) \cdot T(-x_1, -y_1))^{-1}$$

$$= T(x_1, y_1) \cdot S(s_x^{-1}, s_y^{-1}) \cdot R(-\theta) \cdot T(-x_2, -y_2), \tag{5.70}$$

so

$$P^{(5)} = M_{5 \leftarrow 1}P^{(1)} = T(x_1, y_1) \cdot S(s_x^{-1}, s_y^{-1}) \cdot R(-\theta) \cdot T(-x_2, -y_2) \cdot P^{(1)}. \tag{5.71}$$

An important question related to changing coordinate systems is how we change transformations. Suppose $Q^{(j)}$ is a transformation in coordinate system j. It might, for example, be one of the composite transformations derived in previous sections. Suppose we wanted to find the transformation $Q^{(i)}$ in coordinate system i that could be applied to points $P^{(i)}$ in system i and produce exactly the same results as though $Q^{(j)}$ were applied to the corresponding points $P^{(j)}$ in system j. This equality is represented by $Q^{(i)} \cdot P^{(i)} = M_{i \leftarrow j} \cdot Q^{(j)} \cdot P^{(j)}$. Substituting $P^{(i)} = M_{i \leftarrow j} \cdot P^{(j)}$, this expression becomes $Q^{(i)} \cdot M_{i \leftarrow j} \cdot P^{(j)} = M_{i \leftarrow j} \cdot Q^{(j)} \cdot P^{(j)}$. Simplifying, we have $Q^{(i)} = M_{i \leftarrow j} \cdot Q^{(j)} \cdot M^{-1}_{i \leftarrow j}$.

The change-of-coordinate-system point of view is useful when additional information for subobjects is specified in the subobjects' own local coordinate systems. For example, if the front wheel of the tricycle in Fig. 5.28 is made to rotate about its z_{wh} coordinate, all wheels must be rotated appropriately, and we need to know how the tricycle as a whole moves in the world-coordinate system. This problem is complex because several successive changes of coordinate systems occur. First, the tricycle and front-wheel coordinate systems have initial positions in the world-coordinate system. As the bike moves forward, the front wheel rotates about the z axis of the wheel-coordinate system, and simultaneously the wheel- and tricycle-coordinate systems move relative to the world-coordinate system. The wheel- and tricycle-coordinate systems are related to the world-coordinate system by time-varying translations in x and z plus a rotation about y. The tricycle- and wheel-coordinate systems are related to each other by a time-varying rotation about y as the handlebars are turned. (The tricycle-coordinate system is fixed to the frame, rather than to the handlebars.)

To make the problem a bit easier, we assume that the wheel and tricycle axes are parallel to the world-coordinate axes, and that the wheel moves in a straight line parallel to the world-coordinate x axis. As the wheel rotates by an angle α, a point P on the wheel rotates through the distance αr, where r is the radius of the

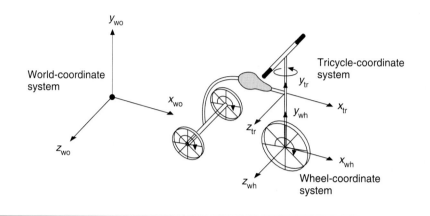

Figure 5.28   A stylized tricycle with three coordinate systems.

wheel. Since the wheel is on the ground, the tricycle moves forward αr units. Therefore, the rim point P on the wheel moves and rotates with respect to the initial wheel-coordinate system with a net effect of translation by αr and rotation by α. Its new coordinates P' in the original wheel-coordinate system are thus

$$P'^{(\text{wh})} = T(\alpha r, 0, 0) \cdot R_z(\alpha) \cdot P^{(\text{wh})}, \tag{5.72}$$

and its coordinates in the new (translated) wheel-coordinate system are given by just the rotation

$$P'^{(\text{wh}')} = R_z(\alpha) \cdot P^{(\text{wh})}. \tag{5.73}$$

To find the points $P^{(\text{wo})}$ and $P'^{(\text{wo})}$ in the world-coordinate system, we transform from the wheel to the world-coordinate system:

$$P^{(\text{wo})} = M_{\text{wo}\leftarrow\text{wh}} \cdot P^{(\text{wh})} = M_{\text{wo}\leftarrow\text{tr}} \cdot M_{\text{tr}\leftarrow\text{wh}} \cdot P^{(\text{wh})}. \tag{5.74}$$

$M_{\text{wo}\leftarrow\text{tr}}$ and $M_{\text{tr}\leftarrow\text{wh}}$ are translations given by the initial positions of the tricycle and wheel.

$P'^{(\text{wo})}$ is computed with Eqs. (5.72) and (5.74):

$$P'^{(\text{wo})} = M_{\text{wo}\leftarrow\text{wh}} \cdot P'^{(\text{wh})} = M_{\text{wo}\leftarrow\text{wh}} \cdot T(\alpha r, 0, 0) \cdot R_z(\alpha) \cdot P^{(\text{wh})}. \tag{5.75}$$

Alternatively, we recognize that $M_{\text{wo}\leftarrow\text{wh}}$ has been changed to $M_{\text{wo}\leftarrow\text{wh}'}$ by the translation of the wheel-coordinate system. We get the same result as Eq. (5.75), but in a different way:

$$P'^{(\text{wo})} = M_{\text{wo}\leftarrow\text{wh}'} \cdot P'^{(\text{wh}')} = (M_{\text{wo}\leftarrow\text{wh}} \cdot M_{\text{wh}\leftarrow\text{wh}'}) \cdot (R_z(\alpha) \cdot P^{(\text{wh})}). \tag{5.76}$$

In general, then, we derive the new $M_{wo \leftarrow wh'}$ and $M_{tr' \leftarrow wh'}$ from their previous values by applying the appropriate transformations from the equations of motion of the tricycle parts. We then apply these updated transformations to updated points in local coordinate systems, and derive the equivalent points in world-coordinate systems.

Exercises

5.1 Prove that we can transform a line by transforming its endpoints and then constructing a new line between the transformed endpoints.

5.2 Prove that two successive 2D rotations are additive: $R(\theta_1) \cdot R(\theta_2) = R(\theta_1 + \theta_2)$.

5.3 Prove that 2D rotation and scaling commute if $s_x = s_y$ or if $\theta = n\pi$ for integral n, and that otherwise they do not.

5.4 Apply the transformations developed in Section 5.8 to the points P_1, P_2, and P_3 to verify that these points transform as intended.

5.5 Rework Section 5.8, assuming that $|P_1P_2| = 1$, $|P_1P_3| = 1$ and that direction cosines of P_1P_2 and P_1P_3 are given (*direction cosines* of a line are the cosines of the angles between the line and the x, y, and z axes). For a line from the origin to (x, y, z), the direction cosines are $(x/d, y/d, z/d)$, where d is the length of the line.

5.6 Show that Eqs. (5.59) and (5.64) are equivalent.

5.7 Given a unit cube with one corner at $(0, 0, 0)$ and the opposite corner at $(1, 1, 1)$, derive the transformations necessary to rotate the cube by θ degrees about the main diagonal (from $(0, 0, 0)$ to $(1, 1, 1)$) in the counterclockwise direction when we are looking along the diagonal toward the origin.

5.8 Suppose that the base of the window is rotated at an angle θ from the x axis, as in the Core System [GSPC79]. What is the window-to-viewport mapping? Verify your answer by applying the transformation to each corner of the window, to see that these corners are transformed to the appropriate corners of the viewport.

5.9 Consider a line from the origin of a right-handed coordinate system to the point $P(x, y, z)$. Find the transformation matrices needed to rotate the line into the positive z axis in two different ways, and show by algebraic manipulation that, in each case, the point P does go to the z axis. For each method, calculate the sines and cosines of the angles of rotation.

a. Rotate about the y axis into the (y, z) plane, then rotate about the x axis into the z axis.

b. Rotate about the z axis into the (x, z) plane, then rotate about the y axis into the z axis.

5.10 An object is to be scaled by a factor S in the direction whose direction cosines are (α, β, γ). Derive the transformation matrix.

5.11 Find the 4×4 transformation matrix that rotates by an angle θ about an arbitrary direction given by the direction vector $U = (u_x, u_y, u_z)$. Do this exercise by composing the transformation matrix that rotates U into the z axis (call this M) with a rotation by $R_z(\theta)$, then composing this result with M^{-1}. The result should be

$$\begin{bmatrix} u_x^2 + \cos\theta(1 - u_x^2) & u_x u_y(1 - \cos\theta) - u_z \sin\theta & u_z u_x(1 - \cos\theta) + u_y \sin\theta & 0 \\ u_x u_y(1 - \cos\theta) + u_z \sin\theta & u_y^2 + \cos\theta(1 - u_y^2) & u_y u_z(1 - \cos\theta) - u_x \sin\theta & 0 \\ u_z u_x(1 - \cos\theta) - u_y \sin\theta & u_y u_z(1 - \cos\theta) + u_x \sin\theta & u_z^2 + \cos\theta(1 - u_z^2) & 0 \\ 0 & 0 & 0 & 1 \end{bmatrix} \quad (5.77)$$

Verify that, if U is a principal axis, the matrix reduces to R_x, R_y, or R_z. See [FAUX79] for a derivation based on vector operations. Note that negating both U and θ leaves the result unchanged. Explain why this result is true.

6 Viewing in 3D

The 3D viewing process is inherently more complex than is the 2D viewing process. In 2D, we simply specify a window on the 2D world and a viewport on the 2D view surface. Conceptually, objects in the world are clipped against the window and are then transformed into the viewport for display. The extra complexity of 3D viewing is caused in part by the added dimension and in part by the fact that display devices are only 2D. Although 3D viewing may seem overwhelming at first, it is less daunting when viewed as a series of easily understood steps, many of which we have prepared for in earlier chapters. Thus, we begin with a précis of the 3D viewing process to help guide you through this chapter.

6.1 THE SYNTHETIC CAMERA AND STEPS IN 3D VIEWING

A useful metaphor for creating 3D scenes is the notion of a **synthetic camera**, a concept illustrated in Fig. 6.1. We imagine that we can move our camera to any location, orient it in any way we wish, and, with a snap of the shutter, create a 2D image of a 3D object—the speedboat, in this case. At our bidding, the camera can become a motion-picture camera, enabling us to create an animated sequence that shows the object in a variety of orientations and magnifications. The camera, of course, is really just a computer program that produces an image on a display screen, and the object is a 3D dataset comprising a collection of points, lines, and surfaces. Figure 6.1 also shows that the camera and the 3D object each have their own coordinate system: u, v, n for the camera, and x, y, z for the object. We shall

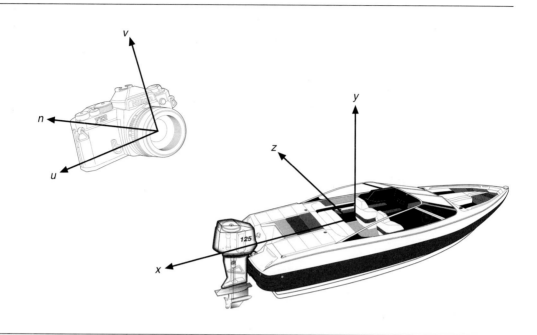

Figure 6.1   A synthetic camera photographing a 3D object.

discuss the significance of these coordinate systems later in this chapter. We note here that they provide an important independence of representation.

While the synthetic camera is a useful concept, there is a bit more to producing an image than just pushing a button. Creation of our "photo" is actually accomplished as a series of steps, which are described now.

■ *Specification of projection type.* We resolve the mismatch between 3D objects and 2D displays by introducing **projections**, which transform 3D objects onto a 2D projection plane. Much of this chapter is devoted to projections: what they are, what their mathematics is, and how they are used in a current graphics subroutine package, PHIGS [ANSI88]. We concentrate on the two most important projections, **perspective** and **parallel orthographic**. The use of projections is also discussed further in Chapter 7.

■ *Specification of viewing parameters.* Once a desired type of projection has been determined, we must specify the conditions under which we want to view the 3D real-world dataset, or the scene to be rendered. Given the world coordinates of the dataset, this information includes the position of the viewer's eye and the location of the viewing plane—the surface where the projection is ultimately displayed. We shall use two coordinate systems—that of the scene and another that we call the **viewing** or **eye coordinate system.** By varying any or all of these parameters, we can achieve any representation of the scene we wish, including viewing its interior, when that makes sense.

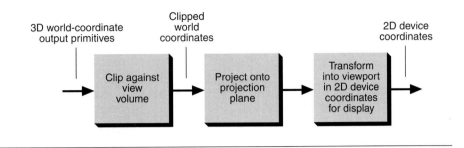

Figure 6.2   Conceptual model of the 3D viewing process.

■ *Clipping in three dimensions.* Just as we must confine the display of a 2D scene to lie within the boundaries of our specified window, so too must we cull out portions of a 3D scene that are not candidates for ultimate display. We may, in fact, want to ignore parts of the scene that are behind us or are too far distant to be clearly visible. This action requires clipping against a view volume— a more complex process than that represented by the algorithms we have studied so far. Because of the wide variability of potential view volumes, we shall invest some effort in defining a canonical **view volume**—one against which we can efficiently apply a standardized clipping algorithm.

■ *Projection and display.* Finally, the contents of the projection of the view volume onto the projection plane, called the **window,** are transformed (mapped) into the viewport for display.

Figure 6.2 shows the major steps in this conceptual model of the 3D viewing process, which is the model presented to the users of numerous 3D graphics subroutine packages. Just as with 2D viewing, a variety of strategies can be used to implement the viewing process. The strategies do not have to be identical to the conceptual model, as long as the results are those defined by the model. A typical implementation strategy for wire-frame line drawings is described in Section 6.6. For graphics systems that perform visible-surface determination and shading, a somewhat different pipeline, discussed in Chapter 14, is used.

6.2 PROJECTIONS

In general, projections transform points in a coordinate system of dimension n into points in a coordinate system of dimension less than n. In fact, computer graphics has long been used for studying n-dimensional objects by projecting them into 2D for viewing [NOLL67]. Here, we shall limit ourselves to the projection from 3D to 2D. The projection of a 3D object is defined by straight projection rays, called **projectors**, emanating from a **center of projection**, passing through each point of the object, and intersecting a **projection plane** to form the projection. In general,

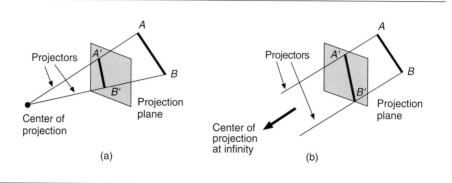

Figure 6.3   Two different projections of the same line. (a) Line *AB* and its perspective projection *A′B′*. (b) Line *AB* and its parallel projection *A′B′*. Projectors *AA′* and *BB′* are parallel.

the center of projection is a finite distance away from the projection plane. For some types of projections, however, it is convenient to think in terms of a center of projection that tends to be infinitely far away; we shall explore this concept further in Section 6.2.1. Figure 6.3 shows two different projections of the same line. Fortunately, the projection of a line is itself a line, so only line endpoints need to be projected.

The class of projections with which we deal here is known as **planar geometric projections,** because the projection is onto a plane rather than onto a curved surface, and uses straight rather than curved projectors. Many cartographic projections are either nonplanar or nongeometric.

Planar geometric projections, hereafter referred to simply as **projections,** can be divided into two basic classes: **perspective** and **parallel.** The distinction lies in the relation of the center of projection to the projection plane. If the distance from the one to the other is finite, then the projection is perspective; as the center of projection moves farther and farther away, the projectors passing through any particular object get closer and closer to being parallel to each other. Figure 6.3 illustrates these two cases. The parallel projection is so named because, with the center of projection infinitely distant, the projectors are parallel. When we define a perspective projection, we explicitly specify its **center of projection**; for a parallel projection, we give its **direction of projection.** The center of projection, being a point, has homogeneous coordinates of the form $(x, y, z, 1)$. Since the direction of projection is a vector (i.e., a difference between points), we can compute it by subtracting two points $d = (x, y, z, 1) - (x', y', z', 1) = (a, b, c, 0)$. Thus, **directions** and **points at infinity** correspond in a natural way. In the limit, a perspective projection whose center of projection tends to a point at infinity becomes a parallel projection.

The visual effect of a perspective projection is similar to that of photographic systems and of the human visual system, and is known as **perspective foreshortening:** The size of the perspective projection of an object varies inversely with the distance of that object from the center of projection. Thus, although the perspective projection of objects tends to look realistic, it is not particularly useful for recording the exact shape and measurements of the objects; distances cannot be taken

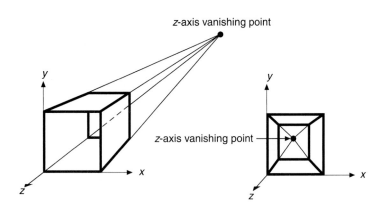

Figure 6.4   One-point perspective projections of a cube onto a plane cutting the z axis, showing vanishing point of lines perpendicular to projection plane.

from the projection, angles are preserved on only those faces of the object parallel to the projection plane, and parallel lines do not in general project as parallel lines.

The parallel projection is a less realistic view because perspective foreshortening is lacking, although there can be different constant foreshortenings along each axis. The projection can be used for exact measurements, and parallel lines do remain parallel. As in the perspective projection, angles are preserved only on faces of the object parallel to the projection plane.

The different types of perspective and parallel projections are discussed and illustrated at length in the comprehensive paper by Carlbom and Paciorek [CARL78]. In Sections 6.2.1 and 6.2.2, we summarize the basic definitions and characteristics of the more commonly used projections; we then move on, in Section 6.3, to understand how the projections are specified to PHIGS.

6.2.1 Perspective Projections

The perspective projections of any set of parallel lines that are not parallel to the projection plane converge to a **vanishing point**. In 3D, the parallel lines meet only at infinity, so the vanishing point can be thought of as the projection of a point at infinity. There is, of course, an infinity of vanishing points, one for each of the infinity of directions in which a line can be oriented.

If the set of lines is parallel to one of the three principal axes, the vanishing point is called an **axis vanishing point**. There are at most three such points, corresponding to the number of principal axes cut by the projection plane. For example, if the projection plane cuts only the z axis (and is therefore normal to it), only the z axis has a principal vanishing point, because lines parallel to either the y or x axes are also parallel to the projection plane and have no vanishing point.

Perspective projections are categorized by their number of principal vanishing points and therefore by the number of axes the projection plane cuts. Figure 6.4

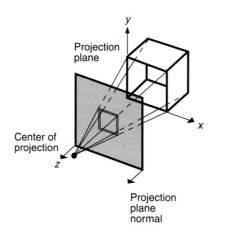

Figure 6.5   Construction of one-point perspective projection of cube onto plane cutting the *z* axis. The projection-plane normal is parallel to *z* axis. (Adapted from [CARL78], Association for Computing Machinery, Inc.; used by permission.)

shows two different one-point perspective projections of a cube. It is clear that they are one-point projections because lines parallel to the *x* and *y* axes do not converge; only lines parallel to the *z* axis do so. Figure 6.5 shows the construction of a one-point perspective with some of the projectors and with the projection plane cutting only the *z* axis.

Figure 6.6 shows the construction of a two-point perspective. Notice that lines parallel to the *y* axis do not converge in the projection. Two-point perspective is commonly used in architectural, engineering, industrial design, and advertising drawings. Three-point perspectives are used less frequently, since they add little realism beyond that afforded by the two-point perspective.

6.2.2 Parallel Projections

Parallel projections are categorized into two types, depending on the relation between the direction of projection and the normal to the projection plane. In **orthographic** parallel projections, these directions are the same (or are the reverse of each other), so the direction of projection is normal to the projection plane. For the **oblique** parallel projection, they are not.

The most common types of orthographic projections are the **front-elevation**, **top-elevation** or **plan-elevation**, and **side-elevation** projections. In all these, the projection plane is perpendicular to a principal axis, which is therefore the direction of projection. Figure 6.7 shows the construction of these three projections; they are often used in engineering drawings to depict machine parts, assemblies, and buildings, because distances and angles can be measured from them. Since each projection depicts only one face of an object, however, the 3D nature of the

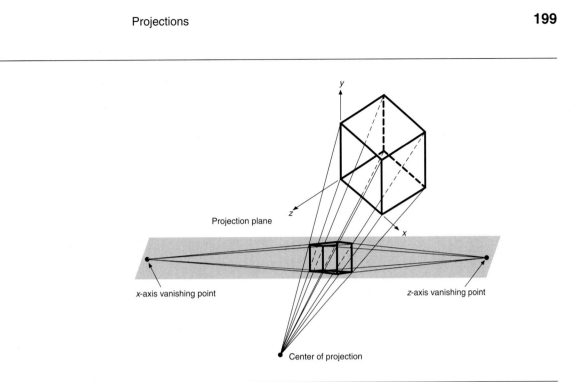

Figure 6.6 Two-point perspective projection of a cube. The projection plane cuts the *x* and *z* axes.

projected object can be difficult to deduce, even if several projections of the same object are studied simultaneously.

Axonometric orthographic projections use projection planes that are not normal to a principal axis and therefore show several faces of an object at once.

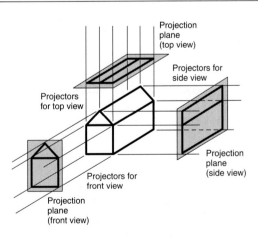

Figure 6.7 Construction of three orthographic projections.

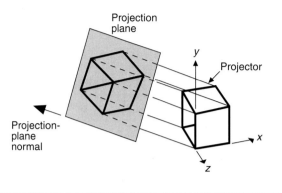

Figure 6.8   Construction of an isometric projection of a unit cube. (Adapted from [CARL78], Association for Computing Machinery, Inc.; used by permission.)

They resemble the perspective projection in this way, but differ in that the foreshortening is uniform, rather than being related to the distance from the center of projection. Parallelism of lines is preserved, but angles are not, and distances can be measured along each principal axis (in general, with different scale factors).

The **isometric projection** is a commonly used axonometric projection. The projection-plane normal (and therefore the direction of projection) makes equal angles with each principal axis. If the projection-plane normal is (d_x, d_y, d_z), then we require that $|d_x| = |d_y| = |d_z|$ or $\pm d_x = \pm d_y = \pm d_z$. There are just eight directions (one in each octant) that satisfy this condition. Figure 6.8 shows the construction of an isometric projection along one such direction, $(1, -1, -1)$.

The isometric projection has the useful property that all three principal axes are equally foreshortened, allowing measurements along the axes to be made to the same scale (hence the name: *iso* for equal, *metric* for measure). In addition, the projections of the principal axes make equal angles of 120° with one another.

Oblique projections, the second class of parallel projections, differ from orthographic projections in that the projection-plane normal and the direction of projection differ. Oblique projections combine properties of the front, top, and side orthographic projections with those of the axonometric projection: the projection plane is normal to a principal axis, so the projection of the face of the object parallel to this plane allows measurement of angles and distances. Other faces of the object project also, allowing distances along principal axes, but not angles, to be measured. Oblique projections are widely, although not exclusively, used in this text because of these properties and because they are easy to draw. Figure 6.9 shows the construction of an oblique projection. Notice that the projection-plane normal and the direction of projection are not the same. Several types of oblique projections are described in [FOLE90].

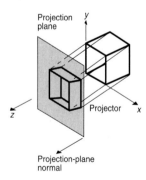

Figure 6.9

Construction of oblique projection. (Adapted from [CARL78], Association for Computing Machinery, Inc.; used by permission.)

Figure 6.10 shows the logical relationships among the various types of projections. The common thread uniting all the projections is that they involve a projection plane and either a center of projection for the perspective projection, or a

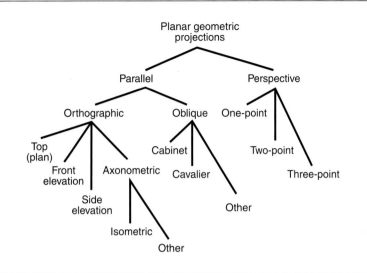

Figure 6.10   The subclasses of planar geometric projections. **Plan view** is another term for a top view. **Front** and **side** are often used without the term **elevation**.

direction of projection for the parallel projection. We can unify the parallel and perspective cases further by thinking of the center of projection as defined by the direction to the center of projection from some reference point, and the distance to the reference point. When this distance increases to infinity, the projection becomes a parallel projection. Hence, we can also say that the common thread uniting these projections is that they involve a projection plane, a direction to the center of projection, and a distance to the center of projection. In Section 6.3, we consider how to integrate some of these types of projections into the 3D viewing process.

6.3 SPECIFICATION OF AN ARBITRARY 3D VIEW

As suggested by Fig. 6.2, 3D viewing involves not just a projection, but also a view volume against which the 3D world is clipped. The projection and view volume together provide all the information that we need to clip and project into 2D space. Then, the 2D transformation into physical device coordinates is straightforward. We now build on the concepts of planar-geometric projection introduced in Section 6.2 to show how to specify a view volume. The viewing approach and terminology presented here is that used in PHIGS.

The projection plane, henceforth called the **view plane** to be consistent with the graphics literature, is defined by a point on the plane called the **view reference point (VRP)** and a normal to the plane called the **view-plane normal (VPN)**. The

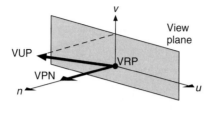

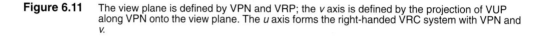

Figure 6.11   The view plane is defined by VPN and VRP; the *v* axis is defined by the projection of VUP along VPN onto the view plane. The *u* axis forms the right-handed VRC system with VPN and *v*.

view plane may be anywhere with respect to the world objects to be projected: It may be in front of, cut through, or be behind the objects.

Given the view plane, a window on the view plane is needed. The window's role is similar to that of a 2D window: Its contents are mapped into the viewport, and any part of the 3D world that projects onto the view plane outside of the window is not displayed. We shall see that the window also plays an important role in defining the view volume.

To define a window on the view plane, we need a means of specifying minimum and maximum window coordinates and the two orthogonal axes in the view plane along which to measure these coordinates. These axes are part of the 3D **viewing-reference coordinate (VRC)** system. The origin of the VRC system is the VRP. One axis of the VRC is VPN; this axis is called the *n* axis. A second axis of the VRC is found from the **view-up vector (VUP)**, which determines the *v*-axis direction on the view plane. The *v* axis is defined such that the projection of VUP parallel to VPN onto the view plane is coincident with the *v* axis. The *u*-axis direction is defined such that *u*, *v*, and *n* form a right-handed coordinate system, as in Fig. 6.11. The VRP and the two direction vectors VPN and VUP are specified in the right-handed world-coordinate system. (Some graphics packages use the *y* axis as VUP, but this convention is too restrictive and fails if VPN is parallel to the *y* axis, in which case VUP is undefined.)

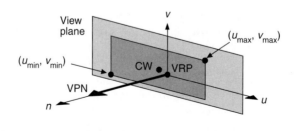

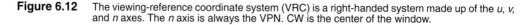

Figure 6.12   The viewing-reference coordinate system (VRC) is a right-handed system made up of the *u*, *v*, and *n* axes. The *n* axis is always the VPN. CW is the center of the window.

With the VRC system defined, the window's minimum and maximum u and v coordinates can be defined, as in Fig. 6.12. This figure illustrates that the window does not have to be symmetrical about the VRP, and explicitly shows the center of the window, CW.

The center of projection and direction of projection (DOP) are defined by a **projection reference point (PRP)** and an indicator of the projection type. If the projection type is perspective, then PRP is the center of projection. If the projection type is parallel, then the DOP is from the PRP to CW. The CW is in general not the VRP, which does not need even to be within the window bounds.

The PRP is specified in the VRC system, not in the world-coordinate system; thus, the position of the PRP relative to the VRP does not change as VUP or VRP is moved. The advantage of this scheme is that the programmer can specify the direction of projection required and then change VPN and VUP (hence changing VRC), without having to recalculate the PRP needed to maintain the desired projection. On the other hand, moving the PRP about to get different views of an object may be more difficult.

The **view volume** bounds that portion of the world that is to be clipped out and projected onto the view plane. For a perspective projection, the view volume is the semi-infinite pyramid with apex at the PRP and edges passing through the corners of the window. Figure 6.13 shows a perspective-projection view volume.

Positions behind the center of projection are not included in the view volume and thus are not projected. In reality, of course, our eyes see an irregularly shaped conelike view volume. However, a pyramidal view volume is mathematically more tractable, and is consistent with the concept of a rectangular viewport.

For parallel projections, the view volume is an infinite parallelepiped with sides parallel to the direction of projection, which is the direction from the PRP to the center of the window. Figure 6.14 shows a parallel-projection view volume and its relation to the view plane, window, and PRP.

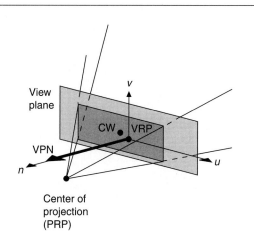

Figure 6.13   Semi-infinite pyramid view volume for perspective projection. CW is the center of the window.

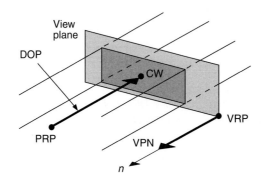

Figure 6.14   Infinite parallelepiped view volume of parallel orthographic projection. The VPN and direction of projection (DOP) are parallel. DOP is the vector from PRP to CW, and is parallel to the VPN.

At times, we might want the view volume to be finite, in order to limit the number of output primitives projected onto the view plane. Figures 6.15 and 6.16 show how the view volume is made finite with a **front clipping plane** and **back clipping plane**. These planes, sometimes called the **hither** and **yon planes,** are parallel to the view plane; their normal is the VPN. The planes are specified by the signed quantities **front distance** (F) and **back distance** (B) relative to the VRP and along the VPN, with positive distances in the direction of the VPN. For the view volume to be nonempty, the front distance must be algebraically greater than the back distance.

Limiting the view volume in this way can be useful to eliminate extraneous objects and to allow the user to concentrate on a particular portion of the world. Dynamic modification of either the front or rear distances can give the viewer a

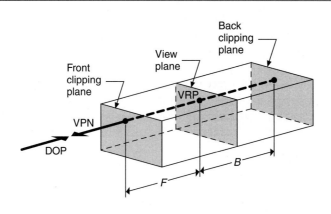

Figure 6.15   Truncated view volume for an orthographic parallel projection. DOP is the direction of projection.

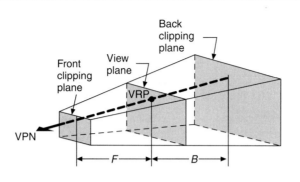

Figure 6.16   Truncated view volume for a perspective projection.

good sense of the spatial relationships between different parts of the object as these parts appear and disappear from view (see Chapter 12). For perspective projections there is an additional motivation. An object very distant from the center of projection projects onto the view surface as a "blob" of no distinguishable form. In displaying such an object on a plotter, the pen can wear through the paper; on a vector display, the CRT phosphor can be burned by the electron beam; and on a vector film recorder, the high concentration of light causes a fuzzy white area to appear. Also, an object very near the center of projection may extend across the window like so many disconnected pick-up sticks, with no discernible structure. Specifying the view volume appropriately can eliminate such problems.

How are the contents of the view volume mapped onto the display surface? First, consider the unit cube extending from 0 to 1 in each of the three dimensions of **normalized projection coordinates (NPC)**. The view volume is transformed into the rectangular solid of NPC, which extends from x_{min} to x_{max} along the x axis, from y_{min} to y_{max} along the y axis, and from z_{min} to z_{max} along the z axis. The front clipping plane becomes the z_{max} plane, and the back clipping plane becomes the z_{min} plane. Similarly, the u_{min} side of the view volume becomes the x_{min} plane, and the u_{max} side becomes the x_{max} plane. Finally, the v_{min} side of the view volume becomes the y_{min} plane, and the v_{max} side becomes the y_{max} plane. This rectangular solid portion of NPC, called a **3D viewport**, is within the unit cube.

The $z = 1$ face of this unit cube, in turn, is mapped into the largest square that can be inscribed on the display. To create a wire-frame display of the contents of the 3D viewport (which are the contents of the view volume), the z-component of each output primitive is simply discarded, and the output primitive is displayed. We shall see in Chapter 13 that hidden-surface removal simply uses the z-component to determine which output primitives are closest to the viewer and hence are visible.

PHIGS uses two 4×4 matrices, the view orientation matrix and the view mapping matrix, to represent the complete set of viewing specifications. The VRP, VPN, and VUP are combined to form the **view orientation matrix**, which transforms positions represented in world coordinates into positions represented in

VRC. This transformation takes the u, v, and n axes into the x, y, and z axes, respectively.

The view-volume specifications, given by PRP, u_{min}, u_{max}, v_{min}, v_{max}, F, and B, along with the 3D viewport specification, given by x_{min}, x_{max}, y_{min}, y_{max}, z_{min}, and z_{max}, are combined to form the **view mapping matrix**, which transforms points in VRC to points in normalized projection coordinates. The subroutine calls that form the view orientation matrix and view mapping matrix are discussed in Section 7.3.4.

In Section 6.4, we see how to obtain various views using the concepts introduced in this section. In Section 6.5, the basic mathematics of planar geometric projections is introduced, whereas in Section 6.6, the mathematics and algorithms needed for the entire viewing operation are developed.

6.4 EXAMPLES OF 3D VIEWING

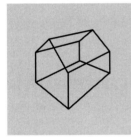

Figure 6.17
Two-point perspective projection of a house.

In this section, we consider how we can apply the basic viewing concepts introduced in Section 6.3 to create a variety of projections, such as that shown in Fig. 6.17. Because the house shown in this figure is used throughout this section, it will be helpful to remember its dimensions and position, which are indicated in Fig. 6.18. For each view discussed, we give a table showing the VRP, VPN, VUP, PRP, window, and projection type (perspective or parallel). The 3D viewport default, which is the unit cube in NPC, is assumed throughout this section. The notation (WC) or (VRC) is added to the table as a reminder of the coordinate system in which the viewing parameter is given. The form of the table is illustrated here for the default viewing specification used by PHIGS. The defaults are shown in Fig. 6.19(a). The view volume corresponding to these defaults is shown in Fig. 6.19(b). If the type of projection is perspective rather than parallel, then the view volume is the pyramid shown in Fig. 6.19(c).

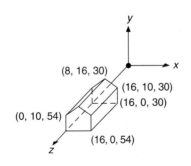

Figure 6.18   This house is used as an example of a world-coordinate dataset throughout this chapter. Its coordinates extend from 30 to 54 in z, from 0 to 16 in x, and from 0 to 16 in y.

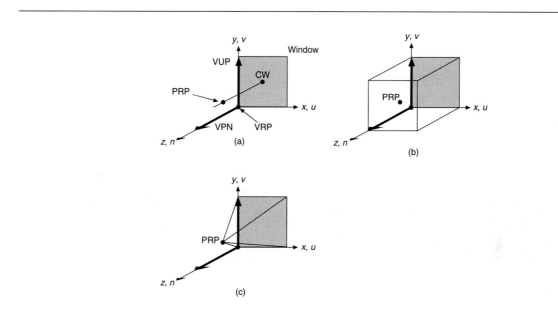

Figure 6.19   The relation between viewing reference and world coordinates. (a) The default viewing specification: VRP is at the origin, VUP is the *y* axis, and VPN is the *z* axis. This arrangement makes the VRC system of *u*, *v*, and *n* coincide with the *x*, *y*, *z* world-coordinate system. The window extends from 0 to 1 along *u* and *v*, and PRP is at (0.5, 0.5, 1.0). (b) Default parallel-projection view volume. (c) View volume if default projection were perspective.

Viewing Parameter	Value	Comments
VRP(WC)	(0, 0, 0)	origin
VPN(WC)	(0, 0, 1)	*z* axis
VUP(WC)	(0, 1, 0)	*y* axis
PRP(VRC)	(0.5, 0.5, 1.0)	
window (VRC)	(0, 1, 0, 1)	
projection type	parallel	

6.4.1 Perspective Projections

To obtain the front one-point perspective view of the house shown in Fig. 6.20 (this figure and all similar figures were made with the SPHIGS program, discussed in Chapter 7), we position the center of projection (which can be thought of as the position of the viewer) at $x = 8$, $y = 6$, and $z = 84$. The x value is selected to be at the horizontal center of the house and the y value is selected to correspond to the approximate eye level of a viewer standing on the (x, z) plane; the z value is arbitrary. In this case, z is removed 30 units from the front of the house ($z = 54$ plane). The window has been made large, to guarantee that the house fits within the view volume. All other viewing parameters have their default values, so the overall set of viewing parameters is as follows:

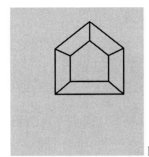

Figure 6.20
One-point perspective projection of the house.

VRP(WC)	(0, 0, 0)
VPN(WC)	(0, 0, 1)
VUP(WC)	(0, 1, 0)
PRP(VRC)	(8, 6, 84)
window(VRC)	(−50, 50, −50, 50)
projection type	perspective

Although the image in Fig. 6.20 is indeed a perspective projection of the house, it is very small and is not centered on the view surface. We would prefer a more centered projection of the house that more nearly spans the entire view surface, as in Fig. 6.21. We can produce this effect more easily if the view plane and the front plane of the house coincide. Now, because the front of the house extends from 0 to 16 in both x and y, a window extending from −1 to 17 in x and y produces reasonable results.

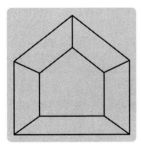

Figure 6.21
Centered perspective projection of a house.

We place the view plane on the front face of the house by placing the VRP anywhere in the $z = 54$ plane; (0, 0, 54), the lower-left front corner of the house, is fine. For the center of projection to be the same as in Fig. 6.20, the PRP, which is in the VRC system, needs to be at (8, 6, 30). Figure 6.22 shows this new arrangement of the VRC, VRP, and PRP, which corresponds to the following set of viewing parameters:

VRP(WC)	(0, 0, 54)
VPN(WC)	(0, 0, 1)
VUP(WC)	(0, 1, 0)
PRP(VRC)	(8, 6, 30)
window(VRC)	(−1, 17, −1, 17)
projection type	perspective

This same result can be obtained in many other ways. For instance, with the VRP at (8, 6, 54), as in Fig. 6.23, the center of projection, given by the PRP, becomes (0, 0, 30). The window also must be changed, because its definition is based on the VRC system, the origin of which is the VRP. The appropriate window extends from −9 to 9 in u and from −7 to 11 in v. With respect to the house, this is the same window as that used in the previous example, but it is now specified in a different VRC system. Because the view-up direction is the y axis, the u axis and x axis are parallel, as are the v and y axes. In summary, the following viewing parameters, shown in Fig. 6.23, also produce Fig. 6.21:

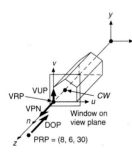

Figure 6.22
The viewing situation for Fig. 6.21.

VRP(WC)	(8, 6, 54)
VPN(WC)	(0, 0, 1)
VUP(WC)	(0, 1, 0)
PRP(VRC)	(0, 0, 30)
window(VRC)	(−9, 9, −7, 11)
projection type	perspective

Next, let us try to obtain the two-point perspective projection shown in Fig. 6.17. The center of projection is analogous to the position of a camera that takes

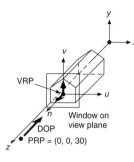

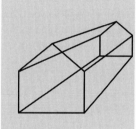

Figure 6.23
An alternative viewing
situation for Fig. 6.21.

snapshots of world-coordinate objects. With this analogy in mind, the center of projection in Fig. 6.17 seems to be somewhat above and to the right of the house, as viewed from the positive z axis. The exact center of projection is (36, 25, 74). Now, if the corner of the house at (16, 0, 54) is chosen as the VRP, then this center of projection is at (20, 25, 20) relative to it. With the view plane coincident with the front of the house (the $z = 54$ plane), a window ranging from −20 to 20 in u and from −5 to 35 in v is certainly large enough to contain the projection. Hence, we can specify the view of Fig. 6.24 with the viewing parameters:

VRP(WC)	(16, 0, 54)
VPN(WC)	(0, 0, 1)
VUP(WC)	(0, 1, 0)
PRP(VRC)	(20, 25, 20)
window(VRC)	(−20, 20, −5, 35)
projection type	perspective

This view is similar to, but clearly is not the same as, that in Fig. 6.17. One difference is that Fig. 6.17 is a two-point perspective projection, whereas Fig. 6.24 is a one-point perspective. It is apparent that simply moving the center of projection is not sufficient to produce Fig. 6.17. In fact, we need to reorient the view plane such that it cuts both the x and z axes, by setting VPN to (1, 0, 1). Thus, the viewing parameters for Fig. 6.17 are as follows:

VRP(WC)	(16, 0, 54)
VPN(WC)	(1, 0, 1)
VUP(WC)	(0, 1, 0)
PRP(VRC)	$(0, 25, 20\sqrt{2})$
window(VRC)	(−20, 20, −5, 35)
projection type	perspective

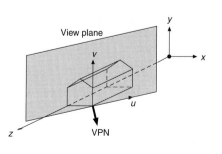

Figure 6.24
Perspective projection of a
house from (36, 25, 74) with
VPN parallel to the z axis.

Figure 6.25 shows the view plane established with this VPN. The $20\sqrt{2}$ n component of the PRP is used so that the center of projection is a distance $20\sqrt{2}$ away from the VRP in the (x, y) plane, as shown in Fig. 6.26.

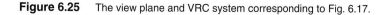

Figure 6.25   The view plane and VRC system corresponding to Fig. 6.17.

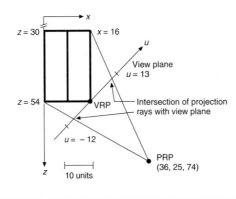

Figure 6.26   Top (plan) view of a house for determining an appropriate window size.

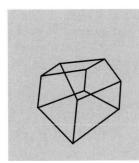

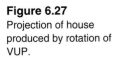
Figure 6.27
Projection of house
produced by rotation of
VUP.

There are two ways to choose a window that completely surrounds the projection, as does the window in Fig. 6.17. We can estimate the size of the projection of the house onto the view plane using a sketch, such as Fig. 6.26, to calculate the intersections of projectors with the view plane. A better alternative, however, is to allow the window bounds to be variables in a program that are determined interactively via a valuator or locator device.

Figure 6.27 is obtained from the same projection as is Fig. 6.17, but the window has a different orientation. In all previous examples, the v axis of the VRC system was parallel to the y axis of the world-coordinate system; thus, the window (two of whose sides are parallel to the v axis) was nicely aligned with the vertical sides of the house. Figure 6.27 has exactly the same viewing parameters as does Fig. 6.17, except that VUP has been rotated away from the y axis by about 10°.

Example 6.1

Problem: Once a VRC system has been established, all subsequent graphics processing is done in that coordinate system, a procedure that we shall explore in more detail in Section 6.6. Prior to those processing steps, we must transform the world coordinates of our dataset to VRC coordinates. This transformation can be done with a single matrix, which accomplishes both rotation and translation. What is the general form of this matrix? What specific values would its elements have for the viewing situation depicted in Fig. 6.17?

Answer: The approach that we shall take was suggested in Section 5.8 and illustrated by Eqs. (5.60) through (5.64). There, an arbitrary set of lines was translated and rotated to assume a new position in the x, y, z coordinate system by composing a translation matrix T and a rotation matrix R to form the matrix M. We want to follow the same procedure, but in this case we want to reorient the u, v, n coordinate system to coincide with the world-coordinate system. The matrix that accomplishes that transformation is the one we are seeking.

First, we must translate the VRC system to the origin. Following Section 5.8, we accomplish this translation by the matrix T, which is simply

$$T = \begin{bmatrix} 1 & 0 & 0 & -\text{VRP}_x \\ 0 & 1 & 0 & -\text{VRP}_y \\ 0 & 0 & 1 & -\text{VRP}_z \\ 0 & 0 & 0 & 1 \end{bmatrix}.$$

The approach taken in Section 5.8, in which we found a rotation matrix (a special orthogonal matrix) by determining where it sent the three principal axes, is what we shall use here. The components of the unit vectors that lie along the u, v, and n directions constitute the elements of such a matrix. Thus, we can find the elements of the rotation matrix, R, by noting that the VPN vector is to be rotated into the z axis, the u axis is perpendicular to VUP and VPN, and the v axis is perpendicular to n and u. Thus,

$$n = \frac{\text{VPN}}{\| \text{VPN} \|}, \quad u = \frac{\text{VUP} \times \text{VPN}}{\| \text{VUP} \times \text{VPN} \|}, \quad v = n \times u,$$

where u, v, and n represent unit vectors. The resulting rotation matrix is

$$R = \begin{bmatrix} u_x & u_y & u_z & 0 \\ v_x & v_y & v_z & 0 \\ n_x & n_y & n_z & 0 \\ 0 & 0 & 0 & 1 \end{bmatrix}.$$

The single matrix that we are seeking is therefore

$$M = R \cdot T = \begin{bmatrix} u_x & u_y & u_z & -(u_x \cdot \text{VRP}_x + u_y \cdot \text{VRP}_y + u_z \cdot \text{VRP}_z) \\ v_x & v_y & v_z & -(v_x \cdot \text{VRP}_x + v_y \cdot \text{VRP}_y + v_z \cdot \text{VRP}_z) \\ n_x & n_y & n_z & -(n_x \cdot \text{VRP}_x + n_y \cdot \text{VRP}_y + n_z \cdot \text{VRP}_z) \\ 0 & 0 & 0 & 1 \end{bmatrix}.$$

Now, for the specific values that apply to Fig. 6.17, we find that $n = [\frac{\sqrt{2}}{2}, 0, \frac{\sqrt{2}}{2}]^T$, $u = [\frac{\sqrt{2}}{2}, 0, -\frac{\sqrt{2}}{2}]^T$, and $v = [0, 1, 0]^T$. Since the components of VRP are 16.0, 0.0, and 54.0, we find that the translation terms in M are 26.8701, 0.0, and -49.4975.

6.4.2 Parallel Projections

We create a front parallel projection of the house (Fig. 6.28) by making the direction of projection parallel to the z axis. Recall that the direction of projection is determined by the PRP and by the center of the window. With the default VRC system and a window of $(-1, 17, -1, 17)$, the center of the window is $(8, 8, 0)$. A PRP of $(8, 8, 100)$ provides a direction of projection parallel to the z axis. Figure 6.29 shows the viewing situation that creates Fig. 6.28. The viewing parameters are as follows:

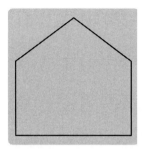

VRP(WC)	(0, 0, 0)
VPN(WC)	(0, 0, 1)
VUP(WC)	(0, 1, 0)
PRP(VRC)	(8, 8, 100)
window(VRC)	(−1, 17,−1, 17)
projection type	parallel

Figure 6.28
Front parallel projection of
the house.

To create a side view we would use a viewing situation with the (*y*, *z*) plane (or any plane parallel to it) as the view plane. We create a top view of the house by using the (*x*, *z*) plane as the view plane and VPN as the *y* axis. The default view-up direction of +*y* must be changed, however. We would use the negative *x* axis instead.

See [FOLE90] for a full treatment of the side- and top-view cases, as well as for examples of oblique projections.

6.4.3 Finite View Volumes

In all the examples so far, the view volume has been assumed to be infinite. The front and back clipping planes, described in Section 6.3, help to determine a **finite view volume**. These planes, both of which are parallel to the view plane, are at distances *F* and *B*, respectively, from the VRP, measured from VRP along VPN. To avoid a negative view volume, we must ensure that *F* is algebraically greater than *B*.

A front perspective view of the house with the rear wall clipped away (Fig. 6.30) results from the following viewing specification, in which *F* and *B* have been added. If a distance is given, then clipping against the corresponding plane is assumed; otherwise, it is not. The viewing specification is as follows:

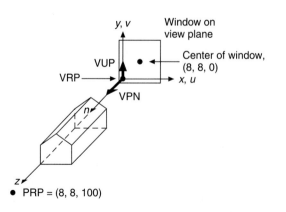

Figure 6.29   Viewing situation that creates Fig. 6.28, a front view of the house. The PRP could be any point with *x* = 8 and *y* = 8.

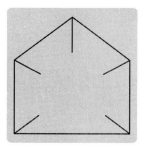

VRP(WC)	$(0, 0, 54)$	lower-left of house
VPN(WC)	$(0, 0, 1)$	z axis
VUP(WC)	$(0, 1, 0)$	y axis
PRP(VRC)	$(8, 6, 30)$	
window(VRC)	$(-1, 17, -1, 17)$	
projection type	perspective	
F(VRC)	$+1$	one unit in front of house, at $z = 54 + 1 = 55$
B(VRC)	-23	one unit from back of house, at $z = 54 - 23 = 31$

Figure 6.30
Perspective projection of
the house with back
clipping plane at $z = 31$.

The viewing situation for this case is the same as that in Fig. 6.22, except for the addition of the clipping planes.

If the front and back clipping planes are moved dynamically, the 3D structure of the object being viewed often can be discerned more readily than it can with a static view.

6.5 THE MATHEMATICS OF PLANAR GEOMETRIC PROJECTIONS

Here we introduce the basic mathematics of planar geometric projections. For simplicity, we start by assuming that, in the perspective projection, the projection plane is normal to the z axis at $z = d$, and that, in the parallel projection, the projection plane is the $z = 0$ plane. Each of the projections can be defined by a 4×4 matrix. This representation is convenient, because the projection matrix can be composed with transformation matrices, allowing two operations (transform, then project) to be represented as a single matrix. In Section 6.6, we discuss arbitrary projection planes.

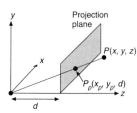

In this section, we derive 4×4 matrices for several projections, beginning with a projection plane parallel to the xy-plane at location $z = d$, and therefore at a distance $|d|$ from the origin, and a point P to be projected onto it. To calculate $P_p = (x_p, y_p, z_p)$, the perspective projection of (x, y, z) onto the projection plane at $z = d$, we use the similar triangles in Fig. 6.31 to write the ratios

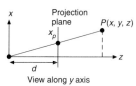

View along y axis

$$\frac{x_p}{d} = \frac{x}{z}; \quad \frac{y_p}{d} = \frac{y}{z}. \tag{6.1}$$

Multiplying each side by d yields

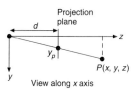

View along x axis

Figure 6.31
Perspective projection.

$$x_p = \frac{d \cdot x}{z} = \frac{x}{z/d}, \quad y_p = \frac{d \cdot y}{z} = \frac{y}{z/d}. \tag{6.2}$$

The distance d is just a scale factor applied to x_p and y_p. The division by z causes the perspective projection of more distant objects to be smaller than that of closer objects. All values of z are allowable except $z = 0$. Points can be behind the center of projection on the negative z axis or between the center of projection and the projection plane.

The transformation of Eq. (6.2) can be expressed as a 4×4 matrix:

$$M_{\text{per}} = \begin{bmatrix} 1 & 0 & 0 & 0 \\ 0 & 1 & 0 & 0 \\ 0 & 0 & 1 & 0 \\ 0 & 0 & 1/d & 0 \end{bmatrix}. \tag{6.3}$$

Multiplying the point $P = [x \ y \ z \ 1]^{\text{T}}$ by the matrix M_{per} yields a general homogeneous point $[X \ Y \ Z \ W]^{\text{T}}$:

$$\begin{bmatrix} X \\ Y \\ Z \\ W \end{bmatrix} = M_{\text{per}} \cdot P = \begin{bmatrix} 1 & 0 & 0 & 0 \\ 0 & 1 & 0 & 0 \\ 0 & 0 & 1 & 0 \\ 0 & 0 & 1/d & 0 \end{bmatrix} \cdot \begin{bmatrix} x \\ y \\ z \\ 1 \end{bmatrix}, \tag{6.4}$$

or

$$[X \quad Y \quad Z \quad W]^{\text{T}} = \left[x \quad y \quad z \quad \frac{z}{d}\right]^{\text{T}}. \tag{6.5}$$

Now, dividing by W (which is z/d) and dropping the fourth coordinate to come back to 3D, we have

$$\left(\frac{X}{W}, \frac{Y}{W}, \frac{Z}{W}\right) = (x_p, y_p, z_p) = \left(\frac{x}{z/d}, \frac{y}{z/d}, d\right); \tag{6.6}$$

these equations are the correct results of Eq. (6.1), plus the transformed z coordinate of d, which is the position of the projection plane along the z axis.

An alternative formulation for the perspective projection places the projection plane at $z = 0$ and the center of projection at $z = -d$, as in Fig. 6.32. Similarity of the triangles now gives

$$\frac{x_p}{d} = \frac{x}{z+d}, \quad \frac{y_p}{d} = \frac{y}{z+d}. \tag{6.7}$$

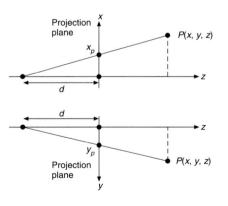

Figure 6.32   Alternative perspective projection.

Multiplying by d, we get

$$x_p = \frac{d \cdot x}{z + d} = \frac{x}{(z/d) + 1}, \qquad y_p = \frac{d \cdot y}{z + d} = \frac{y}{(z/d) + 1}. \qquad (6.8)$$

The matrix is

$$M'_{per} = \begin{bmatrix} 1 & 0 & 0 & 0 \\ 0 & 1 & 0 & 0 \\ 0 & 0 & 0 & 0 \\ 0 & 0 & 1/d & 1 \end{bmatrix}. \qquad (6.9)$$

This formulation allows d, the distance to the center of projection, to tend to infinity.

The orthographic projection onto a projection plane at $z = 0$ is straightforward. The direction of projection is the same as the projection-plane normal—the z axis, in this case. Thus, point P projects as

$$x_p = x, \qquad y_p = y, \qquad z_p = 0. \qquad (6.10)$$

This projection is expressed by the matrix

$$M_{ort} = \begin{bmatrix} 1 & 0 & 0 & 0 \\ 0 & 1 & 0 & 0 \\ 0 & 0 & 0 & 0 \\ 0 & 0 & 0 & 1 \end{bmatrix}. \qquad (6.11)$$

Notice that as d in Eq. (6.9) tends to infinity, Eq. (6.9) becomes Eq. (6.11). This is because the orthographic projection is a special case of the perspective projection.

M_{per} applies only in the special case in which the center of projection is at the origin; M_{ort} applies only when the direction of projection is parallel to the z axis. A more general formulation, cited in [FOLE90], not only removes these restrictions, but also integrates parallel and perspective projections into a single formulation.

In this section, we have seen how to formulate M_{per}, M'_{per}, and M_{ort}, all of which are cases where the projection plane is perpendicular to the z axis. In Section 6.6, we remove this restriction and consider the clipping implied by finite view volumes.

Example 6.2

Problem: The matrix M_{per} defines a one-point perspective projection. Describe a matrix that defines a two-point perspective projection, and its relationship to the matrix M_{per} that we just derived. What is the form of the matrix that defines a three-point perspective?

Answer: As suggested in Section 6.4.1, we need to orient the view plane such that it cuts more than one axis–the z axis, in this case. For example, we shall specify a rotation about the y axis so that the view plane will cut both the x and z axes. We obtain the new matrix by postmultiplying M_{per} with the matrix

$$\begin{bmatrix} \cos\theta & 0 & \sin\theta & 0 \\ 0 & 1 & 0 & 0 \\ -\sin\theta & 0 & \cos\theta & 0 \\ 0 & 0 & 0 & 1 \end{bmatrix},$$

where θ is the angle of rotation about the y axis. The resulting matrix is

$$\begin{bmatrix} \cos\theta & 0 & \sin\theta & 0 \\ 0 & 1 & 0 & 0 \\ -\sin\theta & 0 & \cos\theta & 0 \\ -\sin\theta/d & 0 & \cos\theta/d & 0 \end{bmatrix}.$$

Note the appearance of a non-zero term in the a_{41} position in the composed matrix. This indicates a vanishing point on the x axis. If we were to perform a similar composition with a rotation about the x axis, a nonzero term in the a_{42} position would indicate a vanishing point on the y axis. Combined rotations about the x and y axes would produce a three-point perspective.

6.6 IMPLEMENTATION OF PLANAR GEOMETRIC PROJECTIONS

Given a view volume and a projection, let us consider how the *viewing operation* of clipping and projecting is applied. As suggested by the conceptual model for viewing (Fig. 6.2), we could clip lines against the view volume by calculating their intersections with each of the six planes that define the view volume. Lines remaining after clipping would be projected onto the view plane, by solution of simultaneous equations for the intersection of the projectors with the view plane. The coordinates would then be transformed from 3D world coordinates to 2D device coordinates. However, the large number of calculations required for this process, repeated for many lines, involves considerable computing. Happily, there is a more efficient procedure, based on the divide-and-conquer strategy of breaking down a difficult problem into a series of simpler ones.

Certain view volumes are easier to clip against than is the general one (clipping algorithms are discussed in Section 6.6.3). For instance, it is simple to calculate the intersections of a line with each of the planes of a parallel-projection view volume defined by the six planes

$$x = -1, \quad x = 1, \quad y = -1, \quad y = 1, \quad z = 0, \quad z = -1. \tag{6.12}$$

This situation is also true of the perspective-projection view volume defined by the planes

$$x = z, \quad x = -z, \quad y = z, \quad y = -z, \quad z = -z_{\min}, \quad z = -1. \tag{6.13}$$

These **canonical view volumes** are shown in Fig. 6.33.

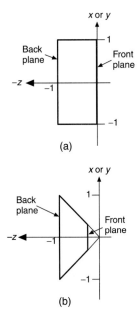

(a)

(b)

Figure 6.33
The two canonical view volumes, for the (a) parallel and (b) perspective projections.

Our strategy is to find the **normalizing transformations** N_{par} and N_{per} that transform an arbitrary parallel- or perspective-projection view volume into the parallel and perspective canonical view volumes, respectively. Then, clipping is performed, followed by projection into 2D, via the matrices in Section 6.5. This strategy risks investing effort in transforming points that are subsequently discarded by the clip operation, but at least the clipping is easy to do.

Figure 6.34 shows the sequence of processes involved here. We can reduce it to a transform–clip–transform sequence by combining steps 3 and 4 into a single transformation matrix. With perspective projections, a division is also needed to map from homogeneous coordinates back to 3D coordinates. This division follows the second transformation of the combined sequence. An alternative strategy, clipping in homogeneous coordinates, is discussed in Section 6.6.4.

Readers familiar with PHIGS will notice that the canonical view volumes of Eqs. (6.12) and (6.13) are different from the **default view volumes** of PHIGS: the unit cube from 0 to 1 in x, y, and z for parallel projection, and the pyramid with apex at $(0.5, 0.5, 1.0)$ and sides passing through the unit square from 0 to 1 in x and y on the $z = 0$ plane for perspective projection. The canonical view volumes are defined to simplify the clipping equations and to provide the consistency between parallel and perspective projections discussed in Section 6.6.4. On the other hand, the PHIGS default view volumes are defined to make 2D viewing a special case of 3D viewing.

In Sections 6.6.1 and 6.6.2, we derive the normalizing transformations for perspective and parallel projections, which are used as the first step in the transform–clip–transform sequence.

6.6.1 The Parallel Projection Case

In this section, we derive the normalizing transformation N_{par} for parallel projections in order to transform world-coordinate positions such that the view volume is transformed into the canonical view volume defined by Eq. (6.12). The transformed coordinates are clipped against this canonical view volume, and the clipped results are projected onto the $z = 0$ plane, and then transformed into the viewport for display.

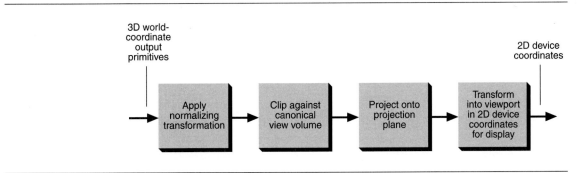

Figure 6.34 Implementation of 3D viewing.

Transformation N_{par} is derived for the most general case, the oblique (rather than orthographic) parallel projection. N_{par} thus includes a shear transformation that causes the direction of projection in viewing coordinates to be parallel to z, even though in (u, v, n) coordinates it is not parallel to VPN. By including this shear, we can do the projection onto the $z = 0$ plane simply by setting $z = 0$. If the parallel projection is orthographic, the shear component of the normalization transformation becomes the identity.

The series of transformations that make up N_{par} is as follows:

1. Translate the VRP to the origin.
2. Rotate VRC such that the n axis (VPN) becomes the z axis, the u axis becomes the x axis, and the v axis becomes the y axis.
3. Shear such that the direction of projection becomes parallel to the z axis.
4. Translate and scale into the parallel-projection canonical view volume of Eq. (6.12).

In PHIGS, steps 1 and 2 define the **view-orientation matrix**, and steps 3 and 4 define the **view-mapping matrix**.

Figure 6.37 shows this sequence of transformations as applied to a parallel-projection view volume and to an outline of a house; Fig. 6.35 shows the parallel projection that results.

Step 1 is just the translation $T(-VRP)$. For step 2, we use the properties of special orthogonal matrices discussed in Sections 5.3 and 5.7 and illustrated in the derivation of Eqs. (5.64) and (5.65). The row vectors of the rotation matrix to perform step 2 are the unit vectors that are rotated by R into the x, y, and z axes. VPN is rotated into the z axis, so

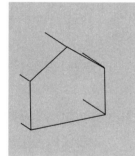

Figure 6.35
Final parallel projection of the clipped house.

$$R_z = \frac{VPN}{\| VPN \|}. \tag{6.14}$$

The u axis, which is perpendicular to VUP and to VPN and is hence the cross-product of the unit vector along VUP and R_z (which is in the same direction as VPN), is rotated into the x axis, so

$$R_x = \frac{VUP \times R_z}{\| VUP \times R_z \|}. \tag{6.15}$$

Similarly, the v axis, which is perpendicular to R_z and R_x, is rotated into the y axis, so

$$R_y = R_z \times R_x. \tag{6.16}$$

Hence, the rotation in step 2 is given by the matrix

$$R = \begin{bmatrix} r_{1x} & r_{2x} & r_{3x} & 0 \\ r_{1y} & r_{2y} & r_{3y} & 0 \\ r_{1z} & r_{2z} & r_{3z} & 0 \\ 0 & 0 & 0 & 1 \end{bmatrix}, \tag{6.17}$$

where r_{1x} is the first element of R_x, and so on.

The third step is to shear the view volume along the z axis such that all of its planes are normal to one of the coordinate system axes. We do this step by determining the shear to be applied to the direction of projection (DOP) to make DOP coincident with the z axis. Recall that DOP is the vector from PRP to the center of the window (CW), and that PRP is specified in the VRC system. The first two transformation steps have brought VRC into correspondence with the world-coordinate system, so the PRP is now itself in world coordinates. Hence, DOP is CW − PRP. Given

$$
\text{DOP} = \begin{bmatrix} dop_x \\ dop_y \\ dop_z \\ 0 \end{bmatrix}, \quad
\text{CW} = \begin{bmatrix} \dfrac{u_{max} + u_{min}}{2} \\ \dfrac{v_{max} + v_{min}}{2} \\ 0 \\ 1 \end{bmatrix}, \quad
\text{PRP} = \begin{bmatrix} prp_u \\ prp_v \\ prp_n \\ 1 \end{bmatrix}, \quad (6.18)
$$

then

$$
\text{DOP} = \text{CW} - \text{PRP}
$$

$$
= \begin{bmatrix} \dfrac{u_{max} + u_{min}}{2} & \dfrac{v_{max} + v_{min}}{2} & 0 & 1 \end{bmatrix}^{\text{T}} - \begin{bmatrix} prp_u & prp_v & prp_n & 1 \end{bmatrix}^{\text{T}}. \quad (6.19)
$$

Figure 6.36 shows the DOP so specified, and the desired transformed DOP′.

The shear can be accomplished with the (x, y) shear matrix from Section 5.7 Eq. (5.45). With coefficients shx_{par} and shy_{par}, the matrix is

$$
SH_{par} = SH_{xy}(shx_{par}, shy_{par}) = \begin{bmatrix} 1 & 0 & shx_{par} & 0 \\ 0 & 1 & shy_{par} & 0 \\ 0 & 0 & 1 & 0 \\ 0 & 0 & 0 & 1 \end{bmatrix}. \quad (6.20)
$$

As described in Section 5.7, SH_{xy} leaves z unaffected, while adding to x and y the terms $z \cdot shx_{par}$ and $z \cdot shy_{par}$. We want to find shx_{par} and shy_{par} such that

$$
\text{DOP}' = \begin{bmatrix} 0 & 0 & dop_z & 0 \end{bmatrix}^{\text{T}} = SH_{par} \cdot \text{DOP}. \quad (6.21)
$$

Performing the multiplication of Eq. (6.21) followed by algebraic manipulation shows that the equality occurs if

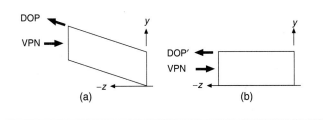

(a)　　　(b)

Figure 6.36　Illustration of shearing using side view of view volume as example. The parallelogram in (a) is sheared into the rectangle in (b); VPN is unchanged because it is parallel to the z axis.

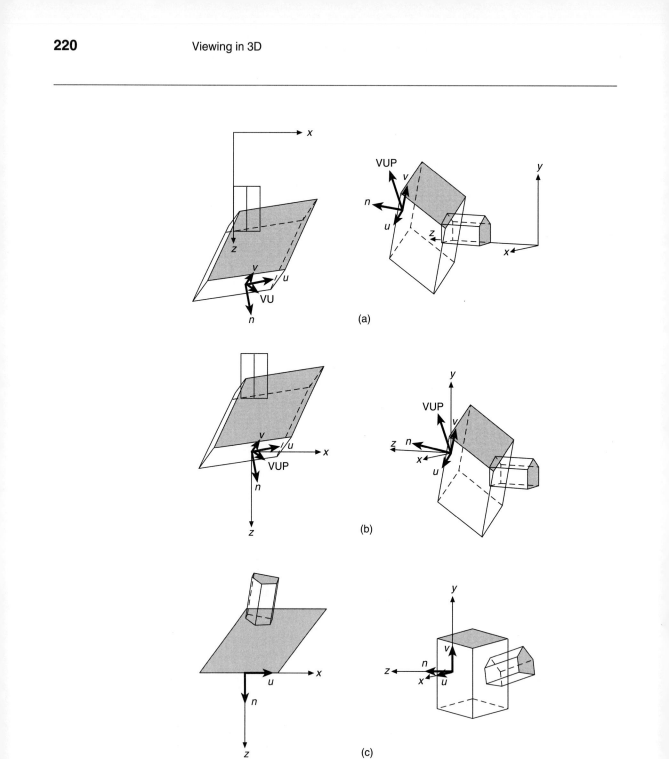

(a)

(b)

(c)

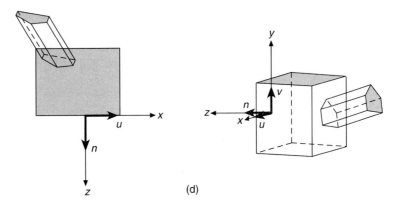

(d)

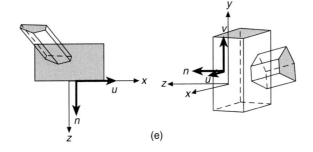

(e)

Figure 6.37   Results at various stages in the parallel-projection viewing pipeline. A top and off-axis parallel projection are shown in each case. (a) The original viewing situation is shown. (b) The VRP has been translated to the origin. (c) The (u, v, n) coordinate system has been rotated to be aligned with the (x, y, z) system. (d) The view volume has been sheared such that the direction of projection (DOP) is parallel to the z axis. (e) The view volume has been translated and scaled into the canonical parallel-projection view volume. The viewing parameters are VRP = (0.325, 0.8, 4.15), VPN = (0.227, 0.267, 1.0), VUP = (0.293, 1.0, 0.227), PRP = (0.6, 0.0, −1.0), Window = (−1.425, 1.0, −1.0, 1.0), $F = 0.0$, $B = −1.75$. (Figures made with program written by L. Lu, The George Washington University.)

$$shx_{par} = -\frac{dop_x}{dop_z}, \qquad shy_{par} = -\frac{dop_y}{dop_z}. \qquad (6.22)$$

Notice that, for an orthographic projection, $dop_x = dop_y = 0$, so $shx_{par} = shy_{par} = 0$, and the shear matrix reduces to the identity.

Figure 6.38 shows the view volume after these three transformation steps have been applied. The bounds of the volume are

$$u_{min} \le x \le u_{max}, \qquad v_{min} \le y \le v_{max}, \qquad B \le z \le F; \qquad (6.23)$$

here F and B are the distances from VRP along the VPN to the front and back clipping planes, respectively.

The fourth and last step in the process is transforming the sheared view volume into the canonical view volume. We accomplish this step by translating the front center of the view volume of Eq. (6.23) to the origin, then scaling to the $2 \times 2 \times 1$ size of the final canonical view volume of Eq. (6.12). The transformations are

$$T_{par} = T\left(-\frac{u_{max} + u_{min}}{2}, \ -\frac{v_{max} + v_{min}}{2}, \ -F\right), \qquad (6.24)$$

$$S_{par} = S\left(\frac{2}{u_{max} + u_{min}}, \ \frac{2}{v_{max} + v_{min}}, \ \frac{1}{F - B}\right). \qquad (6.25)$$

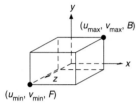

Figure 6.38
View volume after
transformation steps 1 to 3.

If F and B have not been specified (because front- and back-plane clipping are off), then any values that satisfy $B \le F$ can be used. Values of 0 and 1 are satisfactory.

In summary, we have

$$N_{par} = S_{par} \cdot T_{par} \cdot SH_{par} \cdot R \cdot T(-VRP). \qquad (6.26)$$

N_{par} transforms an arbitrary parallel-projection view volume into the parallel-projection canonical view volume, and hence permits output primitives to be clipped against the parallel-projection canonical view volume.

6.6.2 The Perspective Projection Case

We now develop the normalizing transformation N_{per} for perspective projections. N_{per} transforms world-coordinate positions such that the view volume becomes the perspective-projection canonical view volume, the truncated pyramid with apex at the origin defined by Eq. (6.13). After N_{per} is applied, clipping is done against this canonical volume and the results are projected onto the view plane using M_{per} (derived in Section 6.5).

The series of transformations making up N_{per} is as follows:

1. Translate VRP to the origin.
2. Rotate VRC such that the n axis (VPN) becomes the z axis, the u axis becomes the x axis, and the v axis becomes the y axis.
3. Translate such that the center of projection (COP), given by the PRP, is at the origin.

4. Shear such that the center line of the view volume becomes the z axis.

5. Scale such that the view volume becomes the canonical perspective view volume, the truncated right pyramid defined by the six planes of Eq. (6.13).

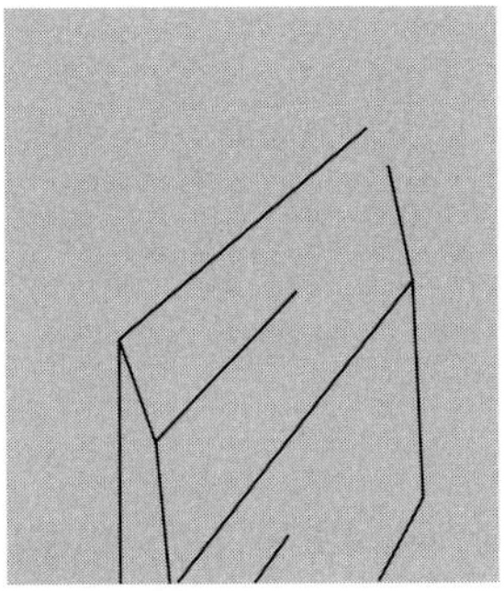

Figure 6.41 shows this sequence of transformations being applied to a perspective-projection view volume and to a house. Figure 6.39 shows the resulting perspective projection.

Steps 1 and 2 are the same as those for the parallel projection: $R \cdot T(-\text{VRP})$. Step 3 is a translation of the center of projection (COP) to the origin, as required for the canonical perspective view volume. COP is specified relative to VRP in VRC by the PRP = (prp_u, prp_v, prp_n). VRCs have been transformed into world coordinates by steps 1 and 2, so the specification for COP in VRC is now also in world coordinates. Hence, the translation for step 3 is just $T(-\text{PRP})$.

To compute the shear for step 4, we examine Fig. 6.40 which shows a side view of the view volume after transformation steps 1 through 3. Notice that the center line of the view volume, which goes through the origin and the center of the window, is not the same as the $-z$ axis. The purpose of the shear is to transform the center line into the $-z$ axis. The center line of the view volume goes from PRP (which is now at the origin) to CW, the center of the window. It is hence the same as the direction of projection for the parallel projection—that is, CW $-$ PRP. Therefore, the shear matrix is SH_{par}, the same as that for the parallel projection! Another way to think of this situation is that the translation by $-$PRP in step 3, which took the center of projection to the origin, also translated CW by $-$PRP; so, after step 3, the center line of the view volume goes through the origin and CW $-$ PRP.

After the shear is applied, the window (and hence the view volume) is centered on the z axis. The bounds of the window on the projection plane are

$$-\frac{u_{\max} - u_{\min}}{2} \le x \le \frac{u_{\max} - u_{\min}}{2}, \tag{6.27}$$

$$-\frac{v_{\max} - v_{\min}}{2} \le y \le \frac{v_{\max} - v_{\min}}{2}.$$

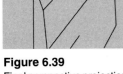

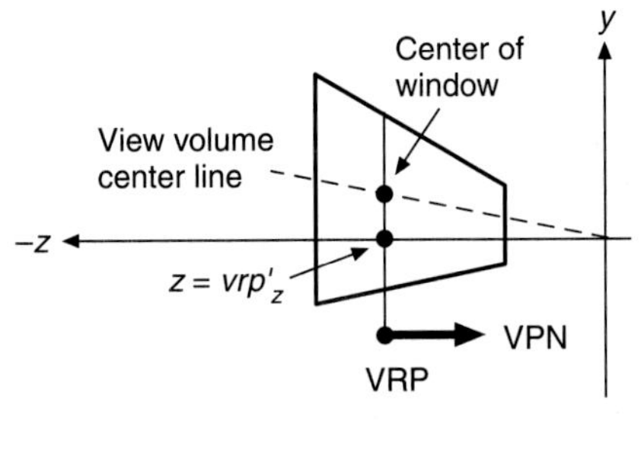

Figure 6.39
Final perspective projection of the clipped house.

Figure 6.40   Cross-section of view volume after transformation steps 1 through 3.

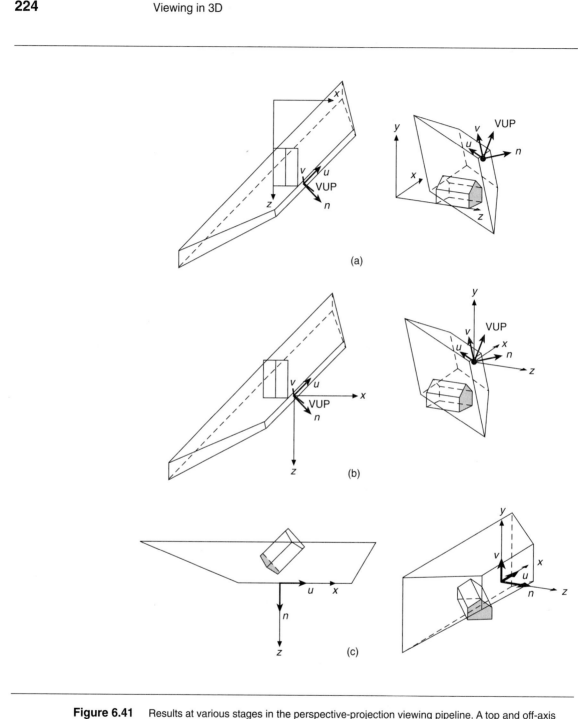

Figure 6.41   Results at various stages in the perspective-projection viewing pipeline. A top and off-axis parallel projection are shown in each case. (a) The original viewing situation is shown. (b) The VRP has been translated to the origin. (c) The (u, v, n) coordinate system has been rotated to be aligned with the (x, y, z) system. (d) The center of projection (COP) has been translated to the origin. (e) The view volume has been sheared, so the direction of projection (DOP) is parallel to the z axis. (f) The view volume has been scaled into the canonical perspective-

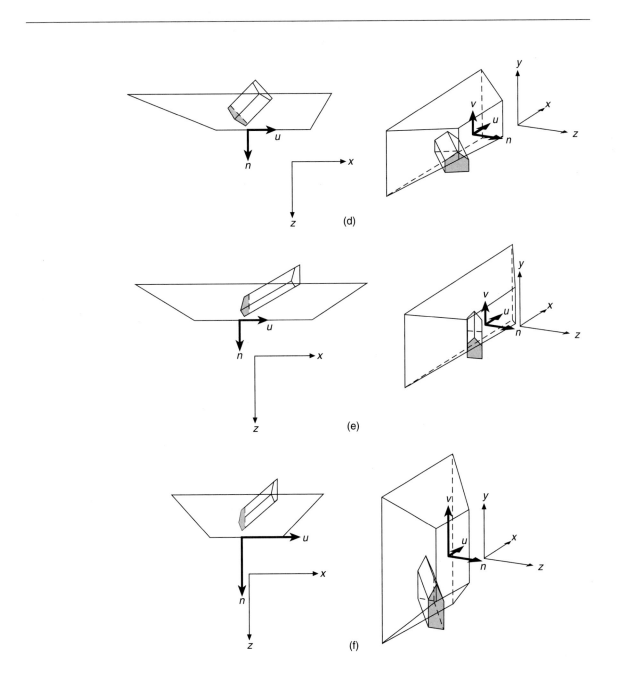

projection view volume. The viewing parameters are VRP = (1.0, 1.275, 2.6), VPN = (1.0, 0.253, 1.0), VUP = (0.414, 1.0, 0.253), PRP = (1.6, 0.0, 1.075), Window = (−1.325, 2.25, −0.575, 0.575), $F = 0$, $B = −1.2$. (Figures made with program written by L. Lu, The George Washington University.)

The VRP, which before step 3 was at the origin, has now been translated by step 3 and sheared by step 4. Defining VRP′ as VRP after the transformations of steps 3 and 4,

$$\text{VRP}' = SH_{\text{par}} \cdot T(-\text{PRP}) \cdot [0 \ 0 \ 0 \ 1]^{\text{T}}. \tag{6.28}$$

The z component of VRP′, designated as vrp_z', is equal to $-prp_n$, because the (x, y) shear SH_{par} does not affect z coordinates.

The final step is a scaling along all three axes to create the canonical view volume defined by Eq. (6.13), and shown in Fig. 6.42. Thus, scaling is best thought of as being done in two substeps. In the first substep, we scale differentially in x and y, to give the sloped planes bounding the view-volume unit slope. We perform this substep by scaling the window so its half-height and half-width are both $-vrp_z'$. The appropriate x and y scale factors are $-2 \cdot vrp_z'/(u_{\text{max}} - u_{\text{min}})$ and $-2 \cdot vrp_z'/(v_{\text{max}} - v_{\text{min}})$, respectively. In the second substep, we scale uniformly along all three axes (to maintain the unit slopes) such that the back clipping plane at $z = vrp_z' + B$ becomes the $z = -1$ plane. The scale factor for this substep is $-1/(vrp_z' + B)$. The scale factor has a negative sign so that the scale factor will be positive, since $vrp_z' + B$ is itself negative.

Bringing together these two substeps, we get the perspective scale transformation:

$$S_{\text{per}} = $$
$$S\left(\frac{2vrp_z'}{(u_{\text{max}} - u_{\text{min}})(vrp_z' + B)}, \frac{2vrp_z'}{(v_{\text{max}} - v_{\text{min}})(vrp_z' + B)}, \frac{-1}{vrp_z' + B} \right). \tag{6.29}$$

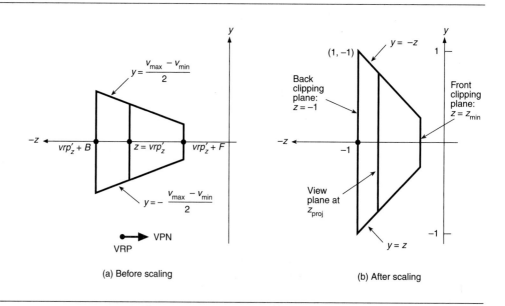

(a) Before scaling   (b) After scaling

Figure 6.42   Cross-section of view volume (a) before scaling. (b) After final scaling steps. In this example, F and B have opposite signs, so the front and back planes are on opposite sides of VRP.

Applying the scale to z changes the positions of the projection plane and clipping planes to the new positions:[1]

$$z_{proj} = -\frac{vrp'_z}{vrp'_z + B}, \quad z_{min} = -\frac{vrp'_z + F}{vrp'_z + B}, \quad z_{max} = -\frac{vrp'_z + B}{vrp'_z + B} = -1. \quad (6.30)$$

In summary, the normalizing viewing transformation that takes the perspective-projection view volume into the perspective-projection canonical view volume is

$$N_{per} = S_{per} \cdot SH_{par} \cdot T(-PRP) \cdot R \cdot T(-VRP). \quad (6.31)$$

Similarly, recall the normalizing viewing transformation that takes the parallel-projection view volume into the parallel-projection canonical view volume:

$$N_{par} = S_{par} \cdot T_{par} \cdot SH_{par} \cdot R \cdot T(-VRP). \quad (6.26)$$

These transformations occur in homogeneous space. Under what conditions can we now come back to 3D to clip? The answer is, as long as we know that $W > 0$. This condition is easy to understand. A negative W implies that, when we divide by W, the signs of Z and z will be opposite. Points with negative Z will have positive z and might be displayed even though they should have been clipped.

When can we be sure that we will have $W > 0$? Rotations, translations, scales, and shears (as defined in Chapter 5) applied to points, lines, and planes will keep $W > 0$; in fact, they will keep $W = 1$. Hence, neither N_{per} nor N_{par} affects the homogeneous coordinate of transformed points, so division by W will not normally be necessary to map back into 3D, and clipping against the appropriate canonical view volume can be performed. After clipping against the perspective-projection canonical view volume, the perspective-projection matrix M_{per}, which involves division, must be applied.

It is possible to get $W < 0$ if output primitives include curves and surfaces that are represented as functions in homogeneous coordinates and are displayed as connected straight-line segments. If, for instance, the sign of the function for W changes from one point on the curve to the next while the sign of X does not change, then X/W will have different signs at the two points on the curve. The rational B-splines discussed in Chapter 9 are an example of such behavior. Negative W can also result from using some transformations other than those discussed in Chapter 5, such as with "fake" shadows [BLIN88]. In the next section, several algorithms for clipping in 3D are discussed. Then, in Section 6.6.4, we discuss how to clip when we cannot ensure that $W > 0$.

6.6.3 Clipping Against a Canonical View Volume in 3D

The canonical view volumes are $2 \times 2 \times 1$ prism for parallel projections and the truncated right regular pyramid for perspective projections. Both the Cohen–Sutherland and Cyrus–Beck clipping algorithms discussed in Chapter 3 readily extend to 3D.

---

[1] z_{min} and z_{max} are named based on their absolute value relationship, as z_{min} is algebraically greater than z_{max}.

The extension of the 2D Cohen–Sutherland algorithm for the canonical parallel view volume uses an outcode of 6 bits; a bit is true (1) when the appropriate condition is satisfied:

bit 1—point is above view volume	$y > 1$
bit 2—point is below view volume	$y < -1$
bit 3—point is right of view volume	$x > 1$
bit 4—point is left of view volume	$x < -1$
bit 5—point is behind view volume	$z < -1$
bit 6—point is in front of view volume	$z > 0$

As in 2D, a line is trivially accepted if both endpoints have a code of all zeros, and is trivially rejected if the bit-by-bit logical **and** of the codes is not all zeros. Otherwise, the process of line subdivision begins. Up to six intersections may have to be calculated, one for each side of the view volume.

The intersection calculations use the parametric representation of a line from $P_0(x_0, y_0, z_0)$ to $P_1(x_1, y_1, z_1)$

$$x = x_0 + t(x_1 - x_0), \tag{6.32}$$

$$y = y_0 + t(y_1 - y_0), \tag{6.33}$$

$$z = z_0 + t(z_1 - z_0) \qquad 0 \le t \le 1. \tag{6.34}$$

As t varies from 0 to 1, the three equations give the coordinates of all points on the line, from P_0 to P_1.

To calculate the intersection of a line with the $y = 1$ plane of the view volume, we replace the variable y of Eq. (6.33) with 1 and solve for t to find $t = (1 - y_0)/(y_1 - y_0)$. If t is outside the 0 to 1 interval, the intersection is on the infinite line through points P_0 and P_1 but is not on the portion of the line between P_0 and P_1 and hence is not of interest. If t is in [0, 1], then its value is substituted into the equations for x and z to find the intersection's coordinates:

$$x = x_0 + \frac{(1 - y_0)(x_1 - x_0)}{y_1 - y_0}, \qquad z = z_0 + \frac{(1 - y_0)(z_1 - z_0)}{y_1 - y_0}. \tag{6.35}$$

The algorithm uses outcodes to make the t in [0, 1] test unnecessary.

The outcode bits for clipping against the canonical perspective view volume are as follows:

bit 1—point is above view volume	$y > -z$
bit 2—point is below view volume	$y < z$
bit 3—point is right of view volume	$x > -z$
bit 4—point is left of view volume	$x < z$
bit 5—point is behind view volume	$z < -1$
bit 6—point is in front of view volume	$z > z_{min}$

Calculating the intersections of lines with the sloping planes is simple. On the $y = z$ plane, for which Eq. (6.33) must be equal to Eq. (6.34), $y_0 + t(y_1 - y_0) = z_0 + t(z_1 - z_0)$. Then,

$$t = \frac{z_0 - y_0}{(y_1 - y_0) - (z_1 - z_0)} \cdot \qquad (6.36)$$

Substituting t into Eqs. (6.32) and (6.33) for x and y gives

$$x = x_0 + \frac{(x_1 - x_0)(z_0 - y_0)}{(y_1 - y_0) - (z_1 - z_0)}, \qquad y = y_0 + \frac{(y_1 - y_0)(z_0 - y_0)}{(y_1 - y_0) - (z_1 - z_0)} \cdot \qquad (6.37)$$

We know that $z = y$. The reason for choosing this canonical view volume is now clear: The unit slopes of the planes make the intersection computations simpler than would arbitrary slopes.

There are other clipping algorithms [CYRU78; LIAN84] that are based on parametric expressions for lines, and these can be more efficient than the simple Cohen-Sutherland algorithm. See Chapters 6 and 19 of [FOLE90].

6.6.4 Clipping in Homogeneous Coordinates

There are two reasons to clip in homogeneous coordinates. The first has to do with efficiency: It is possible to transform the perspective-projection canonical view volume into the parallel-projection canonical view volume, so a single clip procedure, optimized for the parallel-projection canonical view volume, can always be used. However, the clipping must be done in homogeneous coordinates to ensure correct results. This kind of single clip procedure is typically provided in hardware implementations of the viewing operation. The second reason is that points that can occur as a result of unusual homogeneous transformations and from use of rational parametric splines (Chapter 9) can have negative W and can be clipped properly in homogeneous coordinates but not in 3D.

With regard to clipping, it can be shown that the transformation from the perspective-projection canonical view volume to the parallel-projection canonical view volume is

$$M = \begin{bmatrix} 1 & 0 & 0 & 0 \\ 0 & 1 & 0 & 0 \\ 0 & 0 & \dfrac{1}{1 + z_{min}} & \dfrac{-z_{min}}{1 + z_{min}} \\ 0 & 0 & -1 & 0 \end{bmatrix}, \qquad 0 > z_{min} > -1. \qquad (6.38)$$

Recall from Eq. (6.30) that $z_{min} = -(vrp'_z + F)/(vrp'_z + B)$, and from Eq. (6.28) that $VRP' = SH_{par} \cdot T(-PRP) \cdot [0\ 0\ 0\ 1]^T$. Figure 6.43 shows the results of applying M to the perspective-projection canonical view volume.

The matrix M is integrated with the perspective-projection normalizing transformation N_{per}:

$$N'_{per} = M \cdot N_{per} = M \cdot S_{per} \cdot SH_{par} \cdot T(-PRP) \cdot R \cdot T(-VRP). \qquad (6.39)$$

By using N'_{per} instead of N_{per} for perspective projections, and by continuing to use N_{par} for parallel projections, we can clip against the parallel-projection canonical view volume rather than against the perspective-projection canonical view volume.

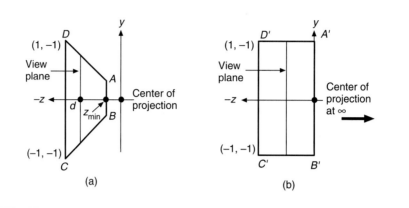

Figure 6.43   Side views of normalized perspective view volume before (a) and after (b) application of matrix M.

The 3D parallel-projection view volume is defined by $-1 \le x \le 1$, $-1 \le y \le 1$, $-1 \le z \le 0$. We find the corresponding inequalities in homogeneous coordinates by replacing x by X/W, y by Y/W, and z by Z/W, which results in

$$-1 \le X/W \le 1, \quad -1 \le Y/W \le 1, \quad -1 \le Z/W \le 0. \tag{6.40}$$

The corresponding plane equations are

$$X = -W, \quad X = W, \quad Y = -W, \quad Y = W, \quad Z = -W, \quad Z = 0. \tag{6.41}$$

To understand how to use these limits and planes, we must consider separately the cases of $W > 0$ and $W < 0$. In the first case, we can multiply the inequalities of Eq. (6.40) by W without changing the sense of the inequalities. In the second case, the multiplication changes the sense. This result can be expressed as

$$W > 0: \quad -W \le X \le W, \quad -W \le Y \le W, \quad -W \le Z \le 0, \tag{6.42}$$

$$W < 0: \quad -W \ge X \ge W, \quad -W \ge Y \ge W, \quad -W \ge Z \ge 0. \tag{6.43}$$

In the case at hand—that of clipping ordinary lines and points—only the region given by Eq. (6.42) needs to be used, because prior to application of M, all visible points have $W > 0$ (normally $W = 1$).

As we shall see in Chapter 9, however, it is sometimes desirable to represent points directly in homogeneous coordinates with arbitrary W coordinates. Hence, we might have a $W < 0$, meaning that clipping must be done against the regions given by Eqs. (6.42) and (6.43). Figure 6.44 shows these as region A and region B, and also shows why both regions must be used.

The point $P_1 = [1 \ 3 \ 2 \ 4]^T$ in region A transforms into the 3D point $(\frac{1}{4}, \frac{3}{4}, \frac{2}{4})$, which is in the canonical view volume $-1 \le x \le 1$, $-1 \le y \le 1$, $-1 \le z \le 0$. The point $P_2 = -P_1 = [-1 \ -3 \ -2 \ -4]^T$, which is *not* in region A but *is* in region B, transforms into the same 3D point as P_1—namely, $(\frac{1}{4}, \frac{3}{4}, \frac{2}{4})$. If clipping were only to

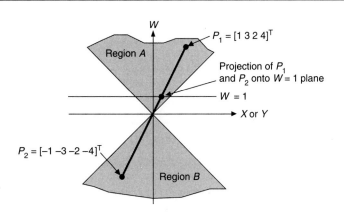

Figure 6.44   The points P_1 and P_2 both map into the same point on the $W = 1$ plane, as do all other points on the line through the origin and the two points. Clipping in homogeneous coordinates against just region A will incorrectly reject P_2.

region A, then P_2 would be discarded incorrectly. This possibility arises because the homogeneous coordinate points P_1 and P_2 differ by a constant multiplier (-1), and we know that such homogeneous points correspond to the same 3D point (on the $W = 1$ plane of homogeneous space).

There are two solutions to this problem of points in region B. One is to clip all points twice, once against each region. But doing two clips is expensive. A better solution is to negate points, such as P_2, with negative W, and then to clip them. Similarly, we can clip properly a line whose endpoints are both in region B of Fig. 6.44 by multiplying both endpoints by -1, to place the points in region A.

Another problem arises with lines such as P_1P_2, shown in Fig. 6.45, whose endpoints have opposite values of W. The projection of the line onto the $W = 1$ plane is two segments, one of which goes to $+\infty$, the other to $-\infty$. The solution now is to clip twice, once against each region, with the possibility that each clip will return a visible line segment. A simple way to do this is to clip the line against region A, to negate both endpoints of the line, and to clip again against region A. This approach preserves one of the original purposes of clipping in homogeneous coordinates: using a single clip region. Interested readers are referred to [BLIN78a] for further discussion.

Given Eq. (6.41), the Cohen–Sutherland or Cyrus–Beck algorithm can be used for the actual clipping. [LIAN84] gives code for the Cyrus–Beck approach. The only difference is that the clipping is in 4D, as opposed to 3D.

6.6.5 Mapping into a Viewport

Output primitives are clipped in the normalized projection coordinate system, which is also called the 3D screen coordinate system. We shall assume for this discussion that the canonical parallel-projection view volume has been used for

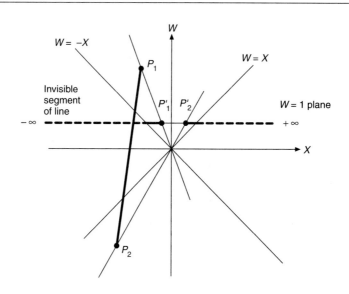

Figure 6.45   The line $P_1 P_2$ projects onto two line segments, one from P_2' to $+\infty$, the other from P_1' to $-\infty$ (shown as solid thick lines where they are in the clip region, and as dashed thick lines where they are outside the clip region). The line must be clipped twice, once against each region.

clipping (the perspective projection M transforms the perspective-projection view volume into the parallel-projection view volume if this assumption is incorrect). Hence, the coordinates of all output primitives that remain are in the view volume $-1 \le x \le 1, -1 \le y \le 1, -1 \le z \le 0$.

The PHIGS programmer specifies a 3D viewport into which the contents of this view volume are mapped. The 3D viewport is contained in the unit cube $0 \le x \le 1, 0 \le y \le 1, 0 \le z \le 1$. The $z = 1$ front face of the unit cube is mapped into the largest square that can be inscribed on the display screen. We assume that the lower-left corner of the square is at $(0, 0)$. For example, on a display device with a horizontal resolution of 1024 and a vertical resolution of 800, the square consists of pixels P at locations (P_x, P_y) with $0 \le P_x \le 799, 0 \le P_y \le 799$. We display points in the unit cube by discarding their z coordinate. Hence, the point $(0.5, 0.75, 0.46)$ would be displayed at the device coordinates $(400, 599)$. In the case of visible-surface determination (Chapter 13), the z coordinate of each output primitive is used to determine which primitives are visible and which are obscured by other primitives with larger z.

Given a 3D viewport within the unit cube, defined by equations $x_{v.min} \le x \le x_{v.max}$, and so forth, the mapping from the canonical parallel-projection view volume into the 3D viewport can be thought of as a three-step process. In the first step, the canonical parallel-projection view volume is translated such that its corner, $(-1, -1, -1)$, becomes the origin. This action is effected by the translation $T(1, 1, 1)$. Next, the translated view volume is scaled into the size of the 3D viewport, with the scale

$$S \left(\frac{x_{v.max} - x_{v.min}}{2}, \frac{y_{v.max} - y_{v.min}}{2}, \frac{z_{v.max} - z_{v.min}}{1} \right).$$

Finally, the properly scaled view volume is translated to the lower-left corner of the viewport by the translation $T(x_{v.min}, y_{v.min}, z_{v.min})$. Hence, the composite canonical view volume to 3D viewport transformation is

$$M_{VV3DV} = T(x_{v.min}, y_{v.min}, z_{v.min}) \cdot S \left(\frac{x_{v.max} - x_{v.min}}{2}, \frac{y_{v.max} - y_{v.min}}{2}, \frac{z_{v.max} - z_{v.min}}{1} \right) \cdot T(1, 1, 1).$$

(6.44)

Note that this transformation is similar to, but not the same as, the window to viewport transformation M_{WV} developed in Section 5.5.

6.6.6 Implementation Summary

There are two generally used implementations of the overall viewing transformation. The first, depicted in Fig. 6.34 and discussed in Sections 6.6.1 through 6.6.3, is appropriate when output primitives are defined in 3D and the transformations applied to the output primitives never create a negative W. Its steps are as follows:

1. Extend 3D coordinates to homogeneous coordinates.
2. Apply normalizing transformation N_{par} or N_{per}
3. Divide by W to map back to 3D (in some cases, it is known that $W = 1$, so the division is not needed).
4. Clip in 3D against the parallel-projection or perspective-projection canonical view volume, whichever is appropriate.
5. Extend 3D coordinates to homogeneous coordinates.
6. Perform parallel projection using M_{ort}, Eq. (6.11), or perform perspective projection, using M_{per}, Eq. (6.3) with $d = -1$.
7. Translate and scale into device coordinates using Eq. (6.44).
8. Divide by W to map from homogeneous to 2D coordinates; the division effects the perspective projection.

Steps 6 and 7 are performed by a single matrix multiplication, and correspond to stages 3 and 4 in Fig. 6.34.

The second way to implement the viewing operation is required whenever output primitives are defined in homogeneous coordinates and might have $W < 0$, when the transformations applied to the output primitives might create a negative W, or when a single clip algorithm is implemented. As discussed in Section 6.6.4, its steps are as follows:

1. Extend 3D coordinates to homogeneous coordinates.
2. Apply normalizing transformation N_{par} or N_{per}' (which includes M, Eq. (6.38)).

3. If $W > 0$, clip in homogeneous coordinates against the volume defined by Eq. (6.42); or else, clip in homogeneous coordinates against the two view volumes defined by Eqs. (6.42) and (6.43).

4. Translate and scale into device coordinates using Eq. (6.44).

5. Divide by W to map from homogeneous coordinates to 2D coordinates; the division effects the perspective projection.

6.7 COORDINATE SYSTEMS

Several different coordinate systems have been used in Chapters 5 and 6. In this section, we summarize all the systems, and also discuss their relationships to one another. Synonyms used in various references and graphics subroutine packages are also given. Figure 6.46 shows the progression of coordinate systems, using the terms generally used in this text; in any particular graphics subroutine package, only some of the coordinate systems are actually used. We have chosen names for the various coordinate systems to reflect common usage; some of the names therefore are not logically consistent with one another. Note that the term *space* is sometimes used as a synonym for *system.*

Starting with the coordinate system that is farthest removed from the actual display device, on the left of Fig. 6.46, individual objects are defined in an **object-coordinate system**. PHIGS calls this the **modeling-coordinate system**; the term **local coordinate system** is also commonly used. As we shall discuss further in Chapter 7, there is often a hierarchy of modeling-coordinate systems.

Objects are transformed into the **world-coordinate system**, the system in which a scene or complete object is represented in the computer, by the **modeling transformation**. This system is sometimes called the **problem-coordinate system** or **application-coordinate system**.

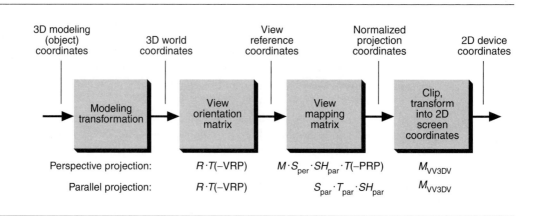

Figure 6.46   Coordinate systems and how they relate to one another. The matrices underneath each stage effect the transformation applied at that stage for the perspective and parallel projections.

The **view-reference coordinate system** is used by PHIGS as a coordinate system to define a view volume. It is also called the (u, v, n) system, or the (u, v, VPN) system. The Core system [GSPC79] used a similar, but unnamed, left-handed system. The left-handed system is used so that, with the eye or camera at the origin looking toward $+z$, increasing values of z are farther away from the eye, x is to the right, and y is up.

Other packages, such as Pixar's RenderMan [PIXA88], place constraints on the view-reference coordinate system, requiring that the origin be at the center of projection and that the view plane normal be the z axis. We call this the **eye-coordinate system;** RenderMan and some other systems use the term **camera-coordinate system.** Referring back to Section 6.6, the first three steps of the perspective-projection normalizing transformation convert from the world-coordinate system into the eye-coordinate system. The eye-coordinate system is sometimes left-handed.

From eye coordinates, we next go to the **normalized-projection coordinate system,** or **3D screen coordinates**, the coordinate system of the parallel-projection canonical view volume (and of the perspective-projection canonical view volume after the perspective transformation). The Core system calls this system **3D normalized device coordinates**. Sometimes the system is called **3D logical device coordinates**. The term *normalized* generally means that all the coordinate values are in either the interval [0, 1] or [−1, 1], whereas the term *logical* generally means that coordinate values are in some other prespecified range, such as [0, 1023], which is typically defined to correspond to some widely available device's coordinate system. In some cases, this system is not normalized.

Projecting from 3D into 2D creates what we call the **2D device-coordinate system**, also called the **normalized device-coordinate system,** the **image-coordinate system** by [SUTH74a], or the **screen-coordinate system** by RenderMan. Other terms used include **screen coordinates, device coordinates, 2D device coordinates, physical device coordinates** (in contrast to the logical device coordinates mentioned previously). RenderMan calls the physical form of the space **raster coordinates**.

Unfortunately, there is no single standard usage for many of these terms. For example, the term **screen-coordinate system** is used by different authors to refer to the last three systems discussed, covering both 2D and 3D coordinates, and both logical and physical coordinates.

Exercises

6.1 Write a program that accepts a viewing specification, calculates either N_{par} or N_{per}, and displays the house whose coordinates are defined in Fig. 6.18.

6.2 Implement 3D clipping algorithms for parallel and perspective projections.

6.3 Show that, for a parallel projection with $F = -\infty$ and $B = +\infty$, the result of clipping in 3D and then projecting to 2D is the same as the result of projecting to 2D and then clipping in 2D.

6.4   Show that, if all objects are in front of the center of projection and if $F = -\infty$ and $B = +\infty$, then the result of clipping in 3D against the perspective-projection canonical view volume followed by perspective projection is the same as first doing a perspective projection into 2D and then clipping in 2D.

6.5   Verify that S_{per} (Section 6.6.2) transforms the view volume of Fig. 6.42(a) into that of Fig. 6.42(b).

6.6   Write the code for 3D clipping against the unit cube. Generalize the code to clip against any rectangular solid with faces normal to the principal axes. Is the generalized code more or less efficient than that for the unit-cube case? Explain your answer.

6.7   Write the code for 3D clipping against the perspective-projection canonical view volume. Now generalize to the view volume defined by

$$-a \cdot z_v \le x_v \le b \cdot z_v, \quad -c \cdot z_v \le y_v \le d \cdot z_v, \quad z_{min} \le z_v \le z_{max}.$$

These relations represent the general form of the view volume after steps 1 through 4 of the perspective normalizing transformation. Which case is more efficient? Explain your answer.

6.8   Write the code for 3D clipping against a general six-faced polyhedral view volume whose faces are defined by

$$A_i x + B_i y + C_i z + D_i = 0, \quad 1 \le i \le 6.$$

Compare the computational effort needed with that required for each of the following:

a.   Clipping against either of the canonical view volumes.
b.   Applying N_{par}, and then clipping against the unit cube.

6.9   Consider a line in 3D going from the world-coordinate points P_1 (6, 10, 3) to P_2 (−3, −5, 2) and a semi-infinite viewing pyramid in the region $-z \le x \le z, -z \le y \le z$, which is bounded by the planes $z = +x, z = -x, z = +y, z = -y$. The projection plane is at $z = 1$.

a.   Clip the line in 3D (using parametric line equations), then project it onto the projection plane. What are the clipped endpoints on the plane?
b.   Project the line onto the plane, then clip the lines using 2D computations. What are the clipped endpoints on the plane?

(*Hint:* If your answers to parts (a) and (b) are not identical, try again!)

6.10   Show what happens when an object *behind* the center of projection is projected by M_{per} and then clipped. Your answer should demonstrate why, in general, we cannot project and then clip.

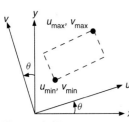

Figure 6.47
A rotated window.

6.11   Consider the 2D viewing operation, with a rotated window. Devise a normalized transformation to transform the window into the unit square. The window is specified by $u_{min}, v_{min}, u_{max}, v_{max}$ in the VRC coordinate system, as in Fig. 6.47. Show that this transformation is the same as that for the general 3D N_{par}, when the projection plane is the (x, y) plane and VUP has an x component of $-\sin \theta$ and a y component of $\cos \theta$ (i.e., the parallel projection of VUP onto the view plane is the v axis).

6.12   What is the effect of applying M_{per} to points whose z coordinate is less than zero?

6.13   Design and implement a set of utility subroutines to generate a 4×4 transformation matrix from an arbitrary sequence of R, S, and T primitive transformations.

6.14   Draw a decision tree to use when you are determining the type of a projection used in creating an image. Apply this decision tree to the figures in this chapter that are projections from 3D.

6.15   The canonical view volume for the parallel projection was taken to be the $2 \times 2 \times 1$ rectangular parallelepiped. Suppose the unit cube in the positive octant, with one corner at the origin, is used instead.

    a.   Find the normalization $N_{par}{}'$ for this view volume.

    b.   Find the corresponding homogeneous-coordinate view volume.

6.16   Give the viewing parameters for top, front, and side views of the house of Fig. 6.18 with the VRP in the middle of the window. Must the PRP be different for each of the views? Explain your answer.

6.17   Stereo pairs are two views of the same scene made from slightly different projection reference points, but with the same VRP. Let d be the stereo separation—that is, the distance between the two reference points. If we think of the reference points as our eyes, then d is the distance between our eyes. Let P be the point midway between our eyes. Given P, d, VRP, VPN, and VUP, derive expressions for the two projection reference points.

7 Object Hierarchy and Simple PHIGS (SPHIGS)

A graphics package is an intermediary between an application program and the graphics hardware. The output primitives and interaction devices that a graphics package supports can range from rudimentary to extremely rich. In Chapter 2, we described the fairly simple and low-level SRGP package, and we noted some of its limitations. In this chapter, we describe a package based on a considerably richer but more complex standard graphics package, **PHIGS** (Programmer's Hierarchical Interactive Graphics System[1]). A **standard graphics package** such as PHIGS or GKS (Graphical Kernel System) implements a specification designated as standard by an official national or international standards body; GKS and PHIGS have been so designated by ANSI (American National Standards Institute) and ISO (International Standards Organization). The main purpose of such standards is to promote portability of application programs and of programmers. Nonofficial industry standards, discussed further in Section 7.11.6, have also proven to be important for interactive graphics. These include Silicon Graphics' OpenGL [NEID93] and Ithaca Software's HOOPS™ [BASS90]. While much has been made of the differences between PHIGS PLUS, OpenGL, and HOOPS, they are far more alike than different, at least in their basic capabilities if not in their procedural Application Program Interface (API). Most of what you will learn in this chapter will apply, with minor changes, to the other packages, since they all support, for example, object hierarchy with transformations.

[1] The term *PHIGS* in this chapter also includes a set of extensions to PHIGS, called PHIGS PLUS, that supports advanced geometric primitives such as polyhedra, curves, and surfaces, as well as rendering techniques that use lighting and shading, discussed in Chapters 12–14.

The package described here is called **SPHIGS** (for Simple PHIGS; pronounced *ess-figs*) because it is essentially a subset of PHIGS. It preserves most of PHIGS's capabilities and power, but simplifies or modifies various features to suit straightforward applications. SPHIGS also includes several enhancements adapted from PHIGS PLUS extensions. Our aim in designing SPHIGS has been to introduce concepts in the simplest possible way, not to provide a package that is strictly upward-compatible with PHIGS. However, an SPHIGS application can easily be adapted to run with PHIGS. Footnotes present some of the important differences between SPHIGS and PHIGS; in general, an SPHIGS feature is also present in PHIGS unless otherwise noted.

There are three major differences between SPHIGS and integer raster packages, such as SRGP or the Xlib package of the X Window System. First, to suit engineering and scientific applications, SPHIGS uses a 3D, floating-point coordinate system, and implements the 3D viewing pipeline discussed in Chapter 6.

The second, further-reaching difference is that SPHIGS maintains a database of structures. A **structure** is a logical grouping of primitives, attributes, and other information. The programmer can modify structures in the database with a few editing commands; SPHIGS ensures that the screen's image is an accurate representation of the contents of the stored database. Structures contain not only specifications of primitives and attributes, but also invocations of subordinate structures. Structures thus exhibit some of the properties of procedures in programming languages. In particular, just as procedure hierarchy is induced by procedures invoking subprocedures, structure hierarchy is induced by structures invoking substructures. Such hierarchical composition is especially powerful when one can control the geometry (position, orientation, size) and appearance (color, style, thickness, etc.) of any invocation of a substructure.

The third difference is that SPHIGS operates in an abstract, 3D world-coordinate system, not in 2D screen space, and therefore does not support direct pixel manipulation. Because of these differences, SPHIGS and SRGP address different sets of needs and applications; as we pointed out in Chapter 2, each has its place—no single graphics package meets all needs.

Because of its ability to support structure hierarchy, SPHIGS is well suited to applications based on models with component–subcomponent hierarchy; indeed, the SPHIGS structure hierarchy can be viewed as a simple special-purpose modeling hierarchy. We therefore look at modeling in general in Section 7.1, before discussing the specifics of geometric modeling with SPHIGS. Sections 7.2 through 7.9 show how to create, display, and edit the SPHIGS structure database. Section 7.10 discusses interaction, particularly pick correlation.

7.1 GEOMETRIC MODELING

You have encountered many examples of models in courses in the physical and social sciences. For example, you are probably familiar with the Bohr model of the atom, in which spheres representing electrons orbit a spherical nucleus containing neutron and proton spheres. Other examples are the exponential unconstrained growth model in biology, and macro- or microeconometric models that purport to describe some aspect of an economy. A model is a representation of some (not necessarily all) features of a concrete or abstract entity. The purpose of a model of an entity is to allow people to visualize and understand the structure or behavior of the entity, and to provide a convenient vehicle for experimentation with and prediction of the effects of inputs or changes to the model. Quantitative models common in physical and social sciences and engineering are usually expressed as systems of equations, and the modeler will experiment by varying the values of independent variables, coefficients, and exponents. Often, models simplify the actual structure or behavior of the modeled entity to make the model easier to visualize or, for those models represented by systems of equations, to make the model computationally tractable.

We restrict ourselves in this book to the discussion of computer-based models—in particular, to those that lend themselves to graphic interpretation. Graphics can be used to create and edit the model, to obtain values for its parameters, and to visualize its behavior and structure. The model and the graphical means for creating and visualizing it are distinct; models such as population models need not have any inherent graphical aspects. Among common types of models for which computer graphics is used are these:

- *Organizational models* are hierarchies representing institutional bureaucracies and taxonomies, such as library classification schemes and biological taxonomies. These models have various directed-graph representations, such as the organization chart.

- *Quantitative models* are equations describing econometric, financial, sociological, demographic, climatic, chemical, physical, and mathematical systems. These are often depicted by graphs or statistical plots.

- *Geometric models* are collections of components with well-defined geometry and, often, interconnections between components, including engineering and architectural structures, molecules and other chemical structures, geographic structures, and vehicles. These models are usually depicted by block diagrams or by pseudorealistic "synthetic photographs."

Computer-assisted modeling allows pharmaceutical drug designers to model the chemical behavior of new compounds that may be effective against particular diseases, aeronautical engineers to predict wing deformation during supersonic flight, pilots to learn to fly, nuclear-reactor experts to predict the effects of various plant malfunctions and to develop the appropriate remedies, and automobile designers to test the integrity of the passenger compartment during crashes. In these and many other instances, it is far easier, cheaper, and safer to experiment with a model than with a real entity. In fact, in many situations, such as training of space-shuttle pilots and studies of nuclear-reactor safety, modeling and simulation are the only feasible method for learning about the system. For these reasons, computer modeling is replacing more traditional techniques, such as wind-tunnel tests. Engineers and scientists now can perform many of their experiments with digital wind tunnels, microscopes, telescopes, and so on. Such numerically based simulation and animation of models is rapidly becoming a new paradigm in science, taking its place beside the traditional branches of theory and physical experimentation. Needless to say, the modeling and simulation are only as good as the model and its inputs—the caution *garbage in, garbage out* pertains especially to modeling.

Models need not necessarily contain intrinsically geometric data; abstractions such as organizational models are not spatially oriented. Nonetheless, most such models can be represented geometrically; for example, an organizational model may be represented by an organization chart, or the results of a clinical drug evaluation may be represented by a histogram. Even when a model represents an intrinsically geometric object, no fixed graphical representation in the model or view of that model is dictated. For example, we can choose whether to represent a robot as a collection of polyhedra or of curved surfaces, and we can specify how the robot is to be "photographed"—from which viewpoint, with which type of geometric projection, and with what degree of realism. Also, we may choose to show either the structure or the behavior of a model pictorially; for instance, we may want to see both a VLSI circuit's physical layout on the chip and its electrical and logical behaviors as functions of inputs and time.

7.1.1 Geometric Models

Geometric or graphical models describe components with inherent geometrical properties and thus lend themselves naturally to graphical representation. Among the ingredients a geometric model may represent are the following:

- Spatial layout and shape of components (i.e., the *geometry* of the entity), and other attributes affecting the appearance of components, such as color
- Connectivity of components (i.e., the structure or *topology* of the entity); note that connectivity information may be specified abstractly (say, in an adjacency matrix for networks or in a tree structure for a hierarchy) or may have its own intrinsic geometry (the dimensions of channels in an integrated circuit)
- Application-specific data values and properties associated with components, such as electrical characteristics or descriptive text.

Associated with the model may be processing algorithms, such as linear-circuit analysis for discrete circuit models, finite-element analysis for mechanical structures, and energy minimization for molecular models.

There is a tradeoff between what is stored explicitly in the model and what must be computed prior to analysis or display—a classic space–time tradeoff. For example, a model of a computer network could store the connecting lines explicitly or could recompute them from a connectivity matrix with a simple graph-layout algorithm each time a new view is requested. Enough information must be kept with the model to allow analysis and display, but the exact format and the choices of encoding techniques depend on the application and on space–time tradeoffs.

7.1.2 Hierarchy in Geometric Models

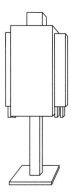

Figure 7.1
Perspective view of simplified android robot.

Geometric models often have a hierarchical structure induced by a bottom-up construction process: Components are used as building blocks to create higher-level entities, which in turn serve as building blocks for yet higher-level entities, and so on. Like large programming systems, hierarchies are seldom constructed strictly bottom-up or top-down; what matters is the final hierarchy, not the exact construction process. Object hierarchies are common because few entities are monolithic (indivisible); once we decompose an entity into a collection of parts, we have created at least a two-level hierarchy. In the uncommon case that each object is included only once in a higher-level object, the hierarchy can be symbolized as a tree, with objects as nodes and inclusion relations between objects as edges. In the more common case of objects included multiple times, the hierarchy is symbolized by a *directed acyclic graph* (DAG). As a simple example of object hierarchy, Fig. 7.1 shows a perspective view of a rudimentary *android* robot; Fig. 7.2(a) shows the robot's structure as a DAG. Note that we can duplicate the multiply included objects to convert the DAG to a tree (Fig. 7.2b). By convention, the arrows are left off as redundant because the ordering relationship between nodes is indicated by the nodes' relative positions in the tree—if node A is above node B, then A includes B.

The robot is composed of an upper body swiveling on a base. The upper body is composed of a head that rotates relative to a trunk; the trunk also has attached to it two identical arms that may rotate independently through a horizontal axis *at the shoulder.* The arm is composed of a fixed part, *the hand,* and a thumb that slides parallel to the hand to form a primitive gripper. Thus, the thumb object is invoked once in the arm, and the arm object is invoked twice in the upper body. We discuss the creation of this robot throughout this chapter; its shape is also presented in three orthographic projections in windows 2–4 of the screen shown in Fig. 7.5(b).

Although an object in a hierarchy is composed of geometric primitives as well as inclusions of lower-level subobjects, the DAG and the tree representing the robot's hierarchy show only references to subobjects. This is analogous to the procedure-hierarchy diagram commonly used to show the calling structure of a program in a high-level procedural language. It is important to note that it is up to the designer to decide exactly how a composite object is hierarchically constructed. For example, the robot could have been modeled as a two-level hierarchy, with a root object consisting of a base, a head and a trunk as geometric primitives (parallelepipeds, say), and two references to an *atomic* arm object composed of geometric primitives only.

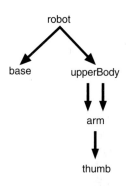

Figure 7.2(a)
Directed acyclic graph (DAG) representation of robot hierarchy.

Many systems, such as computer networks or chemical plants, can be represented by network diagrams, in which objects are not only included multiple times, but are also interconnected arbitrarily. Such networks are also modeled as graphs, possibly even containing cycles, but they can still exhibit properties of object-inclusion hierarchy when subnetworks occur multiple times.

To simplify the task of building complex objects (and their models), we commonly use application-specific atomic components as the basic building blocks. In 2D, these components are often drawn by using plastic or computer

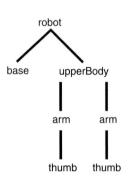

Figure 7.2(b)
Tree representation of robot
hierarchy.

drawn templates of standard symbolic shapes (also called symbols or stencils). In drawing programs, these shapes, in turn, are composed of geometric primitives, such as lines, rectangles, polygons, ellipse arcs, and so on. In 3D, shapes such as cylinders, parallelepipeds, spheres, pyramids, and surfaces of revolution are used as basic building blocks. These 3D shapes may be defined in terms of lower-level geometric primitives, such as 3D polygons; in this case, smoothly curved surfaces must be approximated by polygonal ones, with attendant loss of resolution. Alternatively, in advanced modeling systems that deal directly with free-form surfaces or volumes, shapes such as parametric polynomial surfaces, and solids such as cylinders, spheres, and cones, are themselves geometric primitives and are defined analytically, without loss of resolution—see Chapters 9 and 10. We use the term **object** in this chapter for those 2D or 3D components that are defined in their own modeling coordinate systems in terms of geometric primitives and lower-level objects and that usually have not only geometrical data but also associated application data. An object is thus a (composite) shape and all its data.

A hierarchy, then, is created for a variety of purposes:

- To construct complex objects in a modular fashion, typically by repetitive invocations of building blocks that vary in geometric and appearance attributes

- To increase storage economy, since it suffices to store only references to objects that are used repeatedly, rather than the complete object definition each time

- To allow easy update propagation, because a change in the definition of one building-block object is automatically propagated to all higher-level objects that use that object (since they now refer to an updated version); the analogy between object and procedure hierarchy is useful here, in that a change to the body of a procedure is also reflected in all invocations of that procedure.

The application can use a variety of techniques to encode hierarchical models. For example, a network or relational database can be used to store information on objects and on relationships between objects. Alternatively, a more efficient, customized linked-list structure can be maintained by the application program, with records for objects and pointers for relationships. In some models, connections between objects are objects in their own right; they must also be represented with data records in the model. Yet another alternative is to use an object-oriented database [ZDON90]. Object-oriented programming environments such as SmallTalk [GOLD83], MacApp [SCHM86], and C++ [STRO91] are increasingly being used to store modeling information for the geometric objects in graphics application programs.

Interconnections.   In most networks, objects are placed in specified locations (either interactively by the user or automatically by the application program) and then are interconnected. Interconnections may be abstract and thus of arbitrary shape (e.g., in hierarchy or network diagrams, such as organization charts or project-scheduling charts), or they may have significant geometry of their own (e.g., a VLSI chip). If connections are abstract, we can use various standard conventions for laying out hierarchical or network diagrams, and we can employ attributes such as line style, line width, or color to denote various types of relationships (e.g., *dotted-line responsibility* in an organization chart). Connections whose shape matters, such as the channels connecting transistors and other components of a VLSI circuit, are essentially objects in their own right. Both abstract and nonabstract connections are often **constrained** to have horizontal or vertical orientations (sometimes called the **Manhattan** layout scheme) to simplify visualization and physical construction.

Parameter passing in object hierarchy. Objects invoked as building blocks must be positioned in exactly the right place in their parent objects and, in order to fit, often must be resized and reoriented as well. Homogeneous coordinate matrices were used to transform primitives in Chapter 5 and to normalize the view volume in Chapter 6, and it should come as no surprise that, in a hierarchical model, one frequently applies scaling, rotation, and translation matrices to subobjects. Sutherland first used this capability for graphical modeling in Sketchpad [SUTH63], coining the terms **master** for the definition of an object and **instance** for a geometrically transformed invocation. As discussed in Section 4.3.3, graphics systems using **hierarchical display lists** (also called **structured display files**) implement master–instance hierarchy in hardware, using subroutine jumps and high-speed floating-point arithmetic units for transformations. Because we want to distinguish geometric transformations used in normalizing the view volume from those used in building object hierarchy, we often speak of the latter as **modeling transformations.** Mathematically, of course, there is no difference between modeling and normalizing transformations.

Once again, in analogy with procedure hierarchy, we sometimes speak of a parent object *calling* a child object in a hierarchy, and passing it *geometric parameters* corresponding to its scale, orientation, and position in the parent's coordinate system. As we will see shortly, graphics packages that support object hierarchy, such as SPHIGS, can store, compose, and apply transformation matrices to vertices of primitives, as well as to vertices of instantiated child objects. Furthermore, attributes affecting appearance can also be passed to instantiated objects. In Section 7.5.3, however, we shall see that the SPHIGS parameter-passing mechanism is not as general as is that of a procedural language.

7.1.3 Relationship Among Model, Application Program, and Graphics System

So far, we have looked at models in general, and geometric models with hierarchy and modeling transformations in particular. Before looking at SPHIGS, let's briefly review the conceptual model of graphics first shown in Fig. 1.11 and elaborated in Fig. 3.2, to show the interrelationship among the model, the application program, and the graphics system. In the diagram in Fig. 7.3, application programs are divided into five subsystems, labeled (a) through (e):

    a.   Build, modify, and maintain the model by adding, deleting, and replacing information in it

    b.   Traverse (scan) the model to extract information for display

    c.   Traverse the model to extract information used in the analysis of the model's behavior/performance

    d.   Display both information (e.g., rendering of a geometric model, output of an analysis) and user-interface *tools* (e.g., menus, dialogue boxes)

    e.   Perform miscellaneous application tasks not directly involving the model or display (e.g., housekeeping).

The term **subsystem** does not imply major modules of code—a few calls or a short procedure may be sufficient to implement a given subsystem. Furthermore, a subsystem may be distributed throughout the application program, rather than being gathered in a separate program module. Thus, Fig. 7.3 simply shows logical components, not necessarily program structure components; moreover, while it does differentiate the procedures that build, modify, analyze, or display the model, it is not always clear whether to call a particular module part of the model or part of the model-maintenance code. It could be argued, for example, that a circuit-analysis module is really part of the model's definition because it describes how the circuit behaves. For a programmer using a traditional procedural language such as Pascal or C, Fig. 7.3 works best if one thinks of the model as primarily containing data. People familiar with object-oriented programming languages will find the mixture of data and procedures a natural one.

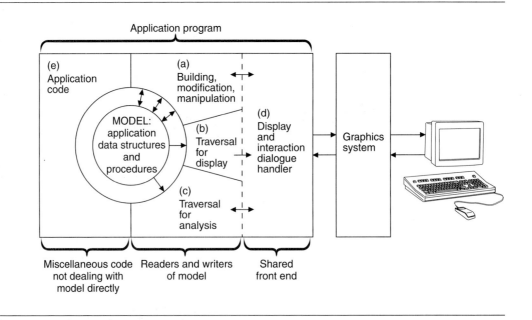

Figure 7.3   The application model and its readers and writers.

In many application programs, especially industrial ones, an 80/20 rule holds: The major portion of the program (80 percent) deals with modeling of entities, and only a minor portion (20 percent) deals with making pictures of them. In other words, in many applications such as CAD, pictorial representation of models is a means to an end, the end being analysis, physical construction, numerically controlled machining, or some other type of postprocessing. Naturally, there are also many applications for which *the picture is the thing*—for example, painting, drafting, film and video production, and animation of scenes for flight simulators. Of these, all but painting also require a model from which the images are rendered. In short, most graphics involve significant modeling (and simulation) and there is considerable support for the saying "graphics *is* modeling"; Chapters 9 and 10 are devoted to that important subject.

7.2 CHARACTERISTICS OF RETAINED-MODE GRAPHICS PACKAGES

In discussing the roles of the application program, the application model, and the graphics package, we glossed over exactly what capabilities the graphics package has and what happens when the model is modified. SRGP, described in Chapter 2, operates in **immediate mode** and keeps no record of the primitives and attributes passed to it. Thus, deletions of and changes to application objects necessitate the removal of information on the screen and therefore either selective modification or complete regeneration of the screen; either of these requires the application to respecify primitives from its model. PHIGS, on the other hand, operates in **retained mode**: It keeps a record of all primitives and other related information to allow subsequent editing and automatic updating of the display, thereby offloading the application program.

7.2.1 Central Structure Storage and Its Advantages

PHIGS stores information in a special-purpose database called the **central structure storage (CSS)**. A **structure** in PHIGS is a sequence of **elements**—primitives, appearance attributes, transformation matrices, and invocations of subordinate structures—whose purpose is to define a coherent geometric object. Thus, PHIGS effectively stores a special-purpose modeling hierarchy, complete with modeling transformations and other attributes passed as *parameters* to subordinate structures. Notice the similarities between the CSS modeling hierarchy and a hardware hierarchical display list that stores a master–instance hierarchy. In effect, PHIGS may be viewed as the specification of a device-independent hierarchical display-list package; a given implementation is, of course, optimized for a particular display device, but the application programmer need not be concerned with that. Whereas many PHIGS implementations are purely software, the most common arrangement is to do CSS manipulation in software and to use a combination of hardware and software for rendering.

As does a display list, the CSS duplicates geometric information stored in the application's more general-purpose model or database to facilitate rapid *display traversal*—that is, the traversal used to compute a new view of the model. The primary advantage of the CSS, therefore, is rapid automatic screen regeneration whenever the application updates the CSS. This feature alone may be worth the duplication of geometric data in the application database and the CSS, especially when the PHIGS implementation uses a separate processor as a *traversal engine* to offload display traversal from the CPU running the application. Small edits, such as changing a transformation matrix, are also done efficiently in PHIGS.

A second advantage of the CSS is automatic pick correlation: The package determines the identity and place within the hierarchy of the primitive picked by the user (see Section 7.10.2). The pick-correlation facility exemplifies a common technique of moving frequently needed functionality into the underlying graphics package.

A third advantage of the CSS is that its editing facilities, in combination with the features of hierarchical modeling, make it easy to create various dynamic effects—for example, motion dynamics—in which time-varying transformations are used to scale, rotate, and position subobjects within parent objects. For example, we can model our simple robot so that each joint is represented by a rotation applied to a substructure (e.g., the arm is a rotated subordinate of the upper body), and dynamically rotate the arm by editing a single rotation matrix.

7.2.2 Limitations of Retained-Mode Packages

Although the CSS (as a special-purpose entity built primarily for display and fast incremental updating) facilitates certain common modeling operations, it is neither necessary nor sufficient for all modeling purposes. It is not necessary because an application can do its own screen regeneration when the model is changed, can do its own pick correlation (albeit with considerable work), and can implement its own object hierarchy via procedures defining objects and accepting transformations and other parameters. The CSS is generally not sufficient because, in most applications, a separately built and updated application data structure is still necessary to record all appropriate data for each application object. Thus, there is duplication of all geometric data, and the two representations must be synchronized properly. For all these reasons, some graphics packages support floating-point coordinates and generalized 2D and 3D viewing facilities without any type of structure storage. The rationale for such immediate-mode packages is that maintaining the CSS is often not worth the overhead, since the application typically maintains an application model sufficient for regenerating the screen image.

For applications in which there is significant structural change between successive images, using a retained-mode package does not pay. For example, in a *digital–wind-tunnel* analysis of an airplane wing, where the surface is represented by a mesh of triangles, most of the vertices shift slightly in position as the wing is subjected to aerodynamic forces. Editing a structure database for such a case makes no sense, since most of the data are replaced for each new image. Indeed, editing the PHIGS structure database is not advised unless the number of elements to be edited is small relative to the size of the networks being displayed. The editing tools provided by PHIGS are rudimentary; for example, it is easy to change a modeling transformation, but to change a vertex of a polygon requires deleting the polygon and respecifying the changed version. Typically, implementations are likely to be optimized for display traversal, since that is the most common operation, rather than for massive editing. Furthermore, the application model must be updated in any case, and it is easier and faster to update just one database than to update two of them.

Because of these limitations, many implementations of PHIGS offer an immediate-mode output facility, or even a hybrid mode in which primitives specified in immediate mode may be combined with retained primitives.

7.3 DEFINING AND DISPLAYING STRUCTURES

The previous section has discussed general properties of PHIGS and SPHIGS. In this section, we begin describing the SPHIGS package in detail; unless otherwise noted, the discussion is generally also applicable to PHIGS. The manipulations permitted on SPHIGS structures include the following:

- Opening (to initiate editing) and closing (to conclude editing)
- Deleting
- Inserting **structure elements** (the three primary types of structure elements are primitives, attributes, including those that specify modeling transformations, and elements that invoke substructures). An element is a data record that is created and inserted into the currently open structure whenever an **element-generator** procedure is called and that stores that procedure's parameters.
- Deleting structure elements
- **Posting** for display (by analogy to posting a snapshot on a bulletin board), subject to a **viewing operation** that specifies how to map the floating-point coordinates to the screen's coordinate system.

7.3.1 Opening and Closing Structures

To create a structure—for example, the collection of primitives and attributes forming the arm component of the robot in Fig. 7.2—we bracket calls to the element-generator functions with calls to

```
void  SPH_openStructure ( int structureID );
void  SPH_closeStructure();
```

These functions do for structures essentially what the standard open- and close-file commands do for disk files. Unlike disk files, however, only one structure may be open at any time, and all elements specified while it is open are stored in it. Once closed, structures may be reopened for editing (see Section 7.9).

We note two additional properties of structures. First, primitives and attributes can be specified only as elements of a structure. There are no rules about how many elements may be stored in a structure; a structure can be empty, or can contain an arbitrarily large number of elements, limited only by memory space. Of course, the elements forming a structure should be, in general, a logically cohesive set defining a single object.

Second, structure IDs are integers. Since they are normally used only by the application program, not by the interactive user, they do not need to have the more general form of character strings, although the application programmer is free to define symbolic constants for structure IDs. Integer IDs also allow a convenient mapping between objects in the application data structure and the objects' corresponding structure IDs.

7.3.2 Specifying Output Primitives and Their Attributes

The functions that generate output-primitive elements look like their SRGP counterparts, but there are important differences. First, points are specified with three floating-point coordinates (x, y, and z). Moreover, these functions place elements in the currently open structure in the CSS rather than directly altering the screen image—displaying structures is a separate operation described in Section 7.3.3. In this chapter, the term **primitive** is used as shorthand for three related entities: an element-generation function, such as SPH_polyLine; the structure element generated by that function (for example, the polyLine element); and the displayed image created when a primitive element is executed during display traversal of central structure storage. SPHIGS **executes** a primitive element by transforming the primitive's coordinates by modeling transformations and a viewing operation, including clipping it to the view volume, and then **rasterizing** it (i.e., converting it to pixels). Attributes are more specialized than in SRGP, in that each type of primitive has its own attributes. Thus, attributes such as color and line style are in effect *typed,* so that the programmer can, for example, reset the current color for lines while preserving the current colors for polyhedra and text.

Primitives.   SPHIGS has fewer output primitives than SRGP does, because the 3D *solid* equivalents of some of SRGP's primitives (e.g., an ellipsoid) are computationally expensive to implement, especially with respect to transformations, clipping, and scan conversion.

Most of the SPHIGS primitives are identical to their SRGP counterparts in their specification methods (except that the points are 3D):

> **void** SPH_polyLine (**int** vertexCount, **pointList** vertices);
> **void** SPH_polyMarker (**int** vertexCount, **pointList** vertices);
> **void** SPH_fillArea (**int** vertexCount, **pointList** vertices);
> /* Like SRGP_polygon */
> **void** SPH_text (**point** origin, **char** *str);
> /* Not fully 3D; see Section 7.7.2 */

Note that SPHIGS does not verify that fill areas (or facets, described next) are planar, and the results are undefined if they are not.

Now, consider the definition of a simple house, shown in Fig. 7.4. We can describe this house to SPHIGS by specifying each face (also called a **facet**) as a fill area, at the cost of unnecessary duplication in the specification and storage (in CSS) of each shared vertex. This duplication also slows down display generation, since the viewing-operation calculation would be performed on a single vertex more than once. It is far more efficient in storage and processing time to specify the facets using indirect references to the shared vertices. We thus think of a polyhedron as a collection of facets, each facet being a list of vertex indexes and each index being a pointer into a list of vertices. We can describe a polyhedron's specification using the following notation:

Polyhedron = {VertexList, FacetList}
VertexList = {V1, V2, V3, V4, V5, V6, V7, V8, V9, V10}
$V1 = (x_1, y_1, z_1)$, $V2 = (x_2, y_2, z_2)$, ...
FacetList = {front = {1, 2, 3, 4, 5}, right = {2, 7, 8, 3}, ... bottom = { ... } }

SPHIGS offers this efficient form of specification with its **polyhedron** primitive. In SPHIGS terminology, a polyhedron is a collection of facets that may or may not enclose a volume. In a closed polyhedron such as our house, vertices are typically shared by at least three facets, so the efficiency of the indirect method of specification is especially high. The appearance of a polyhedron is affected by the same attributes that apply to fill areas.

The list of facets is presented to the polyhedron element generator in the form of a single array of integers (SPHIGS type "vertexIndexList") storing a concatenated set of facet descriptions. Each facet description is a sequence of $(V + 1)$ integers, where V is the number of vertices in the facet. The first V integers are indices into the vertex list; the last integer is (−1) and acts as a sentinel ending the facet specification. Thus, we would specify the facets of the house (via the fourth parameter of the function, described next) by sending the array: 1, 2, 3, 4, 5, −1, 2, 7, 8, 3, −1, ...

void SPH_polyhedron
       (**int** vertexCount, **int** facetCount, **pointList** vertices, **vertexIndexList** facets);

Note that the SPHIGS-rendering algorithms require that a facet's two sides be distinguishable (external versus internal). Thus, the vertices must be specified in counterclockwise (right-hand rule) order, as one examines the external side of the facet.[2]

As a simple example, the following C code creates a structure consisting of a single polyhedron modeling the house of Fig. 7.4:

```
SPH_openStructure (HOUSE_STRUCT);
    SPH_polyhedron (10, 7, houseVertexList, houseFacetDescriptions);
SPH_closeStructure();
```

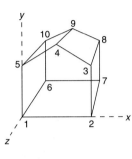

Figure 7.4
A simple house defined as a set of vertices and facets.

---

[2] SPHIGS requires that one side of each facet be deemed *external,* even if the polyhedron's facets do not form a closed object. Furthermore, the *internal* side of a polyhedron facet is never visible.

In essence, SPHIGS supports polygonal geometry only. More advanced 3D modeling primitives will be covered later—polynomially defined smooth curves and surfaces in Chapter 9, and solid primitives in Chapter 10.

Attributes.   The functions listed in Prog. 7.1 generate attribute elements. During display traversal, the execution of an attribute element changes the attribute's value in a modal fashion: The new value stays in effect until it is changed explicitly. Attributes are bound to primitives during display traversal, as discussed in the next section and in Section 7.7.

Program 7.1

Functions generating attribute elements.

polyLine:
> **void** SPH_setLineStyle(**style** CONTINUOUS / DASHED / DOTTED / DOT_DASHED);
> **void** SPH_setLineWidthScaleFactor(**double** scaleFactor);
> **void** SPH_setLineColor(**int** colorIndex);

fill area and polyhedron:
> **void** SPH_setInteriorColor(**int** colorIndex);
> **void** SPH_setEdgeFlag(**flag** EDGE_VISIBLE / EDGE_INVISIBLE);
> **void** SPH_setEdgeStyle(**style** CONTINUOUS / DASHED / DOTTED / DOT_DASHED);
> **void** SPH_setEdgeWidthScaleFactor(**double** scaleFactor);
> **void** SPH_setEdgeColor(**int** colorIndex);

polyMarker:
> **void** SPH_setMarkerStyle(**style** MARKER_CIRCLE / MARKER_SQUARE / ...);
> **void** SPH_setMarkerSizeScaleFactor(**double** scaleFactor);
> **void** SPH_setMarkerColor(**int** colorIndex);

text:
> **void** SPH_setTextFont(**int** fontIndex);
> **void** SPH_setTextColor(**int** colorIndex);

The attributes of fill areas are different from those of polygons in SRGP. Both fill-area and polyhedron primitives have interiors and edges whose attributes are specified separately. The interior has only the color attribute, whereas the edge has style, width, and color attributes. Moreover, the visibility of edges can be turned off via the edge-flag attribute, which is useful for various rendering modes, as discussed in Section 7.8.

Line or edge width and marker size are specified in a *nongeometric* manner: They are not defined using world-coordinate–system units and therefore are not subject to geometric transformations. Thus, modeling transformations and the viewing operation may change a line's apparent length, but not its width. Similarly, the length of dashes in a noncontinuous line style is independent of the transformations applied to the line. However, unlike in SRGP, pixels are not used as the units of measurement, because their sizes are device-dependent. Rather, a nominal width/size has been preset for each device, so that a unit of width/size will have roughly the same appearance on any output device; the SPHIGS application specifies a (noninteger) multiple of that nominal width/size.

SPHIGS does not support patterns, for three reasons. First, SPHIGS reserves patterns to simulate color shading on bilevel systems. Second, smooth shading of patterned areas on a color system is much too computationally intensive for most display systems. Third, the type of geometric pattern called **hatching** in PHIGS is also too time consuming, even for display systems with real-time transformation hardware.

7.3.3 Posting Structures for Display Traversal

SPHIGS records a newly created structure in the CSS, but does not display it until the application *posts* the structure subject to a particular viewing specification.[3] SPHIGS then performs a **display traversal** of the structure's elements in the CSS, executing each element in order from the first to the last. Executing a primitive element contributes to the screen image (if a portion of the primitive is in view). Executing an attribute element (both geometric transformations and appearance attributes) changes the collection of attributes stored in a state vector (the **attribute-traversal state**) that is applied to subsequent primitives as they are encountered, in modal fashion. Thus, attributes are applied to primitives in display-traversal order.

The following function adds a structure to the list of posted structures maintained internally by SPHIGS:

void SPH_postRoot (**int** structureID, **int** viewIndex);

The term *root* indicates that, in posting a structure S that invokes substructures, we are actually posting the hierarchical DAG, called the **structure network,** whose root is S. Even if a posted structure does not invoke substructures, it is called a root; all posted structures are roots.

The *viewIndex* parameter chooses an entry in the table of **views** (discussed in the next section); this entry specifies how the coordinates of the structure's primitives are to be mapped to the screen's integer coordinate space.

We can erase an object's image from the screen by deleting structures (or elements) from the CSS (see Section 7.9) or by using the less drastic SPH_unpostRoot function which removes the root from the list of posted roots without deleting it from the CSS:

void SPH_unpostRoot (**int** structureID, **int** viewIndex);

7.3.4 Viewing

The synthetic camera.   As noted in Chapter 6, it is helpful to think of a 3D graphics package as a synthetic camera that takes *snapshots* of a 3D world inhabited by geometrically defined objects. Creating a structure is equivalent to

---

[3] This way of specifying structure display is the most significant difference between PHIGS and SPHIGS. In PHIGS's more general mechanism, the view specification is a structure element; this allows the view to be changed during display traversal and to be edited like any other element. Many current PHIGS implementations also support the simpler SPHIGS-style posting mechanism.

positioning an object in a photography studio; posting a structure is analogous to activating an instant camera previously set up to point at the scene, and then having the snapshot of the scene posted on a bulletin board. As we see shortly, each time anything changes in the scene, our synthetic camera automatically produces a new, updated image that is posted in place of the old one. To create animation, we show multiple static images in rapid succession, as a movie camera does.

Continuing the metaphor, let's consider how the synthetic picture is produced. First, the camera operator must position and orient the camera, then decide how much of the scene should appear: For example, is the image to be a closeup of a portion of an object of interest, or a long-distance view of the entire scene? Subsequently, the photographer must decide how large a print to make for posting on the bulletin board: Is it to be a wallet-sized print, or a poster? Finally, the place on the bulletin board where the photograph is to be posted must be determined. In SPHIGS, these criteria are represented in a *view* that includes a specification of a viewing operation; this operation's *viewport* specifies the size of the photograph and its position on the bulletin board. Not all objects in the structure database need be photographed with the same *camera setting*. Indeed, multiple views may be specified for the bulletin board, as we shall see shortly.

The viewport.   As discussed in the previous chapter, the viewport specifies a parallelepiped in the (normalized projection coordinate) NPC system to which the contents of the view volume defined in (viewing-reference coordinates) VRC is mapped. Since the NPC system is mapped to the physical device's integer-coordinate system in a fixed manner, the viewport also specifies where the image is to appear on the screen. The 3D NPC system is mapped to the 2D screen coordinate system in this manner: The NPC unit cube having one corner at $(0, 0, 0)$ and the opposing corner at $(1, 1, 1)$ is mapped to the largest square that can be inscribed on the screen, with the z coordinate simply ignored. For example, on a display device having a resolution of 1024 horizontally and 800 vertically, a point $(0.5, 0.75, z)_{\text{NPC}}$ is mapped to $(511, 599)_{\text{DC}}$. For portability, an application should not use NPC space lying outside the unit cube; often, however, the benefits of taking full advantage of a nonsquare screen shape may well be worth the portability cost.

The view table.   SPHIGS maintains a table of views that has an implementation-dependent number of entries. Each view consists of a specification of the view volume and viewport, called the **view representation**, and a list (initially empty) of the roots posted to it. Entry 0 in the table defines a **default view** having the volume described in Fig. 6.19(b), with the front and back planes at $z = 0$ and $z = -\infty$, respectively. The viewport for this default view is the NPC unit cube.

The view representations for all entries in the table (except view 0) may be edited by the application via

```
void SPH_setViewRepresentation(
        int viewIndex, matrix_4x4 voMatrix, matrix_4x4 vmMatrix,
        double NPCviewport_minX, double NPCviewport_maxX,
        double NPCviewport_minY, double NPCviewport_maxY,
        double NPCviewport_minZ, double NPCviewport_maxZ );
```

The two 4×4 homogeneous-coordinate matrices are the view-orientation and view-mapping matrices described in Chapter 6. They are produced by the functions shown in Prog. 7.2.

Program 7.2

Utilities for calculating viewing-transformation matrices.

```
/* To set up UVN Viewing Reference Coordinate System.*/
void  SPH_evaluateViewOrientationMatrix( point_3D viewRefPoint,
            vector_3D viewPlaneNormal, vector_3D viewUpVector,
            matrix_4x4 *voMatrix );

/* To set up View Volume and describe how it is to be mapped to NPC space.*/
void  SPH_evaluateViewMappingMatrix(
      /* First, we specify the view-plane boundaries.*/
         double umin, double umax, double vmin, double vmax,
         int projectionType,          /* PARALLEL / PERSPECTIVE */
         point_3D projectionReferencePoint,            /* In VRC */
         double frontPlaneDistance, double backPlaneDistance,   /* Clip planes */
      /* Then, we specify the NPC viewport.*/
         double NPCvp_minX, double NPCvp_maxX,
         double NPCvp_minY, double NPCvp_maxY,
         double NPCvp_minZ, double NPCvp_maxZ,
         matrix_4x4 *vmMatrix );
```

Multiple views. The view index specified during posting refers to a specific NPC viewport describing where on the screen (bulletin board) the image of the structure (photograph) is to appear. Just as one can tack several photographic prints on a board, an application can divide the screen into a number of viewports. The use of multiple views is powerful in many ways. We can display several different structures simultaneously in individual areas of the screen by posting them with different views. In Fig. 7.5(a), we present a schematic representation of the view table, showing only the pointers to the lists of structure networks posted to each view. We can see that there is one view showing a street scene; also, there are three separate views of a robot. The robot structure was posted three times, each time with a different view index. Figure 7.5(b) shows the resulting screen image. The multiple views of the robot vary not only in their viewport specifications, but also in their view-volume specifications.

The preceding scenario implies that each view has at most one posted structure; in fact, however, any number of roots can be posted to a single view. Thus, we can display different root structures in a single unified picture by posting them together to a view. In this case, our metaphorical camera would take a single composite snapshot of a scene that contains many different objects.

Another property of viewports is that, unlike real snapshots and window-manager windows, they are transparent. In practice, many applications *tile* the viewports to avoid overlapping; however, we can also use overlapping to advantage. For example, we can *compose* two distinct images created by different viewing transformations or showing objects defined in different units of measurement; thus, in building a close-up diagram of an engine part, we could inset a small picture showing the entire engine (for context) overlapping the large close-up picture. (We would do this by selecting an area of the closeup that is just background.)

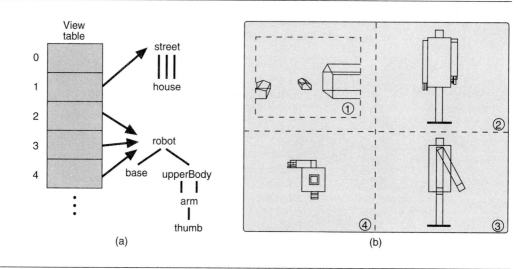

Figure 7.5   Multiple views sharing screen space. (a) Schematic diagram of view table. Each view entry points to a list of the roots posted to that view. (b) Resulting image. Dashed viewport extents and circled numbers show the viewports and their associated view indices.

To regenerate the screen, SPHIGS displays the posted networks by traversing the roots posted to each view in the view table, in increasing order of view index, starting with view 0; thus, the images of objects posted to view N have **display priority** over the images of objects posted to a view with an index less than N, and therefore potentially overlap them. This ordering is significant, of course, only when viewports actually overlap. (Note that this trivial view-priority system is less sophisticated than that of PHIGS, which allows explicit view priorities to be assigned by application.)

Note that an application can manufacture many independent WC spaces and can use any units of measurement desired. In Fig. 7.5, for example, the street structure is defined in a WC space in which each increment on an axis represents 10 yards, whereas the robot is defined in a wholly independent WC space measured in centimeters. Although each root structure is modeled in its own WC space, there is only one NPC space per display device, shared by all posted structures, since that space is an abstraction of the display device.

7.3.5 Graphics Applications Sharing a Screen via Window Management

When the first standard interactive graphics packages were being designed in the early 1970s, only a single graphics application ran at a given time, and it used the entire screen. The design of PHIGS began in the late 1970s, when this mode of operation was still dominant and before window managers were generally available. Thus, the unit cube of the NPC space was traditionally mapped to the screen in its entirety.

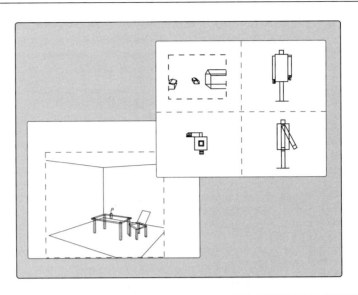

Figure 7.6   Two SPHIGS applications, each running in its own window-manager window. Dashed lines illustrate viewport boundaries.

Modern graphics workstations with multitasking operating systems allow multiple graphics applications to run simultaneously, sharing the workstation's resources, the screen, and the set of input devices, under control of a window manager. In this environment, each application is assigned to its own window, which acts as a *virtual screen*. The user can resize and move these windows by calling on the functionality of the window manager. The primary advantage is that each application can act as though it controls an entire screen; it does not need to know that its screen is only a portion of the actual display device's screen. An SPHIGS application, therefore, need not be modified for a window-manager environment; the package and the window manager cooperate to map NPC space to an assigned window rather than to the entire screen.

Figure 7.6 shows two SPHIGS applications running concurrently on a graphics workstation. Because SPHIGS maps the NPC space to the largest square that fits within the window-manager window, some portion of any nonsquare window is unavailable to the SPHIGS application, as illustrated by the SPHIGS window showing the table and chair scene.

7.4 MODELING TRANSFORMATIONS

Section 7.3.2 contained a C code fragment that created a simple structure modeling a house. For simplicity's sake, we placed one of the house's corners at the origin, aligned the house's sides with the principal axes, and gave it dimensions that were whole units. We shall say that an object defined at the origin and (largely) aligned with the principal axes is *standardized*; not only is it easier to define (determine the vertex coordinates of) a standardized object than it is to define one arbitrarily positioned in space, but also it is easier to manipulate the geometry of a standardized object in order to resize, reorient, or reposition it.

Let us say we want our house to appear at a different location, not near the origin. We could certainly recompute the house's vertices ourselves, and create the house structure using the same C code shown in Section 7.3.2 (changing only the vertex coordinates). Instead, however, we shall examine the powerful technique of transforming a standardized building-block object in order to change its dimensions or placement.

As we saw in Chapter 5, we can transform a primitive such as a polygon by multiplying each vertex, represented as a column vector $[x\ y\ z\ 1]^T$, by a 4×4 homogeneous-coordinate transformation matrix. The following utility functions create such matrices:

```
matrix_4x4 SPH_scale( double scaleX, double scaleY, double scaleZ );
matrix_4x4 SPH_rotateX( double angle );
matrix_4x4 SPH_rotateY( double angle );
matrix_4x4 SPH_rotateZ( double angle );
matrix_4x4 SPH_translate( double deltaX, double deltaY, double deltaZ );
```

A different scale factor may be specified for each of the axes, so an object can be *stretched* or *shrunk* nonuniformly. For rotation, the angle parameter, expressed in degrees, represents counterclockwise motion about the designated principal axis, from the point of view of someone looking along the axis from $+\infty$ toward the origin.

The matrices can be used to create a transformation element to be placed in a structure. The following function is the element generator:

```
void SPH_setLocalTransformation( matrix_4x4 matrix, mode REPLACE /
    PRECONCATENATE / POSTCONCATENATE);
```

The use of the prefix *local* here refers to how SPHIGS displays a structure. As SPHIGS traverses a structure, it stores a *local matrix* as a piece of state information applicable to only the structure being traversed. The local matrix is by default initialized to the identity matrix. Whenever a setLocalTransformation element is encountered, the local matrix is modified in some way: It either is replaced or is changed by a multiplication operation, as specified by the *mode* parameter. Whenever a primitive is encountered during traversal, each of its vertices is transformed by the local matrix and then is subjected to the viewing transformation for display. (As we will see later, hierarchy complicates this rule.)

The following code creates a structure containing our house at an arbitrary location, and posts that structure for display using the default view. The house maintains its original standardized size and orientation.

```
SPH_openStructure (HOUSE_STRUCT);
    SPH_setLocalTransformation (SPH_translate(...), REPLACE);
```

```
        SPH_polyhedron (...);              /* vertices here are standardized as before */
    SPH_closeStructure();
    SPH_postRoot (HOUSE_STRUCT, 0);
```

Simple transformations like this one are uncommon. We typically wish not only to translate the object, but also to affect its size and orientation. When multiple transformations of primitives are desired, the application builds the local matrix by successively concatenating (i.e., composing) individual transformation matrices in the exact order in which they are to be applied. In general, standardized building-block objects are scaled, then rotated, and finally translated to their desired location; as we saw in Chapter 5, this order avoids unwanted translations or shearing.

The following code creates and posts a house structure that is moved away from the origin and is rotated to a position where we see its side instead of its front:

```
    SPH_openStructure (MOVED_HOUSE_STRUCT);
        SPH_setLocalTransformation (SPH_rotate(...), REPLACE);
        SPH_setLocalTransformation (SPH_translate(...), PRECONCATENATE);
        SPH_polyhedron (...);        /* vertices here are standardized as before */
    SPH_closeStructure();
    SPH_postRoot (MOVED_HOUSE_STRUCT, 0);
```

The use of the PRECONCATENATE mode for the translation matrix ensures that premultiplication is used to compose the translation matrix with the rotation matrix, and thus that the translation's effect follows the rotation's. Premultiplication is thus a far more common mode than is postmultiplication, since it corresponds to the order of the individual transformation elements. Since SPHIGS performs scaling and rotation relative to the principal axes, if the programmer wants to transform relative to an arbitrary axis, he must first generate the matrices needed to map that axis to one of the principal axes, then do the transformations, and then map back, as discussed in Chapter 5.

The composition of the transformation elements is performed by SPHIGS at *traversal time*; thus, each time the display is regenerated, the composition must be performed. An alternative method for specifying a contiguous sequence of transformations increases the efficiency of the display-traversal process: Instead of making a structure element for each one, we compose them ourselves at *specification time* and generate a single transformation element. The following function does matrix multiplication at specification time:

matrix_4x4 SPH_composeMatrix(**matrix_4x4** mat1, **matrix_4x4** mat2);

The two setLocalTransformation elements in the preceding code can thus be replaced by

```
    SPH_setLocalTransformation (
        SPH_composeMatrix(SPH_translate(...), SPH_rotate(...)), REPLACE);
```

The disadvantage of this method is that it is no longer possible to make a dynamic change to the size, orientation, or position of a primitive by selectively "editing" the desired member of the sequence of setLocalTransformation elements; rather,

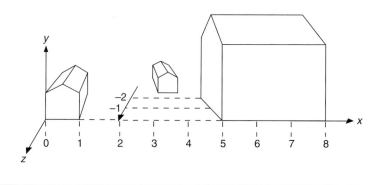

Figure 7.7(a)   Modeling a street with three houses. A perspective view.

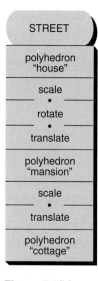

Figure 7.7(b)
Structure of street–house model.

the entire composite must be recomputed and respecified. The rule of thumb for efficiency is thus to use composition at specification time unless the individual transformations are to be updated selectively, in which case they should be specified individually.

Let us create the street structure that contains three copies of our simple house, as first seen in Fig. 7.4. A perspective view of the *house* on the left, the *mansion* on the right, and the *cottage* in the middle is shown in Fig. 7.7(a). We have added dashed lines parallel to the *x* axis and tick marks for the *x* axis to indicate the relative positions of the houses, and have used a display mode of SPHIGS that shows the wireframe edges of polyhedra with hidden edges removed (see Section 7.8). The leftmost house in the figure is an untransformed instance of our standardized house, and the other two copies differ in size, orientation, and position.

The brute-force way to create this street structure is to specify the standardized house polyhedron three times, preceded by the desired transformation elements, as shown in the schematic representation of the structure of Fig. 7.7(b). We show a block of consecutive transformation elements as a single unit; the first element uses REPLACE mode, and all others use PRECONCATENATION mode, with the multiplication symbol (·) separating them to indicate composition. The code generating the structure is shown in Prog. 7.3.

Program 7.3

Code used to generate Fig. 7.7(a).

```
SPH_openStructure(STREET_STRUCT);
   /* Define first house, in standard form. */
   SPH_polyhedron(...);

   /* Mansion is scaled by 2 in x, 3 in y, 1 in z, rotated 90° about y, then translated.
      Note that its left side is subsequently front-facing and lies in the (x, y) plane. */
   SPH_setLocalTransformation(SPH_scale(2.0, 3.0, 1.0), REPLACE);
   SPH_setLocalTransformation(SPH_rotateY(90.0), PRECONCATENATE);
   SPH_setLocalTransformation(SPH_translate(8.0, 0.0, 0.0), PRECONCATENATE);
   SPH_polyhedron(...);
```

```
                      /* Cottage is uniformly scaled by 0.75, unrotated, set back in z and over in x. */
                      SPH_setLocalTransformation(SPH_scale(0.75, 0.75, 0.75), REPLACE);
                      SPH_setLocalTransformation(SPH_translate(3.5, 0.0, −2.5), PRECONCATENATE);
                      SPH_polyhedron(...);
                   SPH_closeStructure();
                   SPH_postRoot(STREET_STRUCT, 0);
```

We can eliminate the redundant specifications of the standardized house polyhedron by defining a C function to perform the call generating the house polyhedron, as shown in the pseudocode of Prog. 7.4. Because the house is defined by a single polyhedron call, the efficiency of this technique is not obvious in this example; however, if our house were more complex and required a series of attribute and primitive specifications, this method clearly would require less C code. Moreover, the technique provides another benefit of modularization: We can change the house's shape or style by editing the House function without having to edit the code that creates the street.

We call a function such as House that generates a sequence of elements defining a standardized building block, and that is made to be used repetitively with arbitrary geometrical transformations, a **template function**. The template function is a convenience for the programmer and also represents good programming practice. Note, however, that although the House function adds a level of function hierarchy to the C program, no structure hierarchy is created—the model of the street is still *flat*. Indeed, the structure network produced by the code of Prog. 7.4 is indistinguishable from that produced by the code of Prog. 7.3. There is no savings in terms of the number of elements produced for the structure.

One change we could make to our template function is to have it accept a transformation matrix as a parameter, which it would then use to specify a setLocalTransformation element. Although in some cases passing transformation parameters would be convenient, this method lacks the generality inherent in our original method of being able to specify an arbitrary number of transformations before calling the template.

Program 7.4

Use of a template function to model the street.

```
void   House()
{
    SPH_polyhedron(...);
}

main()                              /* Mainline */
{
    SPH_openStructure(STREET_STRUCT);
        House();                    /* First  house */
        set local transformation matrix;
        House();                    /* Mansion */
        set local transformation matrix;
        House();                    /* Cottage */
    SPH_closeStructure();
    SPH_postRoot(STREET_STRUCT, 0);
}
```

7.5 HIERARCHICAL STRUCTURE NETWORKS

7.5.1 Two-Level Hierarchy

So far, we have dealt with three types of structure elements: output primitives, appearance attributes, and transformations. Next, we show how the power of SPHIGS derives in large part from structure hierarchy, implemented via an element that *calls* a substructure when executed during traversal. Structure hierarchy should not be confused with the template-procedure hierarchy of the previous section. Template-procedure hierarchy is resolved at specification time, when the CSS is being edited, and produces in-line elements, not substructure invocations. By contrast, structure hierarchy induced by invocation of substructures is resolved when the CSS is traversed for display—the execution of an invocation element acts as a subroutine call.

The **structure-execution element** that invokes a substructure is created by

void SPH_executeStructure(**int** structureID);

Let us replace the template function of the previous section by a function that builds a house structure in the CSS (see Prog. 7.5). This function is called exactly once by the mainline function, and the HOUSE_STRUCT is never posted; rather, its display results from its being invoked as a subobject of the street structure. Note that the only differences in the STREET_STRUCT specification are the addition of the call to the function that builds the house structure and the replacement of each template function call by the generation of an execute structure element. Although the

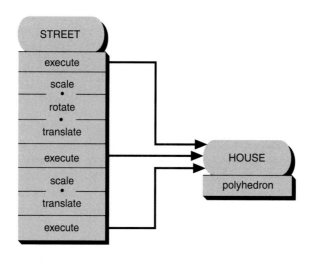

Figure 7.8   Structure network showing invocation of subordinate structure.

displayed image is the same as that of Fig. 7.7(a), the structure network is different, as shown in Fig. 7.8, in which the execute-structure element is depicted as an arrow.

Program 7.5

Use of a subordinate structure to model the street.

```
void   BuildStandardizedHouse()
{
    SPH_openStructure(HOUSE_STRUCT);
    SPH_polyhedron(...);
    SPH_closeStructure;
}

main()                                              /* Mainline */
{
    BuildStandardizedHouse();
    SPH_openStructure(STREET_STRUCT);
        SPH_executeStructure(HOUSE_STRUCT);         /* First house */
        set local transformation matrix;
        SPH_executeStructure(HOUSE_STRUCT);         /* Mansion */
        set local transformation matrix;
        SPH_executeStructure(HOUSE_STRUCT);         /* Cottage */
    SPH_closeStructure();
    SPH_postRoot(STREET_STRUCT);
}
```

Posting STREET_STRUCT tells SPHIGS to update the screen by traversing the STREET_STRUCT structure network; the traversal is in the form of a depth-first tree walk, just as a function/subroutine hierarchy is executed. In the preceding example, the traverser initializes the street structure's local matrix to the identity matrix, and then performs the first invocation of the house substructure, applying the street structure's local matrix to each of the house's vertices as though the house polyhedron were a primitive element in the street structure itself. When it returns from the first invocation, it sets the local matrix to a desired composite transformation, and then performs the second invocation, applying the new composite matrix to the vertices of the house to create the second instantiation of the house. When it returns, the local matrix is again changed; the new composite is applied to the house's vertices to produce the third house instance.

We think of a structure as an independent object, with its primitives defined in its own floating-point modeling-coordinate system (MCS); this way of thinking facilitates the building of low-level standardized building blocks. As we noted in Section 5.9, a transformation maps the vertices in one coordinate system into another; here, SPHIGS uses the local matrix of structure S to transform the primitives of substructures into S's own MCS.

7.5.2 Simple Three-Level Hierarchy

As a simple example of three-level hierarchy, we extend the house in our street example. The new house is composed of the original standardized house (renamed SIMPLE_HOUSE_STRUCT) and a chimney suitably scaled and translated to lie in the

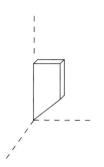

Figure 7.9(a)
Standardized chimney for
three-level street hierarchy.

right place on top of the house. We could revise the house structure by adding the chimney's facets directly to the original polyhedron, or by adding a second polyhedron to the structure, but we choose here to induce three-level hierarchy by decomposing the house into two subobjects. An advantage of this modularization is that we can define the chimney in a standardized manner (at the origin, of unit size) in its own MCS (as shown in Fig. 7.9a) and then use scaling and translation to place it on the roof in the house's MCS. If we had to define the chimney to fit exactly on the roof and to map into the house's MCS without scaling, we would have to do messy calculations to compute the vertices explicitly. With modularity, however, we simply define the standardized chimney such that its bottom facet has the same slope as the roof itself; with that condition met, uniform scaling and arbitrary translation can be applied.

The revised house structure is built via

```
SPH_openStructure (HOUSE_STRUCT);
    SPH_executeStructure (SIMPLE_HOUSE_STRUCT);
    set local matrix to scale/translate standardized chimney onto roof of simple house;
    SPH_executeStructure (CHIMNEY_STRUCT);
SPH_closeStructure();
```

What happens when this two-level house object is instantiated by the street structure with a transformation to yield the three-level hierarchy shown in Fig. 7.9(b)? Since SPHIGS transforms a parent by transforming the latter's component elements and substructures, we are assured that the two component primitives (the simple house and the chimney) are transformed together as a single unified object (Fig. 7.9c). The key point is that the street-structure specification did not need to

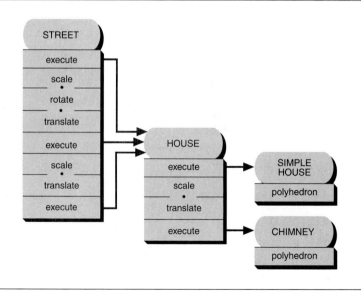

Figure 7.9(b)   Structure network for three-level street hierarchy.

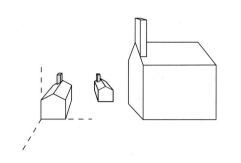

Figure 7.9(c)   Image resulting from application of the three-level hierarchy transformation.

be changed at all. Thus, the designer of the street structure does not need to be concerned with the internal details of how the house is constructed or subsequently edited—it is a black box.

7.5.3 Bottom-Up Construction of the Robot

We shall now look at a more interesting example, our simple robot, which combines the key ideas of modeling using structure hierarchy and of repeated editing of transformations to achieve motion dynamics. A complex object or system hierarchy is usually conceptualized and informally described top-down. For example, a computer-science department building is composed of floors, which are composed of offices and laboratories, which are composed of furniture and equipment, and so on. Recall that our simple android robot is composed of an upper body and a pedestal base; the upper body is composed of a trunk, a head, and two identical arms, each of which is composed of a fixed hand and a *sliding* (translating) thumb as gripper.

Even though we design top-down, we often implement bottom-up, defining building blocks for use in the definitions of higher-level building blocks, and so on, to create the hierarchy of building blocks. Thus, in constructing the robot, we define the thumb building block for the robot's arm, then the arm itself, and then join two instances of the arm building block onto the upper body, and so on, as shown in the symbolic parts hierarchy of Fig. 7.2 and in the more detailed structure network diagram of the upper body in Fig. 7.10.

Let's look at the bottom-up construction process in more detail to see what geometry and transformations are involved. It makes sense to design the arm and thumb in the same units of measurement, so that they fit together easily. We define the thumb structure in a standardized position in its own MCS in which it *hangs* along the y axis (Fig.7.11a). The arm structure is defined with the same unit of measurement as that used for the thumb; it consists of the arm+hand polyhedron (standardized, hanging down along the y axis, as shown in Fig. 7.11b) and a translated invocation of the thumb structure. The translation element preceding the

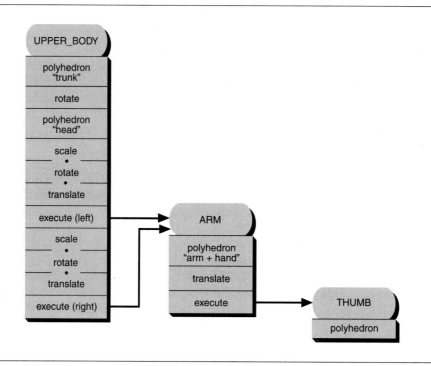

Figure 7.10   Structure hierarchy for robot's upper body.

invocation of the thumb is responsible for moving the thumb from its standardized position at the origin to its proper place on the wrist of the arm as shown in part (c).

The arm-invoking-thumb network is a two-level hierarchy similar to the street–house example. By editing the translation element in the arm structure, we can *slide* the thumb along the wrist of the arm (Fig. 7.11d).[4]

Next, we build the upper body. Since we want to be able to rotate the head, we first specify the trunk polyhedron, then a rotation, and next the head polyhedron (Fig. 7.11e). Our next step is to have the upper-body structure invoke the arm structure twice. What transformations should precede these invocations? If our sole concern is positioning (i.e., translating) each arm correctly in the upper-body MCS, we may produce a picture like Fig. 7.11(f), where the arm and upper body were clearly designed at different scales. This is easy to fix: We can add a scale transformation preceding the translation (Fig. 7.11g). However, a scale and a translation is not enough if we want arms that can swing on the axis connecting the two shoulders (for movement much like that of the arm of a marching soldier); for this we place a rotation element in the structure, preceding the translation. We have completed our definition of the upper-body structure; assembling the full robot is

---

[4] The observant reader may have wondered how the thumb actually slides in this model, since it is not really attached in any way to the arm hand. In fact, none of the components of our robot model is attached to another via objects representing joints.

assigned in Exercise 7.1. Fig. 7.11(h) shows the upper body as it looks when the left arm's rotation element is nonzero.

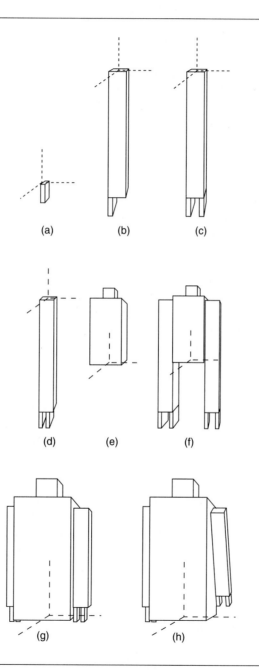

Figure 7.11   Constructing the robot's upper body. (a) Thumb. (b) Fixed arm plus hand. (c) Completed arm. (d) Completed arm with translated thumb. (e) Trunk and head. (f) Upper body with outsized arms. (g) Corrected arms. (h) Left arm rotated.

Because each arm invocation is preceded by an independent sequence of transformations, the motion of each arm can be controlled independently. One arm can be hanging down while the other arm swings, as in Fig. 7.11(h). Indeed, the difference in the transformations is what distinguishes the left and right arms. Notice, however, that the movable thumb is not only on the same side of, but also is the same distance from, the fixed hand on both left and right arms, because it is part of the arm's internal definition. (In fact, if the application simply changes the translation element in the arm structure, all the thumbs on all the robot instances suddenly move!) Thus we must rotate one of the arms 180° about the *y* axis in order to make the arms symmetric. A structure invoking the arm can control the arm's size, orientation, and position only *as a whole*, and cannot alter the arm's internal construction in any way. As we said earlier, a substructure is essentially a black box; the invoker needs to know what geometry is defined by the substructure, but it does not need to know how the substructure was created, and indeed cannot affect any of the substructure's internals.

In summary, in specifying any structure, we deal with only what primitives and lower-level substructures are included in it, what modeling transformations should be used to position its component parts, and what attributes should be used to affect their appearance. We need not, and cannot, deal with the internals of lower-level structures. Furthermore, we design components without concern for how they will be used by invoking structures, since transformations can be used to obtain desired size, orientation, and position. In practice, it is helpful to standardize a component in its local MCS, so that it is easy to scale and rotate about principal axes.

Two additional points must be mentioned. First, a programmer does not need to design purely top-down and to implement purely bottom-up; by analogy to the programming technique of using *stubs and drivers*, dummy substructures can be used in the structure hierarchy. A dummy can be an empty structure; in fact, SPHIGS allows a structure to execute a substructure that has not (yet) been created, in which case SPHIGS automatically creates the referenced substructure and initializes it to be empty. In some cases, it is desirable for the dummy to be a simple object (say, a parallelepiped) of approximately the same size as the more complex version that is specified later. This technique permits top-down debugging of complex structure hierarchies before all components are defined fully. Second, we have not compared structure hierarchy to template-function hierarchy, which is discussed in Section 7.15 of [FOLE90]. We will simply say that structure hierarchy works well if we need to instantiate multiple copies of a building block and to control (to a limited extent) the appearance and placement of each copy but not its internal definition.

7.5.4 Interactive Modeling Programs

Interactive 3D construction and modeling programs facilitate the construction of object hierarchies through the bottom-up assembly process just described. Most such programs offer a palette of icons representing the program's fundamental set of building blocks. If the drawing program is application-specific, so are the building blocks; otherwise, they are such common atoms as polylines, polygons, cubes, parallelepipeds, cylinders, and spheres. The user can select an icon in order to instantiate the associated building block, and can then specify transformations to be applied to the building-block instance. Such specification is typically done via input devices, such as the mouse or control dials, that let the user experiment with the instance's size, orientation, and position until it *looks right*. Since it is difficult to judge spatial relationships in 2D projections of 3D scenes, more sophisticated interaction techniques use 3D grids, numerical scales, potentiometers, sliders of various types, numerical feedback on the position of vertices, and so on (see Section 8.2.5). Some construction programs allow the user to combine instances of fundamental graphical building blocks to create a higher-level building block, which is then added to the building-block palette, to be used in building even higher-level objects.

7.6 MATRIX COMPOSITION IN DISPLAY TRAVERSAL

So far, we have discussed how a programmer constructs a model, using top-down design and (more or less) bottom-up implementation. Regardless of how the model was constructed, SPHIGS displays the model by performing a top-down, depth-first search of the DAG rooted at the posted structure. During traversal, SPHIGS processes all the geometry specified by multiple levels of transformation and invocation. To see what is involved, we observe that, during top-down traversal, when a root structure A invokes structure B, which in turn invokes structure C, this is tantamount to saying that B was constructed bottom-up by transformation of primitives defined in C's MCS to B's MCS, and that A was then similarly constructed by transformation of B's primitives (including any defined via invocation of C) to A's MCS. The net effect was that C's primitives were transformed twice, first from MCS_C to MCS_B and then from MCS_B to MCS_A.

Using the notation developed in Section 5.9 let $M_{B \leftarrow C}$ denote the value of the local matrix for structure B that, at the time of invocation of C, maps vertices in MCS_C to their properly transformed positions in MCS_B. Thus, to map a vertex from MCS_C to MCS_B, we write $V^{(B)} = M_{B \leftarrow C} \cdot V^{(C)}$ (where $V^{(H)}$ indicates the vector representing a vertex whose coordinates are expressed in coordinate-system H), and similarly, $V^{(A)} = M_{A \leftarrow B} \cdot V^{(B)}$. Thus, to mimic the bottom-up construction process, the traverser must successively apply the transformations that map the vertices from C to B and then from B to A:

$$V^{(A)} = M_{A \leftarrow B} \cdot V^{(B)} = M_{A \leftarrow B} \cdot (M_{B \leftarrow C} \cdot V^{(C)}). \qquad (7.1)$$

By matrix associativity, $V^{(A)} = (M_{A \leftarrow B} \cdot M_{B \leftarrow C}) \cdot V^{(C)}$. Therefore, the traverser simply composes the two local matrices and applies the resulting matrix to each of C's vertices.

Using tree notation, let the root be at level 1 and the successive children be at levels 2, 3, 4, ... Then, by induction, for any structure at level j ($j > 4$), we can transform a vertex $V^{(j)}$ in that structure's MCS into the vertex $V^{(1)}$ in the root coordinate system via

$$V^{(1)} = (M_{1 \leftarrow 2} \cdot M_{2 \leftarrow 3} \cdots \cdot M_{(j-1) \leftarrow j}) \cdot V^{(j)}. \tag{7.2}$$

Since SPHIGS allows primitives to be transformed within the local MCS with the local matrix, a vertex $V^{(j)}$ is obtained by applying the local matrix to the coordinate values of the primitive:

$$V^{(j)} = M^{(j)} \cdot V^{(\text{prim})}. \tag{7.3}$$

We use $M^{(j)}$ to denote the local matrix while the structure is being traversed to show that the matrix is being used to transform primitives into the structure's own level-j MCS. If the structure subsequently invokes a subordinate, the matrix's use changes; it is then used to transform the invoked structure at level $j + 1$ into the level-j MCS, and we denote it with $M_{j \leftarrow (j+1)}$. This does not imply that the matrix's value changes—only its use does.

Combining Eqs. (7.2) and (7.3) using associativity, we get

$$V^{(1)} = (M_{1 \leftarrow 2} \cdot M_{2 \leftarrow 3} \cdots \cdot M_{(j-1) \leftarrow j} \cdot M^{(j)}) \cdot V^{(\text{prim})}. \tag{7.4}$$

Thus, to transform a primitive at level j in the hierarchy to the MCS of the root (which is the world-coordinate space), all we need to do is to apply the composition of the current values of the local matrix for each structure from the root down to the structure in which the primitive is defined. This composite of local matrices—the term in parentheses in Eq. (7.4)—is called the **composite modeling transformation matrix** (CMTM). When the state of a traversal is such that a level-j structure's elements are being executed, the CMTM is the composition of j matrices. Only the last of those matrices ($M^{(j)}$) may be changed by the structure, because a structure may modify only its local matrix. Thus, while the structure is active, the first $j - 1$ matrices in the CMTM list are constant. The composite of these $j - 1$ matrices is the **global matrix** (GM)—the term in parentheses in Eq. (7.2)—for the level-j structure being executed. It is convenient for SPHIGS to maintain the GM during the traversal of a structure; when a setLocalTransformation element modifies the local matrix (LM), SPHIGS can easily compute the new CMTM by postconcatenating the new local matrix to the GM.

We can now summarize the traversal algorithm. SPHIGS does a depth-first traversal, saving the CMTM, GM, and LM just before any structure invocation; it then initializes the substructure's GM and CMTM to the inherited CMTM, and its LM to the identity matrix. The CMTM is applied to vertices and is updated by changes to the LM. Finally, when the traverser returns, it restores the CMTM, GM, and LM of the parent structure and continues. Because of the saving and restoring of the matrices, parents affect their children but not vice versa.

Let us watch as SPHIGS traverses the three-level upper-body–arm–thumb hierarchy of Fig. 7.10. We have posted the UPPER_BODY structure as a root. Figure 7.12(a) shows a sequence of snapshots of the traversal state; a snapshot has been created for each point marked with a number in the structure network diagram of Fig. 7.12(b).

The traversal state is maintained via a stack, shown in Fig. 7.12(a) growing downward, with the currently active structure in a solid rectangle and its ancestors in dashed ones. The values of the three state matrices for the currently active structure are shown to the right of the stack diagram. Arcs show the scope of a transformation: The GM arc illustrates that a structure's ancestors contribute to the GM, and the CMTM arc shows that the CMTM is the product of the GM and LM. Recall that in each group of transformations, the first is in REPLACE mode and the rest are PRECONCATENATEd. Thus the first *rotate* in the structure applies only to the head since it will be REPLACEd by the first *scale* that applies to the left arm.

At point 1 in Fig. 7.12(b), the traverser is about to execute the first element in the root. Because a root has no ancestors, its GM is identity; the LM is also identity, as is the case whenever a structure's execution begins. At point 2, the LM is

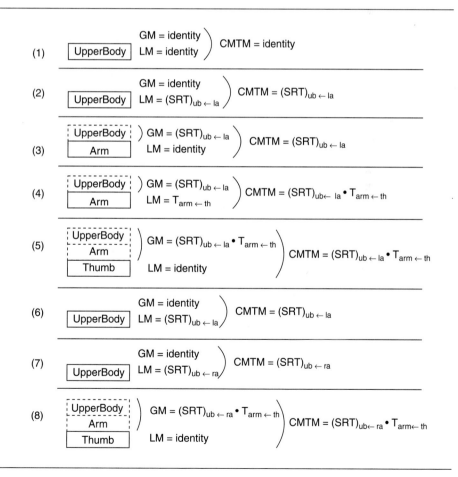

Figure 7.12(a) Snapshots of traversal-state stack in a three-level hierarchy.

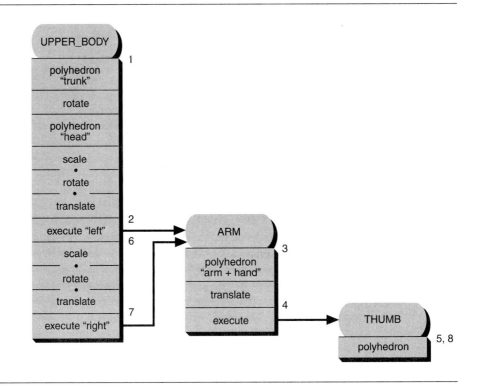

Figure 7.12(b)   Annotated structure network of three-level hierarchy.

set to the composite of the (Scale, Rotate, Translate) transformation triplet. Therefore, the CMTM is updated to the product of the identity GM and the SRT composite, and is then ready for use in transforming the arm subobject to the upper body MCS to become the left arm via $(SRT)_{ub\leftarrow la}$. Next, at point 3, the traverser is about to execute the first element of the arm structure. The GM for the arm execution is, as one would expect for a level–2 instantiation, its parent's LM at the point of invocation.

At point 4, the arm LM is set to position the thumb within the arm $(T_{arm\leftarrow th})$, and the CMTM is updated to the product of the GM and LM. This level–2 CMTM becomes the GM for the level–3 instantiation of the thumb (point 5). Since the LM of the thumb is identity, the CMTM of the thumb has the desired effect of transforming thumb coordinates first to arm coordinates, then to upper-body coordinates. At point 6, the traverser has returned from the thumb and arm invocations, back to the upper body. The matrices for the upper-body structure are as they were before the invocation, since its subordinates cannot change its local matrix. At point 7, the LM of the upper body is replaced with a new composite for the right arm. When we have descended into the thumb structure for the right arm (point 8), the CMTM is almost identical to that at point 5; the only difference is the level–2 matrix that moves the arm into position on the upper body.

To animate a composite object such as the robot, we need only to think about how each child structure is to be affected in its parent, and to define the appropriate transformation elements for each component that can be edited dynamically later. Thus, to make the robot spin about its axis, raise an arm, and open both hands, we change the rotation matrix in the robot structure to affect the upper body, the rotation matrix in the upper-body structure to affect the desired arm, and the translation matrix in the arm structure to affect the thumb. The transformations are done independently at each level of the hierarchy, but the net effect is cumulative. The difficult part of specifying an animation is working backward from a desired result, such as "the robot moves to the northwest corner of the room and picks up a block from the table," to derive the sequence of transformations yielding that result.

7.7 APPEARANCE-ATTRIBUTE HANDLING IN HIERARCHY

7.7.1 Inheritance Rules

The attribute-traversal state is set by attribute elements during traversal and, as in SRGP, is applied modally to all primitives encountered. We saw how parents affect their children via geometric transformations. What rules pertain to appearance attributes? In our street example, the houses all have the default color. To give an object a particular color (e.g., to make a house brown), we can specify that color as an initial element in the object structure itself, but that makes the object's color intrinsic and not changeable during traversal. We would prefer to "pass the color as a parameter," so that the child can inherit it the way a child inherits the CMTM as its GM.

Indeed, in SPHIGS, each substructure inherits the traversal state as the latter exists at the time of the invocation of the substructure, and can then modify that state at will without affecting its ancestors. In other words, attributes and transformations are bound dynamically at traversal time, rather than statically at specification time. This dynamic binding is one of the major features of SPHIGS, making it easy to customize instances of a substructure.

What substructures do with the inherited state depends on the type of data involved. We saw that, for geometric transformations, the substructure inherits the GM but cannot override its inheritance, since it can affect only its own local matrix. Attributes are simpler in that the substructure inherits the parent's attributes as the initial values of its local attribute state but can change its local state subsequently. There is no need to distinguish between global and local attributes, since there is no notion of composing attributes. Note that this mechanism has the same problem we discovered with transformation inheritance—just as our robot's two arm instances cannot have differing thumb transformations, its two arm instances cannot have the same color for the fixed part but differing colors for the thumb.

In the structure network of Fig. 7.13(a), the street structure sets the colors for the house substructure. The resulting image is shown in Fig. 7.13(b), and the code generating the network is shown in Prog. 7.6.

An attribute can be reset within a substructure to override the inherited value. The following code fragment specifies a revised house structure whose chimney is always red:

```
SPH_openStructure (HOUSE_STRUCT);
    SPH_executeStructure (SIMPLE_HOUSE_STRUCT);
    SPH_setInteriorColor (COLOR_RED);
    set up transformations;
    SPH_executeStructure (CHIMNEY_STRUCT);
SPH_closeStructure();
```

Let's use this new house structure in conjunction with the street structure generated by the code in Prog. 7.6. Figure 7.14 shows the structure network and the resulting image. The traverser starts at STREET_STRUCT; the interior- and edge-color attributes have their default values. The edge color is set to white, a value it retains throughout display traversal of this network. The first setInteriorColor causes yellow to be inherited by the first instance of HOUSE_STRUCT, which in turn passes yellow to SIMPLE_HOUSE_STRUCT, whose polyhedron is shown in that color. When the traverser returns from SIMPLE_HOUSE_STRUCT to HOUSE_STRUCT, the interior-color attribute is immediately changed to red by the next element. The invocation of CHIMNEY_STRUCT therefore results in a red chimney with white edges. None of these operations affect the attribute group for STREET_STRUCT, of course; when the traverser returns from HOUSE_STRUCT, STREET_STRUCT's interior-color attribute is restored to yellow. The interior-color attribute is then changed to navy to prepare for drawing two navy houses.

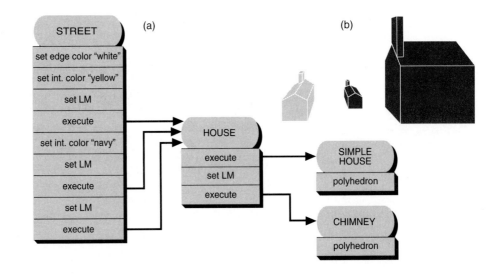

Figure 7.13   Use of attribute inheritance to model street with colored houses. (a) Structure network. (b) Resulting image. (Interior colors are simulated by patterns.)

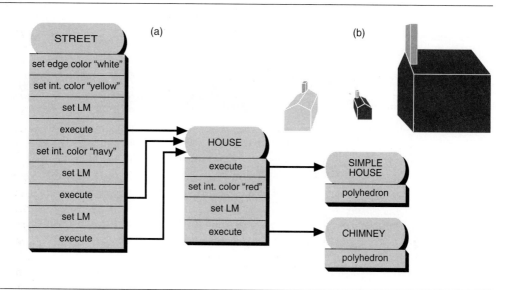

Figure 7.14　Subordinate structure overriding an inherited attribute. (a) Structure network. (b) Resulting view.

Program 7.6

Code used to generate Fig. 7.13.

```
SPH_openStructure (STREET_STRUCT);
    SPH_setEdgeColor (COLOR_WHITE);

    SPH_setInteriorColor (COLOR_YELLOW);
    set up transformations;
    SPH_executeStructure (HOUSE_STRUCT);

    SPH_setInteriorColor(COLOR_NAVY);
    set up transformations;
    SPH_executeStructure (HOUSE_STRUCT);

    set up transformations;
    SPH_executeStructure (HOUSE_STRUCT);
SPH_closeStructure();
```

7.7.2 SPHIGS Attributes and Text Unaffected by Transformations

In true PHIGS implementations, text can be subjected to transformations like any other primitive. Thus, the text characters on the sides of a truck, displayed in perspective, are rotated and shown with appropriate perspective foreshortening, as though the letters were made of individual polylines or fill areas. Similarly, dashes in dashed lines should be subject to geometric transformations and perspective foreshortening. However, just as attributes in SPHIGS are nongeometric for performance reasons, so is text. As in SRGP, the font of the text determines the text's screen size, and a text string cannot even be rotated—the image of a text string is always upright in the plane of the screen, and is never compressed or expanded. Thus, rotation and scaling affect text's origin, but not its size and orientation. SPHIGS's primitive text is thus useful primarily for labeling.

7.8 SCREEN UPDATING AND RENDERING MODES

SPHIGS constantly updates the screen image to match the current status of the CSS and view table. The following actions all can make an arbitrary amount of the screen image obsolete:

- An entry in the view table is changed
- A structure is closed (after having been opened and edited)
- A structure is deleted
- A structure is posted or unposted.

Whenever SPHIGS is called to perform one of these actions, it must regenerate the screen image to display the current state of all posted networks. How SPHIGS chooses to generate the image is a function of the rendering mode the application has selected. These modes present a choice between quality and speed of regeneration: The higher the quality, the longer it takes to render the image. The rendering mode for a specific view is set by

> **void** SPH_setRenderingMode(**int** viewIndex, **int** WIREFRAME / FLAT / LIT_FLAT / GOURAUD);

We summarize the four SPHIGS rendering modes here; they are discussed much more fully in Chapters 12 through 14.

Wireframe rendering mode.   WIREFRAME mode is the fastest but least realistic form of display. Objects are drawn as though made of wire, with only their edges showing. The visible (within the view volume) portions of all edges of all objects are shown in their entirety, with no hidden-edge removal. Primitives are drawn in temporal order—that is, in the order in which the traverser encounters them in the posted structure networks in the database; this order is affected by the display-priority determined by the view index, as mentioned in Section 7.3.4.

All edge attributes affect screen appearance in their designated way in this mode; in fact, when the edge flag is set to EDGE_INVISIBLE, fill areas and polyhedra are entirely invisible in this mode.

Shaded rendering modes.   In its other three rendering modes, SPHIGS displays fill areas and polyhedra in a more realistic fashion by drawing fill areas and facets as filled polygons. The addition of shaded areas to the rendering process increases the complexity significantly, because spatial ordering becomes important—portions of objects that are hidden (because they are obscured by portions of *closer* objects) must not be displayed. Methods for determining visible surfaces (also known as hidden-surface removal) are discussed in Chapter 13.

For the three shaded rendering modes, SPHIGS *shades* the interior pixels of visible portions of the facets; the quality of the rendering varies with the mode. For FLAT shading, the mode used often in this chapter's figures, all facets of a polyhedron are rendered in the current interior color, without being influenced by any light sources in the scene. Visible portions of edges are shown (if the edge flag is EDGE_VISIBLE) as they would appear in WIREFRAME mode. If the interior color is set to match the screen background, only the edges show—this use of FLAT rendering, which produced Figs. 7.7(a) and 7.9(c), simulates wireframe with hidden-edge removal.

The two highest-quality rendering modes produce images illuminated by a light source;[5] illumination and shading models are discussed in Chapter 14. These images are nonuniformly *shaded;* the colors of the pixels are based on, but are not exactly, the value of the interior-color attribute. In LIT_FLAT mode, all the pixels on a facet have the same color, determined by the angle at which the light hits the facet. Because each facet is of a uniform color, the image has a *faceted* look, and the contrast between adjacent faces at their shared edge is noticeable. GOURAUD mode colors the pixels to provide a smooth shaded appearance that eliminates the faceted look.

In FLAT mode, the edge-flag attribute should be set to EDGE_VISIBLE because, without visible edges, the viewer can determine only the silhouette boundary of the object. In the two highest-quality modes, however, edge visibility is usually turned off, since the shading helps the user to determine the shape of the object.

7.9 STRUCTURE NETWORK EDITING FOR DYNAMIC EFFECTS

As with any database, we must be able not only to create and query (in order to display) the SPHIGS structure database, but also to edit it in a convenient way. An application edits a structure via the functions described in this section; if the application also maintains an application model, it must ensure that the two representations are edited in tandem. **Motion dynamics** requires modification of viewing or modeling transformations; **update dynamics** requires changes in or replacement of structures. The programmer may choose to edit a structure's internal element list if the changes are relatively minor; otherwise, for major editing, it is common to delete and then to respecify the structure in its entirety.

In the remainder of this section, we present methods for intrastructure editing; see the SPHIGS reference manual for information on editing operations that affect entire structures (e.g., deletion, emptying), and for more detailed descriptions of the functions presented here.

---

[5] The PHIGS PLUS extension provides many facilities for controlling rendering, including specification of the placement and colors of multiple light sources, of the material properties of objects characterizing their interaction with light, and so on; see Chapters 12 through 14.

7.9.1 Accessing Elements with Indices and Labels

The rudimentary editing facilities of both SPHIGS and PHIGS resemble those of old-fashioned line-oriented program editors that use line numbers. The elements in a structure are indexed from 1 to N; whenever an element is inserted or deleted, the index associated with each higher-indexed element in the same structure is incremented or decremented. The unique **current element** is that element whose index is stored in the **element-pointer** state variable. When a structure is opened with the SPH_openStructure call, the element pointer is set to N (pointing to the last element) or to 0 for an empty structure. The pointer is incremented when a new element is inserted after the current element, and decremented when the current element is deleted. The pointer may also be set explicitly by the programmer using absolute and relative positioning commands:

> **void** SPH_setElementPointer(**int** index);
> **void** SPH_offsetElementPointer(**int** delta);
>   /* + for forward, − for backward */

Because the index of an element changes when a preceding element is added or deleted in its parent structure, using element indices to position the element pointer is liable to error. Thus, SPHIGS allows an application to place *landmark* elements, called **labels**, within a structure. A label element is given an integer identifier when it is generated:

> **void** SPH_label(**int** id);

The application can move the element pointer via

> **void** SPH_moveElementPointerToLabel(**int** id);

The pointer is then moved forward in search of the specified label. If the end of the structure is reached before the label is found, the search terminates unsuccessfully. Thus, it is advisable to move the pointer to the very front of the structure (index 0) before searching for a label.

7.9.2 Intrastructure Editing Operations

The most common editing action is insertion of new elements into a structure. Whenever an element-generating function is called, the new element is placed immediately after the current element, and the element pointer is incremented to point to the new element. Elements are deleted by the following functions:

> **void** SPH_deleteElement();
> **void** SPH_deleteElementsInRange(**int** firstIndex, **int** secondIndex);
> **void** SPH_deleteElementsBetweenLabels(**int** firstLabel, **int** secondLabel);

In all cases, after the deletion is made, the element pointer is moved to the element immediately preceding the ones deleted, and all survivors are renumbered. The first function deletes the current element. The second function deletes the elements lying between and including the two specified elements. The third function is similar, but does not delete the two label elements.

Note that these editing facilities all affect an entire element or a set of elements; there are no provisions for selective editing of data fields within an element. Thus, for example, when a single vertex needs to be updated the programmer must respecify the entire polyhedron.

An editing example.   Let us look at a modification of our simple street example. Our street now consists of only the first house and the cottage, the former being fixed and the latter being movable. We create a label in front of the cottage, so we can subsequently edit the transformation in order to move the cottage.

To move the cottage, we reopen the street structure, move the pointer to the label, and then offset to the transformation element, replace the transformation element, and close the structure. The screen is automatically updated after the structure is closed, to show the cottage in its new position. This code is shown in Prog. 7.7, and its sequence of operations is illustrated in Fig. 7.15.

Program 7.7

Code for editing the street structure in Fig. 7.15.

```
SPH_openStructure(STREET_STRUCT);
    /* When a structure is opened, the element pointer is initially at its end.
    We must first move the pointer to its beginning, so we can search for labels. */
    SPH_setElementPointer(0);
    SPH_moveElementPointerToLabel(COTTAGE_TRANSLATION_LABEL);
    SPH_offsetElementPointer(1);      /* Pointer now points at transform element */
    SPH_deleteElement();              /* Replace here via delete/insert combination */
    SPH_setLocalTransformation(newTranslationMatrix, PRECONCATENATE);
SPH_closeStructure();
```

7.9.3 Instance Blocks for Editing Convenience

The previous editing example suggests that we place a label in front of each element we wish to edit, but creating so many labels is clearly too laborious. There are several techniques for avoiding this tedium. The first is to bracket an editable group of elements with two labels, and to use the labels in deleting or replacing the entire group. Another common technique is to group the set of elements in a fixed format and to introduce the group with a single label. To edit any member of the group, we move the element pointer to the label, then offset the pointer from that label into the group itself. Because the group's format is fixed, the offset is an easily determined small integer.

A special case of this technique is to design a standard way of instantiating substructures by preceding the structure-execution element with a common list of attribute-setting elements. A typical format of such a sequence of elements, called an **instance block**, is shown in Fig. 7.16; first comes the label uniquely identifying the entire block, then an interior-color setting, then the three basic transformations, and finally the invocation of the symbol structure.

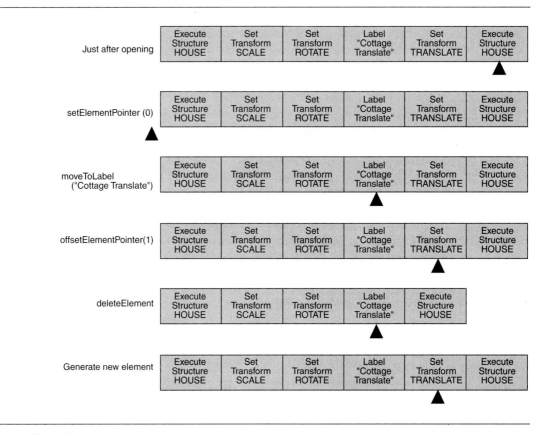

Figure 7.15   Snapshot sequence of structure during editing. The black triangle shows the element pointer's position. (Syntax of calls abbreviated for illustrative purposes.)

We can create a set of symbolic constants to provide the offsets:

```
#define INTERIOR_COLOR_OFFSET    1
#define SCALE_OFFSET             2
#define ROTATION_OFFSET          3
#define TRANSLATION_OFFSET       4
```

Using the fixed format for the block guarantees that a particular attribute is modified in the same way for any instance. To change the rotation transformation of a particular instance, we use the following code:

```
SPH_openStructure (ID of structure to be edited);
    SPH_setElementPointer (0);
    SPH_moveElementPointerToLabel (the desired instance-block label);
    SPH_offsetElementPointer (ROTATION_OFFSET);
    SPH_deleteElement();
    SPH_setLocalTransformation (newMatrix, mode);
SPH_closeStructure();
```

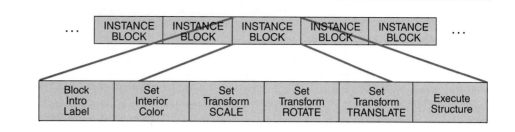

Figure 7.16 Sample instance-block format.

Another nice feature of instance blocks is that the label introducing each block is easy to define: If the application keeps an internal database identifying all instances of objects, as is common, the label can be set to the unique number that the application itself uses to identify the instance internally.

7.9.4 Controlling Automatic Regeneration of the Screen Image

SPHIGS constantly updates the screen image to reflect the current status of its structure storage database and its view table. On occasion, however, we want to inhibit this regeneration, either to increase efficiency or to avoid presenting the user with a continuously changing image that is confusing and that shows irrelevant intermediate stages of editing.

As we have seen, SPHIGS itself suppresses regeneration during the editing of a structure; no matter how many changes are made, an image is regenerated only when the structure is closed. This *batching* of updates is done for efficiency, since any deletion or transformation of a primitive can cause an arbitrary amount of damage to the screen image—damage that requires either selective damage repair or brute-force retraversal of all posted networks in one or more views. It is clearly faster for SPHIGS to calculate the cumulative effect of a number of consecutive edits just once, before regeneration.

A similar situation arises when several consecutive changes are made to different structures—for instance, when a structure and its substructures are deleted via consecutive calls to deleteStructure. To avoid this problem, an application can suppress automatic regeneration before making a series of changes, and allow it again afterward:

> **void** SPH_setImplicitRegenerationMode(**int** ALLOWED / SUPPRESSED);

Even while implicit regeneration is suppressed, the application may explicitly demand a screen regeneration by calling

> **void** SPH_regenerateScreen();

7.10 INTERACTION

Both SRGP's and SPHIGS's interaction modules are based on the PHIGS specification, and thus they have the same facilities for setting device modes and attributes and for obtaining measures. The SPHIGS keyboard device is identical to that of SRGP, except that the echo origin is specified in NPC space with the z coordinate ignored. The SPHIGS locator device's measure has an additional field for the z coordinate, but is otherwise unchanged. SPHIGS also adds two new interaction facilities. The first is **pick correlation**, augmenting the locator functionality to provide identification of an object picked by the user. The second is the **choice** device, described in the reference manual, which supports menus.

7.10.1 Locator

The SPHIGS locator returns the cursor position in NPC coordinates, with $z_{NPC} = 0$. It also returns the index of the highest-priority view whose viewport encloses the cursor.

```
typedef struct {
      point    position;        /* [x, y, 0]NPC screen position */
      int      viewIndex;       /* Index of highest priority view
                                    whose viewport encloses the cursor */
      int      buttonOfMostRecentTransition;
      enum {
         UP, DOWN
      } buttonChord[MAX_BUTTON_COUNT];    /* Typically 1... 3 */
} locatorMeasure;
```

When two viewports overlap and the cursor position lies in the intersection of their bounds, the viewport having the highest index (in the view table) is returned in the second field. Thus, the view index is used to establish view priority for input as well as for output. The view-index field is useful for a variety of reasons. Consider an application that allows the user to specify bounds of a viewport interactively, much as one can move or resize a window manager's windows. In response to a prompt to resize, the user can pick any location within the viewport. The application program can then use the *viewIndex* field to determine which view was picked, rather than do a point-in-rectangle test on viewport boundaries. The view index is also used in applications with some output-only views; such applications can examine the returned view index to determine whether the correlation function even needs to be called.

7.10.2 Pick Correlation

Because the SPHIGS programmer thinks in terms of modeled objects rather than of the pixels composing their images, it is useful for the application to be able to determine the identity of an object whose image a user has picked. The primary use of the locator, therefore, is to provide an NPC point for input to the pick-correlation function discussed in this section. As we saw with SRGP, pick correlation in a flat-earth world is a straightforward matter of detecting **hits**—primitives whose images lie close enough to the locator position to be considered chosen by the user. If there is more than one hit, due to overlapping primitives near the cursor, we disambiguate by choosing the one most recently drawn, since that is the one that lies *on top*. Thus, a 2D pick correlator examines the primitives in inverse temporal order, and picks the first hit. Picking objects in a 3D, hierarchical world is a great deal more complex, for the reasons described next; fortunately, SPHIGS relieves an application of this task.

Picking in a hierarchy.   Consider the complexity introduced by hierarchy. First, what information should be returned by the pick-correlation utility to identify the picked object? A structure ID is not enough, because it does not distinguish between multiple instances of a structure. Only the full **path**—a description of the complete ancestry from root to picked primitive—provides unique identification.

Second, when a particular primitive is picked, which level of the hierarchy did the user mean? For example, if the cursor is placed near one of our robot's thumbs, does the user mean to select the thumb, the arm, the upper body, or the entire robot? At times, the actual primitive is intended, at times the leaf structure is intended, or any other level is possibly intended, up to the very root! Some applications resolve this problem by providing a feedback mechanism allowing the user to step through the levels from primitive to root, in order to specify exactly which level is desired (see Exercise 7.8).

Comparison criterion.   How is proximity to an object defined when the comparison should really be done in 3D? Since the locator device effectively yields a 2D NPC value, there is no basis for comparing the z coordinates of primitives to the locator position. Thus, SPHIGS can compare the cursor position only to the screen images of the primitives, not to the WC locations of the primitives. If a primitive is a hit, it is deemed a *candidate* for correlation. In wireframe mode, SPHIGS picks the very first candidate encountered during traversal; the reason for this strategy is that there is no obvious depth information in a wireframe image, so the user does not expect pick correlation to take relative depth into account. (A side effect of the strategy is that it optimizes pick correlation.) In shaded rendering modes, SPHIGS picks the candidate whose **hit point** (the NPC point, on the primitive's normalized (3D NPC) surface, to which the user pointed directly) is closest to the viewpoint— the one *in front*.

Pick-correlation utility.   To perform pick correlation, the application program calls a SPHIGS pick-correlation utility with an NPC point and a view index, typically returned by a previous interaction with the locator:

```
void SPH_pickCorrelate( point_3D position, int viewIndex,
    pickInformation *pickInfo);
```

The returned information identifies the primitive picked and its ancestry via a *pick path*, as described by C data types in Prog. 7.8.

When no primitive is close enough to the cursor position, the value of *pickLevel* returned is 0 and the *path* field is undefined. When *pickLevel* is greater than 0, it specifies the length of the path from the root to the picked primitive—that is, the primitive's depth within the network. In this latter case, entries [1] through [*pickLevel*] of the *path* array return the identification of the structure elements involved in the path leading from root to picked primitive. At the deepest level (entry [*pickLevel*]), the element identified is the primitive that was picked; at all other levels (entries [*pickLevel*–1] through [1]), the elements are all structure executions. Each entry in *path* identifies one element with a record that gives the structure ID of the structure containing the element, the index of the element in that structure, a code presenting the type of the element, and the pick ID of the element (discussed next).

Figure 7.17 uses the structure network of Fig. 7.10 for the robot's upper body, and shows the pick information returned by several picks within the structure's displayed image.

How does the pick path uniquely identify each instance of a structure that is invoked arbitrarily many times within the hierarchy? For example, how do we distinguish a pick on the robot's left thumb from a pick on its right thumb? The pick paths for the two thumbs are identical except at the root level, as demonstrated by points *a* and *e* in Fig. 7.17.

The *pick identifier* can provide pick correlation at a finer resolution than does a structure ID. Although the element index can be used to identify individual elements, it is subject to change when the structure is edited. Therefore, using the

Program 7.8

Pick-path storage types.

```
typedef struct {
    int    structureID;
    int    elementIndex;
    enum {
        POLYLINE, POLYHEDRON, EXECUTE_STRUCTURE
    } elementType;
    int    pickID;
} pickPathItem;

typedef pickPathItem pickPath[ MAX_HIERARCHY_LEVEL ];

typedef struct {
    int    pickLevel;
    pickPath path;
} pickInformation;
```

pick ID is easier, because the pick ID is not affected by editing of other elements. It has a default value of 0 and is modally set within a structure. One generates a pick-ID element via

```
void SPH_setPickIdentifier( int id );
```

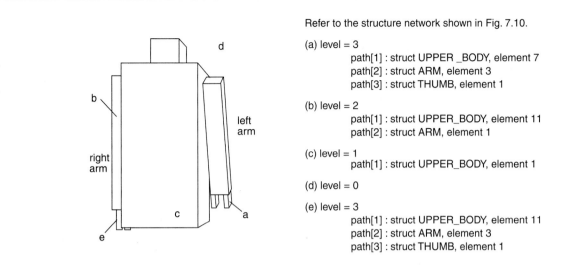

Refer to the structure network shown in Fig. 7.10.

(a) level = 3
> path[1] : struct UPPER _BODY, element 7
> path[2] : struct ARM, element 3
> path[3] : struct THUMB, element 1

(b) level = 2
> path[1] : struct UPPER_BODY, element 11
> path[2] : struct ARM, element 1

(c) level = 1
> path[1] : struct UPPER_BODY, element 1

(d) level = 0

(e) level = 3
> path[1] : struct UPPER_BODY, element 11
> path[2] : struct ARM, element 3
> path[3] : struct THUMB, element 1

Figure 7.17   Example of pick correlation.

The pick-ID element is ignored during display traversal. Also, a pick ID has no notion of inheritance: it is initially 0 when SPHIGS begins the traversal of any structure, whether it is a root or a substructure. Because of these two aspects, pick IDs do not behave like attributes. Multiple primitives within a structure may have unique IDs or share the same one; this permits arbitrarily fine resolution of pick correlation within a structure, as needed by the application. Although labels and pick IDs are thus different mechanisms, the former used for editing and the latter for pick correlation, they are often used in conjunction. In particular, when structures are organized using the instance-block technique described in Section 7.9.2, a pick-ID element is also part of the block, and the pick ID itself is typically set to the same integer value as that of the block label.

Example 7.1

Problem: Enhance the robot animation to provide user interaction. Let there be a number of objects in the room, and allow the user to choose (using the locator) the object that the robot should pick up. To simplify the problem, the robot can be one-armed.

Answer: *User's View.*   The user sees a simple room, with the one-armed robot waiting at the left front side of the room. Toward the rear are suspended rods. By using the mouse, and clicking the left button, the user can select any of these objects, and the robot will dispose of it. The user may quit at any time by hitting the 'q' key.

Placement of the Objects.   We place the objects the robot can manipulate so that a simple strategy will suffice for approaching, grasping, and removing any of them. The objects are evenly spaced laterally (in *x*), and restricted in the depth of the room region in which they may be placed (i.e., restricted in *z*). They float in space at a convenient height. A typical arrangement is shown here.

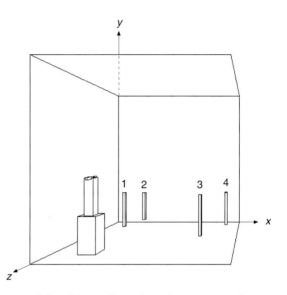

This placement of the objects allows the robot to move along a path parallel to the *x* axis, clearly in front of any of the objects, until it is in line with one of them (aligned in *x*). Then movement toward the object is parallel with the *z* axis, and the amount of forward movement necessary to place the robot within reach of the object is easily determined. From that position, the robot can grasp the object, lift it, then turn, and head back the way it came—forward in a line parallel to the *z* axis. We allow the robot to come forward to a *z* coordinate outside the room (which we suppose to be in a hallway), and then move it away laterally (parallel to the *x* axis). Note that this scheme works for all objects, requiring only the object's *x* and *z* coordinates as parameters. The following sequence of illustrations show the robot approaching a selected rod (3), bending over to grab it, and preparing to leave the room to dispose of the rod it has just selected.

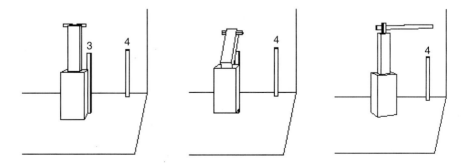

Once the robot is off the screen, the user is unaware of whatever action it performs. Therefore, we want to get rid of the object the robot is carrying as simply as possible and reorient the robot for its return onscreen. To do this, we just detach the object from the robot hierarchy, reset the positions of the thumbs, and let the robot move back to its waiting area.

The C code implementation of this algorithm follows.

Program to provide user interaction to control robot animation.

```c
/* define necessary constants to be used within the program */
/* define the necessary geometry for the room, objects and robot */

main(argc, argv)
int    argc;
char  **argv;
{

/* set inital views, SPHIGS colors and parameters */

    /* Now prepare for event input */
    SPH_setInputMode(KEYBOARD, EVENT);
    SPH_setKeyboardProcessingMode(RAW);

    SPH_setInputMode(LOCATOR, EVENT);
    SPH_setLocatorButtonMask(LEFT_BUTTON_MASK);

    ShowWorld(OUR_ROOM);                    /* display the initial view of room */
    terminate = NO;
    do {
        whichdev = SPH_waitEvent(INDEFINITE);
        switch (whichdev) {
          case KEYBOARD:
            SPH_getKeyboard(keymeasure, KEYMEASURE_SIZE);
            if (keymeasure[0] == 'Q' || keymeasure[0] == 'q')
                terminate = YES;
            break;
          case LOCATOR: {
            SPH_getLocator(&curr_locmeasure);
            /* if button went down, we check for a pick... */
            if (curr_locmeasure.button_chord[LEFT_BUTTON] == DOWN) {
                SPH_pickCorrelate(curr_locmeasure.position,
                        curr_locmeasure.view_index,
                        &pick_info);
                if (pick_info.pickLevel > 2) {      /* object set on second level */
                    if (pick_info.path[1].structureID == OBJECT_SET)
                        MakeAndRunPlan(pick_info.path[1].pickID);
                }
            }
          }
          break;
        }                          /*LOCATOR*/
      }                            /* switch */
    }                              /* do */
```

```
        while (!terminate);
        SPH_end();
    }


    void    MakeAndRunPlan(int object_id)
    {
        double  x, z;

        x = objects_info[object_id].x;
        z = objects_info[object_id].z;

        /* move to align with object in x: */
        MoveRobot(x, Z_WAIT);
        /* face it and approach: */
        SpinRobot(NORTH, CLOCKWISE);
        MoveRobot(x, z + DIST_OF_APPROACH);

        /* get it... */
        LowerArm();
        Grab();
        Pickup(object_id);
        RaiseArm();
        /* got it. */

        /* take it away */
        SpinRobot(EAST, COUNTERCLOCKWISE);
        SpinRobot(SOUTH, COUNTERCLOCKWISE);
        MoveRobot(x, Z_HALL);
        SpinRobot(EAST, CLOCKWISE);
        MoveRobot(X_OFFSCREEN, Z_HALL);

        /* drop it... */
        LowerArm();
        UnGrab();
        Letgo();
        RaiseArm();

        /* and return to the wait area */
        SpinRobot(WEST, CLOCKWISE);
        MoveRobot(X_WAIT, Z_HALL);
        SpinRobot(NORTH, COUNTERCLOCKWISE);
        MoveRobot(X_WAIT, Z_WAIT);
        SpinRobot(EAST, COUNTERCLOCKWISE);
    }

    void  Pickup(int id)
    /* Deletes the appropriate rod object from the room and adds it
       to the hand (arm) of the robot */
    {
        matrix  temp_matrix;                /* transformation matrix */
```

```
SPH_openStructure(OBJECT_SET);
SPH_setElementPointer(0);
SPH_moveElementPointerToLabel(objects_info[id].label);
SPH_offsetElementPointer(1);
SPH_deleteElement();
SPH_executeStructure(NULL_OBJECT);
SPH_closeStructure();

SPH_openStructure(OUR_ARM);
SPH_setElementPointer(0);
SPH_moveElementPointerToLabel(OUR_ARM_DRAW_ROD);
SPH_offsetElementPointer(1);
SPH_deleteElement();
SPH_executeStructure(objects_info[id].struct_id);
SPH_closeStructure();
/* show the frame: */
SPH_regenerateScreen();
}
```

7.11 ADVANCED ISSUES

There are several issues relating to SPHIGS and standard PHIGS that are inappropriate to cover in detail in this book. We will summarize some of the most important points here, but for more detail, see Chapter 7 of [FOLE90].

7.11.1 Additional Output Features

Attribute bundles.   Standard PHIGS provides a mechanism for setting attribute values indirectly. An application can, during its initialization sequence, store a collection of attribute values in an **attribute bundle.** Changing definitions of bundles in the bundle table without changing structure networks is a simple mechanism for dynamically changing the appearance of objects.

Name sets for highlighting and invisibility.   SPHIGS supports two traditional feedback techniques that applications commonly use in conjunction with the SPHIGS picking facility: highlighting objects and making objects invisible. The former technique is typically used to provide feedback when the user picks an object; the latter declutters the screen by showing only desired detail. The SPHIGS reference manual describes structure elements that, when executed during traversal, add names or remove names from the name set.

Picture interchange and metafiles.   Although PHIGS and other standard graphics packages are system- and device-independent to promote portability, a given implementation of such packages in a particular environment is likely to be highly

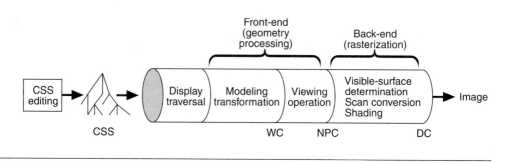

Figure 7.18 The SPHIGS rendering pipeline.

optimized in a nonportable way for performance reasons. The PHIGS archive file, defined by the graphics standards committee, is a portable snapshot of the structure database at a given time and permits different PHIGS implementations to share geometric models. PHIGS implementations may also support the writing of a metafile, which can contain a snapshot of what the application is currently presenting on the display surface.

7.11.2 Implementation Issues

To display a structure network, SPHIGS visits the component structures' elements using a recursive descent, depth-first traversal, and performs the appropriate action for each element, based on the element's type. This display process that maps a model to an image on screen (or hardcopy) is referred to as display traversal in the context of PHIGS, but more generally as **rendering**; its implementation in software and/or hardware is referred to as the **rendering pipeline**.

Traversal. Optimizing regeneration in order to traverse as little of the CSS as possible is quite difficult, because the effect of a trivial operation is potentially enormous. For example, it is difficult to determine how much of the screen must be regenerated due to the editing of a structure.

Rendering. The conceptual rendering pipeline that implements display traversal is illustrated in Fig. 7.18. Its first stage is the actual depth-first traversal of the CSS itself. (Alternatively, if an immediate-mode graphics package is used, the application may traverse the application model or generate primitives and attributes procedurally.) Each primitive encountered during traversal is passed through the remainder of the pipeline: First, the modeling transformations (described in Chapter 5) are applied to map the primitive from modeling coordinates to world coordinates. Then, the viewing operation is applied to transform and clip the primitive to the canonical view volume, and then to map it to the NPC parallelepiped (described in Chapter 6). Since these processes are independent of the display device and deal with vertex geometry in floating-point coordinates, this portion of the pipeline immediately following traversal is often referred to as the geometry-processing subsystem.

The back end of the pipeline takes transformed, clipped primitives and produces pixels; we will refer to this pixel processing as *rasterization*. This process is, of course, straightforward for wireframe mode: The NPC coordinates are easily mapped (via scaling and translating, with z ignored) to integer device coordinates, and then the underlying raster graphics package's line-drawing function is invoked to do the actual scan conversion. Shaded rendering, however, is quite complex, and is composed of three subprocesses: **visible-surface determination** (determining which portions of a primitive are actually visible from the synthetic camera's point of view), **scan conversion** (determining the pixels covered by a primitive's image), and **shading** (determining which color to assign to each covered pixel). The exact order in which these subprocesses are performed varies as a function of the rendering mode and implementation method. Detailed descriptions of the rasterization subprocesses are contained in Chapters 12 through 14.

Optimization via extent checking. The traversal strategy we have presented traverses a network's contents unconditionally. Frequently, however, not all of a network's objects are visible, since modeling and viewing transformations in effect when the traversal is performed can cause large parts of a network to lie outside of the viewing volume. To implement an optimization, we need a simple method for computing the bounds of an arbitrarily complex object, and an efficient way of comparing these bounds to the NPC viewport.

Animation and double-buffering. One side effect of some simple SPHIGS implementations is that, between the *frames* of an animation, viewers see the screen being erased and can (more or less) see the objects being drawn as the traverser performs regeneration. This visual artifact can be reduced by double-buffering: using an offscreen canvas/bitmap to store the next frame while that frame is being drawn; then, when the regeneration is complete, the contents of that canvas can be copied onto the screen.

Pick correlation. In pick correlation, SPHIGS traverses those networks posted to the viewport in which the specified NPC point lies. The traversal is nearly identical to that performed during display; the modeling-transformation matrices are maintained, and much of the rendering pipeline is performed. Pick-correlation traversal can be optimized in a variety of ways, including analytical hit detection and hit detection via clipping. An example of the former is a function PtInPolygon, which is used to test for hits on fill areas and facets in shaded rendering modes. One popular algorithm for determining whether the NPC cursor position lies inside a polygon, based on the odd-parity rule described in Section 2.1.3, casts a ray from the locator position and determines how many times the ray intersects the polygon. The algorithm traverses the edge list, testing for intersections and special cases (e.g., intersections at vertices, edge–ray colinearity). The polygon scan-conversion algorithm described in Section 3.5 tackles a very similar problem and can be adapted for use as a PtInPolygon function.

7.11.3 Optimizing Display of Hierarchical Models

Elision.   We can model a building as a parts hierarchy by saying that it consists of floors, the floors consist of offices, and so on; there are no primitives in the hierarchy's nodes until we get to the level of bricks, planks, and concrete slabs that consist of polyhedra. Although this representation might be useful for construction purposes, it is not as useful for display, where we sometimes wish to see a cruder, simplified picture that eliminates confusing and unneeded details. The term *elision* refers to the decision by a display traverser to refrain from descending into a substructure. Elision can be performed by **pruning, culling**, and by considering **level-of-detail**.

Structure referral.   Certain implementations of PHIGS and PHIGS PLUS allow a nonstandard form of structure execution, called **referral**, that bypasses the expensive state saving and restoring of the ExecuteStructure mechanism. An optimization is to add a ReferStructure operation and to let the programmer use it for those cases in which an invoked child structure does not have any attribute-setting elements.

7.11.4 Limitations of Hierarchical Modeling in PHIGS

Limitations of simple hierarchy.   As mentioned in Section 1.3, some applications have no real structure for their data (e.g., data for scatter plots), or have at most a (partial) ordering in their data (e.g., a function represented algebraically). Many other applications are more naturally expressed as networks—that is, as general (directed) graphs (which may have hierarchical subnets). Among these are circuit and electrical-wiring diagrams, transportation and communications networks, and chemical-plant–piping diagrams. Another example of simple hierarchy's insufficiency for certain types of models is Rubik's cube, a collection of components in which the network and any hierarchy (say of layers, rows, and columns) is fundamentally altered after any transformation.

For other types of models, a single hierarchy does not suffice. For example, the pen holder on an (x, y) plotter is moved by, and therefore "belongs" to, both the horizontal and vertical arms. In short, whether the application model exhibits pure hierarchy, pure network without hierarchy, hierarchy in a network with cross-links, or multiple hierarchies, SPHIGS can be used to display it, but we may not want, or be able, to use structure hierarchy in its full generality.

Limitations of SPHIGS "parameter passing."   The black-box nature of structures is good for modularity but, as shown in our robot example, can be limiting. For example, how can we build a robot with two identical arms and have the robot use its right arm to pick up a cylinder from a table and move away with that cylinder? Structure hierarchy does not support instances of structures differing in the settings of transformations at various hierarchical levels because structure hierarchy has neither the general parameter-passing mechanism of function hierarchy nor general flow-of-control constructs.

7.11.5 Alternative Forms of Hierarchical Modeling

Function hierarchy.   In the spectrum from pure data hierarchy to pure function hierarchy, structure hierarchy is almost all the way at the data end, since it lacks general flow of control. By contrast, a template function (i.e., a function defining a template object, consisting of primitives or of calls to subordinate template functions) can use parameters and arbitrary flow of control.

Data hierarchy.   Unlike function hierarchy, data hierarchy is well suited to dynamic creation. Like template-function hierarchy, it can be used in conjunction with either immediate- or retained-mode graphics packages.

Using database systems.   Since a general-purpose database has more power than does a special-purpose one, we should consider using standard database systems for computer graphics. Unfortunately, such databases are designed to work with large volumes of data in secondary storage and to give response times measured on a human time scale.

7.11.6 Other (Industry) Standards

In Section 7.1 we claimed that many of the features discussed in the context of PHIGS are also available in its competitors such as OpenGL and HOOPS. In this section we briefly cover what is different about these packages, as well as how PEX relates to PHIGS.

First, we need to distinguish between client/server 3D graphics protocols and procedural APIs such as PHIGS used to implement applications. APIs, i.e., application-level libraries or packages, use the lower-level client/server protocols to implement the handshaking required for distributed computing. The X Window System (X) has for some time been the industry standard for 2D graphics applications choosing to work in a client-server environment. Often, the client and server processes run on physically different machines, connected by a local area network (LAN) or a wide area network (WAN). In X, the server process manages the display and the client process contains the application code and the graphics package; the two processes communicate via an interprocess communications protocol (IPC) that has the form of sequences of commands, each consisting in general of an operation and its parameters.

PEX (originally short for "PHIGS Extensions to X," but now not as PHIGS-centric) is the 3D distributed graphics extension to the X Window System. PEX is *output* only; input is handled by the standard X input protocol.

PHIGS, HOOPS and PEXlib are the most common APIs that reside on top of the PEX protocol. PEXlib, by analogy to Xlib for 2D graphics, is a *thin veneer* on top of the PEX protocol that gives access to all protocol functionality but does not support a high degree of abstraction. PHIGS and HOOPS hide the low-level functionality but are less efficient than raw PEXlib calls. OpenGL does not reside on top of PEX but includes its own proprietary protocol for distributed graphics.

OpenGL is a rendering only, vendor-neutral API providing 2D and 3D graphics functions, including modeling, transformations, color, lighting, smooth shading, as well as advanced features like texture mapping (Section 14.3), NURBS (Section 9.2), and motion blur (Section 12.4). Its rendering features are somewhat more advanced than those of PHIGS PLUS because they were originally supported by Silicon Graphics' hardware. OpenGL, like PEX, supports both immediate and retained graphics modes. It is window system- and operating system-independent, and has been integrated with the X Window System under UNIX.

HOOPS differs from PHIGS in several significant ways. Because it is designed and implemented by a single vendor, all implementations are literally compatible, which is not the case for vendor implementations of PHIGS—official standards allow too much flexibility to individual implementations.

HOOPS provides more complete support for fonts, image data and advanced rendering than PHIGS. In addition to the rendering capabilities provided by PHIGS PLUS, HOOPS also supports several forms of global illumination models, including ray tracing, radiosity and a combined ray tracing-radiosity renderer (see Chapter 14).

Like PHIGS, HOOPS supports structure hierarchy, but with a major difference. PHIGS structures contain order dependent lists of graphical elements and attributes. Editing these lists requires that the programmer have detailed knowledge of how, where and when attributes are set and modified. In contrast, all primitives in a HOOPS *segment* have the same attribute state, which is factored out in the segment header. This simplifies the programmer's task, produces more modular, order-independent models and also allows a higher performance implementation by simplifying bookkeeping and eliminating much context switching in the rendering pipeline.

SUMMARY

This chapter has given a general introduction to geometric models, emphasizing hierarchical models that represent parts assemblies. Although many types of data and objects are not hierarchical, most human-made objects are at least partly so. PHIGS, and its alternatives (e.g., OpenGL, HOOPS, and PEXlib) provide a high level of functionality at the cost of considerable complexity. They provide facilities for hierarchical geometric modeling with polygons, polyhedra, curves and surfaces, and can peacefully coexist with window managers and distributed client/server computing such as that provided by the X Window System.

SPHIGS, a subset of PHIGS, is designed to provide efficient and natural representations of geometric objects stored essentially as hierarchies of polygons and polyhedra. Because these packages store an internal database of objects, a programmer can make small changes in the database with little effort, and the package automatically produces an updated view. Thus, the application program builds and edits the database, typically in response to user input, and the package is responsible for producing specified views of the database. These views use a variety of rendering techniques to provide quality–speed tradeoffs. The package also provides locator and choice input devices, as well as pick correlation to allow the selection of objects at any level in a hierarchy. Highlighting and visibility filters can be used for selective enabling and disabling as another form of control over the appearance of objects.

Because the nature of structures and the means for searching and editing them are restricted, such a special-purpose system is best suited to motion dynamics and light update dynamics, especially if the structure database can be maintained in a display subsystem optimized to be a PHIGS peripheral. If much of the structure database must be updated between successive images, or if the application database can be traversed rapidly and there is no bottleneck between the computer and the display subsystem, it is more efficient to use a graphics package in immediate mode, without retaining information.

Structure hierarchy lies between pure data and pure function hierarchy. It has the advantage of dynamic editing that is characteristic of data hierarchy. It also allows a simple form of parameter passing to substructures (of geometric or appearance attributes), using the attribute-traversal state mechanism. Because of the lack of general flow-of-control constructs, however, the parameter-passing mechanism is restricted, and structures cannot selectively set different attributes in different instances of a substructure. Instead, template functions can be used to set up multiple copies of (hierarchical) structures that are identical in structure but that differ in the geometric or appearance attributes of substructures. Alternatively, they can be used to drive an immediate-mode package.

SPHIGS is oriented toward geometric models made essentially from polygons and polyhedra, especially those that exhibit hierarchy; in Chapters 9 and 10, we will look at geometric models that have more complex primitives and combinations of primitives. Before turning to those more advanced modeling topics, we first consider interaction tools, techniques, and user interfaces.

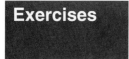

7.1   a.   Complete the robot model of Fig. 7.11 by adding a base on which the upper body swivels, and create a simple animation of its movement through a room.

        b.   Create an SPHIGS application producing an animation in which a one-armed robot approaches a table on which an object lies, picks up the object, and walks off with it.

7.2   Enhance a robot animation so that three views of the animation are shown simultaneously, including one overhead orthographic view and one *robot's eye* view that shows us what the robot itself *sees* as it moves.

7.3   Update our recursive display traverser so that it maintains the MC extent information stored for each structure. Assume that, whenever a structure S is closed after being edited, a Boolean *extentObsolete* field in S's record is set. Assume also that functions are available that, given any primitive, return the primitive's NPC extent.

7.4   Design an algorithm for calculating analytically the hit point of a candidate line, given the line's NPC endpoints and the locator measure.

7.5   Design an algorithm for calculating analytically the hit point of a candidate fill area.

7.6   Design, using pseudocode, a recursive pick-correlation traverser that supports only wireframe mode.

7.7   Implement the function PtInPolygon for use in pick correlation. Treat the special cases of rays that pass through vertices or are coincident with edges. See [PREP85] and [FORR85] for discussion of the subtleties of this problem.

7.8   Design a user interface for picking that lets the user indicate the desired level of a hierarchy. Implement and test your interface with the robot model by writing an application that allows the user to highlight portions of the robot's anatomy, from individual parts to whole subsystems.

8 Input Devices, Interaction Techniques, and Interaction Tasks

High-quality user interfaces are in many ways the *last frontier* in providing computing to a wide variety of users, since hardware and software costs are now low enough to bring significant computing capability to our offices and homes. Just as software engineering has recently given structure to an activity that once was totally ad hoc, so too the new area of user-interface engineering is generating user-interface principles and design methodologies.

The quality of the user interface often determines whether users enjoy or despise a system, whether the designers of the system are praised or damned, whether a system succeeds or fails in the market. The designer of an interactive graphics application must be sensitive to users' desire for easy-to-learn yet powerful interfaces.

The desktop user-interface metaphor, with its windows, icons, and pull-down menus, all making heavy use of raster graphics, is popular because it is easy to learn and requires little typing skill. Most users of such systems are not computer programmers and have little sympathy for the old style, hard-to-learn, keyboard-oriented command-language interfaces that many programmers take for granted. The process of designing, testing, and implementing a user interface is complex; see [FOLE90; SHNE86; MAYH90] for guidelines and methodologies.

We focus in this chapter on input devices, interaction technologies, and interaction tasks. These are the basic building blocks from which user interfaces are constructed. Input devices are the pieces of hardware by which a user enters information into a computer system. We have already discussed many such devices in Chapter 4. In this chapter, we introduce additional devices, and discuss reasons for preferring one device over another. In Section 8.1.6, we describe input devices oriented specifically toward 3D interaction. We continue to use the logical device categories of locator, keyboard, choice, valuator, and pick used by SRGP, SPHIGS, and other device-independent graphics subroutine packages. We also discuss basic elements of user interfaces: **interaction techniques** and **interaction tasks.** Interaction techniques are ways to use input devices to enter information into the computer, whereas interaction tasks classify the fundamental types of information entered with the interaction techniques. Interaction techniques are the primitive building blocks from which a user interface is crafted.

An **interaction task** is the entry of a unit of information by the user. The four basic interaction tasks are **position, text, select,** and **quantify.** The unit of information input in a position interaction task is of course a position. Similarly, the text task yields a text string; the select task yields an object identification; and the quantify task yields a numeric value. Many different **interaction techniques** can be used for a given interaction task. For instance, a selection task can be carried out by using a mouse to select items from a menu, using a keyboard to enter the name of the selection, pressing a function key, or using a speech recognizer. Similarly, a single device can be used for different tasks: A mouse is often used for both positioning and selecting.

Interaction tasks are distinct from the logical input devices discussed in earlier chapters. Interaction tasks are defined by *what* the user accomplishes, whereas logical input devices categorize *how* that task is accomplished by the application program and the graphics package. Interaction tasks are user-centered, whereas logical input devices are a programmer and graphics-package concept.

Many of the topics in this chapter are discussed in much greater depth elsewhere; see the texts by Baecker and Buxton [BAEC87], Hutchins, Hollan, and Norman [HUTC86], Mayhew [MAYH90], Norman [NORM88], Rubenstein and Hersh [RUBE84], Shneiderman [SHNE86], and [FOLE90]; the reference book by Salvendy [SALV87]; and the survey by Foley, Wallace, and Chan [FOLE84].

8.1 INTERACTION HARDWARE

Here, we introduce some interaction devices not covered in Section 4.5, elaborate on how they work, and discuss the advantages and disadvantages of various devices. The presentation is organized around the logical-device categorization of Section 4.5, and can be thought of as a more detailed continuation of that section.

The advantages and disadvantages of various interaction devices can be discussed on three levels: device, task, and dialogue (i.e., sequence of several interaction tasks). The **device level** centers on the hardware characteristics per se, and does not deal with aspects of the device's use controlled by software. At the device level, for example, we note that one mouse shape may be more comfortable to hold than another, and that a data tablet takes up more space than a joystick.

At the **task level**, we might compare interaction techniques using different devices for the same task. Thus, we might assert that experienced users can often enter commands more quickly via function keys or a keyboard than via menu selection, or that users can pick displayed objects more quickly using a mouse than they can using a joystick or cursor control keys.

At the **dialogue level**, we consider not just individual interaction tasks, but also sequences of such tasks. Hand movements between devices take time: Although the positioning task is generally faster with a mouse than with cursor-control keys, cursor-control keys may be faster than a mouse *if* the user's hands are already on the keyboard and will need to be on the keyboard for the next task in sequence after the cursor is repositioned.

Important considerations at the device level, discussed in this section, are the device footprints—(the **footprint** of a piece of equipment is the work area it occupies)—operator fatigue, and device resolution. Other important device issues—such as cost, reliability, and maintainability—change too quickly with technological innovation to be discussed here.

8.1.1 Locator Devices

It is useful to classify locator devices according to three independent characteristics: absolute or relative, direct or indirect, and discrete or continuous.

Absolute devices, such as a data tablet or touch panel, have a frame of reference, or origin, and report positions with respect to that origin. **Relative** devices—such as mice, trackballs, and velocity-control joysticks—have no absolute origin and report only changes from their former position. A relative device can be used to specify an arbitrarily large change in position: A user can move a mouse along the desktop, lift it up and place it back at its initial starting position, and move it again. A data tablet can be programmed to behave as a relative device: The first (x, y) coordinate position read after the pen goes from *far* to *near* state (i.e., close to the tablet) is subtracted from all subsequently read coordinates to yield only the change in x and y, which is added to the previous (x, y) position. This process is continued until the pen again goes to *far* state.

Relative devices cannot be used readily for digitizing drawings, whereas absolute devices can be. The advantage of a relative device is that the application program can reposition the cursor anywhere on the screen.

With a **direct** device—such as a touch screen—the user points directly at the screen with a finger or surrogate finger; with an **indirect** device—such as a tablet, mouse, or joystick—the user moves a cursor on the screen using a device not on the screen. New forms of eye–hand coordination must be learned for the latter; the proliferation of computer games in homes and arcades, however, have created an environment in which many casual computer users have already learned these skills. However, direct pointing can cause arm fatigue, especially among casual users.

A **continuous** device is one in which a smooth hand motion can create a smooth cursor motion. Tablets, joysticks, and mice are all continuous devices, whereas cursor-control keys are **discrete** devices. Continuous devices typically allow more natural, easier, and faster cursor movement than do discrete devices. Most continuous devices also permit easier movement in arbitrary directions than do cursor control keys.

Speed of cursor positioning with a continuous device is affected by the **control-to-display ratio**, commonly called the C/D ratio [CHAP72]; it is the ratio between hand movement (the control) and cursor movement (the display). A large ratio is good for accurate positioning, but makes rapid movements tedious; a small ratio is good for speed but not for accuracy. Fortunately, for a relative positioning device, the ratio need not be constant, but can be changed adaptively as a function of control-movement speed. Rapid movements indicate the user is making a gross hand movement, so a small ratio is used; as the speed decreases, the C/D ratio is increased. This variation of C/D ratio can be set up so that users can use a mouse to position a cursor accurately across a 15-inch screen without repositioning their wrist! For indirect discrete devices (cursor-control keys), there is a similar technique: The distance the cursor is moved per unit time is increased as a function of the time the key has been held down.

Precise positioning is difficult with direct devices, if the arm is unsupported and extended toward the screen. Try writing your name on a blackboard in this pose, and compare the result to your normal signature. This problem can be mitigated if the screen is angled close to horizontal. Indirect devices, on the other hand, allow the heel of the hand to rest on a support, so that the fine motor control of the fingers can be used more effectively. Not all continuous indirect devices are equally satisfactory for drawing, however. Try writing your name with a joystick, a mouse, and a tablet pen stylus. Using the stylus is fastest, and the result is most pleasing.

8.1.2 Keyboard Devices

The well-known QWERTY keyboard has been with us for many years. It is ironic that this keyboard was originally designed to *slow down* typists, so that the typewriter hammers would not be so likely to jam. Studies have shown that the newer Dvořák keyboard [DVOR43], which places vowels and other high-frequency characters under the home positions of the fingers, is somewhat faster than is the QWERTY design [GREE87]. It has not been widely accepted. Alphabetically organized keyboards are sometimes used when many of the users are nontypists. But more and more people are being exposed to QWERTY keyboards, and several experiments have shown no advantage of alphabetic over QWERTY keyboards [HIRS70; MICH71].

Other keyboard-oriented considerations, involving not hardware but software design, are arranging for a user to enter frequently used punctuation or correction characters without needing to press the control or shift keys simultaneously, and assigning dangerous actions (such as delete) to keys that are distant from other frequently used keys.

8.1.3 Valuator Devices

Some valuators are **bounded**, like the volume control on a radio—the dial can be turned only so far before a stop is reached that prevents further turning. A bounded valuator inputs an absolute quantity. A continuous-turn potentiometer, on the other hand, can be turned an **unbounded** number of times in either direction. Given an initial value, the unbounded potentiometer can be used to return absolute values; otherwise, the returned values are treated as relative values. The provision of some sort of echo enables the user to determine what relative or absolute value is currently being specified. The issue of C/D ratio, discussed in the context of positioning devices, also arises in the use of slide and rotary potentiometers to input values.

8.1.4 Choice Devices

Function keys are a common choice device. Their placement affects their usability: Keys mounted on the CRT bezel are harder to use than are keys mounted in the keyboard or in a nearby separate unit. A foot switch can be used in applications in which the user's hands are engaged yet a single switch closure must be frequently made.

8.1.5 Other Devices

Here we discuss some of the less common, and in some cases experimental, 2D interaction devices. Voice recognizers, which are useful because they free the user's hands for other uses, apply a pattern-recognition approach to the waveforms created when we speak a word. The waveform is typically separated into a number of different frequency bands, and the variation over time of the magnitude of the waveform in each band forms the basis for the pattern matching. However, mistakes can occur in the pattern matching, so it is especially important that an application using a recognizer provide convenient correction capabilities.

Voice recognizers differ in whether they must be trained to recognize the waveforms of a particular speaker, and whether they can recognize connected speech as opposed to single words or phrases. Speaker-independent recognizers have vocabularies that include the digits and up to 1000 words.

The data tablet has been extended in several ways. Many years ago, Herot and Negroponte used an experimental pressure-sensitive stylus [HERO76]: High pressure and a slow drawing speed implied that the user was drawing a line with deliberation, in which case the line was recorded exactly as drawn; low pressure and fast speed implied that the line was being drawn quickly, in which case a straight line connecting the endpoints was recorded. A more recent commercially available tablet [WACO93] incorporates such a pressure-sensitive stylus. The resulting three degrees of freedom reported by the tablet can be used in various creative ways.

8.1.6 3D Interaction Devices

Some of the 2D interaction devices are readily extended to 3D. Joysticks can have a shaft that twists for a third dimension (see Fig. 4.15). Trackballs can be made to sense rotation about the vertical axis in addition to that about the two horizontal axes. In both cases, however, there is no direct relationship between hand movements with the device and the corresponding movement in 3-space.

A number of devices can record 3D hand movements. For example, the Polhemus 3SPACE 3D position and orientation sensor uses electromagnetic coupling between three transmitter antennas and three receiver antennas. The transmitter antenna coils, which are at right angles to one another to form a Cartesian coordinate system, are pulsed in turn. The receiver has three similarly arranged receiver antennas; each time a transmitter coil is pulsed, a current is induced in each of the receiver coils. The strength of the current depends both on the distance between the receiver and transmitter and on the relative orientation of the transmitter and receiver coils. The combination of the nine current values induced by the three successive pulses is used to calculate the 3D position and orientation of the receiver. Figure 8.1 shows this device in use for one of its common purposes: digitizing a 3D object.

The DataGlove records hand position and orientation as well as finger movements. As shown in Fig. 8.2, it is a glove covered with small, lightweight sensors. Each sensor is a short length of fiberoptic cable, with a light-emitting diode (LED) at one end and a phototransistor at the other end. The surface of the cable is roughened in the area where it is to be sensitive to bending. When the cable is flexed, some of the LED's light is lost, so less light is received by the phototransistor. In addition, a Polhemus position and orientation sensor records hand movements. Wearing the DataGlove, a user can grasp objects, move and rotate them, and then release them, thus providing very natural interaction in 3D [ZIMM87]. Color Plate 6 illustrates this concept.

Considerable effort has been directed toward creating what are often called **artificial realities** or **virtual realities**; these are completely computer-generated environments with realistic appearance, behavior, and interaction techniques

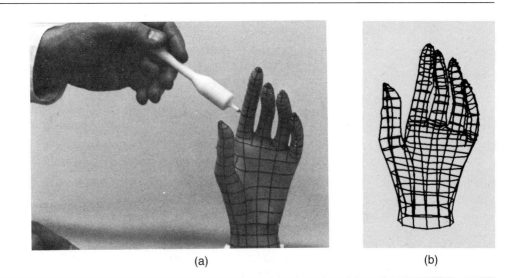

(a)   (b)

Figure 8.1   (a) The Polhemus 3D position sensor being used to digitize a 3D object. (b) A wireframe display of the result. (3Space digitizer courtesy of Polhemus, Inc., Colchester, VT.)

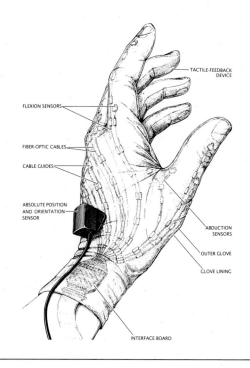

FLEXION SENSORS

FIBER-OPTIC CABLES

CABLE GUIDES

ABSOLUTE POSITION
AND ORIENTATION
SENSOR

TACTILE-FEEDBACK
DEVICE

ABDUCTION
SENSORS

OUTER GLOVE

GLOVE LINING

INTERFACE BOARD

Figure 8.2   The VPL DataGlove, showing the fiberoptic cables that are used to sense finger movements, and the Polhemus position and orientation sensor. (From J. Foley, Interfaces for Advanced Computing, Copyright © 1987 by *Scientific American, Inc.* All rights reserved.)

[FOLE87]. In one version, the user wears a head-mounted stereo display to show proper left- and right-eye views, a Polhemus sensor on the head allows changes in head position and orientation to cause changes to the stereo display, a DataGlove permits 3D interaction, and a microphone is used for issuing voice commands. Color Plate 7 shows this combination of equipment.

Several other technologies can be used to record 3D positions. In one, using optical sensors, LEDs are mounted on the user (either at a single point, such as the fingertip, or all over the body, to measure body movements). Light sensors are mounted high in the corners of a small, semidarkened room in which the user works, and each LED is intensified in turn. The sensors can determine the plane in which the LED lies, and the location of the LED is thus at the intersection of three planes. (A fourth sensor is normally used, in case one of the sensors cannot see the LED.) Small reflectors on the fingertips and other points of interest can replace the LEDs; sensors pick up reflected light rather than the LED's emitted light.

Krueger [KRUE83] has developed a sensor for recording hand and finger movements in 2D. A television camera records hand movements; image-processing techniques of contrast-enhancement and edge detection are used to find the outline of the hand and fingers. Different finger positions can be interpreted as commands, and the user can grasp and manipulate objects, as in Color Plate 8. This technique could be extended to 3D through use of multiple cameras.

8.2 BASIC INTERACTION TASKS

With a basic interaction task, the user of an interactive system enters a unit of information that is meaningful in the context of the application. How large or small is such a unit? For instance, does moving a positioning device a small distance enter a unit of information? Yes, if the new position is put to some application purpose, such as repositioning an object or specifying the endpoint of a line. No, if the repositioning is just one of a sequence of repositionings as the user moves the cursor to place it on top of a menu item: Here, it is the menu choice that is the unit of information.

Basic interaction tasks (BITs) are indivisible; that is, if they were decomposed into smaller units of information, the smaller units would not in themselves be meaningful to the application. BITs are discussed in this section. In Section 8.3, we treat composite interaction tasks (CITs), which are aggregates of the basic interaction tasks described here. If one thinks of BITs as atoms, then CITs are molecules.

A complete set of BITs for interactive graphics is positioning, selecting, entering text, and entering numeric quantities. Each BIT is described in this section, and some of the many interaction techniques for each are discussed. However, there are far too many interaction techniques for us to give an exhaustive list, and we cannot anticipate the development of new techniques. Where possible, the pros and cons of each technique are discussed; remember that a specific interaction technique may be good in some situations and poor in others.

8.2.1 The Position Interaction Task

The positioning task involves specifying an (x, y) or (x, y, z) position to the application program. The customary interaction techniques for carrying out this task involve either moving a screen cursor to the desired location and then pushing a button, or typing the desired position's coordinates on either a real or a simulated keyboard. The positioning device can be direct or indirect, continuous or discrete, absolute or relative. In addition, cursor-movement commands can be typed explicitly on a keyboard, as Up, Left, and so on, or the same commands can be spoken to a voice-recognition unit. Furthermore, techniques can be used together—a mouse controlling a cursor can be used for approximate positioning, and arrow keys can be used to move the cursor a single screen unit at a time for precise positioning.

There are two types of positioning tasks, spatial and linguistic. In a **spatial** positioning task, the user knows where the intended position is, in spatial relation to nearby elements, as in drawing a line between two rectangles or centering an object between two others. In a **linguistic** positioning task, the user knows the numeric values of the (x, y) coordinates of the position. In the former case, the user wants feedback showing the actual position on the screen; in the latter case, the coordinates of the position are needed. If the wrong form of feedback is provided, the user must mentally convert from one form to the other. Both forms of feedback can be provided by displaying both the cursor and its numeric coordinates, as in Fig. 8.3.

8.2.2 The Select Interaction Task—Variable-Sized Set of Choices

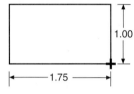

Figure 8.3
Numeric feedback regarding size of an object being constructed. The height and width are changed as the cursor (+) is moved, so the user can adjust the object to the desired size.

The selection task is that of choosing an element from a **choice set**. Typical choice sets are commands, attribute values, object classes, and object instances. For example, the line-style menu in a typical paint program is a set of attribute values, and the object-type (line, circle, rectangle, text, etc.) menu in such programs is a set of object classes. Some interaction techniques can be used to select from any of these four types of choice sets; others are less general. For example, pointing at a visual representation of a set element can serve to select it, no matter what the set type. On the other hand, although function keys often work quite well for selecting from a command, object class, or attribute set, it is difficult to assign a separate function key to each object instance in a drawing, since the size of the choice set is variable, often is large (larger than the number of available function keys), and changes quite rapidly as the user creates and deletes objects.

We use the terms (*relatively*) *fixed-sized choice set* and *varying-sized choice set*. The first term characterizes command, attribute, and object-class choice sets; the second, object-instance choice sets. The modifier *relatively* recognizes that any of these sets can change as new commands, attributes, or object classes (such as symbols in a drafting system) are defined. But the set size does not change frequently, and usually does not change much. Varying-sized choice sets, on the other hand, can become quite large, and can change frequently.

In this section, we discuss techniques that are particularly well suited to potentially large varying-sized choice sets; these include naming and pointing. In Section 8.2.3, we discuss selection techniques particularly well suited to (relatively) fixed-sized choice sets. These sets tend to be small, except for the large (but relatively fixed-sized) command sets found in complex applications. The techniques discussed include typing or speaking the name, abbreviation, or other code that represents the set element; pressing a function key associated with the set element (this can be seen as identical to typing a single character on the keyboard); pointing at a visual representation (textual or graphical) of the set element in a menu; cycling through the set until the desired element is displayed; and making a distinctive motion with a continuous positioning device.

Selecting objects by naming. The user can type the choice's name. The idea is simple, but what if the user does not know the object's name, as could easily happen if hundreds of objects are being displayed, or if the user has no reason to know names? Nevertheless, this technique is useful in several situations. First, if the user is likely to know the names of various objects, as a fleet commander would know the names of the fleet's ships, then referring to them by name is reasonable, and can be faster than pointing, especially if the user might need to scroll through the display to bring the desired object into view. Second, if the display is so cluttered that picking by pointing is difficult *and* if zooming is not feasible (perhaps because the graphics hardware does not support zooming and software zoom is too slow), then naming may be a choice of last resort. If clutter is a problem, then a command to turn object names on and off would be useful.

Typing allows us to make multiple selections through wild-card or don't-care characters, if the choice set elements are named in a meaningful way. Selection by naming is most appropriate for experienced, regular users, rather than for casual, infrequent users.

If naming by typing is necessary, a useful form of feedback is to display, immediately after each keystroke, the list (or partial list, if the full list is too long) of names in the selection set matching the sequence of characters typed so far. This display can trigger memory of how the name is spelled, if the user has recalled the first few characters. As soon as an unambiguous match has been typed, the correct name can be automatically highlighted on the list. Alternatively, the name can be automatically completed as soon as an unambiguous match has been typed. This technique, called **autocompletion**, is sometimes disconcerting to new users, so caution is advisable. A separate strategy for name typein is spelling correction (sometimes called **Do What I Mean**, or DWIM). If the typed name does not match one known to the system, other names that are close to the typed name can be presented to the user as alternatives. Determining closeness can be as simple as searching for single-character errors, or can include multiple-character and missing-character errors.

With a voice recognizer, the user can speak, rather than type, a name, abbreviation, or code. Voice input is a simple way to distinguish commands from data: Commands are entered by voice, the data are entered by keyboard or other means. In a keyboard environment, this feature eliminates the need for special characters or modes to distinguish data and commands.

Selecting objects by pointing.   Any of the pointing techniques mentioned in the introduction to Section 8.2 can be used to select an object, by first pointing and then indicating (typically via a button-push) that the desired object is being pointed at. But what if the object has multiple levels of hierarchy, as did the robot of Chapter 7? If the cursor is over the robot's hand, it is not clear whether the user is pointing at the hand, the arm, or the entire robot. Commands like Select_robot and Select_arm can be used to specify the level of hierarchy. On the other hand, if the level at which the user works changes infrequently, the user will be able to work faster with a separate command, such as Set_selection_level, used to change the level of hierarchy.

A different approach is needed if the number of hierarchical levels is unknown to the system designer and is potentially large (as in a drafting system, where symbols are made up of graphics primitives and other symbols). At least two user commands are required: Up_hierarchy and Down_hierarchy. When the user selects something, the system highlights the lowest-level object seen. If this is what is

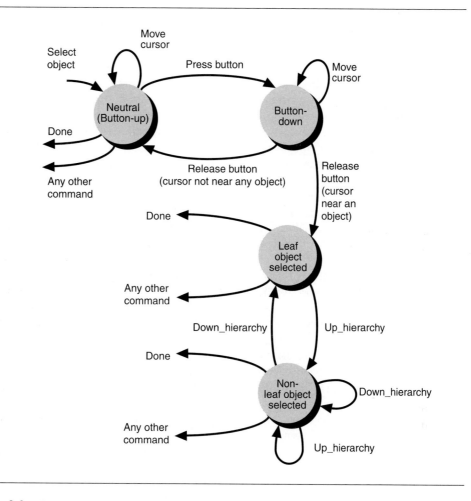

Figure 8.4 State diagram for an object-selection technique for an arbitrary number of hierarchy levels. Up and Down are commands for moving up and down the hierarchy. In the state "Leaf object selected," the Down_hierarchy command is not available. The user selects an object by pointing at it with a cursor, and pressing and then releasing a button.

desired, the user can proceed. If not, the user issues the first command: Up_hierarchy. The entire first-level object of which the detected object is a part is highlighted. If this is not what is wanted, the user travels up again and still more of the picture is highlighted. If the user travels too far up the hierarchy, direction is reversed with the Down_hierarchy command. In addition, a Return_to_lowest_level command can be useful in deep hierarchies, as can a hierarchy diagram in another window, showing where in the hierarchy the current selection is located. The state diagram of Fig. 8.4 shows one approach to hierarchical selection. Alternatively, a single command, say Move_up_hierarchy, can skip back to the originally selected leaf node after the root node is reached.

8.2.3 The Select Interaction Task—Relatively Fixed-Sized Choice Set

Menu selection is one of the richest techniques for selecting from a relatively fixed-sized choice set. Here we discuss several key factors in menu design.

Single-level versus hierarchical design.   One of the most fundamental menu design decisions arises if the choice set is too large to display all at once. Such a menu can be subdivided into a logically structured hierarchy or presented as a linear sequence of choices to be paged or scrolled through. A scroll bar of the type used in many window managers allows all the relevant scrolling and paging commands to be presented in a concise way. A fast keyboard-oriented alternative to pointing at the scrolling commands can also be provided; for instance, the arrow keys can be used to scroll the window, and the shift key can be combined with the arrow keys to move the selection within the visible window, as shown in Fig. 8.5.

With a hierarchical menu, the user first selects from the choice set at the top of the hierarchy, which causes a second choice set to be available. The process is repeated until a leaf node (i.e., an element of the choice set itself) of the hierarchy tree is selected. As with hierarchical object selection, navigation mechanisms need to be provided so that the user can go back up the hierarchy if an incorrect subtree was selected. Visual feedback to give the user some sense of place within the hierarchy is also needed.

Menu hierarchies can be presented in several ways. Of course, successive levels of the hierarchy can replace one another on the display as further choices are made, but this does not give the user much sense of position within the hierarchy. The **cascading hierarchy**, as depicted in Fig. 8.6, is more attractive. Enough of each menu must be revealed that the complete highlighted selection path is visible, and some means must be used to indicate whether a menu item is a leaf node or is the name of a lower-level menu (in the figure, the right-pointing arrow fills this role). Another arrangement is to show just the name of each selection made thus

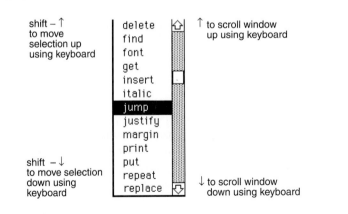

Figure 8.5   A menu within a scrolling window. The user controls scrolling by selecting the up and down arrows or by dragging the square in the scroll bar.

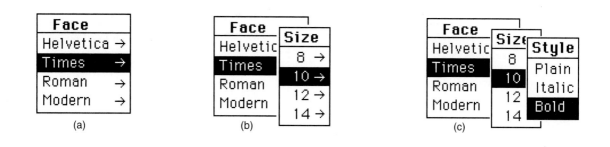

Figure 8.6   A pop-up hierarchical menu. (a) The first menu appears where the cursor is, in response to a button-down action. The cursor can be moved up and down to select the desired typeface. (b) The cursor is then moved to the right to bring up the second menu. (c) The process is repeated for the third menu.

far in traversing down the hierarchy, plus all the selections available at the current level.

When we design a hierarchical menu, the issue of depth versus breadth is always present. Snowberry et al. [SNOW83] found experimentally that selection time and accuracy improve when broader menus with fewer levels of selection are used. Similar results are reported by Landauer and Nachbar [LAND85] and by other researchers. However, these results do not necessarily generalize to menu hierarchies that lack a natural, understandable structure.

Hierarchical menu selection almost demands an accompanying keyboard or function-key accelerator technique to speed up selection for more experienced (so-called **power**) users. This is easy if each node of the tree has a unique name, so that the user can enter the name directly, and the menu system provides a backup should the user's memory fail. If the names are unique only within each level of the hierarchy, the power user must type the complete path name to the desired leaf node.

Menu placement.   Menus shown on the display screen can be static and permanently visible, or can appear dynamically on request (tear-off, appearing, pop-up, pull-down, and pull-out menus).

A pop-up menu appears on the screen when a selection is to be made, either in response to an explicit user action (typically pressing a mouse or tablet puck button), or automatically because the next dialogue step requires a menu selection. The menu normally appears at the cursor location, which is usually the user's center of visual attention, thereby maintaining visual continuity. An attractive feature in pop-up menus is the initial highlighting of the most recently made selection from the choice set *if* the most recently selected item is more likely to be selected a second time than is another item, positioning the menu so the cursor is on that item.

Pop-up and other appearing menus conserve precious screen space—one of the user-interface designer's most valuable commodities. Their use is facilitated by a fast RasterOp instruction, as discussed in Chapter 2.

```
🍎  File  Edit  Style  Font  Layout  Arrange  Fill  Lines  Pen
```

Undo   ⌘Z   . Obj sel state diagram

Cut   ⌘X
Copy   ⌘C
Paste   ⌘U
Clear

Duplicate   ⌘D
Select All   ⌘A

Reshape Arc ⌘R
Smooth
Unsmooth
Round Corners...

Press button   Move Cursor

Button Down

Release button   Release button
(cursor not near any object)

Any Other command

Figure 8.7   A Macintosh pull-down menu. The last menu item is gray rather than black, indicating that it is currently not available for selection (the currently selected object, an arc, does not have corners to be rounded). The Undo command is also gray, because the previously executed command cannot be undone. Abbreviations are accelerator keys for power users. (Copyright 1988 Claris Corporation. All rights reserved.)

Figure 8.8
Radio-button technique for selecting from a set of mutually exclusive alternatives. (Courtesy of NeXT, Inc. © 1989 NeXT, Inc.)

Unlike pop-up menus, pull-down menus are anchored in a menu bar along the top of the screen. All the popular graphical user interfaces—the Apple Macintosh, Microsoft Windows, OPEN LOOK, and Motif—use pull-down menus. Macintosh menus, shown in Fig. 8.7, also illustrate accelerator keys and context sensitivity.

Current selection.   If a system has the concept of *currently selected element* of a choice set, menu selection allows this element to be highlighted. In some cases, an initial default setting is provided by the system and is used unless the user changes it. The currently selected element can be shown in various ways. The **radio-button** interaction technique, patterned after the tuning buttons on car radios, is one way (Fig. 8.8). Again, some pop-up menus highlight the most recently selected item and place it under the cursor, on the assumption that the user is more likely to reselect that item than to select any other entry.

Size and shape of menu items.   Pointing accuracy and speed are affected by the size of each individual menu item. Larger items are faster to select, as predicted by Fitts' law [FITT54; CARD83]; on the other hand, smaller items take less space and permit more menu items to be displayed in a fixed area, but induce more errors during selection. Thus, there is a conflict between using small menu items to preserve screen space versus using larger ones to decrease selection time and to reduce errors.

Pattern recognition.   In selection techniques involving pattern recognition, the user makes sequences of movements with a continuous-positioning device, such as a tablet or mouse. The pattern recognizer automatically compares the sequence with a set of defined patterns, each of which corresponds to an element of the selection set. Proofreader's marks indicating delete, capitalize, move, and so on are attractive candidates for this approach [WOLF87].

Recent advances in character recognition algorithms have led to pen-based operating systems and notepad computers, such as Apple's Newton. Patterns are entered on a tablet, and are recognized and interpreted as commands, numbers, and letters.

Function keys.   Elements of the choice set can be associated with function keys. (We can think of single-keystroke inputs from a regular keyboard as function keys.) Unfortunately, there never seem to be enough keys to go around! The keys can be used in a hierarchical-selection fashion, and their meanings can be altered using chords, say by depressing the keyboard shift and control keys along with the function key itself. For instance, Microsoft Word on the Macintosh uses "shift-option->" to increase point size and the symmetrical "shift-option-<" to decrease point size; "shift-option-I" italicizes plain text and unitalicizes italicized text, whereas "shift-option-U" treats underlined text similarly.

8.2.4 The Text Interaction Task

The text-string input task entails entering a character string to which the application does not ascribe any special meaning. Thus, typing a command name is *not* a text-entry task. In contrast, typing legends for a graph and typing text into a word processor *are* text input tasks. Clearly, the most common text-input technique is use of the QWERTY keyboard.

8.2.5 The Quantify Interaction Task

The quantify interaction task involves specifying a numeric value between some minimum and maximum value. Typical interaction techniques are typing the value, setting a dial to the value, and using an up–down counter to select the value. Like the positioning task, this task may be either linguistic or spatial. When it is linguistic, the user knows the specific value to be entered; when it is spatial, the user seeks to increase or decrease a value by a certain amount, with perhaps an approximate idea of the desired end value. In the former case, the interaction technique clearly must involve numeric feedback of the value being selected (one way to do this is to have the user type the actual value); in the latter case, it is more important to give a general impression of the approximate setting of the value. This is typically accomplished with a spatially oriented feedback technique, such as display of a dial or gauge on which the current (and perhaps previous) value is shown.

One means of entering values is the potentiometer. The decision of whether to use a rotary or linear potentiometer should take into account whether the visual feedback of changing a value is rotary (e.g., a turning clock hand) or linear (e.g., a rising temperature gauge). The current position of one or a group of slide potentiometers is much more easily comprehended at a glance than are those of rotary potentiometers, even if the knobs have pointers. On the other hand, rotary potentiometers are easier to adjust. Availability of both linear and rotary potentiometers

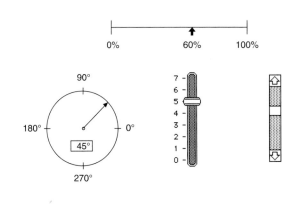

Figure 8.9   Several dials that the user can employ to input values by dragging the control pointer. Feedback is given by the pointer and, in two cases, by numeric displays. (Vertical sliders © Apple Computer, Inc.)

can help users to associate meanings with each device. It is important to use directions consistently: Clockwise or upward movements normally increase a value.

With continuous-scale manipulation, the user points at the current-value indicator on a displayed gauge or scale, presses the selection button, drags the indicator along the scale to the desired value, and then releases the selection button. A pointer is typically used to indicate the value selected on the scale, and a numeric echo may be given. Figure 8.9 shows several such dials and their associated feedback.

8.2.6 3D Interaction Tasks

Two of the four interaction tasks described previously for 2D applications become more complicated in 3D: position and select. The first part of this section deals with a technique for positioning and selecting, which are closely related. In this section, we also introduce an additional 3D interaction task: rotate (in the sense of orienting an object in 3-space). The major reason for the complication is the difficulty of perceiving 3D depth relationships of a cursor or object relative to other displayed objects. This contrasts starkly with 2D interaction, where the user can readily perceive that the cursor is above, next to, or on an object. A secondary complication arises because the commonly available interaction devices, such as mice and tablets, are only 2D devices, and we need a way to map movements of these 2D devices into 3D.

Display of stereo pairs, corresponding to left- and right-eye views, is helpful for understanding general depth relationships, but is of limited accuracy as a precise locating method. Methods for presenting stereo pairs to the eye are discussed in Chapter 12, and in [HODG85]. Other ways to show depth relationships are discussed in Chapters 12–14.

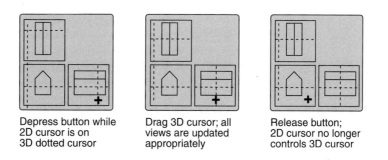

| Depress button while 2D cursor is on 3D dotted cursor | Drag 3D cursor; all views are updated appropriately | Release button; 2D cursor no longer controls 3D cursor |

Figure 8.10 3D positioning technique using three views of the same scene (a house). The 2D cursor (+) is used to select one of the dashed 3D cursor lines.

Figure 8.10 shows a common way to position in 3D. The 2D cursor, under control of, say, a mouse, moves freely among the three views. The user can select any one of the 3D cursor's dashed lines and can drag the line using a button-down–drag–button-up sequence. If the button-down event is close to the intersection of two dashed cursor lines, then both are selected and are moved with the mouse. Although this method may appear restrictive in forcing the user to work in one or two dimensions at a time, it is sometimes advantageous to decompose the 3D manipulation task into simpler lower-dimensional tasks. Selecting as well as locating is facilitated with multiple views: Objects that overlap and hence are difficult to distinguish in one view may not overlap in another view.

As with locating and selecting, the issues in 3D rotation are understanding depth relationships, mapping 2D interaction devices into 3D, and ensuring stimulus-response compatibility (S-R compatibility)[1]. An easily implemented 3D rotation technique provides slider dials or gauges that control rotation about three axes. S-R compatibility suggests that the three axes normally should be in the screen-coordinate system—x to the right, y increasing upward, z out of (or into) the screen [BRIT78]. Of course, the center of rotation either must be explicitly specified as a separate step, or must be implicit (typically the screen-coordinate origin, the origin of the object, or the center of the object). Providing rotation about the screen's x and y axes is especially simple, as suggested in Fig. 8.11(a). The (x, y, z) coordinate system associated with the sliders is rotated as the sliders are moved to show the effect of the rotation. The two-axis rotation approach can be easily generalized to three axes by adding a dial for z-axis rotation (a dial is preferable to a slider for S-R compatibility). Even more S-R compatibility comes from the arrangement of dials on the faces of a cube shown in Fig. 8.11(b), which clearly suggests the axes controlled by each dial. A 3D trackball could be used instead of the dials.

---

[1] The human-factors principle, which states that system responses to user actions must be in the same direction or same orientation, and that the magnitude of the responses should be proportional to the actions.

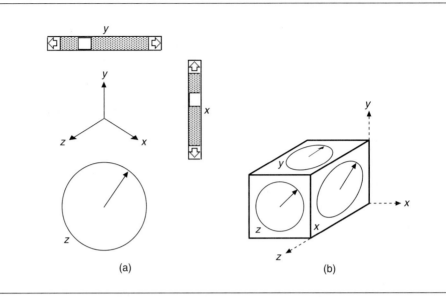

Figure 8.11 Two approaches to 3D rotation. (a) Two slider dials for effecting rotation about the screen's *x* and *y* axes, and a dial for rotation about the screen's *z* axis. The coordinate system represents world coordinates and shows how world coordinates relate to screen coordinates. (b) Three dials to control rotation about three axes. The placement of the dials on the cube provides strong stimulus-response compatibility.

It is often necessary to combine 3D interaction tasks. Thus, rotation requires a select task for the object to be rotated, a position task for the center of rotation, and an orient task for the actual rotation. Specifying a 3D view can be thought of as a combined positioning (where the eye is), orientation (how the eye is oriented), and scaling (field of view, or how much of the projection plane is mapped into the viewport) task. We can create such a task by combining some of the techniques we have discussed, or by designing a *fly-around* capability in which the viewer flies an imaginary airplane around a 3D world. The controls are typically pitch, roll, and yaw, plus velocity to speed up or slow down. With the fly-around concept, the user needs an overview, such as a 2D plan view, indicating the imaginary airplane's ground position and heading.

8.3 COMPOSITE INTERACTION TASKS

Composite interaction tasks (CITs) are built on top of the basic interaction tasks (BITs) described in the previous section, and are actually combinations of BITs integrated into a unit. There are three major forms of CITs: dialogue boxes, used to specify multiple units of information; construction, used to create objects requiring two or more positions; and manipulation, used to reshape existing geometric objects.

8.3.1 Dialogue Boxes

We often need to select multiple elements of a selection set. For instance, text attributes, such as italic, bold, underline, hollow, and all caps, are not mutually exclusive, and the user may want to select two or more at once. In addition, there may be several sets of relevant attributes, such as typeface and font. Some of the menu approaches useful in selecting a single element of a selection set are not satisfactory for multiple selections. For example, pull-down and pop-up menus normally disappear when a selection is made, necessitating a second activation to make a second selection.

This problem can be overcome with dialogue boxes, a form of menu that remains visible until explicitly dismissed by the user. In addition, dialogue boxes can permit selection from more than one selection set, and can also include areas for entering text and values. Selections made in a dialogue box can be corrected immediately. When all the information has been entered into the dialogue box, the box is typically dismissed explicitly with a command. Attributes and other values specified in a dialogue box can be applied immediately, allowing the user to preview the effect of a font or line-style change.

8.3.2 Construction Techniques

One way to construct a line is to have the user indicate one endpoint and then the other; once the second endpoint is specified, a line is drawn between the two points. With this technique, however, the user has no easy way to try out different line positions before settling on a final one, because the line is not actually drawn until the second endpoint is given. With this style of interaction, the user must invoke a command each time an endpoint is to be repositioned.

A far superior approach is **rubberbanding**, discussed in Chapter 2. When the user pushes a button (often the tipswitch on a tablet stylus, or a mouse button), the starting position of the line is established by the cursor (usually but not necessarily controlled by a continuous-positioning device). As the cursor moves, so does the endpoint of the line; when the button is released, the endpoint is frozen. Figure 8.12 shows a rubberband line-drawing sequence. The *rubberband* state is active *only* while a button is held down. It is in this state that cursor movements cause the current line to change.

An entire genre of interaction techniques is derived from rubberband line drawing. The **rubber-rectangle** technique starts by anchoring one corner of a rectangle with a button-down action, after which the opposite corner is dynamically linked to the cursor until a button-up action occurs. The state diagram for this technique differs from that for rubberband line drawing only in the dynamic feedback of a rectangle rather than a line. The **rubber-circle** technique creates a circle that is centered at the initial cursor position and that passes through the current cursor position, or that is within the square defined by opposite corners. All these techniques have in common the user-action sequence of button-down, move locator and see feedback, button-up.

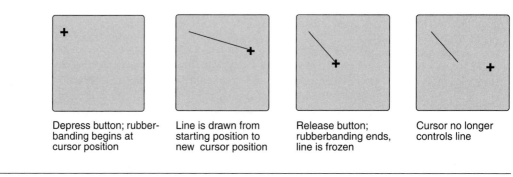

| Depress button; rubber-banding begins at cursor position | Line is drawn from starting position to new cursor position | Release button; rubberbanding ends, line is frozen | Cursor no longer controls line |

Figure 8.12   Rubberband line drawing.

Constraints of various types can be applied to the cursor positions in any of these techniques. For example, Fig. 8.13 shows a sequence of lines drawn using the same cursor positions as in Fig. 8.12, but with a horizontal constraint in effect. A vertical line, or a line at some other orientation, can also be drawn in this manner. Polylines made entirely of horizontal and vertical lines, as in printed circuit boards, VLSI chips, and some city maps, are readily created; right angles are introduced either in response to a user command, or automatically as the cursor changes direction. The idea can be generalized to any shape, such as a circle, ellipse, or any other curve; the curve is initialized at some position, then cursor movements control how much of the curve is displayed. In general, the cursor position is used as input to a constraint function whose output is then used to display the appropriate portion of the object.

8.3.3 Dynamic Manipulation

It is not sufficient to just create lines, rectangles, and so on. In many situations, the user must be able to modify previously created geometric entities.

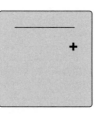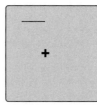

| Depress button; rubberbanding begins at cursor position | Line is drawn from starting position to x coordinate of new cursor position | Release button; rubberbanding ends, line frozen | Cursor no longer controls line |

Figure 8.13   Horizontally constrained rubberband line drawing.

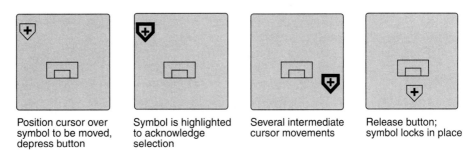

| Position cursor over symbol to be moved, depress button | Symbol is highlighted to acknowledge selection | Several intermediate cursor movements | Release button; symbol locks in place |

Figure 8.14   Dragging a symbol into a new position.

Dragging moves a selected symbol from one position to another under control of a cursor, as in Fig. 8.14. A button-down action typically starts the dragging (in some cases, the button-down is also used to select the symbol under the cursor to be dragged); then, a button-up freezes the symbol in place, so that further movements of the cursor have no effect on it. This button-down–drag–button-up sequence is often called **click-and-drag** interaction.

The concept of **handles** is useful to provide scaling of an object. Figure 8.15 shows an object with eight handles, which are displayed as small squares at the corners and on the sides of the imaginary box surrounding the object. The user selects one of the handles and drags it to scale the object. If the handle is on a corner, then the corner diagonally opposite is locked in place. If the handle is in the middle of a side, then the opposite side is locked in place.

When this technique is integrated into a complete user interface, the handles appear only when the object is selected to be operated on. Handles are also a unique visual code to indicate that an object is selected, since other visual codings (e.g., line thickness, dashed lines, or changed intensity) might also be used as part of the drawing itself.

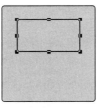 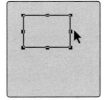 

| Selecting rectangle with cursor causes handles to appear | Button actions on this handle move only right side of rectangle | Button actions on this handle move only corner of rectangle |

Figure 8.15   Handles used to reshape objects.

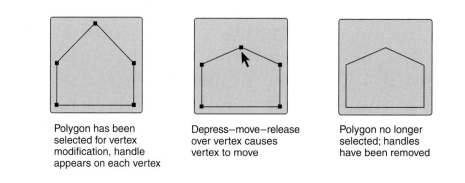

Polygon has been
selected for vertex
modification, handle
appears on each vertex

Depress–move–release
over vertex causes
vertex to move

Polygon no longer
selected; handles
have been removed

Figure 8.16   Handles used to reposition the vertices of a polygon.

Dragging, rotating, and scaling affect an entire object. What if we wish to be able to move individual points, such as the vertices of a polygon? Vertices could be named, and the user could enter the name of a vertex and its new (x, y) coordinates. But the same point-and-drag strategy used to move an entire object is more attractive. In this case, the user points to a vertex, selects it, and drags it to a new position. The vertices adjacent to the one selected remain connected via rubberband lines. To facilitate selecting a vertex, we can make a vertex blink whenever the cursor is near, or we can superimpose handles over each vertex, as in Fig. 8.16. Similarly, the user can move an edge of a polygon by selecting it and dragging, with the edge maintaining its original slope. For smooth curves and surfaces, handles can also be provided to allow the user to manipulate points that control the shape, as discussed further in Chapter 9.

8.4 INTERACTION-TECHNIQUE TOOLKITS

The look and feel of a user–computer interface is determined largely by the collection of interaction techniques provided for it. Recall that interaction techniques implement the hardware binding portion of a user–computer interface design. Designing and implementing a good set of interaction techniques is time consuming: Interaction-technique toolkits, which are subroutine libraries of interaction techniques, are mechanisms for making a collection of techniques available for use by application programmers. This approach, which helps to ensure a consistent look and feel among application programs, is clearly a sound software-engineering practice.

Interaction-technique toolkits can be used not only by application programs, but also by the resident window manager, which is after all just another program. Using the same toolkit across the board is an important and commonly used approach to providing a look and feel that unifies both multiple applications and the windowing environment itself. For instance, the menu style used to select window operations should be the same style used within applications.

A toolkit can be implemented on top of a **window-management system** [FOLE90]. In the absence of a window system, toolkits can be implemented directly on top of a graphics subroutine package; however, because elements of a toolkit include menus, dialogue boxes, scroll bars, and the like, all of which can conveniently be implemented in windows, the window system substrate is normally used. Widely used toolkits include the Macintosh toolkit [APPL85], OSF/Motif [OPEN89] and InterViews [LINT89] for use with the X Window System, and several toolkits that implement OPEN LOOK [SUN89]. Color Plate 9 shows the OSF/Motif interface. Color Plate 10 shows the OPEN LOOK interface.

SUMMARY

We have presented some of the most important concepts of user interfaces: input devices, interaction techniques, and interaction tasks. There are many more aspects of user interface techniques and design, however, that we have not discussed. Among these are the pros and cons of various dialogue styles—such as what you see is what you get (WYSIWYG), command language, and direct manipulation—and window-manager issues that affect the user interface. [FOLE90] has a thorough treatment of those topics.

Exercises

8.1   Examine a user–computer interface with which you are familiar. List each interaction task used. Categorize each task into one of the four BITs of Section 8.2. If an interaction does not fit this classification scheme, try decomposing it further.

8.2   Extend the state diagram of Fig. 8.4 to include a "return to lowest level" command that takes the selection back to the lowest level of the hierarchy, such that whatever was selected first is selected again.

8.3   Implement a menu package on a color raster display that has a look-up table such that the menu is displayed in a strong, bright but partially transparent color, and all the colors underneath the menu are changed to a subdued gray.

8.4   Implement any of the 3D interaction techniques discussed in this chapter.

8.5   Draw the state diagram that controls pop-up hierarchical menus. Draw the state diagram that controls panel hierarchical menus.

9 Representation of Curves and Surfaces

The classic teapot, shown in Fig. 9.1, is perhaps the best-known icon of computer graphics. Since it was modeled in 1975 by Martin Newell [CROW87], it has been used by dozens of researchers as a structure for demonstrating the latest techniques for producing realistic surfaces and textures. Modeling the elegant teapot required specifying its shape as a collection of smooth surface elements, known as **bicubic patches**. Smooth curves and surfaces must be generated in many computer graphics applications. Many real-world objects are inherently smooth, and much of computer graphics involves modeling the real world. Computer-aided design (CAD), high-quality character typefaces, data plots, and artists' sketches all contain smooth curves and surfaces. The path of a camera or object in an animation sequence is almost always smooth; similarly, a path through intensity or color space (Chapters 12 and 11) often must be smooth.

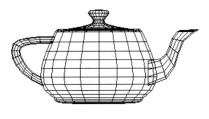

Figure 9.1   The famous *teapot*–a model consisting of an assemblage of smooth, curved surfaces.

The need to represent curves and surfaces arises in two cases: in modeling existing objects (a car, a face, or a mountain) and in modeling *from scratch*, where no preexisting physical object is being represented. In the first case, a mathematical description of the object may be unavailable. Of course, we can use as a model the coordinates of the infinitely many points of the object, but this approach is not feasible for a computer with finite storage. More often, we merely approximate the object with pieces of planes, spheres, or other shapes that are easy to describe mathematically, and require that points on our model be close to corresponding points on the object.

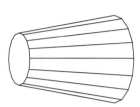

Figure 9.2
A 3D object represented by polygons.

In the second case, when there is no preexisting object to model, the user creates the object in the modeling process; hence, the object matches its representation exactly, because its only embodiment is the representation. To create the object, the user may sculpt the object interactively, describe it mathematically, or give an approximate description to be *filled in* by some program. In CAD, the computer representation is used later to generate physical realizations of the abstractly designed object.

This chapter introduces the general area of **surface modeling.** The area is broad, and only the three most common representations for 3D surfaces are presented here: polygon mesh surfaces, parametric surfaces, and quadric surfaces. We also discuss parametric curves, both because they are interesting in their own right and because parametric surfaces are a generalization of the curves.

Solid modeling, introduced in the next chapter, is the representation of volumes completely surrounded by surfaces, such as a cube, an airplane, or a building. The surface representations discussed in this chapter can be used in solid modeling to define each of the surfaces that bound the volume.

A **polygon mesh** is a set of connected, polygonally bounded planar surfaces. Open boxes, cabinets, and building exteriors can be easily and naturally represented by polygon meshes, as can volumes bounded by planar surfaces. Polygon meshes can be used, although less easily, to represent objects with curved surfaces, as in Fig. 9.2; however, the representation is only approximate. Figure 9.3 shows the cross-section of a curved shape and the polygon mesh representing that shape. We can make the obvious errors in the representation arbitrarily small by using more polygons to create a closer piecewise linear approximation, but this approach increases space requirements and the execution time of algorithms processing the representation. Furthermore, if the image is enlarged, the straight edges again become obvious.

Figure 9.3
A cross-section of a curved shape (dashed line) and its polygonal representation (solid lines).

Parametric polynomial curves define points on a 3D curve by using three polynomials in a parameter t, one for each of x, y, and z. The coefficients of the polynomials are selected such that the curve follows the desired path. Although various degrees of polynomials can be used, we present only the most common case: cubic polynomials (that have powers of the parameter up through the third). The term **cubic curve** will often be used for such curves.

Parametric bivariate (two-variable) **polynomial surface patches** define the coordinates of points on a curved surface by using three bivariate polynomials, one for each of x, y, and z. The boundaries of the patches are parametric polynomial curves. Many fewer bivariate polynomial surface patches than polygonal patches are needed to approximate a curved surface to a given accuracy. The algorithms for working with bivariate polynomials, however, are more complex than are those for polygons. As with curves, polynomials of various degrees can be used, but we discuss here only the common case of polynomials that are cubic in both parameters. The surfaces are accordingly called **bicubic surfaces.**

Quadric surfaces are those defined implicitly by an equation $f(x, y, z) = 0$, where f is a quadric polynomial in x, y, and z. Quadric surfaces are a convenient representation for the familiar sphere, ellipsoid, and cylinder.

Chapter 10, on solid modeling, incorporates these representations into systems to represent not just surfaces, but also bounded (solid) volumes. The surface representations described in this chapter are used, sometimes in combination with one another, to bound a 3D volume.

9.1 POLYGON MESHES

A **polygon mesh** is a collection of edges, vertices, and polygons connected such that each edge is shared by at most two polygons. An edge connects two vertices, and a polygon is a closed sequence of edges. An edge can be shared by two adjacent polygons, a vertex is shared by at least two edges, and every edge is part of *some* polygon. A polygon mesh can be represented in several different ways, each with its advantages and disadvantages. The application programmer's task is to choose the most appropriate representation. Several representations can be used in a single application: one for external storage, another for internal use, and yet another with which the user interactively creates the mesh.

Two basic criteria, space and time, can be used to evaluate different representations. Typical operations on a polygon mesh are finding all the edges incident to a vertex, finding the polygons sharing an edge or a vertex, finding the vertices connected by an edge, finding the edges of a polygon, displaying the mesh, and identifying errors in representation (e.g., a missing edge, vertex, or polygon). In general, the more explicitly the relations among polygons, vertices, and edges are represented, the faster the operations are and the more space the representation requires. Woo [WOO85] has analyzed the time complexity of nine basic access operations and nine basic update operations on a polygon-mesh data structure.

In Sections 9.1.1 and 9.1.2, several issues concerning polygon meshes are discussed: representing polygon meshes, ensuring that a given representation is correct, and calculating the coefficients of the plane of a polygon.

9.1.1 Representing Polygon Meshes

In this section, we discuss three polygon-mesh representations: explicit, pointers to a vertex list, and pointers to an edge list. In the **explicit representation,** each polygon is represented by a list of vertex coordinates:

$$P = ((x_1, y_1, z_1), (x_2, y_2, z_2), \dots, (x_n, y_n, z_n)).$$

The vertices are stored in the order in which we would encounter them were we traveling around the polygon. There are edges between successive vertices in the list and between the last and first vertices. For a single polygon, this representation is space-efficient; for a polygon mesh, however, much space is lost, because the coordinates of shared vertices are duplicated. Even more of a problem, there is no explicit representation of shared edges and vertices. For instance, to drag a vertex and all its incident edges interactively, we must find all polygons that share the vertex. This search requires comparing the coordinate triples of one polygon with those of all other polygons. The most efficient way to do this would be to sort all N coordinate triples, but this process is at best an $N \log_2 N$ one, and even then there is the danger that the same vertex might, due to computational roundoff, have slightly different coordinate values in each polygon, so a correct match might never be made.

With this representation, displaying the mesh either as filled polygons or as polygon outlines necessitates transforming each vertex and clipping each edge of each polygon. If edges are being drawn, each shared edge is drawn twice, which causes problems on pen plotters, film recorders, and vector displays, due to the overwriting. A problem may also be created on raster displays if the edges are drawn in opposite directions, in which case extra pixels may be intensified.

Polygons defined with **pointers to a vertex list,** the method used by SPHIGS, have each vertex in the polygon mesh stored just once, in the vertex list $V = ((x_1, y_1, z_1), \ldots, (x_n, y_n, z_n))$. A polygon is defined by a list of indices (or pointers) into the vertex list. A polygon made up of vertices 3, 5, 7, and 10 in the vertex list would thus be represented as $P = (3, 5, 7, 10)$.

This representation, an example of which is shown in Fig. 9.4, has several advantages over the explicit polygon representation. Since each vertex is stored just once, considerable space is saved. Furthermore, the coordinates of a vertex can be changed easily. On the other hand, it is still difficult to find polygons that share an edge, and shared polygon edges are still drawn twice when all polygon outlines are displayed. We can eliminate these two problems by representing edges explicitly, as in the next method.

When defining polygons by **pointers to an edge list,** we again have the vertex list V, but represent a polygon as a list of pointers not to the vertex list, but rather to an edge list, in which each edge occurs just once. In turn, each edge in the edge list points to the two vertices in the vertex list defining the edge, and also to the one or

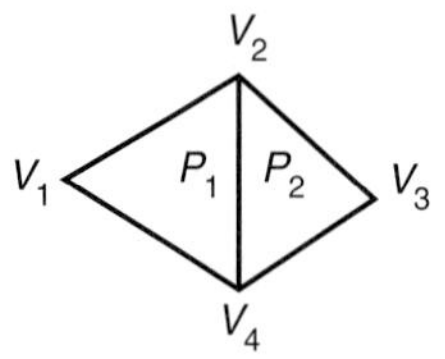

$V = (V_1, V_2, V_3, V_4) = ((x_1, y_1, z_1), \ldots, (x_4, y_4, z_4))$

$P_1 = (1, 2, 4)$

$P_2 = (4, 2, 3)$

Figure 9.4   Polygon mesh defined with indexes into a vertex list.

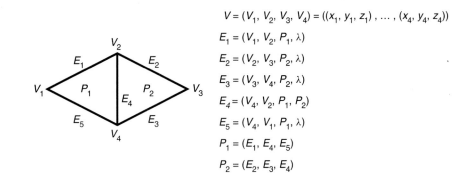

$$V = (V_1, V_2, V_3, V_4) = ((x_1, y_1, z_1), \ldots, (x_4, y_4, z_4))$$
$$E_1 = (V_1, V_2, P_1, \lambda)$$
$$E_2 = (V_2, V_3, P_2, \lambda)$$
$$E_3 = (V_3, V_4, P_2, \lambda)$$
$$E_4 = (V_4, V_2, P_1, P_2)$$
$$E_5 = (V_4, V_1, P_1, \lambda)$$
$$P_1 = (E_1, E_4, E_5)$$
$$P_2 = (E_2, E_3, E_4)$$

Figure 9.5 Polygon mesh defined with edge lists for each polygon (λ represents null).

two polygons to which the edge belongs. Hence, we describe a polygon as $P = (E_1, \ldots, E_n)$, and an edge as $E = (V_1, V_2, P_1, P_2)$. When an edge belongs to only one polygon, either P_1 or P_2 is null. Figure 9.5 shows an example of this representation.

We show polygon outlines by displaying all edges, rather than by displaying all polygons; thus, redundant clipping, transformation, and scan conversion are avoided. Filled polygons are also displayed easily. In some situations, such as the description of a 3D honeycomblike sheet-metal structure, some edges are shared by three polygons. In such cases, the edge descriptions can be extended to include an arbitrary number of polygons: $E = (V_1, V_2, P_1, P_2, \ldots, P_n)$.

In none of these three representations (i.e., explicit polygons, pointers to vertices, pointers to an edge list) is it easy to determine which edges are incident to a vertex: All edges must be inspected. Of course, information can be added explicitly to permit determination of such relationships. For instance, the winged-edge representation used by Baumgart [BAUM75] expands the edge description to include pointers to the two adjoining edges of each polygon, whereas the vertex description includes a pointer to an (arbitrary) edge incident on the vertex, and thus more polygon and vertex information is available.

9.1.2 Plane Equations

When we are working with polygons or polygon meshes, we frequently need to know the equation of the plane in which the polygon lies. In some cases, of course, the equation is known implicitly through the interactive construction methods used to define the polygon. If the equation is not known, we can use the coordinates of three vertices to find the plane. Recall the plane equation

$$Ax + By + Cz + D = 0. \tag{9.1}$$

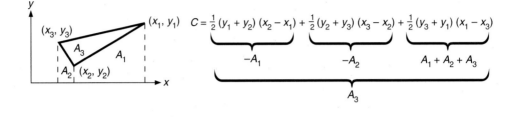

Figure 9.6 Calculating the area C of a triangle using Eq. (9.2).

The coefficients A, B, and C define the normal to the plane, $[A\ B\ C]$. Given points P_1, P_2, and P_3 on the plane, that plane's normal can be computed as the vector cross-product $P_1P_2 \times P_1P_3$ (or $P_2P_3 \times P_2P_1$, etc.). If the cross-product is zero, then the three points are collinear and do not define a plane. Other vertices, if any, can be used instead. Given a nonzero cross-product, we can find D by substituting the normal to $[A\ B\ C]$ and any one of the three points into Eq. (9.1).

If there are more than three vertices, they may be nonplanar, either for numerical reasons or because of the method by which the polygons were generated. Then another technique for finding the coefficients A, B, and C of a plane that comes close to all the vertices is better than the cross-product method. It can be shown that A, B, and C are proportional to the signed areas of the projections of the polygon onto the (y, z), (z, x), and (x, y) planes, respectively. For example, if the polygon is parallel to the (x, y) plane, then $A = B = 0$, as expected: The projections of the polygon onto the (y, z) and (z, x) planes have zero area. This method is better than the cross-product method, because the areas of the projections are a function of the coordinates of all the vertices and so are not sensitive to the choice of a few vertices that might happen not to be coplanar with most or all of the other vertices, or that might happen to be collinear. For instance, the area (and hence coefficient) C of the polygon projected onto the (x, y) plane in Fig. 9.6 is just the area of the trapezoid A_3, minus the areas of A_1 and A_2. In general,

$$C = \frac{1}{2} \sum_{i=1}^{n} (y_i + y_{i \oplus 1})(x_{i \oplus 1} - x_i), \tag{9.2}$$

where the operator $\oplus$ is normal addition except that $n \oplus 1 = 1$. The areas for A and B are given by similar formulae, except the area for B is negated (see Example 9.1).

Eq. (9.2) gives the sum of the areas of all the trapezoids formed by successive edges of the polygons. If $x_{i \oplus 1} < x_i$, the area makes a negative contribution to the sum. The sign of the sum is also useful: If the vertices have been enumerated in a clockwise direction (as projected onto the plane), then the sign is positive; otherwise, it is negative.

Once we determine the plane equation by using all the vertices, we can estimate how nonplanar the polygon is by calculating the perpendicular distance from the plane to each vertex. This distance d for the vertex at (x, y, z) is

$$d = \frac{Ax + By + Cz + D}{\sqrt{A^2 + B^2 + C^2}} . \tag{9.3}$$

This distance is either positive or negative, depending on which side of the plane the point is located. If the vertex is on the plane, then $d = 0$. Of course, to determine only on which side of a plane a point is, only the sign of d matters, so division by the square root is not needed.

The plane equation is not unique; any nonzero multiplicative constant k changes the equation, but not the plane. It is often convenient to store the plane coefficients with a normalized normal; we can do so by choosing

$$k = \frac{1}{\sqrt{A^2 + B^2 + C^2}} , \tag{9.4}$$

which is the reciprocal of the length of the normal. Then, distances can be computed with Eq. (9.3) more easily, since the denominator is 1.

Example 9.1

Problem:　Write a function that calculates the plane equation coefficients, given n vertices of a polygon that is approximately planar. Assume that the polygon vertices are enumerated counterclockwise, as viewed toward the plane from the positive side of the plane. The vertices and the number of vertices are arguments passed to the function.

Answer:　Using Eq. (9.2), and similar equations for A and B, the program is simply:

This function calculates plane equation coefficients.

```
FindPlaneCoefficients(float x[], float y[], float z[], int num_verts,
                      float *a, float *b, float *c, float *d)
{
    float  A, B, C, D;
    int    i, j;

    A = B = C = 0.0;
    for (i = 0; i < num_verts; i++) {
        j = (i + 1) % num_verts;
        A += (z[i] + z[j]) * (y[j] − y[i]);
        B += − (x[i] + x[j]) * (z[j] − z[i]);
        C += (y[i] + y[j]) * (x[j] − x[i]);
    }
    A /= 2.0; B /= 2.0; C /= 2.0;
    D = −(A * x[0] + B * y[0] + C * z[0]);

    *a = A;
    *b = B;
    *c = C;
    *d = D;
}
```

9.2 PARAMETRIC CUBIC CURVES

Polylines and polygons are first-degree, piecewise approximations to curves and surfaces, respectively. Unless the curves or surfaces being approximated are also piecewise linear, large numbers of endpoint coordinates must be created and stored if we are to achieve reasonable accuracy. Interactive manipulation of the data to approximate a shape is tedious, because many points have to be positioned precisely.

In this section, a more compact and more manipulable representation of piecewise smooth curves is developed; in Section 9.3 the mathematical development is generalized to surfaces. The general approach is to use functions that are of a degree higher than that of the linear functions. The functions still generally only approximate the desired shapes, but use less storage and offer easier interactive manipulation than do linear functions.

The higher-degree approximations can be based on one of three methods. First, we can express y and z as *explicit* functions of x, so that $y = f(x)$ and $z = g(x)$. The difficulties with this approach are that (1) it is impossible to get multiple values of y for a single x, so curves such as circles and ellipses must be represented by multiple curve segments; (2) such a definition is not rotationally invariant (to describe a rotated version of the curve requires a great deal of work and may in general require breaking a curve segment into many others); and (3) describing curves with vertical tangents is difficult, because a slope of infinity is difficult to represent.

Second, we can choose to model curves as solutions to *implicit* equations of the form $f(x, y, z) = 0$; this method is fraught with its own perils. First, the given equation may have more solutions than we want. For example, in modeling a circle, we might want to use $x^2 + y^2 = 1$, which is fine. But how do we model one-half of a circle? We must add constraints such as $x \geq 0$, which cannot be contained within the implicit equation. Furthermore, if two implicitly defined curve segments are joined together, it may be difficult to determine whether their tangent directions agree at their join point. Tangent continuity is critical in many applications.

These two mathematical forms do permit rapid determination of whether a point lies on the curve or on which side of the curve the point lies, as was done in Chapter 3. Normals to the curve are also computed easily. Hence, we shall discuss briefly the implicit form in Section 9.4.

The **parametric representation** for curves, $x = x(t)$, $y = y(t)$, $z = z(t)$, overcomes the problems caused by functional or implicit forms and offers a variety of other attractions that will become clear in the remainder of this chapter. Parametric curves replace the use of geometric slopes (which may be infinite) with parametric tangent vectors (which, we shall see, are never infinite). Here a curve is approximated by a **piecewise polynomial curve** instead of by the piecewise linear curve used in Section 9.1. Each segment Q of the overall curve is given by three functions, x, y, and z, which are cubic polynomials in the parameter t.

Cubic polynomials are most often used because lower-degree polynomials give too little flexibility in controlling the shape of the curve, and higher-degree polynomials can introduce unwanted wiggles and also require more computation. No lower-degree representation allows a curve segment to interpolate (pass through) two specified endpoints with specified derivatives at each endpoint. Given a cubic polynomial with its four coefficients, four knowns are used to solve for the unknown coefficients. The four knowns might be the two endpoints and the derivatives at the endpoints. Similarly, the two coefficients of a first-order (straight-line) polynomial are determined by the two endpoints. For a straight line, the derivatives at each end are determined by the line itself and cannot be controlled independently. With quadratic (second-degree) polynomials—and hence three coefficients—two endpoints and one other condition, such as a slope or additional point, can be specified.

Also, parametric cubics are the lowest-degree curves that are nonplanar in 3D. You can see this fact by recognizing that a second-order polynomial's three coefficients can be specified completely by three points and that three points define a plane in which the polynomial lies.

Higher-degree curves require more conditions to determine the coefficients and can *wiggle* back and forth in ways that are difficult to control. Despite these complexities, higher-degree curves are used in applications—such as the design of cars and planes—in which higher-degree derivatives must be controlled to create surfaces that are aerodynamically efficient. In fact, the mathematical development for parametric curves and surfaces is often given in terms of an arbitrary degree n. In this chapter, we fix n at 3.

9.2.1 Basic Characteristics

The cubic polynomials that define a curve segment $Q(t) = [x(t) \ y(t) \ z(t)]^T$ are of the form

$$
\begin{aligned}
x(t) &= a_x t^3 + b_x t^2 + c_x t + d_x, \\
y(t) &= a_y t^3 + b_y t^2 + c_y t + d_y, \\
z(t) &= a_z t^3 + b_z t^2 + c_z t + d_z, \qquad 0 \le t \le 1.
\end{aligned}
\tag{9.5}
$$

To deal with finite segments of the curve, we restrict the parameter t without loss of generality, to the [0, 1] interval.

With $T = [t^3 \ t^2 \ t \ 1]^T$, and defining the matrix of coefficients of the three polynomials as

$$
C = \begin{bmatrix}
a_x & b_x & c_x & d_x \\
a_y & b_y & c_y & d_y \\
a_z & b_z & c_z & d_z
\end{bmatrix},
\tag{9.6}
$$

we can rewrite Eq. (9.5) as

$$
Q(t) = [x(t) \ y(t) \ z(t)]^T = C \cdot T.
\tag{9.7}
$$

This representation provides a compact way to express Eq. (9.5).

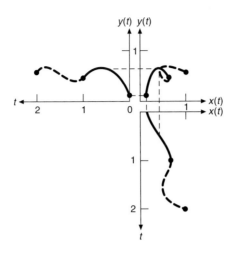

Figure 9.7   Two joined 2D parametric curve segments and their defining polynomials. The dashed lines between the (x, y) plot and the $x(t)$ and $y(t)$ plots show the correspondence between the points on the (x, y) curve and the defining cubic polynomials. The $x(t)$ and $y(t)$ plots for the second segment have been translated to begin at $t = 1$, rather than at $t = 0$, to show the continuity of the curves at their join point.

Figure 9.7 shows two joined parametric cubic curve segments and their polynomials; it also illustrates the ability of parametrics to represent easily multiple values of y for a single value of x with polynomials that are themselves single valued. (This figure of a curve, like all others in this section, shows 2D curves represented by $[x(t)\ y(t)]^T$.)

Continuity between curve segments.   The derivative of $Q(t)$ is the parametric **tangent vector** of the curve. Applying this definition to Eq. (9.7), we have

$$\frac{d}{dt}Q(t) = Q'(t) = \left[\frac{d}{dt}x(t)\quad \frac{d}{dt}y(t)\quad \frac{d}{dt}z(t)\right]^T = \frac{d}{dt}C \cdot T = C \cdot [3t^2\quad 2t\quad 1\quad 0]^T$$

$$= [3a_xt^2 + 2b_xt + c_x\quad 3a_yt^2 + 2b_yt + c_y\quad 3a_zt^2 + 2b_zt + c_z]^T. \qquad (9.8)$$

If two curve segments join together, the curve has G^0 **geometric continuity**. If the directions (but not necessarily the magnitudes) of the two segments' tangent vectors are equal at a join point, the curve has G^1 geometric continuity. In computer-aided design of objects, G^1 continuity between curve segments often is required. G^1 continuity means that the geometric slopes of the segments are equal at the join point. For two tangent vectors TV_1 and TV_2 to have the same direction, it is necessary that one be a scalar multiple of the other: $TV_1 = k \cdot TV_2$, with $k > 0$ [BARS88].

If the tangent vectors of two cubic curve segments are equal (that is, their directions *and* magnitudes are equal) at the segments' join point, the curve has first-degree continuity in the parameter t, or **parametric continuity**, and is said to be C^1 continuous. If the direction and magnitude of $d^n/dt^n[Q(t)]$ through the nth

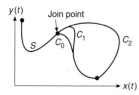

Figure 9.8
Curve segment S joined to segments C_0, C_1, and C_2 with the 0, 1, and 2 degrees of parametric continuity, respectively. The visual distinction between C_1 and C_2 is slight at the join, but obvious away from the join.

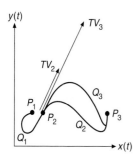

Figure 9.9
Curve segments Q_1, Q_2, and Q_3 join at the point P_2 and are identical except for their tangent vectors at P_2. Q_1 and Q_2 have equal tangent vectors, and hence are both G^1 and C^1 continuous at P_2. Q_1 and Q_3 have tangent vectors in the same direction, but Q_3 has twice the magnitude, so they are only G^1 continuous at P_2. The larger tangent vector of Q_3 means that the curve is pulled more in the tangent-vector direction before heading toward P_3. Vector TV_2 is the tangent vector for Q_2, TV_3 is that for Q_3.

derivative are equal at the join point, the curve is called C^n **continuous**. Figure 9.8 shows curves with three different degrees of continuity. Note that a parametric curve segment is itself everywhere continuous; the continuity of concern here is at the join points.

The tangent vector $Q'(t)$ is the *velocity* of a point on the curve with respect to the parameter t. Similarly, the second derivative of $Q(t)$ is the *acceleration*. Suppose a camera were moving along a parametric cubic curve in equal time steps and recording a picture after each step; the tangent vector gives the velocity of the camera along the curve. So that jerky movements in the resulting animation sequence are avoided, the camera velocity and acceleration at join points should be continuous. It is this continuity of acceleration across the join point in Fig. 9.8 that makes the C^2 curve continue farther to the right than the C^1 curve, before bending around to the endpoint.

In general, C^1 continuity implies G^1, but the converse is generally not true. That is, G^1 continuity is generally less restrictive than is C^1, so curves can be G^1 but not necessarily C^1 continuous. However, join points with G^1 continuity will appear just as smooth as those with C^1 continuity, as seen in Fig. 9.9.

The plot of a parametric curve is distinctly different from the plot of an ordinary function, in which the independent variable is plotted on the x axis and the dependent variable is plotted on the y axis. In parametric curve plots, the independent variable t is never plotted at all. Thus we cannot determine, just by looking at a parametric curve plot, the tangent vector to the curve. It is possible to determine the direction of the vector, but not the magnitude. You can see why if you think about it as follows: If $\gamma(t)$, $0 \le t \le 1$ is a parametric curve, its tangent vector at time 0 is $\gamma'(0)$. If we let $\eta(t) = \gamma(2t)$, $0 \le t \le \frac{1}{2}$, then the parametric plots of γ and η are identical. On the other hand, $\eta'(0) = 2\,\gamma'(0)$. Thus, two curves that have identical plots can have different tangent vectors. This fact is the basis for the definition of **geometric continuity:** For two curves to join smoothly, we require only that their tangent-vector directions match; we do not require that their magnitudes match.

Relation to constraints. A curve segment $Q(t)$ is defined by constraints on endpoints, tangent vectors, and continuity between curve segments. Each cubic polynomial of Eq. (9.5) has four coefficients, so four constraints will be needed, allowing us to formulate four equations in the four unknowns, then solving for the unknowns. The three major types of curves discussed in this section are **Hermite,** defined by two endpoints and two endpoint tangent vectors; **Bézier,** defined by two endpoints and two other points that control the endpoint tangent vectors; and several kinds of **splines,** each defined by four control points. The splines have C^1 and C^2 continuity at the join points and come close to their control points, but generally do not interpolate the points. The types of splines are uniform B-splines and nonuniform B-splines.

To see how the coefficients of Eq. (9.5) can depend on four constraints, we recall that a parametric cubic curve is defined by $Q(t) = C \cdot T$. We rewrite the coefficient matrix as $C = G \cdot M$, where M is a 4×4 **basis matrix,** and G is a four-element matrix of geometric constraints, called the **geometry matrix.** The geometric constraints are just the conditions, such as endpoints or tangent vectors, that define the curve. We use G_x to refer to the row vector of just the x components of the geometry matrix. G_y and G_z have similar definitions. G or M, or both G and M, differ for each type of curve.

The elements of G and M are constants, so the product $G \cdot M \cdot T$ is just three cubic polynomials in t. Expanding the product $Q(t) = G \cdot M \cdot T$ gives

$$Q(t) = \begin{bmatrix} x(t) \\ y(t) \\ z(t) \end{bmatrix} = [G_1 \quad G_2 \quad G_3 \quad G_4] \begin{bmatrix} m_{11} & m_{21} & m_{31} & m_{41} \\ m_{12} & m_{22} & m_{32} & m_{42} \\ m_{13} & m_{23} & m_{33} & m_{43} \\ m_{14} & m_{24} & m_{34} & m_{44} \end{bmatrix} \begin{bmatrix} t^3 \\ t^2 \\ t \\ 1 \end{bmatrix}. \quad (9.9)$$

We can read this equation in a second way: the point $Q(t)$ is a weighted sum of the *columns* of the geometry matrix G, each of which represents a point or a vector in 3-space.

Multiplying out just $x(t) = G_x \cdot M \cdot T$ gives

$$x(t) = (t^3 m_{11} + t^2 m_{21} + t m_{31} + m_{41})g_{1x} + (t^3 m_{12} + t^2 m_{22} + t m_{32} + m_{42})g_{2x}$$
$$+ (t^3 m_{13} + t^2 m_{23} + t m_{33} + m_{43})g_{3x} + (t^3 m_{14} + t^2 m_{24} + t m_{34} + m_{44})g_{4x}. \quad (9.10)$$

Equation (9.10) emphasizes that the curve is a weighted sum of the elements of the geometry matrix. The weights are each cubic polynomials of t, and are called **blending functions.** The blending functions B are given by $B = M \cdot T$. Notice the similarity to a piecewise linear approximation, for which only two geometric constraints (the endpoints of the line) are needed, so each curve segment is a straight line defined by the endpoints G_1 and G_2:

$$x(t) = g_{1x}(1 - t) + g_{2x}(t),$$
$$y(t) = g_{1y}(1 - t) + g_{2y}(t),$$
$$z(t) = g_{1z}(1 - t) + g_{2z}(t). \quad (9.11)$$

Parametric cubics are really just a generalization of straight-line approximations. The cubic curve $Q(t)$ is a combination of the *four* columns of the geometry matrix, just as a straight-line segment is a combination of *two* column vectors.

To see how to calculate the basis matrix M, we turn now to specific forms of parametric cubic curves.

9.2.2 Hermite Curves

The Hermite form (named for the mathematician) of the cubic polynomial curve segment is determined by constraints on the endpoints P_1 and P_4 and tangent vectors at the endpoints R_1 and R_4. (The indices 1 and 4 are used, rather than 1 and 2, for consistency with later sections, where intermediate points P_2 and P_3 will be used, instead of tangent vectors, to define the curve.)

To find the **Hermite basis matrix** M_H, which relates the **Hermite geometry vector** G_H to the polynomial coefficients, we write four equations, one for each of the constraints, in the four unknown polynomial coefficients, and then solve for the unknowns.

Defining G_{H_x}, the x component of the Hermite geometry matrix, as

$$G_{H_x} = [P_{1_x} \quad P_{4_x} \quad R_{1_x} \quad R_{4_x}], \tag{9.12}$$

and rewriting $x(t)$ from Eqs. (9.5) and (9.9) as

$$x(t) = a_x t^3 + b_x t^2 + c_x t + d_x = C_x \cdot T = G_{H_x} \cdot M_H \cdot T = G_{H_x} \cdot M_H \; [t^3 \; t^2 \; t \; 1]^T, \tag{9.13}$$

the constraints on $x(0)$ and $x(1)$ are found by direct substitution into Eq. (9.13) as

$$x(0) = P_{1_x} = G_{H_x} \cdot M_H \; [0 \; 0 \; 0 \; 1]^T, \tag{9.14}$$

$$x(1) = P_{4_x} = G_{H_x} \cdot M_H \; [1 \; 1 \; 1 \; 1]^T. \tag{9.15}$$

Just as in the general case we differentiated Eq. (9.7) to find Eq. (9.8), we now differentiate Eq. (9.13) to get $x'(t) = G_{H_x} \cdot M_H \; [3t^2 \; 2t \; 1 \; 0]^T$. Hence, the tangent-vector–constraint equations can be written as

$$x'(0) = R_{1_x} = G_{H_x} \cdot M_H \; [0 \; 0 \; 1 \; 0]^T, \tag{9.16}$$

$$x'(1) = R_{4_x} = G_{H_x} \cdot M_H \; [3 \; 2 \; 1 \; 0]^T. \tag{9.17}$$

The four constraints of Eqs. (9.14)–(9.17) can be rewritten in matrix form as

$$[P_{1_x} \; P_{4_x} \; R_{1_x} \; R_{4_x}] = G_{H_x} = G_{H_x} \cdot M_H \cdot \begin{bmatrix} 0 & 1 & 0 & 3 \\ 0 & 1 & 0 & 2 \\ 0 & 1 & 1 & 1 \\ 1 & 1 & 0 & 0 \end{bmatrix}. \tag{9.18}$$

For this equation (and the corresponding expressions for y and z) to be satisfied, M_H must be the inverse of the 4×4 matrix in Eq. (9.18):

$$M_H = \begin{bmatrix} 0 & 1 & 0 & 3 \\ 0 & 1 & 0 & 2 \\ 0 & 1 & 1 & 1 \\ 1 & 1 & 0 & 0 \end{bmatrix}^{-1} = \begin{bmatrix} 2 & -3 & 0 & 1 \\ -2 & 3 & 0 & 0 \\ 1 & -2 & 1 & 0 \\ 1 & -1 & 0 & 0 \end{bmatrix}. \tag{9.19}$$

M_H can now be used in $x(t) = G_{H_x} \cdot M_H \cdot T$ to find $x(t)$ based on the geometry vector G_{H_x}. Similarly, $y(t) = G_{H_y} \cdot M_H \cdot T$ and $z(t) = G_{H_z} \cdot M_H \cdot T$, so we can write

$$Q(t) = [x(t) \; y(t) \; z(t)]^T = G_H \cdot M_H \cdot T, \tag{9.20}$$

where G_H is the matrix

$$[P_1 \; P_4 \; R_1 \; R_4].$$

Expanding the product $M_H \cdot T$ in $Q(t) = G_H \cdot M_H \cdot T$ gives the **Hermite blending functions** B_H as the polynomials weighting each element of the geometry matrix:

$$Q(t) = G_H \cdot M_H \cdot T = G_H \cdot B_H$$
$$= (2t^3 - 3t^2 + 1)P_1 + (-2t^3 + 3t^2)P_4 + (t^3 - 2t^2 + t)R_1 + (t^3 - t^2)R_4. \tag{9.21}$$

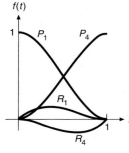

Figure 9.10
The Hermite blending functions, labeled by the elements of the geometry vector that they weight.

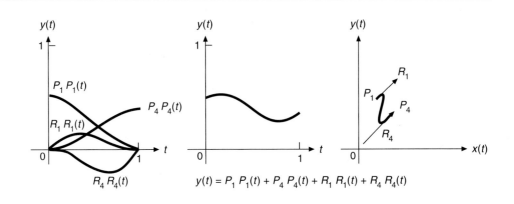

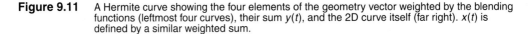

Figure 9.11   A Hermite curve showing the four elements of the geometry vector weighted by the blending functions (leftmost four curves), their sum $y(t)$, and the 2D curve itself (far right). $x(t)$ is defined by a similar weighted sum.

Figure 9.10 shows the four blending functions. Notice that, at $t = 0$, only the function labeled P_1 is nonzero: only P_1 affects the curve at $t = 0$. As soon as t becomes greater than zero, R_1, P_4, and R_4 begin to have an influence. Figure 9.11 shows the four functions weighted by the y components of a specific geometry vector, their sum $y(t)$, and the curve $Q(t)$.

Figure 9.12 shows a series of Hermite curves. The only difference among them is the length of the tangent vector R_1: The directions of the tangent vectors are fixed. The longer the vectors, the greater their effect on the curve. Figure 9.13 is another series of Hermite curves, with constant tangent-vector lengths but with different directions. In an interactive graphics system, the endpoints and tangent vectors of a curve are manipulated interactively by the user to shape the curve. Figure 9.14 shows one way of implementing this type of interaction.

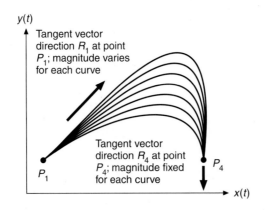

Figure 9.12   Family of Hermite parametric cubic curves. Only R_1, the tangent vector at P_1, varies for each curve, increasing in magnitude for the higher curves.

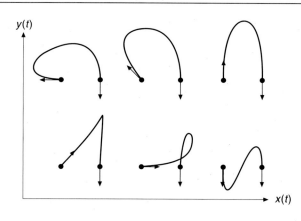

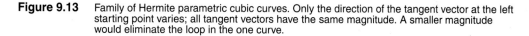

Figure 9.13 Family of Hermite parametric cubic curves. Only the direction of the tangent vector at the left starting point varies; all tangent vectors have the same magnitude. A smaller magnitude would eliminate the loop in the one curve.

Drawing parametric curves. Hermite and other similar parametric cubic curves are simple to display: We evaluate Eq. (9.5) at n successive values of t separated by a step size δ. Program 9.1 gives the code. The evaluation within the { ... } in the **for** loop takes 12 multiplies and 10 additions per 3D point. Use of Horner's rule for factoring polynomials,

$$f(t) = at^3 + bt^2 + ct + d = ((at + b)t + c)t + d, \qquad (9.22)$$

would reduce the effort slightly to 10 multiplies and 10 additions per 3D point.

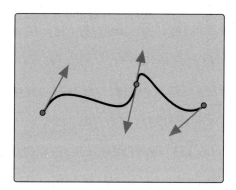

Figure 9.14 Two Hermite cubic curve segments displayed with controls to facilitate interactive manipulation. The user can reposition the endpoints by dragging the dots, and can change the tangent vectors by dragging the arrowheads. The tangent vectors at the join point are constrained to be collinear (to provide C^1 continuity): The user is usually given a command to enforce C^0, C^1, G^1, or no continuity. The tangent vectors at the $t = 1$ end of each curve are drawn in the reverse of the direction used in the mathematical formulation of the Hermite curve, for clarity and for more convenient user interaction.

More efficient ways to display these curves involve forward-difference techniques, as discussed in [FOLE90].

```
typedef float CoefficientArray[4];
void DrawCurve(CoefficientArray cx, CoefficientArray cy,
                    CoefficientArray cz, int n)
    /* cx, cy, and cz are coefficients for x(t), y(t), and z(t) */
    /* e.g., Cx = Gx·M, etc. */
    /* n, number of steps */
{
    float  x, y, z, delta, t, t2, t3;
    int    i;

    MoveAbs3( cx[3], cy[3], cz[3] );
    delta = 1.0 / n;
    for (i = 1; i <= n; i++) {
        t = i * delta;
        t2 = t * t;
        t3 = t2 * t;
        x = cx[0] * t3 + cx[1] * t2 + cx[2] * t + cx[3];
        y = cy[0] * t3 + cy[1] * t2 + cy[2] * t + cy[3];
        z = cz[0] * t3 + cz[1] * t2 + cz[2] * t + cz[3];
        DrawAbs3( x, y, z );
    }
}
```

Because the cubic curves are linear combinations (weighted sums) of the four elements of the geometry vector, as seen in Eq. (9.10), we can transform the curves by transforming the geometry vector and then using it to generate the transformed curve, which is equivalent to saying that the curves are invariant under rotation, scaling, and translation. This strategy is more efficient than is generating the curve as a series of short line segments and then transforming each individual line. The curves are *not* invariant under perspective projection, as will be discussed in Section 9.2.6.

9.2.3 Bézier Curves

The Bézier [BEZI70; BEZI74] form of the cubic polynomial curve segment, named after Pierre Bézier who developed them for use in designing automobiles at Rénault, indirectly specifies the endpoint tangent vector by specifying two intermediate points that are not on the curve; see Fig. 9.15. The starting and ending tangent vectors are determined by the vectors P_1P_2 and P_3P_4 and are related to R_1 and R_4 by

$$R_1 = Q'(0) = 3(P_2 - P_1), \quad R_4 = Q'(1) = 3(P_4 - P_3). \tag{9.23}$$

The Bézier curve interpolates the two end control points and approximates the other two. See Exercise 9.9 to understand why the constant 3 is used in Eq. (9.23). The **Bézier geometry matrix** G_B, consisting of four points, is

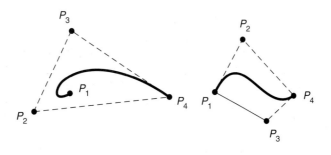

Figure 9.15 Two Bézier curves and their control points. Notice that the convex hulls (the convex polygon formed by the control points), shown as dashed lines, do not need to touch all four control points.

$$G_B = [P_1 \quad P_2 \quad P_3 \quad P_4] . \tag{9.24}$$

Then, the matrix M_{HB} that defines the relation $G_H = G_B \cdot M_{HB}$ between the Hermite geometry matrix G_H and the Bézier geometry matrix G_B is just the 4×4 matrix in the following equation, which rewrites Eq. (9.24) in matrix form:

$$G_H = [P_1 \; P_4 \; R_1 \; R_4] = [P_1 \; P_2 \; P_3 \; P_4]\begin{bmatrix} 1 & 0 & -3 & 0 \\ 0 & 0 & 3 & 0 \\ 0 & 0 & 0 & -3 \\ 0 & 1 & 0 & 3 \end{bmatrix} = G_B \cdot M_{HB}. \tag{9.25}$$

To find the **Bézier basis matrix** M_B, we use Eq. (9.20) for the Hermite form, substitute $G_H = G_B \cdot M_{HB}$, and define $M_B = M_{HB} \cdot M_H$:

$$Q(t) = G_H \cdot M_H \cdot T = (G_B \cdot M_{HB}) \cdot M_H \cdot T = G_B \cdot (M_{HB} \cdot M_H) \cdot T = G_B \cdot M_B \cdot T. \tag{9.26}$$

Carrying out the multiplication $M_B = M_{HB} \cdot M_H$ gives

$$M_B = M_{HB} \cdot M_H = \begin{bmatrix} -1 & 3 & -3 & 1 \\ 3 & -6 & 3 & 0 \\ -3 & 3 & 0 & 0 \\ 1 & 0 & 0 & 0 \end{bmatrix}, \tag{9.27}$$

and the product $Q(t) = G_B \cdot M_B \cdot T$ is

$$Q(t) = (1-t)^3 P_1 + 3t(1-t)^2 P_2 + 3t^2(1-t)P_3 + t^3 P_4. \tag{9.28}$$

The four polynomials $B_B = M_B \cdot T$, which are the weights in Eq. (9.28), are called the **Bernstein polynomials,** and are shown in Fig. 9.16.

Joining of curve segments. Figure 9.17 shows two Bézier curve segments with a common endpoint. G^1 continuity is provided at the endpoint when $P_3 - P_4 = k(P_4 - P_5)$, $k > 0$. That is, the three points P_3, P_4, and P_5 must be distinct and collinear. In the more restrictive case when $k = 1$, there is C^1 continuity in addition to G^1 continuity.

If we refer to the polynomials of two curve segments as x^l (for the left segment) and x^r (for the right segment), we can find the conditions for C^0 and C^1 continuity at their join point:

$$x^l(1) = x^r(0), \quad \frac{d}{dt}x^l(1) = \frac{d}{dt}x^r(0). \tag{9.29}$$

Working with the x component of Eq. (9.29), we have

$$x^l(1) = x^r(0) = P_{4_x}, \frac{d}{dt}x^l(1) = 3(P_{4_x} - P_{3_x}), \frac{d}{dt}x^r(0) = 3(P_{5_x} - P_{4_x}). \tag{9.30}$$

As always, the same conditions are true of y and z. Thus, we have C^0 and C^1 continuity when $P_4 - P_3 = P_5 - P_4$, as expected.

Importance of the convex hull. Examining the four B_B polynomials in Eq. (9.28) and Fig. 9.16, we note that their sum is everywhere unity and that each polynomial is everywhere nonnegative for $0 \le t < 1$. Thus, $Q(t)$ is just a weighted average of the four control points. This condition means that each curve segment, which is just the sum of four control points weighted by the polynomials, is completely contained in the **convex hull** of the four control points. The convex hull for 2D curves is the convex polygon formed by the four control points: Think of it as the polygon that you would form by putting a rubberband around the points (Fig. 9.15). For 3D curves, the convex hull is the convex polyhedron formed by the control points: Think of it as the polyhedron you would form by stretching a rubber sheet around the four points.

This convex-hull property holds for all cubics defined by weighted sums of control points if the blending functions are nonnegative and sum to one. In general, the weighted average of n points falls within the convex hull of the n points; this can be seen intuitively for $n = 2$ and $n = 3$, and the generalization follows. Another consequence of the fact that the four polynomials sum to unity is that we can find the value of the fourth polynomial for any value of t by subtracting the first three from unity—a fact that can be used to reduce computation time.

The convex-hull property is also useful for clipping curve segments: Rather than clip each short line piece of a curve segment to determine its visibility, we first apply a polygonal clip algorithm, for example, the Sutherland–Hodgman

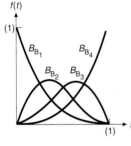

Figure 9.16
The Bernstein polynomials, which are the weighting functions for Bézier curves. At $t = 0$, only B_{B_1} is nonzero, so the curve interpolates P_1; similarly, at $t = 1$, only B_{B_4} is nonzero, and the curve interpolates P_4.

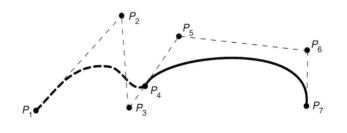

Figure 9.17   Two Bézier curves joined at P_4. Points P_3, P_4, and P_5 are collinear.

algorithm discussed in Chapter 3—to clip the convex hull or its extent against the clip region. If the convex hull (extent) is completely within the clip region, so is the entire curve segment. If the convex hull (extent) is completely outside the clip region, so is the curve segment. Only if the convex hull (extent) intersects the clip region does the curve segment itself need to be examined.

Example 9.2

Problem: Write a program, using SRGP, that allows a user to specify the four control points for a 2D Bézier curve and then draws the curve using the approach of Prog. 9.1. You should provide a way of specifying an arbitrary number of Bézier curves, clearing the SRGP window, and terminating the program.

Answer: We implement the DrawCurve function by using Eq. (9.28), which relates the curve $Q(t)$ to the four control points. In general, this implementation sacrifices efficiency for clarity. We do, however, use the SRGP_polyLine function, which is the most efficient way to draw the curve. The rest of the implementation follows the model of Prog. 9.1.

We have arbitrarily specified the window size and number of steps used to approximate the curve as 400 and 20, respectively. There are many possible ways to implement the interactive part of the program; we have elected to use a combination of locator and keyboard devices. The right locator button is used to specify the beginning of a new sequence of control points, whereas the left button is used to define the remaining three points. A rubber line echo helps to guide the layout of the points. The Bézier curve is drawn as soon as the last point is entered.

Finally, the window is cleared when the user presses the "c" key; pressing the "q" key terminates the program. A typical set of curves produced by the program is shown in the accompanying figure.

Interactive Bézier curve program.

```
#include "srgp.h"
#include <stdio.h>

#define KEYMEASURE_SIZE    80
#define WINDOW_SIZE        400
#define NUM_STEPS          20

void   DrawCurve(point *ControlPoints, int n)
{
    int   i;
    float  t, delta;
    point  CurvePoints[n];

    CurvePoints[0].x = ControlPoints[0].x;      /* Bézier curves interpolate the first */
    CurvePoints[0].y = ControlPoints[0].y;      /* and last control points */
    delta = 1.0 / n;                            /* The curve is to be approximated by n points */
                                                /* t ranges from 0.0 to 1.0 */
    for (i = 1; i <= n; i++) {
        t = i * delta;
        CurvePoints[i].x = ControlPoints[0].x * (1.0 − t) * (1.0 − t) * (1.0 − t)
```

```
            + ControlPoints[1].x * 3.0 * t * (1.0 – t) * (1.0 – t)
            + ControlPoints[2].x * 3.0 * t * t * (1.0 – t)
            + ControlPoints[3].x * t * t * t;

      CurvePoints[i].y = ControlPoints[0].y * (1.0 – t) * (1.0 – t) * (1.0 – t)
            + ControlPoints[1].y * 3.0 * t * (1.0 – t) * (1.0 – t)
            + ControlPoints[2].y * 3.0 * t * t * (1.0 – t)
            + ControlPoints[3].y * t * t * t;
      }
      SRGP_polyLine(n + 1, CurvePoints);              /* Draw the complete curve */
}
```

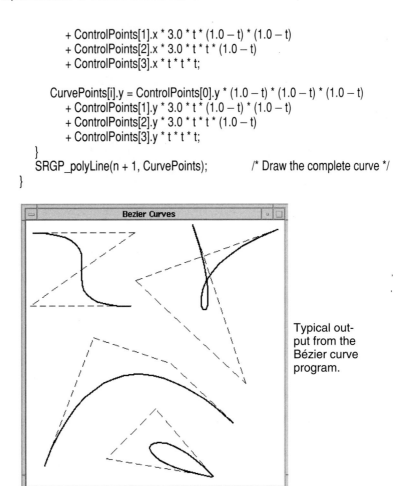

Typical output from the Bézier curve program.

```
main()
{
      locator_measure  locMeasure, pastlocMeasure;
      char    keyMeasure[KEYMEASURE_SIZE];
      int     device;
      int     numCtl;
      boolean terminate;
      rectangle screen;
      point   ControlPoints[4];

      SRGP_begin("Bezier Curves", WINDOW_SIZE, WINDOW_SIZE, 1, FALSE);
      SRGP_setLocatorEchoType(CURSOR);
      SRGP_setLocatorButtonMask(LEFT_BUTTON_MASK|RIGHT_BUTTON_MASK);
      pastlocMeasure.position = SRGP_defPoint(–1, –1);     /* Initialize position to */
      SRGP_setLocatorMeasure(pastlocMeasure.position);     /* arbitrary location */
      SRGP_setKeyboardProcessingMode(RAW);
      SRGP_setInputMode(LOCATOR, EVENT);              /* Both locator (mouse) */
```

```
            SRGP_setInputMode(KEYBOARD, EVENT);          /* and keyboard are active */
            screen = SRGP_defRectangle(0, 0, WINDOW_SIZE – 1, WINDOW_SIZE – 1);

    /* Main event loop */
        terminate = FALSE;
        do {
            device = SRGP_waitEvent(INDEFINITE);
            switch (device) {
            case KEYBOARD:{
                    SRGP_getKeyboard(keyMeasure, KEYMEASURE_SIZE);
                    switch (keyMeasure[0]) {
                    case 'q':                              /* Quitting the program */
                        terminate = TRUE;
                        break;
                    case 'c':                              /* Clearing the window */
                        SRGP_setColor(0);
                        SRGP_fillRectangle(screen);
                        SRGP_setColor(1);
                        break;
                    }
                    break;
                }                                          /* keyboard case  */
            case LOCATOR:{
                    SRGP_getLocator(&locMeasure);
                    switch (locMeasure.buttonOfMostRecentTransition) {
                    case LEFT_BUTTON:          /* Defining remaining control points */
                        if ((locMeasure.buttonChord[LEFT_BUTTON] == DOWN) &&
                            pastlocMeasure.position.x > 0) {
                            SRGP_setLocatorEchoRubberAnchor(locMeasure.position);
                            SRGP_line(pastlocMeasure.position, locMeasure.position);
                            pastlocMeasure = locMeasure;
                            ControlPoints[numCtl] = locMeasure.position;
                            numCtl++;
                            if (numCtl == 4) {
                                SRGP_setLineStyle(CONTINUOUS);        /* To draw curve */
                                SRGP_setLineWidth(2);
                                DrawCurve(ControlPoints, NUM_STEPS);
                                pastlocMeasure.position.x = –1;
                                SRGP_setLocatorEchoType(CURSOR);
                            }
                            break;
                    case RIGHT_BUTTON:          /* Start new set of control points */
                            SRGP_setLocatorEchoRubberAnchor(locMeasure.position);
                            pastlocMeasure = locMeasure;
                            SRGP_setLocatorEchoType(RUBBER_LINE);
                            SRGP_setLineStyle(DASHED);        /* To draw control polygon */
                            SRGP_setLineWidth(1);
                            ControlPoints[0] = locMeasure.position;
                            numCtl = 1;
                            break;
```

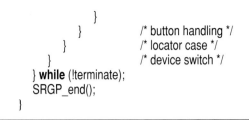

```
                }
            }              /* button handling */
         }                 /* locator case */
      }                    /* device switch */
   } while (!terminate);
   SRGP_end();
}
```

9.2.4 Uniform Nonrational B-Splines

The term **spline** goes back to the long flexible strips of metal used by draftsmen to lay out the surfaces of airplanes, cars, and ships. "Ducks," which are weights attached to the splines, were used to pull the spline in various directions. The metal splines, unless severely stressed, had second-order continuity. The mathematical equivalent of these strips, the **natural cubic spline,** is a C^0, C^1, and C^2 continuous cubic polynomial that interpolates (passes through) the control points. This polynomial has one more degree of continuity than is inherent in the Hermite and Bézier forms. Thus, splines are inherently smoother than are the previous forms.

The polynomial coefficients for natural cubic splines, however, are dependent on all n control points; their calculation involves inverting an $n + 1$ by $n + 1$ matrix [BART87]. This characteristic has two disadvantages: moving any one control point affects the entire curve, and the computation time needed to invert the matrix can interfere with rapid interactive reshaping of a curve.

B-splines, discussed in this section, consist of curve segments whose polynomial coefficients depend on just a few control points. This behavior is called **local control.** Thus, moving a control point affects only a small part of a curve. In addition, the time needed to compute the coefficients is greatly reduced. B-splines have the same continuity as do natural splines, but do not interpolate their control points.

In the following discussion, we change our notation slightly, since we must discuss an entire curve consisting of several curve segments, rather than its individual segments. A curve segment does not need to pass through its control points, and the two continuity conditions on a segment come from the adjacent segments. This behavior results from sharing control points between segments, so it is best to describe the process in terms of all the segments at once.

Cubic B-splines approximate a series of $m + 1$ control points $P_0, P_1, \ldots P_m$, $m \geq 3$, with a curve consisting of $m - 2$ cubic polynomial curve segments $Q_3, Q_4, \ldots, Q_m$. Although such cubic curves might be defined each on its own domain $0 \leq t < 1$, we can adjust the parameter (making a substitution of the form $t = t + k$) such that the parameter domains for the various curve segments are sequential. Thus, we say that the parameter range on which Q_i is defined is $t_i \leq t < t_{i+1}$, for $3 \leq i \leq m$. In the particular case of $m = 3$, there is a single curve segment Q_3 that is defined on the interval $t_3 \leq t < t_4$ by four control points, P_0 to P_3.

For each $i \geq 4$, there is a join point or **knot** between Q_{i-1} and Q_i at the parameter value t_i; the parameter value at such a point is called a **knot value.** The initial

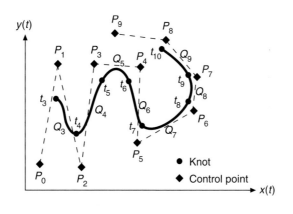

Figure 9.18   A B-spline with curve segments Q_3 through Q_9. This figure and many others in this chapter were created with a program written by Carles Castellsaquè.

and final points at t_3 and t_{m+1} are also called knots, so there are a total of $m - 1$ knots. Figure 9.18 shows a 2D B-spline curve with its knots marked. A closed B-spline curve is easy to create: The control points P_0, P_1, P_2 are repeated at the end of the sequence—$P_0, P_1, \ldots, P_m, P_0, P_1, P_2$.

The term **uniform** means that the knots are spaced at equal intervals of the parameter t. Without loss of generality, we can assume that $t_3 = 0$, and the interval $t_{i+1} - t_i = 1$. Nonuniform nonrational B-splines, which permit unequal spacing between the knots, are discussed in Section 9.2.5. (In fact, the concept of knots is introduced in this section to set the stage for nonuniform splines.) The term **nonrational** is used to distinguish these splines from rational cubic polynomial curves, discussed in Section 9.2.6, where $x(t)$, $y(t)$, and $z(t)$ are each defined as the ratio of two cubic polynomials. The "B" stands for basis, since the splines can be represented as weighted sums of polynomial basis functions, in contrast to the natural splines, for which the weighted-sum property is not true.

Each of the $m - 2$ curve segments of a B-spline curve is defined by four of the $m + 1$ control points. In particular, curve segment Q_i is defined by points P_{i-3}, P_{i-2}, P_{i-1}, and P_i. Thus, the **B-spline geometry matrix** G_{Bs_i} for segment Q_i is

$$G_{\mathrm{Bs}_i} = [P_{i-3} \quad P_{i-2} \quad P_{i-1} \quad P_i], \quad 3 \leq i \leq m. \tag{9.31}$$

The first curve segment, Q_3, is defined by the points P_0 through P_3 over the parameter range $t_3 = 0$ to $t_4 = 1$, Q_4 is defined by the points P_1 through P_4 over the parameter range $t_4 = 1$ to $t_5 = 2$, and the last curve segment, Q_m, is defined by the points $P_{m-3}, P_{m-2}, P_{m-1}$, and P_m over the parameter range $t_m = m - 3$ to $t_{m+1} = m - 2$. In general, curve segment Q_i begins somewhere near point P_{i-2} and ends somewhere near point P_{i-1}. We shall see that the B-spline blending functions are everywhere nonnegative and sum to unity, so the curve segment Q_i is constrained to the convex hull of its four control points.

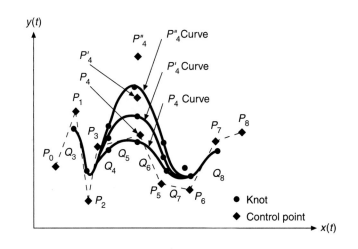

Figure 9.19   A B-spline with control point P_4 in several different locations.

Just as each curve segment is defined by four control points, each control point (except for those at the beginning and end of the sequence $P_0, P_1, \ldots, P_m$) influences four curve segments. Moving a control point in a given direction moves the four curve segments it affects in the same direction; the other curve segments are totally unaffected (see Fig. 9.19). This behavior is the local control property of B-splines and of all the other splines discussed in this chapter.

If we define T_i as the column vector $[(t - t_i)^3 \quad (t - t_i)^2 \quad (t - t_i) \quad 1]^T$, then the B-spline formulation for curve segment i is

$$Q_i(t) = G_{Bs_i} \cdot M_{Bs} \cdot T_i, \quad t_i \le t < t_{i+1}. \tag{9.32}$$

We generate the entire curve by applying Eq. (9.32) for $3 \le i \le m$.

The **B-spline basis matrix**, M_{Bs}, relates the geometrical constraints G_{Bs} to the blending functions and the polynomial coefficients:

$$M_{Bs} = \frac{1}{6} \begin{bmatrix} -1 & 3 & -3 & 1 \\ 3 & -6 & 3 & 0 \\ -3 & 0 & 3 & 0 \\ 1 & 4 & 1 & 0 \end{bmatrix}. \tag{9.33}$$

This matrix is derived in [BART87].

The B-spline blending functions B_{Bs} are given by the product $M_{Bs} \cdot T_i$, analogously to the previous Bézier and Hermite formulations. Note that the blending functions for each curve segment are exactly the same, because, for each segment i, the values of $t - t_i$ range from 0 at $t = t_i$ to 1 at $t = t_{i+1}$. If we replace $t - t_i$ by t, and replace the interval $[t_i, t_{i+1}]$ by $[0, 1]$, we have

$$B_{Bs} = M_{Bs} \cdot T = [B_{Bs-3} \quad B_{Bs-2} \quad B_{Bs-1} \quad B_{Bs0}]^T$$

$$= \frac{1}{6}[-t^3 + 3t^2 - 3t + 1 \quad 3t^3 - 6t^2 + 4 \quad -3t^3 + 3t^2 + 3t + 1 \quad t^3]^T$$

$$= \frac{1}{6}[(1-t)^3 \quad 3t^3 - 6t^2 + 4 \quad -3t^3 + 3t^2 + 3t + 1 \quad t^3]^T, \quad 0 \le t < 1. \quad (9.34)$$

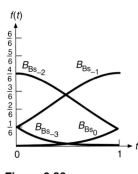

$f(t)$

$\frac{6}{6}$
$\frac{5}{6}$
$\frac{4}{6}$ B_{Bs_2} $B_{Bs_{-1}}$
$\frac{3}{6}$
$\frac{2}{6}$
$\frac{1}{6}$ $B_{Bs_{-3}}$ B_{Bs0}

0   1 t

Figure 9.20
The four B-spline blending functions from Eq. (9.34). At $t = 0$ and $t = 1$, just three of the functions are nonzero.

Figure 9.20 shows the B-spline blending functions B_{Bs}. Because the four functions sum to 1 and are nonnegative, the convex-hull property holds for each curve segment of a B-spline. See [BART87] to understand the relation between these blending functions and the Bernstein polynomial basis functions.

Expanding Eq. (9.32), again replacing $t - t_i$ with t at the second equal-to sign, we have

$$Q_i(t - t_i) = G_{Bs_i} \cdot M_{Bs} \cdot T_i = G_{Bs_i} \cdot M_{Bs} \cdot T$$

$$= G_{Bs_i} \cdot B_{Bs} = P_{i-3} \cdot B_{Bs-3} + P_{i-2} \cdot B_{Bs-2} + P_{i-1} \cdot B_{Bs-1} + P_i \cdot B_{Bs0}$$

$$= \frac{(1-t)^3}{6} P_{i-3} + \frac{3t^3 - 6t^2 + 4}{6} P_{i-2} + \frac{-3t^3 + 3t^2 + 3t + 1}{6} P_{i-1}$$

$$+ \frac{t^3}{6} P_i, \quad 0 \le t < 1. \quad (9.35)$$

It is easy to show that Q_i and Q_{i+1} are C^0, C^1, and C^2 continuous where they join. The additional continuity afforded by B-splines is attractive, but it comes at the cost of less control of where the curve goes. We can force the curve to interpolate specific points by replicating control points; this is useful both at endpoints and at intermediate points on the curve. For instance, if $P_{i-2} = P_{i-1}$, the curve is pulled closer to this point because curve segment Q_i is defined by just three different points, and the point $P_{i-2} = P_{i-1}$ is weighted twice in Eq. (9.35)—once by B_{Bs-2} and once by B_{Bs-1}.

If a control point is used three times—for instance, if $P_{i-2} = P_{i-1} = P_i$—then Eq. (9.35) becomes

$$Q_i(t) = P_{i-3} \cdot B_{Bs-3} + P_i \cdot (B_{Bs-2} + B_{Bs-1} + B_{Bs0}). \quad (9.36)$$

Q_i is clearly a straight line. Furthermore, the point P_{i-2} is interpolated by the line at $t = 1$, where the three weights applied to P_i sum to 1, but P_{i-3} is not in general interpolated at $t = 0$. Another way to think of this behavior is that the convex hull for Q_i is now defined by just two distinct points, so Q_i has to be a line. Figure 9.21 shows the effect of multiple control points at the interior of a B-spline.

Another technique for interpolating endpoints, **phantom vertices,** is discussed in [BARS83; BART87]. We shall see in the next section that, with nonuniform B-splines, endpoints and internal points can be interpolated in a more natural way than they can with the uniform B-splines.

9.2.5 Nonuniform, Nonrational B-Splines

Nonuniform, nonrational B-splines differ from the uniform, nonrational B-splines discussed in Section 9.2.4 in that the parameter interval between successive

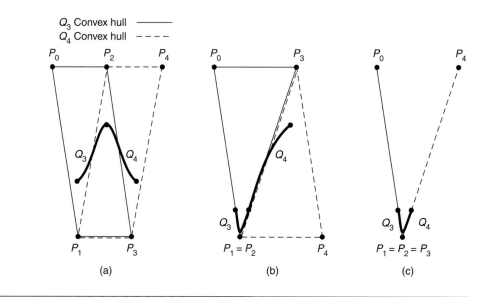

Figure 9.21   The effect of multiple control points on a uniform B-spline curve. In (a), there are no multiple control points. The convex hulls of the two curves overlap; the join point between Q_3 and Q_4 is in the region shared by both convex hulls. In (b), there is a double control point, so the two convex hulls share edge P_2P_3; the join point is therefore constrained to lie on this edge. In (c), there is a triple control point, and the two convex hulls are straight lines that share the triple point; hence, the join point is also at the triple point. Because the convex hulls are straight lines, the two curve segments must also be straight lines. There is C^2 but only G^0 continuity at the join.

knot values is not necessarily uniform. The nonuniform knot-value sequence means that the blending functions are no longer the same for each interval, but rather vary from curve segment to curve segment.

These curves have several advantages over uniform B-splines. First, continuity at selected join points can be reduced from C^2 to C^1 to C^0 to none. If the continuity is reduced to C^0, then the curve interpolates a control point, but without the undesirable effect of uniform B-splines, where the curve segments on either side of the interpolated control point are straight lines. Also, starting and ending points can be easily interpolated exactly, without at the same time introducing linear segments. As is discussed in [FOLE90], it is possible to add an additional knot and control point to nonuniform B-splines, so the resulting curve can be easily reshaped, whereas this modification cannot be done with uniform B-splines.

The increased generality of nonuniform B-splines requires a notation slightly different from that used for uniform B-splines. As before, the spline is a piecewise continuous curve made up of cubic polynomials, approximating the control points P_0 through P_m. The **knot-value sequence** is a nondecreasing sequence of knot values t_0 through t_{m+4} (that is, there are four more knots than there are control points). Because the smallest number of control points is four, the smallest knot sequence has eight knot values and the curve is defined over the parameter interval from t_3 to t_4.

The only restriction on the knot sequence is that it be nondecreasing, which allows successive knot values to be equal. When this occurs, the parameter value is called a **multiple knot** and the number of identical parameter values is called the **multiplicity** of the knot (a single unique knot has multiplicity of 1). For instance, in the knot sequence (0, 0, 0, 0, 1, 1, 2, 3, 4, 4, 5, 5, 5, 5), the knot value 0 has multiplicity 4; value 1 has multiplicity 2; values 2 and 3 have multiplicity 1; value 4 has multiplicity 2; and value 5 has multiplicity 4.

Curve segment Q_i is defined by control points P_{i-3}, P_{i-2}, P_{i-1}, P_i and by blending functions $B_{i-3,4}(t)$, $B_{i-2,4}(t)$, $B_{i-1,4}(t)$, $B_{i,4}(t)$, as the weighted sum

$$Q_i(t) = P_{i-3} \cdot B_{i-3,4}(t) + P_{i-2} \cdot B_{i-2,4}(t) + P_{i-1} \cdot B_{i-1,4}(t) + P_i \cdot B_{i,4}(t)$$

$$3 \leq i \leq m, \quad t_i \leq t < t_{i+1}. \tag{9.37}$$

The curve is not defined outside the interval t_3 through t_{m+1}. When $t_i = t_{i+1}$ (a multiple knot), curve segment Q_i is a single point. It is this notion of a curve segment reducing to a point that provides the extra flexibility of nonuniform B-splines.

There is no single set of blending functions, as there was for other types of splines. The functions depend on the intervals between knot values and are defined recursively in terms of lower-order blending functions. $B_{i,j}(t)$ is the jth-order blending function for weighting control point P_i. Because we are working with fourth-order (that is, third-degree, or cubic) B-splines, the recursive definition ends with $B_{i,4}(t)$ and can be presented easily in its "unwound" form. The recurrence for cubic B-splines is

$$B_{i,1}(t) = \begin{cases} 1, & t_i \leq t < t_{i+1} \\ 0, & \text{otherwise,} \end{cases}$$

$$B_{i,2}(t) = \frac{t - t_i}{t_{i+1} - t_i} B_{i,1}(t) + \frac{t_{i+2} - t}{t_{i+2} - t_{i+1}} B_{i+1,1}(t),$$

$$B_{i,3}(t) = \frac{t - t_i}{t_{i+2} - t_i} B_{i,2}(t) + \frac{t_{i+3} - t}{t_{i+3} - t_{i+1}} B_{i+1,2}(t),$$

$$B_{i,4}(t) = \frac{t - t_i}{t_{i+3} - t_i} B_{i,3}(t) + \frac{t_{i+4} - t}{t_{i+4} - t_{i+1}} B_{i+1,3}(t). \tag{9.38}$$

It can be shown that the blending functions are nonnegative and sum to one, so nonuniform B-spline curve segments lie within the convex hulls of their four control points. For knots of multiplicity greater than one, the denominators can be zero because successive knot values can be equal: Division by zero is defined to yield zero.

Increasing knot multiplicity has two effects. First, the spline, evaluated at any known knot value t_i, will automatically yield a point within the convex hull of the points P_{i-3}, P_{i-2}, and P_{i-1}. If t_i and t_{i+1} are equal, they must lie in the convex hull of P_{i-3}, P_{i-2}, and P_{i-1}, *and* in the convex hull of P_{i-2}, P_{i-1}, and P_i. Thus, they must actually lie on the line segment between P_{i-2} and P_{i-1}. In the same way, if $t_i = t_{i+1} = t_{i+2}$, then this knot must lie *at* P_{i-1}. If $t_i = t_{i+1} = t_{i+2} = t_{i+3}$, then the knot must lie both at P_{i-1} and at P_i—the curve becomes broken. Second, the multiple knots will reduce parametric continuity: from C^2 to C^1 continuity for one extra knot (multiplicity 2); from C^1 to C^0 continuity for two extra knots (multiplicity 3); from C^0 to no continuity for three extra knots (multiplicity 4).

Interactive creation of nonuniform splines typically involves pointing at control points, with multiple control points indicated simply by successive selection of the same point. Another way is to point directly at the curve with a multibutton mouse: A double click on one button can indicate a double control point; a double click on another button can indicate a double knot.

9.2.6 Nonuniform, Rational Cubic Polynomial Curve Segments

General rational cubic curve segments are ratios of polynomials:

$$x(t) = \frac{X(t)}{W(t)}, \quad y(t) = \frac{Y(t)}{W(t)}, \quad z(t) = \frac{Z(t)}{W(t)}, \tag{9.39}$$

where $X(t)$, $Y(t)$, $Z(t)$, and $W(t)$ are all cubic polynomial curves whose control points are defined in homogeneous coordinates. We can also think of the curve as existing in homogeneous space as $Q(t) = [X(t) \quad Y(t) \quad Z(t) \quad W(t)]^T$. As always, moving from homogeneous space to 3-space involves dividing by $W(t)$. We can transform any nonrational curve to a rational curve by adding $W(t) = 1$ as a fourth element. In general, the polynomials in a rational curve can be Bézier, Hermite, or any other type. When they are B-splines, we have nonuniform rational B-splines, sometimes called **NURBS** [FORR80].

Rational curves are useful for two reasons. The first and most important reason is that they are invariant under rotation, scaling, translation, and perspective transformations of the control points (nonrational curves are invariant under only rotation, scaling, and translation). Thus, the perspective transformation needs to be applied to only the control points, which can then be used to generate the perspective transformation of the original curve. The alternative to converting a nonrational curve to a rational curve prior to a perspective transformation is first to generate points on the curve itself, and then to apply the perspective transformation to *each* point—a far less efficient process. An analogous observation is that the perspective transformation of a sphere is not the same as a sphere whose center and radius are the transformed center and radius of the original sphere.

A second advantage of rational splines is that, unlike nonrationals, they can define precisely any of the conic sections. We can only approximate a conic with nonrationals, by using many control points close to the conic. This second property is useful in those applications, particularly CAD, where general curves and surfaces as well as conics are needed. Both types of entities can be defined with NURBS.

For further discussion of conics and NURBS, see [FAUX79; BÖHM84; TILL83].

9.2.7 Fitting Curves to Digitized Points

An engineer or artist often has a nonelectronic representation of a complex shape that can be digitized as a series of discrete points. For example, a paper hardcopy of a shape may be all that is available. For additional manipulation of the shape we might like to fit a smooth curve or series of curves to the (usually) imprecise digitized representation. Various curve-fitting techniques have been published; all have various advantages and disadvantages. Schneider [SCHN90] has developed a method for approximating digitized curves with piecewise Bézier segments. Advantages over previous approaches are geometric continuity, stability, and ease of implementation. A complete C implementation of the algorithm is available in [SCHN90]. Figure 9.22 shows an example of the method applied to a digitized shape.

9.2.8 Comparison of the Cubic Curves

The different types of parametric cubic curves can be compared by several different criteria, such as ease of interactive manipulation, degree of continuity at join points, generality, and speed of various computations using the representations. Of course, it is not necessary to choose a single representation, since it is possible to convert among all representations, as discussed in [FOLE90]. For instance, non-uniform rational B-splines can be used as an internal representation, while the user might interactively manipulate Bézier control points or Hermite control points and tangent vectors. Some interactive graphics editors provide the user with Hermite curves while representing them internally in the Bézier form supported by Post-Script [ADOB85]. In general, the user of an interactive CAD system may be given several choices, such as Hermite, Bézier, uniform B-splines, and nonuniform B-splines. The nonuniform rational B-spline representation is likely to be used internally, because it is the most general.

Table 9.1 compares most of the curve forms mentioned in this section. Ease of interactive manipulation is not included explicitly in the table, because that attribute is quite application specific. *Number of parameters controlling a curve*

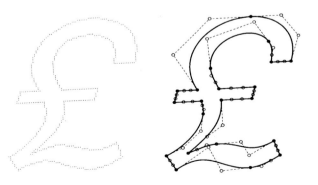

Figure 9.22 A digitized character, showing the original sample, the fitted curves, and the Bézier control points. (Courtesy of Academic Press, Inc.)

Table 9.1

Comparison of Four Different Forms of Parametric Cubic Curves

	Hermite	Bézier	Uniform B-Spline	Nonuniform B-spline
Convex hull defined by control points	N/A	Yes	Yes	Yes
Interpolates some control points	Yes	Yes	No	No
Interpolates all control points	Yes	No	No	No
Ease of subdivision	Good	Best	Average	High
Continuities inherent in representation	C^0 G^0	C^0 G^0	C^2 G^2	C^2 G^2
Continuities achieved easily	C^1 G^1	C^1 G^1	C^2 G^{2*}	C^2 G^{2*}
Number of parameters controlling a curve segment	4	4	4	5

*Except for special case discussed in Section 9.2.

segment is the four geometrical constraints plus other parameters, such as knot spacing for nonuniform splines. *Continuity achieved easily* refers to constraints such as forcing control points to be collinear to allow G^1 continuity. Because C^n continuity is more restrictive than is G^n, any form that can attain C^n can by definition also attain at least G^n.

When only geometric continuity is required, as is often the case for CAD, the choice is narrowed to the various types of splines, all of which can achieve both G^1 and G^2 continuity. Of the three types of splines in the table, uniform B-splines are the most limiting. The possibility of multiple knots afforded by nonuniform B-splines gives more shape control to the user. Of course, a good user interface that allows the user to exploit this power easily is important.

It is customary to provide the user with the ability to drag control points or tangent vectors interactively, continually displaying the updated spline. Figure 9.19 shows such a sequence for B-splines. One of the disadvantages of B-splines in some applications is that the control points are not on the spline itself. It is possible, however, not to display the control points, allowing the user instead to interact with the knots (which must be marked so they can be selected).

9.3 PARAMETRIC BICUBIC SURFACES

Parametric bicubic surfaces are a generalization of parametric cubic curves. Recall the general form of the parametric cubic curve $Q(t) = G \cdot M \cdot T$, where G, the geometry matrix, is a constant. First, for notational convenience, we replace t with s, giving $Q(s) = G \cdot M \cdot S$. If we now allow the points in G to vary in 3D along some path that is parameterized on t, we have

$$Q(s, t) = [G_1(t) \ G_2(t) \ G_3(t) \ G_4(t)] \cdot M \cdot S . \qquad (9.40)$$

Now, for a fixed t_1, $Q(s, t_1)$ is a curve because $G(t_1)$ is constant. Allowing t to take on some new value—say, t_2—where $t_2 - t_1$ is very small, $Q(s, t)$ is a slightly different curve. By repeating this process for arbitrarily many other values of t_2 between 0 and 1, we define an entire family of curves, each member arbitrarily close to another curve. The set of all such curves defines a surface. If the $G_i(t)$ are themselves cubics, the surface is said to be a **parametric bicubic surface.**

Continuing with the case that the $G_i(t)$ are cubics, each can be represented as $G_i(t) = G_i \cdot M \cdot T$, where $G_i = [g_{i1} \ g_{i2} \ g_{i3} \ g_{i4}]$ (the G and g are used to distinguish from the G used for the curve). Hence, g_{i1} is the first element of the geometry matrix for curve $G_i(t)$, and so on.

Now let us transpose the equation $G_i(t) = G_i \cdot M \cdot T$, using the identity $(A \cdot B \cdot C)^T = C^T \cdot B^T \cdot A^T$. The result is $G_i(t) = T^T \cdot M^T \cdot G_i^T = T^T \cdot M^T \cdot [g_{i1} \ g_{i2} \ g_{i3} \ g_{i4}]^T$. If we now substitute this result in Eq. (9.40) for each of the four points, we have

$$Q(s, t) = T^T \cdot M^T \cdot \begin{bmatrix} g_{11} & g_{21} & g_{31} & g_{41} \\ g_{12} & g_{22} & g_{32} & g_{42} \\ g_{13} & g_{23} & g_{33} & g_{43} \\ g_{14} & g_{24} & g_{34} & g_{44} \end{bmatrix} \cdot M \cdot S , \qquad (9.41)$$

or

$$Q(s, t) = T^T \cdot M^T \cdot G \cdot M \cdot S, \quad 0 \le s, t \le 1. \qquad (9.42)$$

Written separately for each of x, y, and z, the form is

$$x(s, t) = T^T \cdot M^T \cdot G_x \cdot M \cdot S,$$

$$y(s, t) = T^T \cdot M^T \cdot G_y \cdot M \cdot S,$$

$$z(s, t) = T^T \cdot M^T \cdot G_z \cdot M \cdot S. \qquad (9.43)$$

Given this general form, we now move on to examine specific ways to specify surfaces using different geometry matrices.

9.3.1 Hermite Surfaces

Hermite surfaces are completely defined by a 4×4 geometry matrix G_H. Derivation of G_H follows the same approach that we used to find Eq. (9.42). We further elaborate the derivation here, applying it just to $x(s, t)$. First, we replace t by s in Eq. (9.13), to get $x(s) = G_{H_x} \cdot M_H \cdot S$. Rewriting this expression further such that the Hermite geometry matrix G_{H_x} is not constant, but is rather a function of t, we obtain

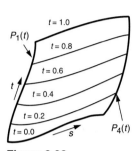

Figure 9.23
Lines of constant parameter values on a bicubic surface: $P_1(t)$ is at $s = 0$, and $P_4(t)$ is at $s = 1$.

$$x(s, t) = G_{H_x}(t) \cdot M_H \cdot S = [P_{1_x}(t) \ \ P_{4_x}(t) \ \ R_{1_x}(t) \ \ R_{4_x}(t)] \cdot M_H \cdot S . \quad (9.44)$$

The functions $P_{1_x}(t)$ and $P_{4_x}(t)$ define the x components of the starting and ending points for the curve in parameter s. Similarly, $R_{1_x}(t)$ and $R_{4_x}(t)$ are the tangent vectors at these points. For any specific value of t, there are two specific endpoints and tangent vectors. Figure 9.23 shows $P_1(t)$, $P_4(t)$, and the cubic in s that is defined when $t = 0.0, 0.2, 0.4, 0.6, 0.8$, and 1.0. The surface patch is essentially a cubic interpolation between $P_1(t) = Q(0, t)$ and $P_4(t) = Q(1, t)$ or, alternatively, between $Q(s, 0)$ and $Q(s, 1)$.

In the special case that the four interpolants $Q(0, t)$, $Q(1, t)$, $Q(s, 0)$, and $Q(s, 1)$ are straight lines, the result is a **ruled surface**. If the interpolants are also coplanar, then the surface is a four-sided planar polygon.

Continuing with the derivation, let each of $P_{1_x}(t)$, $P_{4_x}(t)$, $R_{1_x}(t)$, and $R_{4_x}(t)$ be represented in Hermite form as

$$P_{1_x}(t) = [g_{11} \ g_{12} \ g_{13} \ g_{14}]_x \cdot M_H \cdot T , \quad P_{4_x}(t) = [g_{21} \ g_{22} \ g_{23} \ g_{24}]_x \cdot M_H \cdot T ,$$

$$R_{1_x}(t) = [g_{31} \ g_{32} \ g_{33} \ g_{34}]_x \cdot M_H \cdot T , \quad R_{4_x}(t) = [g_{41} \ g_{42} \ g_{43} \ g_{44}]_x \cdot M_H \cdot T .$$
$$(9.45)$$

These four cubics can be rewritten together as a single equation:

$$[P_{1_x}(t) \ \ P_{4_x}(t) \ \ R_{1_x}(t) \ \ R_{4_x}(t)]^T = G_{H_x} \cdot M_H \cdot T, \quad (9.46)$$

where

$$G_{H_x} = \begin{bmatrix} g_{11} & g_{12} & g_{13} & g_{14} \\ g_{21} & g_{22} & g_{23} & g_{24} \\ g_{31} & g_{32} & g_{33} & g_{34} \\ g_{41} & g_{42} & g_{43} & g_{44} \end{bmatrix}_x . \quad (9.47)$$

Transposing both sides of Eq. (9.46) results in

$$[P_{1_x}(t) \ \ P_{4_x}(t) \ \ R_{1_x}(t) \ \ R_{4_x}(t)] = T^T \cdot M_H^T \cdot \begin{bmatrix} g_{11} & g_{21} & g_{31} & g_{41} \\ g_{12} & g_{22} & g_{32} & g_{42} \\ g_{13} & g_{23} & g_{33} & g_{43} \\ g_{14} & g_{24} & g_{34} & g_{44} \end{bmatrix}_x = T^T \cdot M_H^T \cdot G_{H_x} . \quad (9.48)$$

Substituting Eq. (9.48) into Eq. (9.44) yields

$$x(s, t) = T^T \cdot M_H^T \cdot G_{H_x} \cdot M_H \cdot S; \quad (9.49)$$

similarly,

$$y(s, t) = T^T \cdot M_H^T \cdot G_{H_y} \cdot M_H \cdot S, \quad z(s, t) = T^T \cdot M_H^T \cdot G_{H_z} \cdot M_H \cdot S. \quad (9.50)$$

The three 4×4 matrixes G_{H_x}, G_{H_y}, and G_{H_z} play the same role for Hermite surfaces as did the single matrix G_H for curves.

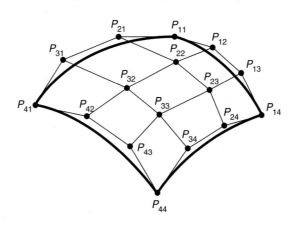

Figure 9.24   Sixteen control points for a Bézier bicubic patch.

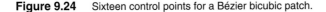

The Hermite bicubic permits C^1 and G^1 continuity from one patch to the next in much the same way the Hermite cubic permits C^1 and G^1 continuity from one curve segment to the next. Details can be found in Chapter 11 of [FOLE90].

9.3.2 Bézier Surfaces

The Bézier bicubic formulation can be derived in exactly the same way as the Hermite cubic. The results are

$$x(s,\,t) = T^{\mathrm{T}} \cdot M_{\mathrm{B}}{}^{\mathrm{T}} \cdot \boldsymbol{G}_{\mathrm{B}_x} \cdot M_{\mathrm{B}} \cdot S,$$

$$y(s,\,t) = T^{\mathrm{T}} \cdot M_{\mathrm{B}}{}^{\mathrm{T}} \cdot \boldsymbol{G}_{\mathrm{B}_y} \cdot M_{\mathrm{B}} \cdot S, \qquad (9.51)$$

$$z(s,\,t) = T^{\mathrm{T}} \cdot M_{\mathrm{B}}{}^{\mathrm{T}} \cdot \boldsymbol{G}_{\mathrm{B}_z} \cdot M_{\mathrm{B}} \cdot S.$$

The Bézier geometry matrix $\boldsymbol{G}$ consists of 16 control points, as shown in Fig. 9.24. Bézier surfaces are attractive in interactive design for the same reason as Bézier curves are: Some of the control points interpolate the surface, giving convenient precise control, whereas tangent vectors also can be controlled explicitly. When Bézier surfaces are used as an internal representation, their convex-hull property is attractive.

We create C^0 and G^0 continuity across patch edges by making the four common control points equal. G^1 continuity occurs when the two sets of four control points on either side of the edge are collinear with the points on the edge. In Fig. 9.25, the following sets of control points are collinear and define four line segments whose lengths all have the same ratio k: $(P_{13},\, P_{14},\, P_{15})$, $(P_{23},\, P_{24},\, P_{25})$, $(P_{33},\, P_{34},\, P_{35})$, and $(P_{43},\, P_{44},\, P_{45})$. The teapot shown in Fig. 9.1 was modeled by 32 Bézier patches, all joined to ensure G^1 continuity.

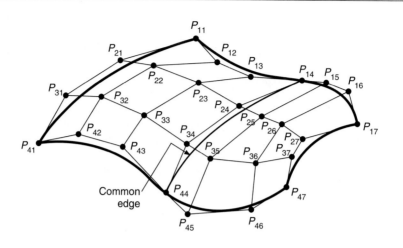

Figure 9.25   Two Bézier patches joined along the edge P_{14}, P_{24}, P_{34}, and P_{44}.

9.3.3 B-Spline Surfaces

B-spline patches are represented as

$$x(s, t) = T^{\mathrm{T}} \cdot M_{\mathrm{Bs}}^{\mathrm{T}} \cdot G_{\mathrm{Bs}_x} \cdot M_{\mathrm{Bs}} \cdot S,$$

$$y(s, t) = T^{\mathrm{T}} \cdot M_{\mathrm{Bs}}^{\mathrm{T}} \cdot G_{\mathrm{Bs}_y} \cdot M_{\mathrm{Bs}} \cdot S, \qquad (9.52)$$

$$z(s, t) = T^{\mathrm{T}} \cdot M_{\mathrm{Bs}}^{\mathrm{T}} \cdot G_{\mathrm{Bs}_z} \cdot M_{\mathrm{Bs}} \cdot S.$$

C^2 continuity across boundaries is automatic with B-splines; no special arrangements of control points are needed, except to avoid duplicate control points, which create discontinuities.

Bicubic nonuniform and rational B-spline surfaces and other rational surfaces are similarly analogous to their cubic counterparts. All the techniques for display carry over directly to the bicubic case.

9.3.4 Normals to Surfaces

The normal to a bicubic surface, needed for shading (Chapter 14), for performing interference detection in robotics, for calculating offsets for numerically controlled machining, and for doing other calculations, is easy to find. From Eq. (9.42), the s tangent vector of the surface $Q(s, t)$ is

$$\frac{\partial}{\partial s} Q(s, t) = \frac{\partial}{\partial s} (T^{\mathrm{T}} \cdot M^{\mathrm{T}} \cdot G \cdot M \cdot S) = T^{\mathrm{T}} \cdot M^{\mathrm{T}} \cdot G \cdot M \cdot \frac{\partial}{\partial s}(S)$$

$$= T^{\mathrm{T}} \cdot M^{\mathrm{T}} \cdot G \cdot M \cdot [3s^2 \ \ 2s \ \ 1 \ \ 0]^{\mathrm{T}}, \qquad (9.53)$$

and the t tangent vector is

$$\frac{\partial}{\partial t}Q(s,t) = \frac{\partial}{\partial t}(T^T \cdot M^T \cdot G \cdot M \cdot S) = \frac{\partial}{\partial t}(T^T) \cdot M^T \cdot G \cdot M \cdot S$$

$$= [3t^2 \ 2t \ 1 \ 0]^T \cdot M^T \cdot G \cdot M \cdot S. \tag{9.54}$$

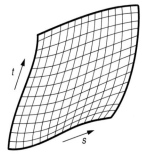

Both tangent vectors are parallel to the surface at the point (s, t), and their cross-product is therefore perpendicular to the surface. Notice that, if both tangent vectors are zero, the cross-product is zero, and there is no meaningful surface normal. Recall that a tangent vector can go to zero at join points that have C^1 but not G^1 continuity.

Each of the tangent vectors is, of course, a 3-tuple, because Eq. (9.42) represents the x, y, and z components of the bicubic. With the notation x_s for the x component of the s tangent vector, y_s for the y component, and z_s for the z component, the normal is

Figure 9.26
A single surface patch displayed as curves of constant s and constant t.

$$\frac{\partial}{\partial s}Q(s,t) \times \frac{\partial}{\partial t}Q(s,t) = [y_s z_t - y_t z_s \quad z_s x_t - z_t x_s \quad x_s y_t - x_t y_s]. \tag{9.55}$$

The surface normal is a biquintic (two-variable, fifth-degree) polynomial and hence is fairly expensive to compute. [SCHW82] gives a bicubic approximation that is satisfactory as long as the patch itself is relatively smooth.

9.3.5 Displaying Bicubic Surfaces

Like curves, surfaces can be displayed by iterative evaluation of the bicubic polynomials. Iterative evaluation is best suited for displaying bicubic patches in the style of Fig. 9.26. Each of the curves of constant s and constant t on the surface is itself a cubic, so display of each of the curves is straightforward, as in Prog. 9.2.

Brute-force iterative evaluation for surfaces is even more expensive than for curves, because the surface equations must be evaluated about $2/\delta^2$ times. For $\delta = 0.1$, this value is 200; for $\delta = 0.01$, it is 20,000. These numbers make the alternative, forward-differencing method even more attractive than it is for curves. This method and other useful ways to display bicubic surfaces are presented in [FOLE90; FORR79].

Program 9.2

Function to display bicubic patch as a grid. Functions X(s,t), Y(s,t), and Z(s,t) evaluate the surface using the coefficient matrix coefficients.

```
typedef float Coeffs[4][4][3];

void  DrawSurface( Coeffs coefficients, int ns, int nt, int n )
    /* the variable coefficients are the coefficients for Q(s,t) */
    /* ns and nt are the number of curves of constant s and t to be drawn */
{
    float  del, dels, delt, s, t;
    int  i, j;
    /* Initialize */
    del = 1.0 / n;          /* Step size to use in drawing each curve */
    dels = 1.0 / (ns – 1);  /* Step size in s when moving to next curve of constant t */
    delt = 1.0 / (nt – 1);  /* Step size in t when moving to next curve of constant s */
```

```
/* Draw ns curves of constant s, for s=0.0, dels, 2dels, ... 1.0 */
for ( i = 0; i < ns; i++ ) {
    s = i * dels;
    /* Draw a curve of constant s, varying t from 0.0 to 1.0 */
    /* X, Y, and Z are functions to evaluate the bicubics for a given s and t */
    MoveAbs3(X(s, 0.0), Y(s, 0.0), Z(s, 0.0));
    for ( j = 0; j < n; j++ ) {
        t = j * del;
        /* n steps are used as t varies from 0.0 to 1.0 for each curve */
        LineAbs3(X(s, t), Y(s, t), Z(s, t));
    }
}

/* Draw nt curves of constant t, for t=0.0, delt, 2delt, ... 1.0 */
for ( i = 0; i < nt; i++ ) {
    t = i * delt;
    /* Draw a curve of constant t, varying s from 0.0 to 1.0 */
    MoveAbs3(X(0.0, t), Y(0.0, t), Z(0.0, t));
    for ( j = 0; j < n; j++ ) {
        s = j * del;
        /* n steps are used as s varies from 0 to 1 for each curve */
        LineAbs3(X(s, t), Y(s, t), Z(s, t));
    }
}
}
```

The functions $X(s, t)$, $Y(s, t)$, and $Z(s, t)$ can be easily developed for a specific type of surface. As an example, we will consider a Bézier surface. From Eq. (9.51), the $x(s, t)$ equation can be rewritten as

$$x(s, t) = [(1 - t)^3 \quad 3t(1 - t)^2 \quad 3t^2(1 - t) \quad t^3] \cdot \boldsymbol{G}_{\mathrm{B}_x} \cdot \begin{bmatrix} (1 - s)^3 \\ 3s(1 - s)^2 \\ 3s^2(1 - s) \\ s^3 \end{bmatrix}, \quad (9.56)$$

just by multiplying out the $T^{\mathrm{T}} \cdot M_{\mathrm{B}}^{\mathrm{T}}$ and $M_{\mathrm{B}} \cdot S$ matrices. Recall that $\boldsymbol{G}_{\mathrm{B}_x}$ is the matrix of the x component of the control points, which are shown in Fig. 9.24, so it can be written as

$$\boldsymbol{G}_{\mathrm{B}_x} = \begin{bmatrix} \boldsymbol{P}_{11} & \boldsymbol{P}_{21} & \boldsymbol{P}_{31} & \boldsymbol{P}_{41} \\ \boldsymbol{P}_{12} & \boldsymbol{P}_{22} & \boldsymbol{P}_{32} & \boldsymbol{P}_{42} \\ \boldsymbol{P}_{13} & \boldsymbol{P}_{23} & \boldsymbol{P}_{33} & \boldsymbol{P}_{43} \\ \boldsymbol{P}_{14} & \boldsymbol{P}_{24} & \boldsymbol{P}_{34} & \boldsymbol{P}_{44} \end{bmatrix}_x.$$

Finally, the completely expanded form of Eq. (9.56) can be written as

$$\begin{aligned} x(s, t) &= (1 - s)^3(\boldsymbol{P}_{11_x}(1 - t)^3 + 3\boldsymbol{P}_{12_x}(1 - t)^2 t + 3\boldsymbol{P}_{13_x}(1 - t)t^2 + \boldsymbol{P}_{14_x}t^3) \\ &+ 3(1 - s)^2 s(\boldsymbol{P}_{21_x}(1 - t)^3 + 3\boldsymbol{P}_{22_x}(1 - t)^2 t + 3\boldsymbol{P}_{23_x}(1 - t)t^2 + \boldsymbol{P}_{24_x}t^3) \\ &+ 3(1 - s)s^2(\boldsymbol{P}_{31_x}(1 - t)^3 + 3\boldsymbol{P}_{32_x}(1 - t)^2 t + 3\boldsymbol{P}_{33_x}(1 - t)t^2 + \boldsymbol{P}_{34_x}t^3) \\ &+ s^3(\boldsymbol{P}_{41_x}(1 - t)^3 + 3\boldsymbol{P}_{42_x}(1 - t)^2 t + 3\boldsymbol{P}_{43_x}(1 - t)t^2 + \boldsymbol{P}_{44_x}t^3) . \end{aligned}$$

The equations for $y(s, t)$ and $z(s, t)$ are derived in an identical fashion. The functions $X(s, t)$, $Y(s, t)$, and $Z(s, t)$, which are required for Prog. 2.2, can be coded directly from the $x(s, t)$, $y(s, t)$, and $z(s, t)$ expressions. Functions for drawing other types of surfaces can be developed just as easily as for the Bézier surface.

9.4 QUADRIC SURFACES

The implicit surface equation of the form

$$f(x, y, z) = ax^2 + by^2 + cz^2 + 2dxy + 2eyz + 2fxz + 2gx + 2hy + 2jz + k = 0 \quad (9.57)$$

defines the family of quadric surfaces. For example, if $a = b = c = -k = 1$ and the remaining coefficients are zero, a unit sphere is defined at the origin. If a through f are zero, a plane is defined. Quadric surfaces are particularly useful in specialized applications such as molecular modeling [PORT79; MAX79] and have also been integrated into solid-modeling systems. Recall, too, that rational cubic curves can represent conic sections; similarly, rational bicubic surfaces can represent quadrics. Hence, the implicit quadratic equation is an alternative to rational surfaces, *if* only quadric surfaces are being represented. Other reasons for using quadrics include ease of

- Computing the surface normal
- Testing whether a point is on the surface [just substitute the point into Eq. (9.57), evaluate, and test for a result within some ϵ of zero]
- Computing z given x and y (important in hidden-surface algorithms—see Chapter 13)
- Calculating intersections of one surface with another.

An alternative representation of Eq. (9.57) is

$$P^{\mathrm{T}} \cdot Q \cdot P = 0, \quad (9.58)$$

with
$$Q = \begin{bmatrix} a & d & f & g \\ d & b & e & h \\ f & e & c & j \\ g & h & j & k \end{bmatrix} \quad \text{and} \quad P = \begin{bmatrix} x \\ y \\ z \\ 1 \end{bmatrix}. \quad (9.59)$$

The surface represented by Q can be easily translated and scaled. Given a 4×4 transformation matrix M of the form developed in Chapter 5, the transformed quadric surface Q' is given by

$$Q' = (M^{-1})^{\mathrm{T}} \cdot Q \cdot M^{-1}. \quad (9.60)$$

The normal to the implicit surface defined by $f(x, y, z) = 0$ is the vector $[df/dx \ df/dy \ df/dz]$. This surface normal is much easier to evaluate than is the surface normal to a bicubic surface discussed in Section 9.3.4.

9.5 SPECIALIZED MODELING TECHNIQUES

In this chapter we have concentrated on geometric models; we will as well in Chapter 10. In a world made entirely of simple geometric objects, these models would suffice. But many natural phenomena are not efficiently represented by geometric models, at least not on a large scale. Fog, for example, is made up of tiny drops of water, but using a model in which each drop must be individually placed is out of the question. Furthermore, this water-drop model does not accurately represent our perception of fog: We see fog as a blur in the air in front of us, not as millions of drops. Our visual perception of fog is based on how fog alters the light reaching our eyes, not on the shape or placement of the individual drops. Thus, to model the perceptual effect of fog efficiently, we need a different model. In the same way, the shape of a leaf of a tree may be modeled with polygons and its stem may be modeled with a spline tube, but to place explicitly every limb, branch, twig, and leaf of a tree would be impossibly time consuming and cumbersome.

You will find a comprehensive discussion of advanced modeling techniques in Chapter 20 of [FOLE90]; here we will discuss two specialized methods, which are surprisingly easy to implement and which produce startlingly realistic images.

9.5.1 Fractal Models

Fractals have recently attracted much attention [VOSS87; MAND82; PEIT86]. The images resulting from them are spectacular, and many different approaches to generating fractals have been developed. The term **fractal** has been generalized by the computer graphics community to include objects outside Mandelbrot's original definition. It has come to mean anything which has a substantial measure of exact or statistical self-similarity, and that is how we use it here, although its precise mathematical definition requires statistical self-similarity at all resolutions. Thus, only fractals generated by infinitely recursive processes are true fractal objects. On the other hand, those generated by finite processes may exhibit no visible change in detail after some stage, so they are adequate approximations of the ideal. What we mean by **self-similarity** is best illustrated by an example, the von Koch snowflake. Starting with a line segment with a bump on it, as shown in Fig. 9.27, we

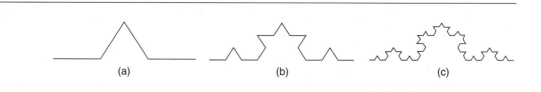

(a)   (b)   (c)

Figure 9.27   Construction of the von Koch snowflake: each segment in (a) is replaced by an exact copy of the entire figure, shrunk by a factor of 3. The same process is applied to the segments in (b) to generate those in (c).

replace each segment of the line by a figure exactly like the original line. This process is repeated: Each segment in part (b) of the figure is replaced by a shape exactly like the entire figure. (It makes no difference whether the replacement is by the shape shown in part (a) or by the shape shown in part (b); if the one in part (a) is used, the result after 2^n steps is the same as the result after n steps if each segment of the current figure is replaced by the entire current figure at each stage.) If this process is repeated infinitely many times, the result is said to be **self-similar**: The entire object is similar (i.e., can be translated, rotated, and scaled) to a subportion of itself.

Associated with this notion of self-similarity is the notion of **fractal dimension**. To define fractal dimension, we shall examine some properties of objects whose dimension we know. A line segment is 1D; if we divide a line into N equal parts, the parts each look like the original line scaled down by a factor of $N = N^{1/1}$. A square is 2D: if we divide it into N parts, each part looks like the original scaled down by a factor of $\sqrt{N} = N^{1/2}$. (For example, a square divides nicely into nine subsquares; each one looks like the original scaled by a factor of $\frac{1}{3}$.) What about the von Koch snowflake? When it is divided into four pieces (the pieces associated with the original four segments in Fig. 9.27(a), each resulting piece looks like the original scaled down by a factor of 3. We would like to say it has a dimension d, where $4^{1/d} = 3$. The value of d must be $\log(4)/\log(3) = 1.26\ldots$. This is the definition of fractal dimension.

The most famous two fractal objects deserve mention here: the Julia–Fatou set and the Mandelbrot set. These objects are generated from the study of the rule $x \rightarrow x^2 + c$ (and many other rules as well—this is the simplest and best known). Here x is a **complex number**,[1] $x = a + bi$. If a complex number has modulus < 1, then squaring it repeatedly makes it go toward zero. If it has a modulus > 1, repeated squaring makes it grow larger and larger. Numbers with modulus 1 still have modulus 1 after repeated squarings. Thus, some complex numbers "fall toward zero" when they are repeatedly squared, some "fall toward infinity," and some do neither—the last group forms the boundary between the numbers attracted to zero and those attracted to infinity.

Suppose we repeatedly apply the mapping $x \rightarrow x^2 + c$ to each complex number x for some nonzero value of c, such as $c = -0.12375 + 0.056805i$; some complex numbers will be attracted to infinity, some will be attracted to finite numbers, and some will go toward neither. Drawing the set of points that go toward neither, we get the Julia–Fatou set shown in Fig. 9.28(a).

Notice that the region in Fig. 9.28(b) is not as well connected as is that in part (a) of the figure. In part (b), some points fall toward each of the three black dots shown, some go to infinity, and some do neither. These last points are the ones drawn as the outline of the shape in part (b). The shape of the Julia–Fatou set evidently depends on the value of the number c. If we compute the Julia sets for all

---

[1] If you are unfamiliar with complex numbers, it suffices to treat i as a special symbol and merely to know the definitions of addition and multiplication of complex numbers. If $z = c + di$ is a second complex number, then $x + z$ is defined to be $(a + c) + (b + d)i$, and xz is defined to be $(ac - bd) + (ad + bc)i$. We can represent complex numbers as points in the plane by identifying the point (a, b) with the complex number $(a + bi)$. The *modulus* of the number $a + bi$ is the real number $(a^2 + b^2)^{1/2}$, which gives a measure of the "size" of the complex number.

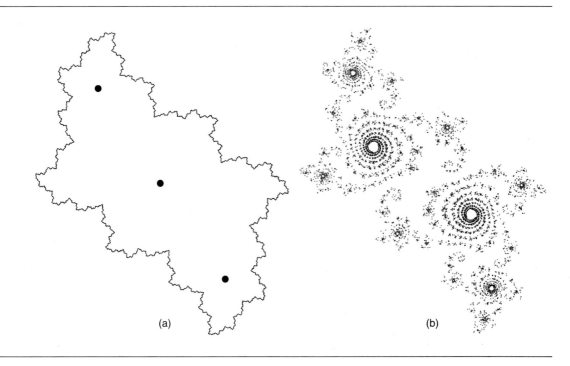

(a)

(b)

Figure 9.28 The Julia–Fatou set. (a) $c = -0.12375 + 0.056805i$. (b) $c = -0.012 + 0.74i$.

possible values of c and color the point c black when the Julia–Fatou set is connected (i.e, is made of one piece, not broken into disjoint "islands") and white when the set is not connected, we get the object shown in Fig. 9.29, which is known as the **Mandelbrot set**. Note that the Mandelbrot set is self-similar in that, around the edge of the large disk in the set, there are several smaller sets, each looking a great deal like the large one scaled down.

Fortunately, there is an easier way to generate approximations of the Mandelbrot set: For each value of c, take the complex number $0 = 0 + 0i$ and apply the process $x \rightarrow x^2 + c$ to it some finite number of times (perhaps 1000). If after this many iterations it is outside the disk defined by modulus < 100, then we color c white; otherwise, we color it black. As the number of iterations and the radius of the disk are increased, the resulting picture becomes a better approximation of the set. Peitgen and Richter [PEIT86] give explicit directions for generating many spectacular images of Mandelbrot and Julia–Fatou sets.

These results are extremely suggestive for modeling natural forms, since many natural objects seem to exhibit striking self-similarity. Mountains have peaks and smaller peaks and rocks and gravel, which all look similar; trees have limbs and branches and twigs, which all look similar; coastlines have bays and inlets and estuaries and rivulets and drainage ditches, which all look similar. Hence, modeling self-similarity at some scale seems to be a way to generate appealing-looking models of natural phenomena. The scale at which the self-similarity breaks down

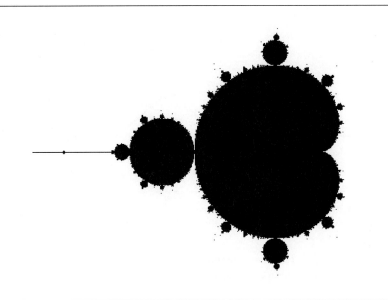

Figure 9.29 The Mandelbrot set. Each point c in the complex plane is colored black if the Julia set for the process $x \to x^2 + c$ is connected.

is not particularly important here, since the intent is modeling rather than mathematics. Thus, when an object has been generated recursively through enough steps that all further changes happen at well below pixel resolution, there is no need to continue.

Fournier, Fussell, and Carpenter [FOUR82] developed a mechanism for generating a class of fractal mountains based on recursive subdivision. It is easiest to explain in 1D. Suppose we start with a line segment lying on the x axis, as shown in Fig. 9.30(a). If we now subdivide the line into two halves and then move the midpoint some distance in the y direction, we get the shape shown in Fig. 9.30(b). To continue subdividing each segment, we compute a new value for the midpoint of the segment from (x_i, y_i) to (x_{i+1}, y_{i+1}) as follows: $x_{new} = \frac{1}{2}(x_i + x_{i+1})$, $y_{new} = \frac{1}{2}(y_i + y_{i+1}) + P(x_{i+1} - x_i) R(x_{new})$, where $P()$ is a function determining the extent of the perturbation in terms of the size of the line being perturbed, and $R()$ is a random number[2] between 0 and 1 selected on the basis of x_{new} (see Fig. 9.30c). If $P(s) = s$, then the first point cannot be displaced by more than 1, each of the next two points (which are at most at height $\frac{1}{2}$ already) cannot be displaced by more than $\frac{1}{2}$, and so on. Hence, all the resulting points fit in the unit square. For $P(s) = s^a$, the shape of the result depends on the value of a; smaller values of a yield larger perturbations, and vice versa. Of course, other functions, such as $P(s) = 2^{-s}$, can be used as well.

---

[2] $R()$ is actually a *random variable*, a function taking real numbers and producing randomly distributed numbers between 0 and 1. If this is implemented by a pseudorandom-number generator, it has the advantage that the fractals are repeatable: We can generate them again by supplying the same seed to the pseudorandom-number generator.

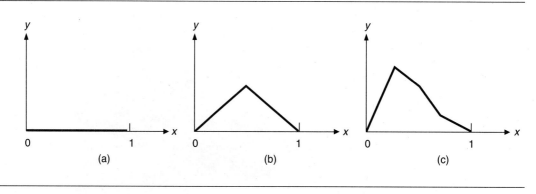

Figure 9.30   A line segment on the x axis. (b) The midpoint of the line has been translated in the y direction by a random amount. (c) The result of one further iteration.

Fournier, Fussell, and Carpenter use this process to modify 2D shapes in the following fashion. They start with a triangle, mark the midpoint of each edge, and connect the three midpoints, as shown in Fig. 9.31(a). The y coordinate of each midpoint is then modified in the manner we have described, so that the resulting set of four triangles looks like Fig. 9.31(b). This process, when iterated, produces quite realistic-looking mountains, as shown in Color Plate 11 (although, in an overhead view, one perceives a very regular polygonal structure).

Notice that we can start with an arrangement of triangles that have a certain shape, then apply this process to generate the finer detail. This ability is particularly important in some modeling applications, in which the layout of objects in a scene may be stochastic at a low level but ordered at a high level: The foliage in an ornamental garden may be generated by a stochastic mechanism, but its arrangement in the garden must follow strict rules. On the other hand, the fact that the

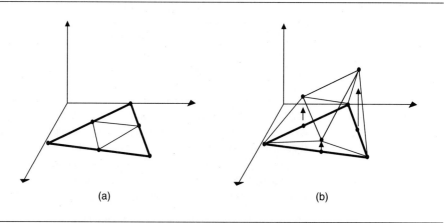

Figure 9.31   (a) The subdivision of a triangle into four smaller triangles. The midpoints of the original triangle are perturbed in the y direction to yield the shape in (b).

high-level structure of the initial triangle arrangement persists in the iterated subdivisions may be inappropriate in some applications (in particular, the fractal so generated does not have all the statistical self-similarities present in fractals based on Brownian motion [MAND82]). Also, since the position of any vertex is adjusted only once and is stationary thereafter, creases tend to develop in the surface along the edges between the original triangles, and these may appear unnatural.

Rendering fractals can be difficult. If the fractals are rendered into a z-buffer, displaying the entire object takes a long time because of the huge number of polygons involved. In scan-line rendering, it is expensive to sort all the polygons so that only those intersecting the scan line are considered. But ray tracing fractals is extremely difficult, since each ray must be checked for intersection with each of the possibly millions of polygons involved. Kajiya [KAJI83] gave a method for ray tracing fractal objects of the class described in [FOUR82], and Bouville [BOUV85] improves this algorithm by finding a better bounding volume for the objects.

9.5.2 Grammar-Based Models

Smith [SMIT84] presents a method for describing the structure of certain plants, originally developed by Lindenmayer [LIND68], by using parallel graph grammar languages (**L-grammars**), which Smith called **graftals**. These languages are described by a grammar consisting of a collection of productions, all of which are applied at once. Lindenmayer extended the languages to include brackets, so the alphabet contained the two special symbols, "[" and "]." A typical example is the grammar with alphabet {A, B, [,]} and two production rules:

1. A → AA
2. B → A[B]AA[B]

Starting from the axiom A, the first few generations are A, AA, AAAA, and so on; starting from the axiom B, the first few generations are

0. B
1. A[B]AA[B]
2. AA[A[B]AA[B]]AAAA[A[B]AA[B]]

and so on. If we say that a word in the language represents a sequence of segments in a graph structure and that bracketed portions represent portions that branch from the symbol preceding them, then the figures associated with these three levels are as shown in Fig. 9.32.

This set of pictures has a pleasing branching structure, but a somewhat more balanced tree would be appealing. If we add the parentheses symbols, "(" and ")," to the language and alter the second production to be A[B]AA(B), then the second generation becomes

2. AA[A[B]AA(B)]AAAA(A[B]AA(B))

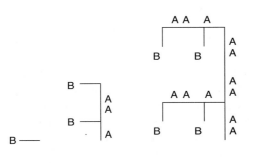

Figure 9.32   Tree representations of the first three words of the language. All branches are drawn to the left of the current main axis.

If we say that square brackets denote a left branch and parentheses denote a right branch, then the associated pictures are as shown in Fig. 9.33. By progressing to later generations in such a language, we get graph structures representing extremely complex patterns. These graph structures have a sort of self-similarity, in that the pattern described by the nth-generation word is contained (repeatedly, in this case) in the $(n + 1)$th-generation word.

Generating an object from such a word is a process separate from that of generating the word itself. Here, the segments of the tree have been drawn at successively smaller lengths, the branching angles have all been 45°, and the branches go to the left or to the right. Choosing varying branching angles for different depth branches, and varying thicknesses for the lines (or even cylinders) representing the segments, gives different results; drawing a "flower" or "leaf" at each terminal node of the tree further enhances the picture. The grammar itself has no inherent geometric content, so using a grammar-based model requires both a grammar and a geometric interpretation of the language.

This sort of enhancement of the languages and the interpretation of words in the language (i.e., pictures generated from words) has been carried out by several

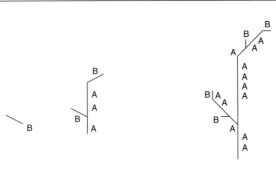

Figure 9.33   Tree representations of the first three words, but in the language with two-sided branching. We have made each segment of the tree shorter as we progress into further generations.

researchers [REFF88; PRUS88]. The grammars have been enriched to allow us to keep track of the "age" of a letter in a word, so that the old and young letters are transformed differently (this recording of ages can be done with rules of the form $A \to B$, $B \to C$, $C \to D$,..., $Q \to QG[Q]$, so that no interesting transitions occur until the plant has "aged"). Much of the work has been concentrated on making grammars that accurately represent the biology of plants during development.

At some point, however, a grammar becomes unwieldy as a descriptor for plants: Too many additional features are added to it or to the interpretation of a word in it. In Reffye's model [REFF88], the simulation of the growth of a plant is controlled by a small collection of parameters that are described in biological terms and that can be cast in an algorithm. The productions of the grammar are applied probabilistically, rather than deterministically.

In this model, we start as before with a single stem. At the tip of this stem is a **bud**, which can undergo one of several transitions: it may die, it may flower and die, it may sleep for some period of time, or it may become an **internode**, a segment of the plant between buds. The process of becoming an internode has three stages: the original bud may generate one or more **axillary buds** (buds on one side of the joint between internodes), a process that is called **ramification**; the internode is added; and the end of the new internode becomes an **apical bud** (a bud at the very end of a sequence of internodes). Figure 9.34(a) shows examples of the transition from bud to internode.

Each of the buds in the resulting object can then undergo similar transitions. If we say the initial segment of the tree is of **order 1**, we can define the order of all other internodes inductively: Internodes generated from the apical bud of an order-i internode are also of order-i; those generated from axillary buds of an order-i internode are of order $(i + 1)$. Thus, the entire trunk of a tree is order 1, the limbs are order 2, the branches on those limbs are order 3, and so on. Figure 9.34(b) shows a more complicated plant and the orders of various internodes in the plant.

Converting this description into an actual image of a tree requires a model for the shapes of its various components: an order-1 internode may be a large tapered cylinder, and an order-7 internode may be a small green line, for example. The sole requirement is that there must be a leaf at each axillary node (although the leaf may fall at some time).

Finally, to simulate the growth of a plant in this model, then, we need the following biological information: the current age of the model, the growth rate of each order of internode, the number of axillary buds at the start of each internode (as a function of the order of the internode), and the probabilities of death, pause, ramification, and reiteration as functions of age, dimension, and order. We also need certain geometric information: the shape of each internode (as a function of order and age), the branching angles for each order and age, and the tropism of each axis (whether each sequence of order-i internodes is a straight line, or curves toward the horizontal or vertical). To draw an image of the plant, we need still more information: the color and texture of each of the entities to be drawn—internodes of various orders, leaves of various ages, and flowers of different ages. Very convincing tree models can be produced by grammar-based models; see Color Plate 12.

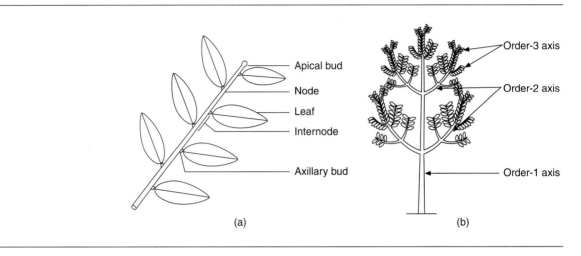

Figure 9.34 Examples of plant growth. (a) The bud at the tip of a segment of the plant can become an internode; in so doing, it creates a new bud (the **axillary bud**), a new segment (**the internode**), and a new bud at the tip (the **apical bud**). (b) A more complex plant, with orders attached to the various internodes.

SUMMARY

This chapter has only touched on important ideas concerning curve and surface representation, but it has given sufficient information so that you can implement interactive systems using these representations. Theoretical treatments of the material can be found in texts such as [BART87; DEBO78; FAUX79; MORT85].

Polygon meshes, which are piecewise linear, are well suited for representing flat-faced objects, but are seldom satisfactory for curve-faced objects. Piecewise continuous parametric cubic curves and bicubic surfaces are widely used in computer graphics and CAD to represent curve-faced objects because they

- Permit multiple values for a single value of x or y
- Represent infinite slopes
- Provide local control, such that changing a control point affects only a local piece of the curve
- Can be made either to interpolate or to approximate control points, depending on application requirements
- Are computationally efficient
- Are easily transformed by transformation of control points.

Although we have discussed only cubics, higher- and lower-order surfaces also can be used. The texts mentioned previously generally develop parametric curves and surfaces for the general case of order n.

We have also discussed briefly some techniques for modeling natural phenomena; in particular, fractal and grammar-based approaches.

Exercises

9.1 Find the geometry matrix and basis matrix for the parametric representation of a straight line given in Eq. (9.11).

9.2 Show that, for a 2D curve $[x(t) \quad y(t)]^T$, G^1 continuity means that the geometric slope dy/dx is equal at the join points between segments.

9.3 Let $\gamma(t) = (t, t^2)$ for $0 \leq t \leq 1$, and let $\eta(t) = (2t + 1, t^3 + 4t + 1)$ for $0 \leq t \leq 1$. Notice that $\gamma(1) = (1, 1) = \eta(0)$, so γ and η join with C^0 continuity.

a. Plot $\eta(t)$ and $\gamma(t)$ for $0 \leq t \leq 1$.

b. Determine whether $\eta(t)$ and $\gamma(t)$ meet with C^1 continuity at the join point. (You will need to compute the vectors $\dfrac{d\gamma}{dt}(1)$ and $\dfrac{d\eta}{dt}(0)$ to check your answer.)

c. Determine whether $\eta(t)$ and $\gamma(t)$ meet with G^1 continuity at the join point.(You will need to check ratios from part(b) to check your answer.)

9.4 Consider the paths

$$\gamma(t) = (t^2 - 2t + 1, t^3 - 2t^2 + t) \quad \text{and} \quad \eta(t) = (t^2 + 1, t^3),$$

both defined on the interval $0 \leq t \leq 1$. The curves join, since $\gamma(1) = (1, 0) = \eta(0)$. Show that they meet with C^1 continuity, but not with G^1 continuity. Plot both curves as functions of t to demonstrate exactly why this behavior occurs.

9.5 Show that the two curves $\gamma(t) = (t^2 - 2t, t)$ and $\eta(t) = (t^2 + 1, t + 1)$ are both C^1 and G^1 continuous where they join at $\gamma(1) = \eta(0)$.

9.6 Analyze the effect on a B-spline of having in sequence four collinear control points.

9.7 Write a program to accept an arbitrary geometry matrix, basis matrix, and list of control points, and to draw the corresponding curve.

9.8 Find the conditions under which two joined Hermite curves have C^1 continuity.

9.9 Suppose that the equations relating the Hermite geometry to the Bézier geometry are of the form $R_1 = \beta(P_2 - P_1)$, $R_4 = \beta(P_4 - P_3)$. Consider the four equally spaced Bézier control points $P_1 = (0, 0)$, $P_2 = (1, 0)$, $P_3 = (2, 0)$, $P_4 = (3, 0)$. Show that, for the parametric curve $Q(t)$ to have constant velocity from P_1 to P_4, the coefficient β must be equal to 3.

9.10 Explain why Eq. (9.35) for uniform B-splines is written as $Q_i(t - t_i)$, whereas Eq. (9.37) for nonuniform B-splines is written as $Q_i(t)$.

9.11 Given a 2D nonuniform B-spline and an (x, y) value on the curve, write a program to find the corresponding value of t. Be sure to consider the possibility that, for a given value of x (or y), there may be multiple values of y (or x).

9.12 Apply the methodology used to derive Eqs. (9.49) and (9.50) for Hermite surfaces to derive Eq. (9.51) for Bézier surfaces.

9.13 Let $t_0 = 0$, $t_1 = 1$, $t_2 = 3$, $t_3 = 4$, $t_4 = 5$. Using these values, compute $B_{0,4}$ and each of the functions used in its definition. Then plot these functions on the interval $-3 \leq t \leq 8$.

9.14 Develop a program, similar to Example 9.2, for displaying Bézier surface patches using the framework of Prog. 9.2. Your program should offer the option of displaying the control points for a specified patch, so that the user can select any one of them (using a locator) and move it to a new location. The patch should then be redrawn to reflect the new geometric constraint. Since the locator input is 2D, how will you associate it with a 3D control point? You can specify your own patch geometry or use existing data, such as that for the teapot in Fig. 9.1. Complete data for the teapot are included in [CROW87].

10 Solid Modeling

The representations discussed in Chapter 9 allow us to describe curves and surfaces in 2D and 3D. Just as a set of 2D lines and curves does not need to describe the boundary of a closed area, a collection of 3D planes and surfaces does not necessarily bound a closed volume. In many applications, however, it is important to distinguish among the inside, outside, and surface of a 3D object and to be able to compute properties of the object that depend on this distinction. In CAD/CAM, for example, if a solid object can be modeled in a way that adequately captures its geometry, then a variety of useful operations can be performed before the object is manufactured. We may wish to determine whether two objects interfere with each other, for example, whether a robot arm will bump into objects in its environment, or whether a cutting tool will cut only the material it is intended to remove. In simulating physical mechanisms, such as a gear train, it may be important to compute properties such as volume and center of mass. Finite-element analysis is applied to solid models to determine response to factors such as stress and temperature through finite-element modeling. A satisfactory representation for a solid object may even make it possible to generate instructions automatically for computer-controlled machine tools to create that object or to rapidly prototype it using a technique such as stereolithography, a process which uses a laser beam to form a hardened object out of a bath of molten plastic. In addition, some graphical techniques, such as modeling refractive transparency, depend on being able to determine where a beam of light enters and exits a solid object. These applications are all examples of **solid modeling**. The need to model objects as solids has resulted in the development of a variety of specialized ways to represent them. This chapter provides a brief introduction to these representations.

10.1 REPRESENTING SOLIDS

A representation's ability to encode things that *look* like solids does not by itself mean that the representation is adequate for representing solids. Consider how we have represented objects so far, as collections of straight lines, curves, polygons, and surfaces. Do the lines of Fig. 10.1(a) define a solid cube? If each set of four lines on each side of the object is assumed to bound a square face, then the figure is a cube. However, there is nothing in the representation given that requires the lines to be interpreted this way. For example, the same set of lines would be used to draw the figure if any or all of the faces were missing. What if we decide that each planar loop of connected lines in the drawing by definition determines a polygonal face? Then, Fig. 10.1(b) would consist of all of the faces of Fig. 10.1(a), plus an extra "dangling" face, producing an object that does not bound a volume. As we shall see in Section 10.5, some extra constraints are needed if we want to ensure that a representation of this sort models only solids.

Requicha [REQU80] provides a list of the properties desirable in a solid representation scheme. The **domain** of representation should be large enough to allow a useful set of physical objects to be represented. Ideally, the representation should be *unambiguous*: There should be no question as to what is being represented, and a given representation should correspond to one and only one solid, unlike the one in Fig. 10.1(a). An unambiguous representation is also said to be **complete**. A representation is *unique* if it can be used to encode any given solid in only one way. If a representation can ensure uniqueness, then operations such as testing two objects for equality are easy. An *accurate* representation allows an object to be represented without approximation. Much as a graphics system that can draw only straight lines forces us to create approximations of smooth curves, some solid modeling representations describe many objects as approximations. Ideally, a representation

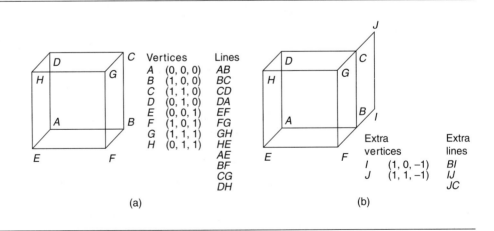

	Vertices	Lines
A	(0, 0, 0)	AB
B	(1, 0, 0)	BC
C	(1, 1, 0)	CD
D	(0, 1, 0)	DA
E	(0, 0, 1)	EF
F	(1, 0, 1)	FG
G	(1, 1, 1)	GH
H	(0, 1, 1)	HE
		AE
		BF
		CG
		DH

(a)

	Extra vertices	Extra lines
I	(1, 0, –1)	BI
J	(1, 1, –1)	IJ
		JC

(b)

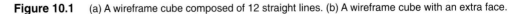

Figure 10.1   (a) A wireframe cube composed of 12 straight lines. (b) A wireframe cube with an extra face.

scheme should make it *impossible to create an invalid representation* (i.e., one that does not correspond to a solid), such as Fig. 10.1(b). In addition, it should be *easy to create a valid representation,* typically with the aid of an interactive solid modeling system. We would like objects to maintain **closure** under rotation, translation, and other operations. Thus, performing these operations on valid solids should yield only valid solids. A representation should be *compact* to save space, which in turn may save communication time in a distributed system. Finally, a representation should allow the use of *efficient* algorithms for computing desired physical properties and, most important for us, for creating pictures.

Designing a representation with all these properties is difficult indeed, and compromises are often necessary. As we discuss the major representations in use today, our emphasis will be on providing enough detail to be able to understand how these representations can be interfaced to graphics software. More detail, with an emphasis on the solid modeling aspects, can be found in [REQU80; MORT85; MÄNT88].

10.2 REGULARIZED BOOLEAN SET OPERATIONS

No matter how we represent objects, we would like to be able to combine them in order to make new ones. One of the most intuitive and popular methods for combining objects is by **Boolean set operations,** such as union, difference, and intersection, as shown in Fig. 10.2. These operations are the 3D equivalents of the familiar 2D Boolean operations. Applying an ordinary Boolean set operation to two solid objects, however, does not necessarily yield a solid object. For example, the ordinary intersection of two cubes that meet at only a single vertex is a point.

Rather than using the ordinary Boolean set operators, we will instead use the **regularized Boolean set operators** [REQU77], denoted ∪*, ∩*, and −*, and defined such that operations on solids always yield solids. For example, the regularized Boolean intersection of two cubes that meet at only a single vertex is the null object.

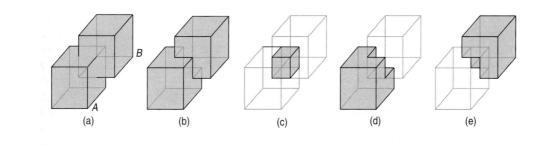

Figure 10.2   Boolean operations. (a) Objects *A* and *B*, (b) *A* ∪ *B*, (c) *A* ∩ *B*, (d) *A* − *B*, and (e) *B* − *A*.

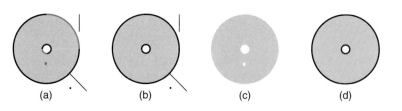

Figure 10.3 Regularizing an object. (a) The object is defined by interior points, shown in light gray, and boundary points. Boundary points that are part of the object are shown in black; the rest of the boundary points are shown in dark gray. The object has dangling and unattached points and lines, and there is a boundary point in the interior that is not part of the object. (b) Closure of the object. All boundary points are part of the object. The boundary point embedded in the interior of part (a) is now part of the interior. (c) Interior of the object. Dangling and unattached points and lines have been eliminated. (d) Regularization of the object is the closure of its interior.

To explore the difference between ordinary and regularized operators, we can consider any object to be defined by a set of points, partitioned into interior points and boundary points, as shown in Fig. 10.3(a). **Boundary points** are those points whose distance from the object and the object's complement is zero. Boundary points need not be part of the object. A **closed set** contains all its boundary points, whereas an **open set** contains none. The union of a set with the set of its boundary points is known as the set's **closure**, as shown in Fig. 10.3(b), which is itself a closed set. The **boundary** of a closed set is the set of its boundary points, whereas the **interior**, shown in Fig. 10.3(c), consists of all of the set's other points, and thus is the complement of the boundary with respect to the object. The **regularization** of a set is defined as the closure of the set's interior points. Figure 10.3(d) shows the closure of the object in Fig. 10.3(c) and, therefore, the regularization of the object in Fig. 10.3(a). A set that is equal to its own regularization is known as a **regular set**. Note that a regular set can contain no boundary point that is not adjacent to some interior point; thus, it can have no "dangling" boundary points, lines, or surfaces. We can define each regularized Boolean set operator in terms of the corresponding ordinary Boolean set operator as

$$A \; op^* \; B = \text{closure}(\text{interior}(A \; op \; B)), \tag{10.1}$$

where *op* is one of ∪, ∩, or −. The regularized Boolean set operators produce only regular sets when applied to regular sets.

We now compare the ordinary and regularized Boolean set operations as performed on regular sets. Consider the two objects of Fig. 10.4(a), positioned as shown in Fig. 10.4(b). The ordinary Boolean intersection of two objects contains the intersection of the interior and boundary of each object with the interior and boundary of the other, as shown in Fig. 10.4(c). In contrast, the regularized Boolean intersection of two objects, shown in Fig. 10.4(d), contains the intersection of their interiors and the intersection of the interior of each with the boundary of the other, but only a subset of the intersection of their boundaries. The criterion used to define this subset determines how regularized Boolean intersection differs from

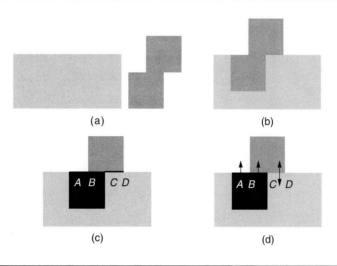

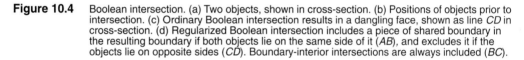

Figure 10.4   Boolean intersection. (a) Two objects, shown in cross-section. (b) Positions of objects prior to intersection. (c) Ordinary Boolean intersection results in a dangling face, shown as line *CD* in cross-section. (d) Regularized Boolean intersection includes a piece of shared boundary in the resulting boundary if both objects lie on the same side of it (*AB*), and excludes it if the objects lie on opposite sides (*CD*). Boundary–interior intersections are always included (*BC*).

ordinary Boolean intersection, in which all parts of the intersection of the boundaries are included.

Intuitively, a piece of the boundary–boundary intersection is included in the regularized Boolean intersection if and only if the interiors of both objects lie on the same side of this piece of shared boundary. Since the interior points of both objects that are directly adjacent to that piece of boundary are in the intersection, the boundary piece must also be included to maintain closure. Consider the case of a piece of shared boundary that lies in coplanar faces of two polyhedra. Determining whether the interiors lie on the same side of a shared boundary is simple if both objects are defined such that their surface normals point outward (or inward). The interiors are on the same side if the normals point in the same direction. Thus, segment *AB* in Fig. 10.4(d) is included. Remember that those parts of one object's boundary that intersect with the other object's interior, such as segment *BC*, are always included.

Consider what happens when the interiors of the objects lie on opposite sides of the shared boundary, as is the case with segment *CD*. In such cases, none of the interior points adjacent to the boundary are included in the intersection. Thus, the piece of shared boundary is not adjacent to any interior points of the resulting object and therefore is not included in the regularized intersection. This additional restriction on which pieces of shared boundary are included ensures that the resulting object is a regular set. The surface normal of each face of the resulting object's boundary is the surface normal of whichever surface(s) contributed that part of the boundary. (As we shall see in Chapter 14, surface normals are important in shading objects.) Having determined which faces lie in the boundary, we include an edge or

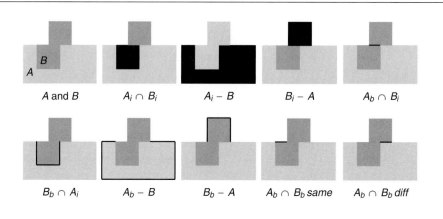

Figure 10.5   Ordinary Boolean operations on subsets of two objects.

vertex of the boundary–boundary intersection in the boundary of the intersection if the edge or vertex is adjacent to one of these faces.

The results of each regularized operator may be defined in terms of the ordinary operators applied to the boundaries and interiors of the objects. Table 10.1 shows how the regularized operators are defined for any objects A and B; Fig. 10.5 shows the results of performing the operations. A_b and A_i are A's boundary and interior, respectively. $A_b \cap B_b$ *same* is that part of the boundary shared by A and B for which A_i and B_i lie on the same side. This result is the case for some point b on the shared boundary if at least one point i adjacent to it is a member of both A_i and B_i. $A_b \cap B_b$ *diff* is that part of the boundary shared by A and B for which A_i and B_i lie on opposite sides. This is true for b if it is adjacent to no such point i. Each regularized operator is defined by the union of the sets associated with those rows that have a bullet (•) in the operator's column.

Table 10.1

Regularized Boolean Set Operations

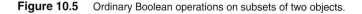

Set	$A \cup^* B$	$A \cap^* B$	$A -^* B$
$A_i \cap B_i$	•	•	
$A_i - B$	•		•
$B_i - A$	•		
$A_b \cap B_i$		•	
$B_b \cap A_i$		•	•
$A_b - B$	•		•
$B_b - A$	•		
$A_b \cap B_b$ *same*	•	•	
$A_b \cap B_b$ *diff*			•

Note that, in all cases, each piece of the resulting object's boundary is on the boundary of one or both of the original objects. When computing $A \cup^* B$ or $A \cap^* B$, the surface normal of a face of the result is inherited from the surface normal of the corresponding face of one or both original objects. In the case of $A -^* B$, however, the surface normal of each face of the result at which B has been used to excavate A must point in the *opposite* direction from B's surface normal at that face. This corresponds to the boundary pieces $A_b \cap B_b$ *diff* and $B_b \cap A_i$. Alternatively, $A -^* B$ may be rewritten as $A \cap^* \bar{B}$. We can obtain $\bar{B}$ (the complement of B) by complementing B's interior and reversing the normals of its boundary.

The regularized Boolean set operators have been used as a user–interface technique to build complex objects from simple ones in most of the representation schemes we shall discuss. These operators are also included explicitly in one of the schemes, constructive solid geometry. In the following sections, we shall describe a variety of ways to represent solid objects unambiguously.

10.3 PRIMITIVE INSTANCING

In **primitive instancing**, the modeling system defines a set of primitive 3D solid shapes that are relevant to the application area. These primitives are typically parameterized not just in terms of the transformations of Chapter 7, but on other properties as well. For example, one primitive object may be a regular pyramid with a user-defined number of faces meeting at the apex. Primitive instances are similar to parameterized objects, such as the menus of Chapter 2, except that the objects are solids. A parameterized primitive may be thought of as defining a family of parts whose members vary in a few parameters, an important CAD concept known as **group technology**. Primitive instancing is often used for relatively complex objects, such as gears or bolts, that are tedious to define in terms of Boolean combinations of simpler objects, yet are readily characterized by a few high-level

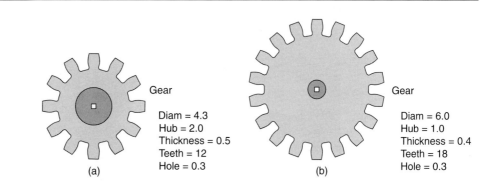

Gear

Diam = 4.3
Hub = 2.0
Thickness = 0.5
Teeth = 12
Hole = 0.3

(a)

Gear

Diam = 6.0
Hub = 1.0
Thickness = 0.4
Teeth = 18
Hole = 0.3

(b)

Figure 10.6   Two gears defined by primitive instancing.

parameters. For example, a gear may be parameterized by its diameter or number of teeth, as shown in Fig. 10.6.

Although we can build up a hierarchy of primitive instances, each leaf-node instance is still a separately defined object. In primitive instancing, no provisions are made for combining objects to form a new higher-level object, using, for example, the regularized Boolean set operations. Thus, the only way to create a new kind of object is to write the code that defines it. Similarly, the routines that draw the objects or determine their mass properties must be written individually for each primitive.

10.4 SWEEP REPRESENTATIONS

Sweeping an object along a trajectory through space defines a new object, called a **sweep**. The simplest kind of sweep is defined by a 2D area swept along a linear path normal to the plane of the area to create a volume. This process is known as a **translational sweep**, or **extrusion**, and is a natural way to represent objects made by extruding metal or plastic through a die with the desired cross-section. In these simple cases, each sweep's volume is simply the swept object's area times the length of the sweep. Simple extensions involve scaling the cross-section as it is swept to produce a tapered object or sweeping the cross-section along a linear path that is not normal to it. **Rotational sweeps** are defined by rotating an area about an

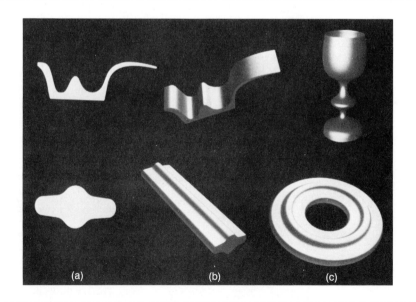

Figure 10.7   Sweeps of (a) 2D areas are used to define (b) translational sweeps and (c) rotational sweeps. (Created using the Alpha_1 modeling system. Courtesy of the University of Utah.)

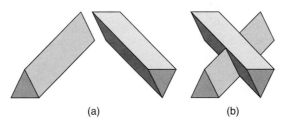

(a)   (b)

Figure 10.8   (a) Two simple sweeps of 2D objects (triangles). (b) The union of the sweeps shown in (a) is not itself a simple sweep of a 2D object.

axis. Figure 10.7 shows two objects and simple translational and rotational sweeps generated using them.

The object being swept does not need to be 2D. Sweeps of solids are useful in modeling the region swept out by a machine-tool cutting head or robot following a path. Sweeps whose generating area or volume changes in size, shape, or orientation as they are swept and that follow an arbitrary curved trajectory are called **general sweeps**. General sweeps of 2D cross-sections are known as **generalized cylinders** in computer vision [BINF71] and are usually modeled as parameterized 2D cross-sections swept at right angles along an arbitrary curve. General sweeps are particularly difficult to model efficiently. For example, the trajectory and object shape may make the swept object intersect itself, making volume calculations complicated. As well, general sweeps do not always generate solids. For example, sweeping a 2D area in its own plane generates another 2D area.

In general, it is difficult to apply regularized Boolean set operations to sweeps without first converting to some other representation. Even simple sweeps are not closed under regularized Boolean set operations. For example, the union of two simple sweeps is in general not a simple sweep, as shown in Fig. 10.8. Despite problems of closure and calculation, however, sweeps are a natural and intuitive way to construct a variety of objects. For this reason, many solid modeling systems allow users to construct objects as sweeps, but store the objects in one of the other representations that we shall discuss.

10.5 BOUNDARY REPRESENTATIONS

Boundary representations (also known as **b-reps**) resemble the naive representations that we discussed in Section 10.1, in that they describe an object in terms of its surface boundaries: vertices, edges, and faces. Some b-reps are restricted to planar, polygonal boundaries, and may even require faces to be convex polygons or triangles. Determining what constitutes a face can be particularly difficult if curved surfaces are allowed, as shown in Fig. 10.9. Curved faces are often approximated with polygons. Alternatively, curved surfaces can also be represented as surface patches if the algorithms that process the representation can treat the resulting intersection curves, which will, in general, be of higher order than the original surfaces. B-reps grew out of the simple vector representations used in earlier chapters and are used in many current modeling systems. Because of their prevalence in graphics, a number of efficient techniques have been developed to create smooth shaded pictures of polygonal objects; many of these techniques are discussed in Chapter 14.

Many b-rep systems support only solids whose boundaries are **2-manifolds**. By definition, every point on a 2-manifold has some arbitrarily small neighborhood of points around it that can be considered topologically the same as a disk in the plane. This means that there is a continuous one-to-one correspondence between the neighborhood of points and the disk, as shown in Fig. 10.10(a) and (b). For example, if more than two faces share an edge, as in Fig. 10.10(c), any neighborhood of a point on that edge contains points from each of those faces. It is intuitively obvious that there is no continuous one-to-one correspondence between this neighborhood and a disk in the plane, although the mathematical proof is by no means trivial. Thus, the surface in Fig. 10.10(c) is not a 2-manifold. Although some current systems do not have this restriction, we limit our discussion of b-reps to 2-manifolds, except where we state otherwise.

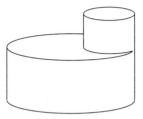

Figure 10.9
How many faces does this object have?

10.5.1 Polyhedra and Euler's Formula

A **polyhedron** is a solid that is bounded by a set of polygons whose edges are each a member of an even number of polygons (exactly two polygons in the case of 2-manifolds) and that satisfies some additional constraints (discussed later). A **simple polyhedron** is one that can be deformed into a sphere—that is, a polyhedron that, unlike a torus, has no holes. The b-rep of a simple polyhedron satisfies Euler's formula, which expresses an invariant relationship among the number of vertices, edges, and faces of a simple polyhedron:

$$V - E + F = 2, \tag{10.2}$$

where V is the number of vertices, E is the number of edges, and F is the number of faces. Figure 10.11 shows some simple polyhedra and their numbers of vertices,

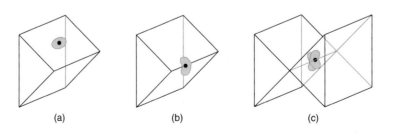

(a) (b) (c)

Figure 10.10 On a 2-manifold, each point, shown as a black dot, has a neighborhood of surrounding points that is a topological disk, shown in gray in (a) and (b). (c) If an object is not a 2-manifold, then it has points that do not have a neighborhood that is a topological disk.

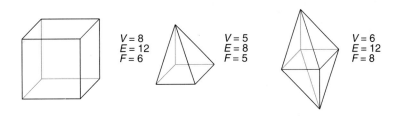

Figure 10.11   Some simple polyhedra with their V, E, and F values. In each case $V - E + F = 2$.

edges, and faces. Note that the formula still applies if curved edges and nonplanar faces are allowed. Euler's formula by itself states necessary but not sufficient conditions for an object to be a simple polyhedron. One can construct objects that satisfy the formula but do not bound a volume, by attaching one or more dangling faces or edges to an otherwise valid solid, as in Fig. 10.1(b). Additional constraints are needed to guarantee that the object is a solid: Each edge must connect two vertices and be shared by exactly two faces, at least three edges must meet at each vertex, and faces must not interpenetrate.

A generalization of Euler's formula applies to 2-manifolds that have faces with holes:

$$V - E + F - H = 2(C - G), \tag{10.3}$$

where H is the number of holes in the faces, G is the number of holes that pass through the object, and C is the number of separate components (parts) of the object, as shown in Fig. 10.12. If an object has a single component, its G is known as its **genus;** if it has multiple components, then its G is the sum of the genera of its components. As before, additional constraints are also needed to guarantee that the objects are solids.

Baumgart introduced the notion of a set of **Euler operators** that operate on objects satisfying Euler's formula in order to transform the objects into new

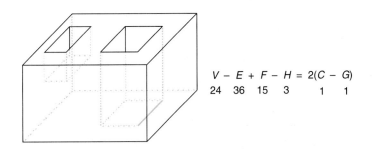

$$
\begin{array}{cccccc}
V & - & E & + & F & - & H & = & 2(C & - & G) \\
24 & & 36 & & 15 & & 3 & & 1 & & 1
\end{array}
$$

Figure 10.12   A polyhedron classified according to Eq. (10.3), with two holes in its top face and one hole in its bottom face.

objects that obey the formula as well, by adding and removing vertices, edges, and faces[BAUM74]. Braid, Hillyard, and Stroud [BRAI78] show how a small number of Euler operators can be composed to transform objects, provided that intermediate objects are not required to be valid solids, whereas Mäntylä [MÄNT88] proves that all valid b-reps can be constructed by a finite sequence of Euler operators. Other operators that do not affect the number of vertices, edges, or faces may be defined that *tweak* an object by moving the existing vertices, edges, or faces.

Perhaps the simplest possible b-rep is a list of polygonal faces, each represented by a list of vertex coordinates. To represent the direction in which each polygon faces, we list a polygon's vertices in clockwise order, as seen from the exterior of the solid. To avoid replicating coordinates shared by faces, we may instead represent each vertex of a face by an index into a list of coordinates. In this representation, edges are represented implicitly by the pairs of adjacent vertices in the polygon vertex lists. Edges may instead be represented explicitly as pairs of vertices, with each face now defined as a list of indices into the list of edges. These representations were discussed in more detail in Section 9.1.1.

10.5.2 Boolean Set Operations

B-reps may be combined, using the regularized Boolean set operators, to create new b-reps [REQU85]. Sarraga [SARR83] and Miller [MILL87] discuss algorithms that determine the intersections between quadric surfaces. Algorithms for combining polyhedral objects are presented in [TURN84; REQU85; PUTN86; LAID86], and Thibault and Naylor [THIB87] describe a method based on the binary space-partitioning tree representation of solids discussed in Section 10.6.4.

One approach [LAID86] is to inspect the polygons of both objects, splitting them if necessary to ensure that the intersection of a vertex, edge, or face of one object with any vertex, edge, or face of another is a vertex, edge, or face of both. The polygons of each object are then classified relative to the other object to determine whether they lie inside, outside, or on its boundary. Referring back to Table 10.1, we note that since this is a b-rep, we are concerned with only the last six rows, each of which represents some part of one or both of the original object boundaries, A_b and B_b. After splitting, each polygon of one object is either wholly inside the other object ($A_b \cap B_i$ or $B_b \cap A_i$), wholly outside the other object ($A_b - B$ or $B_b - A$), or part of the shared boundary ($A_b \cap B_b$ *same* or $A_b \cap B_b$ *diff*).

A polygon may be classified by the ray-casting technique discussed in Section 13.4.1. Here, we construct a vector in the direction of the polygon's surface normal from a point in the polygon's interior, and then find the closest polygon that intersects the vector in the other object. If no polygon is intersected, the original polygon is outside the other object. If the closest intersecting polygon is coplanar with the original polygon, then this intersection is a boundary–boundary one, and comparing polygon normals indicates what kind of intersection it is ($A_b \cap B_b$ *same* or $A_b \cap B_b$ *diff*). Otherwise, the dot product of the two polygons' normals is inspected. A positive dot product indicates that the original polygon is inside the other object, whereas a negative dot product indicates that the original polygon is outside. A zero dot product occurs if the vector is in the plane of the intersected polygon; in this case, the vector is perturbed slightly and is intersected again with the other object's polygons.

Vertex-adjacency information can be used to avoid the overhead of classifying each polygon in this way. If a polygon is adjacent to (i.e., shares vertices with) a classified polygon and does not meet the surface of the other object, then the polygon is assigned the same classification. All vertices on the common boundary between objects can be marked during the initial polygon-splitting phase. Whether a polygon meets the other object's surface can be determined by checking whether it has boundary vertices.

Each polygon's classification determines whether the polygon is retained or discarded in the operation creating the composite object, as described in Section 10.2. For example, in forming the union, the operation discards any polygon belonging to one object that is inside the other object. The operation retains any polygon from either object that is not inside the other, except in the case of coplanar polygons. Coplanar polygons are discarded if they have opposite surface normals, and only one of a pair is retained if the directions of the surface normals are the same. Deciding which polygon to retain is important if the objects are made of different materials. Although $A \cup^* B$ has the same geometric meaning as $B \cup^* A$, the two may have visibly different results in this case, so the operation may be defined to favor one of its operands in the case of coplanar polygons.

10.6 SPATIAL-PARTITIONING REPRESENTATIONS

In **spatial-partitioning** representations, a solid is decomposed into a collection of adjoining, nonintersecting solids that are more primitive than, although not necessarily of the same type as, the original solid. Primitives may vary in type, size, position, parameterization, and orientation, much like the different-shaped blocks in a child's block set. How far we decompose objects depends on how primitive the solids must be in order to perform readily the operations of interest.

10.6.1 Cell Decomposition

One of the most general forms of spatial partitioning is called **cell decomposition**. Each cell-decomposition system defines a set of primitive cells that are typically parameterized and are often curved. Cell decomposition differs from primitive instancing in that we can compose more complex objects from simple, primitive ones in a bottom-up fashion by "gluing" them together. The *glue* operation can be thought of as a restricted form of union in which the objects must not intersect. Further restrictions on gluing cells often require that two cells share a single point, edge, or face. Although cell-decomposition representation of an object is unambiguous, it is not necessarily unique, as shown in Fig. 10.13. Cell decompositions are also difficult to validate, since each pair of cells must potentially be tested for intersection. Nevertheless, cell decomposition is an important representation for use in finite-element analysis.

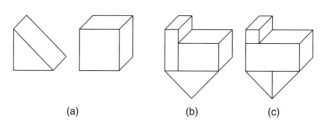

(a)   (b)   (c)

Figure 10.13   The cells shown in (a) may be transformed to construct the same object shown in (b) and (c) in different ways. Even a single cell type is enough to cause ambiguity.

10.6.2 Spatial-Occupancy Enumeration

Spatial-occupancy enumeration is a special case of cell decomposition in which the solid is decomposed into identical cells arranged in a fixed, regular grid. These cells are often called **voxels** (volume elements), in analogy to pixels. Figure 10.14 shows an object represented by spatial-occupancy enumeration. The most common cell type is the cube, and the representation of space as a regular array of cubes is called a **cuberille**. When representing an object using spatial-occupancy enumeration, we control only the presence or absence of a single cell at each position in the grid. To represent an object, we need only to decide which cells are occupied and which are not. The object can thus be encoded by a unique and unambiguous list of occupied cells. It is easy to find out whether a cell is inside or outside of the solid, and determining whether two objects are adjacent is simple as well. Spatial-occupancy enumeration is often used in biomedical applications to represent volumetric data obtained from sources such as computerized axial tomography (CAT) scans.

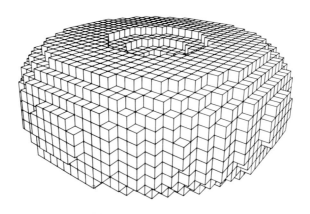

Figure 10.14   Torus represented by spatial-occupancy enumeration. [By A.H.J. Christensen, SIGGRAPH '80 Conference Proceedings, *Computer Graphics* (14)3, July 1980. Courtesy of Association for Computing Machinery, Inc.]

For all of its advantages, however, spatial-occupancy enumeration has a number of obvious failings that parallel those of representing a 2D shape by a 1-bit-deep bitmap. There is no concept of *partial* occupancy. Thus, many solids can be only approximated; the torus of Fig. 10.14 is an example. If the cells are cubes, then the only objects that can be represented exactly are those whose faces are parallel to the cube sides and whose vertices fall exactly on the grid. Like pixels in a bitmap, cells may, in principle, be made as small as desired to increase the accuracy of the representation. Space becomes an important issue, however, since up to n^3 occupied cells are needed to represent an object at a resolution of n voxels in each of three dimensions.

10.6.3 Octrees

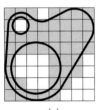

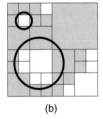

(a)

(b)

Figure 10.15

An object represented using (a) spatial-occupancy enumeration to derive (b) a quadtree.

Octrees are a hierarchical variant of spatial-occupancy enumeration, designed to address that approach's demanding storage requirements. Octrees in turn are derived from **quadtrees,** a 2D representation format used to encode images. As detailed in Samet's comprehensive survey [SAME84], both representations appear to have been discovered independently by a number of researchers: quadtrees in the late 1960s to early 1970s [e.g., WARN69; KLIN71] and octrees in the late 1970s to early 1980s [e.g., HUNT78; REDD78; JACK80; MEAG80; MEAG82].

The fundamental idea behind both the quadtree and the octree is the divide-and-conquer power of binary subdivision. A quadtree is derived by successively subdividing a 2D plane in both dimensions to form quadrants, as shown in Fig. 10.15. When a quadtree is used to represent an area in the plane, each quadrant may be full, partially full, or empty (also called black, gray, and white, respectively), depending on how much of the quadrant intersects the area. A partially full quadrant is recursively subdivided into subquadrants. Subdivision continues until all quadrants are homogeneous (either full or empty) or until a predetermined cutoff depth is reached. Whenever four sibling quadrants are uniformly full or empty, they are deleted and their partially full parent is replaced with a full or empty node. (A bottom-up approach can be used instead to avoid this deletion and merging process [SAME90b].) In Fig. 10.15, any partially full node at the cutoff depth is classified as full. The successive subdivisions can be represented as a tree with partially full quadrants at the internal nodes and full and empty quadrants at the leaves, as shown in Fig. 10.16. This idea can be compared to the Warnock area-subdivision algorithm discussed in Section 13.5.2. If the criteria for classifying a node as homogeneous are relaxed to allow nodes that are above or below some threshold to be classified as full or empty, then the representation becomes more compact, although less accurate. The octree is similar to the quadtree, except that the octree's three dimensions are recursively subdivided into octants, as shown in Fig. 10.17.

Quadrants are often referred to by the numbers 0 to 3, and octants by numbers from 0 to 7. Since no standard numbering scheme has been devised, mnemonic names are also used. Quadrants are named according to their compass direction relative to the center of their parent: NW, NE, SW, and SE. Octants are named

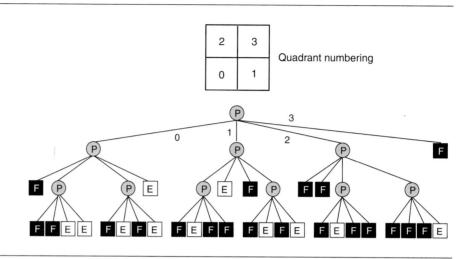

Figure 10.16   Quadtree data structure for the object in Fig. 10.15. F = full, P = partially full. E = empty.

similarly, distinguishing between left (L) and right (R), up (U) and down (D), and front (F) and back (B): LUF, LUB, LDF, LDB, RUF, RUB, RDF, and RDB.

With the exception of a few worst cases, it can be shown that the number of nodes in a quadtree or octree representation of an object is proportional to the object's perimeter or surface, respectively [HUNT78; MEAG80]. This relation holds because node subdivision arises only from the need to represent the boundary of the object being encoded. The only internal nodes that are split are those through which part of the boundary passes. Thus, any operation on one of these data structures that is linear in the number of nodes it contains also executes in time proportional to the size of its perimeter or area.

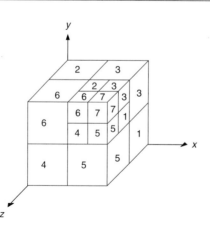

Figure 10.17   Octree enumeration. Octant zero is not visible.

Boolean set operations and transformations. Much work has been done on developing efficient algorithms for storing and processing quadtrees and octrees [SAME84; SAME90a; SAME90b]. For example, Boolean set operations are straightforward for both quadtrees and octrees [HUNT79]. To compute the union or intersection U of two trees, S and T, we traverse both trees top-down in parallel.

Figure 10.18 shows the operations for quadtrees; the generalization to octrees is straightforward. Each matching pair of nodes is examined. Consider the case of union. If either of the nodes in the pair is black, then a corresponding black node is added to U. If one of the pair's nodes is white, then the corresponding node is created in U with the value of the other node in the pair. If both nodes of the pair are gray, then a gray node is added to U, and the algorithm is applied recursively to the pair's children. In this last case, the children of the new node in U must be inspected after the algorithm has been applied to them. If they are all black, they are deleted and their parent in U is changed from gray to black.

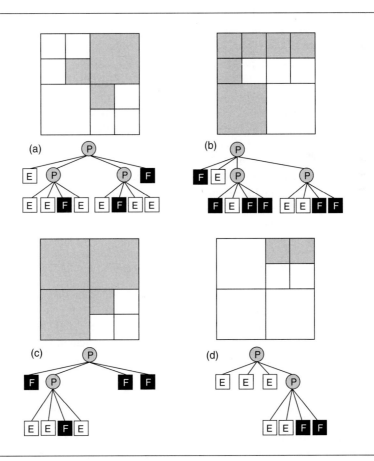

Figure 10.18 Performing Boolean set operations on quadtrees. (a) Object S and its quadtree. (b) Object T and its quadtree. (c) $S \cup T$. (d) $S \cap T$

It is easy to perform simple transformations on quadtrees and octrees. For example, rotation about an axis by multiples of 90° is accomplished by recursively rotating the children at each level. Scaling by powers of 2 and reflections are also straightforward. Translations are somewhat more complex, as are general transformations. In addition, as in spatial-occupancy enumeration in general, the problem of aliasing under general transformations is severe.

Neighbor finding. One important operation in quadtrees and octrees is finding a node's *neighbor*, that is, finding a node that is adjacent to the original node (sharing a face, edge, or vertex) and of equal or greater size. A quadtree node has neighbors in eight possible directions. Its N, S, E, W neighbors are neighbors along a common edge, whereas its NW, NE, SW, and SE neighbors are neighbors along a common vertex. An octree node has neighbors in 26 possible directions: 6 neighbors along a face, 12 neighbors along an edge, and 8 neighbors along a vertex.

Samet [SAME89a] describes a way to find a node's neighbor in a specified direction. The method starts at the original node and ascends the quadtree or octree until the first common ancestor of the original node and neighbor is found. Traversal then continues downward to find the desired neighbor. Two problems must be solved efficiently here: finding the common ancestor and determining which of its descendants is the neighbor. The simplest case is finding an octree node's neighbor in the direction d of one of its faces: L, R, U, D, F, or B. As we ascend the tree starting at the original node, the common ancestor will be the first node that is not reached from a child on the node's d side. For example, if the search is for an L neighbor, then the first common ancestor is the first node that is not reached from an LUF, LUB, LDF, or LDB child. This is true because a node that has been reached from one of these children cannot have any child that is left of (is an L neighbor of) the original node. When the common ancestor is found, its subtree is descended in a mirror image of the path from the original node to the ancestor, reflected about the common border. Only part of the reflected path is followed if the neighbor is larger than the original node.

10.6.4 Binary Space-Partitioning Trees

Octrees recursively divide space by planes that are always mutually perpendicular and that bisect all three dimensions at each level of the tree. In contrast, **binary space-partitioning (BSP) trees** recursively divide space into pairs of subspaces, each separated by a plane of arbitrary orientation and position. The binary-tree data structure created was originally used in determining visible surfaces in graphics, as described in Section 13.5. Thibault and Naylor [THIB87] later introduced the use of BSP trees to represent arbitrary polyhedra. Each internal node of the BSP tree is associated with a plane and has two child pointers, one for each side of the plane. Assuming that normals point out of an object, the left child is behind or inside the plane, whereas the right child is in front of or outside the plane. If the half-space on a side of the plane is subdivided further, then its child is the root of a subtree; if the half-space is homogeneous, then its child is a leaf, representing a region either entirely inside or entirely outside the polyhedron. These homogeneous

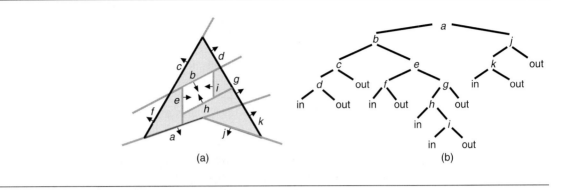

(a)

(b)

Figure 10.19   A BSP tree representation in 2D. (a) A concave polygon bounded by black lines. Lines defining the half-spaces are dark gray, and *in* cells are light gray. (b) The BSP tree.

regions are called *in* cells and *out* cells. To account for the limited numerical precision with which operations are performed, each node also has a *thickness* associated with its plane. Any point lying within this tolerance of the plane is considered to be *on* the plane.

The subdivision concept behind BSP trees, like that underlying octrees and quadtrees, is dimension-independent. Thus, Fig. 10.19(a) shows a concave polygon in 2D, bordered by black lines. *In* cells are shaded light gray, and the lines defining the half-spaces are shown in dark gray, with normals pointing to the outside. The corresponding BSP tree is shown in Fig. 10.19(b). In 2D, the *in* and *out* regions form a convex polygonal tessellation of the plane; in 3D, the *in* and *out* regions form a convex polyhedral tessellation of 3-space. Thus, a BSP tree can represent an arbitrary concave solid with holes as a union of convex *in* regions.

Consider the task of determining whether a point lies inside, outside, or on a solid, a problem known as **point classification** [TILO80]. A BSP tree may be used to classify a point by filtering that point down the tree, beginning at the root. At each node, the point is substituted into the node's plane equation and is passed recursively to the left child if it lies behind (inside) the plane, or to the right child if it lies in front of (outside) the plane. If the node is a leaf, then the point is given the leaf's value, either *out* or *in*. If the point lies on a node's plane, then it is passed to both children, and the classifications are compared. If they are the same, then the point receives that value; if they are different, then the point lies on the boundary between *out* and *in* regions and is classified as *on*. This approach can be extended to classify lines and polygons. Unlike a point, however, a line or polygon may lie partially on both sides of a plane. Therefore, at each node whose plane intersects the line or polygon, the line or polygon must be divided (clipped) into those parts that are in front of, in back of, or on the plane, and the parts classified separately.

Thibault and Naylor describe algorithms for building a BSP tree from a b-rep, for performing Boolean set operations to combine a BSP tree with a b-rep, and for determining those polygonal pieces that lie on a BSP tree's boundary [THIB87]. These algorithms operate on BSP trees whose nodes are each associated with a list of polygons embedded in the node's plane. Polygons are inserted into the tree using a variant of the BSP tree-building algorithm sketched in Section 13.5.

Although BSP trees provide an elegant and simple representation, polygons are subdivided as the tree is constructed and as Boolean set operations are performed, making the notation potentially less compact than other representations. By taking advantage of the BSP tree's inherent dimension-independence, however, we can develop a closed Boolean algebra for 3D BSP trees that recursively relies on representing polygons as 2D trees, edges as 1D trees, and points as 0D trees [NAYL90].

10.7 CONSTRUCTIVE SOLID GEOMETRY

In **constructive solid geometry** (CSG), simple primitives are combined by means of regularized Boolean set operators that are included directly in the representation. An object is stored as a tree with operators at the internal nodes and simple primitives at the leaves (Fig. 10.20). Some nodes represent Boolean operators, whereas others perform translation, rotation, and scaling, much like the hierarchies of Chapter 7. Since Boolean operations are not, in general, commutative, the edges of the tree are ordered.

To determine physical properties or to make pictures, we must be able to combine the properties of the leaves to obtain the properties of the root. The general processing strategy is a depth-first tree walk up the tree, as in Chapter 7, to combine nodes from the leaves. The complexity of this task depends on the representation in which the leaf objects are stored and on whether a full representation of the composite object at the tree's root must actually be produced. For example, the

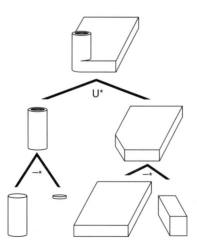

Figure 10.20   An object defined by CSG and its tree.

regularized Boolean set operation algorithms for b-reps, discussed in Section 10.5, combine the b-reps of two nodes to create a third b-rep and are difficult to implement. The much simpler CSG algorithm, discussed in Chapter 15 of [FOLE90], on the other hand, produces a picture by processing the representations of the leaves without explicitly combining them.

In some implementations, the primitives are simple solids, such as cubes or spheres, ensuring that all regularized combinations are valid solids as well. In other systems, primitives include half-spaces, which themselves are not bounded solids. For example, a cube can be defined as the intersection of six half-spaces, or a finite cylinder as an infinite cylinder that is capped off at the top and bottom by planar half-spaces. Using half-spaces introduces a validity problem, since not all combinations produce solids. Half-spaces are useful, however, for operations such as slicing an object by a plane, an operation that might otherwise be performed by using the face of another solid object. Without half-spaces, extra overhead is introduced, since the regularized Boolean set operations must be performed with the full object doing the slicing, even if only a single slicing face is of interest.

We can think of the cell-decomposition and spatial-occupancy enumeration techniques as special cases of CSG in which the only operator is the implicit glue operator: the union of two objects that may touch but must have disjoint interiors (i.e., the objects must have a null regularized Boolean intersection).

CSG does not provide a unique representation. This characteristic can be particularly confusing in a system that lets the user manipulate the leaf objects with tweaking operators. Applying the same operation to two objects that are initially the same can yield two different results, as shown in Fig. 10.21. Nevertheless, the ability to edit models by deleting, adding, replacing, and modifying subtrees, coupled with the relatively compact form in which models are stored, has made CSG one of the dominant solid modeling representations.

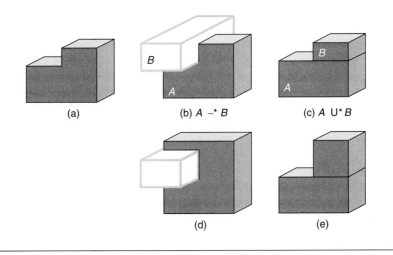

(a)

(b) $A -^* B$

(c) $A \cup^* B$

(d)

(e)

Figure 10.21   The object shown in (a) may be defined by different CSG operations, as shown in (b) and (c). Tweaking the top face of (b) and (c) upward yields different objects, shown in (d) and (e).

10.8 COMPARISON OF REPRESENTATIONS

We have discussed five main kinds of representations: primitive instancing, sweeps, b-reps, spatial partitioning (including cell decomposition, spatial-occupancy enumeration, octrees, and BSP trees), and CSG. Let us compare them on the basis of the criteria introduced in Section 10.1.

- *Accuracy.* Spatial-partitioning and polygonal b-rep methods produce only approximations for many objects. In some applications, such as finding a path for a robot, this limitation is not a drawback, as long as the approximation is computed to an adequate (often relatively coarse) resolution. The resolution needed to produce visually pleasing graphics or to calculate object interactions with sufficient accuracy, however, may be too high to be practical. The smooth shading techniques discussed in Chapter 14 do not fix the visual artifacts caused by the all-too-obvious polygonal edges. Therefore, systems that support high-quality graphics often use CSG with nonpolyhedral primitives and b-reps that allow curved surfaces. Primitive instancing also can produce high-quality pictures, but does not allow two simpler objects to be combined with Boolean set operators.

- *Domain.* The domain of objects that can be represented by both primitive instancing and sweeps is limited. In comparison, spatial-partitioning approaches can represent any solid, although often only as an approximation. By providing other kinds of faces and edges in addition to polygons bounded by straight lines, b-reps can be used to represent a very wide class of objects. Many b-rep systems, however, are restricted to simple surface types and topologies. For example, they may be able to encode only combinations of quadrics that are 2-manifolds.

- *Uniqueness.* Only octree and spatial-occupancy–enumeration approaches guarantee the uniqueness of a representation: There is only one way to represent an object with a specified size and position. In the case of octrees, some processing must be done to ensure that the representation is fully reduced (i.e., that no gray node has all black children or all white children). Primitive instancing does not guarantee uniqueness in general; for example, a sphere may be represented by both a spherical and an elliptical primitive. If the set of primitives is chosen carefully, however, uniqueness can be ensured.

- *Validity.* Among all the representations, b-reps stand out as being the most difficult to validate. Not only may vertex, edge, and face data structures be inconsistent, but also faces or edges may intersect. In contrast, any BSP tree represents a valid spatial set, but not necessarily a bounded solid. Only simple, local syntactic checking needs to be done to validate a CSG tree (which is always bounded, if its primitives are bounded) or an octree, and no checking is needed for spatial-occupancy enumeration.

- *Closure*. Primitives created using primitive instancing cannot be combined at all, and simple sweeps are not closed under Boolean operations. Therefore, neither is typically used as an internal representation in modeling systems. Although particular b-reps may suffer from closure problems under Boolean operations (e.g., the inability to represent other than 2-manifolds), these problem cases can often be avoided.

- *Compactness and efficiency.* Representation schemes are often classified by whether they produce *evaluated* or *unevaluated* models. *Unevaluated* models contain information that must be processed (or evaluated) further in order to perform basic operations, such as determining an object's boundary. With regard to the use of Boolean operations, CSG creates unevaluated models, in that each time computations are performed, we must walk the tree, evaluating the expressions. Consequently, the advantages of CSG are its compactness and the ability to record Boolean operations and changes of transformations quickly, and to undo all of these quickly since they involve only tree-node building. Octrees and BSP trees can also be considered unevaluated models, as can a sequence of Euler operators that creates a b-rep. B-reps and spatial-occupancy enumeration, on the other hand, are often considered *evaluated* models insofar as any Boolean operations used to create an object have already been performed. Note that the use of these terms is relative; if the operation to be performed is determining whether a point is inside an object, for example, more work may be done evaluating a b-rep than evaluating the equivalent CSG tree.

  As discussed in Chapter 13, a number of efficient algorithms exist for generating pictures of objects encoded using b-reps. Although spatial-occupancy enumeration and octrees can provide only coarse approximations for most objects, the algorithms used to manipulate them are in general simpler than the equivalents for other representations. They have thus been used in hardware-based solid modeling systems intended for applications in which the increased speed with which Boolean set operations can be performed on them outweighs the coarseness of the resulting images.

Some systems use multiple representations because some operations are more efficient with one representation than with another. For example, GMSOLID [BOYS82] uses CSG for compactness and a b-rep for quick retrieval of useful data not explicitly specified in CSG, such as connectivity. Although GMSOLID's CSG representation always reflects the current state of the object being modeled, its b-rep is updated only when the operations that require it are executed. In addition to systems that maintain two completely separate representations, deriving one from the other when needed, there are also hybrid systems that go down to some level of detail in one scheme, then switch to another, but never duplicate information. Some of the issues raised by the use of multiple representations and hybrid representations are addressed in [MILL89].

As pointed out in Section 10.1, wireframe representations containing only vertex and edge information, with no reference to faces, are inherently ambiguous. Markowsky and Wesley, however, have developed an algorithm for deriving all polyhedra that could be represented by a given wireframe [MARK80] and a companion algorithm that generates all polyhedra that could produce a given 2D projection [WESL81].

10.9 USER INTERFACES FOR SOLID MODELING

Developing the user interface for a solid modeling system provides an excellent opportunity to put into practice the interface design techniques discussed in Chapter 8. A variety of techniques lend themselves well to graphical interfaces, including the direct application of regularized Boolean set operators, tweaking, and Euler operators. In CSG systems, the user may be allowed to edit the object by modifying or replacing one of the leaf solids or subtrees. Blending and chamfering operations may be defined to smooth the transition from one surface to another. The user interfaces of successful systems are largely independent of the internal representation chosen. Primitive instancing is an exception, however, since it encourages users to think of objects in terms of special-purpose parameters.

In Chapter 9, we noted that there are many equivalent ways to describe the same curve. For example, the user interface to a curve-drawing system can let the user enter curves by controlling Hermite tangent vectors or by specifying Bézier control points, while storing curves only as Bézier control points. Similarly, a solid modeling system may let the user create objects in terms of several different representations, while storing them in yet another. As with curve representations, each different input representation may have some expressive advantage that makes it a natural choice for creating the object.

The precision with which objects must be specified often dictates that some means be provided to determine measurements accurately—for example, through a locator device or through numeric entry. Because the position of one object often depends on those of others, interfaces often provide the ability to constrain one object by another. A related technique is to give the user the ability to define grid lines to constrain object positions.

Some of the most fundamental problems of designing a solid modeling interface are those caused by the need to manipulate and display 3D objects with what are typically 2D interaction devices and displays. These general issues were discussed in Chapter 8. Many systems address some of these problems by providing multiple display windows that allow the user to view the object simultaneously from different positions.

SUMMARY

As we have seen, solid modeling is important in both CAD/CAM and graphics. Although useful algorithms and systems exist that handle the objects described so far, many difficult problems remain unsolved. One of the most important is the issue of robustness. Solid modeling systems are typically plagued by numerical instabilities. Commonly used algorithms require more precision to hold intermediate floating-point results than is available in hardware. For example, Boolean set operation algorithms may fail when presented with two objects, one of which is a very slightly transformed copy of the first.

Representations are needed for nonrigid, flexible, jointed objects. Many objects cannot be specified with total accuracy; rather, their shapes are defined by parameters constrained to lie within a range of values. Known as *toleranced* objects, they correspond to real objects turned out by machines such as lathes and stampers [REQU84]. New representations are being developed to encode toleranced objects [GOSS88].

Common to all designed objects is the concept of *features*, such as holes and chamfers, that are designed for specific purposes. One current area of research is exploring the possibility of recognizing features automatically and inferring the designer's intent for what each feature should accomplish [PRAT84]. This process will allow the design to be checked to ensure that the features perform as intended. For example, if certain features are designed to give a part strength under pressure, then their ability to perform this function could be validated automatically. Future operations on the object could also be checked to ensure that the features' functionality was not compromised.

Exercises

10.1   Define the results of performing $\cup^*$ and $-^*$ for two polyhedral objects in the same way as the result of performing $\cap^*$ was defined in Section 10.2. Explain how the resulting object is constrained to be a regular set, and specify how the normal is determined for each of the object's faces.

10.2   Consider the task of determining whether a legal solid is the null object (which has no volume). How difficult is it to perform this test in each of the representations discussed?

10.3   Consider a system whose objects are represented as sweeps and can be operated on using the regularized Boolean set operators. What restrictions must be placed on the objects to ensure closure?

10.4   Explain why an implementation of Boolean set operations on quadtrees or octrees does not need to address the distinction between the ordinary and regularized operations described in Section 10.2.

10.5   Although the geometric implications of applying the regularized Boolean set operators are unambiguous, it is less clear how object properties should be treated. For example, what properties should be assigned to the intersection of two objects made of different materials? In modeling actual objects, this question is of little importance, but in the artificial world of graphics, it is possible to intersect any two materials. What solutions do you think would be useful?

10.6   Explain how a quadtree or an octree could be used to speed up 2D or 3D picking in a graphics package.

10.7   Describe how to perform point classification in primitive instancing, b-rep, spatial occupancy enumeration, and CSG.

11 Achromatic and Colored Light

It is crucial that the student of modern computer graphics understand the theory and application of light and color. Even the judicious use of just a few shades of gray can greatly enhance the appearance of a rendered object. But it is the use of color that is responsible for much of the impact of the images that appear in the Color Plates section. Color is an immensely complex subject—one that draws on concepts and results from physics, physiology, psychology, art, and graphic design. In this chapter, we introduce the areas of color that are most relevant to computer graphics.

The color of an object depends not only on the object itself, but also on the light source illuminating the object, on the color of the surrounding area, and on the human visual system. Furthermore, certain objects reflect light (wall, desk, paper), whereas others also transmit light (cellophane, glass). When a surface that reflects only pure blue light is illuminated with pure red light, it appears black. Similarly, a pure green light viewed through glass that transmits only pure red will also appear black. We postpone consideration of some of these issues by starting our discussion with achromatic sensations—that is, those described as black, gray, and white.

11.1 ACHROMATIC LIGHT

Achromatic (literally, the absence of color) light is what we see on a black-and-white television set or computer display. An observer of achromatic light experiences none of the sensations we associate with red, blue, yellow, and so on.

Quantity of light is the only attribute of achromatic light. Quantity of light can be discussed in the physics sense of energy, in which case the terms **intensity** and **luminance** are used, or in the psychological sense of perceived intensity, in which case the term **brightness** is used. As we shall discuss shortly, these two concepts are related but are not the same. It is useful to associate a scalar with different intensity levels, defining 0 as black and 1 as white with intensity levels between 0 and 1 representing different grays.

A black-and-white television can produce many different intensities at a single pixel position. Line printers, pen plotters, and electrostatic plotters produce only two levels: the white (or light gray) of the paper and the black (or dark gray) of the ink or toner deposited on the paper. Certain techniques, discussed in later sections, allow such inherently **bilevel** devices to produce additional intensity levels.

11.1.1 Selection of Intensities

Suppose that we want to display 256 different intensities. We select this number because the brightness of each pixel of many images is represented by 8 bits of data. Which 256 intensity levels should we use? We surely do not want 128 in the range of 0 to 0.1 and 128 more in the range of 0.9 to 1.0, since the transition from 0.1 to 0.9 would certainly appear discontinuous. We might initially distribute the levels evenly over the range 0 to 1, but this choice ignores an important character-istic of the eye: that it is sensitive to ratios of intensity levels, rather than to abso-lute values of intensity. That is, we perceive the intensities 0.10 and 0.11 as differing just as much as the intensities 0.50 and 0.55. (This nonlinearity is easy to observe: Cycle through the settings on a three-way 50–100–150-watt lightbulb; you will see that the step from 50 to 100 seems much greater than the step from 100 to 150.) On a brightness (that is, perceived intensity) scale, the difference between intensities of 0.10 and 0.11 and that between intensities of 0.50 and 0.55 are equal. Therefore, the intensity levels should be spaced logarithmically rather than linearly, to achieve equal steps in brightness.

To find 256 intensities starting with the lowest attainable intensity I_0 and going to a maximum intensity of 1.0, with each intensity r times higher than the preceding intensity, we use the following relations:

$$I_0 = I_0, I_1 = rI_0, I_2 = rI_1 = r^2I_0, I_3 = rI_2 = r^3I_0, \dots, I_{255} = r^{255}I_0 = 1. \quad (11.1)$$

Therefore,

$$r = (1/I_0)^{1/255}, I_j = r^jI_0 = (1/I_0)^{j/255} I_0 = I_0^{(255-j)/255} \qquad \text{for } 0 \le j \le 255, \quad (11.2)$$

and, in general, for $n + 1$ intensities,

$$r = (1/I_0)^{1/n}, I_j = I_0^{(n-j)/n} \qquad \text{for } 0 \le j \le n. \quad (11.3)$$

With just four intensities ($n = 3$) and an I_0 of $\frac{1}{8}$ (an unrealistically large value cho-sen for illustration only), Eq. (11.3) tells us that $r = 2$, yielding intensity values of $\frac{1}{8}, \frac{1}{4}, \frac{1}{2}$, and 1.

The minimum attainable intensity I_0 for a CRT is anywhere from about $\frac{1}{200}$ up to $\frac{1}{40}$ of the maximum intensity of 1.0. Therefore, typical values of I_0 are between 0.005 and 0.025. The minimum is not 0, because of light reflection from the phosphor within the CRT. The ratio between the maximum and minimum intensities is called the **dynamic range**. We can find the exact value for a specific CRT by displaying a square of white on a field of black and measuring the two intensities with a photometer. We take this measurement in a completely darkened room, so that reflected ambient light does not affect the intensities. With an I_0 of 0.02, corresponding to a dynamic range of 50, Eq. (11.2) yields $r = 1.0154595 \ldots$, and the first few and last two intensities of the 256 intensities from Eq. (11.1) are 0.0200, 0.0203, 0.0206, 0.0209, 0.0213, 0.0216,..., 0.9848, 1.0000.

Correctly displaying the intensities defined by Eq. (11.1) on a CRT is a tricky process, and recording them on film is even more difficult, because of the nonlinearities in the CRT and film. These difficulties can be overcome by using a technique called **gamma correction**, which involves loading the lookup table of a raster display with compensatory values. Details of procedure are in [FOLE90].

A natural question is, "How many intensities are enough?" By "enough," we mean the number needed to reproduce a continuous-tone black-and-white image such that the reproduction appears to be continuous. This appearance is achieved when the ratio r is 1.01 or less (below this ratio, the eye cannot distinguish between intensities I_j and I_{j+1}) [WYSZ82, p. 569]. Thus, we find the appropriate value for n, the number of intensity levels, by equating r to 1.01 in Eq. (11.3):

$$r = (1/I_0)^{1/n} \quad \text{or} \quad 1.01 = (1/I_0)^{1/n}. \tag{11.4}$$

Solving for n gives

$$n = \log_{1.01}(1/I_0), \tag{11.5}$$

where $1/I_0$ is the dynamic range of the device.

The dynamic range $1/I_0$ for several display media, and the corresponding n, which is the number of intensity levels needed to maintain $r = 1.01$ and at the same time to use the full dynamic range, are shown in Table 11.1. These are theoretical

Table 11.1

Dynamic Range($1/I_0$) and Number of Required Intensities $n = \log_{1.01}(1/I_0)$ For Several Display Media.

Display Media	Typical Dynamic Range	Number of Intensities, n
CRT	50–200	400–530
Photographic prints	100	465
Photographic slides	1000	700
Coated paper printed in B/W*	100	465
Coated paper printed in color	50	400
Newsprint printed in B/W	10	234

*B/W = black and white

Figure 11.1   A continuous-tone photograph.

values, assuming perfect reproduction processes. In practice, slight blurring due to ink bleeding and small amounts of random noise in the reproduction decreases n considerably for print media. For instance, in Fig. 11.1 shows a continuous-tone photograph; and Fig. 11.2 reproduces the same photograph at 4 and 32 intensity levels. With four levels, the transitions or contours between one intensity level and the next are quite conspicuous, because the ratio r between successive intensities is considerably greater than the ideal 1.01 . Contouring is barely detectable with 32

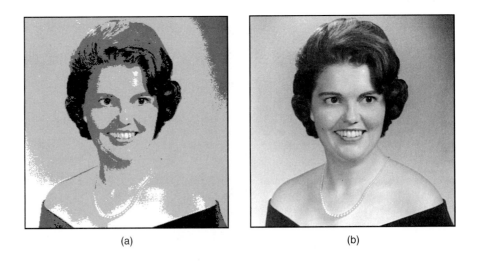

(a)   (b)

Figure 11.2   The effect of intensity levels on image reproduction. (a) A continuous-tone photograph reproduced with four intensity levels. (b) A continuous-tone photograph reproduced with 32 intensity levels. (Courtesy of Alan Paeth, University of Waterloo Computer Graphics Lab.)

levels, and for these particular images would disappear with 64. This observation suggests that 64 intensity levels is the absolute minimum needed for contour-free printing of continuous-tone black-and-white images on paper such as that used in this book. For a well-adjusted CRT in a perfectly black room, however, the higher dynamic range demands that many more levels be used.

11.1.2 Halftone Approximation

Many displays and hardcopy devices are bilevel—they produce just two intensity levels—and even 2- or 3-bit-per-pixel raster displays produce fewer intensity levels than we might desire. How can we expand the range of available intensities? The answer lies in the **spatial integration** that our eyes perform. If we view a small area from a sufficiently large viewing distance, our eyes average fine detail within the small area and record only the overall intensity of the area.

This phenomenon is exploited in printing of black-and-white photographs in newspapers, magazines, and books, by a technique called **halftoning** (also called **clustered-dot ordered dither** in computer graphics). Each small resolution unit is imprinted with a circle of black ink whose area is proportional to the blackness $1 - I$ (where I = intensity) of the area in the original photograph. Figure 11.3 shows part of a halftone pattern, greatly enlarged. Note that the pattern makes a 45° angle with the horizontal, called the **screen angle.** Newspaper halftones use 60 to 80 variable-sized and variable-shaped areas [ULIC87] per inch, whereas halftones in magazines and books use 110 to 200 per inch.

Graphics output devices can approximate the variable-area circles of halftone reproduction. For example, a 2×2 pixel area of a bilevel display can be used to produce five different intensity levels at the cost of halving the spatial resolution

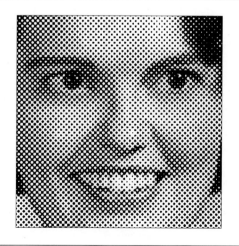

Figure 11.3   Halftoning effectively expands the number of intensities available to media with a small dynamic range. In this enlarged halftone pattern, we can see that dot sizes vary inversely with intensity of the original photograph (see Fig. 11.1). (Courtesy of Alan Paeth, University of Waterloo Computer Graphics Lab.)

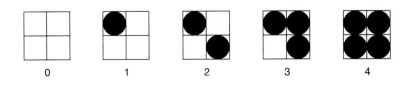

0	1	2	3	4

Figure 11.4   Five intensity levels approximated with four 2 × 2 dither patterns.

along each axis. The patterns shown in Fig. 11.4 can be used to fill the 2×2 areas with the number of *on* pixels that is proportional to the desired intensity. Figure 11.5 shows a face digitized as a 351×351 image array and displayed with 2×2 patterns.

An $n \times n$ group of bilevel pixels can provide $n^2 + 1$ intensity levels. In general, there is a tradeoff between spatial resolution and intensity resolution. The use of a 3×3 pattern cuts spatial resolution by one-third on each axis, but provides 10 intensity levels. Of course, the tradeoff choices are limited by our visual acuity (about 1 minute of arc in normal lighting), the distance from which the image is viewed, and the dots-per-inch resolution of the graphics device.

Halftone approximation is not limited to bilevel displays. Consider a display with 2 bits per pixel and hence four intensity levels. The halftone technique can be used to increase the number of intensity levels. If we use a 2×2 pattern, we have a total of 4 pixels at our disposal, each of which can take on three values in addition to black; this fact allows us to display $4 \times 3 + 1 = 13$ intensities.

The techniques presented thus far have assumed that the image array being shown is smaller than the display device's pixel array, so multiple display pixels

Figure 11.5   A continuous-tone photograph, digitized to a resolution of 351 × 351 and displayed using the 2 × 2 patterns of Fig. 11.4. (Courtesy of Alan Paeth, University of Waterloo Computer Graphics Lab.)

can be used for one image pixel. What if the image and display device arrays are the same size? One approach is to use **error diffusion**, a technique developed by Floyd and Steinberg [FLOY75]. The visual results of applying error diffusion are often satisfactory. The error (i.e., the difference between the exact pixel value and the approximated value actually displayed) is added to the values of the four image-array pixels to the right of and below the pixel in question: $\frac{7}{16}$ of the error to the pixel to the right, $\frac{3}{16}$ to the pixel below and to the left, $\frac{5}{16}$ to the pixel immediately below, and $\frac{1}{16}$ to the pixel below and to the right. This strategy has the effect of spreading, or diffusing, the error over several pixels in the image array. Figure 11.6 was created using this method.

Given a picture S to be displayed in the intensity matrix I, the modified values in S and the displayed values in I are computed for pixels in scan-line order, working downward from the topmost scan line:

```
K = Approximate(S[x][y]);     /* Approximate S to nearest displayable intensity */
I [x][y] = K;                 /* Draw the pixel at (x, y) */
error = S[x][y] – K;          /* Error term. Must be of type float */
```

/* Step 1: spread $\frac{7}{16}$ of error into the pixel to the right, at $(x + 1, y)$ */
```
S[x + 1][y] += 7 * error /16;
```

/* Step 2: spread $\frac{3}{16}$ of error into pixel below and to the left */
```
S[x – 1][y – 1] += 3 * error /16;
```

/* Step 3: spread $\frac{5}{16}$ of error into pixel below */
```
S[x][y – 1] += 5 * error /16;
```

/* Step 4: spread $\frac{1}{16}$ of error below and to the right */
```
S[x + 1][y – 1] += error /16;
```

Figure 11.6 A continuous-tone photograph reproduced with Floyd–Steinberg error diffusion. (Courtesy of Alan Paeth, University of Waterloo Computer Graphics Lab.)

To avoid introducing visual artifacts into the displayed image, we must ensure that the four errors sum exactly to *error*; no roundoff errors can be allowed. We can meet this constraint by calculating the step 4 error term as *error* minus the error terms from the first three steps. The function *Approximate* returns the displayable intensity value closest to the actual pixel value. For a bilevel display, the value of *S* is simply rounded to 0 or 1.

We can obtain even better results by alternately scanning left to right and right to left; on a right-to-left scan, the left–right directions for errors in steps 1, 2, and 4 are reversed. For a detailed discussion of this and other error-diffusion methods, see [ULIC87]. Other approaches are discussed in [KNUT87].

11.2 CHROMATIC COLOR

The visual sensations caused by colored light are much richer than those caused by achromatic light. Discussions of color perception usually involve three quantities, known as hue, saturation, and lightness. **Hue** distinguishes among colors such as red, green, purple, and yellow. **Saturation** refers to how far a color is from a gray of equal intensity. Red is highly saturated; pink is relatively unsaturated; royal blue is highly saturated; sky blue is relatively unsaturated. Pastel colors are relatively unsaturated; unsaturated colors include more white light than do the vivid, saturated colors. **Lightness** embodies the achromatic notion of perceived intensity of a reflecting object. **Brightness**, a fourth term, is used instead of **lightness** to refer to the perceived intensity of a self-luminous (i.e., emitting rather than reflecting light) object, such as a light bulb, the sun, or a CRT.

It is necessary to specify and measure colors if we are to use them precisely in computer graphics. For reflected light, we can do these tasks by visually comparing a sample of unknown color against a set of *standard* samples. The unknown and sample colors must be viewed under a standard light source, since the perceived color of a surface depends both on the surface and on the light under which the surface is viewed. The widely used Munsell color-order system includes sets of published standard colors [MUNS76] organized in a 3D space of hue, value (what we have defined as lightness), and chroma (saturation). Each color is named, and is ordered so as to have an equal perceived *distance* in color space (as judged by many observers) from its neighbors. [KELL76] gives an extensive discussion of standard samples, charts depicting the Munsell space, and tables of color names.

In the printing industry and graphic-design profession, colors are typically specified by their match to printed color samples, such as those provided by the PANTONE MATCHING SYSTEM® [PANT91].

Artists often specify color as different tints, shades, and tones of strongly saturated, or pure, pigments. A **tint** results when white pigment is added to a pure pigment, thereby decreasing saturation. A **shade** comes from adding a black pigment to a pure pigment, thereby decreasing lightness. A **tone** is the consequence of adding both black and white pigments to a pure pigment. All these steps produce different colors of the same hue, with varying saturation and lightness. Mixing just black and white pigments creates grays. Figure 11.7 shows the relationship of tints, shades, and tones. The percentage of pigments that must be mixed to match a color can be used as a color specification. The Ostwald [OSTW31] color-order system is similar to the artist's model of tints, shades, and tones.

11.2.1 Psychophysics

The Munsell and artist's pigment-mixing methods are subjective: They depend on the human observers' judgments, the lighting, the size of the sample, the surrounding color, and the overall lightness of the environment. An objective, quantitative way of specifying colors is needed; to meet this need we turn to the branch of physics known as **colorimetry.** Important terms in colorimetry are dominant wavelength, excitation purity, and luminance.

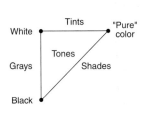

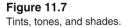

Figure 11.7
Tints, tones, and shades.

Dominant wavelength is the wavelength of the color we "see" when viewing the light, and corresponds to the perceptual notion of hue; **excitation purity** corresponds to the saturation of the color; **luminance** is the amount or intensity of light. The excitation purity of a colored light is the proportion of pure light of the dominant wavelength and of white light needed to define the color. A completely pure color is 100-percent saturated and thus contains no white light, whereas mixtures of a pure color and white light have saturations somewhere between 0 and 100 percent. White light and hence grays are 0-percent saturated, containing no color of any dominant wavelength. The correspondences between these perceptual and colorimetry terms are as follows:

Perceptual term	**Colorimetry**
Hue	Dominant wavelength
Saturation	Excitation purity
Lightness (reflecting objects)	Luminance
Brightness (self-luminous objects)	Luminance

Basically, light is electromagnetic energy in the 400- to 700-nm wavelength part of the spectrum, which is perceived as the colors from violet through indigo, blue, green, yellow, and orange to red. The amount of energy present at each wavelength is represented by a spectral energy distribution $P(\lambda)$, such as shown in Fig. 11.8.

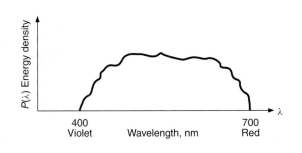

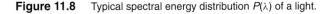

Figure 11.8   Typical spectral energy distribution $P(\lambda)$ of a light.

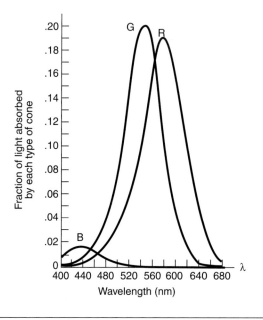

Figure 11.9   Spectral-response functions of each of the three types of cones on the human retina.

The distribution represents an infinity of numbers, one for each wavelength in the visible spectrum (in practice, the distribution is represented by a large number of sample points on the spectrum, as measured by a spectroradiometer). Fortunately, we can describe the visual effect of any spectral distribution much more concisely by the triple [dominant wavelength, excitation purity, luminance]. This implies that many different spectral energy distributions produce the same color: They "look" the same. Hence the relationship between spectral distributions and colors is many-to-one.

How does this discussion relate to the red, green, and blue phosphor dots on a color CRT? And how does it relate to the **tristimulus theory** of color perception, which is based on the hypothesis that the retina has three kinds of color sensors (called cones), with peak sensitivity to red, green, or blue lights? Experiments based on this hypothesis produce the spectral-response functions of Fig. 11.9. The peak blue response is around 440 nm; that for green is about 545 nm; that for red is about 580 nm. (The terms *red* and *green* are somewhat misleading here, as the 545-nm and 580-nm peaks are actually in the yellow range.) The curves suggest that the eye's response to blue light is much less strong than is its response to red or green.

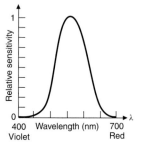

Figure 11.10
Luminous-efficiency
function for the human eye.

Figure 11.10 shows the **luminous-efficiency function**—the eye's response to light of constant luminance—as the dominant wavelength is varied: our peak sensitivity is to yellow-green light of wavelength around 550 nm. There is experimental evidence that this curve is just the sum of the three curves shown in Fig. 11.9.

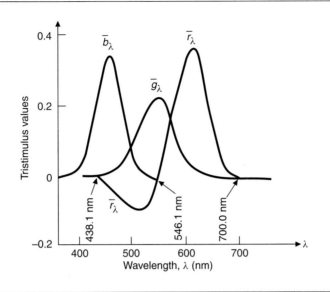

Figure 11.11 Color-matching functions, showing the amounts of three primaries needed to match all the wavelengths of the visible spectrum.

The tristimulus theory is intuitively attractive because it corresponds loosely to the notion that colors can be specified by positively weighted sums of red, green, and blue (the so-called primary colors). This notion is almost true: The three color-matching functions in Fig. 11.11 show the amounts of red, green, and blue light needed by an average observer to match a color of constant luminance, for all values of dominant wavelength in the visible spectrum.

A negative value in Fig. 11.11 means that we cannot match the color by adding together the primaries. However, if one of the primaries is added to the color sample, the sample can then be matched by a mixture of the other two primaries. Hence, negative values in Fig. 11.11 indicate that the primary was added to the color being matched. The need for negative values does not mean that the notion of mixing red, green, and blue to obtain other colors is invalid; on the contrary, a huge range of colors can be matched by positive amounts of red, green, and blue. Otherwise, the color CRT would not work! It does mean, however, that certain colors cannot be produced by RGB mixes, and hence cannot be shown on an ordinary CRT.

The human eye can distinguish hundreds of thousands of different colors in color space, when different colors are judged side by side by different viewers who state whether the colors are the same or different. When colors differ only in hue, the wavelength between just noticeably different colors varies from more than 10 nm at the extremes of the spectrum to less than 2 nm around 480 nm (blue) and 580 nm (yellow) [BEDF58]. Except at the spectrum extremes, however, most distinguished hues are within 4 nm. Altogether, about 128 fully saturated hues can be distinguished.

The eye is less sensitive to hue changes in less saturated light, while sensitivity to changes in saturation for a fixed hue and lightness is greater at the extremes of the visible spectrum, where about 23 distinguishable steps exist.

11.2.2 The CIE Chromaticity Diagram

Matching and therefore defining a colored light with a mixture of three fixed primaries is a desirable approach to specifying color, but the need for negative weights suggested by Fig. 11.11 is awkward. In 1931, the *Commission Internationale de l'Éclairage (CIE)* defined three standard primaries, called **X**, **Y**, and **Z**, to replace red, green, and blue in this matching process. The three corresponding color-matching functions, $\bar{x}_\lambda$, $\bar{y}_\lambda$, and $\bar{z}_\lambda$, are shown in Fig. 11.12. The primaries can be used to match, with only positive weights, all the colors we can see. The **Y** primary was intentionally defined to have a color-matching function $\bar{y}_\lambda$ that exactly matches the luminous-efficiency function of Fig. 11.10. Note that $\bar{x}_\lambda$, $\bar{y}_\lambda$, and $\bar{z}_\lambda$ are not the spectral distributions of the **X**, **Y**, and **Z** colors, just as the curves in Fig. 11.11 are not the spectral distributions of red, green, and blue. They are merely auxiliary functions used to compute how much of **X**, **Y**, and **Z** should be mixed together to generate a spectral distribution of any visible color.

The amounts of **X**, **Y**, and **Z** primaries needed to match a color with a spectral energy distribution $P(\lambda)$ are

$$X = k \int P(\lambda)\bar{x}_\lambda d\lambda, \quad Y = k \int P(\lambda)\bar{y}_\lambda d\lambda, \quad Z = k \int P(\lambda)\bar{z}_\lambda d\lambda. \quad (11.6)$$

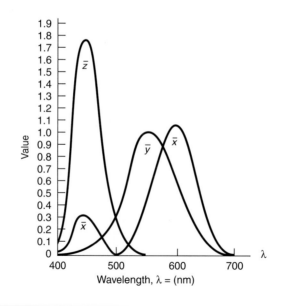

Figure 11.12   The color-matching functions $\bar{x}_\lambda$, $\bar{y}_\lambda$, and $\bar{z}_\lambda$, for the 1931 CIE **X**, **Y**, **Z** primaries.

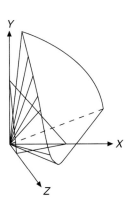

Figure 11.13
The cone of visible colors in CIE color space, shown by the lines radiating from the origin. The $X + Y + Z = 1$ plane is shown. (Courtesy of Gary Meyer, Program of Computer Graphics, Cornell University, 1978.)

For self-luminous objects such as a CRT, k is 680 lumens per watt. For reflecting objects, k is usually selected such that bright white has a Y value of 100; then, other Y values will be in the range of 0 to 100.

Figure 11.13 shows the cone-shaped volume of XYZ space that contains visible colors. The volume extends out from the origin into the positive octant, and is capped at the smooth curved line terminating the cone.

Let (X, Y, Z) be the weights applied to the CIE primaries to match a color **C**, as found using Eq. (11.6). Then $\mathbf{C} = X\,\mathbf{X} + Y\,\mathbf{Y} + Z\,\mathbf{Z}$. We define **chromaticity** values (which depend on only dominant wavelength and saturation, and are independent of the amount of luminous energy) by normalizing against $X + Y + Z$, which can be thought of as the total amount of light energy:

$$x = \frac{X}{(X + Y + Z)}, \quad y = \frac{Y}{(X + Y + Z)}, \quad z = \frac{Z}{(X + Y + Z)}. \tag{11.7}$$

Notice that $x + y + z = 1$. That is, x, y, and z are on the $(X + Y + Z = 1)$ plane of Fig. 11.13. Color Plate 14 shows the $X + Y + Z = 1$ plane as part of CIE space, and also shows an orthographic view of the plane along with the projection of the plane onto the (X, Y) plane. This latter projection is just the CIE chromaticity diagram.

If we specify x and y, then z is determined by $z = 1 - x - y$. We cannot recover X, Y, and Z from x and y, however. To recover them, we need one more piece of information, typically Y, which carries luminance information. Given (x, y, Y), the transformation to the corresponding (X, Y, Z) is

$$X = \frac{x}{y}Y, \quad Y = Y, \quad Z = \frac{1 - x - y}{y}Y. \tag{11.8}$$

Chromaticity values depend on only dominant wavelength and saturation, and are independent of the amount of luminous energy. By plotting x and y for all visible colors, we obtain the CIE chromaticity diagram shown in Fig. 11.14, which is the projection onto the (X, Y) plane of the $(X + Y + Z = 1)$ plane of Fig. 11.13. The interior and boundary of the horseshoe-shaped region represent all visible chromaticity values. (All perceivable colors with the same chromaticity but different luminances map into the same point within this region.) The 100 percent spectrally pure colors of the spectrum are on the curved part of the boundary. A standard white light, meant to approximate sunlight, is formally defined by a light source **illuminant C**, marked by the center dot. It is near, but not at, the point where $x = y = z = \frac{1}{3}$. Illuminant C was defined by specification of a spectral power distribution that is close to daylight at a correlated color temperature of 6774° kelvin.

The CIE chromaticity diagram is useful in many ways. For one, it allows us to measure the dominant wavelength and excitation purity of any color by matching the color with a mixture of the three CIE primaries. Now suppose the matched color is at point A in Fig. 11.15. When two colors are added together, the new color lies somewhere on the straight line in the chromaticity diagram connecting the two colors being added. Therefore, color A can be thought of as a mixture of "standard" white light (illuminant C) and the pure spectral light at point B. Thus, B defines the dominant wavelength. The ratio of length AC to length BC, expressed as a percentage, is the excitation purity of A. The closer A is to C, the more white light A includes and the less pure it is.

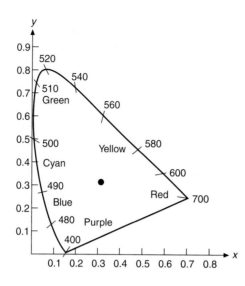

Figure 11.14   The CIE chromaticity diagram. Wavelengths around the periphery are in nanometers. The dot marks the position of illuminant C.

The chromaticity diagram factors out luminance, so color sensations that are luminance-related are excluded. For instance, brown, which is an orange-red chromaticity at very low luminance relative to its surrounding area, does not appear. It

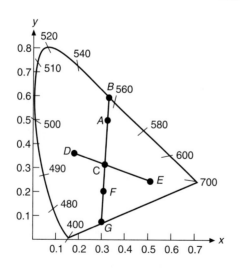

Figure 11.15   Colors on the chromaticity diagram. The dominant wavelength of color *A* is that of color *B*. Colors *D* and *E* are complementary colors. The dominant wavelength of color *F* is defined as the complement of the dominant wavelength of color *A*.

is thus important to remember that the chromaticity diagram is not a full color palette. There is an infinity of planes in (X, Y, Z) space, each of which projects onto the chromaticity diagram and each of which loses luminance information in the process. The colors found on each such plane are all different.

Complementary colors are those that can be mixed to produce white light (such as D and E in Fig. 11.15). Some colors (such as F in Fig. 11.15) cannot be defined by a dominant wavelength and are thus called **nonspectral**. In this case, the dominant wavelength is said to be the complement of the wavelength at which the line through F and C intersects the horseshoe part of the curve at point B, and is designated by a "c" (here about 555 nm c). The excitation purity is still defined by the ratio of lengths (here CF to CG). The colors that must be expressed by using a complementary dominant wavelength are the purples and magentas; they occur in the lower part of the CIE diagram.

Another use of the CIE chromaticity diagram is to define **color gamuts**, or color ranges, that show the effect of adding colors together. We can add any two colors, say I and J in Fig. 11.16, to produce any color along their connecting line by varying the relative amounts of the two colors being added. A third color K (see Fig. 11.16) can be used with various mixtures of I and J to produce the gamut of all colors in triangle IJK, again by varying relative amounts. The shape of the diagram shows why visible red, green, and blue cannot be mixed additively to match all colors: No triangle whose vertices are within the visible area can cover the visible area completely.

The chromaticity diagram is also used to compare the gamuts available on various color display and hardcopy devices. Color Plate 15 shows the gamuts for a color television monitor, film, and print. The smallness of the print gamut with

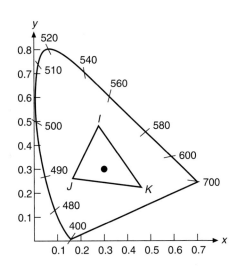

Figure 11.16   Mixing colors. We can create all colors on the line IJ by mixing colors I and J; we can create all colors in the triangle IJK by mixing colors I, J, and K.

respect to the color-monitor gamut suggests that, if images originally seen on a monitor must be reproduced faithfully by printing, a reduced gamut of colors should be used with the monitor. Otherwise, accurate reproduction will not be possible. If, however, the goal is to make a pleasing rather than an exact reproduction, small differences in color gamuts are less important. A discussion of color-gamut compression can be found in [HALL89].

With this background on color, we now turn our attention to color in computer graphics.

11.3 COLOR MODELS FOR RASTER GRAPHICS

A **color model** is a specification of a 3D color coordinate system and a visible subset in the coordinate system within which all colors in a particular color gamut lie. For instance, the RGB color model is the unit cube subset of the 3D Cartesian coordinate system.

The purpose of a color model is to allow convenient specification of colors within some color gamut. Our primary interest is the gamut for color CRT monitors, as defined by the RGB (red, green, blue) primaries in Color Plate 15. As we see in this color plate, a color gamut is a subset of all visible chromaticities. Hence, a color model cannot be used to specify all visible colors.

Three hardware-oriented color models are RGB, used with color CRT monitors; YIQ, the broadcast TV color system; and CMY (cyan, magenta, yellow) used for certain color-printing devices. Unfortunately, none of these models are particularly easy to use, because they do not relate directly to intuitive color notions of hue, saturation, and brightness. Therefore, another class of models has been developed with ease of use as a goal. Several such models are described in [GSPC79; JOBL78; MEYE80; SMIT78]. We discuss just one, the HSV (sometimes called HSB) model.

For each model there is a means of converting to another specification. We show how to convert between RGB and both HSV and CMY, and between RGB and YIQ. Additional conversion algorithms are included in [FOLE90].

11.3.1 The RGB Color Model

The RGB color model used in color CRT monitors and color raster graphics employs a Cartesian coordinate system. The RGB primaries are **additive** primaries; that is, the individual contributions of each primary are added together to yield the result, as suggested in Color Plate 16. The subset of interest is the unit cube shown in Fig. 11.17. The main diagonal of the cube, with equal amounts of each primary, represents the gray levels: black is (0, 0, 0); white is (1, 1, 1).

The color gamut covered by the RGB model is defined by the chromaticities of a CRT's phosphors. Two CRTs with different phosphors will cover different gamuts. To convert colors specified in the gamut of one CRT to the gamut of

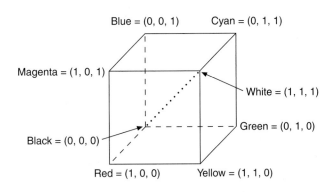

Blue = (0, 0, 1)   Cyan = (0, 1, 1)

Magenta = (1, 0, 1)

White = (1, 1, 1)

Green = (0, 1, 0)

Black = (0, 0, 0)

Red = (1, 0, 0)   Yellow = (1, 1, 0)

Figure 11.17   The RGB cube. Grays are on the dotted main diagonal.

another CRT, we use the transformations from the RGB color space of each monitor to the (X, Y, Z) color space. See [FOLE90] for details.

11.3.2 The CMY Color Model

Cyan, magenta, and yellow are the complements of red, green, and blue, respectively. When used as filters to subtract color from white light, they are called **subtractive** primaries. The subset of the Cartesian coordinate system for the CMY model is the same as that for RGB except that white (full light) instead of black (no light) is at the origin. Colors are specified by what is removed or subtracted from white light, rather than by what is added to blackness.

A knowledge of CMY is important when you are dealing with hardcopy devices that deposit colored pigments onto paper, such as electrostatic and ink-jet plotters. When a surface is coated with cyan ink, no red light is reflected from the surface. Cyan subtracts red from the reflected white light, which is itself the sum of red, green, and blue. Hence, in terms of the additive primaries, cyan is white minus red—that is, blue plus green. Similarly, magenta absorbs green, so it is red plus blue; yellow absorbs blue, so it is red plus green. A surface coated with cyan and yellow absorbs red and blue, leaving only green to be reflected from illuminating white light. A cyan, yellow, and magenta surface absorbs red, green, and blue, and therefore is black. These relations, diagrammed in Fig. 11.18, can be seen in Color Plate 17 and are represented by the following equation:

$$\begin{bmatrix} C \\ M \\ Y \end{bmatrix} = \begin{bmatrix} 1 \\ 1 \\ 1 \end{bmatrix} - \begin{bmatrix} R \\ G \\ B \end{bmatrix}. \tag{11.9}$$

The unit column vector is the RGB representation for white and the CMY representation for black.

The conversion from RGB to CMY is then

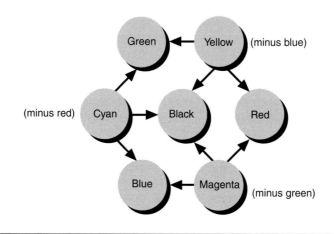

Figure 11.18   Subtractive primaries (cyan, magenta, yellow) and their mixtures. For instance, cyan and yellow combine to green.

$$\begin{bmatrix} R \\ G \\ B \end{bmatrix} = \begin{bmatrix} 1 \\ 1 \\ 1 \end{bmatrix} - \begin{bmatrix} C \\ M \\ Y \end{bmatrix}. \qquad (11.10)$$

These straightforward transformations can be used for converting the eight colors that can be achieved with binary combinations of red, green, and blue into the eight colors achievable with binary combinations of cyan, magenta, and yellow. This conversion is relevant for use on ink-jet and xerographic color printers.

Another color model, CMYK, uses black (denoted by K) as a fourth color. CMYK is used in the four-color printing process of printing presses and certain hardcopy devices. Given a CMY specification, black is used in place of equal amounts of C, M, and Y, according to the following relations:

K = min(C,M,Y),
C = C – K,
M= M – K,
Y = Y – K.   (11.11)

This subject is discussed further in [STON88].

11.3.3 The YIQ Color Model

The YIQ model is used in U.S. commercial color-TV broadcasting and is therefore closely related to color raster graphics. YIQ is a recoding of RGB for transmission efficiency and for downward compatibility with black-and-white television. The recoded signal is transmitted using the National Television System Committee (NTSC) standard [PRIT77].

The Y component of YIQ is not yellow, but rather is luminance; it is defined to be the same as the CIE **Y** primary. Only the Y component of a color TV signal is shown on black-and-white televisions: The chromaticity is encoded in I and Q. The YIQ model uses a 3D Cartesian coordinate system, with the visible subset being a convex polyhedron that maps into the RGB cube.

The RGB-to-YIQ mapping is defined as follows:

$$\begin{bmatrix} Y \\ I \\ Q \end{bmatrix} = \begin{bmatrix} 0.299 & 0.587 & 0.114 \\ 0.596 & -0.275 & -0.321 \\ 0.212 & -0.528 & 0.311 \end{bmatrix} \begin{bmatrix} R \\ G \\ B \end{bmatrix}. \tag{11.12}$$

The quantities in the first row reflect the relative importance of green and red and the relative unimportance of blue in brightness. The inverse of the RGB-to-YIQ matrix is used for the YIQ-to-RGB conversion.

Specifying colors with the YIQ model solves a potential problem with material being prepared for broadcast television: Two different colors shown side by side on a color monitor will appear to be different, but, when converted to YIQ and viewed on a monochrome monitor, they may appear to be the same. We can avoid this problem by specifying the two colors with different Y values in the YIQ color model space (i.e., by adjusting only the Y value to disambiguate them).

The YIQ model exploits two useful properties of our visual system. First, the system is more sensitive to changes in luminance than to changes in hue or saturation; that is, our ability to discriminate color information spatially is weaker than our ability to discriminate monochrome information spatially. This observation suggests that more bits of bandwidth should be used to represent Y than are used to represent I and Q, so as to provide higher resolution in Y. Second, objects that cover an extremely small part of our field of view produce a limited color sensation, which can be specified adequately with one rather than two color dimensions. This fact suggests that either I or Q can have a lower bandwidth than the other. The NTSC encoding of YIQ into a broadcast signal uses these properties to maximize the amount of information transmitted in a fixed bandwidth: 4 MHz is assigned to Y, 1.5 MHz to I, and 0.6 MHz to Q. Further discussion of YIQ can be found in [SMIT78; PRIT77].

11.3.4 The HSV Color Model

The RGB, CMY, and YIQ models are hardware-oriented. By contrast, Smith's HSV (hue, saturation, value) model [SMIT78] (also called the HSB model, with B for brightness) is user-oriented, being based on the intuitive appeal of the artist's model of tint, shade, and tone. The coordinate system is cylindrical, and the subset of the space within which the model is defined is a **hexcone**, or six-sided pyramid, as shown in Fig. 11.19. The top of the hexcone corresponds to $V = 1$, which contains the relatively bright colors. The colors of the $V = 1$ plane are *not* all of the same perceived brightness, however.

Hue, or H, is measured by the angle around the vertical axis, with red at $0°$, green at $120°$, and so on (see Fig. 11.19). Complementary colors in the HSV

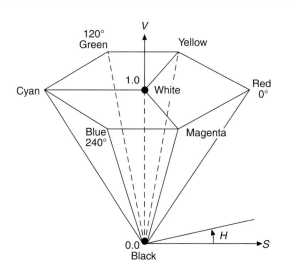

Figure 11.19   Single-hexcone HSV color model. The $V = 1$ plane contains the RGB model's $R = 1$, $G = 1$, and $B = 1$ planes in the regions shown.

hexcone are 180° opposite each other. The value of S is a ratio ranging from 0 on the center line (V axis) to 1 on the triangular sides of the hexcone. Saturation is measured relative to the color gamut represented by the model, which is, of course, a subset of the entire CIE chromaticity diagram. Therefore, saturation of 100 percent in the model is less than 100 percent excitation purity.

The hexcone is 1 unit high in V, with the apex at the origin. The point at the apex is black and has a V coordinate of 0. At this point, the values of H and S are irrelevant. The point $S = 0$, $V = 1$ is white. Intermediate values of V for $S = 0$ (on the center line) are the grays. When $S = 0$, the value of H is irrelevant (called by convention UNDEFINED). When S is not zero, H is relevant. For example, pure red is at $H = 0$, $S = 1$, $V = 1$. Indeed, any color with $V = 1$, $S = 1$ is akin to an artist's pure pigment used as the starting point in mixing colors. Adding white pigment corresponds to decreasing S (without changing V). We create shades by keeping $S = 1$ and decreasing V. We create tones by decreasing both S and V. Of course, changing H corresponds to selecting the pure pigment with which to start. Thus, H, S, and V correspond to concepts from the artist's color system, and are not exactly the same as the similar terms introduced in Section 11.2.

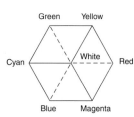

Figure 11.20

RGB color cube viewed along the principal diagonal. Visible edges of the cube are solid; invisible edges are dashed.

The top of the HSV hexcone corresponds to the projection that we can see by looking along the principal diagonal of the RGB color cube from white toward black, as shown in Fig. 11.20. The RGB cube has subcubes, as illustrated in Fig. 11.21. Each subcube, when viewed along its main diagonal, is like the hexagon in Fig. 11.20, except smaller. Each plane of constant V in HSV space corresponds to such a view of a subcube in RGB space. The main diagonal of RGB space becomes the V axis of HSV space. Thus, we can see intuitively the correspondence between RGB and HSV. The algorithms of Progs. 11.1 and 11.2 define the correspondence precisely by providing conversions from one model to the other.

Program 11.1

Algorithm for converting from RGB to HSV color space.

```
void   RGB_To_HSV(float r, float g, float b, float *h, float *s, float *v)
{
/* Given:  r,g,b,each in [0,1].
    Desired: h in [0,360], s and v in [0,1] except if s = 0, then h = UNDEFINED, which
    is some constant defined with a value outside the interval [0,360] */
    float  max, min, delta;

    max = MAX(r, g, b);
    min = MIN(r, g, b);
    *v = max;                          /*This is the value v */
    /*Next calculate saturation, s.*/
    if (max != 0.0)
        *s = (max − min) / max;        /* s is the saturation */
    else
        *s = 0.0;                      /* Saturation is 0 if red, green and blue are all 0 */
    if (*s == 0.0) {
        *h = UNDEFINED;
        return;
    }
    /* Chromatic case:Saturation is not 0, so determine hue */
    delta = max − min;
    if (r == max)                      /* Resulting color is between magenta and cyan */
        *h = (g − b) / delta;          /* Resulting color is between yellow and magenta */
    else if (g == max)
        *h = 2.0 + (b − r) / delta;    /* Resulting color is between cyan and yellow */
    else if (b == max)
        *h = 4.0 + (r − g) / delta;
    *h *= 60.0;                        /* Convert hue to degrees */
    if (*h < 0.0)
        *h += 360.0;                   /* Make sure hue is nonnegative */
}
```

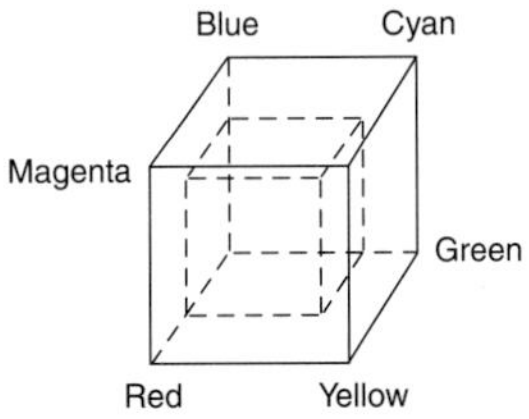

Figure 11.21
RGB cube and a subcube.

Program 11.2

Algorithm for converting from HSV to RGB color space.

```
void   HSV_To_RGB(float *r, float *g, float *b, float h, float s, float v)
{
/* Given: h in [0,360] or UNDEFINED, s and v in [0,1].
    Desired: r,g,b,each in [0,1] */
    float  f, p, q, t;
    int    i;

    if (s == 0.0) {                    /* The color is on the black-and-white center line */
        if (h != UNDEFINED) {          /* Achromatic color:  There is no hue */
            Error();                   /*By our convention, error if s = 0 and h has a value.*/
            return;
        }
        *r = v;
        *g = v;
        *b = v;
```

```
        return;
    }

    if (h == 360.0)            /* Chromatic color: s ≠ 0, so there is a hue */
        h = 0.0;               /* 360° is equivalent to 0° */
    h /= 60.0;                 /* h is now in [0,6] */
    i = floor(h);              /* floor returns the largest integer ≤ h */
    f = h - i;                 /* f is the fractional part of h */
    p = v * (1 - s);
    q = v * (1 - s * f);
    t = v * (1 - s * (1 - f));

    switch (i) {
    case 0:
        *r = v;
        *g = t;
        *b = p;
        break;

    case 1:
        *r = q;
        *g = v;
        *b = p;
        break;

    case 2:
        *r = p;
        *g = v;
        *b = t;
        break;

    case 3:
        *r = p;
        *g = q;
        *b = v;
        break;

    case 4:
        *r = t;
        *g = p;
        *b = v;
        break;

    case 5:
        *r = v;
        *g = p;
        *b = q;
        break;
    }
}
```

11.3.5 Interactive Specification of Color

Many application programs allow the user to specify colors of areas, lines, text, and so on. If only a small set of colors is provided, menu selection from samples of the available colors is appropriate. But what if the set of colors is larger than can be displayed reasonably in a menu?

The basic choices are to use English-language names, to specify the numeric coordinates of the color in a color space (either by typing or with slider dials), or to interact directly with a visual representation of the color space. Naming is in general unsatisfactory because it is ambiguous and subjective (a light navy blue with a touch of green), and it is also the antithesis of graphic interaction. On the other hand, [BERK82] describes CNS, a fairly well-defined color-naming scheme that uses terms such as greenish yellow, green-yellow, and yellowish green to distinguish three hues between green and yellow. In an experiment, users of CNS were able to specify colors more precisely than were users who entered numeric coordinates in either RGB or HSV space.

Coordinate specification can be done with slider dials, using any of the color models. If the user understands how each dimension affects the color, this technique works well. Probably the best interactive coordinate specification method is to let the user interact directly with a representation of the color space, as shown in Fig. 11.22. The line on the circle (representing the $V = 1$ plane) can be dragged around to determine which slice of the HSV volume is displayed in the triangle. The cursor on the triangle can be moved around to specify saturation and value. As the line or the cursor is moved, the numeric readouts change value. When the user types new values directly into the numeric readouts, the line and cursor are repositioned. The color sample box shows the currently selected color. However, a person's perception of color is affected by surrounding colors and the sizes of colored areas; hence the color as perceived in the feedback area will probably differ from the color as perceived in the actual display. It is thus important that the user also see the actual display while the colors are being set.

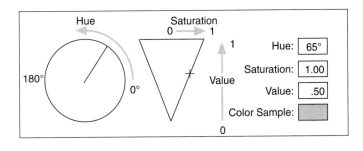

Figure 11.22   A convenient way to specify colors in HSV space. Saturation and value are shown by the cursor in the triangular area, and hue by the line in the circular area. The user can move the line and cursor indicators on the diagrams, causing the numeric readouts to be updated. Alternatively, the user can type new values, causing the indicators to change. Slider dials for *H, S,* and *V* could also be added, giving the user accurate control over a single dimension at a time, without the need to type values.

11.3.6 Interpolation in Color Space

Color interpolation is necessary in at least three situations: for Gouraud shading (Section 14.2.4), for antialiasing (Section 3.14), and for blending two images together, as for a fade-in, fade-out sequence. The results of the interpolation depend on the color model in which the colors are interpolated; thus, we must take care to select an appropriate model.

If the conversion from one color model to another transforms a straight line (representing the interpolation path) in one color model into a straight line in the other color model, then the results of linear interpolation in both models will be the same. This situation is the case for the RGB, CMY, YIQ, and CIE color models, all of which are related by simple affine transformations. However, a straight line in the RGB model does *not* in general transform into a straight line in the HSV model. Color Plate 19 shows the results of interpolating linearly between the same two colors in the HSV, RGB, and YIQ color spaces. Consider the interpolation between red and green. In RGB, red = (1, 0, 0) and green = (0, 1, 0). Their interpolation (with both weights equal to 0.5 for convenience) is (0.5, 0.5, 0). Applying algorithm RGB_To_HSV (Prog. 11.1) to this result, we have (60°, 1, 0.5). Now, representing red and green in HSV, we have (0°, 1, 1) and (120°, 1, 1). But interpolating with equal weights in HSV, we have (60°, 1, 1); thus, the value differs by 0.5 from the same interpolation in RGB.

As a second example, consider interpolating red and cyan in the RGB and HSV models. In RGB, we start with (1, 0, 0) and (0, 1, 1), respectively, and interpolate to (0.5, 0.5, 0.5), which in HSV is represented as (UNDEFINED, 0, 0.5). In HSV, red and cyan are (0°, 1, 1) and (180°, 1, 1). Interpolating, we have (90°, 1, 1); a new hue at maximum value and saturation has been introduced, whereas the *correct* result of combining equal amounts of complementary colors is a gray value. Here, again, interpolating and then transforming gives different results from transforming and then interpolating.

For Gouraud shading, any of the models can be used, because the two interpolants are generally so close together that the interpolation paths between the colors are close together as well. When two images are blended—as in a fade-in, fade-out sequence or for antialiasing—the colors may be distant, and an additive model, such as RGB, is appropriate. If, on the other hand, the objective is to interpolate between two colors of fixed hue (or saturation) and to maintain the fixed hue (or saturation) for all interpolated colors, then HSV is preferable.

11.4 USE OF COLOR IN COMPUTER GRAPHICS

We use color for aesthetics, to establish a tone or mood, for realism, as a highlight, to identify associated areas as being associated, and for coding. With care, color can be used effectively for each of these purposes. In addition, users tend to like color, even when there is no quantitative evidence that its use improves their performance.

Careless use of color can make the display less useful or less attractive than a corresponding monochrome presentation. In one experiment, introduction of meaningless color reduced user performance to about one-third of what it was without color [KREB79]. Color should be employed conservatively. Any decorative use of color should be subservient to the functional use, so that the color cannot be misinterpreted as having an underlying meaning. Thus, the use of color, like all other aspects of a user–computer interface, must be tested with real users so that problems can be identified and remedied. Of course, people may have different preferences, so it is common practice to provide defaults chosen on the basis of color-usage rules, with a means for the user to change the defaults. A conservative approach to color selection is to design first for a monochrome display, to ensure that color use is purely redundant. This option avoids creating problems for users whose color vision is impaired and also means that the application can be used on a monochrome display. Color choices used in window managers, such as that shown in Color Plates 9 and 10, are often conservative. Color is not used as a unique code for button status, for selected menu item, and so forth.

Many books have been written on the use of color for aesthetic purposes, including [BIRR61]; we state here just a few of the simpler rules that help to produce color harmony. The most fundamental rule of color aesthetics is to select colors according to some method, typically by traversing a smooth path in a color model or by restricting the colors to planes or hexcones in a color space. This guideline might mean using colors of constant lightness or value. Furthermore, colors are best spaced at equal *perceptual* distances, which is not the same as being at equally spaced increments of a coordinate, and can be difficult to implement. Recall too that linear interpolation (as in Gouraud shading) between two colors produces different results in different color spaces (see Exercise 11.6 and Color Plate 19).

A random selection of different hues and saturations is usually garish. Alvy Ray Smith performed an informal experiment in which a 16×16 grid was filled with randomly generated colors. Not unexpectedly, the grid was unattractive. Sorting the 256 colors according to their H, S, and V values and redisplaying them on the grid in their new order improved the appearance of the grid remarkably.

More specific instances of these rules suggest that, if a chart contains just a few colors, the complement of one of the colors should be used as the background. A neutral (gray) background should be used for an image containing many different colors, since it is both harmonious and inconspicuous. If two adjoining colors are not particularly harmonious, we can use a thin black border to set them apart. This use of borders is also more effective for the achromatic (black-and-white) visual channel, since shape detection is facilitated by the black outline. Certain of these rules are encoded in ACE (A Color Expert), an expert system for selecting user-interface colors [MEIE88]. In general, it is good to minimize the number of different colors being used (except for shading of realistic images).

Color can be used for encoding information, as illustrated by Color Plate 20. However, several cautions are in order. First, color codes can easily carry unintended meanings. Displaying the earnings of company A as red and those of company B as green might well suggest that company A is in financial trouble, because of our learned association of red with financial deficits. Bright, saturated colors stand out more strongly than do dimmer, paler colors, and may give unintended emphasis. Two elements of a display that have the same color may be seen as related by the same color code, even if they are not.

This last problem often arises when color is used both to group menu items and to distinguish display elements, such as different layers of a printed circuit board or VLSI chip; for example, users tend to associate green display elements with menu items of the same color. This tendency is one of the reasons that use of color in user-interface elements—such as menus, dialog boxes, and window borders—should be restrained. (Another reason is to leave free as many colors as possible for the application program itself.)

Various color usage rules are based on physiological, rather than aesthetic, considerations. For example, because the eye is more sensitive to spatial variation in intensity than it is to variation in chromaticity, the lines, text, and other fine detail should vary from the background not just in chromaticity, but also in brightness (perceived intensity)—especially for colors containing blue, since relatively few cones are sensitive to blue. Thus, the edge between two equal-brightness colored areas that differ only in the amount of blue will be fuzzy. On the other hand, blue-sensitive cones spread out farther on the retina than do red- and green-sensitive ones, so our peripheral color vision is more acute for blue, which is why many police-car flashers are now blue instead of red.

Blue and black differ little in brightness, and are thus a particularly bad combination. Similarly, yellow on white is relatively hard to distinguish, because both colors are bright. Color Plate 10 shows an effective use of yellow to highlight black text on a white background. The yellow contrasts well with the black text and also stands out. In addition, the yellow highlight is not as overpowering as a black highlight with reversed text (i.e., with the highlighted text in white on a black highlight), as is common on monochrome displays.

White text on a blue background provides a good contrast that is less harsh than white on black. It is best to avoid reds and greens with low saturation and luminance, as these are the colors confused by those of us who are red–green color blind, the most common form of color-perception deficiency. Meyer and Greenberg describe effective ways to choose colors for color-blind viewers [MEYE88].

The human eye cannot distinguish the color of very small objects, as already remarked in connection with the YIQ NTSC color model, so color coding should not be applied to small objects. In particular, judging the color of objects subtending less than 20 to 40 minutes of arc is error-prone [BISH60, HAEU76]. An object 0.1 inch high, viewed from 24 inches (a typical viewing distance), subtends this much arc, which corresponds to about 7 pixels of height on a 1024-line display with a vertical height of 15 inches. It is clear that the color of a single pixel is difficult to discern (see Exercise 11.10).

The perceived color of a colored area is affected by the color of the surrounding area; this effect is particularly problematic if colors are used to encode information. The effect is minimized when the surrounding areas are a shade of gray or are a relatively unsaturated color.

The color of an area can affect that area's perceived size. Cleveland and

McGill discovered that a red square is perceived as larger than a green square of equal size [CLEV83]. This effect could well cause the viewer to attach more importance to the red square than to the green one.

If a user stares at a large area of highly saturated color for several seconds and then looks elsewhere, he will see an afterimage of the large area. This effect is disconcerting, and causes eye strain. Use of large areas of saturated colors is hence unwise. Also, large areas of different colors can appear to be at different distances from the viewer, because the index of refraction of light depends on wavelength. The eye changes its focus as the viewer's gaze moves from one colored area to another, and this change in focus gives the impression of differing depths. Red and blue, which are at opposite ends of the spectrum, have the strongest depth-disparity effect, with red appearing closer and blue more distant. Hence, simultaneously using blue for foreground objects and red for the background is unwise; using the converse is fine.

With all these perils and pitfalls of color usage, is it surprising that one of our first-stated rules was to apply color conservatively?

SUMMARY

The importance of color in computer graphics will continue to increase as color monitors and color hardcopy devices become the norm in many applications. In this chapter, we have introduced those color concepts most relevant to computer graphics; for more information, see the vast literature on color, such as [BILL81; BOYN79; GREG66; HUNT87; JUDD75; WYSZ82]. More background on artistic and aesthetic issues in the use of color in computer graphics can be found in [FROM84; MARC82; MEIE88; MURC85]. The difficult problems of calibrating monitors precisely, and of matching the colors appearing on monitors with printed colors, are discussed in [COWA83; STON88].

Exercises

11.1 Derive an equation for the number of intensities that can be represented by $m \times m$ pixel patterns, where each pixel has w bits.

11.2 Write an algorithm to display a pixel array on a bilevel output device. The inputs to the algorithm are an $m \times m$ array of pixel intensities, with w bits per pixel, and an $n \times n$ growth sequence matrix, i.e. a matrix where any pixel intensified for intensity level j is also intensified for all levels $k > j$. Assume that the output device has resolution of $m \cdot n \times m \cdot n$.

11.3 Write an algorithm to display a filled polygon on a bilevel device by using an $n \times n$ filling pattern.

11.4 When certain patterns are used to fill a polygon being displayed on an interlaced raster display, all the *on* bits fall on either the odd or the even scan lines, introducing a slight amount of flicker. Revise the algorithm from Exercise 11.3 to permute rows of the $n \times n$ pattern so that alternate replications of the pattern will alternate use of the odd and even scan lines. Figure 11.23 shows the results we obtain by using intensity level 1 from Fig. 11.4, with and without this alternation.

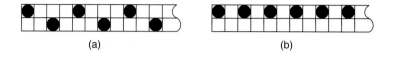

Figure 11.23   Results obtained when intensity level 1 from Fig. 11.4 is used in two ways: (a) with alternation (intensified pixels are on both scan lines), and (b) without alternation (all intensified pixels are on the same scan line).

11.5   Plot the locus of points of the constant luminance values 0.25, 0.50, and 0.75, defined by $Y = 0.299R + 0.587G + 0.114B$, on the RGB cube and the HSV hexcone.

11.6   Express, in terms of R, G, and B, the I of YIQ and the V of HSV. Note that I and V are not the same.

11.7   Discuss the design of a raster display that uses HSV, instead of RGB, as its color specification.

11.8   Rewrite the HSV-to-RGB conversion algorithm to make it more efficient. Replace the assignment statements for p, q, and t with $vs = v * s$; $vsf = vs * f$; $p = v - vs$; $q = v - vsf$; $t = p + vsf$. Also assume that R, G, and B are in the interval [0, 255], and see how many of the computations can be converted to integer.

11.9   Write a program that displays, side by side, two 16×16 grids. Fill each grid with colors. The left grid will have 256 colors randomly selected from HSV color space (create it by using a random-number generator to choose one out of 10 equally spaced values for each of H, S, and V). The right grid contains the same 256 colors, sorted on H, S, and V. Experiment with the results that you obtain by varying which of H, S, and V is used as the primary sort key.

11.10   Write a program to display on a gray background small squares colored orange, red, green, blue, cyan, magenta, and yellow. Each square is separated from the others and is of size $n \times n$ pixels, where n is an input variable. How large must n be so that the user can judge unambiguously the colors of each square from distances of 24 and of 48 inches? What should be the relation between the two values of n? What effect, if any, do different background colors have on this result?

11.11   Calculate the number of bits of look-up-table accuracy needed to store 256 different intensity levels given dynamic intensity ranges of 50, 100, and 200.

11.12   Write a program to interpolate linearly between two colors in RGB and HSV. Accept the two colors as input, allowing them to be specified in any of these three models.

12 The Quest for Visual Realism

In previous chapters, we discussed graphics techniques involving simple 2D and 3D primitives. The pictures that we produced, such as the wireframe houses of Chapter 6, represent objects that in real life are significantly more complex in both structure and appearance. In this chapter, we introduce an increasingly important application of computer graphics: creating realistic images of 3D scenes.

What is a *realistic* image? In what sense a picture—whether painted, photographed, or computer-generated—can be said to be *realistic* is a subject of much scholarly debate [HAGE86]. We use the term rather broadly to refer to a picture that captures many of the effects of light interacting with real physical objects. Thus, we treat realistic images as a continuum and speak freely of pictures, and of the techniques used to create them, as being *more* or *less* realistic. At one end of the continuum are examples of what is often called **photographic realism** (or **photorealism**). These pictures attempt to synthesize the field of light intensities that would be focused on the film plane of a camera aimed at the objects depicted. As we approach the other end of the continuum, we find images that provide successively fewer of the visual cues we shall discuss.

You should bear in mind that a more realistic picture is not necessarily a more desirable or useful one. If the ultimate goal of a picture is to convey information, then a picture that is free of the complications of shadows and reflections may well be more successful than a *tour de force* of photographic realism. In addition, in many applications of the techniques outlined in the following chapters, reality is intentionally altered for aesthetic effect or to fulfill a naive viewer's expectations. Such techniques are done for the same reasons that science-fiction films feature the sounds of weapon blasts in outer space—an impossibility in a vacuum. For example, in depicting Uranus in Color Plate 23, Blinn shined an extra light on the night side of the planet and stretched the contrast to make all features visible simultaneously—the night side of the planet would have been black otherwise. Taking liberties with physics can result in attractive, memorable, and useful pictures!

Creating realistic pictures involves a number of stages that are treated in detail in the following chapters. Although these stages are often thought of as forming a conceptual pipeline, the order in which they are performed can vary, as we shall see, depending on the algorithms used. The first stage generates models of the objects, using methods discussed in Chapters 9 and 10. Next, we select a viewing specification (as developed in Chapter 6) and lighting conditions. Those surfaces visible to the viewer are then determined using algorithms discussed in Chapter 13. The color assigned to each pixel in a visible surface's projection is a function of the light reflected and transmitted by the objects and is determined by methods treated in Chapter 14. The resulting picture can then be combined with previously generated ones (e.g., to reuse a complex background) by using compositing techniques. Finally, if we are producing an animated sequence, we must define time-varying changes in the models, lighting, and viewing specifications. The process of creating images from models is often called **rendering**. The term **rasterization** is also used to refer specifically to those steps that involve determining pixel values from input geometric primitives.

This chapter presents realistic rendering from a variety of perspectives. First, we look at some of the applications in which realistic images have been used. Then, we examine, in roughly historical progression, a series of techniques that make it possible to create successively more realistic pictures. Each technique is illustrated by a picture of a standard scene, with the new technique applied to it. Finally, we conclude with suggestions about how to approach the following chapters.

12.1 WHY REALISM?

The creation of realistic pictures is an important goal in fields such as simulation, design, entertainment and advertising, research and education, and command and control.

Simulation systems present images that not only are realistic, but also change dynamically. For example, a flight simulator shows the view that would be seen from the cockpit of a moving plane. To produce the effect of motion, the system generates and displays a new, slightly different view many times per second. Simulators have been used to train the pilots of spacecraft, airplanes, and boats—and, more recently, drivers of cars.

Designers of 3D objects such as automobiles, airplanes, and buildings want to see how their preliminary designs look. Creating realistic computer-generated images is often an easier, less expensive, and more effective way to see preliminary results than is building models and prototypes, and also allows the consideration of additional alternative designs. If the design work itself is also computer-based, a digital description of the object may already be available to use in creating the images. Ideally, the designer can also interact with the displayed image to modify the design. Automotive-design systems have been developed to determine what a car will look like under a variety of lighting conditions. Realistic graphics is often coupled with programs that analyze other aspects of the object being designed, such as its mass properties or its response to stress.

Computer-generated imagery is used extensively in the entertainment world, both in traditional animated cartoons and in realistic and surrealistic images for logos, advertisements, and science-fiction movies. Computer-generated cartoons can mimic traditional animation, but can also transcend manual techniques by introducing more complicated motion and richer or more realistic imagery. Some complex realistic images can be produced at less cost than filming them from physical models of the objects. Other images have been generated that would have been extremely difficult or impossible to stage with real models. Special-purpose hardware and software created for use in entertainment include sophisticated paint systems and real-time systems for generating special effects and for combining images. As technology improves, home and arcade video games generate increasingly realistic images.

Realistic images are becoming an essential tool in research and education. A particularly important example is the use of graphics in molecular modeling, as shown in Color Plate 22. It is interesting how the concept of realism is stretched here: The realistic depictions are not of "real" atoms, but rather of stylized ball-and-stick and volumetric models that allow larger structures to be built than are feasible with physical models, and that permit special effects, such as animated vibrating bonds and color changes representing reactions. On a macroscopic scale, movies made at JPL show NASA space-probe missions, depicted in Color Plate 23.

Another application for realistic imagery is in command and control, in which the user needs to be informed about and to control the complex process represented by the picture. Unlike simulations, which attempt to mimic what a user would actually see and feel in the simulated situation, command and control applications often create symbolic displays that emphasize certain data and suppress others to aid in decision making.

12.2 FUNDAMENTAL DIFFICULTIES

A fundamental difficulty in achieving total visual realism is the complexity of the real world. Observe the richness of your environment. There are many surface textures, subtle color gradations, shadows, reflections, and slight irregularities in the surrounding objects. Think of patterns on wrinkled cloth, the texture of skin, tousled hair, scuff marks on the floor, and chipped paint on the wall. These all combine to create a *real* visual experience. The computational costs of simulating these effects can be high: Some of the pictures shown in the color plates required many minutes or even hours for creation on powerful computers.

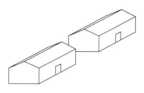

Figure 12.1
Line drawing of two houses.

A more easily met subgoal in the quest for realism is to provide sufficient information to let the viewer understand the 3D spatial relationships among several objects. This subgoal can be achieved at a significantly lower cost and is a common requirement in CAD and in many other application areas. Although highly realistic images convey 3D spatial relationships, they usually convey much more as well. For example, Fig. 12.1, a simple line drawing, suffices to persuade us that one building is partially behind the other. There is no need to show building surfaces filled with shingles and bricks, or shadows cast by the buildings. In fact, in some contexts, such extra detail may only distract the viewer's attention from more important information being depicted.

One long-standing difficulty in depicting spatial relationships is that most display devices are 2D. Therefore, 3D objects must be projected into 2D, with considerable attendant loss of information—which can sometimes create ambiguities in the image. Some of the techniques introduced in this chapter can be used to add back information of the type normally found in our visual environment, so that human depth-perception mechanisms resolve the remaining ambiguities properly.

Consider the Necker cube illusion of Fig. 12.2(a), a 2D projection of a cube; we do not know whether it represents the cube in part (b) or that in part (c) of this figure. Indeed, the viewer can easily "flip-flop" between the alternatives, because Fig. 12.2(a) does not contain enough visual information for an unambiguous interpretation.

The more the viewers know about the object being displayed, the more readily they can form what Gregory calls an **object hypothesis** [GREG70]. Figure 12.3 shows the Schröder stairway illusion—are we looking down a stairway, or looking up from underneath it? We are likely to choose the former interpretation, probably because we see stairways under our feet more frequently than over our heads and therefore *know* more about stairways viewed from above. With a small stretch of the imagination, however, we can visualize the alternative interpretation of the figure. Nevertheless, with a blink of the eye, a reversal occurs for most viewers, and the stairway again appears to be viewed from above. Of course, additional context, such as a person standing on the steps, will resolve the ambiguity.

In the following sections, we list some of the steps along the path toward realistic images. The path has actually been a set of intertwined trails, rather than a single straight road, but we have linearized it for the sake of simplicity, providing a purely descriptive introduction to the detailed treatment in subsequent chapters.

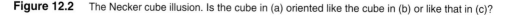

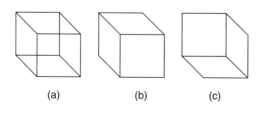

(a)   (b)   (c)

Figure 12.2   The Necker cube illusion. Is the cube in (a) oriented like the cube in (b) or like that in (c)?

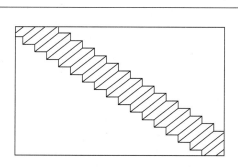

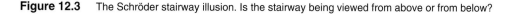

Figure 12.3   The Schröder stairway illusion. Is the stairway being viewed from above or from below?

We first mention techniques applicable to static line drawings. These methods concentrate on ways to present the 3D spatial relationships among several objects on a 2D display. Next come techniques for shaded images, made possible by raster graphics hardware, that concentrate on the interaction of objects with light. Next, we discuss the issues of increased model complexity and dynamics, applicable to both line and shaded pictures. Finally, we discuss the possibilities of true 3D images, advances in display hardware, and the future place of picture generation in the context of full, interactive environmental synthesis.

12.3 RENDERING TECHNIQUES FOR LINE DRAWINGS

In this section, we focus on a subgoal of realism: showing 3D depth relationships on a 2D surface. This goal is served by the planar geometric projections defined in Chapter 6.

12.3.1 Multiple Orthographic Views

Figure 12.4
Front, top, and side orthographic projections of the block letter "L."

The easiest projections to create are parallel orthographics, such as plan and elevation views, in which the projection plane is perpendicular to a principal axis. Since depth information is discarded, plan and elevations are typically shown together, as with the top, front, and side views of a block letter "L" in Fig. 12.4. This particular drawing is not difficult to understand; however, understanding drawings of complicated manufactured parts from a set of such views may require many hours of study. Training and experience sharpen our interpretive powers, of course, and familiarity with the types of objects being represented hastens the formulation of a correct object hypothesis. Still, scenes as complicated as that of our *standard scene* shown in Color Plate 24 are often confusing when shown in only three such projections. Although a single point may be unambiguously located from three mutually perpendicular orthographics, multiple points and lines may conceal one another when so projected.

12.3.2 Perspective Projections

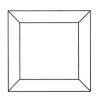

Figure 12.5
Perspective projection of a cube.

In perspective projections, an object's size is scaled in inverse proportion to its distance from the viewer. The perspective projection of a cube shown in Fig. 12.5 reflects this scaling. There is still ambiguity, however; the projection could just as well be a picture frame, or the parallel projection of a truncated pyramid, or the perspective projection of a rectangular parallelepiped with two equal faces. If our object hypothesis is a truncated pyramid, then the smaller square represents the face closer to the viewer; if the object hypothesis is a cube or rectangular parallelepiped, then the smaller square represents the face farther from the viewer.

Our interpretation of perspective projections is often based on the assumption that a smaller object is farther away. In Fig. 12.6, we would probably assume that the larger house is nearer to the viewer. However, the house that appears larger (a mansion, perhaps) may actually be more distant than the one that appears smaller (a cottage, for example), at least as long as there are no other cues, such as trees and windows. When the viewer knows that the projected objects have many parallel lines, perspective further helps to convey depth, because the parallel lines seem to converge at their vanishing points. This convergence may actually be a stronger depth cue than the effect of decreasing size. Color Plate 25 shows a perspective projection of our standard scene.

12.3.3 Depth Cueing

The depth (distance) of an object can be represented by the intensity of the image: Parts of objects that are intended to appear farther from the viewer are displayed at lower intensity. This effect is known as **depth cueing.** Depth cueing exploits the fact that distant objects appear dimmer than closer objects, especially if seen through haze. Such effects can be sufficiently convincing that artists refer to the use of changes in intensity (as well as in texture, sharpness, and color) to depict distance as **aerial perspective.** Thus, depth cueing may be seen as a simplified version of the effects of atmospheric attenuation.

In vector displays, depth cueing is implemented by interpolating the intensity of the beam along a vector as a function of its starting and ending z coordinates. Color graphics systems usually generalize the technique to support interpolating

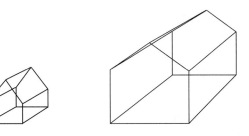

Figure 12.6   Perspective projection of two houses.

between the color of a primitive and a user-specified depth-cue color, which is typically the color of the background. To restrict the effect to a limited range of depths, PHIGS PLUS allows the user to specify front and back depth-cueing planes between which depth cueing is to occur. A separate scale factor associated with each plane indicates the proportions of the original color and the depth-cue color to be used in front of the front plane and behind the back plane. The color of points between the planes is linearly interpolated between these two values. The eye's intensity resolution is lower than its spatial resolution, so depth cueing is not useful for accurately depicting small differences in distance. It is quite effective, however, in depicting large differences, or as an exaggerated cue in depicting small ones.

12.3.4 Depth Clipping

Further depth information can be provided by **depth clipping.** The back clipping plane is placed so as to cut through the objects being displayed. Partially clipped objects are then known by the viewer to be cut by the clipping plane. A front clipping plane may also be used. By allowing the position of one or both planes to be varied dynamically, the system can convey more depth information to the viewer. Back-plane depth clipping can be thought of as a special case of depth cueing: In ordinary depth cueing, intensity is a smooth function of z; in depth clipping, it is a step function. A technique related to depth clipping is highlighting of all points on the object intersected by some plane. This technique is especially effective when the slicing plane is shown moving through the object dynamically, and has even been used to help illustrate depth along a fourth dimension [BANC77].

12.3.5 Texture

Simple vector textures, such as **cross-hatching,** may be applied to an object. These textures follow the shape of an object and delineate it more clearly. Texturing one of a set of otherwise identical faces can clarify a potentially ambiguous projection. Texturing is especially useful in perspective projections, as it adds yet more lines whose convergence and foreshortening may provide useful depth cues.

12.3.6 Color

Color may be used symbolically to distinguish one object from another by assigning a different color to each object in the scene. Color can also be used in line drawings to provide other information. For example, the color of each vector of an object may be determined by interpolating colors that encode the temperatures at the vector's endpoints.

12.3.7 Visible-Line Determination

The last line-drawing technique we mention is **visible-line determination** or **hidden-line removal**, which results in the display of only visible (i.e., unobscured) lines or parts of lines. Only surfaces, bounded by edges (lines), can obscure other lines. Thus, objects that are to block others must be modeled either as collections of surfaces or as solids.

Color Plate 26 shows the usefulness of hidden-line removal (also using color as described in Section 12.3.6). Because hidden-line–removed views conceal *all* the internal structure of opaque objects, they are not necessarily the most effective way to show depth relations. Hidden-line–removed views convey less depth information than do exploded and cutaway views. Showing hidden lines as dashed lines can be a useful compromise.

12.4 RENDERING TECHNIQUES FOR SHADED IMAGES

The techniques mentioned in Section 12.3 can be used to create line drawings on both vector and raster displays. The techniques introduced in this section exploit the ability of raster devices to display shaded areas. When pictures are rendered for raster displays, problems are introduced by the relatively coarse grid of pixels on which smooth contours and shading must be reproduced. The simplest ways to render shaded pictures fall prey to the problem of aliasing, first encountered in Section 3.14. Because of the fundamental role that antialiasing plays in producing high-quality pictures, all the pictures in this section have been created with antialiasing.

12.4.1 Visible-Surface Determination

By analogy to visible-line determination, **visible-surface determination** or **hidden-surface removal,** entails displaying only those parts of surfaces that are visible to the viewer. As we have seen, simple line drawings can often be understood without visible-line determination. When there are few lines, those in front may not seriously obstruct our view of those behind them. In raster graphics, on the other hand, if surfaces are rendered as opaque areas, then visible-surface determination is essential for the picture to make sense. Color Plate 27 shows an example in which all faces of an object are painted the same color.

12.4.2 Illumination and Shading

One problem with Color Plate 27 is that each object appears as a flat silhouette. Our next step toward achieving realism is therefore to shade the visible surfaces. Ultimately, each surface's appearance should depend on the types of light sources illuminating it, its properties (color, texture, reflectance), and its position and orientation with respect to the light sources, viewer, and other surfaces.

In many real visual environments, a considerable amount of *ambient light* impinges from all directions. Ambient light is the easiest kind of light source to model, because in a simple lighting model it is assumed to produce constant illumination on all surfaces, regardless of their position or orientation. Using ambient light by itself produces very unrealistic images, however, since few real environments are illuminated solely by uniform ambient light. Color Plate 27 is an example of a picture shaded this way.

A *point source,* whose rays emanate from a single point, can approximate a small incandescent bulb. A *directional source,* whose rays all come from the same direction, can be used to represent the distant sun by approximating it as an infinitely distant point source. Modeling these sources requires additional work because their effect depends on the surface's orientation. If the surface is *normal* (perpendicular) to the incident light rays, it is brightly illuminated; the more oblique the surface is to the light rays, the less its illumination. This variation in illumination is, of course, a powerful cue to the 3D structure of an object. Finally, a *distributed,* or *extended, source,* whose surface area emits light, such as a bank of fluorescent lights, is even more complex to model, since its light comes from neither a single direction nor a single point. Color Plate 28 shows the effect of illuminating our scene with ambient and point light sources, and shading each polygon separately.

12.4.3 Interpolated Shading

Interpolated shading is a technique in which shading information is computed for each polygon vertex and interpolated across the polygons to determine the shading at each pixel. This method is especially effective when a polygonal object description is intended to approximate a curved surface. In this case, the shading information computed at each vertex can be based on the surface's actual orientation at that point and is used for all of the polygons that share that vertex. Interpolating among these values across a polygon approximates the smooth changes in shade that occur across a curved, rather than planar, surface.

Even objects that are supposed to be polyhedral, rather than curved, can benefit from interpolated shading, since the shading information computed for each vertex of a polygon may differ, although typically much less dramatically than for a curved object. When shading information is computed for a true polyhedral object, the value determined for a polygon's vertex is used only for that polygon and not for others that share the vertex. Color Plate 29 shows Gouraud shading, a kind of interpolated shading discussed in Section 14.2.

12.4.4 Material Properties

Realism is further enhanced if the **material properties** of each object are taken into account when its shading is determined. Some materials are dull and disperse reflected light about equally in all directions, like a piece of chalk; others are shiny and reflect light only in certain directions relative to the viewer and light source, like a mirror. Color Plate 31 shows what our scene looks like when some objects are modeled as shiny. Phong shading, a more accurate interpolated shading method (Section 14.2), was used.

12.4.5 Modeling Curved Surfaces

Although interpolated shading vastly improves the appearance of an image, the object geometry is still polygonal. Color Plate 32 uses object models that include curved surfaces. Full shading information is computed at each pixel in the image.

12.4.6 Improved Illumination and Shading

One of the most important reasons for the "unreal" appearance of most computer graphics images is the failure to model accurately the many ways that light interacts with objects. Color Plate 33 uses better illumination models. Section 14.1.7 discusses progress toward the design of efficient, physically correct illumination models.

12.4.7 Texture

Object texture not only provides additional depth cues, as discussed in Section 12.3.5, but also can mimic the surface detail of real objects. Color Plate 35 shows a variety of ways in which texture may be simulated, ranging from varying the surface's color (as was done with the patterned ball), to actually deforming the surface geometry (as was done with the striated torus and crumpled cone).

12.4.8 Shadows

We can introduce further realism by reproducing shadows cast by objects on one another. Note that this technique is the first we have met in which the appearance of an object's visible surfaces is affected by other objects. Color Plate 35 shows the shadows cast by the lamp at the rear of the scene. Shadows enhance realism and provide additional depth cues: If object *A* casts a shadow on surface *B*, then we know that *A* is between *B* and a direct or reflected light source. A point light source casts sharp shadows, because from any point it is either totally visible or invisible. An extended light source casts *soft* shadows, since there is a smooth transition from those points that see all of the light source, through those that see only part of it, to those that see none of it.

12.4.9 Transparency and Reflection

Thus far, we have dealt with opaque surfaces only. Transparent surfaces can also be useful in picture making. Simple models of transparency do not include the refraction (bending) of light through a transparent solid. Lack of refraction can be a decided advantage, however, if transparency is being used not so much to simulate reality as to reveal an object's inner geometry. More complex models include refraction, diffuse translucency, and the attenuation of light with distance. Similarly, a model of light reflection may simulate the sharp reflections of a perfect mirror reflecting another object or the diffuse reflections of a less highly polished surface. Color Plate 36 shows the effect of reflection from the floor and teapot; Color Plate 41 shows transparency.

Like modeling shadows, modeling transparency or reflection requires knowledge of other surfaces besides the surface being shaded. Furthermore, refractive transparency is the first effect we have mentioned that requires objects actually to be modeled as solids rather than just as surfaces! We must know something about the materials through which a light ray passes and the distance it travels to model its refraction properly.

12.4.10 Improved Camera Models

All the pictures shown so far are based on a camera model with a pinhole lens and an infinitely fast shutter: All objects are in sharp focus and represent the world at one instant in time. It is possible to model more accurately the way that we (and cameras) see the world. For example, by modeling the focal properties of lenses, we can produce pictures, such as Color Plate 37, that show **depth of field:** Some parts of objects are in focus, whereas closer and farther parts are out of focus. See [POTM82] for details. Other techniques allow the use of special effects, such as fish-eye lenses. The lack of depth-of-field effects is responsible in part for the surreal appearance of many early computer-generated pictures.

Moving objects look different from stationary objects in a picture taken with a regular still or movie camera. Because the shutter is open for a finite period of time, visible parts of moving objects are blurred across the film plane. This effect, called **motion blur,** can be simulated convincingly [KORE83]. Motion blur not only captures the effects of motion in stills, but is of crucial importance in producing high-quality animation, as described in Chapter 21 of [FOLE90].

12.5 IMPROVED OBJECT MODELS

Independent of the rendering technology used, the search for realism has concentrated, in part, on ways of building more convincing models, both static and dynamic. Some researchers have developed models of special kinds of objects such as gases, waves, mountains, and trees; see, for example, Color Plates 11, 12, and 13. Techniques for producing these objects are based on fractals, grammar-based approaches, and particle systems. Other investigators have concentrated on advanced modeling with splines, procedural models, volume rendering, physically-based modeling, and modeling of humans. Another important topic is automating the positioning of large numbers of objects, such as trees in a forest, which would be too tedious to do by hand. Witkin and Kass [WITK88] describe an automated placement method which they applied to animating a model of *Luxo Jr.* The images of *Luxo Jr.* that appear on the cover of this book, however, are from a Pixar animation [PIXA86] whose production did not use automated placement methods. Some of these techniques are discussed in Section 9.5, while a detailed treatment can be found in Chapter 20 of [FOLE90].

12.6 DYNAMICS AND ANIMATION

12.6.1 The Value of Motion

By **dynamics,** we mean changes that spread across a sequence of pictures, including changes in position, size, material properties, lighting, and viewing specification—indeed, changes in any parts of the scene or the techniques applied to it. The benefits of dynamics can be examined independently of the progression toward more realistic static images.

Perhaps the most popular kind of dynamics is motion dynamics, ranging from simple transformations performed under user control to complex animation. Motion has been an important part of computer graphics since the field's inception. In the early days of slow raster graphics hardware, motion capability was one of the strong competitive selling points of vector graphics systems. If a series of projections of the same object, each from a slightly different viewpoint around the object, is displayed in rapid succession, then the object appears to rotate. By integrating the information across the views, the viewer creates an object hypothesis.

A perspective projection of a rotating cube, for instance, provides several types of information. There is the series of different projections, which are themselves useful. This information is supplemented by the motion effect, in which the maximum linear velocity of points near the center of rotation is lower than that of points distant from the center of rotation. This difference can help to clarify the relative distance of a point from the center of rotation. Also, the changing sizes of different parts of the cube as they change distance under perspective projection provide additional cues about the depth relationships. Motion becomes even more powerful when it is under the interactive control of the viewer. By selectively transforming an object, viewers may be able to form an object hypothesis more quickly.

In contrast to the use of simple transformations to clarify complex models, surprisingly simple models look extremely convincing if they move in a realistic fashion. For example, just a few points positioned at key parts of a human model, when moved naturally, can provide a convincing illusion of a person in motion. The points themselves do not *look like* a person, but they do inform the viewer that a person is present. It is also well known that objects in motion can be rendered with less detail than is needed to represent static objects, because the viewer has more difficulty picking out details when an object is moving. Television viewers, for example, are often surprised to discover how poor and grainy an individual television frame appears.

12.6.2 Animation

To *animate* is, literally, to bring to life. Although people often think of animation as synonymous with motion, it covers all changes that have a visual effect. It thus includes the time-varying position (**motion dynamics**), shape, color, transparency,

Plate 5. *Hard Drivin'* Arcade video game. (Courtesy of Atari Games Corporation, copyright © 1988 Atari Games Corporation.)

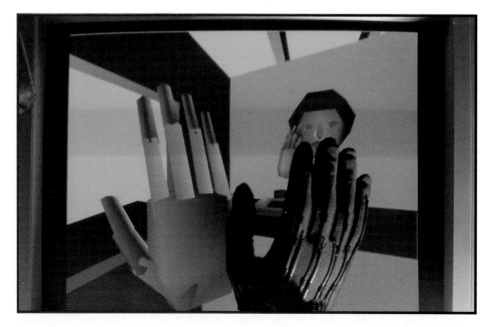

Plate 6. A DataGlove (right) and computer image of the glove. The DataGlove measures finger movements and hand orientation and position. The computer image of the hand tracks the changes. (Courtesy of Jaron Lanier, VPL.)

Plate 7. A User wearing a head-mounted stereo display, DataGloves, and microphone for issuing commands. These devices are used to create virtual reality for the user, by changing the stereo display presentation as the head is moved, with the DataGloves used to manipulate computer-generated objects. (Courtesy of Michael McGreevey and Scott Fisher, NASA Ames Research Center, Moffett Field, CA.)

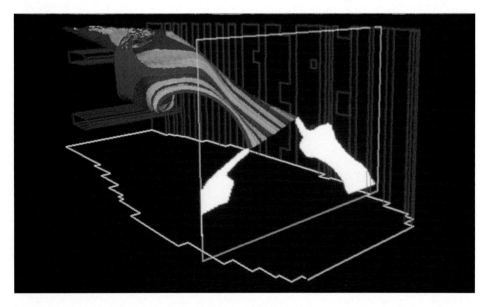

Plate 8. Krueger's Videotouch system, in which a user's hand movements are used to manipulate an object. The hand's outlines are displayed along with the objects to provide natural feedback. (Courtesy of Myron Krueger, Artificial Reality Corp.)

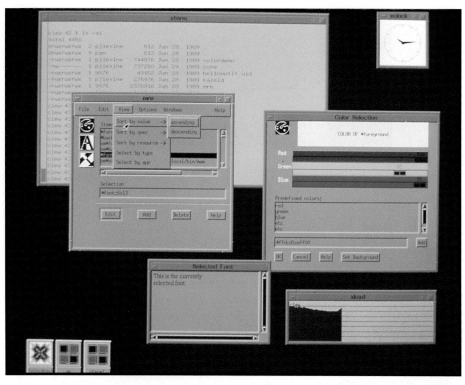

Plate 9. The OSF/Motif user interface. The color slider bars are used to define colors for use in windows. Notice the use of shading on the edges of buttons, menus, and so forth, to create a 3D effect. (Courtesy of Open Software Foundation.)

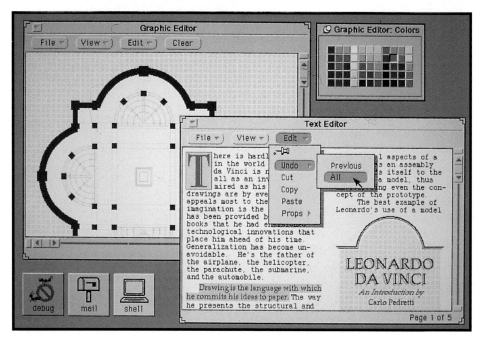

Plate 10. The OPEN LOOK user interface. Yellow is used to highlight selected text. Subdued shades are used for the background and window borders. (Courtesy of Sun Microsystems.)

Plate 12. Simple trees modeled using probabilistic grammers: (a) a palm tree; (b) and (c) fir trees. (Courtesy of Atelier de Modilisation et d'Archetecture des Plantes, © AMAP.)

Plate 13. A beach at sunset. (Courtesy of Bill Reeves, Pixar, and Alan Fournier, University of Toronto.)

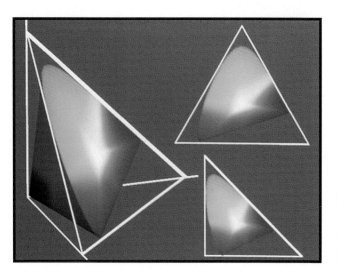

Plate 14. Several views of the $X+Y+Z = 1$ plane of CIE space. Left: the plane embedded in CIE space. Top right: a view perpendicular to the plane. Bottom right: the projection onto the (X, Y) plane (that is, the $Z = 0$ plane), which is the chromaticity diagram. (Courtesy of Barbara Meier, Brown University.)

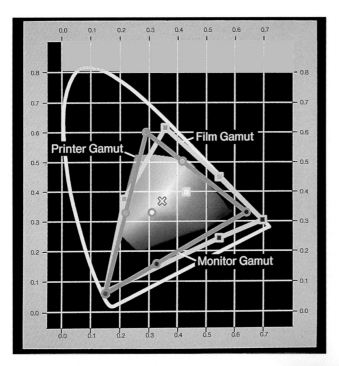

Plate 15. The CIE chromaticity diagram, showing typical color gamuts for an offset printing press, a color monitor, and for slide film. The print colors represent the Graphic Arts Technical Foundation S.W.O.P. standard colors measured under a graphic arts light with a color temperature of 5000° K. The color monitor is a Barco CTVM 3/51 with a white point set to 6500° K. and the slide film is Kodak Ektachrome 5017 ISO 64 as characterized under CIE source A: a 2653° K. black body that closely approximates a Tungsten lamp. The x, circle, and square indicate the white points for the print, color monitor, and film gamuts, respectively. (Courtesy of M. Stone, Xerox Palo Alto Research Center. Film gamut measured by A. Paeth, Computer Graphics Lab, University of Waterloo: see also the first appendix of [PAET89]).

Plate 16. Additive colors. Red plus green form yellow, red plus blue form magenta, green plus blue form cyan, red plus green plus blue form white.

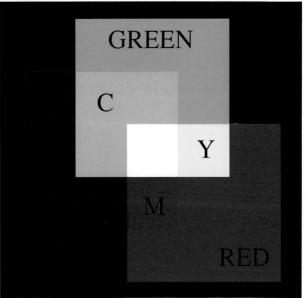

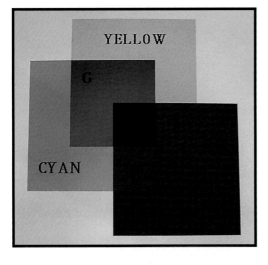

Plate 17. Subtractive colors. Yellow and magenta subtracted from white form red, yellow and cyan subtracted from white form green, cyan and magenta subtracted from white form blue.

Plate 18. An interaction technique used on the Macintosh to specify colors in the HSV space. Hue and saturation are shown in the circular area, and the value by the slider dial. The user can move the mark in the circular area and change the slider dial, or can type in new HSV or RGB values. The square color area (upper left) shows the current color and the new color.

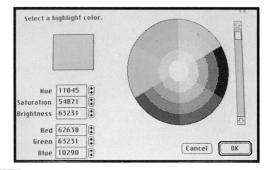

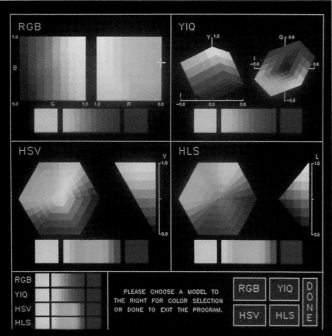

Plate 19. An interactive program that allows the user to specify and interpolate colors in four different color spaces: RGB, YIQ, HSV, and HLS. The starting and ending colors for a linear interpolation are specified by pointing at the various projections of the color spaces. The interpolation is shown below each color space, and together for comparison in the lower left. (Courtesy of Paul Charlton, The George Washington University.)

Plate 20. A pseudo-color image showing the topography of Venus. The color scale on the left indicates altitudes from -22 km to +2 km above or below an average radius for Venus of 6052 km. Data were calculated by the Lunar and Planetary Institute from radar altimetry observations by NASA's Pioneer Venus Orbiter spacecraft. The image was created with the National Space Science Data Center Graphics System. (Courtesy of Lloyd Treinish, NASA Goddard Space Flight Center.)

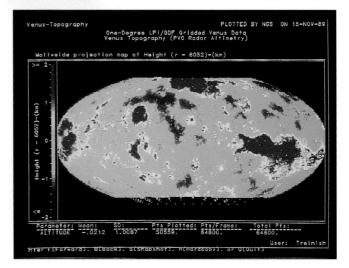

Plate 21. Chevrolet Camaro lit by five lights with Warn's lighting controls. (Courtesy of David R. Warn, General Motors Research Laboratories.)

Plate 22. Stereo pair of Polio virus capsid, imaged by placing a sphere of 0.5 nm radius at each alpha carbon position. One pentamer is removed to reveal the interior. Coordinates courtesy of J. Hogle. (Courtesy of David Goodsell and Arthur Olsen. Copyright © 1989, Research Institute of Scripps Clinic.)

Plate 23. Simulated flyby of Uranus with rings and orbit. (Courtesy of Jim Blinn, Computer Graphics Lab, Jet Propulsion Lab, California Institute of Technology.)

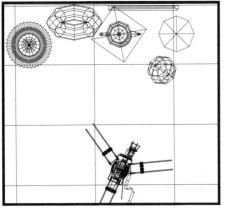

Plate 24. *Shutterbug.* Living room scene with movie camera. Orthographic projections (Sections 6.2.2 and 12.3.1). (a) Plan view. (b) Front view. (c) Side view. Polygonal models generated from spline patches. (Copyright © 1990, Pixar. Rendered by Thomas Williams and H.B. Siegal using Pixar's PhotoRealistic Renderman™ software.)

(a)

(b)

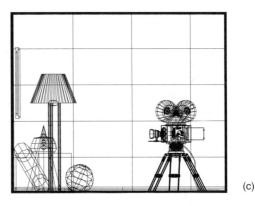

(c)

Plate 25. *Shutterbug.* Perspective Projection (Sections 6.2.1 and 12.3.2).Copyright © 1990, Pixar. Rendered by Thomas Williams and H.B. Siegal using Pixar's PhotoRealistic Renderman™ software.)

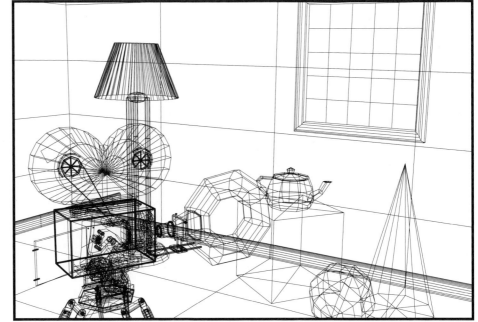

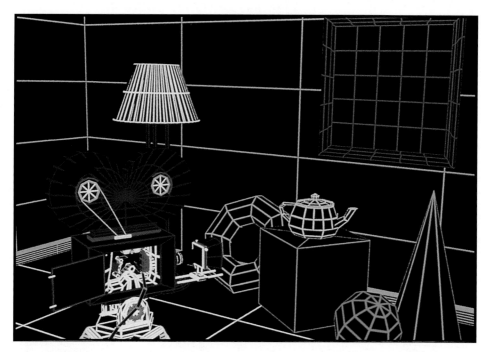

Plate 26. *Shutterbug.* Visible-line determination (Section 12.3.7). (Copyright © 1990, Pixar. Rendered by Thomas Williams and H.B. Siegal using Pixar's PhotoRealistic Renderman™ software.)

Plate 27. *Shutterbug.* Visible-surface determination with ambient illumination only (Sections 12.4.1 and 14.1.1). (Copyright © 1990, Pixar. Rendered by Thomas Williams and H.B. Siegal using Pixar's PhotoRealistic Renderman™ software.)

Plate 28. *Shutterbug.* Individually shaded polygons with diffuse reflection (Sections 12.4.2 and 14.2.3). (Copyright © 1990, Pixar. Rendered by Thomas Williams and H.B. Siegal using Pixar's PhotoRealistic Renderman™ software.)

Plate 29. *Shutterbug.* Gouraud shaded polygons with diffuse reflection (Sections 12.4.2 and 14.2.3). (Copyright © 1990, Pixar. Rendered by Thomas Williams and H.B. Siegal using Pixar's PhotoRealistic Renderman™ software.)

Plate 30. *Shutterbug.* Gouraud shaded polygons with specular reflection (Sections 12.4.4 and 14.2.4). (Copyright © 1990, Pixar. Rendered by Thomas Williams and H.B. Siegal using Pixar's PhotoRealistic Renderman™ software.)

Plate 31. *Shutterbug.* Phong shaded polygons with specular reflection (Sections 12.4.4 and 14.2.5). (Copyright © 1990, Pixar. Rendered by Thomas Williams and H.B. Siegal using Pixar's PhotoRealistic Renderman™ software.)

Plate 32. *Shutterbug.* Curved surfaces with specular reflection (Section 12.4.5). (Copyright © 1990, Pixar. Rendered by Thomas Williams and H.B. Siegal using Pixar's PhotoRealistic Renderman™ software.)

Plate 33. *Shutterbug.* Improved illumination model and multiple lights (Sections 12.4.6 and 14.1). (Copyright © 1990, Pixar. Rendered by Thomas Williams and H.B. Siegal using Pixar's PhotoRealistic Renderman™ software.)

Plate 34. *Shutterbug.* Texture mapping (Sections 12.4.7 and 14.3.2). (Copyright © 1990, Pixar. Rendered by Thomas Williams and H.B. Siegal using Pixar's PhotoRealistic Renderman™ software.)

Plate 35. *Shutterbug.* Displacement mapping (Sections 12.4.7 and 14.3.4). (Copyright © 1990, Pixar. Rendered by Thomas Williams and H.B. Siegal using Pixar's PhotoRealistic Renderman™ software.)

Plate 36.
Shutterbug.
Reflection mapping
(Section 12.4.9).
(Copyright © 1990,
Pixar. Rendered by
Thomas Williams
and H.B. Siegal
using Pixar's
PhotoRealistic
Renderman™
software.)

(a)

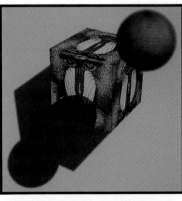

(b)

Plate 37. Depth of field, implemented by postprocessing
(Section 12.4.10). (a) Focused at cube (550 mm), f/11
aperture. (b) Focused at sphere (290 mm), f/11 aperture.
(Courtesy of Michael Potmesil and Indranil Chakravarty, RPI.)

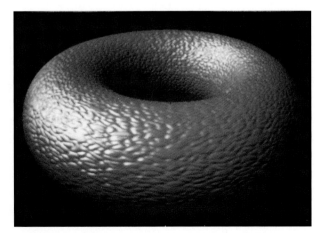

Plate 38. A torus bump mapped with a hand-generated
bump function (Section 14.3.3). (By Jim Blinn. Courtesy of
University of Utah.)

Plate 39. A strawberry bump mapped with a hand-generated bump function (Section 14.3.3). (By Jim Blinn. Courtesy of University of Utah.)

(a)   (b)

Plate 40. Two vases rendered with the Cook-Torrance illumination model (Section 14.1.7). Both are lit by two lights with $I_{i_1} = I_{i_2}$ = CIE standard illuminant D6500, $d\omega_{i_1}$ = 0.0001, and $d\omega_{i_2}$ = 0.0002; I_a = 0.01I_{i_1}; ρ = the bidirectional reflectivity of copper for normal incidence; $\rho_a = \pi\rho_d$. (a) Copper-colored plastic: k_s = 0.1; F = reflectivity of a vinyl mirror; D = Beckmann function with m = 0.15; k_d = 0.9 (b) Copper metal: k_s = 1.0; F = reflectivity of a copper mirror; D = Beckmann function with m_1 = 0.4, w_1 = 0.4, m_2 = 0.2, w_2 = 0.6, k_d = 0.0. (By Robert Cook, Program of Computer Graphics, Cornell University.)

Plate 41. Spheres and checkerboard. An early image produced with recursive ray tracing (Section 14.7). (Courtesy of Turner Whitted, Bell Laboratories.)

structure, and texture of an object (**update dynamics**), and changes in lighting, camera position, orientation, and focus, and even changes of rendering technique.

Animation is used widely in the entertainment industry, and is also being applied in education, in industrial applications such as control systems and heads-up displays and flight simulators for aircraft, and in scientific research. The scientific applications of computer graphics, and especially of animation, have come to be grouped under the heading **scientific visualization**. Visualization is more than the mere application of graphics to science and engineering, however; it can involve other disciplines, such as signal processing, computational geometry, and database theory. Often, the animations in scientific visualization are generated from simulations of scientific phenomena. The results of the simulations may be large datasets representing 2D or 3D data (e.g., in the case of fluid-flow simulations); these data are converted into images that then constitute the animation. At the other extreme, the simulation may generate positions and locations of physical objects, which must then be rendered in some form to generate the animation. This happens, for example, in chemical simulations, where the positions and orientations of the various atoms in a reaction may be generated by simulation, but the animation may show a ball-and-stick view of each molecule, or may show overlapping smoothly shaded spheres representing each atom. In some cases, the simulation program will contain an embedded animation language, so that the simulation and animation processes are simultaneous.

If some aspect of an animation changes too quickly relative to the number of animated frames displayed per second, **temporal aliasing** occurs. Examples of this are wagon wheels that apparently turn backward and the jerky motion of objects that move through a large field of view in a short time. Videotape is shown at 30 frames per second (fps), and photographic film speed is typically 24 fps, and both of these provide adequate results for many applications. Of course, to take advantage of these rates, we must create a new image for each videotape or film frame. If, instead, the animator records each image on two videotape frames, the result will be an effective 15 fps, and the motion will appear jerkier.

Traditional animation (i.e., noncomputer animation) is a discipline in itself, and we discuss few of its aspects. Rather, here we summarize the basic concepts of computer-based animation. We begin by discussing conventional animation and the ways in which computers have been used to assist in its creation. We then move on to animation produced principally by computer. Since much of this is 3D animation, many of the techniques from traditional 2D character animation no longer apply directly. Also, controlling the course of an animation is more difficult when the animator is not drawing the animation directly: it is often more difficult to describe *how* to do something than it is to do that action directly. Thus, after mentioning animation languages, we examine several animation control techniques. We conclude by discussing a few general rules for animation, and problems peculiar to animation.

Conventional and computer-assisted animation.   A conventional animation is created in a fairly fixed sequence: The story for the animation is written (or perhaps merely conceived), then a **storyboard** is laid out. A storyboard is an animation in outline form—a high-level sequence of sketches showing the structure and ideas of the animation. Next, the soundtrack (if any) is recorded, a detailed layout is produced (with a drawing for every scene in the animation), and the soundtrack is read—that is, the instants at which significant sounds occur are recorded in order. The detailed layout and the soundtrack are then correlated. Next, certain **key frames** of the animation are drawn—these are the frames in which the entities being animated are at extreme or characteristic positions, from which their intermediate positions can be inferred. The intermediate frames are then filled in (this is called **inbetweening**), and a trial film is made (a **pencil test**). The pencil-test frames are then transferred to **cels** (sheets of acetate film), either by hand copying in ink or by photocopying directly onto the cels. The cels are colored in or painted and are assembled into the correct sequence; then, they are filmed. Because of the use of key frames and inbetweening, this type of animation is called **key-frame animation.** The name is also applied to computer-based systems that mimic this process.

Many stages of conventional animation seem ideally suited to computer assistance, especially inbetweening and coloring, which can be done using a seed-fill technique [SMIT79]. Before the computer can be used, however, the drawings must be digitized. Digitizing can be done by using optical scanning, by tracing the drawings with a data tablet, or by producing the original drawings with a drawing program in the first place. The drawings may need to be postprocessed (e.g., filtered) to clean up any glitches arising from the input process (especially optical scanning) and to smooth the contours somewhat.

Animation languages.   Many different languages have been developed for describing animation, ranging from special stand-alone notations to procedure packages for use with conventional languages. (See Chapter 21 of [FOLE90].) Some animation languages are mingled with modeling languages, so the descriptions of the objects in an animation and of the animations of these objects are done at the same time.

Methods of controlling animation.   Controlling an animation is somewhat independent of the language used for describing it—most control mechanisms can be adapted for use with various types of languages. Animation-control mechanisms range from full explicit control—in which the animator explicitly describes the position and attributes of every object in a scene by means of translations, rotations, and other position- and attribute-changing operators—to the highly automated control provided by knowledge-based systems—which take high-level descriptions of an animation ("make the character walk out of the room") and generate the explicit controls that effect the changes necessary to produce the animation. Some of the more recent techniques for controlling animation are described in [FOLE90].

Basic rules of animation.   Traditional character animation developed from an art form to an industry at Walt Disney Studio between 1925 and the late 1930s. At the beginning, animation entailed little more than drawing a sequence of cartoon panels—a collection of static images that, taken together, made an animated image. As the techniques of animation developed, certain basic principles evolved that became the fundamental rules for character animation and are still in use today [LAYB79; LASS87]. Despite their origins in cartoon-character animation, many of these principles apply equally to realistic 3D animations. These rules, together with their application to 3D character animation, are surveyed in [LASS87]. It is important to recognize, however, that these rules are not absolute. Just as much of modern art has moved away from the traditional rules for drawing, many modern animators have moved away from traditional rules of animation, often with excellent results (see, e.g., [LEAF74; LEAF77]). Among the rules are *squash and stretch*, which indicates physical properties of an object by distortions of shape; *slow-in and slow-out* movements, to provide smooth transitions; and proper *staging*, or choosing a view that projects the most information about events taking place in the animation.

Problems peculiar to animation. Just as moving from 2D to 3D graphics introduced many new problems and challenges, the change from 3D to 4D (the addition of the time dimension) poses special problems as well. One of these problems is *temporal aliasing*. Just as the aliasing problems in 2D and 3D graphics are partially solved by increasing the screen resolution, the temporal aliasing problems in animation can be partially solved by increasing temporal resolution. Of course, another aspect of the 2D solution is antialiasing; the corresponding solution in 3D is temporal antialiasing.

12.7 STEREOPSIS

All the techniques we have discussed thus far present the same image to both eyes of the viewer. Now conduct an experiment: Look at your desk or table top first with one eye, then with the other. The two views differ slightly because our eyes are separated from each other by a few inches, as shown in Fig. 12.7. The *binocular disparity* caused by this separation provides a powerful depth cue called **stereopsis,** or **stereo vision.** Our brain fuses the two separate images into one that is interpreted as being in 3D. The two images are called a *stereo pair*; stereo pairs were used in the stereo viewers popular around the turn of the century and are used today in the common toy, the View-Master. Color Plate 22 shows a stereo pair of a molecule. You can fuse the two images into one 3D image by viewing them such that each eye sees only one image; you can do this, for example, by placing a stiff piece of paper between the two images perpendicular to the page. Some people can see the effect without any need for the piece of paper, and a small number of people cannot see it at all.

A variety of other techniques exists for providing different images to each eye, including glasses with polarizing filters and holography. Some of these techniques make possible true 3D images that occupy space, rather than being projected on a single plane. These displays can provide an additional 3D depth cue: Closer

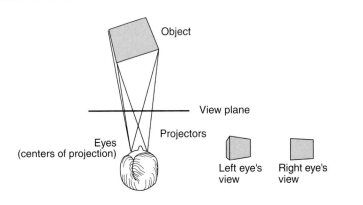

Figure 12.7   Binocular disparity.

objects actually are closer, just as in real life, so the viewer's eyes focus differently on different objects, depending on each object's proximity. The mathematics of stereo projection is described in Exercise 6.17.

12.8 IMPROVED DISPLAYS

In addition to improvements in the software used to design and render objects, improvements in the displays themselves have heightened the illusion of reality. The history of computer graphics is, in part, that of a steady improvement in the visual quality achieved by display devices. Still, a modern monitor's color gamut and its dynamic intensity range are both a small subset of what we can see. We have a long way to go before the image on our display can equal the crispness and contrast of a well-printed professional photograph! Limited display resolution makes it impossible to reproduce extremely fine detail. Artifacts such as a visible phosphor pattern, glare from the screen, geometric distortion, and the stroboscopic effect of frame-rate flicker are ever-present reminders that we are viewing a display. The display's relatively small size, compared with our field of vision, also helps to remind us that the display is a window on a world, rather than a world itself.

12.9 INTERACTING WITH OUR OTHER SENSES

Perhaps the final step toward realism is the integration of realistic imagery with information presented to our other senses. Computer graphics has a long history of programs that rely on a variety of input devices to allow user interaction. Flight simulators are a current example of the coupling of graphics with realistic engine sounds and motion, all offered in a mocked-up cockpit to create an entire environment. Wearing a head-worn simulator, which monitors head motion, makes possible another important 3D depth cue called *head-motion parallax*: When the user moves his or her head from side to side, perhaps to try to see more of a partially hidden object, the view changes as it would in real life. Other active work on head-mounted displays centers on the exploration of *virtual worlds,* such as the insides of molecules or of buildings that have not yet been constructed [CHUN89].

Many current arcade games feature a car or plane that the player rides, moving in time to a simulation that includes synthesized or digitized images, sound, and force feedback. This use of additional output and input modalities points the way to systems of the future that will provide complete immersion of all the senses, including hearing, touch, taste, and smell.

SUMMARY

In this chapter, we provided a high-level introduction to the techniques used to produce realistic images. In the following chapters, we discuss in detail how these techniques can be implemented. There are four key questions that you should bear in mind when you read about the algorithms presented in later chapters:

1. *Is the algorithm general or special purpose?* Some techniques work best only in specific circumstances; others are designed to be more general. For example, some algorithms assume that all objects are convex polyhedra and derive part of their speed and relative simplicity from this assumption.

2. *What is the algorithm's space–time performance?* How is the algorithm affected by factors such as the size or complexity of the database, or the resolution at which the picture is rendered?

3. *How convincing are the effects generated?* For example, is refraction modeled correctly, does it look right only in certain special cases, or is it not modeled at all? Can additional effects, such as shadows or specular reflection, be added? How convincing will they be? Sacrificing the accuracy with which an effect is rendered may make possible significant improvements in a program's space or time requirements.

4. *Is the algorithm appropriate, given the purpose for which the picture is created?* The philosophy behind many of the pictures in the following chapters can be summed up by the credo, "If it looks good, do it!" This directive can be interpreted two ways. A simple or fast algorithm may be used if it produces attractive effects, even if no justification can be found in the laws of physics. On the other hand, a shockingly expensive algorithm may be used if it is the only known way to render certain effects.

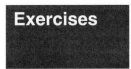

12.1   Suppose you had a graphics system that could draw any of the color plates referenced in this chapter in real time. Consider several application areas with which you are (or would like to be) familiar. For each area, list those effects that would be most useful, and those that would be least useful.

12.2   Show that you cannot infer the direction of rotation from orthographic projections of a monochrome, rotating, wireframe cube. Explain how additional techniques can help to make the direction of rotation clear without changing the projection.

13 Visible-Surface Determination

Given a set of 3D objects and a viewing specification, we wish to determine which lines or surfaces of the objects are visible, either from the center of projection (for perspective projections) or along the direction of projection (for parallel projections), so that we can display only the visible lines or surfaces. This process is known as **visible-line** or **visible-surface determination,** or **hidden-line** or **hidden-surface elimination.** In visible-line determination, lines are assumed to be the edges of opaque surfaces that may obscure the edges of other surfaces farther from the viewer. Therefore, we shall refer to the general process as **visible-surface determination**.

Although the statement of this fundamental idea is simple, its implementation requires significant processing power, and consequently involves large amounts of computer time on conventional machines. These requirements have encouraged the development of numerous carefully structured visible-surface algorithms, many of which are described in this chapter. In addition, many special-purpose architectures have been designed to address the problem, some of which are discussed in Chapter 18 of [FOLE90]. The need for this attention can be seen from an analysis of two fundamental approaches to the problem. In both cases, we can think of each object as comprising one or more polygons (or more complex surfaces).

The first approach determines which of n objects is visible at each pixel in the image. The pseudocode for this approach looks like this:

```
for ( each pixel in the image ) {
    determine the object closest to the viewer that is pierced by
        the projector through the pixel;
```

> *draw the pixel in the appropriate color;*
> }

A straightforward, brute-force way of doing this for 1 pixel requires examining all n objects to determine which is closest to the viewer along the projector passing through the pixel. For p pixels, the effort is proportional to np, where p is over 1 million for a high-resolution display.

The second approach is to compare objects directly with each other, eliminating entire objects or portions of them that are not visible. Expressed in pseudocode, this becomes

> **for** (*each object in the world*) {
>   *determine those parts of the object whose view is unobstructed*
>   *by other parts of it or any other object;*
>   *draw those parts in the appropriate color;*
> }

We can do this naively by comparing each of the n objects to itself and to the other objects, and discarding invisible portions. The computational effort here is proportional to n^2. Although this second approach might seem superior for $n < p$, its individual steps are typically more complex and time consuming, as we shall see, so it is often slower and more difficult to implement.

We shall refer to these prototypical approaches as **image-precision** and **object-precision** algorithms, respectively. Image-precision algorithms are typically performed at the resolution of the display device, and determine the visibility at each pixel. Object-precision algorithms are performed at the precision with which each object is defined, and they determine the visibility of each object.[1] Since object-precision calculations are done without regard to a particular display resolution, they must be followed by a step in which the objects are actually displayed at the desired resolution. Only this final display step needs to be repeated if the size of the finished image is changed, for example, to cover a different number of pixels on a raster display. The reason that the geometry of each visible object's projection is represented at the full object database resolution. In contrast, consider enlarging an image created by an image-precision algorithm. Since visible-surface calculations were performed at the original lower resolution, they must be done again if we wish to reveal further detail. Thus, image-precision algorithms fall prey to aliasing in computing visibility, whereas object-precision algorithms do not.

Object-precision algorithms were first developed for vector graphics systems. On these devices, hidden-line removal was most naturally accomplished by turning the initial list of lines into one in which lines totally hidden by other surfaces

---

[1] The terms *image space* and *object space,* popularized by Sutherland, Sproull, and Schumacker [SUTH74a], are often used to draw the same distinction. Unfortunately, these terms have also been used quite differently in computer graphics. For example, *image space* has been used to refer to objects after perspective transformation [CATM75] or after projection onto the view plane [GILO78], but still at their original precision. To avoid confusion, we have opted for our slightly modified terms. We refer explicitly to an object's perspective transformation or projection, when appropriate, and reserve the terms *image precision* and *object precision* to indicate the precision with which computations are performed. For example, intersecting two objects' projections on the view plane is an object-precision operation if the precision of the original object definitions is maintained.

were removed, and partially hidden lines were clipped to one or more visible line segments. All processing was performed at the precision of the original list and resulted in a list in the same format. In contrast, image-precision algorithms were first written for raster devices to take advantage of the relatively small number of pixels for which the visibility calculations had to be performed. This was an understandable partitioning. Vector displays had a large address space (4096×4096 even in early systems) and severe limits on the number of lines and objects that could be displayed. Raster displays, on the other hand, had a limited address space (256×256 in early systems) and the ability to display a potentially unbounded number of objects. Later algorithms often combine both object- and image-precision calculations, with object-precision calculations chosen for accuracy and image-precision ones chosen for speed.

In this chapter, we first introduce a variety of issues relating to the efficiency of general visible-surface algorithms. Then, we present the major approaches to determining visible surfaces.

13.1 TECHNIQUES FOR EFFICIENT VISIBLE-SURFACE ALGORITHMS

The formulations of typical image-precision and object-precision algorithms can require a number of potentially costly operations. These operations include determining for a projector and an object, or for two objects' projections, whether or not they intersect and where they intersect. Then, for each set of intersections, it is necessary to compute the object that is closest to the viewer and therefore visible. To minimize the time that it takes to create a picture, we must organize visible-surface algorithms so that costly operations are performed as efficiently and as infrequently as possible. The following sections describe some general ways to do this.

13.1.1 Coherence

Sutherland, Sproull, and Schumacker [SUTH74a] point out how visible-surface algorithms can take advantage of **coherence**—the degree to which parts of an environment or its projection exhibit local similarities. Environments typically contain objects whose properties vary smoothly from one part to another. In fact, it is the less-frequent discontinuities in properties (such as depth, color, and texture), and the effects that they produce in pictures, that let us distinguish between objects. We exploit coherence when we reuse calculations made for one part of the environment or picture for other nearby parts, either without changes or with incremental changes that are more efficient to make than recalculating the information from scratch. Many different kinds of coherence have been identified [SUTH74a], which we list here and refer to later:

- **Object coherence.** If one object is entirely separate from another, comparisons may need to be done only between the two objects, not between their component faces or edges. For example, if all parts of object A are farther from the viewer than are all parts of object B, none of A's faces need be compared with B's faces to determine whether they obscure B's faces.

- **Face coherence.** Surface properties typically vary smoothly across a face, allowing computations for one part of a face to be modified incrementally to apply to adjacent parts. In some models, faces can be guaranteed not to interpenetrate.

- **Edge coherence.** An edge may change visibility only where it crosses behind a visible edge or penetrates a visible face.

- **Implied edge coherence.** If one planar face penetrates another, their line of intersection (the implied edge) can be determined from two points of intersection.

- **Scan-line coherence.** The set of visible object spans determined for one scan line of an image typically differs little from the set on the previous line.

- **Area coherence.** A group of adjacent pixels is often covered by the same visible face. A special case of area coherence is **span coherence,** which refers to a face's visibility over a span of adjacent pixels on a scan line.

- **Depth coherence.** Adjacent parts of the same surface are typically close in depth, whereas different surfaces at the same screen location are typically separated farther in depth. Once the depth at one point of the surface is calculated, the depth of points on the rest of the surface can often be determined by a simple difference equation.

- **Frame coherence.** Pictures of the same environment at two successive points in time are likely to be quite similar, despite small changes in objects and viewpoint. Calculations made for one picture can be reused for the next in a sequence.

13.1.2 The Perspective Transformation

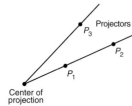

Figure 13.1
If two points P_1 and P_2 are on the same projector, then the closer one obscures the other; otherwise, it does not (e.g., P_1 does not obscure P_3).

Visible-surface determination clearly must be done in a 3D space prior to the projection into 2D that destroys the depth information needed for depth comparisons. Regardless of the kind of projection chosen, the basic depth comparison at a point can be typically reduced to the following question: Given points $P_1 = (x_1, y_1, z_1)$ and $P_2 = (x_2, y_2, z_2)$, does either point obscure the other? This question is the same: Are P_1 and P_2 on the same projector (see Fig. 13.1)? If the answer is yes, z_1 and z_2 are compared to determine which point is closer to the viewer. If the answer is no, then neither point can obscure the other.

Depth comparisons are typically done after the normalizing transformation (Chapter 6) has been applied, so that projectors are parallel to the z axis in parallel projections or emanate from the origin in perspective projections. For a parallel projection, the points are on the same projector if $x_1 = x_2$ and $y_1 = y_2$. For a perspective projection, we must unfortunately perform four divisions to determine whether $x_1/z_1 = x_2/z_2$ and $y_1/z_1 = y_2/z_2$, in which case the points are on the same

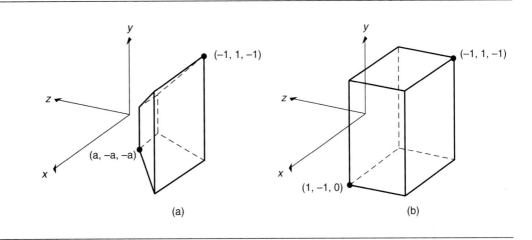

(a)   (b)

Figure 13.2   The normalized perspective view volume (a) before and (b) after perspective transformation.

projector, as shown in Fig. 13.1. Moreover, if P_1 is later compared against some P_3, two more divisions are required.

Unnecessary divisions can be avoided by first transforming a 3D object into the 3D screen-coordinate system, so that the parallel projection of the transformed object is the same as the perspective projection of the untransformed object. Then the test for one point obscuring another is the same as for parallel projections. This perspective transformation distorts the objects and moves the center of projection to infinity on the positive z axis, making the projectors parallel. Figure 13.2 shows the effect of this transformation on the perspective view volume; Fig. 13.3 shows how a cube is distorted by the transformation.

The essence of such a transformation is that it preserves relative depth, straight lines, and planes, and at the same time performs the perspective foreshortening. The division that accomplishes the foreshortening is done just once per point, rather than each time two points are compared. The matrix

$$M = \begin{bmatrix} 1 & 0 & 0 & 0 \\ 0 & 1 & 0 & 0 \\ 0 & 0 & \dfrac{1}{1+z_{min}} & \dfrac{-z_{min}}{1+z_{min}} \\ 0 & 0 & -1 & 0 \end{bmatrix}, \qquad 0 > z_{min} > -1 \qquad (13.1)$$

transforms the normalized perspective view volume into the rectangular parallelepiped bounded by

$$-1 \le x \le 1, \qquad -1 \le y \le 1, \qquad -1 \le z \le 0. \qquad (13.2)$$

Clipping can be done against the normalized truncated-pyramid view volume before M is applied, but then the clipped results must be multiplied by M. A more attractive alternative is to incorporate M into the perspective normalizing

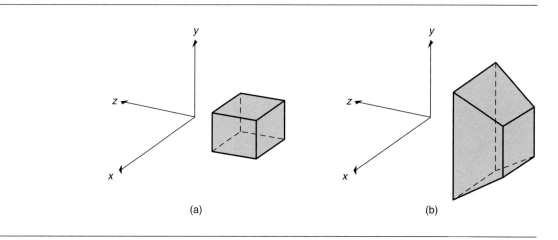

Figure 13.3   A cube (a) before and (b) after perspective transformation.

transformation N_{per} from Chapter 6, so that just a single matrix multiplication is needed, and then to clip in homogeneous coordinates prior to the division. If we call the results of that multiplication (X, Y, Z, W), then, for $W > 0$, the clipping limits become

$$-W \leq X \leq W, \qquad -W \leq Y \leq W, \qquad -W \leq Z \leq 0. \qquad (13.3)$$

These limits are derived from Eq. (13.2) by replacing x, y, and z by X/W, Y/W, and Z/W, respectively, to reflect the fact that x, y, and z in Eq. (13.2) result from division by W. After clipping, we divide by W to obtain (x_p, y_p, z_p). Note that M assumes that the view volume is in the negative z half-space. For notational convenience, however, our examples will often use decreasing positive z values, rather than decreasing negative z values, to indicate increasing distance from the viewer. In contrast, many graphics systems transform their right-handed world into a left-handed viewing coordinate system, in which increasing positive z values correspond to increasing distance from the viewer.

We can now proceed with visible-surface determination unfettered by the complications suggested by Fig. 13.1. Of course, when a parallel projection is specified, the perspective transformation M is unnecessary, because the normalizing transformation N_{par} for parallel projections makes the projectors parallel to the z axis.

13.1.3 Extents and Bounding Volumes

Screen extents, introduced in Chapter 3 as a way to avoid unnecessary clipping, are also commonly used to avoid unnecessary comparisons between objects or their projections. Figure 13.4 shows two objects (3D polygons, in this case), their projections, and the upright rectangular screen extents surrounding the projections.

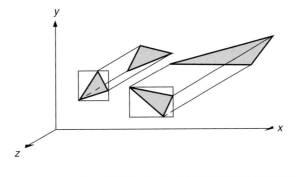

Figure 13.4 Two objects, their projections onto the (x, y) plane, and the extents surrounding the projections.

The objects are assumed to have been transformed by the perspective transformation matrix M of Section 13.1.2. Therefore, for polygons, orthographic projection onto the (x, y) plane is done trivially by ignoring each vertex's z coordinate. In Fig. 13.4, the extents do not overlap, so the projections do not need to be tested for overlap with one another. If the extents overlap, one of two cases occurs, as shown in Fig. 13.5: Either the projections also overlap, as in part (a), or they do not, as in part (b). In both cases, more comparisons must be performed to determine whether the projections overlap. In part (b), the comparisons will establish that the two projections really do not intersect; in a sense, the overlap of the extents was a false alarm. Extent testing thus provides a service similar to that of trivial reject testing in clipping.

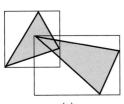

(a)

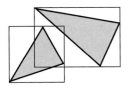

(b)

Figure 13.5
Extents bounding object projections. (a) Extents and projections overlap. (b) Extents overlap, but projections do not.

Rectangular-extent testing is also known as **bounding-box** testing. Extents can be used as in Chapter 7 to surround the objects themselves rather than their projections: In this case, the extents become solids and are also known as **bounding volumes**. Alternatively, extents can be used to bound a single dimension, in order to determine, say, whether or not two objects overlap in z. Figure 13.6 shows the use of extents in such a case; here, an extent is the infinite volume bounded by the minimum and maximum z values for each object. There is no overlap in z if

$$z_{max2} < z_{min1} \quad \text{or} \quad z_{max1} < z_{min2}. \tag{13.4}$$

Comparing against minimum and maximum bounds in one or more dimensions is also known as **minmax** testing. When comparing minmax extents, the most complicated part of the job is finding the extent itself. For polygons (or for other objects that are wholly contained within the convex hull of a set of defining points), an extent may be computed by iterating through the list of point coordinates and recording the largest and smallest values for each coordinate.

Extents and bounding volumes are used not only to compare two objects or their projections with each other, but also to determine whether or not a projector intersects an object. This involves computing the intersection of a point with a 2D projection or a vector with a 3D object, as described in Section 13.4.

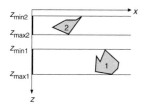

Figure 13.6
Using 1D extents to
determine whether objects
overlap.

Although we have discussed only minmax extents so far, other bounding volumes are possible. What is the best bounding volume to use? Not surprisingly, the answer depends on both the expense of performing tests on the bounding volume itself and on how well the volume protects the enclosed object from tests that do not yield an intersection. Weghorst, Hooper, and Greenberg [WEGH84] treat bounding-volume selection as a matter of minimizing the total cost function T of the intersection test for an object. This may be expressed as

$$T = bB + oO, \tag{13.5}$$

where b is the number of times the bounding volume is tested for intersection, B is the cost of performing an intersection test on the bounding volume, o is the number of times the object is tested for intersection (the number of times the bounding volume is actually intersected), and O is the cost of performing an intersection test on the object.

Since the object intersection test is performed only when the bounding volume is actually intersected, $o \leq b$. Although O and b are constant for a particular object and set of tests to be performed, B and o vary as a function of the bounding volume's shape and size. A *tighter* bounding volume, which minimizes o, is typically associated with a greater B. A bounding volume's effectiveness may also depend on an object's orientation or the kind of objects with which that object will be intersected.

13.1.4 Back-Face Culling

If an object is approximated by a solid polyhedron, then its polygonal faces completely enclose its volume. Assume that all the polygons have been defined such that their surface normals point out of their polyhedron. If none of the polyhedron's interior is exposed by the front clipping plane, then those polygons whose surface normals point away from the observer lie on a part of the polyhedron whose visibility is completely blocked by other closer polygons, as shown in Fig. 13.7. Such invisible **back-facing** polygons can be eliminated from further processing, a technique known as **back-face culling.** By analogy, those polygons that are not back-facing are often called **front-facing**.

In eye coordinates, a back-facing polygon may be identified by the nonnegative dot product that its surface normal forms with the vector from the center of projection to any point on the polygon. (Strictly speaking, the dot product is positive for a back-facing polygon; a zero dot product indicates a polygon being viewed on edge.) Assuming that the perspective transformation has been performed or that an orthographic projection onto the (x, y) plane is desired, then the direction of projection is $(0, 0, -1)$. In this case, the dot-product test reduces to selecting a polygon as back-facing only if its surface normal has a negative z coordinate. If the environment consists of a single convex polyhedron, back-face culling is the only visible-surface calculation that needs to be performed. Otherwise, there may be front-facing polygons, such as C and E in Fig. 13.7, that are partially or totally obscured.

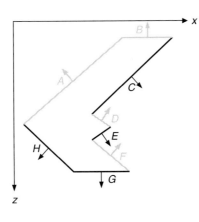

Figure 13.7   Back-face culling. Back-facing polygons (*A,B,D,F*), shown in gray, are eliminated, whereas front-facing polygons (*C,E,G,H*) are retained.

If the polyhedra have missing or clipped front faces, or if the polygons are not part of polyhedra at all, then back-facing polygons may still be given special treatment. If culling is not desired, the simplest approach is to treat a back-facing polygon as though it were front-facing, flipping its normal in the opposite direction. In PHIGS PLUS, the user can specify a completely separate set of properties for each side of a surface.

Note that a projector passing through a polyhedron intersects the same number of back-facing polygons as of front-facing ones. Thus, a point in a polyhedron's projection lies in the projections of as many back-facing polygons as front-facing ones. Back-face culling therefore halves the number of polygons to be considered for each pixel in an image-precision visible surface algorithm. On average, approximately one-half of a polyhedron's polygons are back-facing. Thus, back-face culling also typically halves the number of polygons to be considered by the remainder of an object-precision visible-surface algorithm. (Note, however, that this is true only on average. For example, a pyramid's base may be that object's only back- or front-facing polygon.)

13.1.5 Spatial Partitioning

Spatial partitioning (also known as **spatial subdivision**) allows us to break down a large problem into a number of smaller ones. The basic approach is to assign objects or their projections to spatially coherent groups as a preprocessing step. For example, we can divide the projection plane with a coarse, regular 2D rectangular grid and determine in which grid spaces each object's projection lies. Projections need to be compared for overlap with only those other projections that fall within their grid boxes. This technique is used by [ENCA72; MAHN73; FRAN80;

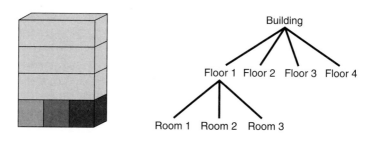

Figure 13.8   Hierarchy can be used to restrict the number of object comparisons needed. Only if a projector intersects the building and floor does it need to be tested for intersection with rooms 1 through 3.

HEDG82]. Spatial partitioning can be used to impose a regular 3D grid on the objects in the environment. The process of determining which objects intersect with a projector can then be sped up by first determining which partitions the projector intersects and then testing only the objects lying within those partitions (Section 13.4).

If the objects being depicted are unequally distributed in space, it may be more efficient to use **adaptive partitioning**, in which the size of each partition varies. One approach to adaptive partitioning is to subdivide space recursively until some termination criterion is fulfilled for each partition. For example, subdivision may stop when there are fewer than some maximum number of objects in a partition [TAMM82]. The quadtree, octree, and BSP-tree data structures of Section 10.6 are particularly attractive for this purpose.

13.1.6 Hierarchy

As we saw in Chapter 7, hierarchies can be useful for relating the structure and motion of different objects. A nested hierarchical model, in which each child is considered part of its parent, can also be used to restrict the number of object comparisons needed by a visible-surface algorithm [CLAR76; RUBI80; WEGH84]. An object on one level of the hierarchy can serve as an extent for its children if they are entirely contained within it, as shown in Fig. 13.8. In this case, if two objects in the hierarchy fail to intersect, the lower-level objects of one do not need to be tested for intersection with those of the other. Similarly, only if a projector is found to penetrate an object in the hierarchy must it be tested against the object's children. This use of hierarchy is an important instance of object coherence.

In the rest of this chapter, we discuss the rich variety of algorithms developed for visible-surface determination. We concentrate here on computing which parts of an object's surfaces are visible, leaving the determination of surface color to Chapter 14. In describing each algorithm, we emphasize its application to polygons, but point out when it can be generalized to handle other objects.

13.2 THE z-BUFFER ALGORITHM

The **z-buffer**, or **depth-buffer**, image-precision algorithm, developed by Catmull [CATM74], is one of the simplest visible-surface algorithms to implement in either software or hardware. It requires that we have available not only a frame buffer F in which color values are stored, but also a z-**buffer** Z, with the same number of entries, in which a z value is stored for each pixel. The z-buffer is initialized to zero, representing the z value at the back clipping plane, and the frame buffer is initialized to the background color. The largest value that can be stored in the z-buffer represents the z of the front clipping plane. Polygons are scan-converted into the frame buffer in arbitrary order. During the scan-conversion process, if the polygon point being scan-converted at (x, y) is no farther from the viewer than is the point whose color and depth are currently in the buffers, then the new point's color and depth replace the old values. The pseudocode for the z-buffer algorithm is shown in Prog. 13.1. The WritePixel and ReadPixel procedures introduced in Chapter 3 are supplemented here by WriteZ and ReadZ procedures that write and read the z-buffer.

Program 13.1

Pseudocode for the z-buffer algorithm.

```
void zBuffer()
{
    int  pz;                                /* Polygon's z at pixel coords (x, y) */
        for (y = 0; y < YMAX; y++) {
            for (x = 0; x < XMAX; x++) {
                WritePixel (x, y, BACKGROUND_VALUE);
                WriteZ (x, y, 0);
            }
        }
        for (each polygon ) {
            for (each pixel in polygon's projection) {
                pz = polygon's z-value at pixel coords (x, y);
                if (pz >= ReadZ (x, y)) {        /* New point is not farther */
                    WriteZ (x, y, pz);
                    WritePixel (x, y, polygon's color at pixel coords (x, y));
                }
            }
        }
}
```

No presorting is necessary and no object–object comparisons are required. The entire process is no more than a search over each set of pairs $\{Z_i(x, y), F_i(x, y)\}$ for fixed x and y, to find the largest Z_i. The z-buffer and the frame buffer record the information associated with the largest z encountered thus far for each (x, y). Thus, polygons appear on the screen in the order in which they are processed. Each polygon may be scan-converted one scan line at a time into the buffers, as described in Section 3.5. Figure 13.9 shows the addition of two polygons to an image. Each pixel's shade is shown by its color; its z is shown as a number.

Remembering our discussion of depth coherence, we can simplify the calculation of z for each point on a scan line by exploiting the fact that a polygon is planar. Normally, to calculate z, we would solve the plane equation $Ax + By + Cz + D = 0$ for the variable z:

$$z = \frac{-D - Ax - By}{C}. \tag{13.6}$$

Now, if at (x, y) Eq. (13.6) evaluates to z_1, then at $(x + \Delta x, y)$ the value of z is

$$z_1 - \frac{A}{C}(\Delta x). \tag{13.7}$$

Only one subtraction is needed to calculate $z(x + 1, y)$ given $z(x, y)$, since the quotient A/C is constant and $\Delta x = 1$. A similar incremental calculation can be performed to determine the first value of z on the next scan line, decrementing by B/C for each Δy. Alternatively, if the surface has not been determined or if the polygon is not planar (see Section 9.1.2), $z(x, y)$ can be determined by interpolating the z coordinates of the polygon's vertices along pairs of edges, and then across each scan line, as shown in Fig. 13.10. Incremental calculations can be used here as well. Note that the color at a pixel does not need to be computed if the conditional determining the pixel's visibility is not satisfied. Therefore, if the shading computation is time consuming, additional efficiency can be gained by performing a rough front-to-back depth sort of the objects to display the closest objects first. The z-buffer algorithm does not require that objects be polygons. Indeed, one of its most powerful attractions is that it can be used to render any object if a shade and a z value can be determined for each point in its projection; no explicit intersection algorithms need to be written.

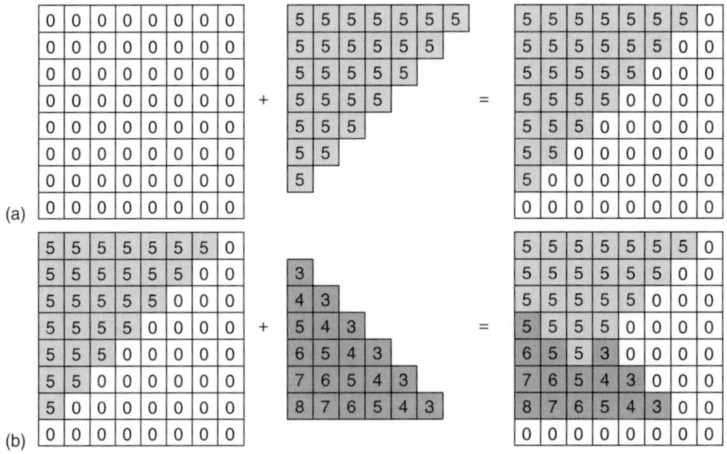

Figure 13.9   The z-buffer. A pixel's shade is shown by its color, its z value is shown as a number. (a) Adding a polygon of constant z to the empty z-buffer. (b) Adding another polygon that intersects the first.

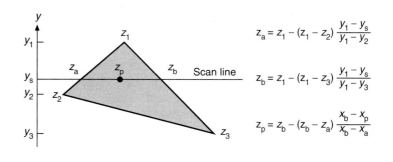

$$z_a = z_1 - (z_1 - z_2) \frac{y_1 - y_s}{y_1 - y_2}$$

$$z_b = z_1 - (z_1 - z_3) \frac{y_1 - y_s}{y_1 - y_3}$$

$$z_p = z_b - (z_b - z_a) \frac{x_b - x_p}{x_b - x_a}$$

Figure 13.10   Interpolation of z values along polygon edges and scan lines. z_a is interpolated between z_1 and z_2; z_b between z_1 and z_3; z_p between z_a and z_b.

The z-buffer algorithm performs radix sorts in x and y, requiring no comparisons, and its z sort takes only one comparison per pixel for each polygon containing that pixel. The time taken by the visible-surface calculations tends to be independent of the number of polygons in the objects because, on the average, the number of pixels covered by each polygon decreases as the number of polygons in the view volume increases. Therefore, the average size of each set of pairs being searched tends to remain fixed. Of course, it is also necessary to take into account the scan-conversion overhead imposed by the additional polygons.

Although the z-buffer algorithm requires a large amount of space for the z-buffer, it is easy to implement. If memory is at a premium, the image can be scan-converted in strips, so that only enough z-buffer for the strip being processed is required, at the expense of performing multiple passes through the objects. Because of the z-buffer's simplicity and the lack of additional data structures, decreasing memory costs have inspired a number of hardware and firmware implementations of the z-buffer. Because the z-buffer algorithm operates in image precision, however, it is subject to aliasing. The A-buffer algorithm [CARP84] addresses this problem by using a discrete approximation to unweighted area sampling.

The z-buffer is often implemented with 16- through 32-bit integer values in hardware, but software (and some hardware) implementations may use floating point values. Although a 16-bit z-buffer offers an adequate range for many CAD/CAM applications, 16 bits do not have enough precision to represent environments in which objects defined with millimeter detail are positioned a kilometer apart. To make matters worse, if a perspective projection is used, the compression of distant z values resulting from the perspective divide has a serious effect on the depth ordering and intersections of distant objects. Two points that would transform to different integer z values if close to the view plane may transform to the same z value if they are farther back (see Exercise 13.9 and [HUGH89]).

The z-buffer's finite precision is responsible for another aliasing problem. Scan-conversion algorithms typically render two different sets of pixels when drawing the common part of two collinear edges that start at different endpoints. Some of those pixels shared by the rendered edges may also be assigned slightly different z values because of numerical inaccuracies in performing the z interpolation. This effect is most noticeable at the shared edges of a polyhedron's faces. Some of the visible pixels along an edge may be part of one polygon, while the rest come from the polygon's neighbor. The problem can be fixed by inserting extra vertices to ensure that vertices occur at the same points along the common part of two collinear edges.

Even after the image has been rendered, the z-buffer can still be used to advantage. Since it is the only data structure used by the visible-surface algorithm proper, it can be saved along with the image and used later to merge in other objects whose z can be computed. The algorithm can also be coded so as to leave the z-buffer contents unmodified when rendering selected objects. If the z-buffer is masked off this way, then a single object can be written into a separate set of overlay planes with hidden surfaces properly removed (if the object is a single-valued function of x and y) and then erased without affecting the contents of the z-buffer. Thus, a simple object, such as a ruled grid, can be moved about the image in x, y, and z, to serve as a *3D cursor* that obscures and is obscured by the objects in the environment. Cutaway views can be created by making the z-buffer and framebuffer writes contingent on whether the z value is behind a cutting plane. If the objects being displayed have a single z value for each (x, y), then the z-buffer contents can also be used to compute area and volume.

Rossignac and Requicha [ROSS86] discuss how to adapt the z-buffer algorithm to handle objects defined by CSG. Each pixel in a surface's projection is written only if it is both closer in z and on a CSG object constructed from the surface. Instead of storing only the point with closest z at each pixel, Atherton suggests saving a list of all points, ordered by z and accompanied by each surface's identity, to form an **object buffer** [ATHE81]. A postprocessing stage determines how the image is displayed. A variety of effects, such as transparency, clipping, and Boolean set operations, can be achieved by processing each pixel's list, without any need to re–scan convert the objects.

13.3 SCAN-LINE ALGORITHMS

Scan-line algorithms, first developed by Wylie, Romney, Evans, and Erdahl [WYLI67], Bouknight [BOUK70a; BOUK70b], and Watkins [WATK70], operate at image precision to create an image one scan line at a time. The basic approach is an extension of the polygon scan-conversion algorithm described in Section 3.5, and thus uses a variety of forms of coherence, including scan-line coherence and edge coherence. The difference is that we deal not with just one polygon, but rather with a set of polygons. The first step is to create an **edge table** (ET) for all nonhorizontal edges of all polygons projected on the view plane. As before, horizontal edges are ignored. Entries in the ET are sorted into buckets based on each edge's smaller y coordinate, and within buckets are ordered by increasing x coordinate of their lower endpoint. Each entry contains:

1. The x coordinate of the end with the smaller y coordinate.
2. The y coordinate of the edge's other end.
3. The x increment, Δx, used in stepping from one scan line to the next (Δx is the inverse slope of the edge).
4. The polygon identification number, indicating the polygon to which the edge belongs.

Also required is a **polygon table** (PT) that contains at least the following information for each polygon, in addition to its ID:

1. The coefficients of the plane equation.
2. Shading or color information for the polygon.
3. An in–out Boolean flag, initialized to *false* and used in scan-line processing.

Figure 13.11 shows the projection of two triangles onto the (x, y) plane; hidden edges are shown as dashed lines. The sorted ET for this figure contains entries for *AB, AC, FD, FE, CB,* and *DE*. The PT has entries for *ABC* and *DEF*.

The **active-edge table** (AET) used in Section 3.5 is needed here also. It is always kept in order of increasing x. Figure 13.12 shows ET, PT, and AET entries. By the time the algorithm has progressed upward to the scan line $y = \alpha$, the AET contains *AB* and *AC*, in that order. The edges are processed from left to right. To process *AB*, we first invert the in–out flag of polygon *ABC*. In this case, the flag becomes *true*; thus, the scan is now *in* the polygon, so the polygon must be considered. Now, because the scan is *in* only one polygon (*ABC*), it must be visible, so the shading for *ABC* is applied to the *span* from edge *AB* to the next edge in the AET, edge *AC*. This is an instance of span coherence. At this edge the flag for *ABC* is inverted to false, so that the scan is no longer *in* any polygons. Furthermore, because *AC* is the last edge in the AET, the scan-line processing is completed. The

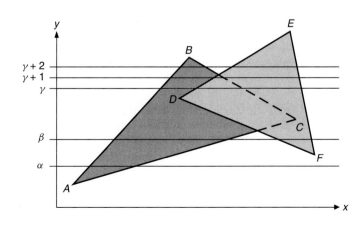

Figure 13.11   Two polygons being processed by a scan-line algorithm.

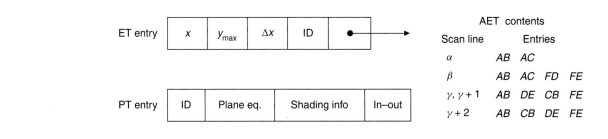

ET entry	x	y_{max}	Δx	ID	● →	

PT entry	ID	Plane eq.	Shading info	In–out

AET contents

Scan line	Entries			
α	AB	AC		
β	AB	AC	FD	FE
$\gamma, \gamma + 1$	AB	DE	CB	FE
$\gamma + 2$	AB	CB	DE	FE

Figure 13.12   ET, PT, AET for the scan-line algorithm.

AET is updated from the ET and is again ordered on x because some of its edges may have crossed, and the next scan line is processed.

When the scan line $y = \beta$ is encountered, the ordered AET is *AB, AC, FD,* and *FE.* Processing proceeds much as before. There are two polygons on the scan line, but the scan is *in* only one polygon at a time.

For scan line $y = \gamma$, things are more interesting. Entering *ABC* causes its flag to become *true. ABC*'s shade is used for the span up to the next edge, *DE.* At this point, the flag for *DEF* also becomes *true,* so the scan is *in* two polygons. (It is useful to keep an explicit list of polygons whose in–out flag is *true,* and also to keep a count of how many polygons are on the list.) We must now decide whether *ABC* or *DEF* is closer to the viewer, which we determine by evaluating the plane equations of both polygons for z at $y = \gamma$ and with x equal to the intersection of $y = \gamma$ with edge *DE.* This value of x is in the AET entry for *DE.* In our example, *DEF* has a larger z and thus is visible. Therefore, assuming nonpenetrating polygons, the shading for *DEF* is used for the span to edge *CB,* at which point *ABC*'s flag becomes *false* and the scan is again *in* only one polygon *DEF* whose shade continues to be used up to edge *FE.* Figure 13.13 shows the relationship of the two

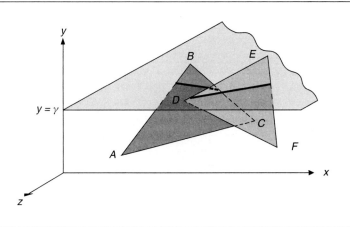

Figure 13.13   Intersections of polygons *ABC* and *DEF* with the plane $y = \gamma$.

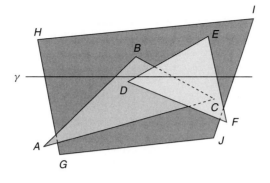

Figure 13.14   Three nonpenetrating polygons. Depth calculations do not need to be made when scan line γ leaves the obscured polygon *ABC*, since nonpenetrating polygons maintain their relative *z* order.

polygons and the $y = \gamma$ plane; the two thick lines are the intersections of the polygons with the plane.

Suppose there is a large polygon *GHIJ* behind both *ABC* and *DEF*, as in Fig. 13.14. Then, when the $y = \gamma$ scan line comes to edge *CB*, the scan is still *in* polygons *DEF* and *GHIJ*, so depth calculations are performed again. These calculations can be avoided, however, if we assume that none of the polygons penetrate another. This assumption means that, when the scan leaves *ABC*, the depth relationship between *DEF* and *GHIJ* cannot change, and *DEF* continues to be in front. Therefore, depth computations are unnecessary when the scan leaves an obscured polygon, and are required only when it leaves an obscuring polygon.

To use this algorithm properly for penetrating polygons, as shown in Fig. 13.15, we break up *KLM* into *KLL′M′* and *L′MM′*, introducing the *false edge M′L′*. Alternatively, the algorithm can be modified to find the point of penetration on a scan line as the scan line is processed.

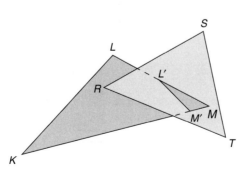

Figure 13.15   Polygon *KLM* pierces polygon *RST* at the line *L′M′*.

Another modification to this algorithm uses *depth coherence*. Assuming that polygons do not penetrate one another, Romney noted that, if the same edges are in the AET on one scan line as are on the immediately preceding scan line, and if they are in the same order, then no changes in depth relationships have occurred on any part of the scan line and no new depth computations are needed [ROMN69]. The record of visible spans on the previous scan line then defines the spans on the current scan line. Such is the case for scan lines $y = \gamma$ and $y = \gamma + 1$ in Fig. 13.11, for both of which the spans from *AB* to *DE* and from *DE* to *FE* are visible. The depth coherence in this figure is lost, however, as we go from $y = \gamma + 1$ to $y = \gamma + 2$, because edges *DE* and *CB* change order in the AET (a situation that the algorithm must accommodate). The visible spans therefore change and, in this case, become *AB* to *CB* and *DE* to *FE*. Hamlin and Gear [HAML77] show how depth coherence can sometimes be maintained even when edges do change order in the AET.

We have not yet discussed how to treat the background. The simplest way is to initialize the frame buffer to the background color, so the algorithm needs to process only scan lines that intersect edges. Another way is to include in the scene definition a large enough polygon that is farther back than any others are, is parallel to the projection plane, and has the desired shading. A final alternative is to modify the algorithm to place the background color explicitly into the frame buffer whenever the scan is not *in* any polygon.

Although the algorithms presented so far deal with polygons, the scan-line approach has been used extensively for more general surfaces, as described in Section 13.5.3. To accomplish this, the ET and AET are replaced by a **surface table** and **active-surface table,** sorted by the surfaces' (x, y) extents. When a surface is moved from the surface table to the active-surface table, additional processing may be performed. For example, the surface may be decomposed into a set of approximating polygons, which would then be discarded when the scan leaves the surface's y extent; this eliminates the need to maintain all surface data throughout the rendering process. Pseudocode for this general scan-line algorithm is shown in Prog. 13.2. Atherton [ATHE83] discusses a scan-line algorithm that renders polygonal objects combined using the regularized Boolean set operations of constructive solid geometry.

Program 13.2

Pseudocode for a general scan-line algorithm.

```
add surfaces to surface table;
initialize active-surface table;

for ( each scan line ) {
    update active-surface table;

    for ( each pixel on scan line ) {
        determine surfaces in active-surface table that project to pixel;
        find closest such surface;
        determine closest surface's shade at pixel;
    }
}
```

A scan-line approach that is appealing in its simplicity uses a *z*-buffer to resolve the visible-surface problem [MYER75]. A single-scan-line frame buffer and z-buffer are cleared for each new scan line and are used to accumulate the spans. Because only one scan line of storage is needed for the buffers, extremely high-resolution images are readily accommodated.

13.4 VISIBLE-SURFACE RAY TRACING

Ray tracing, also known as **ray casting**, determines the visibility of surfaces by tracing imaginary rays of light from the viewer's eye to the objects in the scene.[2] This is exactly the prototypical image-precision algorithm discussed at the beginning of this chapter. A center of projection (the viewer's eye) and a window on an arbitrary view plane are selected. The window may be thought of as being divided into a regular grid whose elements correspond to pixels at the desired resolution. Then, for each pixel in the window, an **eye ray** is fired from the center of projection through the pixel's center into the scene, as shown in Fig. 13.16. The pixel's color is set to that of the object at the closest point of intersection. The pseudocode for this simple ray tracer is shown in Prog. 13.3.

Program 13.3

Pseudocode for a simple ray tracer.

```
select center of projection and window on viewplane;
for ( each scan line in image ) {
    for ( each pixel in scan line ) {
        determine ray from center of projection through pixel;
        for ( each object in scene ) {
            if (object is intersected and is closest considered thus far)
                record intersection and object name;
        }
        set pixel's color to that at closest object intersection;
    }
}
```

Ray tracing was first developed by Appel [APPE68] and by Goldstein and Nagel [MAGI68; GOLD71]. Appel used a sparse grid of rays to determine shading, including whether a point was in shadow. Goldstein and Nagel originally used their algorithm to simulate the trajectories of ballistic projectiles and nuclear particles; only later did they apply it to graphics. Appel was the first to ray trace shadows, whereas Goldstein and Nagel pioneered the use of ray tracing to evaluate Boolean set operations. Whitted [WHIT80] and Kay [KAY79a] extended ray tracing to handle specular reflection and refraction. We discuss shadows, reflection, and refraction—the effects for which ray tracing is best known—in Section 14.7, where we describe a full recursive ray-tracing algorithm that integrates both visible-surface determination and shading. Here, we treat ray tracing only as a visible-surface algorithm.

---

[2] Although *ray casting* and *ray tracing* are often used synonymously, sometimes *ray casting* is used to refer to only this section's visible-surface algorithm, and *ray tracing* is reserved for the recursive algorithm of Section 14.7.

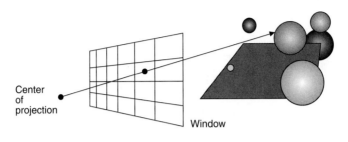

Figure 13.16   A ray is fired from the center of projection through each pixel to which the window maps, to determine the closest object intersected.

13.4.1 Computing Intersections

At the heart of any ray tracer is the task of determining the intersection of a ray with an object. To do this task, we use the same parametric representation of a vector introduced in Chapter 3. Each point (x, y, z) along the ray from (x_0, y_0, z_0) to (x_1, y_1, z_1) is defined by some value t such that

$$x = x_0 + t\,(x_1 - x_0), \qquad y = y_0 + t\,(y_1 - y_0), \qquad z = z_0 + t\,(z_1 - z_0). \quad (13.8)$$

For convenience, we define Δx, Δy, and Δz such that

$$\Delta x = x_1 - x_0, \qquad \Delta y = y_1 - y_0, \qquad \Delta z = z_1 - z_0. \qquad (13.9)$$

Thus,

$$x = x_0 + t\,\Delta x, \qquad y = y_0 + t\,\Delta y, \qquad z = z_0 + t\,\Delta z. \qquad (13.10)$$

If (x_0, y_0, z_0) is the center of projection and (x_1, y_1, z_1) is the center of a pixel on the window, then t ranges from 0 to 1 between these points. Negative values of t represent points behind the center of projection, whereas values of t greater than 1 correspond to points on the side of the window farther from the center of projection. We need to find a representation for each kind of object that enables us to determine t at the object's intersection with the ray. One of the easiest objects for which to do this is the sphere, which accounts for the plethora of spheres observed in typical ray-traced images! The sphere with center (a, b, c) and radius r may be represented by the equation

$$(x - a)^2 + (y - b)^2 + (z - c)^2 = r^2. \qquad (13.11)$$

The intersection is found by expanding Eq. (13.11), and substituting the values of x, y, and z from Eq. (13.10) to yield

$$x^2 - 2ax + a^2 + y^2 - 2by + b^2 + z^2 - 2cz + c^2 = r^2, \qquad (13.12)$$

$$(x_0 + t\Delta x)^2 - 2a(x_0 + t\Delta x) + a^2 + (y_0 + t\Delta y)^2 - 2b(y_0 + t\Delta y) + b^2 \qquad (13.13)$$

$$+ (z_0 + t\Delta z)^2 - 2c(z_0 + t\Delta z) + c^2 = r^2,$$

$$x_0^2 + 2x_0\Delta xt + \Delta x^2 t^2 - 2ax_0 - 2a\Delta xt + a^2 \tag{13.14}$$

$$+ y_0^2 + 2y_0\,\Delta yt + \Delta y^2 t^2 - 2by_0 - 2b\Delta yt + b^2$$

$$+ z_0^2 + 2z_0\,\Delta zt + \Delta z^2 t^2 - 2cz_0 - 2c\Delta zt + c^2 = r^2.$$

Collecting terms gives

$$(\Delta x^2 + \Delta y^2 + \Delta z^2)t^2 + 2t[\Delta x(x_0 - a) + \Delta y(y_0 - b) + \Delta z(z_0 - c)] \tag{13.15}$$

$$+ (x_0^2 - 2ax_0 + a^2 + y_0^2 - 2by_0 + b^2 + z_0^2 - 2cz_0 + c^2) - r^2 = 0,$$

$$(\Delta x^2 + \Delta y^2 + \Delta z^2)t^2 + 2t[\Delta x\,(x_0 - a) + \Delta y(y_0 - b) + \Delta z(z_0 - c)] \tag{13.16}$$

$$+ (x_0 - a)^2 + (y_0 - b)^2 + (z_0 - c)^2 - r^2 = 0.$$

Equation (13.16) is a quadratic in t, with coefficients expressed entirely in constants derived from the sphere and ray equations, so it can be solved using the quadratic formula. If there are no real roots, then the ray and sphere do not intersect; if there is one real root, then the ray grazes the sphere. Otherwise, the two roots are the points of intersection with the sphere; the one that yields the smallest positive t is the closest. It is also useful to normalize the ray so that the distance from (x_0, y_0, z_0) to (x_1, y_1, z_1) is 1. This gives a value of t that measures distance in WC units, and simplifies the intersection calculation, since the coefficient of t^2 in Eq. (13.16) becomes 1. We can obtain the intersection of a ray with the general quadric surfaces introduced in Chapter 9 in a similar fashion.

As we shall see in Chapter 14, we must determine the surface normal at the point of intersection in order to shade the surface. This is particularly easy in the case of the sphere, since the (unnormalized) normal is the vector from the center to the point of intersection: The sphere with center (a, b, c) has a surface normal $((x - a)/r, (y - b)/r, (z - c)/r)$ at the point of intersection (x, y, z).

Finding the intersection of a ray with a polygon is somewhat more difficult. We can determine where a ray intersects a polygon by first determining whether the ray intersects the polygon's plane and then whether the point of intersection lies within the polygon. Since the equation of a plane is

$$Ax + By + Cz + D = 0, \tag{13.17}$$

substitution from Eq. (13.10) yields

$$A(x_0 + t\Delta x) + B(y_0 + t\Delta y) + C(z_0 + t\Delta z) + D = 0, \tag{13.18}$$

$$t(A\Delta x + B\Delta y + C\Delta z) + (Ax_0 + By_0 + Cz_0 + D) = 0, \tag{13.19}$$

$$t = -\frac{(Ax_0 + By_0 + Cz_0 + D)}{(A\Delta x + B\Delta y + C\Delta z)}. \tag{13.20}$$

If the denominator of Eq. (13.20) is 0, then the ray and plane are parallel and do not intersect. An easy way to determine whether the point of intersection lies within the polygon is to project the polygon and point orthographically onto one

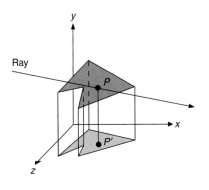

Figure 13.17   Determining whether a ray intersects a polygon. The polygon and the ray's point of
intersection *P* with the polygon's plane are projected onto one of the three planes defining the
coordinate system. Projected point *P'* is tested for containment within the projected polygon.

of the three planes defining the coordinate system, as shown in Fig. 13.17. To
obtain the most accurate results, we should select the axis along which to project
that yields the largest projection. This corresponds to the coordinate whose coefficient in the polygon's plane equation has the largest absolute value. The orthographic projection is accomplished by dropping this coordinate from the polygon's
vertices and from the point. The polygon-containment test for the point can then be
performed entirely in 2D, using the point-in-polygon algorithm sketched in Section 7.11.2.

Like the z-buffer algorithm, ray tracing has the attraction that the only intersection operation performed is that of a projector with an object. There is no need
to determine the intersection of two objects in the scene directly. The z-buffer algorithm approximates an object as a set of z values along the projectors that intersect
the object. Ray tracing approximates objects as the set of intersections along each
projector that intersects the scene. We can extend a z-buffer algorithm to handle a
new kind of object by writing a scan-conversion and z-calculation routine for it.
Similarly, we can extend a visible-surface ray tracer to handle a new kind of object
by writing a ray-intersection routine for it. In both cases, we must also write a routine to calculate surface normals for shading. Intersection and surface-normal algorithms have been developed for algebraic surfaces [HANR83] and parametric
surfaces [KAJI82; SEDE84; TOTH85; JOY86]. Surveys of these algorithms are
provided in [HAIN89; HANR89].

13.4.2 Efficiency Considerations for Visible-Surface Ray Tracing

At each pixel, the z-buffer algorithm computes information only for those objects
that project to that pixel, taking advantage of coherence. In contrast, the simple but
expensive version of the visible-surface ray tracing algorithm that we have discussed intersects each of the rays from the eye with each of the objects in the

scene. A 1024×1024 image of 100 objects would therefore require 100M intersection calculations. It is not surprising that Whitted found that 75–95 percent and more of his system's time was spent in the intersection routine for typical scenes [WHIT80]. Consequently, the approaches to improving the efficiency of visible-surface ray tracing we discuss here attempt to speed up individual intersection calculations, or to avoid them entirely. As we shall see in Section 14.7, recursive ray tracers trace additional rays from the points of intersection to determine a pixel's shade. Therefore, several of the techniques developed in Section 13.1, such as the perspective transformation and back-face culling, are not useful in general, since all rays do not emanate from the same center of projection.

Optimizing intersection calculations.   Many of the terms in the equations for object–ray intersection contain expressions that are constant either throughout an image or for a particular ray. These can be computed in advance, as can, for example, the orthographic projection of a polygon onto a plane. With care and mathematical insight, fast intersection methods can be developed; even the simple intersection formula for a sphere given in Section 13.4.1 can be improved [HAIN89]. If rays are transformed to lie along the z axis, then the same transformation can be applied to each candidate object, so that any intersection occurs at $x = y = 0$. This step simplifies the intersection calculation and allows the closest object to be determined by a z sort. The intersection point can then be transformed back for use in shading calculations via the inverse transformation.

Bounding volumes provide a particularly attractive way to decrease the amount of time spent on intersection calculations. An object that is relatively expensive to test for intersection may be enclosed in a bounding volume whose intersection test is less expensive, such as a sphere [WHIT80], ellipsoid [BOUV85], or rectangular solid [RUBI80; TOTH85]. The object does not need to be tested if the ray fails to intersect with its bounding volume.

Hierarchies.   Although bounding volumes do not by themselves determine the order or frequency of intersection tests, bounding volumes may be organized in nested hierarchies with objects at the leaves and internal nodes that bound their children [RUBI80; WEGH84; KAY86]. A child volume is guaranteed not to intersect with a ray if its parent does not. Thus, if intersection tests begin with the root, many branches of the hierarchy (and hence many objects) may be trivially rejected.

Spatial partitioning.   Bounding-volume hierarchies organize objects bottom-up; in contrast, spatial partitioning subdivides space top-down. The bounding box of the scene is calculated first. In one approach, the bounding box is then divided into a regular grid of equal-sized extents, as shown in Fig. 13.18. Each partition is associated with a list of objects it contains, either wholly or in part. The lists are filled by assigning each object to the one or more partitions that contain it. Now, as shown in 2D in Fig. 13.19, a ray needs to be intersected with only those objects that are contained within the partitions through which it passes. In addition, the partitions can be examined in the order in which the ray passes through them; thus, as soon as a partition is found in which there is an intersection, no more partitions

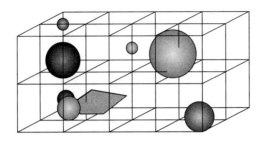

Figure 13.18   The scene is partitioned into a regular grid of equal-sized volumes.

need to be inspected. Note that we must consider all the remaining objects in the partition, to determine the one whose intersection is closest. Since the partitions follow a regular grid, each successive partition lying along a ray may be calculated using a 3D version of the line-drawing algorithm discussed in Section 3.2.2, modified to list every partition through which the ray passes [FUJI85; AMAN87].

If a ray intersects an object in a partition, it is also necessary to check whether the intersection itself lies in the partition; it is possible that the intersection that was found may be farther along the ray in another partition and that another object may have a closer intersection. For example, in Fig. 13.20, object B is intersected in partition 3 although it is encountered in partition 2. We must continue traversing the partitions until an intersection is found in the partition currently being traversed, in this case with A in partition 3. To avoid recalculating the intersection of a ray with an object that is found in multiple partitions, the point of intersection and the ray's ID can be cached with the object when the object is first encountered.

Dippé and Swensen [DIPP84] discuss an adaptive subdivision algorithm that produces unequal-sized partitions. An alternative adaptive spatial-subdivision method divides the scene using an octree [GLAS84]. In this case, the octree neighbor-finding algorithm sketched in Section 10.6.3 may be used to determine the successive partitions lying along a ray [SAME89b]. Octrees, and other hierarchical

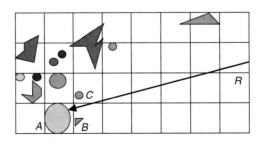

Figure 13.19   Spatial partitioning. Ray R needs to be intersected with only objects A, B, and C, since the other partitions through which it passes are empty.

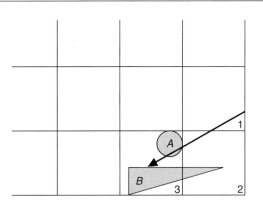

Figure 13.20   An object may be intersected in a different voxel than the current one.

spatial partitionings, can be thought of as a special case of hierarchy in which a node's children are guaranteed not to intersect each other. Because these approaches allow adaptive subdivision, the decision to subdivide a partition further can be sensitive to the number of objects in the subdivision or the cost of intersecting the objects. This is advantageous in heterogeneous, unevenly distributed environments.

13.5 OTHER APPROACHES

13.5.1 List-Priority Algorithms

List-priority algorithms determine a visibility ordering for objects, ensuring that a correct picture results if the objects are rendered in that order. For example, if no object overlaps another in z, then we need only to sort the objects by increasing z, and to render them in that order. Farther objects are obscured by closer ones as pixels from the closer polygons overwrite those of the more distant ones. If objects overlap in z, we may still be able to determine a correct order, as in Fig. 13.21(a). If objects cyclically overlap each other, as in Figs. 13.21(b) and (c), or penetrate each other, then there is no correct order. In these cases, it will be necessary to split one or more objects to make a linear order possible.

List-priority algorithms are hybrids that combine both object-precision and image-precision operations. Depth comparisons and object splitting are done with object precision. Only scan conversion, which relies on the ability of the graphics device to overwrite the pixels of previously drawn objects, is done with image precision. Because the list of sorted objects is created with object precision, however, it can be redisplayed correctly at any resolution. As we shall see, list-priority algorithms differ in how they determine the sorted order, as well as in which objects get split and when the splitting occurs. The sort need not be on z, some objects may be split that neither cyclically overlap nor penetrate others, and the splitting may even be done independent of the viewer's position.

The depth-sort algorithm.   The basic idea of the **depth-sort algorithm**, developed by Newell, Newell, and Sancha [NEWE72], is to paint the polygons into the frame buffer in order of decreasing distance from the viewpoint. Three conceptual steps are performed:

1.   Sort all polygons according to the smallest (farthest) z coordinate of each.
2.   Resolve any ambiguities that sorting may cause when the polygons' z extents overlap, splitting polygons if necessary.
3.   Scan convert each polygon in ascending order of smallest z coordinate (i.e., back to front).

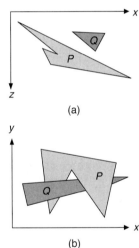

(a)

Consider the use of explicit priority, such as that associated with views in SPHIGS. The explicit priority takes the place of the minimum z value, and there can be no depth ambiguities, because each priority is thought of as corresponding to a different plane of constant z. This simplified version of the depth-sort algorithm is often known as the **painter's algorithm,** in reference to how a painter might paint closer objects over more distant ones. Environments whose objects each exist in a plane of constant z, such as those of VLSI layout, cartography, and window management, are said to be $2\frac{1}{2}$D and can be correctly handled with the painter's algorithm. The painter's algorithm may be applied to a scene in which each polygon is not embedded in a plane of constant z, by sorting the polygons by their minimum z coordinate or by the z coordinate of their centroid, ignoring step 2. Although scenes can be constructed using this approach, it does not in general produce a correct ordering.

(b)

Figure 13.21 shows some of the types of ambiguities that must be resolved as part of step 2. How is this done? Let the polygon currently at the far end of the sorted list of polygons be called P. Before this polygon is scan-converted into the frame buffer, it must be tested against each polygon Q whose z extent overlaps the z extent of P, to prove that P cannot obscure Q and that P can therefore be written before Q. Up to five tests are performed, in order of increasing complexity. As soon as one succeeds, P has been shown not to obscure Q and the next polygon Q overlapping P in z is tested. If all such polygons pass, then P is scan-converted and the next polygon on the list becomes the new P. The five tests follow:

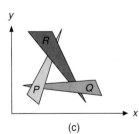

(c)

Figure 13.21
Some cases in which z extents of polygons overlap.

1.   Do the polygons' x extents not overlap?
2.   Do the polygons' y extents not overlap?
3.   Is P entirely on the opposite side of Q's plane from the viewpoint? [This is not the case in Fig. 13.21(a), but is true for Fig. 13.22(a).]
4.   Is Q entirely on the same side of P's plane as the viewpoint? [This is not the case in Fig. 13.21(a), but is true for Fig. 13.22(b).]
5.   Do the projections of the polygons onto the (x, y) plane not overlap? (This can be determined by comparing the edges of one polygon to the edges of the other.)

If all five tests fail, we assume for the moment that P actually obscures Q, and we therefore test whether Q can be scan-converted before P. Tests 1, 2, and 5 do not need to be repeated, but new versions of tests 3 and 4 are used, with the polygons reversed:

3′. Is Q entirely on the opposite side of P's plane from the viewpoint?

4′. Is P entirely on the same side of Q's plane as the viewpoint?

In the case of Fig. 13.21(a), test 3′ succeeds. Therefore, we move Q to the end of the list, and it becomes the new P. In the case of Fig 13.21(b), however, the tests are still inconclusive; in fact, there is no order in which P and Q can be scan-converted correctly. Instead, either P or Q must be split by the plane of the other (see Section 3.11 on polygon clipping, treating the clip edge as a clip plane). The original unsplit polygon is discarded, its pieces are inserted in the list in proper z order, and the algorithm proceeds as before.

Figure 13.21(c) shows a more subtle case. It is possible for P, Q, and R to be oriented such that each polygon can always be moved to the end of the list to place it in the correct order relative to one, but not both, of the other polygons. This would result in an infinite loop. To avoid looping, we must modify our approach by marking each polygon that is moved to the end of the list. Then, whenever the first five tests fail and the current polygon Q is marked, we do not try tests 3′ and 4′. Instead, we split either P or Q (as if tests 3′ and 4′ had both failed) and reinsert the pieces.

Binary space-partitioning trees. The binary space-partitioning (BSP) tree algorithm was developed by Fuchs, Kedem, and Naylor [FUCH80; FUCH83], based on work of Schumacker [SCHU69]. The BSP tree algorithm is an extremely efficient method for calculating the visibility relationships among a static group of 3D polygons as seen from an arbitrary viewpoint. It trades off an initial time- and space-intensive preprocessing step against a linear display algorithm that is executed whenever a new viewing specification is desired. Thus, the algorithm is well suited for applications in which the viewpoint changes but the objects do not.

The BSP tree algorithm is based on the observation that a polygon will be scan-converted correctly (i.e., will not overlap incorrectly or be overlapped incorrectly by other polygons) if all polygons on the other side of it from the viewer are scan-converted first, followed by it, and then all polygons on the same side of it as the viewer. We need to ensure that this is so for each polygon.

The algorithm makes it easy to determine a correct order for scan conversion by building a binary tree of polygons, the **BSP tree**. The BSP tree's root is a polygon selected from those to be displayed; the algorithm works correctly no matter which is picked. The root polygon is used to partition the environment into two half-spaces. One half-space contains all remaining polygons in front of the root polygon, relative to its surface normal; the other contains all polygons behind the root polygon. Any polygon lying on both sides of the root polygon's plane is split by the plane, and its front and back pieces are assigned to the appropriate half-space. One polygon each from the root polygon's front and back half-spaces becomes its front and back children, and each child is recursively used to divide

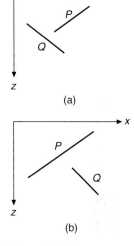

Figure 13.22
Possible polygon orientations. (a) Test 3 is true. (b) Test 3 is false, but test 4 is true.

the remaining polygons in its half-space in the same fashion. The algorithm terminates when each node contains only a single polygon.

Remarkably, the BSP tree can be traversed in a modified in-order tree walk to yield a correct priority-ordered polygon list for an arbitrary viewpoint. Consider the root polygon. It divides the remaining polygons into two sets, each of which lies entirely on one side of the root's plane. Thus, the algorithm needs only to guarantee that the sets are displayed in the correct relative order to ensure both that one set's polygons do not interfere with the other's and that the root polygon is displayed properly and in the correct order relative to the others. If the viewer is in the root polygon's front half-space, then the algorithm must first display all polygons in the root's rear half-space (those that could be obscured by the root), then the root, and finally all polygons in its front half-space (those that could obscure the root). Alternatively, if the viewer is in the root polygon's rear half-space, then the algorithm must first display all polygons in the root's front half-space, then the root, and finally all polygons in its rear half-space. If the polygon is seen on edge, either display order suffices. Back-face culling may be accomplished by not displaying a polygon if the eye is in its rear half-space. Each of the root's children is recursively processed by this algorithm. Pseudocode for both the tree-building phase and the display phase is given in [FOLE90].

Like the depth-sort algorithm, the BSP tree algorithm performs intersection and sorting entirely at object precision, and relies on the image-precision overwrite capabilities of a raster device. Unlike depth sort, it performs all polygon splitting during a preprocessing step that must be repeated only when the environment changes. Note that more polygon splitting may occur than in the depth-sort algorithm.

List-priority algorithms allow the use of hardware polygon scan converters that are typically much faster than are those that check the z at each pixel. The depth-sort and BSP tree algorithms display polygons in a back-to-front order, possibly obscuring more distant ones later. Thus, like the z-buffer algorithm, shading calculations may be computed more than once for each pixel. Alternatively, polygons can instead be displayed in a front-to-back order, and each pixel in a polygon can be written only if it has not yet been.

If a list-priority algorithm is used for hidden-line removal, special attention must be paid to the new edges introduced by the subdivision process. If these edges are scan-converted like the original polygon edges, they will appear in the picture as unwelcome artifacts, and they thus should be flagged so that they will not be scan-converted.

13.5.2 Area-Subdivision Algorithms

Area-subdivision algorithms all follow the divide-and-conquer strategy of spatial partitioning in the projection plane. An area of the projected image is examined. If it is easy to decide which polygons are visible in the area, they are displayed. Otherwise, the area is subdivided into smaller areas to which the decision logic is applied recursively. As the areas become smaller, fewer polygons overlap each area, and ultimately a decision becomes possible. This approach exploits area

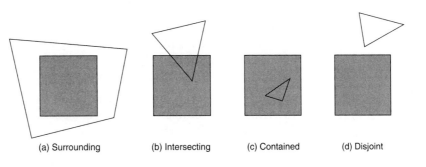

(a) Surrounding　　　　(b) Intersecting　　　　(c) Contained　　　　(d) Disjoint

Figure 13.23　　The four relations of polygon projections to an area element: (a) surrounding, (b) intersecting, (c) contained, and (d) disjoint.

coherence, since sufficiently small areas of an image will be contained in at most a single visible polygon.

Warnock's algorithm.　The area-subdivision algorithm developed by Warnock [WARN69] subdivides each area into four equal squares. At each stage in the recursive-subdivision process, the projection of each polygon has one of four relationships to the area of interest (see Fig. 13.23):

1. **Surrounding polygons** completely contain the (shaded) area of interest (Fig. 13.23a).
2. **Intersecting polygons** intersect the area (Fig. 13.23b).
3. **Contained polygons** are completely inside the area (Fig. 13.23c).
4. **Disjoint polygons** are completely outside the area (Fig. 13.23d).

Disjoint polygons clearly have no influence on the area of interest. The part of an intersecting polygon that is outside the area is also irrelevant, whereas the part of an intersecting polygon that is interior to the area is the same as a contained polygon and can be treated as such.

In four cases, a decision about an area can be made easily, so the area does not need to be divided further to be conquered:

1. All the polygons are disjoint from the area. The background color can be displayed in the area.
2. There is only one intersecting or only one contained polygon. The area is first filled with the background color, and then the part of the polygon contained in the area is scan-converted.
3. There is a single surrounding polygon, but no intersecting or contained polygons. The area is filled with the color of the surrounding polygon.
4. More than one polygon is intersecting, contained in, or surrounding the area, but one is a surrounding polygon that is in front of all the other polygons.

Determining whether a surrounding polygon is in front is done by computing the z coordinates of the planes of all surrounding, intersecting, and contained polygons at the four corners of the area; if there is a surrounding polygon whose four corner z coordinates are larger (closer to the viewpoint) than are those of any of the other polygons, then the entire area can be filled with the color of this surrounding polygon.

Cases 1, 2, and 3 are simple to understand. Case 4 is further illustrated in Fig. 13.24. In part (a), the four intersections of the surrounding polygon are all closer to the viewpoint (which is at infinity on the $+z$ axis) than are any of the other intersections. Consequently, the entire area is filled with the surrounding polygon's color. In part (b), no decision can be made, even though the surrounding polygon seems to be in front of the intersecting polygon, because on the left the plane of the intersecting polygon is in front of the plane of the surrounding polygon. Note that the depth-sort algorithm accepts this case without further subdivision if the intersecting polygon is wholly on the side of the surrounding polygon that is farther from the viewpoint. Warnock's algorithm, however, always subdivides the area to simplify the problem. After subdivision, only contained and intersecting polygons need to be reexamined: Surrounding and disjoint polygons of the original area are surrounding and disjoint polygons of each subdivided area.

Up to this point, the algorithm has operated at object precision, with the exception of the actual scan conversion of the background and clipped polygons in the four cases. These image-precision scan-conversion operations, however, can be replaced by object-precision operations that output a precise representation of the visible surfaces: either a square of the area's size (cases 1, 3, and 4) or a single polygon clipped to the area, along with its Boolean complement relative to the area, representing the visible part of the background (case 2). What about the cases that are not one of these four? One approach is to stop subdividing when the resolution of the display device is reached. Thus, on a 1024×1024 raster display, at

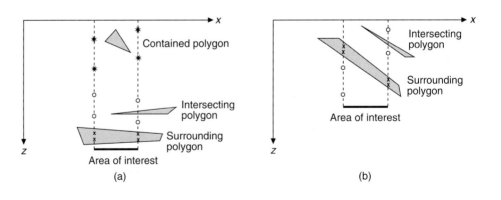

Figure 13.24   Two examples of case 4 in recursive subdivision. (a) Surrounding polygon is closest at all corners of area of interest. (b) Intersecting polygon plane is closest at left side of area of interest. × marks the intersection of surrounding polygon plane; ○ marks the intersection of intersecting polygon plane; * marks the intersection of contained polygon plane.

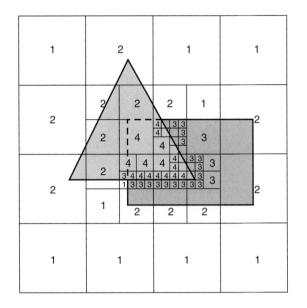

Figure 13.25   Area subdivision into squares.

most 10 levels of subdivision are needed. If, after this maximum number of subdivisions, none of cases 1 to 4 have occurred, then the depth of all relevant polygons is computed at the center of this pixel-sized, indivisible area. The polygon with the closest z coordinate defines the shading of the area. Alternatively, for antialiasing, several further levels of subdivision can be used to determine a pixel's color by weighting the color of each of its subpixel-sized areas by its size. It is these image-precision operations, performed when an area is not one of the simple cases, that makes this an image-precision approach.

Figure 13.25 shows a simple scene and the subdivisions necessary for that scene's display. The number in each subdivided area corresponds to one of the four cases; in unnumbered areas, none of the four cases are true. Compare this approach to the 2D spatial partitioning performed by quadtrees (Section 10.6.3).

13.5.3 Algorithms for Curved Surfaces

All the algorithms presented thus far, with the exception of the z-buffer, have been described only for objects defined by polygonal faces. Objects such as the curved surfaces of Chapter 9 must first be approximated by many small facets before polygonal versions of any of the algorithms can be used. Although this approximation can be done, it is often preferable to scan-convert curved surfaces directly, eliminating polygonal artifacts and avoiding the extra storage required by polygonal approximation.

Quadric surfaces, discussed in Section 9.4, are a popular choice in computer graphics. Visible-surface algorithms for quadrics have been developed by Weiss [WEIS66], Woon [WOON71], Mahl [MAHL72], Levin [LEVI76], and Sarraga [SARR83]. They all find the intersections of two quadrics, yielding a fourth-order equation in x, y, and z whose roots must be found numerically. Levin reduces this to a second-order problem by parameterizing the intersection curves. Spheres, a special case of quadrics, are easier to work with, and are of particular interest because molecules are often displayed as collections of colored spheres (see Color Plate 22). A number of molecular display algorithms have been developed [KNOW77; STAU78; MAX79; PORT79; FRAN81; MAX84]. Section 13.4 discusses how to render spheres using ray tracing.

Even more flexibility can be achieved with the parametric spline surfaces introduced in Chapter 9, because they are more general and allow tangent continuity at patch boundaries. Catmull [CATM74; CATM75] developed the first display algorithm for bicubics. In the spirit of Warnock's algorithm, a patch is recursively subdivided in s and t into four patches until its projection covers no more than one pixel. A z-buffer algorithm determines whether the patch is visible at this pixel. If it is, a shade is calculated for it and is placed in the frame buffer. The pseudocode for this algorithm is shown in Prog. 13.4. Since checking the size of the curved patch itself is time consuming, a quadrilateral defined by the patch's corner vertices may be used instead.

Program 13.4

Pseudocode for the Catmull recursive-subdivision algorithm.

```
for (each patch) {
    push patch onto stack;
    while (stack not empty) {
        pop patch from stack;
        if (patch covers ≤ 1 pixel) {
            if (patch's pixel closer in z)
                determine shade and draw;
        }
        else {
            subdivide patch into 4 subpatches;
            push subpatches onto stack;
        }
    }
}
```

Another approach is based on the adaptive subdivision of each bicubic patch until each subdivided patch is within some given tolerance of being flat. This tolerance depends on the resolution of the display device and on the orientation of the area being subdivided with respect to the projection plane, so unnecessary subdivisions are eliminated. The patch needs to be subdivided in only one direction if it is already flat enough in the other. Once subdivided sufficiently, a patch can be treated like a quadrilateral. The small polygonal areas defined by the four corners of each patch are processed by a scan-line algorithm, allowing polygonal and bicubic surfaces to be readily intermixed. Algorithms that use this basic idea have been developed by Lane and Carpenter [LANE80], and by Clark [CLAR79]; they are described in [FOLE90].

SUMMARY

Sutherland, Sproull, and Schumacker [SUTH74a] stress that the heart of visible-surface determination is sorting. Indeed, we have seen many instances of sorting and searching in the algorithms, and efficient sorting is vital to efficient visible-surface determination. Equally important is avoiding any more sorting than is absolutely necessary, a goal typically achieved by exploiting coherence. For example, the scan-line algorithms use scan-line coherence to eliminate the need for a complete sort on x for each scan line.

Algorithms can be classified by the order in which they sort. The depth-sort algorithm sorts on z and then on x and y (by use of extents in tests 1 and 2); it is thus called a zxy algorithm. Scan-line algorithms sort on y (with a bucket sort), then sort on x (initially with an insertion sort, then with a bubble sort as each scan line is processed), and finally search in z for the polygon nearest the viewpoint; therefore, they are yxz algorithms. Warnock's algorithm does a parallel sort on x and y, and then searches in z, and hence is an $(xy)z$ algorithm (sorting on a combination of dimensions is indicated by parentheses). The z-buffer algorithm does no explicit sorting and searches only in z; it is called an (xyz) algorithm.

Sancha has argued that the order of sorting is unimportant: There is no intrinsic benefit in sorting along any particular axis first as opposed to another because, at least in principle, the *average* object is equally complex in all three dimensions [SUTH74a]. On the other hand, a graphics scene, like a Hollywood set, may be constructed to look best from a particular viewpoint, and this may entail building in greater complexity along one axis than along another. Even if we assume roughly symmetric object complexity, however, all algorithms are still not equally efficient: They differ in how effectively coherence is used to avoid sorting and other computation and in the use of space–time tradeoffs. The results reported in [SUTH74a, Table VII], which compare the estimated performance of four of the basic algorithms we have presented, are summarized in Table 13.1. The authors suggest that, because these are only estimates, small differences should be ignored, but that "we feel free to make order of magnitude comparisons between the various algorithms to learn something about the effectiveness of the various methods" [SUTH74a, p. 52].

Table 13.1   Relative Estimated Performance of Four Algorithms for Visible-Surface Determination

Algorithm	Number of Polygonal Faces in Scene		
	100	2500	60,000
Depth sort	1 *	10	507
z-buffer	54	54	54
Scan line	5	21	100
Warnock area subdivision	11	64	307

*Entries are normalized such that this case is unity.

The depth-sort algorithm is efficient for small numbers of polygons because the simple overlap tests almost always suffice to decide whether a polygon can be scan-converted. With more polygons, the more complex tests are needed more frequently and polygon subdivision is more likely to be required. The z-buffer algorithm has constant performance because, as the number of polygons in a scene increases, the number of pixels covered by a single polygon decreases. On the other hand, its memory needs are high. The individual tests and calculations involved in the Warnock area-subdivision algorithm are relatively complex, so it is generally slower than are the other methods. In addition to these informal estimates, there has been some work on formalizing the visible-surface problem and analyzing its computational complexity [GILO78; FOUR88; FIUM89]. For example, Fiume [FIUM89] proves that object-precision visible-surface algorithms have a lower bound that is worse than that of sorting.

In general, comparing visible-surface algorithms is difficult because not all algorithms compute the same information with the same accuracy. For example, we have discussed algorithms that restrict the kinds of objects, relationships among objects, and even the kinds of projections that are allowed. As we shall see in the following chapter, the choice of a visible-surface algorithm is also influenced by the kind of shading desired. If an expensive shading procedure is being used, it is better to choose a visible-surface algorithm that shades only parts of objects that are visible, such as a scan-line algorithm. Depth sort would be a particularly bad choice in this case, since it draws all objects in their entirety. When interactive performance is important, hardware z-buffer approaches are popular. The BSP-tree algorithm, on the other hand, can generate new views of a static environment quickly, but requires additional processing whenever the environment changes. Scan-line algorithms allow extremely high resolution because data structures need to represent fully elaborated versions only of primitives that affect the line being processed. As with any algorithm, the time spent implementing the algorithm and the ease with which it can be modified (e.g., to accommodate new primitives) is also a major factor.

One important consideration in implementing a visible-surface algorithm is the kind of hardware support available. If a parallel machine is available, we must recognize that, at each place where an algorithm takes advantage of coherence, it depends on the results of previous calculations. Exploiting parallelism may entail ignoring some otherwise useful form of coherence. Ray tracing has been a particularly popular candidate for parallel implementation because, in its simplest form, each pixel is computed independently.

Exercises

13.1   Prove that the transformation M in Section 13.1.2 preserves (a) straight lines, (b) planes, and (c) depth relationships.

13.2   Given a plane $Ax + By + Cz + D = 0$, apply M from Section 13.1.2 and find the new coefficients of the plane equation.

13.3   How can a scan-line algorithm be extended to deal with polygons with shared edges? Should a shared edge be represented once, as a shared edge, or twice, once for each polygon it borders, with no record kept that it is a shared edge? When the depth of two polygons is evaluated at their common shared edge, the depths will, of course, be equal. Which polygon should be declared visible, given that the scan is entering both?

13.4   Explain, for the z-buffer, depth-sort, Warnock, and BSP-tree algorithms, how piercing polygons would be handled. Are they a special case that must be treated explicitly, or are they accommodated by the basic algorithm?

13.5   How can the algorithms mentioned in Exercise 13.4 be adapted to work with polygons containing holes?

13.6   One of the advantages of the z-buffer algorithm is that primitives may be presented to it in any order. Does this mean that two images created by sending primitives in different orders will have identical values in their z-buffers and in their frame buffers? Explain your answer.

13.7   Consider merging two images of identical size, represented by their frame-buffer and z-buffer contents. If you know the z_{min} and z_{max} of each image and the values of z to which they originally corresponded, can you merge the images properly? Is any additional information needed?

13.8   Section 13.2 mentions the z-compression problems caused by rendering a perspective projection using an integer z-buffer. Choose a perspective viewing specification and a small number of object points. Show how, in the perspective transformation, two points near the center of projection are mapped to different z values, whereas two points separated from each other by the same distance, but farther from the center of projection, are mapped to a single z value.

13.9   a. Suppose that the view volume V has front and back clipping planes at distances F and B (both positive!), respectively, from the VRP, measured along the direction DOP. Suppose that the distance from the COP to the VRP, measured along the DOP, is w, and furthermore suppose that the front clipping plane is between the VRP and the COP, and that the VRP is between the COP and the back clipping plane (just as shown in Fig. 6.16). Define $f = w - F$ and $b = w + B$, so that f is the distance from the COP to the front plane, and b is the distance from the COP to the back plane. Now do this again with a view volume V', and define f' and b' similarly. After transformation to the canonical perspective view volume, the back clipping plane of V goes to $z = -1$, and the front plane goes to $z = A$. Similarly, for the volume V', the front plane will go to $z = A'$. Show that if $f/b = f'/b'$, then $A = A'$, and vice versa. In short, the range of z values after transforming to the canonical view-volume is dependent only on the ratio between the distances from the COP to the front and back planes.

b. Part (a) shows that, in considering the effect of perspective, we need to consider only the ratio of backplane to frontplane distance (from the COP). We can therefore simply study the canonical view volume with various values of the frontplane distance. Suppose, then, that we have a canonical-perspective view volume, with front clipping plane $z = A$ and back clipping plane $z = -1$, and we transform it, through the perspective transformation, to the parallel view volume between $z = 0$ and $z = -1$. Write down the formula for the transformed z coordinate in terms of the original z coordinate. (Your answer will depend on A, of course.) Suppose that the transformed z values in the parallel view volume are multiplied by 2^n and then are rounded to integers (i.e., they are mapped to an integer z-buffer). Find two values of z that are as far apart as possible, but that map, under this transformation, to the same integer. (Your answer will depend on n and A.)

c. Suppose you want to make an image in which the ratio of f to b is R, and objects that are more than distance Q apart (in z) must map to different values in the z-buffer. Using your work in part (b), write a formula for the number of bits of z-buffer needed.

13.10 When ray tracing is performed, it is typically necessary to compute only whether a ray intersects an extent, not what the actual points of intersection are. Complete the ray–sphere intersection equation (Eq. 13.16), using the quadratic formula, and show how it can be simplified to determine only whether the ray and sphere intersect.

13.11 Ray tracing can also be used to determine the mass properties of objects through numerical integration. The full set of intersections of a ray with an object gives the total portion of the ray that is inside the object. Show how you can estimate an object's volume by firing a regular array of parallel rays through that object.

13.12 Derive the intersection of a ray with a quadric surface. Modify the method used to derive the intersection of a ray with a sphere in Eqs. (13.12) through (13.15) to handle the definition of a quadric given in Section 9.4.

13.13 Implement one of the polygon visible surface algorithms in this chapter, such as a z-buffer algorithm or scan-line algorithm.

13.14 Implement a simple ray tracer for spheres and polygons. (Choose one of the illumination models from Section 14.1.) Improve your program's performance through the use of spatial partitioning or hierarchies of bounding volumes.

14 Illumination and Shading

In this chapter, we discuss how to shade surfaces based on the position, orientation, and characteristics of the surfaces and the light sources illuminating them. We develop a number of different **illumination models** that express the factors determining a surface's color at a given point. Illumination models are also frequently called **lighting models** or **shading models.** Here, however, we reserve the term **shading model** for the broader framework in which an illumination model fits. The shading model determines when the illumination model is applied and what arguments it will receive. For example, some shading models invoke an illumination model for every pixel in the image, whereas others invoke an illumination model for only some pixels and shade the remaining pixels by interpolation.

When we compared the accuracy with which the visible-surface calculations of the previous chapter are performed, we distinguished between algorithms that use the actual object geometry and those that use polyhedral approximations, between object-precision and image-precision algorithms. In all cases, however, the single criterion for determining the direct visibility of an object at a pixel is whether something lies between the object and the observer along the projector through the pixel. In contrast, the interaction between lights and surfaces is a good deal more complex. Graphics researchers have often approximated the underlying rules of optics and thermal radiation, either to simplify computation or because more accurate models were not known in the graphics community. Consequently, many of the illumination and shading models traditionally used in computer graphics include a multitude of kludges, "hacks," and simplifications that have no firm grounding in theory, but that work well in practice. The first part of this chapter covers these simple models, which are still in common use because they can produce attractive and useful results with minimal computation.

We begin, in Section 14.1, with a discussion of simple illumination models that take into account an individual point on a surface and the light sources directly illuminating it. We first develop illumination models for monochromatic surfaces and lights and then show how the computations can be generalized to handle the color systems discussed in Chapter 11. Section 14.2 describes the most common shading models that are used with these illumination models. In Section 14.3, we expand these models to simulate textured surfaces.

Modeling refraction, reflection, and shadows requires additional computation that is very similar to, and often is integrated with, hidden-surface elimination. Indeed, these effects occur because some of the *hidden surfaces* are not really hidden at all—they are seen through, reflected from, or cast shadows on the surface being shaded! Sections 14.4 and 14.5 discuss how to model some of these effects.

Sections 14.6 through 14.8 describe **global illumination models** that attempt to take into account the interchange of light between all surfaces: recursive ray tracing and radiosity methods. Recursive ray tracing extends the visible-surface ray-tracing algorithm introduced in the previous chapter to interleave the determination of visibility, illumination, and shading at each pixel. Radiosity methods model the energy equilibrium in a system of surfaces; they determine the illumination of a set of sample points in the environment in a view-independent fashion before visible-surface determination is performed from the desired viewpoint. More detailed treatments of many of the illumination and shading models covered here may be found in [GLAS89; HALL89].

Finally, in Section 14.9, we look at several different graphics pipelines that integrate the rasterization techniques discussed in this and the previous chapters. We examine some ways to implement these capabilities to produce systems that are both efficient and extensible.

14.1 ILLUMINATION MODELS

14.1.1 Ambient Light

Perhaps the simplest illumination model possible is that used implicitly in this book's earliest chapters: Each object is displayed using an intensity intrinsic to it. We can think of this model, which has no external light source, as describing a rather unrealistic world of nonreflective, self-luminous objects. Each object appears as a monochromatic silhouette, unless its individual parts, such as the polygons of a polyhedron, are given different shades when the object is created. Color Plate 27 demonstrates this effect.

An illumination model can be expressed by an **illumination equation** in variables associated with the point on the object being shaded. The illumination equation that expresses this simple model is

$$I = k_i,$$
(14.1)

where I is the resulting intensity and the coefficient k_i is the object's intrinsic intensity. Since this illumination equation contains no terms that depend on the position of the point being shaded, we can evaluate it once for each object. The process of evaluating the illumination equation at one or more points on an object is often referred to as **lighting** the object.

Now imagine, instead of self-luminosity, that there is a diffuse, nondirectional source of light, the product of multiple reflections of light from the many surfaces present in the environment. This is known as **ambient** light. If we assume that ambient light impinges equally on all surfaces from all directions, then our illumination equation becomes

$$I = I_a k_a. \tag{14.2}$$

I_a is the intensity of the ambient light, assumed to be constant for all objects. The amount of ambient light reflected from an object's surface is determined by k_a, the **ambient-reflection coefficient,** which ranges from 0 to 1. The ambient-reflection coefficient is a **material property**. Along with the other material properties that we will discuss, it may be thought of as characterizing the material from which the surface is made. Like some of the other properties, the ambient-reflection coefficient is an empirical convenience and does not correspond directly to any physical property of real materials. Furthermore, ambient light by itself is not of much interest. As we see later, it is used to account for all the complex ways in which light can reach an object that are not otherwise addressed by the illumination equation. Color Plate 27 also demonstrates illumination by ambient light.

14.1.2 Diffuse Reflection

Although objects illuminated by ambient light are more or less brightly lit in direct proportion to the ambient intensity, they are still uniformly illuminated across their surfaces. Now consider illuminating an object by a **point light source,** whose rays emanate uniformly in all directions from a single point. The object's brightness varies from one part to another, depending on the direction of and distance to the light source.

Lambertian reflection.   Dull, matte surfaces, such as chalk, exhibit **diffuse reflection,** also known as **Lambertian reflection.** These surfaces appear equally bright from all viewing angles because they reflect light with equal intensity in all directions. For a given surface, the brightness depends only on the angle θ between the direction $\overline{L}$ to the light source and the surface normal $\overline{N}$ of Fig. 14.1. Let us examine why this occurs. There are two factors at work here. First, Fig. 14.2 shows that a beam that intercepts a surface covers an area whose size is inversely proportional to the cosine of the angle θ that the beam makes with $\overline{N}$. If the beam has an infinitesimally small cross-sectional differential area dA, then the beam intercepts an area $dA / \cos \theta$ on the surface. Thus, for an incident light beam, the amount of light energy that falls on dA is proportional to $\cos \theta$. This is true for any surface, independent of its material.

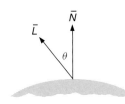

Figure 14.1
Diffuse reflection.

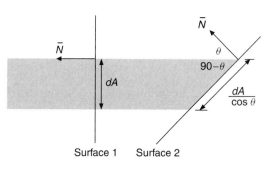

Figure 14.2   Beam (shown in 2D cross-section) of infinitesimal cross-sectional area dA at angle of incidence θ intercepts area of $dA/\cos\,\theta$.

Second, we must consider the amount of light seen by the viewer. Lambertian surfaces have the property, often known as Lambert's law, that the amount of light reflected from a unit differential area dA toward the viewer is directly proportional to the cosine of the angle between the direction to the viewer and $\overline{N}$. Since the amount of surface area seen is inversely proportional to the cosine of this angle, these two factors cancel out. For example, as the viewing angle increases, the viewer sees more surface area, but the amount of light reflected at that angle per unit area of surface is proportionally less. Thus, for Lambertian surfaces, the amount of light seen by the viewer is independent of the viewer's direction and is proportional only to $\cos\theta$, the angle of incidence of the light.

The diffuse illumination equation is

$$I = I_p k_d \cos\theta. \tag{14.3}$$

I_p is the point light source's intensity; the material's **diffuse-reflection coefficient** k_d is a constant between 0 and 1 and varies from one material to another. The angle θ must be between 0° and 90° if the light source is to have any direct effect on the point being shaded. This means that we are treating the surface as **self-occluding**, so that light cast from behind a point on the surface does not illuminate it. Rather than include a max($\cos\theta$, 0) term explicitly here and in the following equations, we assume that θ lies within the legal range. When we want to light self-occluding surfaces, we can use abs($\cos\theta$) to invert their surface normals. This causes both sides of the surface to be treated alike, as though the surface were lit by two opposing lights.

Assuming that the vectors $\overline{N}$ and $\overline{L}$ have been normalized (see Section 5.1), we can rewrite Eq. (14.3) by using the dot product:

$$I = I_p k_d\,(\overline{N}\,\cdot\,\overline{L}\,). \tag{14.4}$$

The surface normal $\overline{N}$ can be calculated using the methods discussed in Chapter 9. If polygon normals are precomputed and transformed with the same matrix used

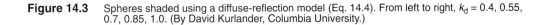

Figure 14.3　Spheres shaded using a diffuse-reflection model (Eq. 14.4). From left to right, $k_d = 0.4$, 0.55, 0.7, 0.85, 1.0. (By David Kurlander, Columbia University.)

for the polygon vertices, it is important that nonrigid modeling transformations, such as shears or differential scaling, not be performed; these transformations do not preserve angles and may cause some normals to no longer be perpendicular to their polygons. The proper method to transform normals when objects undergo arbitrary transformations is described in Section 5.7. In any case, the illumination equation must be evaluated in the WC system (or in any coordinate system isometric to it), since both the normalizing and perspective transformations will modify θ.

If a point light source is sufficiently distant from the objects being shaded, it makes essentially the same angle with all surfaces sharing the same surface normal. In this case, the light is called a **directional light source,** and $\overline{L}$ is a constant for the light source.

Figure 14.3 shows a series of pictures of a sphere illuminated by a single point source. The shading model calculated the intensity at each pixel at which the sphere was visible using the illumination model of Eq. (14.4). Objects illuminated in this way look harsh, as when a flashlight illuminates an object in an otherwise dark room. Therefore, an ambient term is commonly added to yield a more realistic illumination equation:

$$I = I_a k_a + I_p k_d\,(\overline{N}\,\cdot\,\overline{L}\,). \qquad (14.5)$$

Equation (14.5) was used to produce Fig. 14.4.

Figure 14.4　Spheres shaded using ambient and diffuse reflection (Eq. 14.5). For all spheres, $I_a = I_p = 1.0$, $k_d = 0.4$. From left to right, $k_a = 0.0$, 0.15, 0.30, 0.45, 0.60. (By David Kurlander, Columbia University.)

Light-source attenuation. If the projections of two parallel surfaces of identical material, lit from the eye, overlap in an image, Eq. (14.5) will not distinguish where one surface leaves off and the other begins, no matter how different are their distances from the light source. To do this, we introduce a light-source attenuation factor, f_{att}, yielding

$$I = I_a k_a + f_{att} I_p k_d (\overline{N} \cdot \overline{L}).\qquad(14.6)$$

An obvious choice for f_{att} takes into account the fact that the energy from a point light source that reaches a given part of a surface falls off as the inverse square of d_L, the distance the light travels from the point source to the surface. In this case,

$$f_{att} = \frac{1}{d_L^2}.\qquad(14.7)$$

In practice, however, this often does not work well. If the light is far away, $1 / d_L^2$ does not vary much; if it is very close, it varies widely, giving considerably different shades to surfaces with the same angle θ between $\overline{N}$ and $\overline{L}$. Although this behavior is correct for a point light source, the objects we see in real life typically are not illuminated by point sources and are not shaded using the simplified illumination models of computer graphics. To complicate matters, early graphics researchers often used a single point light source positioned right at the viewpoint. They expected f_{att} to approximate some of the effects of atmospheric attenuation between the viewer and the object (see Section 14.1.3), as well as the energy density falloff from the light to the object. A useful compromise, which allows a richer range of effects than simple square-law attenuation, is

$$f_{att} = \min \left(\frac{1}{c_1 + c_2 d_L + c_3 d_L^2}, 1 \right).\qquad(14.8)$$

Here c_1, c_2, and c_3 are user-defined constants associated with the light source. The constant c_1 keeps the denominator from becoming too small when the light is close, and the expression is clamped to a maximum of 1 to ensure that it always attenuates. Figure 14.5 uses this illumination model with different constants to show a range of effects.

Colored lights and surfaces. So far, we have described monochromatic lights and surfaces. Colored lights and surfaces are commonly treated by writing separate equations for each component of the color model. We represent an object's **diffuse color** by one value of O_d for each component. For example, the triple (O_{dR}, O_{dG}, O_{dB}) defines an object's diffuse red, green, and blue components in the RGB color system. In this case, the illuminating light's three primary components, I_{pR}, I_{pG}, and I_{pB}, are reflected in proportion to $k_d O_{dR}$, $k_d O_{dG}$, and $k_d O_{dB}$, respectively. Therefore, for the red component,

$$I_R = I_{aR} k_a O_{dR} + f_{att} I_{pR} k_d O_{dR} (\overline{N} \cdot \overline{L}).\qquad(14.9)$$

Similar equations are used for I_G and I_B, the green and blue components. The use of a single coefficient to scale an expression in each of the equations allows the

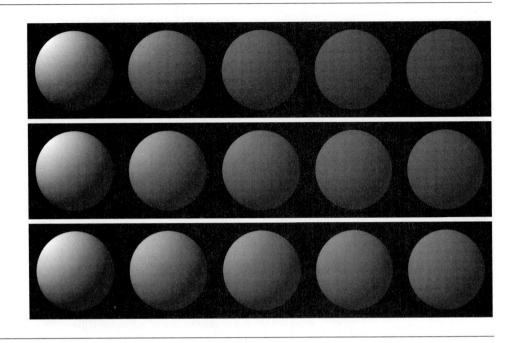

Figure 14.5 Spheres shaded using ambient and diffuse reflection with a light-source-attenuation term (Eqs. 14.6 and 14.8). For all spheres, $I_a = I_p = 1.0$, $k_a = 0.1$, $k_d = 0.9$. From left to right, sphere's distance from light source is 1.0, 1.375, 1.75, 2.125, 2.5. Top row: $c_1 = c_2 = 0.0$, $c_3 = 1.0$ $(1/d_L^2)$. Middle row: $c_1 = c_2 = 0.25$, $c_3 = 0.5$. Bottom row: $c_1 = 0.0$, $c_2 = 1.0$, $c_3 = 0.0$ $(1/d_L)$. (By David Kurlander, Columbia University.)

user to control the amount of ambient or diffuse reflection, without altering the proportions of its components. An alternative formulation that is more compact, but less convenient to control, uses a separate coefficient for each component, for example, substituting k_{aR} for $k_a O_{dR}$ and k_{dR} for $k_d O_{dR}$.

A simplifying assumption is made here that a three-component color model can completely model the interaction of light with objects. This assumption is wrong, but it is easy to implement and often yields acceptable pictures. In theory, the illumination equation should be evaluated continuously over the spectral range being modeled; in practice, it is evaluated for some number of discrete spectral samples. Rather than restrict ourselves to a particular color model, we explicitly indicate those terms in an illumination equation that are wavelength-dependent by subscripting them with a λ. Thus, Eq. (14.9) becomes

$$I_\lambda = I_{a\lambda} k_a O_{d\lambda} + f_{att} I_{p\lambda} k_d O_{d\lambda} (\overline{N} \cdot \overline{L}). \tag{14.10}$$

14.1.3 Atmospheric Attenuation

To simulate the atmospheric attenuation from the object to the viewer, many systems provide **depth cueing.** In this technique, which originated with vector-graphics hardware, more distant objects are rendered with lower intensity than are closer ones. The PHIGS PLUS standard recommends a depth-cueing approach that also makes it possible to approximate the shift in colors caused by the intervening atmosphere. Front and back depth-cue reference planes are defined in NPC; each of these planes is associated with a scale factor, s_f and s_b, respectively, that ranges between 0 and 1. The scale factors determine the blending of the original intensity with that of a depth-cue color, $I_{dc\lambda}$. The goal is to modify a previously computed I_λ to yield the depth-cued value I'_λ that is displayed. Given z_o, the object's z coordinate, a scale factor s_o is derived that will be used to interpolate between I_λ and $I_{dc\lambda}$, to determine

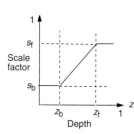

Figure 14.6

Computing the scale factor for atmospheric attenuation.

$$I'_\lambda = s_o I_\lambda + (1 - s_o)I_{dc\lambda}. \tag{14.11}$$

If z_o is in front of the front depth-cue reference plane's z coordinate z_f, then $s_o = s_f$. If z_o is behind the back depth-cue reference plane's z coordinate z_b, then $s_o = s_b$. Finally, if z_o is between the two planes, then

$$s_o = s_b + \frac{(z_o - z_b)(s_f - s_b)}{z_f - z_b}. \tag{14.12}$$

The relationship between s_o and z_o is shown in Fig. 14.6. Figure 14.7 shows spheres shaded with depth cueing. To avoid complicating the equations, we ignore depth cueing as we develop the illumination model further.

14.1.4 Specular Reflection

Specular reflection can be observed on any shiny surface. Illuminate an apple with a bright white light: The highlight is caused by specular reflection, whereas the light reflected from the rest of the apple is the result of diffuse reflection. Also note that, at the highlight, the apple appears not to be red, but white, the color of the incident light. Objects such as waxed apples or shiny plastics have a transparent surface; plastics, for example, are typically composed of pigment particles embedded in a transparent material. Light specularly reflected from the colorless surface has much the same color as that of the light source.

Figure 14.7 Spheres shaded using depth cueing (Eqs. 14.5, 14.11, and 14.12). Distance from light is constant. For all spheres, $I_a = I_p = 1.0$, $k_a = 0.1$, $k_d = 0.9$, $z_f = 1.0$, $z_b = 0.0$, $s_f = 1.0$, $s_b = 0.1$, radius = 0.09. From left to right, z at front of sphere is 1.0, 0.77, 0.55, 0.32, 0.09. (By David Kurlander, Columbia University.)

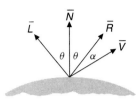

Figure 14.8
Specular reflection.

Now move your head and notice how the highlight also moves. It does so because shiny surfaces reflect light unequally in different directions; on a perfectly shiny surface, such as a perfect mirror, light is reflected *only* in the direction of reflection $\overline{R}$, which is $\overline{L}$ mirrored about $\overline{N}$. Thus the viewer can see specularly reflected light from a mirror only when the angle α in Fig. 14.8 is zero; α is the angle between $\overline{R}$ and the direction to the viewpoint $\overline{V}$.

The Phong illumination model.   Phong Bui-Tuong [BUIT75] developed a popular illumination model for nonperfect reflectors, such as the apple. The model assumes that maximum specular reflectance occurs when α is zero and falls off sharply as α increases. This rapid falloff is approximated by $\cos^n \alpha$, where n is the material's **specular-reflection exponent.** Values of n typically vary from 1 to several hundred, depending on the surface material being simulated. A value of 1 provides a broad, gentle falloff, whereas higher values simulate a sharp, focused highlight (Fig. 14.9). For a perfect reflector, n would be infinite. As before, we treat a negative value of $\cos \alpha$ as zero. Phong's illumination model is based on earlier work by researchers such as Warnock [WARN69], who used a $\cos^n \theta$ term to model specular reflection with the light at the viewpoint. Phong, however, was the first to account for viewers and lights at arbitrary positions.

The amount of incident light specularly reflected depends on the angle of incidence θ. If $W(\theta)$ is the fraction of specularly reflected light, then Phong's model is

$$I_\lambda = I_{a\lambda}k_aO_{d\lambda} + f_{att}I_{p\lambda}\ [k_dO_{d\lambda}\ \cos \theta + W(\theta)\cos^n \alpha].\qquad(14.13)$$

If the direction of reflection $\overline{R}$ and the viewpoint direction $\overline{V}$ are normalized, then $\cos \alpha = \overline{R} \cdot \overline{V}$. In addition, $W(\theta)$ is typically set to a constant k_s, the material's **specular-reflection coefficient,** which ranges between 0 and 1. The value of k_s is selected experimentally to produce aesthetically pleasing results. Then, Eq. (14.13) can be rewritten as

$$I_\lambda = I_{a\lambda}k_aO_{d\lambda} + f_{att}I_{p\lambda}[k_dO_{d\lambda}(\overline{N} \cdot \overline{L}) + k_s(\overline{R} \cdot \overline{V})^n].\qquad(14.14)$$

Note that the color of the specular component in Phong's illumination model is *not* dependent on any material property; thus, this model does a good job of modeling

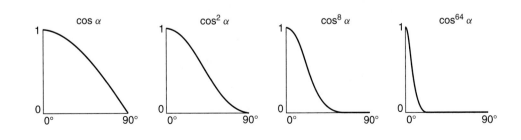

Figure 14.9   Different values of $\cos^n \alpha$ used in the Phong illumination model.

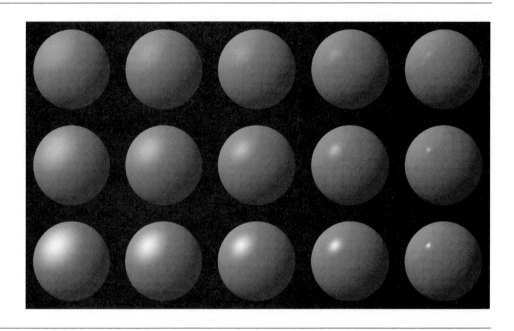

Figure 14.10   Spheres shaded using Phong's illumination model (Eq. 14.14) and different values of k_s and n. For all spheres, $I_a = I_p = 1.0$, $k_a = 0.1$, $k_d = 0.45$. From left to right, $n = 3.0, 5.0, 10.0, 27.0, 200.0$. From top to bottom, $k_s = 0.1, 0.25, 0.5$. (By David Kurlander, Columbia University.)

specular reflections from plastic surfaces. As we discuss in Section 14.1.7, specular reflection is affected by the properties of the surface itself and, in general, may have a different color than diffuse reflection when the surface is a composite of several materials. We can accommodate this effect to a first approximation by modifying Eq. (14.14) to yield

$$I_\lambda = I_{a\lambda}k_aO_{d\lambda} + f_{att}I_{p\lambda}[k_dO_{d\lambda}(\overline{N} \cdot \overline{L}) + k_sO_{s\lambda}(\overline{R} \cdot \overline{V})^n], \quad (14.15)$$

where $O_{s\lambda}$ is the object's **specular color.** Figure 14.10 shows a sphere illuminated using Eq. (14.14) with different values of k_s and n.

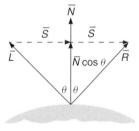

Figure 14.11

Calculating the reflection vector.

Calculating the reflection vector. Calculating $\overline{R}$ requires mirroring $\overline{L}$ about $\overline{N}$. As shown in Fig. 14.11, this can be accomplished with some simple geometry. Since $\overline{N}$ and $\overline{L}$ are normalized, the projection of $\overline{L}$ onto $\overline{N}$ is $\overline{N}\cos\theta$. Note that $\overline{R} = \overline{N}\cos\theta + \overline{S}$, where $|\overline{S}|$ is $\sin\theta$. But, by vector subtraction and congruent triangles, $\overline{S}$ is just $\overline{N}\cos\theta - \overline{L}$. Therefore, $\overline{R} = 2\overline{N}\cos\theta - \overline{L}$. Substituting $\overline{N} \cdot \overline{L}$ for $\cos\theta$ and $\overline{R} \cdot \overline{V}$ for $\cos\alpha$ yields

$$\overline{R} = 2\overline{N}(\overline{N} \cdot \overline{L}) - \overline{L}, \quad (14.16)$$

$$\overline{R} \cdot \overline{V} = (2\overline{N}(\overline{N} \cdot \overline{L}) - \overline{L}) \cdot \overline{V}. \quad (14.17)$$

If the light source is at infinity, $\overline{N} \cdot \overline{L}$ is constant for a given polygon, whereas $\overline{R} \cdot \overline{V}$ varies across the polygon. For curved surfaces or for a light source not at infinity, both $\overline{N} \cdot \overline{L}$ and $\overline{R} \cdot \overline{V}$ vary across the surface.

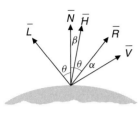

Figure 14.12
$\overline{H}$, the halfway vector, is halfway between the direction of the light source and the viewer.

The halfway vector. An alternative formulation of Phong's illumination model uses the **halfway vector** $\overline{H}$, so called because its direction is halfway between the directions of the light source and the viewer, as shown in Fig. 14.12. $\overline{H}$ is also known as the direction of maximum highlights. If the surface were oriented so that its normal were in the same direction as $\overline{H}$, the viewer would see the brightest specular highlight, since $\overline{R}$ and $\overline{V}$ would also point in the same direction. The new specular-reflection term can be expressed as $(\overline{N} \cdot \overline{H})^n$, where $\overline{H} = (\overline{L} + \overline{V})/|\overline{L} + \overline{V}|$. When the light source and the viewer are both at infinity, then the use of $\overline{N} \cdot \overline{H}$ offers a computational advantage, since $\overline{H}$ is constant. Note that β, the angle between $\overline{N}$ and $\overline{H}$, is not equal to α, the angle between $\overline{R}$ and $\overline{V}$, so the same specular exponent n produces different results in the two formulations (see Exercise 14.1). Although using a $\cos^n$ term allows the generation of recognizably glossy surfaces, you should remember that it is based on empirical observation, not on a theoretical model of the specular-reflection process.

14.1.5 Improving the Point-Light-Source Model

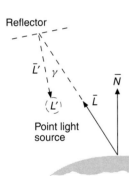

Figure 14.13
Warn's lighting model. A light is modeled as the specular reflection from a single point illuminated by a point light source.

Real light sources do not radiate equally in all directions. Warn [WARN83] has developed easily implemented lighting controls that can be added to any illumination equation to model some of the directionality of the lights used by photographers. In Phong's model, a point light source has only an intensity and a position. In Warn's model, a light L is modeled by a point on a hypothetical specular reflecting surface, as shown in Fig. 14.13. This surface is illuminated by a point light source L' in the direction $\overline{L}\,'$. Assume that $\overline{L}\,'$ is normal to the hypothetical reflecting surface. Then, we can use the Phong illumination equation to determine the intensity of L at a point on the object in terms of the angle γ between $\overline{L}$ and $\overline{L}\,'$. If we further assume that the reflector reflects only specular light and has a specular coefficient of 1, then the light's intensity at a point on the object is

$$I_{L'\lambda} \cos^p \gamma, \tag{14.18}$$

where $I_{L'\lambda}$ is the intensity of the hypothetical point light source, p is the reflector's specular exponent, and γ is the angle between $-\overline{L}$ and the hypothetical surface's normal, $\overline{L}\,'$, which is the direction to L'. Equation (14.18) models a symmetric directed light source whose axis of symmetry is $\overline{L}\,'$, the direction in which the light may be thought of as pointing. Using dot products, we can write Eq. (14.18) as

$$I_{L'\lambda} (-\overline{L} \cdot \overline{L}\,')^p. \tag{14.19}$$

Once again, we treat a negative dot product as zero. Equation (14.19) can thus be substituted for the light-source intensity $I_{p\lambda}$ in the formulation of Eq. (14.15) or any other illumination equation. The larger the value of p, the more the light is

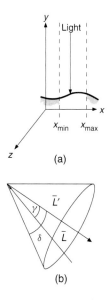

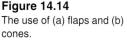

(b)

Figure 14.14
The use of (a) flaps and (b) cones.

concentrated along $\overline{L}\,'$. Thus, a large value of p can simulate a highly directional spotlight, whereas a small value of p can simulate a more diffuse floodlight. If p is 0, then the light acts like a uniformly radiating point source. Figure 14.15(a–c) shows the effects of different values of p.

To restrict a light's effects to a limited area of the scene, Warn implemented **flaps** and **cones**. Flaps, modeled loosely after the "barn doors" found on professional photographic lights, confine the effects of the light to a designated range in x, y, and z world coordinates. Each light has six flaps, corresponding to user-specified minimum and maximum values in each coordinate. When a point's shade is determined, the illumination model is evaluated for a light only if the point's coordinates are within the range specified by the minimum and maximum coordinates of those flaps that are on. For example, if $\overline{L}\,'$ is parallel to the y axis, then the x and z flaps can restrict the light's effects sharply, much like the photographic light's barn doors. Figure 14.14(a) shows the use of x flaps in this situation. The y flaps can also be used here to restrict the light in a way that has no physical counterpart, allowing only objects within a specified range of distances from the light to be illuminated. In Fig. 14.15(d) the cube is aligned with the coordinate system, so two pairs of flaps can produce the effects shown.

Warn makes it possible to create a sharply delineated spotlight through the use of a cone whose apex is at the light source and whose axis lies along $\overline{L}\,'$. As shown in Fig. 14.14(b), a cone with a generating angle of δ may be used to restrict the light source's effects by evaluating the illumination model only when $\gamma < \delta$ (or when $\cos\gamma > \cos\delta$, since $\cos\gamma$ has already been calculated). The PHIGS PLUS illumination model includes the Warn $\cos^p\gamma$ term and cone angle δ. Figure 14.15(e) demonstrates the use of a cone to restrict the light of Fig. 14.15(c). Color Plate 21 shows a car rendered with Warn's lighting controls.

14.1.6 Multiple Light Sources

If there are m light sources, then the terms for each light source are summed:

$$I_\lambda = I_{a\lambda}k_aO_{d\lambda} + \sum_{1 \le i \le m} f_{att_i}I_{p\lambda_i}[k_dO_{d\lambda}(\overline{N}\cdot\overline{L}_i) + k_sO_{s\lambda}(\overline{R}_i\cdot\overline{V})^n]. \qquad (14.20)$$

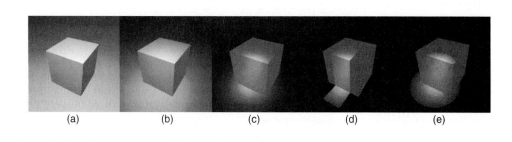

(a)   (b)   (c)   (d)   (e)

Figure 14.15 Cube and plane illuminated using Warn lighting controls. (a) Uniformly radiating point source (or $p = 0$). (b) $p = 4$. (c) $p = 32$. (d) Flaps. (e) Cone with $\delta = 18°$. (By David Kurlander, Columbia University.)

The summation harbors a new possibility for error in that I_λ can now exceed the maximum displayable pixel value. (Although this can also happen for a single light, we can easily avoid it by an appropriate choice of f_{att} and the material.) Several approaches can be used to avoid overflow. The simplest is to clamp each I_λ individually to its maximum value. Another approach considers all of a pixel's I_λ values together. If at least one is too big, each is divided by the largest to maintain the hue and saturation at the expense of the value. If all the pixel values can be computed before display, image-processing transformations can be applied to the entire picture to bring the values within the desired range. Hall [HALL89] discusses the tradeoffs of these and other techniques.

14.1.7 Physically Based Illumination Models

The illumination models discussed in the previous sections are largely the result of a common sense, practical approach to graphics. Although the equations used approximate some of the ways light interacts with objects, they do not have a physical basis. In this section, we touch upon physically based illumination models, relying in part on the work of Cook and Torrance [COOK82].

Thus far, we have used the word *intensity* without defining it, referring informally to the intensity of a light source, of a point on a surface, or of a pixel. It is time now to formalize our terms by introducing the radiometric terminology used in the study of thermal radiation, which is the basis for our understanding of how light interacts with objects [NICO77; SPARR78; SIEG81; IES87]. We begin with **flux**, which is the rate at which light energy is emitted and is measured in watts (W). To refer to the amount of flux emitted in or received from a given direction, we need the concept of a **solid angle**, which is the angle at the apex of a cone. Solid angle is measured in terms of the area on a sphere intercepted by a cone whose apex is at the sphere's center. A **steradian** (sr) is the solid angle of such a cone that intercepts an area equal to the square of the sphere's radius r. If a point is on a surface, we are concerned with the hemisphere above it. Since the area of a sphere is $4\pi r^2$, there are $4\pi r^2 / 2r^2 = 2\pi$ sr in a hemisphere. Imagine projecting an object's shape onto a hemisphere centered about a point on the surface that serves as the center of projection. The solid angle ω subtended by the object is the area on the hemisphere occupied by the projection, divided by the square of the hemisphere's radius (the division eliminates dependence on the size of the hemisphere).

Radiant intensity is the flux radiated into a unit solid angle in a particular direction and is measured in W / sr. When we used the word *intensity* in reference to a point source, we were referring to its radiant intensity.

Radiance is the radiant intensity per unit foreshortened surface area, and is measured in W / (sr · m^2). **Foreshortened surface area**, also known as **projected surface area**, refers to the projection of the surface onto the plane perpendicular to the direction of radiation. The foreshortened surface area is found by multiplying the surface area by $\cos \theta_r$, where θ_r is the angle of the radiated light relative to the surface normal. A small solid angle $d\omega$ may be approximated as the object's foreshortened surface area divided by the square of the distance from the object to the point at which the solid angle is being computed. When we used the word *intensity* in reference to a surface, we were referring to its radiance. Finally, **irradiance**, also known as **flux density**, is the incident flux per (unforeshortened) unit surface area and is measured in W / m^2.

In graphics, we are interested in the relationship between the light incident on a surface and the light reflected from and transmitted through that surface. Consider Fig. 14.16. The irradiance of the incident light is

$$E_i = I_i(\overline{N} \cdot \overline{L})\,d\omega_i,$$

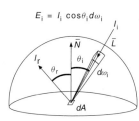

where I_i is the incident light's radiance, and $\overline{N} \cdot \overline{L}$ is $\cos\theta_i$. Since irradiance is expressed per unit area, whereas radiance is expressed per unit foreshortened area, multiplying by $\overline{N} \cdot \overline{L}$ converts it to the equivalent per unit unforeshortened area.

It is not enough to consider just I_i (the incident radiance) when determining I_r (the reflected radiance); E_i (the incident irradiance) must instead be taken into account. For example, an incident beam that has the same radiant intensity (W / sr) as another beam but a greater solid angle has proportionally greater E_i and causes the surface to appear proportionally brighter. The ratio of the reflected radiance (intensity) in one direction to the incident irradiance (flux density) responsible for it from another direction is known as the **bidirectional reflectivity**, ρ, which is a function of the directions of incidence and reflection,

$$\rho = \frac{I_r}{E_i}.$$

Figure 14.16
Reflected radiance and incident irradiance.

As we have seen, it is conventional in computer graphics to consider bidirectional reflectivity as composed of diffuse and specular components. Therefore,

$$\rho = k_d\rho_d + k_s\rho_s,$$

where ρ_d and ρ_s are respectively the diffuse and specular bidirectional reflectivities, and k_d and k_s are respectively the diffuse and specular reflection coefficients introduced earlier in this chapter.

The Torrance–Sparrow surface model [TORR66; TORR67], developed by applied physicists, is a physically based model of a reflecting surface. Blinn was the first to adapt the Torrance–Sparrow model to computer graphics, giving the mathematical details and comparing it to the Phong model in [BLIN77a]; Cook and Torrance [COOK82] were the first to approximate the spectral composition of reflected light in an implementation of the model.

In the Torrance–Sparrow model, the surface is assumed to be an isotropic collection of planar microscopic facets, each a perfectly smooth reflector. The geometry and distribution of these **microfacets** and the direction of the light (assumed to emanate from an infinitely distant source, so that all rays are parallel) determine the intensity and direction of specular reflection as a function of I_p (the point light source intensity), $\overline{N}$, $\overline{L}$, and $\overline{V}$. Experimental measurements show a very good correspondence between the actual reflection and the reflection predicted by this model [TORR67].

For the specular component of the bidirectional reflectivity, Cook and Torrance use

$$\rho_s = \frac{F_\lambda}{\pi} \frac{DG}{(\overline{N} \cdot \overline{V})(\overline{N} \cdot \overline{L})}, \tag{14.21}$$

where D is a distribution function of the microfacet orientations, G is the **geometrical attenuation factor,** which represents the masking and shadowing effects of the microfacets on each other, and F_λ is the Fresnel term computed by Fresnel's equation, which, for specular reflection, relates incident light to reflected light for the smooth surface of each microfacet. The π in the denominator is intended to account for surface roughness (but see [JOY88, pp. 227–230] for an overview of how the equation is derived). The $\overline{N} \cdot \overline{V}$ term makes the equation proportional to the surface area (and hence to the number of microfacets) that the viewer sees in a unit piece of foreshortened surface area, whereas the $\overline{N} \cdot \overline{L}$ term makes the equation proportional to the surface area that the light sees in a unit piece of foreshortened surface area. Details of the constituent terms of Eq. (14.21) are in Section 16.7 of [FOLE90]; here we only present results.

Color Plate 40 shows two copper vases rendered with the Cook–Torrance model, both of which use the bidirectional reflectance of copper for the diffuse term. The first vase models the specular term using the reflectance of a vinyl mirror and represents results similar to those obtained with the original Phong illumination model of Eq. (14.14). The second models the specular term with the reflectance of a copper mirror. Note how accounting for the dependence of the specular highlight color on both angle of incidence and surface material produces a more convincing image of a metallic surface.

In general, the ambient, diffuse, and specular components are the color of the material for both dielectrics and conductors. Composite objects, such as plastics, typically have diffuse and specular components that are different colors. Metals typically show little diffuse reflection and have a specular component color that ranges between that of the metal and that of the light source as θ_i approaches 90°. This observation suggests a rough approximation to the Cook–Torrance model that uses Eq. (14.15) with $O_{s\lambda}$ chosen by interpolating from a look-up table based on θ_i.

There have been several enhancements and generalizations to the Cook–Torrance illumination model; see, for example, [KAJI85; CABR87; WOLF90]. Recent work by He et al. [HE92] demonstrates a fast and accurate method for applying such physically based models. It is interesting to note that [HE92] is a multimedia publication that allows the reader to explore interactively the effect of many of the terms in Eq. (14.21).

14.2 SHADING MODELS FOR POLYGONS

It should be clear that we can shade any surface by calculating the surface normal at each visible point and applying the desired illumination model at that point. Unfortunately, this brute-force shading model is expensive. In this section, we describe more efficient shading models for surfaces defined by polygons and polygon meshes.

14.2.1 Constant Shading

The simplest shading model for a polygon is **constant shading,** also known as **faceted shading** or **flat shading.** This approach applies an illumination model once to determine a single intensity value that is then used to shade an entire polygon. In essence, we are sampling the value of the illumination equation once for each polygon, and holding the value across the polygon to reconstruct the polygon's shade. This approach is valid if several assumptions are true:

1. The light source is at infinity, so $\overline{N} \cdot \overline{L}$ is constant across the polygon face.
2. The viewer is at infinity, so $\overline{N} \cdot \overline{V}$ is constant across the polygon face.
3. The polygon represents the actual surface being modeled and is not an approximation to a curved surface.

If a visible-surface algorithm is used that outputs a list of polygons, such as one of the list-priority algorithms, constant shading can take advantage of the ubiquitous single-color 2D polygon primitive.

If either of the first two assumptions is wrong, then if we are to use constant shading, we need some method to determine a single value for each of $\overline{L}$ and $\overline{V}$. For example, values may be calculated for the center of the polygon, or for the polygon's first vertex. Of course, constant shading does not produce the variations in shading across the polygon that should occur in this situation.

14.2.2 Interpolated Shading

As an alternative to evaluating the illumination equation at each point on the polygon, Wylie, Romney, Evans, and Erdahl [WYLI67] pioneered the use of **interpolated shading,** in which shading information is linearly interpolated across a triangle from values determined for its vertices. Gouraud [GOUR71] generalized this technique to arbitrary polygons. This method is particularly easy for a scan-line algorithm that already interpolates the z value across a span from interpolated z values computed for the span's endpoints.

For increased efficiency, a difference equation may be used, like that developed in Section 13.2 to determine the z value at each pixel. Although z interpolation is physically correct (assuming that the polygon is planar), note that interpolated shading is not, since it only approximates evaluating the illumination model at each point on the polygon.

Our final assumption, that the polygon accurately represents the surface being modeled, is most often the one that is incorrect, which has a much more substantial effect on the resulting image than does the failure of the other two assumptions. Many objects are curved, rather than polyhedral, yet representing them as a polygon mesh allows the use of efficient polygon visible-surface algorithms. We discuss next how to render a polygon mesh so that it looks as much as possible like a curved surface.

14.2.3 Polygon-Mesh Shading

Suppose that we wish to approximate a curved surface by a polygonal mesh. If each polygonal facet in the mesh is shaded individually, it is easily distinguished from neighbors whose orientation is different, producing a "faceted" appearance, as shown in Color Plate 28. This is true if the polygons are rendered using constant shading, interpolated shading, or even per-pixel illumination calculations, because two adjacent polygons of different orientation have different intensities along their borders. The simple solution of using a finer mesh turns out to be surprisingly ineffective, because the perceived difference in shading between adjacent facets is accentuated by the Mach band effect (discovered by Mach in 1865 and described in detail in [RATL72]), which exaggerates the intensity change at any edge where there is a discontinuity in magnitude or slope of intensity. At the border between two facets, the dark facet looks darker and the light facet looks lighter. Figure 14.17 shows, for two separate cases, the actual and perceived changes in intensity along a surface.

Mach banding is caused by **lateral inhibition** of the receptors in the eye. The more light a receptor receives, the more that receptor inhibits the response of the receptors adjacent to it. The response of a receptor to light is inhibited by its adjacent receptors in inverse relation to the distance to the adjacent receptor. Receptors directly on the brighter side of an intensity change have a stronger response than do those on the brighter side that are farther from the edge, because they receive less inhibition from their neighbors on the darker side. Similarly, receptors immediately to the darker side of an intensity change have a weaker response than do those farther into the darker area, because they receive more inhibition from their neighbors on the brighter side. The Mach band effect is quite evident in Color Plate 28, especially between adjacent polygons that are close in color.

The polygon-shading models we have described determine the shade of each polygon individually. Two basic shading models for polygon meshes take advantage of the information provided by adjacent polygons to simulate a smooth surface. In order of increasing complexity (and realistic effect), they are known as

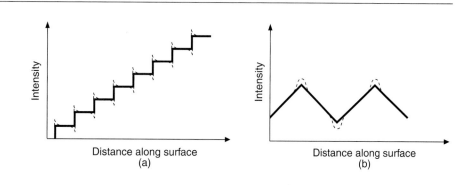

Figure 14.17   Two examples of actual and perceived intensities in the Mach band effect. Dashed lines are perceived intensity; solid lines are actual intensity.

Gouraud shading and Phong shading, after the researchers who developed them. Current 3D graphics workstations typically support one or both of these approaches through a combination of hardware and firmware.

14.2.4 Gouraud Shading

Gouraud shading [GOUR71], also called **intensity interpolation shading** or **color interpolation shading,** eliminates intensity discontinuities. Color Plate 29 uses Gouraud shading. Although most of the Mach banding of Color Plate 28 is no longer visible in Color Plate 29, the bright ridges on objects such as the torus and cone are Mach bands caused by a rapid, although not discontinuous, change in the slope of the intensity curve; Gouraud shading does not completely eliminate such intensity changes.

Gouraud shading extends the concept of interpolated shading applied to individual polygons by interpolating polygon vertex illumination values that take into account the surface being approximated. The Gouraud shading process requires that the normal be known for each vertex of the polygonal mesh. Gouraud was able to compute these **vertex normals** directly from an analytical description of the surface. Alternatively, if the vertex normals are not stored with the mesh and cannot be determined directly from the actual surface, then, Gouraud suggested, we can approximate them by averaging the surface normals of all polygonal facets sharing each vertex (Fig. 14.18). If an edge is meant to be visible (as at the joint between a plane's wing and body), then we find two vertex normals, one for each side of the edge, by averaging the normals of polygons on each side of the edge separately.

The next step in Gouraud shading is to find **vertex intensities** by using the vertex normals with any desired illumination model. Finally, each polygon is shaded by linear interpolation of vertex intensities along each edge and then between edges along each scan line (Fig. 14.19) in the same way that we described interpolating z values in Section 13.2. The term *Gouraud shading* is frequently

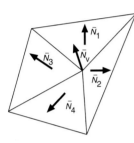

Figure 14.18

Normalized polygon surface normals may be averaged to obtain vertex normals.

Averaged normal $\bar{N}_v$ is

$$\Sigma_{1 \le i \le n}\, \bar{N}_i \,/\, |\,\Sigma_{1 \le i \le n}\, \bar{N}_i\,|.$$

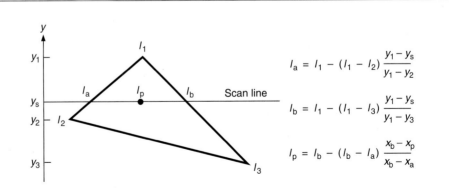

$$I_a = I_1 - (I_1 - I_2)\,\frac{y_1 - y_s}{y_1 - y_2}$$

$$I_b = I_1 - (I_1 - I_3)\,\frac{y_1 - y_s}{y_1 - y_3}$$

$$I_p = I_b - (I_b - I_a)\,\frac{x_b - x_p}{x_b - x_a}$$

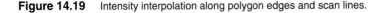

Figure 14.19   Intensity interpolation along polygon edges and scan lines.

generalized to refer to intensity interpolation shading of even a single polygon in isolation, or to the interpolation of arbitrary colors associated with polygon vertices.

The interpolation along edges can easily be integrated with the scan-line visible-surface algorithm of Section 13.3. With each edge, we store for each color component the starting intensity and the change of intensity for each unit change in y. A visible span on a scan line is filled in by interpolating the intensity values of the two edges bounding the span. As in all linear-interpolation algorithms, a difference equation may be used for increased efficiency.

14.2.5 Phong Shading

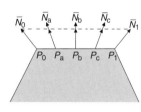

Figure 14.20
Normal vector interpolation. (After [BUIT75].)

Phong shading [BUIT75], also known as **normal-vector interpolation shading**, interpolates the surface normal vector $\overline{N}$, rather than the intensity. Interpolation occurs across a polygon span on a scan line, between starting and ending normals for the span. These normals are themselves interpolated along polygon edges from vertex normals that are computed, if necessary, just as in Gouraud shading. The interpolation along edges can again be done by means of incremental calculations, with all three components of the normal vector being incremented from scan line to scan line. At each pixel along a scan line, the interpolated normal is normalized and is backmapped into the WC system or one isometric to it, and a new intensity calculation is performed using any illumination model. Figure 14.20 shows two edge normals and the normals interpolated from them, before and after normalization.

Color Plates 30 and 31 were generated using Gouraud shading and Phong shading, respectively, and an illumination equation with a specular-reflectance term. Phong shading yields substantial improvements over Gouraud shading when such illumination models are used, because highlights are reproduced more faithfully, as shown in Fig. 14.21. Consider what happens if n in the Phong $\cos^n \alpha$ illumination term is large and one vertex has a very small α, but each of its adjacent vertices has a large α. The intensity associated with the vertex that has a small α

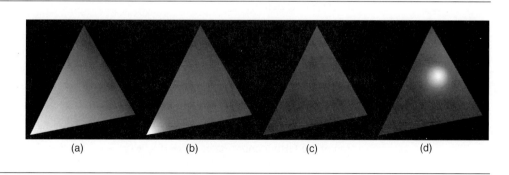

(a) (b) (c) (d)

Figure 14.21 A specular-reflection illumination model used with Gouraud shading and Phong shading. Highlight falls at left vertex: (a) Gouraud shading, (b) Phong shading. Highlight falls in polygon interior: (c) Gouraud shading, (d) Phong shading. (By David Kurlander, Columbia University.)

will be appropriate for a highlight, whereas the other vertices will have nonhighlight intensities. If Gouraud shading is used, then the intensity across the polygon is linearly interpolated between the highlight intensity and the lower intensities of the adjacent vertices, spreading the highlight over the polygon (Fig. 14.21a). Contrast this with the sharp drop from the highlight intensity that is computed if linearly interpolated normals are used to compute the $\cos^n \alpha$ term at each pixel (Fig. 14.21b). Furthermore, if a highlight fails to fall at a vertex, then Gouraud shading may miss it entirely (Fig. 14.21c), since no interior point can be brighter than the brightest vertex from which it is interpolated. In contrast, Phong shading allows highlights to be located in a polygon's interior (Fig. 14.21d). Compare the highlights on the ball in Color Plates 30 and 31.

Even with an illumination model that does not take into account specular reflectance, the results of normal-vector interpolation are in general superior to intensity interpolation, because an approximation to the normal is used at each point. This reduces Mach-band problems in most cases, but greatly increases the cost of shading in a straightforward implementation, since the interpolated normal must be normalized every time it is used in an illumination model. Duff [DUFF79] has developed a combination of difference equations and table lookup to speed up the calculation. Bishop and Weimer [BISH86] provide an excellent approximation of Phong shading by using a Taylor series expansion that offers even greater increases in shading speed.

14.2.6 Problems with Interpolated Shading

There are many problems common to all these interpolated-shading models, several of which we list here.

Polygonal silhouette.   No matter how good an approximation an interpolated shading model offers to the actual shading of a curved surface, the silhouette edge of the mesh is still clearly polygonal. We can improve this situation by breaking the surface into a greater number of smaller polygons, but at a corresponding increase in expense.

Perspective distortion.   Anomalies are introduced because interpolation is performed after perspective transformation in the 3D screen-coordinate system, rather than in the WC system. For example, linear interpolation causes the shading information in Fig. 14.19 to be incremented by a constant amount from one scan line to another along each edge. Consider what happens when vertex 1 is more distant than vertex 2. Perspective foreshortening means that the difference from one scan line to another in the untransformed z value along an edge increases in the direction of the farther coordinate. Thus, if $y_s = (y_1 + y_2) / 2$, then $I_s = (I_1 + I_2) / 2$, but z_s will not equal $(z_1 + z_2) / 2$. This problem can also be reduced by using a larger number of smaller polygons. Decreasing the size of the polygons increases the number of points at which the information to be interpolated is sampled, and therefore increases the accuracy of the shading.

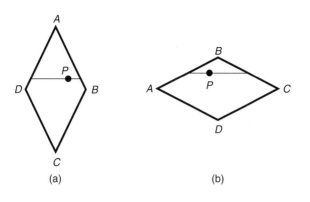

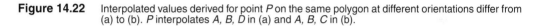

Figure 14.22   Interpolated values derived for point *P* on the same polygon at different orientations differ from (a) to (b). *P* interpolates *A, B, D* in (a) and *A, B, C* in (b).

Orientation dependence.   The results of interpolated-shading models are not independent of the projected polygon's orientation. Since values are interpolated between vertices and across horizontal scan lines, the results may differ when the polygon is rotated (see Fig. 14.22). This effect is particularly obvious when the orientation changes slowly between successive frames of an animation. A similar problem can also occur in visible-surface determination when the *z* value at each point is interpolated from the *z* values assigned to each vertex. Both problems can be solved by decomposing polygons into triangles (see Exercise 14.2). Alternatively, Duff [DUFF79] suggests rotation-independent, but expensive, interpolation methods that solve this problem without the need for decomposition.

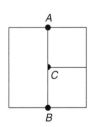

Figure 14.23
Vertex *C* is shared by the two polygons on the right, but not by the larger rectangular polygon on the left.

Problems at shared vertices.   Shading discontinuities can occur when two adjacent polygons fail to share a vertex that lies along their common edge. Consider the three polygons of Fig. 14.23, in which vertex *C* is shared by the two polygons on the right, but not by the large polygon on the left. The shading information determined directly at *C* for the polygons at the right will typically not be the same as the information interpolated at that point from the values at *A* and *B* for the polygon at the left. As a result, there will be a discontinuity in the shading. The discontinuity can be eliminated by inserting in the polygon on the left an extra vertex that shares *C*'s shading information. We can preprocess a static polygonal database to eliminate this problem; alternatively, if polygons will be split on the fly (e.g., using the BSP-tree visible-surface algorithm), then extra bookkeeping can be done to introduce a new vertex in a polygon that shares an edge that is split.

Unrepresentative vertex normals.   Computed vertex normals may not represent the surface's geometry adequately. For example, if we compute vertex normals by averaging the normals of the surfaces sharing a vertex, all of the vertex normals of Fig. 14.24 will be parallel to one another, resulting in little or no variation in shade

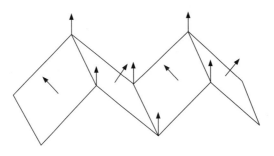

Figure 14.24   Problems with computing vertex normals. Vertex normals are all parallel.

if the light source is distant. Subdividing the polygons further before vertex normal computation will solve this problem.

Although these problems have prompted much work on rendering algorithms that handle curved surfaces directly, polygons are sufficiently faster (and easier) to process that they still form the core of most rendering systems.

14.3 SURFACE DETAIL

Applying any of the shading models we have described so far to planar or bicubic surfaces produces smooth, uniform surfaces—in marked contrast to most of the surfaces we see and feel. We discuss next a variety of methods developed to simulate this missing surface detail.

14.3.1 Surface-Detail Polygons

The simplest approach adds gross detail through the use of *surface-detail polygons* to show features (such as doors, windows, and lettering) on a base polygon (such as the side of a building). Each surface-detail polygon is coplanar with its base polygon, and is flagged so that it does not need to be compared with other polygons during visible-surface determination. When the base polygon is shaded, its surface-detail polygons and their material properties take precedence for those parts of the base polygon that they cover.

14.3.2 Texture Mapping

As detail becomes finer and more intricate, explicit modeling with polygons or other geometric primitives becomes less practical. An alternative is to map an image, either digitized or synthesized, onto a surface, a technique pioneered by Catmull [CATM74] and refined by Blinn and Newell [BLIN76]. This approach is

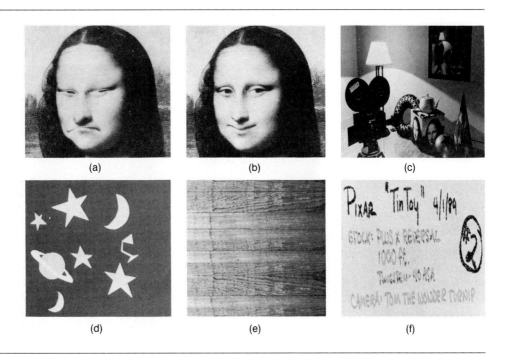

Figure 14.25   Textures used to create Color Plate 34. (a) Frowning Mona. (b) Smiling Mona. (c) Painting. (d) Wizard's cap. (e) Floor. (f) Film label. (Copyright ©1990, Pixar. Images rendered by Thomas Williams and H. B. Siegel using Pixar's PhotoRealistic RenderMan™ software.)

known as **texture mapping** or **pattern mapping;** the image is called a **texture map**, and its individual elements are often called **texels.** The rectangular texture map resides in its own (u, v) texture coordinate space. Alternatively, the texture may be defined by a procedure. Color Plate 34 shows several examples of texture mapping, using the textures shown in Fig. 14.25. At each rendered pixel, selected texels are used either to substitute for or to scale one or more of the surface's material properties, such as its diffuse color components. One pixel is often covered by a number of texels. To avoid aliasing problems, we must consider all relevant texels.

As shown in Fig. 14.26, texture mapping can be accomplished in two steps. A simple approach starts by mapping the four corners of the pixel onto the surface. For a bicubic patch, this mapping naturally defines a set of points in the surface's (s, t) coordinate space. Next, the pixel's corner points in the surface's (s, t) coordinate space are mapped into the texture's (u, v) coordinate space. The four (u, v) points in the texture map define a quadrilateral that approximates the more complex shape into which the pixel may actually map due to surface curvature. We compute a value for the pixel by summing all texels that lie within the quadrilateral, weighting each by the fraction of the texel that lies within the quadrilateral. If a transformed point in (u, v) space falls outside of the texture map, the texture map may be thought of as being replicated, like the patterns of Section 2.1.3. Rather

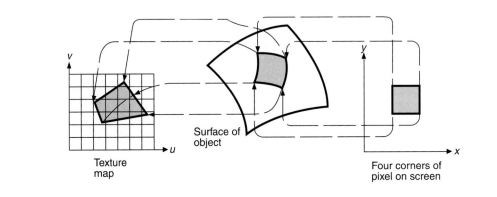

Figure 14.26   Texture mapping from pixel to the surface to the texture map.

than always use the identity mapping between (s, t) and (u, v), we can define a correspondence between the four corners of the 0-to-1 (s, t) rectangle and a quadrilateral in (u, v). When the surface is a polygon, it is common to assign texture map coordinates directly to its vertices. Since, as we have seen, linearly interpolating values across arbitrary polygons is orientation-dependent, polygons may be decomposed into triangles first. Even after triangulation, however, linear interpolation will cause distortion in the case of perspective projection. This distortion will be more noticeable than that caused when interpolating other shading information, since texture features will not be correctly foreshortened. We can obtain an approximate solution to this problem by decomposing polygons into smaller ones, or an exact solution, at greater cost, by performing the perspective division while interpolating. Heckbert [HECK86b] provides a thorough survey of texture-mapping methods.

14.3.3 Bump Mapping

Texture mapping affects a surface's shading, but the surface continues to appear geometrically smooth. If the texture map is a photograph of a rough surface, the surface being shaded will not look quite right, because the direction to the light source used to create the texture map is typically different from the direction to the light source illuminating the surface. Blinn [BLIN78b] developed a way to provide the appearance of modified surface geometry that avoids explicit geometrical modeling. His approach involves perturbing the surface normal before it is used in the illumination model, just as slight roughness in a surface would perturb the surface normal. This method is known as **bump mapping**, and is based on texture mapping.

A **bump map** is an array of displacements, each of which can be used to simulate displacing a point on a surface a little above or below that point's actual position. The results of bump mapping can be quite convincing. Viewers often fail to notice that an object's texture does not affect its silhouette edges. Color Plates 38 and 39 show two examples of bump mapping.

14.3.4 Other Approaches

Although 2D mapping can be effective in many situations, it often fails to produce convincing results. Textures frequently betray their 2D origins when mapped onto curved surfaces, and problems are encountered at texture *seams*. For example, when a wood-grain texture is mapped onto the surface of a curved object, the object will look as if it were painted with the texture. Peachey [PEAC85] and Perlin [PERL85] have investigated the use of solid textures for proper rendering of objects *carved* of wood or marble. In this approach, described in Chapter 20 of [FOLE90], the texture is a 3D function of its position in the object.

Other surface properties can be mapped as well. For example, Cook has implemented **displacement mapping,** in which the actual surface is displaced, instead of only the surface normals [COOK84]; this process, which must be carried out before visible-surface determination, was used to modify the surfaces of the cone and torus in Color Plate 35. Using fractals to create richly detailed geometry from an initial simple geometric description is discussed in Section 9.5.1.

So far, we have made the tacit assumption that the process of shading a point on an object is unaffected by the rest of that object or by any other object. But an object might in fact be shadowed by another object between it and a light source; might transmit light, allowing another object to be seen through it; or might reflect other objects, allowing another object to be seen because of it. In the following sections, we describe how to model some of these effects.

14.4 SHADOWS

Visible-surface algorithms determine which surfaces can be seen from the viewpoint; shadow algorithms determine which surfaces can be "seen" from the light source. Thus, visible-surface algorithms and shadow algorithms are essentially the same. The surfaces that are visible from the light source are not in shadow; those that are not visible from the light source are in shadow. When there are multiple light sources, a surface must be classified relative to each of them.

Here, we consider shadow algorithms for point light sources; extended light sources are discussed in [FOLE90], Chapter 16. Visibility from a point light source is, like visibility from the viewpoint, all or nothing. When a point on a surface cannot be seen from a light source, then the illumination calculation must be adjusted to take it into account. The addition of shadows to the illumination equation yields

$$I_\lambda = I_{a\lambda}k_aO_{d\lambda} + \sum_{1\leq i\leq m} S_i f_{\text{att}_i} I_{p\lambda_i} [k_dO_{d\lambda}(\overline{N} \cdot \overline{L}_i) + k_sO_{s\lambda}(\overline{R}_i \cdot \overline{V})^n], \qquad (14.22)$$

where

$$S_i = \begin{cases} 0, & \text{if light } i \text{ is blocked at this point;} \\ 1, & \text{if light } i \text{ is not blocked at this point.} \end{cases}$$

Note that areas in the shadow of all point light sources are still illuminated by the ambient light.

Although computing shadows requires computing visibility from the light source, as we have pointed out, it is also possible to generate "fake" shadows without performing any visibility tests. These shadows can be created efficiently by transforming each object into its polygonal projection from a point light source onto a designated ground plane, without clipping the transformed polygon to the surface that it shadows or checking whether it is blocked by intervening surfaces [BLIN88]. These shadows are then treated as surface-detail polygons. For the general case, in which these fake shadows are not adequate, various approaches to shadow generation are possible. We could perform all shadow processing first, interleave it with visible-surface processing in a variety of ways, or even do it after visible-surface processing has been performed. Here we examine two classes of shadow algorithms. Later, in Sections 14.7 and 14.8, we discuss how shadows are handled in global illumination approaches. Other shadow algorithms are surveyed in [FOLE90]. To simplify the explanations, we shall assume that all objects are polygons unless otherwise specified.

14.4.1 Scan-Line Generation of Shadows

One of the oldest methods for generating shadows is to augment a scan-line algorithm to interleave shadow and visible-surface processing [APPE68; BOUK70b]. Using the light source as a center of projection, the edges of polygons that might potentially cast shadows are projected onto the polygons intersecting the current scan line. When the scan crosses one of these shadow edges, the colors of the image pixels are modified accordingly.

A brute-force implementation of this algorithm must compute all $n(n-1)$ projections of every polygon on every other polygon. Bouknight and Kelley [BOUK70b] instead use a clever preprocessing step in which all polygons are projected onto a sphere surrounding the light source, with the light source as center of projection. Pairs of projections whose extents do not overlap can be eliminated, and a number of other special cases can be identified to limit the number of polygon pairs that need be considered by the rest of the algorithm. The authors then compute the projection from the light source of each polygon onto the plane of each of those polygons that they have determined it could shadow, as shown in Fig. 14.27. Each of these shadowing polygon projections has associated information about the polygon's casting and potentially receiving the shadow. While the scan-line algorithm's regular scan keeps track of which regular polygon edges are being crossed, a separate, parallel shadow scan keeps track of which shadowing polygon projection edges are crossed, and thus which shadowing polygon projections the shadow scan is currently *in*. When the shade for a span is computed, it is in shadow if the shadow scan is *in* one of the shadow projections cast on the polygon's plane. Thus span *bc* in Fig. 14.27 is in shadow, while spans *ab* and *cd* are not. Note that

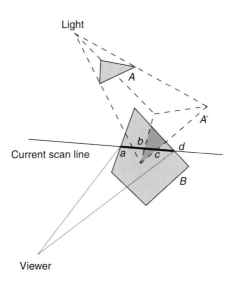

Light

A

A'

b
a c d
Current scan line

B

Viewer

Figure 14.27 A scan-line shadow algorithm using the Bouknight and Kelley approach. Polygon *A* casts shadow *A'* on plane of *B*.

the algorithm does not need to clip the shadowing polygon projections analytically to the polygons being shadowed.

14.4.2 Shadow Volumes

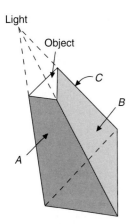

Light

Object

C

B

A

Figure 14.28
A shadow volume is defined by a light source and an object.

Crow [CROW77] describes how to generate shadows by creating for each object a **shadow volume** that the object blocks from the light source. A shadow volume is defined by the light source and an object and is bounded by a set of invisible **shadow polygons.** As shown in Fig. 14.28, there is one quadrilateral shadow polygon for each silhouette edge of the object relative to the light source. Three sides of a shadow polygon are defined by a silhouette edge of the object and the two lines emanating from the light source and passing through that edge's endpoints. Each shadow polygon has a normal that points out of the shadow volume. Shadow volumes are generated only for polygons facing the light. In the implementation described by Bergeron [BERG86a], the shadow volume—and hence each of its shadow polygons—is capped on one end by the original object polygon and on the other end by a scaled copy of the object polygon whose normal has been inverted. This scaled copy is located at a distance from the light beyond which its attenuated energy density is assumed to be negligible. We can think of this distance as the light's **sphere of influence.** Any point outside of the sphere of influence is effectively in shadow and does not require any additional shadow processing. In fact, there is no need to generate a shadow volume for any object wholly outside the sphere of influence. We can generalize this approach to apply to nonuniformly

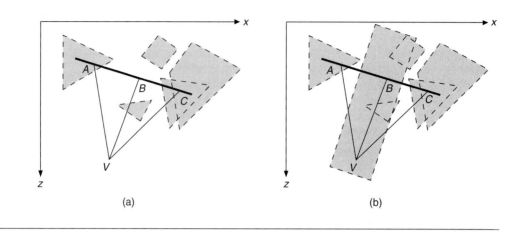

Figure 14.29   Determining whether a point is in shadow for a viewer at *V.* Dashed lines define shadow
volumes (shaded in gray). (a) *V* is not in shadow. Points *A* and *C* are shadowed; point *B* is lit.
(b) *V* is in shadow. Points *A*, *B*, and *C* are shadowed.

radiating sources by considering a **region of influence**, for example, by culling
objects outside of a light's flaps and cone. The shadow volume may also be further
clipped to the view volume if the view volume is known in advance. The cap polygons are also treated as shadow polygons by the algorithm.

Shadow polygons are not rendered themselves, but are used to determine
whether the other objects are in shadow. Relative to the observer, a front-facing
shadow polygon (polygon *A* or *B* in Fig. 14.28) causes those objects behind it to be
shadowed; a back-facing shadow polygon (polygon *C*) cancels the effect of a
front-facing one. Consider a vector from the viewpoint *V* to a point on an object.
The point is in shadow if the vector intersects more front-facing than back-facing
shadow polygons. Thus, points *A* and *C* in Fig. 14.29(a) are in shadow. This is the
only case in which a point is shadowed when *V* is not shadowed; therefore, point *B*
is lit. If *V* is in shadow, there is one additional case in which a point is shadowed:
when all the back-facing shadow polygons for the object polygons shadowing the
eye have not yet been encountered. Thus, points *A*, *B*, and *C* in Fig. 14.29(b) are in
shadow, even though the vector from *V* to *B* intersects the same number of front-
facing and back-facing shadow polygons as it does in part (a).

We can compute whether a point is in shadow by assigning to each front-facing (relative to the viewer) shadow polygon a value of +1 and to each back-facing
shadow polygon a value of −1. A counter initially is set to the number of shadow
volumes that contain the eye and is incremented by the values associated with all
shadow polygons between the eye and the point on the object. The point is in
shadow if the counter is positive at the point. The number of shadow volumes containing the eye is computed only once for each viewpoint, by taking the negative of
the sum of the values of all shadow polygons intercepted by an arbitrary projector
from the eye to infinity.

Multiple light sources can be handled by building a separate set of shadow volumes for each light source, marking the volume's shadow polygons with their light source identifier, and keeping a separate counter for each light source. Brotman and Badler [BROT84] have implemented a z-buffer version of the shadow-volume algorithm, and Bergeron [BERG86a] discusses a scan-line implementation that efficiently handles arbitrary polyhedral objects containing nonplanar polygons. Chin and Feiner [CHIN89] describe an object-precision algorithm that builds a single shadow volume for a polygonal environment, using the BSP-tree solid modeling representation discussed in Section 10.6.4.

14.5 TRANSPARENCY

Much as surfaces can have specular and diffuse reflection, those that transmit light can be transparent or translucent. We can usually see clearly through **transparent** materials, such as glass, although in general the rays are refracted (bent). Diffuse transmission occurs through **translucent** materials, such as frosted glass. Rays passing through translucent materials are jumbled by surface or internal irregularities, and thus objects seen through translucent materials are blurred.

14.5.1 Nonrefractive Transparency

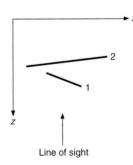

Line of sight

Figure 14.30
Cross section of two polygons.

The simplest approach to modeling transparency ignores refraction, so light rays are not bent as they pass through the surface. Thus, whatever is visible on the line of sight through a transparent surface also is located geometrically on that line of sight. Although refractionless transparency is not realistic, often it can be a more useful effect than can refraction. For example, it can provide a distortionless view through a surface. As we have noted before, total photographic realism is not always the objective in making pictures.

Two different methods have been used commonly to approximate the way in which the colors of two objects are combined when one object is seen through the other. We shall refer to these as **interpolated** and **filtered** transparency.

Interpolated transparency. Consider what happens when transparent polygon 1 is between the viewer and opaque polygon 2, as shown in Fig. 14.30. **Interpolated transparency** determines the shade of a pixel in the intersection of two polygons' projections by linearly interpolating the individual shades calculated for the two polygons:

$$I_\lambda = (1 - k_{t_1})I_{\lambda_1} + k_{t_1}I_{\lambda_2}. \qquad (14.23)$$

The **transmission coefficient** k_{t_1} measures the **transparency** of polygon 1, and ranges between 0 and 1. When k_{t_1} is 0, the polygon is opaque and transmits no light; when k_{t_1} is 1, the polygon is perfectly transparent and contributes nothing to the intensity I_λ; The value $1 - k_{t_1}$ is called the polygon's **opacity**. Interpolated transparency may be thought of as modeling a polygon that consists of a fine mesh of opaque material through which other objects may be seen; k_{t_1} is the fraction of the mesh's surface that can be seen through. A totally transparent polygon that is processed this way will not have any specular reflection. For a more realistic effect, we can interpolate only the ambient and diffuse components of polygon 1 with the full shade of polygon 2, and then add in polygon 1's specular component [KAY79b].

Another approach, often called **screen-door transparency,** literally implements a mesh by rendering only some of the pixels associated with a transparent object's projection. The low-order bits of a pixel's (x, y) address are used to index into a transparency bit mask. If the indexed bit is 1, then the pixel is written; otherwise, it is suppressed, and the next closest polygon at that pixel is visible.

Filtered transparency.   **Filtered transparency** treats a polygon as a transparent filter that selectively passes different wavelengths; it can be modeled by

$$I_\lambda = I_{\lambda_1} + k_{t_1} O_{t\lambda} I_{\lambda_2},$$ (14.24)

where $O_{t\lambda}$ is polygon 1's **transparency color**. A colored filter may be modeled by choosing a different value of $O_{t\lambda}$ for each λ. In either interpolated or filtered transparency, if additional transparent polygons are in front of these polygons, then the calculation is invoked recursively for polygons in back-to-front order, each time using the previously computed I_λ as I_{λ_2}.

Implementing transparency.   Several visible-surface algorithms can be adapted readily to incorporate transparency, including scan-line and list-priority algorithms. In list-priority algorithms, the color of a pixel about to be covered by a transparent polygon is read back and used in the illumination model while the polygon is being scan-converted.

Most z-buffer–based systems support screen-door transparency because it allows transparent objects to be intermingled with opaque objects and to be drawn in any order. Adding transparency effects that use Eqs. (14.23) or (14.24) to the z-buffer algorithm is more difficult, because polygons are rendered in the order in which they are encountered. Imagine rendering several overlapping transparent polygons, followed by an opaque one. We would like to slip the opaque polygon behind the appropriate transparent ones. Unfortunately, the z-buffer does not store the information needed to determine which transparent polygons are in front of the opaque polygon, or even the polygons' relative order. One simple, although incorrect, approach is to render transparent polygons last, combining their colors with those already in the frame buffer, but not modifying the z-buffer; when two transparent polygons overlap, however, their relative depth is not taken into account.

Kay and Greenberg [KAY79b] have implemented a useful approximation to the increased attenuation that occurs near the silhouette edges of thin curved surfaces, where light passes through more material. They define k_t in terms of a nonlinear function of the z component of the surface normal after perspective transformation,

$$k_t = k_{t_{min}} + (k_{t_{max}} - k_{t_{min}})(1 - (1 - z_N)^m),$$

where $k_{t_{min}}$ and $k_{t_{max}}$ are the object's minimum and maximum transparencies, z_N is the z component of the normalized surface normal at the point for which k_t is being computed, and m is a power factor (typically 2 or 3). A higher m models a thinner surface. This new value of k_t may be used as k_{t_1} in either Eq. (14.23) or (14.24).

14.5.2 Refractive Transparency

Refractive transparency is significantly more difficult to model than is nonrefractive transparency, because the geometrical and optical lines of sight are different. If refraction is considered in Fig. 14.31, object A is visible through the transparent object along the line of sight shown; if refraction is ignored, object B is visible. The relationship between the angle of incidence θ_i and the angle of refraction θ_t is given by Snell's law

$$\frac{\sin \theta_i}{\sin \theta_t} = \frac{\eta_{t\lambda}}{\eta_{i\lambda}}, \qquad (14.25)$$

where $\eta_{i\lambda}$ and $\eta_{t\lambda}$ are the **indices of refraction** of the materials through which light passes. A material's index of refraction is the ratio of the speed of light in a vacuum to the speed of light in the material. This index varies with the wavelength of the light and even with temperature. A vacuum has an index of refraction of 1.0, as does the atmosphere to close approximation; all materials have higher values. The index of refraction's wavelength-dependence is evident in many instances of refraction as **dispersion**—the familiar, but difficult to model, phenomenon of refracted light being spread into its spectrum [THOM86; MUSG89].

Calculating the refraction vector. The unit vector in the direction of refraction, $\overline{T}$, can be calculated as

$$\overline{T} = \sin \theta_t \, \overline{M} - \cos \theta_t \, \overline{N}, \qquad (14.26)$$

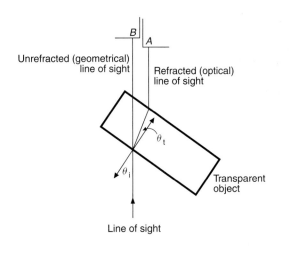

Figure 14.31   Refraction.

where $\overline{M}$ is a unit vector perpendicular to $\overline{N}$ in the plane of the incident ray $\overline{I}$ and $\overline{N}$ [HECK84] (Fig. 14.32). Recalling the use of $\overline{S}$ in calculating the reflection vector $\overline{R}$ in Section 14.1.4, we see that $\overline{M} = (\overline{N} \cos \theta_i - \overline{I}) / \sin \theta_i$. By substitution,

$$\overline{T} = \frac{\sin \theta_t}{\sin \theta_i}(\overline{N} \cos \theta_i - \overline{I}) - \cos \theta_t \overline{N} \cdot \tag{14.27}$$

If we let $\eta_{r\lambda} = \eta_{i\lambda} / \eta_{t\lambda} = \sin \theta_t / \sin \theta_i$, then after rearranging terms

$$\overline{T} = (\eta_{r\lambda} \cos \theta_i - \cos \theta_t) \overline{N} - \eta_{r\lambda} \overline{I}. \tag{14.28}$$

Note that $\cos \theta_i$ is $\overline{N} \cdot \overline{I}$, and $\cos \theta_t$ can be computed as

$$\cos \theta_t = \sqrt{1 - \sin^2 \theta_t} - \sqrt{1 - \eta_{r\lambda}^2 \sin^2 \theta_i} = \sqrt{1 - \eta_{r\lambda}^2(1 - (\overline{N} \cdot \overline{I})^2)} \cdot \tag{14.29}$$

Thus,

$$\overline{T} = \left(\eta_{r\lambda}(\overline{N} \cdot \overline{I}) - \sqrt{1 - \eta_{r\lambda}^2(1 - (\overline{N} \cdot \overline{I})^2)} \right) \overline{N} - \eta_{r\lambda} \overline{I} \cdot \tag{14.30}$$

Total internal reflection. When light passes from one medium into another whose index of refraction is lower, the angle θ_t of the transmitted ray is greater than the angle θ_i. If θ_i becomes sufficiently large, then θ_t exceeds 90° and the ray is reflected from the interface between the media, rather than being transmitted. This

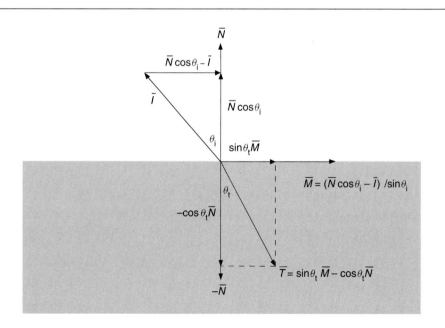

Figure 14.32   Calculating the refraction vector.

phenomenon is known as **total internal reflection,** and the smallest θ_i at which it occurs is called the **critical angle**. You can observe total internal reflection easily by looking through the front of a filled fish tank and trying to see your hand through a side wall. When the viewing angle is greater than the critical angle, the only visible parts of your hand are those pressed firmly against the tank, with no intervening layer of air (which has a lower index of refraction than glass or water). The critical angle is the value of θ_i at which $\sin \theta_t$ is 1. If $\sin \theta_t$ is set to 1 in Eq. (14.25), we can see that the critical angle is $\sin^{-1}(\eta_{t\lambda} / \eta_{i\lambda})$. Total internal reflection occurs when the square root in Eq. (14.30) is imaginary.

Section 14.7 discusses the use of Snell's law in modeling transparency with ray tracing.

14.6 GLOBAL ILLUMINATION ALGORITHMS

An illumination model computes the color at a point in terms of light directly emitted by light sources and of light that reaches the point after reflection from and transmission through its own and other surfaces. This indirectly reflected and transmitted light is often called **global illumination.** In contrast, **local illumination** is light that comes directly from the light sources to the point being shaded. Thus far, we have modeled global illumination by an ambient illumination term that was held constant for all points on all objects. It did not depend on the positions of the object or the viewer, or on the presence or absence of nearby objects that could block the ambient light. In addition, we have seen some limited global illumination effects made possible by shadows and transparency.

Much of the light in real-world environments does not come from direct light sources. Two different classes of algorithms have been used to generate pictures that emphasize the contributions of global illumination. Section 14.7 discusses extensions to the visible-surface ray-tracing algorithm that interleave visible-surface determination and shading to depict shadows, reflection, and refraction. Thus, global specular reflection and transmission supplement the local specular, diffuse, and ambient illumination computed for a surface. In contrast, the radiosity methods discussed in Section 14.8 completely separate shading and visible-surface determination. They model all an environment's interactions with light sources, first in a view-independent stage, and then compute one or more images for the desired viewpoints using conventional visible-surface and interpolation shading algorithms.

The distinction between view-dependent algorithms, such as ray tracing, and view-independent ones, such as radiosity, is an important one. **View-dependent** algorithms discretize the view plane to determine points at which to evaluate the illumination equation, given the viewer's direction. In contrast, **view-independent** algorithms discretize the environment, and process it in order to provide enough information to evaluate the illumination equation at any point and from any viewing direction. View-dependent algorithms are well suited for handling specular phenomena that are highly dependent on the viewer's position, but these algorithms may perform extra work when modeling diffuse phenomena that change little over large areas of an image or between images made from different viewpoints. On the other hand, view-independent algorithms model diffuse phenomena efficiently but require overwhelming amounts of storage to capture enough information about specular phenomena.

Ultimately, all these approaches attempt to solve what Kajiya [KAJI86] has referred to as the **rendering equation,** which expresses the light being transferred from one point to another in terms of the intensity of the light emitted from the first point to the second and the intensity of light emitted from all other points that reaches the first and is reflected from the first to the second. The light transferred from each of these other points to the first is, in turn, expressed recursively by the rendering equation. Kajiya presents the rendering equation as

$$I(x, x') = g(x, x') \left[\epsilon(x, x') + \int_S \rho(x, x', x'')\, I(x', x'')dx'' \right], \qquad (14.31)$$

where x, x', and x'' are points in the environment; $I(x, x')$ is related to the intensity passing from x' to x; $g(x, x')$ is a geometry term that is 0 when x and x' are occluded from each other, and $1 / r^2$ when they are visible to each other, where r is the distance between them; and $\epsilon(x, x')$ is related to the intensity of light that is emitted from x' to x. The initial evaluation of $g(x, x')\epsilon(x, x')$ for x at the viewpoint accomplishes visible-surface determination in the sphere about x. The integral is over all points on all surfaces S. $\rho(x, x', x'')$ is related to the intensity of the light reflected (including both specular and diffuse reflection) from x'' to x from the surface at x'. Thus, the rendering equation states that the light from x' that reaches x consists of light emitted by x' itself and light scattered by x' to x from all other surfaces, which themselves emit light and recursively scatter light from other surfaces.

As we shall see, how successful an approach is at solving the rendering equation depends in large part on how it handles the remaining terms and the recursion, on what combinations of diffuse and specular reflectivity it supports, and on how well the visibility relationships between surfaces are modeled.

14.7 RECURSIVE RAY TRACING

In this section, we extend the basic ray-tracing algorithm of Section 13.4 to handle shadows, reflection, and refraction. This simple algorithm determined the color of a pixel at the closest intersection of an eye ray with an object, by using any of the illumination models described previously. To calculate shadows, we fire an additional ray from the point of intersection to each of the light sources. This is shown for a single light source in Fig.14.33, which is reproduced from a paper by Appel [APPE68]—the first paper published on ray tracing for computer graphics. If one of these **shadow rays** intersects any object along the way, then the object is in shadow at that point and the shading algorithm ignores the contribution of the shadow ray's light source.

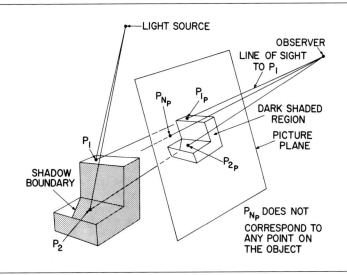

Figure 14.33 Determining whether a point on an object is in shadow. (Courtesy of Arthur Appel, IBM T.J. Watson Research Center.).

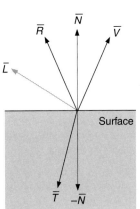

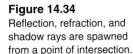

Figure 14.34
Reflection, refraction, and shadow rays are spawned from a point of intersection.

The illumination model developed by Whitted [WHIT80] and Kay [KAY79a] fundamentally extended ray tracing to include specular reflection and refractive transparency. Color Plate 41 is an early picture generated with these effects. In addition to shadow rays, Whitted's recursive ray-tracing algorithm conditionally spawns **reflection rays** and **refraction rays** from the point of intersection, as shown in Fig. 14.34. The shadow, reflection, and refraction rays are often called **secondary rays**, to distinguish them from the **primary rays** from the eye. If the object is specularly reflective, then a reflection ray is reflected about the surface normal in the direction of $\overline{R}$, which may be computed as in Section 14.1.4. If the object is transparent, and if total internal reflection does not occur, then a refraction ray is sent into the object along $\overline{T}$ at an angle determined by Snell's law, as described in Section 14.5.2. (Note that your incident ray may be oppositely oriented to those in these sections.)

Each of these reflection and refraction rays may, in turn, recursively spawn shadow, reflection, and refraction rays, as shown in Fig. 14.35. The rays thus form a **ray tree,** such as that of Fig. 14.36. In Whitted's algorithm, a branch is terminated if the reflected and refracted rays fail to intersect an object, if some user-specified maximum depth is reached or if the system runs out of storage. The tree is evaluated bottom-up, and each node's intensity is computed as a function of its children's intensities.

We can represent Whitted's illumination equation as

$$I_\lambda = I_{a\lambda}k_a O_{d\lambda} + \sum_{1 \le i \le m} S_i f_{\text{att}_i} I_{p\lambda_i}[k_d O_{d\lambda}(\overline{N} \cdot \overline{L}_i) + k_s(\overline{N} \cdot \overline{H}_i)^n] + k_s I_{r\lambda} + k_t I_{t\lambda} , \quad (14.32)$$

where $I_{r\lambda}$ is the intensity of the reflected ray, k_t is the **transmission coefficient**

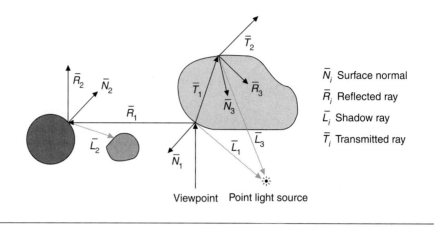

Figure 14.35   Rays recursively spawn other rays.

ranging between 0 and 1, and $I_{t\lambda}$ is the intensity of the refracted transmitted ray. Values for $I_{r\lambda}$ and $I_{t\lambda}$ are determined by recursively evaluating Eq. (14.32) at the closest surface that the reflected and transmitted rays intersect. To approximate attenuation with distance, Whitted multiplied the I_{λ} calculated for each ray by the inverse of the distance traveled by the ray. Rather than treating S_i as a delta function, as in Eq. (14.22), he also made it a continuous function of the k_t of the objects intersected by the shadow ray, so that a transparent object obscures less light than an opaque one at those points it shadows.

Prog.14.1 shows pseudocode for a simple recursive ray tracer. RT_trace determines the closest intersection the ray makes with an object and calls RT_shade to determine the shade at that point. First, RT_shade determines the intersection's ambient color. Next, a shadow ray is spawned to each light on the side of the surface being shaded to determine its contribution to the color. An opaque object blocks the light totally, whereas a transparent one scales the light's contribution. If we are not too deep in the ray tree, then recursive calls are made to RT_trace to handle reflection rays for reflective objects and refraction rays for transparent objects. Since the indices of refraction of two media are needed to determine the direction of the refraction ray, the index of refraction of the material in which a ray is traveling can be included with each ray. RT_trace retains the ray tree only long enough to determine the current pixel's color. If the ray trees for an entire image can be preserved, then surface properties can be altered and a new image recomputed relatively quickly, at the cost of only reevaluating the trees. Sequin and Smyrl [SEQU89] present techniques that minimize the time and space needed to process and store ray trees.

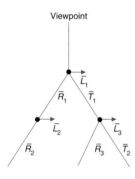

Figure 14.36
The ray tree for Fig. 14.35.

Program 14.1

Pseudocode for simple recursive ray tracing without antialiasing.

select center of projection and window on view plane;
for (*each scan line in image*) {
    for (*each pixel in scan line*) {
       determine ray from center of projection through pixel;

```
            pixel = RT_trace (ray, 1);
        }
    }
```

/* Intersect ray with objects and compute shade at closest intersection. */
/* Depth is current depth in ray tree. */

```
RT_color RT_trace ( RT_ray ray, int depth )
{
    determine closest intersection of ray with an object;
    if ( object hit ) {
            compute normal at intersection;
            return RT_shade (closest object hit, ray, intersection, normal, depth);
    }
    else
        return BACKGROUND_VALUE;
}
```

/* Compute shade at point on object, tracing rays for shadows, reflection, refraction.*/

```
RT_color RT_shade (
        RT_object  object ,             /* Object intersected */
        RT_ray  ray,                    /* Incident ray */
        RT_point  point ,               /* Point of intersection to shade */
        RT_normal  normal,              /* Normal at point */
        int  depth )                    /* Depth in ray tree */
{
RT_color  color;                /* Color of ray */
RT_ray  rRay, tRay, sRay;       /* Reflected, refracted, and shadow rays */
RT_color  rColor, tColor;       /* Reflected and refracted ray colors */

    color = ambient term;
    for ( each light ) {
        sRay = ray to light from point;
        if ( dot product of normal and direction to light is positive ) {
            compute how much light is blocked by opaque and transparent surfaces,
            and use to scale diffuse and specular terms before adding them to color;
        }
    }
    if ( depth < maxDepth ) {          /* Return if depth is too deep. */
        if ( object is reflective ) {
            rRay = ray in reflection direction from point;
            rColor = RT_trace (rRay, depth + 1);
            scale rColor by specular coefficient and add to color;
        }
        if ( object is transparent ) {
            tRay = ray in refraction direction from point;
            if ( total internal reflection does not occur ) {
                tColor = RT_trace (tRay, depth + 1);
                scale tColor by transmission coefficient and add to color;
```

```
          }
        }
      }
      return color;      /* Return color of ray. */
    }
```

Figure 14.35 shows a basic problem with how ray tracing models refraction: The shadow ray $\overline{L}_3$ is not refracted on its path to the light. In fact, if we were to simply refract $\overline{L}_3$ from its current direction at the point where it exits the large object, it would not end at the light source. In addition, when the paths of rays that are refracted are determined, a single index of refraction is used for each ray.

Ray tracing is particularly prone to problems caused by limited numerical precision. These show up when we compute the objects that intersect with the secondary rays. After the x, y, and z coordinates of the intersection point on an object visible to an eye ray have been computed, they are then used to define the starting point of the secondary ray for which we must determine the parameter t (Section 13.4.1). If the object that was just intersected is intersected with the new ray, it will often have a small, nonzero t because of numerical-precision limitations. If not dealt with, this false intersection can result in visual problems. For example, if the ray were a shadow ray, then the object would be considered as blocking light from itself, resulting in splotchy pieces of incorrectly "self-shadowed" surface. A simple way to solve this problem for shadow rays is to treat as a special case the object from which a secondary ray is spawned, so that intersection tests are not performed on it. Of course, this does not work if objects are supported that really could obscure themselves or if transmitted rays have to pass through the object and be reflected from the inside of the same object. A more general solution is to compute abs(t) for an intersection, to compare it with a small tolerance value, and to ignore it if it is below the tolerance.

The paper Whitted presented at *SIGGRAPH '79* [WHIT80], and the movies he made using the algorithm described there, started a renaissance of interest in ray tracing. Recursive ray tracing makes possible a host of impressive effects—such as shadows, specular reflection, and refractive transparency—that were difficult or impossible to obtain previously. In addition, a simple ray tracer is quite easy to implement. Consequently, much effort has been directed toward improving both the algorithm's efficiency and its image quality. For more detail, see Section 16.12 of [FOLE90] and [GLAS89].

14.8 RADIOSITY METHODS

Although ray tracing does an excellent job of modeling specular reflection and dispersionless refractive transparency, it still makes use of a directionless ambient lighting term to account for all other global lighting contributions. Approaches based on thermal-engineering models for the emission and reflection of radiation eliminate the need for the ambient-lighting term by providing a more accurate treatment of interobject reflections. First introduced by Goral, Torrance,

Greenberg, and Battaile [GORA84] and by Nishita and Nakamae [NISH85], these algorithms assume the conservation of light energy in a closed environment. All energy emitted or reflected by every surface is accounted for by its reflection from or absorption by other surfaces. The rate at which energy leaves a surface, called its **radiosity,** is the sum of the rates at which the surface emits energy and reflects or transmits it from that surface or other surfaces. Consequently, approaches that compute the radiosities of the surfaces in an environment have been named **radiosity methods.** Unlike conventional rendering algorithms, radiosity methods first determine all the light interactions in an environment in a view-independent way. Then, one or more views are rendered, with only the overhead of visible-surface determination and interpolative shading.

14.8.1 The Radiosity Equation

In the shading algorithms considered previously, light sources have always been treated separately from the surfaces they illuminate. In contrast, radiosity methods allow any surface to emit light; thus, all light sources are modeled inherently as having area. Imagine breaking up the environment into a finite number n of discrete patches, each of which is assumed to be of finite size, emitting and reflecting light uniformly over its entire area. If we consider each patch to be an opaque Lambertian diffuse emitter and reflector, then, for surface i,

$$B_i = E_i + \rho_i \sum_{1 \leq j \leq n} B_j F_{j-i} \frac{A_j}{A_i}. \tag{14.33}$$

B_i and B_j are the radiosities of patches i and j, measured in energy/unit time/unit area (i.e., W/m^2). E_i is the rate at which light is emitted from patch i and has the same units as radiosity. ρ_i is patch i's reflectivity and is dimensionless. F_{j-i} is the dimensionless **form factor** or **configuration factor,** which specifies the fraction of energy leaving the entirety of patch j that arrives at the entirety of patch i, taking into account the shape and relative orientation of both patches and the presence of any obstructing patches. A_i and A_j are the areas of patches i and j.

Equation (14.33) states that the energy leaving a unit area of surface is the sum of the light emitted plus the light reflected. The reflected light is computed by scaling the sum of the incident light by the reflectivity. The incident light is in turn the sum of the light leaving the entirety of each patch in the environment scaled by the fraction of that light reaching a unit area of the receiving patch. $B_j F_{j-i}$ is the amount of light leaving a unit area of A_j that reaches all of A_i. Therefore, it is necessary to multiply by the area ratio A_j / A_i to determine the light leaving all of A_j that reaches a unit area of A_i.

Conveniently, a simple reciprocity relationship holds between form factors in diffuse environments,

$$A_i F_{i-j} = A_j F_{j-i}. \tag{14.34}$$

Thus, Eq. (14.33) can be simplified, yielding

$$B_i = E_i + \rho_i \sum_{1 \le j \le n} B_j F_{i-j} . \tag{14.35}$$

Rearranging terms,

$$B_i - \rho_i \sum_{1 \le j \le n} B_j F_{i-j} = E_i . \tag{14.36}$$

Therefore, the interaction of light among the patches in the environment can be stated as a set of simultaneous equations:

$$
\begin{bmatrix}
1 - \rho_1 F_{1-1} & -\rho_1 F_{1-2} & \cdots & -\rho_1 F_{1-n} \\
-\rho_2 F_{2-1} & 1 - \rho_2 F_{2-2} & \cdots & -\rho_2 F_{2-n} \\
\cdot & \cdot & \cdots & \cdot \\
\cdot & \cdot & \cdots & \cdot \\
\cdot & \cdot & \cdots & \cdot \\
-\rho_n F_{n-1} & -\rho_n F_{n-2} & \cdots & 1 - \rho_n F_{n-n}
\end{bmatrix}
\begin{bmatrix}
B_1 \\ B_2 \\ \cdot \\ \cdot \\ \cdot \\ B_n
\end{bmatrix}
=
\begin{bmatrix}
E_1 \\ E_2 \\ \cdot \\ \cdot \\ \cdot \\ E_n
\end{bmatrix}
. \tag{14.37}
$$

Note that a patch's contribution to its own reflected energy must be taken into account (e.g., it may be concave); so, in the general case, each term along the diagonal is not merely 1. Equation (14.37) must be solved for each band of wavelengths considered in the lighting model, since ρ_i and E_i are wavelength-dependent. The form factors, however, are independent of wavelength and are solely a function of geometry, and thus do not need to be recomputed if the lighting or surface reflectivity changes.

Equation (14.37) may be solved using Gauß–Seidel iteration [PRES88], yielding a radiosity for each patch. The patches can then be rendered from any desired viewpoint with a conventional visible-surface algorithm; the set of radiosities computed for the wavelength bands of each patch are that patch's intensities. Instead of using faceted shading, we can compute vertex radiosities from the patch radiosities to allow intensity interpolation shading.

Cohen and Greenberg [COHE85] suggest the following approach for determining vertex radiosities. If a vertex is interior to a surface, it is assigned the average of the radiosities of the patches that share it. If it is on the edge, then the nearest interior vertex v is found. The radiosity of the edge vertex when averaged with B_v should be the average of the radiosities of the patches that share the edge vertex. Consider the patches in Fig. 14.37. The radiosity for interior vertex e is B_e = $(B_1 + B_2 + B_3 + B_4) / 4$. The radiosity for edge vertex b is computed by finding its nearest interior vertex, e, and noting that b is shared by patches 1 and 2. Thus, to determine B_b, we use the preceding definition: $(B_b + B_e) / 2 = (B_1 + B_2) / 2$. Solving for B_b, we get $B_b = B_1 + B_2 - B_e$. The interior vertex closest to a is also e, and a is part of patch 1 alone. Thus, since $(B_a + B_e) / 2 = B_1$, we get $B_a = 2B_1 - B_e$. Radiosities for the other vertices are computed similarly.

The first radiosity method was implemented by Goral et al. [GORA84], who used contour integrals to compute exact form factors for convex environments with no occluded surfaces, as shown in Color Plate 43. Note the correct *color-bleeding*

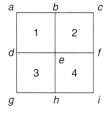

Figure 14.37
Computing vertex radiosities from patch radiosities.

effects due to diffuse reflection between adjacent surfaces, visible in both the model and the rendered image: Diffuse surfaces are tinged with the colors of other diffuse surfaces that they reflect. For radiosity methods to become practical, however, ways to compute form factors between occluded surfaces had first to be developed.

14.8.2 Computing Form Factors

Cohen and Greenberg [COHE85] adapted an image-precision visible-surface algorithm to approximate form factors for occluded surfaces efficiently. Consider the two patches shown in Fig. 14.38. The form factor from differential area dA_i to differential area dA_j is

$$dF_{di-dj} = \frac{\cos\theta_i \cos\theta_j}{\pi r^2} H_{ij} dA_j . \qquad (14.38)$$

For the ray between differential areas dA_i and dA_j in Fig. 14.38, θ_i is the angle that the ray makes with A_i's normal, θ_j is the angle that it makes with A_j's normal, and r is the ray's length. H_{ij} is either 1 or 0, depending on whether or not dA_j is visible from dA_i. To determine F_{di-j}, the form factor from differential area dA_i to finite area A_j, we need to integrate over the area of patch j. Thus,

$$F_{di-j} = \int_{A_j} \frac{\cos\theta_i \cos\theta_j}{\pi r^2} H_{ij} dA_j . \qquad (14.39)$$

Finally, the form factor from A_i to A_j is the area average of Eq. (14.39) over patch i:

$$F_{i-j} = \frac{1}{A_i} \int_{Ai} \int_{Aj} \frac{\cos\theta_i \cos\theta_j}{\pi r^2} H_{ij} dA_j dA_i . \qquad (14.40)$$

If we assume that the center point on a patch typifies the patch's other points, then F_{i-j} can be approximated by F_{di-j} computed for dA_i at patch i's center.

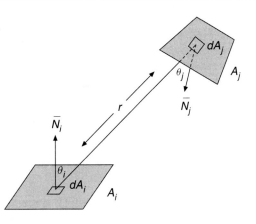

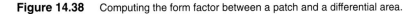

Figure 14.38 Computing the form factor between a patch and a differential area.

Nusselt has shown [SIEG81] that computing F_{di-j} is equivalent to projecting those parts of A_j that are visible from dA_i onto a unit hemisphere centered about dA_i, projecting this projected area orthographically down onto the hemisphere's unit circle base, and dividing by the area of the circle (Fig. 14.39). Projecting onto the unit hemisphere accounts for $\cos \theta_j / r^2$ in Eq. (14.39), projecting down onto the base corresponds to a multiplication by $\cos \theta_i$, and dividing by the area of the unit circle accounts for the π in the denominator.

Rather than analytically projecting each A_j onto a hemisphere, Cohen and Greenberg developed an efficient image-precision algorithm that projects onto the upper half of a cube centered about dA_i, with the cube's top parallel to the surface (Fig. 14.40). Each face of this **hemicube** is divided into a number of equal-sized square cells. (Resolutions used in pictures included in this book range from 50×50 to several hundred on a face.) All the other patches are clipped to the view-volume frusta defined by the center of the cube and each of its upper five faces, and then each of the clipped patches is projected onto the appropriate face of the hemicube. An **item-buffer** [WEGH84] algorithm is used that records the identity of the closest intersecting patch at each cell. These item buffers can be computed by performing the z-buffer algorithm for each side of the hemicube, recording the closest patch id in each cell, rather than a shade. Each of the hemicube cells is associated with a precomputed *delta form factor* based on its position. For any patch j, F_{di-j} can be approximated by summing the values of the delta

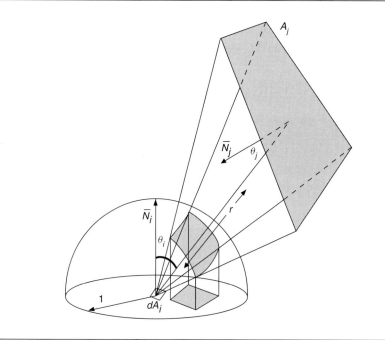

Figure 14.39   Determining the form factor between a differential area and a patch using Nusselt's method. The ratio of the area projected onto the hemisphere's base to the area of the entire base is the form factor. (After [SIEG81].)

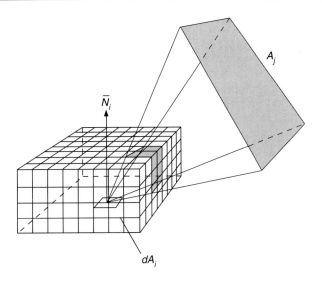

Figure 14.40   The hemicube is the upper half of a cube centered about the patch. (After [COHE85].)

form factors associated with all hemicube cells that contain patch j's id. Because much of the computation performed using the hemicube involves computing item buffers, it can take advantage of existing z-buffer hardware. On the other hand, because it uses image-precision operations, the hemicube is prone to aliasing.

14.8.3 Progressive Refinement

Given the high costs of executing the radiosity algorithm described thus far, it makes sense to ask whether it is possible to approximate the algorithm's results incrementally. Can we produce a useful, although perhaps inaccurate, image early on, which can be successively refined to greater accuracy as more time is allocated? The radiosity approach described in the previous sections will not let us do this for two reasons. First, an entire Gauss–Seidel iteration must take place before an estimate of the patch radiosities becomes available. Second, form factors are calculated between all patches at the start and must be stored throughout the computation, requiring $O(n^2)$ time and space. Cohen, Chen, Wallace, and Greenberg [COHE88] have developed a progressive-refinement radiosity algorithm that addresses both of these issues.

Consider the approach described thus far. Evaluating the ith row of Eq. (14.37) provides an estimate of patch i's radiosity, B_i, expressed in Eq. (14.35), based on the estimates of the other patch radiosities. Each term of the summation in Eq. (14.35) represents patch j's effect on the radiosity of patch i:

$$B_i \text{ due to } B_j = \rho_i B_j F_{i-j}, \qquad \text{for all } j. \qquad (14.41)$$

Thus, this approach *gathers* the light from the rest of the environment. In contrast, the progressive-refinement approach *shoots* the radiosity from a patch into the environment. A straightforward way to do this is to modify Eq. (14.41) to yield

$$B_j \text{ due to } B_i = \rho_j B_i F_{j-i}, \qquad \text{for all } j. \tag{14.42}$$

Given an estimate of B_i, the contribution of patch i to the rest of the environment can be determined by evaluating Eq. (14.42) for each patch j. Unfortunately, this will require knowing F_{j-i} for each j, each value of which is determined with a separate hemicube. This imposes the same overwhelmingly large space–time overhead as does the original approach. By using the reciprocity relationship of Eq. (14.34), however, we can rewrite Eq. (14.42) as

$$B_j \text{ due to } B_i = \rho_j B_i F_{i-j} \frac{A_i}{A_j}, \qquad \text{for all } j \cdot \tag{14.43}$$

Evaluating this equation for each j requires only the form factors calculated using a single hemicube centered about patch i. If the form factors from patch i can be computed quickly (e.g., by using z-buffer hardware), then they can be discarded as soon as the radiosities shot from patch i have been computed. Thus, only a single hemicube and its form factors need to be computed and stored at a time.

As soon as a patch's radiosity has been shot, another patch is selected. A patch may be selected to shoot again after new light has been shot to it from other patches. Therefore, it is not patch i's total estimated radiosity that is shot, but rather ΔB_i, the amount of radiosity that patch i has received since the last time that it shot. The algorithm iterates until the desired tolerance is reached. Rather than choose patches in random order, it makes sense to select the patch that will make the most difference. This is the patch that has the most energy left to radiate. Since radiosity is measured per unit area, a patch i is picked for which $\Delta B_i A_i$ is the greatest. Initially, $B_i = \Delta B_i = E_i$ for all patches, which is nonzero only for light sources. The pseudocode for a single iteration is shown in Prog. 14.2.

Program 14.2

Pseudocode for shooting radiosity from a patch.

```
select patch i;

calculate F_{i-j} for each patch j;

for ( each patch j ) {
        ΔRadiosity =  ρ_j ΔB_i F_{i-j} A_i/A_j;
        ΔB_j += ΔRadiosity;
        B_j += ΔRadiosity;
}

ΔB_i = 0;
```

Each execution of the pseudocode in Prog. 14.2 will cause another patch to shoot its unshot radiosity into the environment. Thus, the only surfaces that are illuminated after the first execution are those that are light sources and those that are illuminated directly by the first patch whose radiosity is shot. If a new picture is rendered at the end of each execution, the first picture will be relatively dark, and those following will get progressively brighter. To make the earlier pictures more useful, we can add an ambient term to the radiosities. With each additional pass through the loop, the ambient term will be decreased, until it disappears. Color Plate 44, which is rendered using an ambient term, depicts stages in the creation of an image after 1, 2, 24, and 100 iterations.

14.9 THE RENDERING PIPELINE

Now that we have seen a variety of different ways to perform visible-surface determination, illumination, and shading, we shall review how these processes fit into the standard graphics pipeline introduced in Chapter 7. For simplicity, we assume polygonal environments, unless otherwise specified. Chapter 18 of [FOLE90] provides a more detailed discussion of how some of these pipelines may be implemented in hardware.

14.9.1 Local Illumination Pipelines

z-buffer and Gouraud shading.   Perhaps the most straightforward modification to the pipeline occurs in a system that uses the z-buffer visible-surface algorithm to render Gouraud-shaded polygons, as shown in Fig. 14.41. The z-buffer algorithm has the advantage that primitives may be presented to it in any order. Therefore, as before, primitives are obtained by traversing the database, and are transformed by the modeling transformation into the WC system.

Primitives may have associated surface normals that were specified when the model was built. Since the lighting step will require the use of surface normals, it is important to remember that normals must be transformed correctly. Furthermore, we cannot just ignore stored normals and attempt to recompute new ones later using the correctly transformed vertices. The normals defined with the objects may represent the true surface geometry, or may specify user-defined surface blending effects, rather than just being the averages of the normals of shared faces in the polygonal mesh approximation.

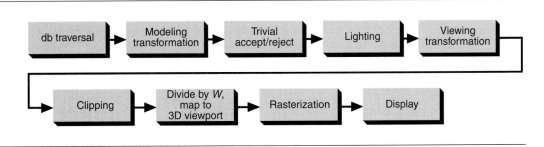

Figure 14.41   Rendering pipeline for *z*-buffer and Gouraud shading.

Our next step is to cull primitives that fall entirely outside of the window and to perform back-face culling. This trivial-reject phase is typically performed now because we want to eliminate unneeded processing in the lighting step that follows. Now, because we are using Gouraud shading, the illumination equation is evaluated at each vertex. This operation must be performed in the WC system (or in any coordinate system isometric to it), before the viewing transformation (which may include skew and perspective transformations), to preserve the correct angle and distance from each light to the surface. If vertex normals were not provided with the object, they may be computed immediately before lighting the vertices. Culling and lighting are often performed in a lighting coordinate system that is a rigid body transformation of WC (e.g., VRC when the view orientation matrix is created with the standard PHIGS utilities).

Next objects are transformed to NPC by the viewing transformation, and clipped to the view volume. Division by W is performed, and objects are mapped to the viewport. If an object is partially clipped, correct intensity values must be calculated for vertices created during clipping. At this point, the clipped primitive is submitted to the z-buffer algorithm, which performs rasterization, interleaving scan conversion with the interpolation needed to compute the z value and color-intensity values for each pixel. If a pixel is determined to be visible, its color-intensity values may be further modified by depth cueing (Eq. 14.11), not shown here.

Although this pipeline may seem straightforward, there are many new issues that must be dealt with to provide an efficient and correct implementation. For example, consider the problems raised by handling curved surfaces, such as B-spline patches, which must be tessellated. Tessellation should occur after transformation into a coordinate system in which screen size can be determined. This enables tessellation size to be determined adaptively, and limits the amount of data that are transformed. On the other hand, tessellated primitives must be lit in a coordinate system isometric to world coordinates. Abi-Ezzi [ABIE89] addresses these issues, proposing a more efficient, yet more complex, formulation of the pipeline that incorporates feedback loops. This new pipeline uses a lighting coordinate system that is an isometric (i.e., rigid or Euclidean) transformation of WC, yet is computationally close to DC to allow tessellation decisions to be made efficiently.

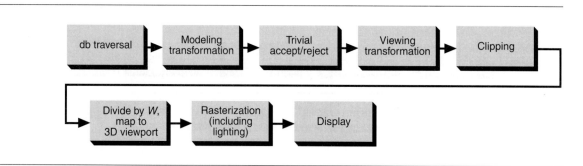

Figure 14.42   Rendering pipeline for z-buffer and Phong shading.

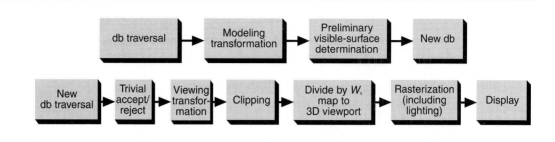

Figure 14.43   Rendering pipeline for list-priority algorithm and Phong shading.

z-**buffer and Phong shading.**   This simple pipeline must be modified if we wish to accommodate Phong shading, as shown in Fig. 14.42. Because Phong shading interpolates surface normals, rather than intensities, the vertices cannot be lit early in the pipeline. Instead, each object must be clipped (with properly interpolated normals created for each newly created vertex), transformed by the viewing transformation, and passed to the *z*-buffer algorithm. Finally, lighting is performed with the interpolated surface normals that are derived during scan conversion. Thus, each point and its normal must be backmapped into a coordinate system that is isometric to WC to evaluate the illumination equation.

List-priority algorithm and Phong shading.   When a list-priority algorithm is used, primitives obtained from traversal and processed by the modeling transformation are inserted in a separate database, such as a BSP tree, as part of preliminary visible-surface determination. Figure 14.43 presents the pipeline for the BSP tree algorithm, whose preliminary visible-surface determination is view-independent. As we noted in Chapter 7, the application program and the graphics package may each keep separate databases. Here, we see that rendering can require yet another database. Since, in this case, polygons are split, correct shading information must be determined for the newly created vertices. The rendering database can now be traversed to return primitives in a correct, back-to-front order. The overhead of building this database can, of course, be applied toward the creation of multiple pictures. Therefore, we have shown it as a separate pipeline whose output is a new database. Primitives extracted from the rendering database are clipped and normalized, and are presented to the remaining stages of the pipeline. These stages are structured much like those used for the *z*-buffer pipeline, except that the only visible-surface process they need to perform is to guarantee that each polygon will correctly overwrite any previously scan-converted polygon that it intersects.

14.9.2 Global Illumination Pipelines

Thus far, we have ignored global illumination. As we have noted before, incorporating global illumination effects requires information about the geometric relationships between the object being rendered and the other objects in the world. In the case of shadows, which depend only on the position of the light source, and not

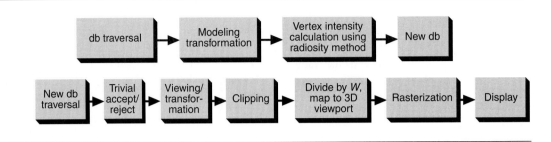

Figure 14.44   Rendering pipeline for radiosity and Gouraud shading.

on that of the viewer, preprocessing the environment to add surface-detail polygon shadows allows the use of an otherwise conventional pipeline.

Radiosity.   Radiosity algorithms offer an interesting example of how to take advantage of the conventional pipeline to achieve global-illumination effects. The algorithms of Section 14.8 process objects and assign to them a set of view-independent vertex intensities. These objects may then be presented to a modified version of the pipeline for z-buffer and Gouraud shading, depicted in Fig. 14.44, that eliminates the lighting stage.

Ray tracing.   Finally, we consider ray tracing, whose pipeline, shown in Fig. 14.45, is the simplest because those objects that are visible at each pixel and their illumination are determined entirely in WC. Once objects have been obtained from the database and transformed by the modeling transformation, they are loaded into the ray tracer's WC database, which is carefully implemented to support efficient ray intersection calculations.

14.9.3 Progressive Refinement

One interesting modification to the pipelines that we have discussed takes advantage of the fact that the image is viewed for a finite time. Instead of attempting to render a final version of a picture all at once, we can first render the picture coarsely, and then progressively refine it, to improve it. For example, a first image might have no antialiasing, simpler object models, and simpler shading. As the user views an image, idle cycles may be spent improving its quality [FORR85]. If

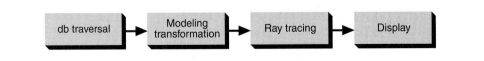

Figure 14.45   Rendering pipeline for ray tracing.

there is some metric by which to determine what to do next, then refinement can occur adaptively. Bergman, Fuchs, Grant, and Spach [BERG86b] have developed such a system that uses a variety of heuristics to determine how it should spend its time. For example, a polygon is Gouraud-shaded, rather than constant-shaded, only if the range of its vertex intensities exceeds a threshold. Ray-tracing [PAIN89] and radiosity [COHE88] algorithms are both amenable to progressive refinement.

SUMMARY

In this chapter, we encountered many different illumination models, some inspired primarily by the need for efficiency, others that attempt to account for the physics of how surfaces actually interact with light. We saw how interpolation could be used in shading models, both to minimize the number of points at which the illumination equation is evaluated, and to allow curved surfaces to be approximated by polygonal meshes. We contrasted local illumination approaches that consider in isolation each surface point and the lights illuminating each point directly, with global approaches that support refraction and reflection of other objects in the environment.

As we have stressed throughout this chapter, the wide range of illumination and shading algorithms gives rise to a corresponding diversity in the images that can be produced of the same scene with the same viewing specification. The decision about which algorithms should be used depends on many factors, including the purposes for which an image is to be rendered. Although photorealism is often sacrificed in return for efficiency, advances in algorithms and hardware will soon make real-time implementations of physically correct, global illumination models a reality. When efficiency is no longer an issue, however, we may still choose to render some images without texture, shadows, or refraction, because in some cases this will remain the best way to communicate the desired information to the viewer.

Exercises

14.1   (a) Describe the difference in appearance you would expect between a Phong illumination model that used $(\bar{N} \cdot \bar{H})^n$ and one that used $(\bar{R} \cdot \bar{V})^n$. (b) Show that $\alpha = 2\beta$ when all vectors of Fig. 14.12 are coplanar. (c) Show that this relationship is *not* true in general.

14.2   Prove that the results of interpolating vertex information across a polygon's edges and scan lines are independent of orientation in the case of triangles.

14.3   Suppose there are polygons A, B, and C intersecting the same projector in order of increasing distance from the viewer. Show that, in general, if polygons A and B are transparent, the color computed for a pixel in the intersection of their projections will depend on whether Eq. (14.23) is evaluated with polygons A and B treated as polygons 1 and 2 or as polygons 2 and 1.

14.4 Consider the use of texture mapping to modify or replace different material properties. List the effects you can produce by mapping properties singly or in combination.

14.5 What other lighting effects can you think of that would generalize Warn's flaps and cones?

14.6 Implement a simple recursive ray tracer based on the material in Sections 13.4 and 14.7.

14.7 Explain why lighting must be done before clipping in the pipeline of Fig. 14.41.

14.8 Implement a testbed for experimenting with local illumination models. Store an image that contains for each pixel its visible surface's index into a table of material properties, the surface normal, the distance from the viewer, and the distance from a normalized vector to one or more light sources. Allow the user to modify the illumination equation, the intensity and color of the lights, and the surface properties. Each time a change is made, render the surface. Use Eq. (14.20) with light-source attenuation (Eq. 14.8) and depth-cueing (Eq. 14.11).

Bibliography

What follows is an extensive bibliography in computer graphics. In addition to being a list of references from the various chapters, it is also a fine place to browse. Just looking at the titles of the books and articles can give you a good idea of where research in the field has been and where it is going.

Since certain journals are referenced frequently, we have abbreviated them here. The most important of these are the ACM SIGGRAPH Conference Proceedings, published each year as an issue of *Computer Graphics,* and the *ACM Transactions on Graphics.* These two sources make up more than one-third of the bibliography.

Abbreviations

ACM TOG	*Association for Computing Machinery, Transactions on Graphics*
CACM	*Communications of the ACM*
CG & A	*IEEE Computer Graphics and Applications*
CGIP	*Computer Graphics and Image Processing*
CVGIP	*Computer Vision, Graphics, and Image Processing (formerly CGIP)*
FJCC	*Proceedings of the Fall Joint Computer Conference*
JACM	*Journal of the ACM*
NCC	*Proceedings of the National Computer Conference*
SJCC	*Proceedings of the Spring Joint Computer Conference*

SIGGRAPH 76   *Proceedings of SIGGRAPH '76 (Philadelphia, Pennsylvania, July 14–16, 1976).* In *Computer Graphics,* 10(2), Summer 1976, ACM SIGGRAPH, New York.

SIGGRAPH 77   *Proceedings of SIGGRAPH '77 (San Jose, California, July 20–22, 1977).* In *Computer Graphics,* 11(2), Summer 1977, ACM SIGGRAPH, New York.

SIGGRAPH 78   *Proceedings of SIGGRAPH '78 (Atlanta, Georgia, August 23–25, 1978).* In *Computer Graphics,* 12(3), August 1978, ACM SIGGRAPH, New York.

SIGGRAPH 79   *Proceedings of SIGGRAPH '79 (Chicago, Illinois, August 8–10, 1979).* In *Computer Graphics,* 13(2), August 1979, ACM SIGGRAPH, New York.

SIGGRAPH 80   *Proceedings of SIGGRAPH '80 (Seattle, Washington, July 14–18, 1980).* In *Computer Graphics,* 14(3), July 1980, ACM SIGGRAPH, New York.

SIGGRAPH 81   *Proceedings of SIGGRAPH '81 (Dallas, Texas, August 3–7, 1981).* In *Computer Graphics,* 15(3), August 1981, ACM SIGGRAPH, New York.

SIGGRAPH 82   *Proceedings of SIGGRAPH '82 (Boston, Massachusetts, July 26–30, 1982).* In *Computer Graphics,* 16(3), July 1982, ACM SIGGRAPH, New York.

SIGGRAPH 83   *Proceedings of SIGGRAPH '83 (Detroit, Michigan, July 25–29, 1983).* In *Computer Graphics,* 17(3), July 1983, ACM SIGGRAPH, New York.

SIGGRAPH 84   *Proceedings of SIGGRAPH '84 (Minneapolis, Minnesota, July 23–27, 1984).* In *Computer Graphics,* 18(3), July 1984, ACM SIGGRAPH, New York.

SIGGRAPH 85   *Proceedings of SIGGRAPH '85 (San Francisco, California, July 22–26, 1985).* In *Computer Graphics,* 19(3), July 1985, ACM SIGGRAPH, New York.

SIGGRAPH 86   *Proceedings of SIGGRAPH '86 (Dallas, Texas, August 18–22, 1986).* In *Computer Graphics,* 20(4), August 1986, ACM SIGGRAPH, New York.

SIGGRAPH 87   *Proceedings of SIGGRAPH '87 (Anaheim, California, July 27–31, 1987).* In *Computer Graphics,* 21(4), July 1987, ACM SIGGRAPH, New York.

SIGGRAPH 88   *Proceedings of SIGGRAPH '88 (Atlanta, Georgia, August 1–5, 1988).* In *Computer Graphics,* 22(4), August 1988, ACM SIGGRAPH, New York.

SIGGRAPH 89   *Proceedings of SIGGRAPH '89 (Boston, Massachusetts, July 31–August 4, 1989).* In *Computer Graphics,* 23(3), July 1989, ACM SIGGRAPH, New York.

ABIE89   Abi-Ezzi, S.S., *The Graphical Processing of B-Splines in a Highly Dynamic Environment,* Ph.D. Thesis, Rensselaer Polytechnic Institute, Troy, NY, May 1989.

ADOB85   Adobe Systems, Inc., *PostScript Language Reference Manual,* Addison-Wesley, Reading, MA, 1985.

AMAN87   Amanatides, J., and A. Woo, "A Fast Voxel Traversal Algorithm for Ray Tracing," in Kunii, T.L., ed., *Computer Graphics 87: Proceedings of Computer Graphics International 87, London, October 1987,* Springer, Tokyo, 1987, 149–155.

ANSI85   ANSI (American National Standards Institute), *American National Standard for Information Processing Systems—Computer Graphics—Graphical Kernel System (GKS) Functional Description,* ANSI X3.124-1985, ANSI, New York, 1985.

ANSI88   ANSI (American National Standards Institute), *American National Standard for Information Processing Systems—Programmer's Hierarchical Interactive Graphics System (PHIGS) Functional Description, Archive File Format, Clear-Text Encoding of Archive File,* ANSI, X3.144-1988, ANSI, New York, 1988.

APPE68   Appel, A., "Some Techniques for Shading Machine Renderings of Solids," *SJCC,* 1968, 37–45.

APPL85   Apple Computer, Inc., *Inside Macintosh,* Addison-Wesley, Reading, MA, 1985.

APT85   Apt, C., "Perfecting the Picture," *IEEE Spectrum,* 22(7), July 1985, 60–66.

ATHE81   Atherton, P.R., "A Method of Interactive Visualization of CAD Surface Models on a Color Video Display," *SIGGRAPH 81,* 279–287.

ATHE83   Atherton, P.R., "A Scan-Line Hidden Surface Removal Procedure for Constructive Solid Geometry," *SIGGRAPH 83,* 73–82.

BAEC87   Baecker, R., and B. Buxton, *Readings in Human-Computer Interaction,* Morgan Kaufmann, Los Altos, CA, 1987.

BALD85   Baldauf, D., "The Workhorse CRT: New Life," *IEEE Spectrum,* 22(7), July 1985, 67–73.

BANC77   Banchoff, T.F., and C.M. Strauss, *The Hypercube: Projections and Slicings,* Film, International Film Bureau, 1977.

BANC83   Banchoff, T., and J. Wermer, *Linear Algebra Through Geometry,* Springer-Verlag, New York, 1983.

BARS83   Barsky, B., and J. Beatty, "Local Control of Bias and Tension in Beta-Splines," *ACM TOG,* 2(2), April 1983, 109–134.

BARS88   Barsky, B., *Computer Graphics and Geometric Modeling Using Beta-splines,* Springer-Verlag, New York, 1988.

BART87   Bartels, R., J. Beatty, and B. Barsky, *An Introduction to Splines for Use in Computer Graphics and Geometric Modeling,* Morgan Kaufmann, Los Altos, CA, 1987.

BASS90   Bass, C., M. Capsimalis, N. Jeske, A. Look, S, Sheppard, and G. Wiegand, *HOOPS Graphics System User Guides,* Ithaca Software, 1990.

BAUM74   Baumgart, B.G., *Geometric Modeling for Computer Vision,* Ph.D. Thesis, Report AIM-249, STAN-CS-74-463, Computer Science Department, Stanford University, Palo Alto, CA, October 1974.

BAUM75   Baumgart, B.G., "A Polyhedron Representation for Computer Vision," *NCC 75,* 589–596.

BAYE73   Bayer, B.E., "An Optimum Method for Two-Level Rendition of Continuous-Tone Pictures," in *Conference Record of the International Conference on Communications,* 1973, 26-11–26-15.

BEAT82   Beatty, J.C., and K.S. Booth, eds., *Tutorial: Computer Graphics,* Second Edition, IEEE Comp. Soc. Press, Silver Spring, MD 1982.

BEDF58   Bedford, R., and G. Wyszecki, "Wavelength Discrimination for Point Sources," *Journal of the Optical Society of America,* 48, 1958, 129–ff.

BERG86a   Bergeron, P., "A General Version of Crow's Shadow Volumes," *CG & A,* 6(9), September 1986, 17–28.

BERG86b   Bergman, L., H. Fuchs, E. Grant, and S. Spach, "Image Rendering by Adaptive Refinement," *SIGGRAPH 86,* 29–37.

BERK82   Berk, T., L. Brownston, and A. Kaufman, "A New Color-Naming System for Graphics Languages," *CG & A,* 2(3), May 1982, 37–44.

BEZI70   Bézier, P., *Emploi des Machines á Commande Numérique*, Masson et Cie, Paris, 1970. Translated by Forrest, A. R., and A. F. Pankhurst as Bézier, P., *Numerical Control —Mathematics and Applications*, Wiley, London, 1972.

BEZI74   Bézier, P., "Mathematical and Practical Possibilities of UNISURF," in Barnhill, R. E., and R. F. Riesenfeld, eds., *Computer Aided Geometric Design*, Academic Press, New York, 1974.

BILL81   Billmeyer, F., and M. Saltzman, *Principles of Color Technology*, second edition, Wiley, New York, 1981.

BINF71   Binford, T., in *Visual Perception by Computer, Proceedings of the IEEE Conference on Systems and Control,* Miami, FL, December 1971.

BIRR61   Birren, R., *Creative Color*, Van Nostrand Reinhold, New York, 1961.

BISH60   Bishop, A., and M. Crook, *Absolute Identification of Color for Targets Presented Against White and Colored Backgrounds*. Report WADD TR 60-611, Wright Air Development Division, Wright Patterson AFB, Dayton, Ohio, 1960.

BISH86   Bishop, G., and D.M. Weimer, "Fast Phong Shading," *SIGGRAPH 86,* 103–106.

BLIN76   Blinn, J.F., and M.E. Newell, "Texture and Reflection in Computer Generated Images," *CACM,* 19(10), October 1976, 542–547. Also in BEAT82, 456–461.

BLIN77a   Blinn, J.F., "Models of Light Reflection for Computer Synthesized Pictures," *SIGGRAPH 77,* 192–198. Also in FREE80, 316–322.

BLIN77b   Blinn, J.F., "A Homogeneous Formulation for Lines in 3-Space," *SIGGRAPH 77,* 237–241.

BLIN78a   Blinn, J.F., and M.E. Newell, "Clipping Using Homogeneous Coordinates," *SIGGRAPH 78,* 245–251.

BLIN78b   Blinn, J.F., "Simulation of Wrinkled Surfaces," *SIGGRAPH 78,* 286–292.

BLIN88   Blinn, J.F., "Me and My (Fake) Shadow," *CG & A,* 9(1), January 1988, 82–86.

BOUK70a   Bouknight, W.J., "A Procedure for Generation of Three-Dimensional Half-Toned Computer Graphics Presentations," *CACM,* 13(9), September 1970, 527–536. Also in FREE80, 292–301.

BOUK70b   Bouknight, W.J., and K.C. Kelly, "An Algorithm for Producing Half-Tone Computer Graphics Presentations with Shadows and Movable Light Sources," *SJCC,* AFIPS Press, Montvale, NJ, 1970, 1–10.

BOUV85   Bouville, C., "Bounding Ellipsoids for Ray-Fractal Intersection," *SIGGRAPH 85,* 45–52.

BOYN79   Boynton, R.M., *Human Color Vision*, Holt, Rinehart, and Winston, New York, 1979.

BOYS82   Boyse, J.W., and J.E. Gilchrist, "GMSolid: Interactive Modeling for Design and Analysis of Solids," *CG & A,* 2(2), March 1982, 27–40.

BÖHM80   Böhm, W., "Inserting New Knots into B-spline Curves," *Computer Aided Design*, 12(4), July 1980, 199–201.

BÖHM84   Böhm, W., G. Farin, and J. Kahmann, "A Survey of Curve and Surface Methods in CAGD," *Computer Aided Geometric Design*, 1(1), July 1984, 1–60.

BRAI78   Braid, I.C., R.C. Hillyard, and I.A. Stroud, *Stepwise Construction of Polyhedra in Geometric Modelling,* CAD Group Document No. 100, Cambridge University, Cambridge, England, 1978. Also in K.W. Brodlie, ed., *Mathemat-*

ical Methods in Computer Graphics and Design, Academic Press, New York, 1980, 123–141.

BRES65   Bresenham, J.E., "Algorithm for Computer Control of a Digital Plotter," *IBM Systems Journal,* 4(1), 1965, 25–30.

BRES77   Bresenham, J.E. "A Linear Algorithm for Incremental Digital Display of Circular Arcs," *Communications of the ACM,* 20(2), February 1977, 100–106.

BRES83   Bresenham, J.E., D.G. Grice, and S.C. Pi, "Bi-Directional Display of Circular Arcs," US Patent 4,371,933, February 1, 1983.

BRIT78   Britton, E., J. Lipscomb, and M. Pique, "Making Nested Rotations Convenient for the User," *SIGGRAPH 78,* 222–227.

BROT84   Brotman, L.S., and N.I. Badler, "Generating Soft Shadows with a Depth Buffer Algorithm," *CG & A,* 4(10), October 1984, 5–12.

BUIT75   Bui-Tuong, Phong, "Illumination for Computer Generated Pictures," *CACM,* 18(6), June 1975, 311–317. Also in BEAT82, 449–455.

CABR87   Cabral, B., N. Max, and R. Springmeyer, "Bidirectional Reflection Functions from Surface Bump Maps," *SIGGRAPH 87,* 273–281.

CACM84   "An Interview with Andries van Dam," *CACM,* 27(7), August 1984.

CARD83   Card, S., T. Moran, and A. Newell, *The Psychology of Human-Computer Interaction,* Lawrence Erlbaum Associates, Hillsdale, NJ, 1983.

CARL78   Carlbom, I., and J. Paciorek, "Planar Geometric Projections and Viewing Transformations," *Computing Surveys,* 10(4), December 1978, 465–502.

CARP84   Carpenter, L., "The A-buffer, an Antialiased Hidden Surface Method," *SIGGRAPH 84,* 103–108.

CATM74   Catmull, E., *A Subdivision Algorithm for Computer Display of Curved Surfaces,* Ph.D. Thesis, Report UTEC-CSc-74-133, Computer Science Department, University of Utah, Salt Lake City, UT, December 1974.

CATM75   Catmull, E., "Computer Display of Curved Surfaces," in *Proc. IEEE Conf. on Computer Graphics, Pattern Recognition and Data Structures,* May 1975. Also in FREE80, 309–315.

CHAP72   Chapanis, A., and R. Kinkade, "Design of Controls," in Van Cott, H., and R. Kinkade, eds., *Human Engineering Guide to Equipment Design,* U.S. Government Printing Office, 1972.

CHAS81   Chasen, S.H., "Historical Highlights of Interactive Computer Graphics," *Mechanical Engineering,* 103, ASME, November 1981, 32–41.

CHIN89   Chin, N., and S. Feiner, "Near Real-Time Shadow Generation Using BSP Trees," *SIGGRAPH 89,* 99–106.

CHIN90   Chin, N., *Near Real-Time Object-Precision Shadow Generation Using BSP Trees,* M.S. Thesis, Department of Computer Science, Columbia University, New York, 1990.

CHUN89   Chung, J.C., *et al.,* "Exploring Virtual Worlds with Head-Mounted Displays," *Proc. SPIE Meeting on Non-Holographic True 3-Dimensional Display Technologies,* 1083, Los Angeles, Jan. 15–20, 1989.

CLAR76   Clark, J.H., "Hierarchical Geometric Models for Visible Surface Algorithms," *CACM,* 19(10), October 1976, 547–554. Also in BEAT82, 296–303.

CLAR79   Clark, J., "A Fast Scan-Line Algorithm for Rendering Parametric Surfaces," abstract in *SIGGRAPH 79,* 174. Also in Whitted, T., and R. Cook, eds., *Image Rendering Tricks, Course Notes 16 for SIGGRAPH 86,* Dallas, TX, August 1986. Also in JOY88, 88–93.

CLEV83   Cleveland, W., and R. McGill, "A Color-Caused Optical Illusion on a Statistical Graph," *The American Statistician*, 37(2), May 1983, 101–105.

COHE85   Cohen, M.F., and D.P. Greenberg, "The Hemi-Cube: A Radiosity Solution for Complex Environments," *SIGGRAPH 85*, 31–40.

COHE88   Cohen, M.F., S.E. Chen, J.R. Wallace, and D.P. Greenberg, "A Progressive Refinement Approach to Fast Radiosity Image Generation," *SIGGRAPH 88*, 75–84.

CONR85   Conrac Corporation, *Raster Graphics Handbook*, second edition, Van Nostrand Reinhold, New York, 1985.

COOK82   Cook, R., and K. Torrance, "A Reflectance Model for Computer Graphics," *ACM TOG*, 1(1), January 1982, 7–24.

COOK84   Cook, R.L., "Shade Trees," *SIGGRAPH 84*, 223–231.

COWA83   Cowan, W., "An Inexpensive Scheme for Calibration of a Colour Monitor in Terms of CIE Standard Coordinates," *SIGGRAPH 83*, 315–321.

CROW77   Crow, F.C., "Shadow Algorithms for Computer Graphics," *SIGGRAPH 77*, 242–247. Also in BEAT82, 442–448.

CROW87   Crow, F.C., "The Origins of the Teapot," *CG & A*, 7(1), January 1987, 8–19.

CYRU78   Cyrus, M. and J. Beck, "Generalized Two- and Three-Dimensional Clipping," *Computers and Graphics*, 3(1), 1978, 23–28.

DEBO78   de Boor, C., *A Practical Guide to Splines*, Applied Mathematical Sciences Volume 27, Springer-Verlag, New York, 1978.

DIPP84   Dippé, M., and J. Swensen, "An Adaptive Subdivision Algorithm and Parallel Architecture for Realistic Image Synthesis," *SIGGRAPH 84*, 149–158.

DUFF79   Duff, T., "Smoothly Shaded Renderings of Polyhedral Objects on Raster Displays," *SIGGRAPH 79*, 270–275.

DURB88   Durbeck, R., and S. Sherr, eds., *Output Hardcopy Devices*, Academic Press, New York, 1988.

DUVA90   Duvanenko, V., W.E. Robbins, and R.S. Gyurcsik, "Improved Line Segment Clipping," *Dr. Dobb's Journal*, July 1990, 36–45, 98–100.

DVOR43   Dvořák, A., "There Is a Better Typewriter Keyboard," *National Business Education Quarterly*, 12(2), 1943, 51–58.

ENCA72   Encarnação, J., and W. Giloi, "PRADIS—An Advanced Programming System for 3-D-Display," *SJCC*, AFIPS Press, Montvale, NJ, 1972, 985–998.

ENGE68   Englebart, D.C., and W.K. English, *A Research Center for Augmenting Human Intellect, FJCC*, Thompson Books, Washington, D.C., 1968, 395.

FAUX79   Faux, I.D., and M.J. Pratt, *Computational Geometry for Design and Manufacture*, Wiley, New York, 1979.

FITT54   Fitts, P., "The Information Capacity of the Human Motor System in Controlling Amplitude of Motion," *Journal of Experimental Psychology*, 47(6), June 1954, 381–391.

FIUM89   Fiume, E.L., *The Mathematical Structure of Raster Graphics*, Academic Press, San Diego, 1989.

FLOY75   Floyd, R., and Steinberg, L., "An Adaptive Algorithm for Spatial Gray Scale," in *Society for Information Display 1975 Symposium Digest of Technical Papers*, 1975, 36.

FOLE82   Foley, J., and A. van Dam, *Fundamentals of Interactive Computer Graphics*, Addison-Wesley, Reading, MA, 1982.

FOLE84 Foley, J., V. Wallace, and P. Chan, "The Human Factors of Computer Graphics Interaction Techniques," *CG & A*, 4(11), November 1984, 13–48.

FOLE87 Foley, J., "Interfaces for Advanced Computing," *Scientific American*, 257(4), October 1987, 126–135.

FOLE90 Foley, J., A. van Dam, S. Feiner, and J. Hughes, *Computer Graphics: Principles and Practice, Second Edition*, Addison-Wesley, Reading, MA, 1990.

FORR79 Forrest, A.R., "On the Rendering of Surfaces," *SIGGRAPH 79*, 253–259.

FORR80 Forrest, A.R., "The Twisted Cubic Curve: A Computer-Aided Geometric Design Approach," *Computer Aided Design*, 12(4), July 1980, 165–172.

FORR85 Forrest, A.R., "Antialiasing in Practice," in Earnshaw, R.A., ed., *Fundamental Algorithms for Computer Graphics*, NATO ASI Series F: Computer and Systems Sciences, Vol. 17, Springer-Verlag, New York, 1985, 113–134.

FOUR82 Fournier, A., D. Fussell, and L. Carpenter, "Computer Rendering of Stochastic Models," *CACM*, 25(6), June 1982, 371–384.

FOUR88 Fournier, A. and D. Fussell, "On the Power of the Frame Buffer," *ACM TOG*, 7(2), April 1988, 103–128.

FRAN80 Franklin, W.R., "A Linear Time Exact Hidden Surface Algorithm," *SIGGRAPH 80*, 117–123.

FRAN81 Franklin, W.R., "An Exact Hidden Sphere Algorithm that Operates in Linear Time," *CGIP*, 15(4), April 1981, 364–379.

FREE80 Freeman, H. ed., *Tutorial and Selected Readings in Interactive Computer Graphics*, IEEE Comp. Soc. Press, Silver Spring, MD 1980.

FROM84 Fromme, F., "Improving Color CAD Systems for Users: Some Suggestions from Human Factors Studies," *IEEE Design and Test of Computers*, 1(1), February 1984, 18–27.

FUCH80 Fuchs, H., Z.M. Kedem, and B.F. Naylor, "On Visible Surface Generation by A Priori Tree Structures," *SIGGRAPH 80*, 124–133.

FUCH83 Fuchs, H., G.D. Abram, and E.D. Grant, "Near Real-Time Shaded Display of Rigid Objects," *SIGGRAPH 83*, 65–72.

FUJI85 Fujimura, K., and Kunii, T. L., "A Hierarchical Space Indexing Method," in Kunii, T.L., ed., *Computer Graphics: Visual Technology and Art, Proceedings of Computer Graphics Tokyo '85 Conference*, Springer-Verlag, 1985, 21–34.

GILO78 Giloi, W.K., *Interactive Computer Graphics—Data Structures, Algorithms, Languages*, Prentice-Hall, Englewood Cliffs, NJ, 1978.

GLAS84 Glassner, A.S., "Space Subdivision for Fast Ray Tracing," *CG & A*, 4(10), October 1984, 15–22.

GLAS89 Glassner, A.S., ed., *An Introduction to Ray Tracing*, Academic Press, London, 1989.

GOLD71 Goldstein, R.A., and R. Nagel, "3-D Visual Simulation," *Simulation*, 16(1), January 1971, 25–31.

GOLD83 Goldberg, A., and D. Robson, *SmallTalk 80: The Language and Its Implementation*, Addison-Wesley, Reading, MA, 1983.

GORA84 Goral, C.M., K.E. Torrance, D.P. Greenberg, and B. Battaile, "Modeling the Interaction of Light Between Diffuse Surfaces," *SIGGRAPH 84*, 213–222.

GOSS88 Gossard, D., R. Zuffante, and H. Sakurai, "Representing Dimensions, Tolerances, and Features in MCAE Systems," *CG & A*, 8(2), March 1988, 51–59.

GOUR71 Gouraud, H., "Continuous Shading of Curved Surfaces," *IEEE Trans. on Computers*, C-20(6), June 1971, 623–629. Also in FREE80, 302–308.

GREE87   Greenstein, J. and L. Arnaut, "Human Factors Aspects of Manual Computer Input Devices," in Salvendy, G., ed., *Handbook of Human Factors*, Wiley, New York, 1987, 1450–1489.

GREG66   Gregory, R.L., *Eye and Brain— The Psychology of Seeing*, McGraw-Hill, New York, 1966.

GREG70   Gregory, R.L., *The Intelligent Eye,* McGraw-Hill, London, 1970.

GSPC77   Graphics Standards Planning Committee, "Status Report of the Graphics Standards Planning Committee," *Computer Graphics*, 11, 1977.

GSPC79   Graphics Standards Planning Committee, "Status Report of the Graphics Standards Planning Committee," *Computer Graphics,* 13(3), August 1979.

HAEU76   Haeusing, M., "Color Coding of Information on Electronic Displays," in *Proceedings of the Sixth Congress of the International Ergonomics Association,* 1976, 210–217.

HAGE86   Hagen, M., *Varieties of Realism,* Cambridge University Press, Cambridge, England, 1986.

HAIN89   Haines, E., "Essential Ray Tracing Algorithms," in Glassner, A.S., ed., *An Introduction to Ray Tracing,* Academic Press, London, 1989, 33–77.

HALL89   Hall, R., *Illumination and Color in Computer Generated Imagery,* Springer-Verlag, New York, 1989.

HAML77   Hamlin, G., Jr., and C.W. Gear, "Raster-Scan Hidden Surface Algorithm Techniques," *SIGGRAPH 77,* 206–213. Also in FREE80, 264–271.

HANR83   Hanrahan, P., "Ray Tracing Algebraic Surfaces," *SIGGRAPH 83,* 83–90.

HANR89   Hanrahan, P., "A Survey of Ray-Surface Intersection Algorithms," in Glassner, A.S., ed., *An Introduction to Ray Tracing,* Academic Press, London, 1989, 79–119.

HE92   He, X., P. Heynen, R. Phillips, K. Torrance, D. Salesin, and D. Greenberg, "A Fast and Accurate Light Reflection Model," *SIGGRAPH 92,* 253–254.

HECK84   Heckbert, P.S., and P. Hanrahan, "Beam Tracing Polygonal Objects," *SIGGRAPH 84,* 119–127.

HECK86a   Heckbert, P.S., "Filtering by Repeated Integration," *SIGGRAPH 86,* 315–321.

HECK86b   Heckbert, P.S., "Survey of Texture Mapping," *CG & A,* 6(11), November 1986, 56–67.

HEDG82   Hedgley, D.R., Jr., *A General Solution to the Hidden-Line Problem,* NASA Reference Publication 1085, NASA Scientific and Technical Information Branch, 1982.

HERO76   Herot, C., "Graphical Input Through Machine Recognition of Sketches," *SIGGRAPH 76,* 97–102.

HIRS70   Hirsch, R., "Effects of Standard vs. Alphabetical Keyboard Formats on Typing Performance," *Journal of Applied Psychology*, 54, December 1970, 484–490.

HODG85   Hodges, L., and D. McAllister, "Stereo and Alternating-Pair Techniques for Display of Computer-Generated Images," *CG & A,* 5(9), September 1985, 38–45.

HOFF61   Hoffman, K., and R. Kunze, *Linear Algebra,* Prentice–Hall, Englewood Cliffs, NJ, 1961.

HUGH89   Hughes, J., *Integer and Floating-Point Z-Buffer Resolution,* Department of Computer Science Technical Report, Brown University, Providence, RI, 1989.

HUNT78   Hunter, G.M., *Efficient Computation and Data Structures for Graphics,* Ph.D. Thesis, Department of Electrical Engineering and Computer Science, Princeton University, Princeton, NJ, 1978.

HUNT79   Hunter, G.M. and K. Steiglitz, "Operations on Images Using Quad Trees," *IEEE Trans. Pattern Anal. Mach. Intell.,* 1(2), April 1979, 145–153.

HUNT87   Hunt, R.W., *The Reproduction of Colour,* fourth edition, Fountain Press, Tolworth, England, 1987.

HUTC86   Hutchins, E., J. Hollan, and D. Norman, "Direct Manipulation Interfaces," in Norman, D., and S. Draper, eds., *User Centered System Design,* Erlbaum, Hillsdale, NJ, 1986, 87–124.

IES87   Illuminating Engineering Society, Nomenclature Committee, *ANSI/IES RP-16-1986: American National Standard: Nomenclature and Definitions for Illuminating Engineering,* Illuminating Engineering Society of North America, New York, 1987.

INGA81   Ingalls, D., "The SmallTalk Graphics Kernel," *BYTE,* 6(8), August 1981.

INTE85   Interaction Systems, Inc., *TK-1000 Touch System,* Interaction Systems, Inc., Newtonville, MA, 1985.

INTE88   International Standards Organization, *International Standard Information Processing Systems*—Computer Graphics—Graphical Kernel System for Three Dimensions (GKS–3D) Functional Description, ISO Document Number 8805:1988(E), American National Standards Institute, New York, 1988.

JACK64   Jacks, E., "A Laboratory for the Study of Man–Machine Communication," in *FJCC 64,* AFIPS, Montvale, NJ, 1964, 343–350.

JACK80   Jackins, C., and S.L. Tanimoto, "Oct-Trees and Their Use in Representing Three-Dimensional Objects," *CGIP,* 14(3), November 1980, 249–270.

JARV76a   Jarvis, J.F., C.N. Judice, and W.H. Ninke, "A Survey of Techniques for the Image Display of Continuous Tone Pictures on Bilevel Displays," *CGIP,* 5(1), March 1976, 13–40.

JARV76b   Jarvis, J.F., and C.S. Roberts, "A New Technique for Displaying Continuous Tone Images on a Bilevel Display," *IEEE Trans.,* COMM-24(8), August 1976, 891–898.

JOBL78   Joblove, G.H., and D. Greenberg, "Color Spaces for Computer Graphics," *SIGGRAPH 78,* 20–27.

JOY86   Joy, K.I., and M.N. Bhetanabhotla, "Ray Tracing Parametric Surface Patches Utilizing Numerical Techniques and Ray Coherence," *SIGGRAPH 86,* 279–285.

JOY88   Joy, K., C. Grant, N. Max, and L. Hatfield, *Tutorial: Computer Graphics: Image Synthesis,* IEEE Computer Society, Washington, DC, 1988.

JUDD75   Judd, D., and G. Wyszecki, *Color in Business, Science, and Industry,* Wiley, New York, 1975.

JUDI74   Judice, J.N., J.F. Jarvis, and W. Ninke, "Using Ordered Dither to Display Continuous Tone Pictures on an AC Plasma Panel," *Proceedings of the Society for Information Display,* Q4 1974, 161–169.

KAJI82   Kajiya, J.T., "Ray Tracing Parametric Patches," *SIGGRAPH 82,* 245–254.

KAJI83   Kajiya, J., "New Techniques for Ray Tracing Procedurally Defined Objects," *SIGGRAPH 83,* 91–102.

KAJI85   Kajiya, J.T., "Anisotropic Reflection Models," *SIGGRAPH 85,* 15–21.

KAJI86   Kajiya, J.T., "The Rendering Equation," *SIGGRAPH 86,* 143–150.

KAPP85   Kappel, M.R., "An Ellipse-Drawing Algorithm for Raster Displays," in Earnshaw, R., ed., *Fundamental Algorithms for Computer Graphics*, NATO ASI Series, Springer-Verlag, Berlin, 1985, 257–280.

KAY79a   Kay, D.S., *Transparency, Refraction and Ray Tracing for Computer Synthesized Images,* M.S. Thesis, Program of Computer Graphics, Cornell University, Ithaca, NY, January 1979.

KAY79b   Kay, D.S., and D. Greenberg, "Transparency for Computer Synthesized Images," *SIGGRAPH 79,* 158–164.

KAY86   Kay, T.L., and J.T. Kajiya, "Ray Tracing Complex Scenes," *SIGGRAPH 86,* 269–278.

KELL76   Kelly, K., and D. Judd, *COLOR—Universal Language and Dictionary of Names,* National Bureau of Standards Spec. Publ. 440, 003-003-01705-1, U.S. Government Printing Office, Washington, DC, 1976.

KLIN71   Klinger, A., "Patterns and Search Statistics," in Rustagi, J., ed., *Optimizing Methods in Statistics,* Academic Press, New York, 1971, 303–337.

KNOW77   Knowlton, K., and L. Cherry, "ATOMS—A Three-D Opaque Molecule System for Color Pictures of Space-Filling or Ball-and-Stick Models," *Computers and Chemistry,* 1, 1977, 161–166.

KNUT87   Knuth, D., "Digital Halftones by Dot Diffusion," *ACM TOG,* 6(4), October 1987, 245–273.

KORE83   Korein, J., and N. Badler, "Temporal Anti-Aliasing in Computer Generated Animation," *SIGGRAPH 83,* 377–388.

KREB79   Krebs, M., and J. Wolf, "Design Principles for the Use of Color in Displays," *Proceedings of the Society for Information Display,* 20, 1979, 10–15.

KRUE83   Krueger, M., *Artificial Reality,* Addison-Wesley, Reading, MA, 1983.

LAID86   Laidlaw, D.H., W.B. Trumbore, and J.F. Hughes, "Constructive Solid Geometry for Polyhedral Objects," *SIGGRAPH 86,* 161–170.

LAND85   Landauer, T., and D. Nachbar, "Selection from Alphabetic and Numeric Menu Trees Using a Touch-Sensitive Screen: Breadth, Depth, and Width," in *Proceedings CHI '85 Human Factors in Computing Systems Conference,* ACM, New York, 1985, 73–78.

LANE80   Lane, J., L. Carpenter, T. Whitted, and J. Blinn, "Scan Line Methods for Displaying Parametrically Defined Surfaces," *CACM,* 23(1), January 1980, 23–34. Also in BEAT82, 468–479.

LASS87   Lasseter, J., "Principles of Traditional Animation Applied to 3D Computer Animation," *SIGGRAPH 87,* 35–44.

LAYB79   Laybourne, K., *The Animation Book,* Crown, New York, 1979.

LEAF74   Leaf, C., *The Owl Who Married a Goose,* film, National Film Board of Canada, 1974.

LEAF77   Leaf, C., *The Metamorphosis of Mr. Samsa,* film, National Film Board of Canada, 1977.

LEVI76   Levin, J., "A Parametric Algorithm for Drawing Pictures of Solid Objects Composed of Quadric Surfaces," *CACM,* 19(10), October 1976, 555–563.

LIAN84   Liang, Y-D., and Barsky, B., "A New Concept and Method for Line Clipping," *ACM TOG,* 3(1), January 1984, 1–22.

LIND68   Lindenmayer, A, "Mathematical Models for Cellular Interactions in Development, Parts I and II," *J. Theor. Biol.,* 18, 1968, 280–315.

LINT89   Linton, M., J. Vlissides, and P. Calder, "Composing User Interfaces with InterViews," *IEEE Computer,* 22(2), February 1989, 8–22.

MACH78   Machover, C., "A Brief Personal History of Computer Graphics," *Computer*, 11(11), November 1978, 38–45.

MAGI68   Mathematical Applications Group, Inc., "3-D Simulated Graphics Offered by Service Bureau," *Datamation*, 13(1), February 1968, 69.

MAHL72   Mahl, R., "Visible Surface Algorithms for Quadric Patches," *IEEE Trans. on Computers*, C-21(1), January 1972, 1–4.

MAHN73   Mahnkopf, P., and J.L. Encarnação, *FLAVIS—A Hidden Line Algorithm for Displaying Spatial Constructs Given by Point Sets*, Technischer Bericht Nr. 148, Heinrich Hertz Institut, Berlin, 1973.

MAMM89   Mammen, A., "Transparency and Antialiasing Algorithms Implemented with the Virtual Pixel Maps Technique," *CG & A*, 9(4), July 1989, 43–55.

MAND82   Mandelbrot, B., Technical Correspondence, *CACM*, 25(8), August 1982, 581–583.

MÄNT88   Mäntylä, M. *Introduction to Solid Modeling*, Computer Science Press, Rockville, MD, 1988.

MARC82   Marcus, A., "Color: A Tool for Computer Graphics Communication," in Greenberg, D., A. Marcus, A. Schmidt, and V. Gorter, *The Computer Image*, Addison-Wesley, Reading, MA, 1982, 76–90.

MARK80   Markowsky, G., and M.A. Wesley, "Fleshing Out Wire Frames," *IBM Journal of Research and Development*, 24(5), September 1980, 582–597.

MARS85   Marsden, J., and A. Weinstein, *Calculus I, II, and III*, second edition, Springer Verlag, New York, 1985.

MAX79   Max, N.L., "ATOMLLL: ATOMS with Shading and Highlights," *SIGGRAPH 79*, 165–173.

MAX84   Max, N.L., "Atoms with Transparency and Shadows," *CVGIP*, 27(1), July 1984, 46–63.

MAXW46   Maxwell, E.A., *Methods of Plane Projective Geometry Based on the Use of General Homogeneous Coordinates*, Cambridge University Press, Cambridge, England, 1946.

MAXW51   Maxwell, E.A., *General Homogeneous Coordinates in Space of Three Dimensions*, Cambridge University Press, Cambridge, England, 1951.

MAYH90   Mayhew, D., *Principles and Guidelines in User Interface Design*, Prentice-Hall, Englewood Cliffs, NJ, 1990.

MEAG80   Meagher, D., *Octree Encoding: A New Technique for the Representation, Manipulation, and Display of Arbitrary 3-D Objects by Computer*, Technical Report IPL-TR-80-111, Image Processing Laboratory, Rensselaer Polytechnic Institute, Troy, NY, October 1980.

MEAG82   Meagher, D., "Geometric Modeling Using Octree Encoding," *CGIP*, 19(2), June 1982, 129–147.

MEIE88   Meier, B., "ACE: A Color Expert System for User Interface Design," in *Proceedings of the ACM SIGGRAPH Symposium on User Interface Software*, ACM, New York, 117–128, 1988.

MEYE80   Meyer, G.W., and D.P. Greenberg, "Perceptual Color Spaces for Computer Graphics," *SIGGRAPH 80*, 254–261.

MEYE88   Meyer, G., and Greenberg, D., "Color-defective Vision and Computer Graphic Displays," *CG & A*, 8(5), September 1988, 28–40.

MICH71   Michaels, S., "QWERTY Versus Alphabetical Keyboards as a Function of Typing Skill," *Human Factors*, 13(5), October 1971, 419–426.

MICR89   Microsoft Corporation, *Presentation Manager*, Microsoft Corporation, Bellevue, WA, 1989.

MILL87   Miller, J.R., "Geometric Approaches to Nonplanar Quadric Surface Intersection Curves," *ACM TOG*, 6(4), October 1987, 274–307.

MILL89   Miller, J.R., "Architectural Issues in Solid Modelers," *CG & A*, 9(5), September 1989, 72–87.

MORT85   Mortenson, M., *Geometric Modeling*, Wiley, New York, 1985.

MUNS76   Munsell Color Company, *Book of Color*, Munsell Color Company, Baltimore, MD, 1976.

MURC85   Murch, G., "Using Color Effectively: Designing to Human Specifications," *Technical Communications*, Q4 1985, Tektronix Corporation, Beaverton, OR, 14–20.

MUSG89   Musgrave, F.K., "Prisms and Rainbows: A Dispersion Model for Computer Graphics," in *Proceedings of Graphics Interface '89*, London, Ontario, June 19–23, 1989, 227–234.

MYER68   Myer, T., and I. Sutherland, "On the Design of Display Processors," *CACM*, 11(6), June 1968, 410–414.

MYER75   Myers, A.J., *An Efficient Visible Surface Program*, Report to the National Science Foundation, Computer Graphics Research Group, Ohio State University, Columbus, OH, July 1975.

NAYL90   Naylor, B.F., "Binary Space Partitioning Trees as an Alternative Representation of Polytopes," *CAD*, 22(4), May 1990, 250–253.

NEID93   Neider, J., T. Davis, and M. Woo, *OpenGL Programming Guide*, Addison-Wesley, Reading, MA, 1993.

NEWE72   Newell, M.E., R.G. Newell, and T.L. Sancha, "A Solution to the Hidden Surface Problem," in *Proceedings of the ACM National Conference 1972*, 443–450. Also in FREE80, 236–243.

NICH87   Nicholl, T.M., D.T. Lee, and R.A. Nicholl, "An Efficient New Algorithm for 2-D Line Clipping: Its Development and Analysis," *SIGGRAPH 87*, 253–262.

NICO77   Nicodemus, F.E., J.C. Richmond, J.J. Hsia, I.W. Ginsberg, and T. Limperis, *Geometrical Considerations and Nomenclature for Reflectance*, NBS Monograph 160, U.S. Department of Commerce, Washington DC, October 1977.

NISH85   Nishita, T., and E. Nakamae, "Continuous Tone Representation of Three-Dimensional Objects Taking Account of Shadows and Interreflection," *SIGGRAPH 85*, 23–30.

NOLL67   Noll, M., "A Computer Technique for Displaying N-dimensional Hyperobjects," *CACM*, 10(8), August 1967, 469–473.

NORM88   Norman, D., *The Psychology of Everyday Things*, Basic Books, New York, 1988.

OPEN89   Open Software Foundation, *OSF/MOTIF™ Manual*, Open Software Foundation, Cambridge, MA, 1989.

OSTW31   Ostwald, W., *Colour Science*, Winsor & Winsor, London, 1931.

PAIN89   Painter, J., and K. Sloan, "Antialiased Ray Tracing by Adaptive Progressive Refinement," *SIGGRAPH 89*, 281–288.

PALA88   Palay, A., W. Hansen, M. Kazar, M. Sherman, M. Wadlow, T. Neuendorffer, Z. Stern, M. Bader, and T. Peters, "The Andrew Toolkit: An Overview," in *Proceedings 1988 Winter USENIX*, February 1988, 9–21.

PANT91   Pantone, Inc., *PANTONE Color Formula Guide 1000*, © Pantone, Inc., 1991.

PEAC85   Peachey, D.R., "Solid Texturing of Complex Surfaces," *SIGGRAPH 85,* 279–286.

PEIT86   Peitgen, H.-O., and P.H. Richter, *The Beauty of Fractals: Images of Complex Dynamical Systems,* Springer-Verlag, Berlin, 1986.

PERL85   Perlin, K., "An Image Synthesizer," *SIGGRAPH 85,* 287–296.

PERR85   Perry, T., and P. Wallach, "Computer Displays: New Choices, New Trade-offs," *IEEE Spectrum,* 22(7), July 1985, 52–59.

PHIG88   PHIGS+ Committee, Andries van Dam, chair, "PHIGS+ Functional Description, Revision 3.0," *Computer Graphics,* 22(3), July 1988, 125–218.

PHIG92   Programmer's Hierarchical Interactive Graphics System (PHIGS) Part 4–Plus Lumierè und Surfaces (PHIGS PLUS), ISO/IEC 9592-4:1992(E).

PHIL91   Phillips, R.L., "MediaView: A General Multimedia Digital Publishing System," *CACM,* 34(7), July 1991, 75–83.

PHIL92   Phillips, R.L., "Opportunities for Multimedia in Education," in S. Cunningham and R. Hubbold, *Interactive Learning Through Visualization,* Springer-Verlag, Berlin, 1992, 25–35.

PITT67   Pitteway, M.L.V., "Algorithm for Drawing Ellipses or Hyperbolae with a Digital Plotter," *Computer J.,* 10(3), November 1967, 282–289.

PIXA86   Pixar Corporation, *Luxo, Jr.,* film, Pixar Corporation, San Rafael, CA, 1986.

PIXA88   Pixar Corporation, *The RenderMan Interface,* Version 3.0, Pixar Corporation, San Rafael, CA, May 1988.

PORT79   Porter, T., "The Shaded Surface Display of Large Molecules," *SIGGRAPH 79,* 234–236.

POTM82   Potmesil, M., and I. Chakravarty, "Synthetic Image Generation with a Lens and Aperture Camera Model," *ACM TOG,* 1(2), April 1982, 85–108.

PRAT84   Pratt, M., "Solid Modeling and the Interface Between Design and Manufacture," *CG & A,* 4(7), July 1984, 52–59.

PREP85   Preparata, F. P., and M.I. Shamos, *Computational Geometry: An Introduction,* Springer-Verlag, New York, 1985.

PRES88   Press, W.H., B.P. Flannery, S.A. Teukolskym, and W.T. Vetterling, *Numerical Recipes in C: The Art of Scientific Computing,* Cambridge University Press, Cambridge, England, 1988.

PRIN71   Prince, D., *Interactive Graphics for Computer Aided Design,* Addison-Wesley, Reading, MA, 1971.

PRIT77   Pritchard, D.H., "U.S. Color Television Fundamentals—A Review," *IEEE Transactions on Consumer Electronics,* CE-23(4), November 1977, 467–478.

PRUS88   Prusinkiewicz, P., A. Lindenmayer, and J. Hanan, "Developmental Models of Herbaceous Plants for Computer Imagery Purposes," *SIGGRAPH 88,* 141–150.

PUTN86   Putnam, L.K., and P.A. Subrahmanyam, "Boolean Operations on *n*-Dimensional Objects," *CG & A,* 6(6), June 1986, 43–51.

RATL72   Ratliff, F., "Contour and Contrast," *Scientific American,* 226(6), June 1972, 91–101. Also in BEAT82, 364–375.

REDD78   Reddy, D., and S. Rubin, *Representation of Three-Dimensional Objects,* CMU-CS-78-113, Computer Science Department, Carnegie-Mellon University, Pittsburgh, PA, 1978.

REFF88   de Reffye, P., C. Edelin, J. Françon, M. Jaeger, and C. Puech, "Plant Models Faithful to Botanical Structure and Development," *SIGGRAPH 88,* 151–158.

REQU77   Requicha, A.A.G., *Mathematical Models of Rigid Solids,* Tech. Memo 28, Production Automation Project, University of Rochester, Rochester, NY, 1977.

REQU80   Requicha, A.A.G., "Representations for Rigid Solids: Theory, Methods, and Systems," *ACM Computing Surveys,* 12(4), December 1980, 437–464.

REQU84   Requicha, A.A.G., "Representation of Tolerances in Solid Modeling: Issues and Alternative Approaches," in Pickett, M., and J. Boyse, eds., *Solid Modeling by Computers,* Plenum Press, New York, 1984, 3–22.

REQU85   Requicha, A.A.G., and H.B. Voelcker, "Boolean Operations in Solid Modeling: Boundary Evaluation and Merging Algorithms," *Proc. IEEE,* 73(1), January 1985, 30–44.

ROBE65   Roberts, L.G., *Homogeneous Matrix Representations and Manipulation of N-Dimensional Constructs*, Document MS 1405, Lincoln Laboratory, MIT, Cambridge, MA, 1965.

ROMN69   Romney, G.W., G.S. Watkins, and D.C. Evans, "Real Time Display of Computer Generated Half-Tone Perspective Pictures," in *Proceedings 1968 IFIP Congress,* North Holland Publishing Co., 1969, 973–978.

ROSE85   Rose, C., B. Hacker, R. Anders, K. Wittney, M. Metzler, S. Chernicoff, C. Espinosa, A. Averill, B. Davis, and B. Howard, *Inside Macintosh,* I, Addison-Wesley, Reading, MA, 1985, I-35–I-213.

ROSS86   Rossignac, J.R., and A.A.G. Requicha, "Depth-Buffering Display Techniques for Constructive Solid Geometry," *CG & A,* 6(9), September 1986, 29–39.

RUBE84   Rubenstein, R., and H. Hersh, *The Human Factor—Designing Computer Systems for People*, Digital Press, Burlington, MA, 1984.

RUBI80   Rubin, S.M., and T. Whitted, "A 3-Dimensional Representation for Fast Rendering of Complex Scenes," *SIGGRAPH 80,* 110–116.

SALV87   Salvendy, G., ed., *Handbook of Human Factors*, Wiley, New York, 1987.

SAME84   Samet, H., "The Quadtree and Related Hierarchical Data Structures," *ACM Comp. Surv.,* 16(2), June 1984, 187–260.

SAME89a   Samet, H., "Neighbor Finding in Images Represented by Octrees," *CVGIP,* 46(3), June 1989, 367–386.

SAME89b   Samet, H. and R. Webber, "Hierarchical Data Structures and Algorithms for Computer Graphics, Part II: Applications," *CG & A,* 8(4), July 1988, 59–75.

SAME90a   Samet, H., *Design and Analysis of Spatial Data Structures,* Addison-Wesley, Reading, MA, 1990.

SAME90b   Samet, H., *Applications of Spatial Data Structures: Computer Graphics, Image Processing and GIS,* Addison-Wesley, Reading, MA, 1990.

SARR83   Sarraga, R.F., "Algebraic Methods for Intersections of Quadric Surfaces in GMSOLID," *CVGIP,* 22(2), May 1983, 222–238.

SCHE88   Scheifler, R.W., J. Gettys, and R. Newman, *X Window System,* Digital Press, 1988.

SCHM86   Schmucker, K., "MacApp: An Application Framework," *Byte,* 11(8), August 1986, 189–193.

SCHN90   Schneider, P., "An Algorithm for Automatically Fitting Digitized Curves," *Graphics Gems*, Ed: A. Glassner, Academic Press, 1990, 612–626.

SCHU69   Schumacker, R., B. Brand, M. Gilliland, and W. Sharp, *Study for Applying Computer-Generated Images to Visual Simulation,* Technical Report AFHRL-TR-69-14, NTIS AD700375, U.S. Air Force Human Resources Lab., Air Force Systems Command, Brooks AFB, TX, September 1969.

SCHW82   Schweitzer, D., and E. Cobb, "Scanline Rendering of Parametric Surfaces," *SIGGRAPH 82,* 265–271.

SEDE84   Sederberg, T.W., and D.C. Anderson, "Ray Tracing of Steiner Patches," *SIGGRAPH 84,* 159–164.

SEQU89   Séquin, C.H., and E.K. Smyrl, "Parameterized Ray Tracing," *SIGGRAPH 89,* 307–314.

SHER93   Sherr, S., *Electronic Displays, Second Edition,* Wiley, New York, 1993.

SHNE86   Shneiderman, B., *Designing the User Interface: Strategies for Effective Human-Computer Interaction,* Addison-Wesley, Reading, MA, 1986.

SIEG81   Siegel, R., and J. Howell, *Thermal Radiation Heat Transfer,* second edition, Hemisphere, Washington, DC, 1981.

SMIT78   Smith, A.R., "Color Gamut Transform Pairs," *SIGGRAPH 78,* 12–19.

SMIT79   Smith, A.R., "Tint Fill," *SIGGRAPH 79,* 276–283.

SMIT84   Smith, A.R., "Plants, Fractals and Formal Languages," *SIGGRAPH 84,* 1–10.

SNOW83   Snowberry, K., S. Parkinson, and N. Sisson, "Computer Display Menus," *Ergonomics,* 26(7), July 1983, 699–712.

SPAR78   Sparrow, E.M., and R.D. Cess, *Radiation Heat Transfer,* Hemisphere, Washington, DC, 1978.

SPRO82   Sproull, R.F., "Using Program Transformations to Derive Line-Drawing Algorithms," *ACM TOG,* 1(4), October 1982, 259–273.

STAU78   Staudhammer, J., "On Display of Space Filling Atomic Models in Real Time," *SIGGRAPH 78,* 167–172.

STON88   Stone, M., W. Cowan, and J. Beatty, "Color Gamut Mapping and the Printing of Digital Color Images," *ACM TOG,* 7(3), October 1988, 249–292.

STOV82   Stover, H., "True Three-Dimensional Display of Computer Data," in *Proceedings of SPIE,* 367, August 1982, 141–144.

STRO91   Stroustrup, B., *The C++ Programming Language,* second edition, Addison-Wesley, Reading, MA, 1991.

SUN89   Sun Microsystems, *OPEN LOOK Graphical User Interface,* Sun Microsystems, Mountain View, CA, 1989.

SUTH63   Sutherland, I.E., "Sketchpad: A Man–Machine Graphical Communication System," in *SJCC,* Spartan Books, Baltimore, MD, 1963.

SUTH74a   Sutherland, I.E., R.F. Sproull, and R.A. Schumacker, "A Characterization of Ten Hidden-Surface Algorithms," *ACM Computing Surveys,* 6(1), March 1974, 1–55. Also in BEAT82, 387–441.

SUTH74b   Sutherland, I.E., and Hodgman, G.W., "Reentrant Polygon Clipping," *CACM,* 17(1), January 1974, 32–42.

TAMM82   Tamminen, M., and R. Sulonen, "The EXCELL Method for Efficient Geometric Access to Data," in *Proc. 19th ACM IEEE Design Automation Conf.,* Las Vegas, June 14–16, 1982, 345–351.

TANN85   Tannas, L. Jr., ed., *Flat-Panel Displays and CRTs,* Van Nostrand Reinhold, New York, 1985.

THIB87   Thibault, W.C., and B.F. Naylor, "Set Operations on Polyhedra Using Binary Space Partitioning Trees," *SIGGRAPH 87,* 153–162.

THOM86   Thomas, S.W., "Dispersive Refraction in Ray Tracing," *The Visual Computer,* 2(1), January 1986, 3–8.

TILL83   Tiller, W., "Rational B-Splines for Curve and Surface Representation," *CG & A,* 3(6), September 1983, 61–69.

TILO80   Tilove, R.B., "Set Membership Classification: A Unified Approach to Geometric Intersection Problems," *IEEE Trans. on Computers,* C-29(10), October 1980, 847–883.

TORR66   Torrance, K.E., E.M. Sparrow, and R.C. Birkebak, "Polarization, Directional Distribution, and Off-Specular Peak Phenomena in Light Reflected from Roughened Surfaces," *J. Opt. Soc. Am.,* 56(7), July 1966, 916–925.

TORR67   Torrance, K., and E.M. Sparrow, "Theory for Off-Specular Reflection from Roughened Surfaces," *J. Opt. Soc. Am.,* 57(9), September 1967, 1105–1114.

TOTH85   Toth, D.L., "On Ray Tracing Parametric Surfaces," *SIGGRAPH 85,* 171–179.

TURN84   Turner, J.A., *A Set-Operation Algorithm for Two and Three-Dimensional Geometric Objects,* Architecture and Planning Research Laboratory, College of Architecture, University of Michigan, Ann Arbor, MI, August 1984.

ULIC87   Ulichney, R., *Digital Halftoning*, MIT Press, Cambridge, MA, 1987.

VANA84   Van Aken, J. R., "An Efficient Ellipse-Drawing Algorithm," *CG & A*, 4(9), September 1984, 24–35.

VANA85   Van Aken, J.R., and M. Novak, "Curve-Drawing Algorithms for Raster Displays," *ACM TOG,* 4(2), April 1985, 147–169.

VOSS87   Voss, R., "Fractals in Nature: Characterization, Measurement, and Simulation," in *Course Notes 15 for SIGGRAPH 87*, Anaheim, CA, July 1987.

WACO93   Wacom Technology Corporation, *Wacom Cordless Digitizer Specification Sheet*, Wacom Technology Corporation, Vancouver, WA, 1993.

WARE87   Ware, C., and J. Mikaelian, "An Evaluation of an Eye Tracker as a Device for Computer Input," in *Proceedings of CHI + GI 1987*, ACM, New York, 183–188.

WARN69   Warnock, J., *A Hidden-Surface Algorithm for Computer Generated Half-Tone Pictures,* Technical Report TR 4-15, NTIS AD-753 671, Computer Science Department, University of Utah, Salt Lake City, UT, June 1969.

WARN83   Warn, D.R., "Lighting Controls for Synthetic Images," *SIGGRAPH 83,* 13–21.

WATK70   Watkins, G.S., *A Real Time Visible Surface Algorithm,* Ph.D. Thesis, Technical Report UTEC-CSc-70-101, NTIS AD-762 004, Computer Science Department, University of Utah, Salt Lake City, UT, June 1970.

WEGH84   Weghorst, H., G. Hooper, and D.P. Greenberg, "Improved Computational Methods for Ray Tracing," *ACM TOG,* 3(1), January 1984, 52–69.

WEIL77   Weiler, K., and P. Atherton, "Hidden Surface Removal Using Polygon Area Sorting," *SIGGRAPH 77,* 214–222.

WEIS66   Weiss, R.A., "BE VISION, A Package of IBM 7090 FORTRAN Programs to Draw Orthographic Views of Combinations of Plane and Quadric Surfaces," *JACM,* 13(2), April 1966, 194–204. Also in FREE80, 203–213.

WESL81   Wesley, M.A., and G. Markowsky, "Fleshing Out Projections," *IBM Journal of Research and Development*, 25(6), November 1981, 934–954.

WHIT80   Whitted, T., "An Improved Illumination Model for Shaded Display," *CACM,* 23(6), June 1980, 343–349.

WHIT84   Whitton, M., "Memory Design for Raster Graphics Displays," *CG & A,* 4(3), March 1984, 48–65.

WITK88   Witkin, A., and M. Kass, "Spacetime Constraints," *SIGGRAPH 88,* 159–168.

WOLF87   Wolf, C., and P. Morel-Samuels, "The Use of Hand-Drawn Gestures for Text Editing," *International Journal of Man-Machine Studies*, 27(1), July 1987, 91-102.

WOLF90   Wolff, L., and D. Kurlander, "Ray Tracing with Polarization Parameters," *CG & A,* 10(6), November 1990, 44–55.

WOLF91   Wolfram, S., *Mathematica: A System for Doing Mathematics by Computer*, second edition, Addison-Wesley, Reading, MA, 1991.

WOO85   Woo, T., "A Combinatorial Analysis of Boundary Data Structure Schemata," *CG & A,* 5(3), March 1985, 19–27.

WOON71   Woon, P.Y., and H. Freeman, "A Procedure for Generating Visible-Line Projections of Solids Bounded by Quadric Surfaces," in *IFIP 1971,* North-Holland Pub. Co., Amsterdam, 1971, pp. 1120–1125. Also in FREE80, 230–235.

WU87   Wu, X., and J.G. Rokne, "Double-Step Incremental Generation of Lines and Circles," *CVGIP,* (37), 1987, 331-334.

WYLI67   Wylie, C., G.W. Romney, D.C. Evans, and A.C. Erdahl, "Halftone Perspective Drawings by Computer," *FJCC 67,* Thompson Books, Washington, DC, 1967, 49–58.

WYSZ82   Wyszecki, G., and W. Stiles, *Color Science: Concepts and Methods, Quantitative Data and Formulae*, second edition, Wiley, New York, 1982.

WYVI88   Wyvill, B., "The Great Train Rubbery," *ACM SIGGRAPH 88 Electronic Theater and Video Review,* 26, 1988.

WYVI90   Wyvill, B., "Symmetric Double Step Line Algorithm," *Graphics Gems*, Ed. A. Glassner, Academic Press, 1990, 101–104.

ZDON90   Zdonik, S.B., and D. Maier, *Readings in Object-Oriented Database Systems*, Morgan Kaufmann, San Mateo, CA, 1990.

ZIMM87   Zimmerman, T., J. Lanier, C. Blanchard, S. Bryson, and Y. Harvill, "A Hand Gesture Interface Device," in *Proceedings of the CHI + GI 1987 Conference*, ACM, New York, 189–192.

Index

Accelerator keys, 309
ACE, 419
Achromatic light, 395
ACM, 12
Active-edge table (AET), 91, 455
Active-surface table, 458
Adaptive subdivision, *see* Spatial partitioning
Additive color primaries, 410
Address space, 141, 151
    single, 150–151
Addressability, 130
Aerial perspective, 428
Aliasing, 119, 430, 437, 442, 453, *see also*
    Antialiasing
  artifact, 10
  sliver polygons, 90
  temporal, 435, 437
Alignment
  for patterns, 94
α (angle between $\overline{R}$ and $\overline{V}$), 487
Ambient light, 430, 478–479
Ambient reflection coefficient (k_a), 479
American National Standards Institute, *see* ANSI
Anchor, of pattern, 94
Animation, 6, 434–437
  basic rules, 436–437
  cartoon-character, 436
  control, 436
  conventional, 435–436
  graphical languages, 435
  key-frame, 436

  staging of, 437
Animation control
  explicit, 436
  key-frame, 436
ANSI (American National Standards Institute),
  12, 239
Antialiasing, 10, 66, 70, 79, 119, 125, 419, *see*
  also Area sampling
  temporal, 435, 437
Application
  database, 16
  model, 15–16
  program, 15
Area sampling
  unweighted, 120
  weighted, 122
Area subdivision algorithm, Warnock, 383
Area subdivision algorithms, 468
Artificial reality, *see* Virtual world
Atmospheric attenuation, 483
Attribute bundle, PHIGS, 289
Attributes, 27
  inheritance, 273
  nongeometric, 252, 275
  object, 16
  output primitives, 27–33
  SRGP, 27–29,
Autocompletion, command, 306

B (radiosity), 515

545

Graphics Software Packages: SRGP and SPHIGS

The SRGP and SPHIGS graphics packages described in this book are archived in multiple formats, and are available on the World Wide Web free for your use.

http//:www.aw.com/cseng/authors/foley/compgrafix/compgrafix.sup.html

These formats allow you to run the packages on many PC, Apple Macintosh, and UNIX platforms. The files are identical across platforms except for the method used in compressing or archiving them. The website indicated above includes specific directions for accessing each format.

PLEASE NOTE BELOW THE SPECIFIC PLATFORMS REQUIRED FOR EACH FORMAT. THE SOFTWARE MAY NOT INSTALL OR RUN PROPERLY ON ANY OTHER PLATFORM—UNDER SOME OTHER C COMPILER, FOR EXAMPLE. WE REGRET THAT WE ARE UNABLE TO OFFER ANY USER SUPPORT IN SUCH CASES.

Requirements:

UNIX Worksations: Requires a workstation running UNIX and the X Window System; X11 release R4 or later; an ANSII C Compiler (gcc is recommended); v4.3 or 4.4 BSD, System V UNIX, or Solaris 2.0.

Apple Macintosh: Requires any model Apple Macintosh with a minimum of 1 megabyte of RAM; 2 megabytes of RAM are required to run the debugger; System Software v7.0 or later; Metrowerks CodeWarrior v.10 or later.

Microsoft Windows for the PC Family: Requires any PC using an 80826 or higher microprocessor with a minimum of 1 megabyte of RAM (combined conventional and extended memory); Hercules monochrome adapter, or EGA color monitor or better; Microsoft Mouse or compatible pointing device; Microsoft Windows v3.1, Windows95, or DOS v5.0 or later; Microsoft Software Development Kit for Windows; Borland Turbo C v2.0 or later.

Instructors Note: Instructors who adopt this book may obtain a free copy of the Apple Macintosh or Microsoft Windows files on a diskette. Contact your local Addison Wesley Longman representative, send e-mail to aw.cse@aw.com, or (in the U.S.) call 1-800-322-1377. Be sure to specify the format you need.

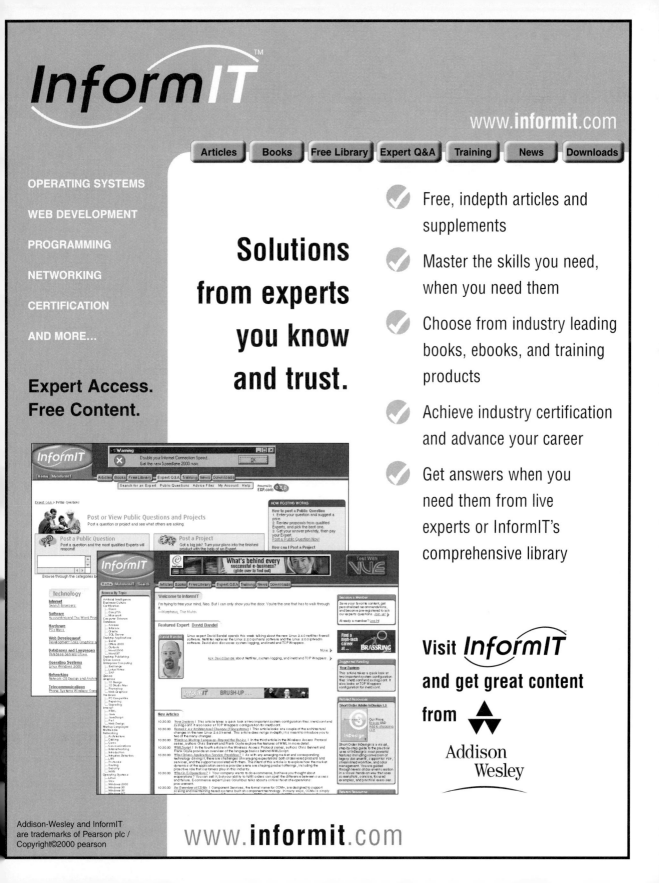

Plate 42. Ray-traced images.(Section 14.7) (a) Scene from short film *Quest* (1985). (Michael Sciulli, James Arvo, and Melissa White. © Hewlett-Packard.) (b) "Haute Air." Functions were used to modify color, surface normals, and transparency at nearly every pixel. (Courtesy of David Kurlander, Columbia University, 1986)

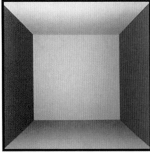

(a)

(b)

Plate 43. Radiosity (section 14.8.1). Cube with six diffuse walls (emmissive white front wall is not shown). (a) Photograph of actual cube. (b) Model rendered with 49 patches per side, using constant shading. (c) Model rendered with 49 patches per side, using interpolated shading. (Cindy M. Goral, Kenneth E. Torrance, Donald P. Greenberg, and Bennett Battaile, Program of Computer Graphics, Cornell University, 1984.)

(a)

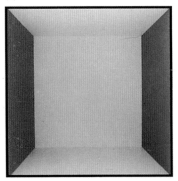

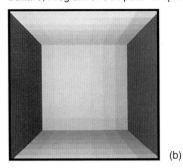

(b)

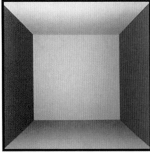

(c)